SOCIALLY RESPONSIBLE AND SUSTAINABLE BUSINESS AROUND THE GLOBE: THE NEW AGE OF CORPORATE SOCIAL RESPONSIBILITY

JONATHAN H. WESTOVER, EDITOR

SOCIALLY RESPONSIBLE AND SUSTAINABLE BUSINESS AROUND THE GLOBE: THE NEW AGE OF CORPORATE SOCIAL RESPONSIBILITY

JONATHAN H. WESTOVER, EDITOR

COMMON GROUND

First published in 2013 in Champaign, Illinois, USA
by Common Ground Publishing LLC
as part of The Organization Book Series

Library of Congress Cataloging-in-Publication Data

Socially responsible and sustainable business around the globe: the new age of corporate social responsibility / edited by Jonathan H. Westover

p. cm.
ISBN 978-1-61229-080-5 (pbk: alk. Paper) — ISBN 978-1-61229-081-2 (pdf)
1. Social responsibility of business. 2. Sustainable development–Social aspects. I. Westover, Jonathan H.

HD60.S637 2012
658.4'08–dc23

2012034122

Table of Contents

Acknowledgements

I want to thank Common Ground Publishing for providing me with a venue for publishing this edited compilation. Additionally, I would like to thank the many individuals who contributed their own research to this edited work. Of course, this book would not be possible without each of their important contributions. Most of all, I would like to publically thank my beloved wife, Jacque, and my five wonderful children (Sara, Amber, Lia, Kaylie, and David) for all of their love and support!

Contributor Information

(In Order of Contribution Appearance)

Jonathan H. Westover, Ph.D.

Jonathan H. Westover is an Assistant Professor of Business at Utah Valley University, specializing in international human resource management and organizational behavior. Additionally, he recently received the prestigious Fulbright Scholar award to be visiting faculty in the MBA program at Belarusian State University (Minsk, Belarus) and is a visiting faculty member in the MBA program at the University of Science and Technology of China (Hefei, China). He received a Master's of Public Administration with an emphasis in Human Resource Management and Organizational Behavior from the Marriott School of Management at Brigham Young University. As a sociology doctoral student at the University of Utah, his research interests combined comparative international sociology and the sociology of work and organizations. His ongoing research examines issues of globalization, labor transformation, social entrepreneurship, work-quality characteristics, and the determinants of job satisfaction cross-nationally.

Dr. Michele Simms

Dr. Michele Simms is Associate Professor in Management and the Director and Cullen Trust Endowed Chair of the Center for Business Ethics, Cameron School of Business at the University of St. Thomas, Houston, Texas. Her areas of expertise are in organizational and professional ethics, creating sustainable business-public health partnerships and corporate social responsibility. She is recognized in the Who’s Who in Business Higher Education and the Worldwide Registry of Global Business Leaders.

Gerald David Flint, Ph.D.

Gerald David Flint is a Clinical Associate Professor in the Management Department of the Mays Business School at Texas A&M University while maintaining private industry directorships and ownership interests in several firms as well as board positions in non-profit organizations. Dr. Flint began his business entrepreneurial endeavors in 1983 in the software development industry. The success of the initial firm led to additional business endeavors involving commercial real estate, insurance, importation of consumer goods, logistics technologies, and language education. The desire to better understand the global business environment led him to complete a Masters in International Management from Thunderbird and a doctoral program in Management from Mays Business School. His research interests span the areas of strategic management, international management, entrepreneurship, and the intersection of business and society.

Dr. Gregory R. Berry

Dr. Gregory R. Berry is Professor of Management and Organization at Central Connecticut State University, teaching Entrepreneurship and Management. Greg received his Ph.D. in Organizational Analysis from the University of Alberta in 1997, and has taught in Canada, Australia and five US states. Greg's research focus is on corporate discretionary environmental and citizenship behaviors, effective virtual teaming, and experiential learning and teaching. Greg regularly presents at the Academy of Management, and is well published in peer-reviewed journals.

Ling Wong

Ling Wong is a research associate at the Institute for Sustainable Leadership in Sydney, Australia and serves on the Institute's advisory board. She completed her MBA at Macquarie Graduate School of Management (MGSM), Macquarie University, in 2008. Her research interest is in sustainable leadership, change process, organisational behaviour and sustainability. She has published on sustainable leadership and has extensive management experience in major corporations. She established a practice, Leading Light in Leadership, which advises, consults, educates and facilitates in sustainable leadership and management.

Prof. Gayle C Avery

Professor Gayle Avery heads the Institute for Sustainable Leadership at Macquarie Graduate School of Management in Sydney, Australia. At MGSM since 1997, she teaches elective MBA subjects in leadership and takes the annual European Study Tour to Germany and Switzerland to examine best practices in sustainability. She is author of many papers and books on leadership and sustainability, including Leadership for Sustainable Futures and Understanding Leadership. Gayle Avery is consultant to major organisations in Australia and the Asia Pacific Region.

Dr. Mohammad E. Ansari

Dr. Mohammad E. Ansari is a Associate professor of management department at faculty of Administrative Sciences and Economics at University of Isfahan, Iran. His fields of interest are Human Resource Management and Organizational Behavior. He has published several books and research article in local and international journals.

Dr. Hadi Teimouri

Dr. Hadi Teimouri is a Assistant professor of management department at faculty of Administrative Sciences and Economics at University of Isfahan, Iran. His fields of interest are Human Resource Management, Organizational Behavior and Strategic Management. He has published several books and research article in local and international journals.

Dr. Johanna Maksimainen, Ph.D.

Johanna Maksimainen is a post-doctoral researcher in Department of Computer Science and Information Systems, Faculty of Information Technology, University of Jyväskylä, Finland. She holds Phil.Lic. in art history and Ph.D. in cognitive science. Johanna has carried out multidisciplinary research and related teaching in the areas of human-computer interaction and ICT-ethics. Her main areas of research interests are technology consumption, user experience, mental representation, well-being, sustainable development and CSR. She is the author of several peer-reviewed articles and reviewer in scientific journals.

Dr. Pertti Saariluoma

Pertti Saariluoma is a professor of cognitive science in the University of Jyväskylä, Finland. He has studied and visited over the year in Oxford University, Carnegie-Mellon University, Cambridge University, IIASA, Luxemburg and University of Granada.

Dr Hadrian G. Djajadikerta

Dr Hadrian G. Djajadikerta is an Associate Professor of Accounting at the School of Accounting, Finance & Economics, and the Associate Leader of the Centre for Innovative Practice at Edith Cowan University in Australia.

Dr Terri Trireksani

Dr Terri Trireksani is the Deputy Academic Chair for UG Programmes at Murdoch Business School in Australia.

Brynn Harrington

Brynn Harrington is an organizational change/sustainability consultant in the San Francisco Bay Area. Her professional expertise is in internal/external communications, program design, organizational strategy, and individual/organizational behavior change. She has consulted with a range of private and public sector clients, most recently NetApp, Blu Skye Sustainability Consulting, Walmart, and the Taproot Foundation. She received her M.S. in Learning and Organizational Change from Northwestern University and her B.A. from the University of Wisconsin-Madison.

Dr. Gail Ann Berger

Gail Berger is a Lecturer at Northwestern University in the School of Education and Social Policy, Kellogg School of Management, and McCormick School of Engineering. She brings academic and professional experience in the areas of conflict resolution, leadership development, succession planning and team building. She has consulted to small firms, Fortune 500 companies, and non-profit organizations. Her consulting work focuses on executive assessments, succession planning, leadership development and teambuilding. Some of the organizations she has worked with include Driehaus Capital Management, Grant Thornton, Jewish Federation of Chicago, Lockheed Martin, Masco, McDonalds, and Safer Foundation. Professor Berger has won several teaching awards and her research has been presented at national conferences and published in leading journals. She received her Ph.D. in Management and Organizations from the Kellogg School of Management, Northwestern University. She also holds a M.Ed. in Administration and Supervision from Loyola University and a B.A./B.S. in Psychology and Elementary Education from Boston University

Dr. Mindy Douthit

Mindy Douthit is an Adjunct Professor at Northwestern University in the School of Education & Social Policy's Master of Learning & Organizational Change program. She brings both professional and academic expertise in the areas of organizational development and change and social network analysis. She spent several years with Anderson Consulting working in the areas of organization analysis and design, human-computer interaction, and training design and development. As Manager with The International Forum, she designed senior executive educational programs for a global clientele. She holds a PhD in Organization Theory and Strategy from the University of Chicago Graduate School of Business. Her research and teaching interests include organizational change and innovation, entrepreneurship, competitive strategy and cooperative behavior within organizations.

Dr. Johannes Boon

Dr. Johannes (Jan) Boon is an emeritus scientist with Natural Resources Canada. He has had a long career in research and research management, which included leadership of provincial and federal geological survey organizations. He has also been an associate professor of physical chemistry at a Venezuelan University. During his career, Dr. Boon has been a member and chair of the Boards of many community and professional organizations, and co-chair of the Canada-Japan Joint Panel on Earth Sciences and the Environment. Currently he is a member of the Prospectors and Developers Association of Canada (PDAC) International Affairs Committee and of the Centre for Excellence in Corporate Social Responsibility (CSR) Executive Committee. Dr. Boon holds a Ph. D. in geochemistry as well as professional certificates in intercultural studies and conflict management. After his retirement in 2007 he completed the Master's Program in Globalization and International Development at the University of Ottawa, and is currently enrolled in the Ph. D. Program in Sociology at Carleton University (Ottawa, Canada). His research deals with CSR in the mineral exploration industry.

Naci Polat

Naci Polat is an Assistant Professor of Business at Dumlupınar University (Turkey) specializing in Tourism Management and Sustainability. He finished his master studies in Development Policy with focus on Non-Governmental Organizations at the University of Bremen (Germany) with an emphasis in protection of climate in aviation sector and their political instruments. As an European Union Jean Monnet Scholar, he did also researches on ecological management and audit scheme (EMAS) at the University of Trier (Germany). He is the member of International Association of Scientific Experts in Tourism (AIEST) and World Leisure Organization (WLO). His ongoing EU-project (KNOWNET) examines sustainability and competitiveness of small and medium sized tourism enterprises (SMEs) and creates a knowledge network with other 7 European partners.

Dr. Leon Zurawicki

Dr. Leon Zurawicki is a Full Professor at the College of Management, University of Massachusetts-Boston. His research interests center on the Foreign Direct Investment theory and practice, ethical issues in international business, and applications of neuroscience to research in consumer behavior. In addition to his academic activities, Professor Zurawicki has also been a consultant to various institutions including the OECD, Ministry of Finance of Nicaragua, Ministry of Privatization in Poland and several private companies like American Express Bank, ARCOR (Argentina), Ferroatlantica (Spain).He is a member of the Advisory Board of the Chief Marketing Officers' Council. Dr. Zurawicki is an author of four books and numerous articles in the top tier journals such as Journal of World Business, Journal of International Business Studies, Journal of Business Research. Dr. Zurawicki holds academic degrees in international business and economics from the University of Warsaw, the Netherlands School of Economics and the College of Europe (Bruges).

Mohsin Habib

Abbas Ameli-Renani

Abbas Ameli-Renani is an Emerging Markets Strategist at RBS Markets & International Banking in the City of London. His focus is on the fundamental economic drivers of global emerging economies, with a special attention to Central & Eastern European currencies, rates and credit. He is a graduate of University of Cambridge, where he completed a BA Honours in Economics, and a graduate of University of Warwick, where he completed a Master of Science in Economics. Abbas Ameli-Renani's academic focus has been on Monetary Policy, having dedicated his postgraduate dissertation to the in-depth study of the bank-lending channel of monetary policy transmission mechanism. He has published in and is an associate editor of 'The International Journal of Environmental, Cultural, Economic and Social Sustainability'. His broader interests include fiscal and public policy. Since 2010 Abbas has also been a contributing columnist for Iran's best-selling financial daily newspaper, Donya-e-eqtesad.

Dr. Cynthia Cann

Cynthia Cann serves as a faculty member in the Arthur J. Kania School of Management at the University of Scranton, where she is an Associate Professor in the Department of Management/Marketing. She holds a PhD from the State University of New York at Binghamton. Her research interests include: sustainability, sustainable strategic management, strategic marketing, sustainable marketing and environmental business. She has developed the cornerstone course for the Scranton MBA program, Responsibility, Sustainability and Justice, as well as an undergraduate course Sustainable Marketing. Dr. Cann is co-author of a chapter in China's Environment: the Challenges of Sustainable Development and has authored or co-authored a number of papers in the area of sustainability and marketing. Dr. Cann is committed to sustainability education and is part of a Task Force on Sustainability at The University of Scranton.

Natalya Parente Boock

Natalya Parente Boock received her MBA from the Arthur J. Kania School of Management at the University of Scranton in 2004. She currently serves as Marketing Director for CampusWorks Inc., a higher education technology consulting firm based in Sarasota Florida.

Paul Ziek

Paul Ziek is an Assistant Professor in the Department of Media, Communications, and Visual Arts at Pace University. His primary research interest is how and why organizations communicate CSR. Where extant theories explain CSR communication in terms of resource dependence or institutions, Paul examines how the communication-information-media matrix shapes CSR communication. Paul has a B.A. from Rutgers, M.A. from New York University, and a Ph.D. from Rutgers.

Jennifer Davis

Jennifer Davis completed her Master's in Business Administration at the Telfer School of Management in the University of Ottawa. Her research during that time focused on the challenges and opportunities that businesses face as they consider the journey to business sustainability and the organizational change processes that businesses would need to consider in order to achieve cultural change and to "green" their operations. Jennifer now works as a consultant with Stratos Inc., Canada's leading sustainability consultancy.

Sharon Leiba O'Sullivan

Sharon Leiba O'Sullivan is an associate professor of international human resources and cross-cultural management at the Telfer School of Management, University of Ottawa. Her current research program, funded by the Social Sciences and Humanities Research Council of Canada, addresses the international human resource management challenges in international development non-governmental organizations (INGOs). Sharon has published in several journals, including the Journal of International Business Studies, Human Relations, International Journal of Human Resource Management, Human Resource Management, International Business Review, Career Development International, and International Journal of Manpower.

Rumaisa Shaukat

Rumaisa Shaukat is a contract professor and a doctoral candidate at the University of Ottawa, Canada. Her research interests lay within the field of organizational studies, specifically related to the topics of organizational change, program implementation, performance management and organizational behaviour. Her doctoral research is centered on diverse institutional responses to government-initiated organizational changes.

Dr. Leah Ritchie

Leah E. Ritchie earned a Ph.D. in communication from the University of Maryland, College Park in 1999. She was awarded the top dissertation in the field of organizational communication in May of 2000. She is currently an Associate

Professor and Chairperson of the Management Department at Salem State College where she teaches courses in management, organizational behavior, conflict management, and negotiation skills. She has focused her research and teaching on promoting democratic practices in corporations. She sits on the editorial board of the Journal of Workplace Rights and was recently invited to co-convene a workshop on emancipation and organizational democracy at the Academy of Management. Dr. Ritchie also volunteers in the district court system as a certified mediator.

David Humphreys

David Humphreys is Senior Lecturer in Environmental Policy at The Open University in the United Kingdom. His book *Logjam: Deforestation and the Crisis of Global Governance* won the International Studies Association's Harold and Margaret Sprout Award of 2008 for the best book on international environmental problems.

Cisil Sohodol Bir

Cisil Sohodol Bir graduated from Ege University, in Izmir- Turkey, Faculty of Communication in 2000. She received her Ph.D. in public relations from Ege University in 2008. She worked as an assistant professor at Bahcesehir University, Istanbul, between 2008-2011. Then she was appointed to associate professor in 2011. She teaches courses on public relations, corporate social responsibility, reputation management and corporate communication. She is the author of two books and numerous articles in the public relations field.

Nicola H. J. Swan

Nicola works as a management consultant in the sphere of sustainable rural development. She has a PhD from the University of Reading and an MBA from Henley Management College, UK, as well as post graduate qualifications in research methodology and law. Previously, she was CEO for the Queensland Rural Medical Support Agency in Australia during its set up years. She is the Programme administrator for the Arkleton Trust. This Trust was established to study new approaches to rural education and development, and foster better communication between academics, rural communities, practitioners and policy makers. Other current appointments include: Parish Chairman for the rural village of Streatley; Director and Chairman for the International Rural Network (IRN). The IRN is an inclusive and interdisciplinary network of academics, rural community practitioners and activists, and policy makers who are engaged in rural community development, health and education in any country of the world. The aim of the network is as a means of sharing knowledge, research and experience, building capacities, and establishing mutual assistance. Nicola's practical management interests cover rural health, education and forestry from a management and community view point. Her academic interests focus on governance and corporate social responsibility particularly as both are implemented in developing and emerging economies.

Dr. Bahram Ranjbarian

University of Isfahan, Iran (Islamic Republic of)

Hadi Teimouri
University of Isfahan, Iran (Islamic Republic of)

Maria Lai-Ling Ling
Maria Lai-ling Ling is Professor of Business Administration at Malone University, Canton, Ohio, U.S. She holds the degrees of Bachelor of Business Administration, Master of Business Administration, Master of Art in Religion Studies, from the Chinese University of Hong Kong, and a Ph.D. in Business Administration from George Washington University. She has more than twenty years of professional experience in marketing and organization behavior in China business. She is a fellow of International Academy of Intercultural Research; and a member of several professional bodies. She has published one book and more than 30 peer-reviewed articles. Some articles are in the Journal of Business Ethics, Management Research Review, Journal of International Business Research and Practice, Journal of Biblical Integration in Business, International Journal of Sustainable Development, the International Journal of Humanities. Her research interest is corporate social responsibility development in China, cross-cultural negotiation, and business education.

Alice Lai-Heung Lam
Alice Lai-heung Lam holds the degree of Bachelor of Arts and Master of Arts in Public Policy and Management and Master of Arts in Arbitration and Dispute Resolution from the City University of Hong Kong. She has been awarded an external law degree by University of London(2010) and the Post Advanced Graduate Certificate in career counseling issued by University of Hong Kong (2011). She has worked in Hong Kong Government for more than twenty years as Housing Officer and Executive. She has conducted research about human rights movement in Hong Kong since 1998. She has worked as a consultant to AJ-GREAT Limited for providing consulting services in the field of rehabilitation, medical and sports products and equipment.

Lewis Hon-Chung Lam
Lewis Hon-Chung Lam is a researcher. He holds the degree of Bachelor of Arts in Social Science from the University of Hong Kong. He has conducted fieldwork about non-government organizations in Hong Kong and mainland China for more than seven years.

Prof. Phd Michela Cortini
Prof. Phd Michela Cortini teaches "Work and organizational psychology" at the University G. d'Annunzio of Chieti Pescara (Italy). Her main research interests are in organizational communication, organizational wellbeing and mixed-methods for I/O psychology.

Dr. Ulla Kotonen
Dr. Ulla Kotonen is a head of Master's Degree Programmes and a principal lecturer of Research and Development at the Faculty of Business Studies, Lahti University of Applied Sciences. She has previously worked as a professor of accounting at School of Business, Lappeenranta University of Technology. Her

current research interests include corporate social responsibility (CSR) and sustainability reporting, corporate governance issues as well as local and regional development. Her resent studies are related especially to Finnish companies CSR reporting and regional responsibility. Her resent CSR and sustainability articles are published in The Journal of Applied Accounting Research, The International Journal of Environmental, Cultural, Economic and Social Sustainability, and Social Responsibility Journal. In 2011 she organised 11th International Conference on Corporate Social Responsibility in conjunction with the Social Responsibility Research Network (SRRNet).

Thomas Kern

Thomas Kern lectures in financial accounting in the Department of Accounting and Corporate Governance at Macquarie University, Australia. His research interests are in the areas of corporate social responsibility of financial institutions and accounting education. He has previously held positions at the University of Canterbury, New Zealand and Saarland University, Saarbruecken, Germany. During this time, he taught in advanced professional programmes offered at the Frankfurt School of Finance and Management, Academy of Administration and Commerce Rheinland-Pfalz and the Saarland Academy of Labour and Welfare. Thomas' research interests have led to publications in leading academic and professional journals, editorial roles both in social and environmental accounting and education, successful awarding of research grants and Co-Chair of the Scientific Technical Committee of the 2009 Australasian Corporate Social and Environmental Accounting Research (CSEAR) Conference. Prior to returning to academia, Thomas was Head of the International Financial Reporting Standards (IFRS) Competence Centre of an international commercial bank based in Hamburg, Germany where he took shared responsibility for the technical implementation of IFRS.

Nicholas McGuigan

Nicholas McGuigan is a lecturer in accounting at Macquarie University. He is directly involved in applied research focussing on the enhancement of educational and professional development programmes of accountants. His research interests include threshold concepts and conceptualisations, development of generic learning skills in accounting graduates, student perceptions and learning approaches towards accounting, mobile learning technology and innovative teaching practice. His research interests have led to the awarding of competitive research grant funding both nationally and internationally. Nicholas has published in leading international accounting education journals, presented at numerous national and international conferences and invited to present to professional accounting bodies. He is an Associate Editor of *Higher Education and Research (HERD) Journal* and American Accounting Association *Issues in Accounting Education Journal*. He further acts as an Editorial Board Member for *Accounting Education*, *Global Perspectives on Accounting Education* and *Education* Research and Reviews. Nicholas has further assisted as Co-Editor of a themed issue of *Accounting Forum* on Social and Environmental Accounting and Accountability and has Co-Chaired the Scientific Technical Committee of the 2009 Australasian CSEAR Conference. He has also published in the field of

This book is comprised of 16 core chapters and 9 additional CSR research papers on specific topics in specific regions around the globe, divided into seven parts: (1) Overview of Corporate Social Responsibility, (2) Organizations and Corporate Social Responsibility, (3) Corporate Social Responsibility and Economic Development, (4) Corporate Social Responsibility and Sustainable Development, (5) Corporate Social Responsibility and Environmental Sustainability, (6) What is next for Corporate Social Responsibility?, and (7) Additional Research in Corporate Social Responsibility. Each part starts with a brief overview, outlining the overall theme of the section and specific chapters that it contains.

Chapters 1 and 2 make up Part 1 of the book, which provides a general overview to corporate social responsibility. Chapter 1 looks at emerging trends and ethics in corporate social responsibility. Chapter 2 explores corporate social responsibility within the framework of a global economy.

Chapters 3-7 make up Part 2 of the book, which focuses on organizations and corporate social responsibility. Chapter 3 looks at creating sustainability in organizations. Chapter 4 explores the role of corporate social responsibility strategy on success of multi-national organizations. Chapter 5 explores how human resource management and human capital management influence corporate social responsibility. Chapter 6 looks at executive perceptions of CSR. Chapter 7 looks at employee perceptions of CSR.

Chapters 8-10 make up Part 3 of the book, which focuses on corporate social responsibility and economic development. Chapter 8 explores the role of CSR in development. Chapter 9 explores the interaction between multinational companies and development countries. Chapter 10 looks at cooperation between the government and business in CSR development efforts.

Chapters 11 and 12 make of Part 4 of the book, which focuses on corporate social responsibility and sustainable development. Chapter 11 explores targeting demand instead of supply when looking at the economics of sustainability. Chapter 12 looks at the role of CSR assurance reporting.

Chapters 13 and 14 make up Part 5 of the book, which focuses on corporate social responsibility and environmental sustainability. Chapter 13 examines the role of interorganizational alliances in environmental sustainability. Chapter 14 looks at corporate greening initiatives.

Chapters 15 and 16 make up Part 6 of the book, which asks the question, "What is next for CSR?" Chapter 15 explores new directions in CSR. Chapter 16 explores the possibility of moving beyond CSR, to the democratic regulation of transnational corporations.

Part 7 of the book is made up 9 additional CSR research papers on specific topics in specific regions around the globe: (1) CSR in Turkey, (2) CSR Lessons from India, (3) Iranian Culture and CSR, (4) NGO Influence on CSR in China, (5) Intercorporate Social Responsibility, (6) Third-Party Assurance of CSR in Finland, (7) Socially Responsible Lending in Australasian Banks, (8) Teaching Sustainability in Australian Higher Education, and (9) CSR and Potentially Harmful Products in the Gaming Industry.

Part I: An Overview of Corporate Social Responsibility

Chapters 1 and 2 make up Part 1 of the book, which provides a general overview to corporate social responsibility. Chapter 1 looks at emerging trends and ethics in corporate social responsibility. Chapter 2 explores corporate social responsibility within the framework of a global economy.

Chapter 1: Emerging Trends and Ethics in Corporate Social Responsibility

Emerging Trends and Ethics in Corporate Responsibility

Michele Simms, Department of Business Administration and Marketing, United States of America

Abstract: Industrial and technological advances mobilized the global and environmental movements challenging business and societal perspectives on human nature and nature itself (Hoffman, 2002). The positive growth that accompanied the exploration, production and knowledge exchange of these movements also resulted in numerous negative effects on the natural environment. Corporate social responsibility (CSR) and corporate citizenship have evolved in parallel with the market changes brought on by globalization and the environmental movement. Identifying best practice ethics of CSR reveals the relationship between business and society in the era of globalization and environmentalism. Part I of this paper introduces trends in CSR and identifies three areas of best practice ethics: human rights, sustainability and healthy societies. Part II provides models emerging from the CSR-related field and concludes with discussion on the future roles and challenges of business in society.

Industrial and technological advances mobilized the global and environmental movements challenging business and societal perspectives on human nature and nature itself (Hoffman, 2002). The positive growth that accompanied the exploration, production and knowledge exchange of these movements also resulted in numerous negative effects on the natural environment: air, land and water pollution, toxic waste, and depletion of natural resources. Consequently, the concepts of corporate social responsibility (CSR) and corporate citizenship have evolved in parallel with market changes brought on by globalization and the environmental movement.

Identifying the trends and best practice ethics of CSR reveals the relationship between business and society in the era of globalization and environmentalism. The link between business and society has been a controversial and complex relationship. Part 1 of this paper introduces trends in CSR and identifies three areas of best practice ethics: human rights, sustainable development and healthy societies. Part II provides models emerging from the CSR-related field and concludes with discussion on the future roles and challenges of business in society.

Part I: Trends in Corporate Social Responsibility

Introduction

Corporate citizenship responsibilities and expectations related to corporate social responsibility, social accounting and marketing, business ethics, compliance and reputation management have evolved over the past five decades. Many large US conglomerates following WW II dominated the global economy. Due to the relative lack of global competitors, few formal governance practices were in place to act as restraints. The economic turmoil of the 1970s and 1980s resulted in a business focus on core competencies and the elevation of product diversity. The late 1980s and the1990s brought new focus on efficiency and productivity with models emerging on Total Quality Management and reengineering (Kolarik, 2000; Hammer, 1993). The technological advances of the 1990s, the globalization of the market place, and civil society and stakeholder demand shifted the business focus to include social justice and corporate citizenship practices while managing global economies. Corporate social responsibility subsumed the relationship between business and society with strategic intent to fulfil economic, legal, ethical and philanthropic social responsibilities expected by shareholders and stakeholders alike (Harrison and Freeman, 1999; Marsden, 2000; Donaldson and Dunfee, 1999).

With globalization came the international focus on corporate citizenship although many business shareholders question the validity of its practices (Bakan, 2004; Jennings, 1999; Matten, Crane and Chapple, 2003; Connor, 2001). Progressive global businesses realize the shared bottom line that comes from partnering among all stakeholders, a central tenet in CSR and corporate citizenship. These concepts evolved at a time of dramatic gains in knowledge and technological change challenging the role and obligation of business to social issues. The exploration, production and exchange of knowledge brought economic gains, improved living conditions and an enhanced quality of life for many both locally and globally (Armstrong and Bennett, 2001). But this has also resulted in numerous negative effects to the natural environment: air, land and water pollution, toxic waste and depletion of natural resources.

The cost-benefits of technology, which includes the consequences of industry and commerce on the environment, contribute to the complex relationship between technology and nature. Attitudes toward technology and nature have religious and philosophical underpinnings as well, and ultimately lead to discussions on human nature. Identifying trends and best practices in CSR begins, then, within this context of environmentalism and environmental ethics.

Linking Environment, Ecology and Economy

Questions of technology and the environment are jointly considered because of the capacity and will to control and predict natural events (Hoffman, 2002). These advances have typically come through experimentation and technological innovation, market forces, and analytic science, not through any symbiotic relationship with nature. One of the major costs of technological innovation is the degradation of the natural environment, which consequently spawned the environmental movement in the 1970s. Three categories of questions emerged (Heath, 2002). Scientific questions involved knowing the extent of the damage and identifying the long-term consequences for humans and natural systems. Questions of ethics considered the value of nature and whether this value is tied only to human well-being. Political questions considered whether private or public tools and processes were best designed and/or used to preserve natural resources.

A response to these questions is tied to one's perspective on nature and human value (Heath, 2002). An anthropocentric view regards the world in terms of human value and experiences. The extensionist view extends the anthropomorphic perspective to include the animal world; the capacity to feel pleasure or pain determines value. Finally, the biocentric view maintains a deep ecology that states nature has an intrinsic value independent of any human value, purpose or utility.

Thus, emerging themes of the environmental movement are questions of nature, human nature, and what it means to be human. Questions of science, ethics and politics are social questions as well, at a time when technology has come of age not just as technical capability but as social phenomenon (Hoffman, 2002; Kavanaugh, 2001; Hanson, 2001; Fukuyama, 2002; Naess, 1998; Goodpaster, 1982). This social phenomenon includes questions of markets and economics. Are markets the best institutions for preserving the environment and avoiding harm to nature (Hoffman, 2002)? To what extent are environmental problems understood as economic problems?

People and communities involved in defending the rights of the poor identify, as one link, the economic problem of poverty with the destruction of the ecological environment (Assemblee des eveques du Quebec, 2001). The words "economy" and "ecology" share the same Greek root: *oixia*, meaning home. Ecology is the science of the environment (or human home) and economy is the control or management of this environment. To re-establish the connection between economy and ecology involves factoring the ecological and the social costs into the calculation of economic costs. Particularly with the impact of economic globalization, the profound connection between ecology and social issues is emerging (Assemblee des eveques du Quebec, 2001; Panayotou, 2000) implying that environmental problems are social problems. The "cry of the earth is the cry of the poor; there is no true separation between how we support life economically and ecologically" (Assemblee des eveques du Quebec, 2001;

Hawken et. al., 2003). To this end, the ecological crisis is a moral problem that requires a "common responsibility" (Centesimus Annus, 1990).

The scientific, ethical and political categories of questions emerging from environmentalism and the corresponding anthropocentric, extensionist and biocentric models also inform business practice. These categories of questions and perspectives on human value and human nature illuminate the concept of corporate citizenship and the business-to-society link. The environmental movement is driving many of the questions and making visible the invisible on related issues of poverty, economy and ecology. These are deep moral questions that concern business regarding leadership, responsibility, human rights and practices, management strategies and the role of business in helping shape the future.

Corporate response to environmentalism results in emerging ethical and structural shifts toward human rights, sustainability and healthy societies.

Best Practice Ethics: Human Rights, Sustainability and Healthy Societies

On Human Rights

Human rights are rights all persons possess despite particular customs and laws but are not necessarily universally recognized, honored or allowed to be exercised. Human rights standards were established in 1948 by international agreement based on universal norms, applicable to every society, through the adoption of The Universal Declaration of Human Rights.

In the first four decades following its adoption, human rights were considered a state issue requiring state action; the private sector was not involved. With the Cold War effectively at an end, the world perspective shifted and the World Trade Organization meeting in Seattle in 1998 was obvious indication that human rights is a business concern. Several events occurred marking the convergence between the human rights movement and corporate response.

First, the concept of corporate responsibility had its genesis in the 1970s with events related to the environmental movement; to the 1970s and 1980s with nuclear weapon proliferation and the Nestle Infant Formula marketing case; followed by the sweatshop and child labor issues of the 1990s that continue today. The scope of issues that evoked a corporate social response emerged consequent to the human rights movement tracking the same issues.

A second area of convergence followed the human rights movement itself, which moved beyond the political and civil aspects to include broader cultural and economic issues. Accordingly, the role and impact of business expanded with the growth of multinational companies, deemed by the human rights community as "the most powerful non-state actors in the world" (Freeman, 2001).

A third area of convergence between business and human rights was globalization which demands a constituency of global companies and "civil society forces" (Freeman, 2001) to develop and enforce human rights practices.

Two documents providing business guidelines for a human rights agenda are the *Declaration of Fundamental Principles at Work* and *The Voluntary Principles.* [1]

These events culminated in businesses recognizing their impact on individuals, communities and the environment and the corresponding role of corporate social responsibility. "It is clear that one of the central measures of a company's social responsibility is its respect for human rights. And while most companies recognize the moral imperative to operate consistently with human rights principles, recognition is growing that respect for human rights also can be a tool for improving business performance" (UNCHR, 2001).

Human rights are increasingly viewed as a means of building support and trust with stakeholder groups, a way of managing risk and safe-guarding a reputation, and as part of corporate sustainability.

On Sustainability

Although definitions of sustainability vary, the movement toward sustainability began in the late 1980s and culminated in 1991 with the drafting of the *Declaration of the World Business Council for Sustainable Development* (WBCSD). This movement intensified throughout the 1990s given the understanding and support by the United Nations, local communities and business that the current global system of relationships between people, the environment and the marketplace were not sustainable.

Like the human rights movement, concepts of sustainability overlapped with, and became defined as part of, existing trends in environmental management. Environmental management systems were designed to monitor and reduce material wastage and use; consequently, 'sustainable development' and 'environmental performance' were often used synonymously.

Current thinking stresses, however, that addressing environmental consequences are "necessary but not sufficient to assure a sustainable future" (Armstrong and Bennett, 2001). Economic and social imbalances along with growing populations need to be added to the equation of human activities and the environment. Today, sustainability as a desired end, and the sustainable development as the means to achieving that goal, reflects the broader thinking of relating business to economic, environmental and social impacts: the triple bottom line of accountability or 'the three pillars'. This definition reflects the "core ethic of intergenerational equity, emphasizing the current generation's moral obligation to insure that future generations enjoy at least as good a quality of life as the current generation has now" (Pezzey, 1989).

The mix of assets that support sustainability (i.e., human, natural, physical and social) continues to evolve thus shaping business response in the form of

---

[1] Both are supported by a number of major American and British-based oil and mining companies (BP, Shell, Chevron, Texaco, Conic, Freeport, McMoran, Rio Tinto); NGOs (Human Rights Watch, Amnesty International, International Alert, Lawyers Committee for Human Rights, the Fund for Peace); corporate responsibility groups (Business for Social Responsibility, Prince of Wales Business Leaders Forum, the Council on Economic Priorities) and the International Federation of Chemical, Energy, Mine and General Worker's Union.

corporate citizenship, corporate social responsibility and strategic philanthropic practices. Business is viewed "as the entity most accountable for achieving sustainability" (World Development Report, 2003) because business has the resources and means for global reach, is a contributor to the problem vis-à-vis waste and usage, and has a vested interest. Consequently, businesses are publicly reporting progress on the environmental, health and safety issues, with increased screening by investors for sustainable performance, making business a key player on many global issues (Gunther, 2004).

Embedded in the vision of sustainability of "ensuring a better quality of life for everyone, now and for generations to come" (UK Strategy for Sustainable Development) leads to a third best practice: healthy societies.

On Healthy Societies

The potential of globalization to enhance sustainable human development is frequently thwarted due its predominant focus on economic benefits without equal consideration devoted to its social and environmental consequences, although this is changing. By not having social adjustment policies in place, the economic dislocation and marginalization of the poor harms the health of local societies. This phenomenon has been coined as "the race to the bottom":

Downward leveling affects people in all parts of the world and in rich and poor countries alike. Loss of job security in the US, growing unemployment in Europe, mushrooming poverty in the Third World, falling living standards in Eastern Europe and the former Soviet Union, and denial of human and labor rights in much of Asia are all aggravated by downward leveling (Brecher and Costello, 1994).

This phenomenon manifests the role of economic insecurity, disruption, and poverty in undermining human relationships, traditional lifestyles and social values resulting in the antithesis of sustainability. Insuring sustainable practices involves linking the management of environmental concerns with the management of social problems locally, nationally and globally. Social and environmental issues are often public health issues: poverty, widening inequality, increasing air, water and soil pollution and degradation; and their related issues of disappearing biodiversity, destroyed forests and declining fisheries.

Two decades of research establishes a causal link between the environment and disease (McEwen and Schmeck, 1994; Seeman and McEwen, 1996; Marmot, Bobak and Smith, 1995; MacIntyre, 1994; Wilkinson, 1986; Evans, 1994; Amick, Levine and Tarlov, 1995; Blaine, Brunne, and Wilkinson, 1996). Public health is at the forefront of this research with its population-based/community perspective to reduce disease and early death. Health risks are viewed as common problems that affect entire communities. There is a collective approach to developing policy that includes institutionalising health and safety issues. Public health solutions are aimed toward sustaining communities through cohesive and meaningful political involvement.

Understanding the impact of society on health reinforces the interdependencies of government, workplace and economic structures (Brecher and Costello, 1994) in an era of globalization and environmentalism. What emerges is an ethic of health and healthy society, which is related to sustainability and human rights. Taken together, the trends and best practice ethics that comprise CSR result in creating new social and economic structures (Korten, 2001; Brecher and Costello, 1994; Annas, 1998; Kavanaugh, 2001; Beauchamp and Steinbock, 1999; Lebacqz, 1987; Callahan, 1998; Hanson, 2001; Pelligrino and Faden, 1999; Simms, 2004). Part II identifies the new thinking that informs these new structures.

Part II: New Thinking / New Models

Model Guidelines

Several model guidelines exist that integrate human rights, sustainability and healthy societies and serve as frameworks for business. The first are NGOs (Non-governmental Organizations). The number of internationally recognized NGOs has grown from 6000 to 26,000 in the 1990s (Economist, 1999). NGOs are cited as an emerging business model based on their focus on cross-sectoral, alliance-building relationships, public accountability and addressing environmental issues. Natural capitalism and economic democracy are two emerging paradigms that redefine economics. The essence of natural capitalism rests on one proposition: "that all capital be valued" (Hawken et. al., 2003). "Capital" includes money, goods, people, and culture and represents a new form of economics (Hawken et.al., 2003). Economic Democracy has been cited as "the next step for CSR" with its focus on system design and stakeholder theory with the goal of creating structures of justice and checks and balances (Kelly, 2002). At its core, economic democracy views corporations not as objects but as human communities thus linking sustainable futures to corporate citizenship (Renesh, 2001; Korten, 2001; Kelly, 2002).

Corporate humanism and the role of spirituality in management introduce practices that emphasize the person and the role of community in redefining business. Corporate humanism derives from corporate moral agency, a construct to describe those corporations that acknowledge the premises of natural rights or human rights in the workplace (French, 1979; Goodpaster, 1982; Keeley, 1988; May, 1987; Phillips, 1992; Velasquez, 1983; Werhane, 1995). Corporations are viewed as a society of persons (Mele, 2001), and the business enterprise is "morally justified, indeed, they are morally praiseworthy, to the extent that the products and services business enterprises provide promote the fundamental goods that fulfil human nature" (Valasquez, 1983). Current questions on human dignity, life, health and meaning have resulted in what is the fastest growing area in business today: spirituality and management (Mitroff and Denton, 1999). Incorporating the spiritual component in business practice recognizes how values of dignity, life and the person "cannot be separated from economic development and interests" (Stackhouse et. al., 1995; Novak, 1990; 1996).

Finally, The World Development Report 2003, *Pathways to Sustainability*, outlines two guidelines for business. The first involves the design of innovative institutional approaches, for example creating think-and-do tanks and enhancing capacity building in developing worlds through research and development. A second area is the implementation of national and international Codes of Conduct, which facilitate and foster economic, environmental and social growth.

Each of these models, paradigms, practices and guidelines are a response to the environmental movement in its broadest context. The next section provides examples in business, selected for their work that integrates the trends and ethical practices of human rights, sustainability and healthy societies.

CSR in Action

Dupont, ABB, Proctor & Gamble and Baxter International

The Conference Board cites these four global companies as recognized sustainability leaders (Armstrong and Bennett, 2001). All firms adhere to the following tenets: sustainable development as the most viable course for multinational businesses; virtually all aspects of corporate operations designed toward sustainability; and transparency in reporting. The differences in focus across industries shows there is not "one right way" to define operational practices of sustainable development. Dupont's focus is on social and economic growth while reducing to zero the depletion of natural resources through its energy, emissions and safety programs. ABB (Asea Brown Boveri, Ltd.), a utility, energy and manufacturing company, has divested many of its traditional energy holdings and is working toward alternative energy production. Baxter International, a leader in bioscience and medication delivery, focuses on a triple-bottom line of accountability, ethical behavior, eco-efficiency and NGO involvement. Proctor and Gamble focuses on water, health and hygiene for all people, particularly those in lesser-developed nations.

The Mondragon Cooperatives of Spain

The genesis of the Mondragon Cooperatives occurred in 1941 when Father Hose Maria Arizmediarrieta incorporated Catholic social teaching with its technical curriculum. Today Cooperatives are involved in manufacturing, retail and wholesale food business catering with 100 banks that offer full service insurance including social security and health benefits. Mondragon is often cited as the premier example of democracy in the workplace with its attention to economic development, helping people reach their full potential, focus on the common good and enhancing human dignity. (See http://www.justpeace.org/mondragon for details).

South Shore Bank

As a grassroots enterprise, South Shore Bank in Chicago, Illinois provided residential mortgages and small business loans to an indigent African-American neighborhood and organized initiatives in commercial development and housing rehabilitation. Through these services, the bank was able to help finance and redevelop the neighborhood's infrastructure by funding 30 percent of the residential apartments. (See Brecher and Costello, 1994 for details).

Curitiba

Curitiba is a southeastern city in Brazil whose 2.5 million population quadrupled in the past two decades. Private companies in partnership with local communities instituted hundreds of multipurpose, "cheap, fast, simple, home-grown, people-centered initiatives" rather than the typical model of a few economic mega-projects. The city is an example of applied natural capitalism concepts: an integrated design process, strong public and business participation, and a widely shared public vision orchestrated under the Governor's leadership. (See Hawken et.al., 2003 for details).

Enviro-Capitalists / Nature's Entrepreneurs

Enviro-capitalists attract venture capital and contract with private landowners to hire labor and develop market product for profit, or not. Enviro-captialists view private solutions as part of the effort to manage and conserve natural resources and as one alternative to government regulation of market demand for environmental protection. (See Property and Environmental Research Center at www.perc.org for details).

Implications: Business Roles and Challenges

The best practice ethics of CSR emerged within the context of environmentalism and environmental ethics. The scientific, political and ethical questions that shaped the environmental movement became the same provocations for business. Analysis of CSR yields four challenges, and their corresponding shift in thinking and practice, that are shaping the future role of business.

Challenge One/ Comprehensive Planning: The business community faces increasing demands across a number of areas: globalization, shorter product life-cycles, information technology that alters time perspective, overcapacity, complex regulations, currency volatility and changing governmental policies (Drucker, 2000; Hamel, 2000; Korten, 2001; Hawken et.al., 2003; Kelly, 2002). Shift: Typically, government and business avoid integrating policies related to the environment and society because the timeframes are distant and not measurable. Today, there are continuous efforts to engage a long-term perspective responsible to current events while complementing future events.

Challenge Two/ Integrating Social Dynamics: "Globalization from below" or the race to the bottom generated by a global corporate environment impacts economic, social and environmental concerns (Brecher and Costello, 1994; World Bank, 2003; Panayotou, 2000; Zarsky, 1991.) Shift: The emerging common interests of "shared pain, and evolving global norms of human rights, economic justice and environmental sustainability" (Assemblee des eveques du Quebec, 2001) have led to identifying alternatives to the predominant economic corporate agenda toward a global human agenda.

Challenge Three / Regulations: Formal regulations are unable to keep pace with current pressure from communities, customers, shareholders and employers on environmental issues leaving industry to voluntarily self-regulate (Panayotou, 2000). Shift: The growing public environmental awareness and rapidly spreading information about industry's environmental performance are helping give rise to a global environmental ethic (Koehn, 2001).

Challenge Four / Cross-Sector Alliances: All activities and their effects have typically been addressed by compartmentalizing across sectors of energy, trade, and agriculture within broad areas of environmental, economic and social domains. Shift: Global crises have captured public concern or at least public attention with its corresponding understanding that the crisis of energy, trade and agriculture are connected and require a cross-sector approach for resolution (Assemblee des eveques du Quebec, 2001).

Each challenge culminates into a corresponding shift in thinking that requires new or different mental models. The significant opportunity for CSR, as presented in the best practices, is "identifying the true nature of man, corporations and of society as a whole" (Mele and Sison, 1993). How will business incorporate eco-models into operational practices that value natural and human capital along with financial and manufacturing capital (Hawken et.al., 2003)? How will those in business integrate the role of human relationship to natural systems (Korten, 2001)? Businesses, and society in general, have yet to answer these questions satisfactorily, although current research suggests the shift in thinking is occurring.

Conclusion

This paper introduces trends and best practice ethics that comprise corporate social responsibility. Several model guidelines exist that integrate human rights, sustainability and healthy societies and serve as frameworks for business. How business defines CSR is a dynamic process, as highlighted in the eight examples. Future opportunity for business, at a minimum, is to integrate practices certain to shape current and future agendas on human rights, sustainable development and healthy societies. At an ambitious level, business can be the leader by initiating new innovative institutions comprised of efforts between the government, the private sector and society-at-large. Ultimately, the work of CSR offers a deeper call and a calling to deep change.

References

Amick, B., S. Levine and A. Tarlov: 1995, *Society and Health*, Oxford University Press, NY.

Annas, G.: 1998, *Some Choice: Law, Medicine and The Market*, Oxford University Press, NY.

Armstrong, M. and C. Bennett: 2001, *The Road to Sustainability: Business' First Steps*, The Conference Board, NY.

Assemblee des eveques du Quebec, *Cry of the Earth, Cry of the Poor*, Message of May 1, 2001. www.eveques.qc.ca

Bakan, J: 2004, *The Corporation*, Constable, London.

Beauchamp, D. and B. Steinbock: 1999, *New Ethics for the Public's Health*, Oxford University Press, NY.

Blaine, D., E. Brunne and R. Wilkinson: 1996, *Health and Social Organization: Towards a Health Policy for the 21st Century*, Routledge, London.

Brecher, J. and T. Costello: 1994, *Global Village or Global Pillage: Economic Reconstruction from the Bottom Up,* South End Press, MA.

Callahan, D.: 1998, *False Hopes: Why America's Quest for Perfect Health Is A Recipe for Failure,* Simon & Schuster, NY.

Centesimus Annus: On the Hundredth Anniversary of Rerum Novarum, John Paul II: 1990, United States Catholic Conference, Washington, D.C.

Connor, T.: 2001, *Still Waiting for Nike To Do It*, Global Exchange, CA.

Donaldson T. and T. Dunfee: 1999, *Ties That Bind: A Social Contracts Approach to Business,* Harvard Business School Press, MA.

Drucker, P.: 2000, *Management Challenges of the 21st Century,* JosseyBass, NY.

Evans, R.G.: 1994, *Why Are Some People Healthy and Others Not? The Determinants of Health of Population,* Aldine de Gruyter, NY.

Freeman, B. 2001: 'Corporate Responsibility and Human Rights,' http://www.globaldimesnions.net

French, P.: 1979, 'The Corporation as a Moral Person', *American Philosophical Quarterly*, **16**, 207-215.

Fukuyama, F.: 2002, *Our Postmodern Future: Consequences of the Biotechnology Revolution,* FSG, NY.

Goodpaster, K.: 1982, 'Morality and Organizations', In Donaldson, T. and P. Werhane (Eds.), *Ethical Issues in Business (2nd Ed.),* Englewood Cliffs, NJ., 137-145.

Gunther, M.: 2004, 'Bottom Line: Do The Right Thing', Houston Chronicle, November 21, E4.

Hamel, G.: 2000, *Leading the Revolution: How To Thrive in Turbulent Times by Making Innovation A Way of Life,* Harvard University Press, MA.

Hammer, M. and J. Champy: 1993, *Reengineering the Corporation: A Manifesto for Business Revolution*, Harper-Business, NY.

Hanson, M.: 2001, *Claiming Power Over Life: Religion and Biotechnology Policy*, Georgetown University Press, Washington D.C.

Harrison, J. and E. Freeman: 1999, 'Stakeholders, Social Responsibility, and Performance: Empirical Evidence and Theoretical Perspectives', *Academy of Management Journal,* **42**, October, 479.

Hawken, P., A. Lovins and L. Lovins: 2003, *Creating the Next Industrial Revolution: Natural Capitalism,* Rocky Mountain Institute, CO.

Heath, E.: 2002, *Morality and the Market: Ethics and Virtue in the Conduct of Business,* McGraw Hill, NY.

Hoffman, M.: 2002, 'Business and Environmental Ethics', In Heath, E. (Ed.) *Morality and the Markets: Ethics and Virtue in the Conduct of Business*, McGraw-Hill, MA., 667-673.

Jennings, M.: 1999, 'Stakeholder Theory: Letting Anyone Who's Interested Run the Business—No Investment Required', In Koehn, D. (Ed.) Corporate Governance: Ethics Across the Board, Center for Business Ethics, University of St. Thomas, Houston, Texas, 57-70.

Kavanaugh, J.: 2001, *Who Count as Persons? Human Identity and the Ethics of Killing',* Georgetown University Press, Washington D.C.

Keeley, M.: 1988, A *Social Contract Theory of Organizations,* Notre Dame University Press, IN.

Kelly, M.: 2002, *The Divine Right of Capital,* Berrett-Koehler, VT.

Koehn, D.: 2001, *Local Insights, Global Ethics*, Rodopi.

Kolarik, W.J.: 2000, *Creating Quality: Process Design for Results*, McGraw Hill, NY.

Korten, D.: 2001, *When Corporations Rule The World*, Berrett-Koehler, CA.

Lebacqz, K.: 1987, 'Bioethics: Some Challenges from a Liberation Perspective', In Lammers, S. and A. Verhey (Eds.) *On Moral Medicine: Theological Perspectives in Medical Ethics,* Eerdmans, MI., pp. 64-69.

Lippman, A.: 1991, 'Prenatal Genetic Testing and Screening: Constructing Needs and Reinforcing Inequities', *American Journal of Law and Medicine*, XVII, 19-36, 44-49.

MacIntyre, S.: 1994, 'Understanding the Social Patterning of Health: The Role of the Social Sciences', *Journal of Public Health Medicine*, **16**, 53.

Marmot, M., M. Bobak, and D. Smith: 1995, 'Explanations for Social Inequalities in Health', In Amick, B., S. Levine and A. Tarlov (Eds.): 1995 *Society and Health,* University Press, NY.

Marsden, C.: 2000, 'The New Corporate Citizenship of Big Business: Part of the Solution to Sustainability?' *Business and Society Review*, 105 (Spring), 9-25.

Matten, D., A. Crane and W. Chapple: 2003, 'Behind the Mask: Revealing the True Face of Corporate Citizenship', *Journal of Business Ethics*, **45**, 109-120.

May, L.: 1987, *The Morality of Groups*, Notre Dame University Press, IN.

McEwen, B.S. and H. Schmeck: 1994, *The Hostage Brain,* Rockefeller University Press, NY.

Mele, D.: 2002: 'A Humanistic Framework of the Corporation of the 21st Century', Paper presented for the Center for Business Ethics/University of St. Thomas, Houston TX.

_______ and A. Sison: 1993, 'Corporations and the Social Contract: A Reply to Professor Thomas Donaldson', IESE, University of Navarra, Spain.

Mitroff, I. and E. Denton: 1999, *A Spiritual Audit of Corporate America*, Josses-Bass, CA.

Naess, A.: 1998, 'Identification as a Source of Deep Ecological Attitudes', In Tobias, M. (Ed.) *Deep Ecology,* Avant Books, CA., 266.

Novak, M.: 1990, *Toward a Theology of the Corporation,* University Press of America, MD.

_____ 1996, *Business as Calling,* The Free Press, NY.

Panayotou, T.: 2000, 'Globalization and Environment', CID Working Paper No. 53, July. http://www.cid.harvard.edu

Pellegrino, E. and A. Faden: 1999, *Jewish and Catholic Bioethics: An Ecumenical Dialogue*, Georgetown University Press, Washington, D.C.

Pezzey, J.: 1989, 'Economic Analysis of Sustainable Growth and Sustainable Development', World Bank Environment Department Working Paper 15, Washington D.C.

Phillips, M.: 1992, 'Corporate Moral Personhood and Three Conceptions of the Corporation', *Business Ethics Quarterly*, 1992.

Renesch, J.: 2000, *Getting to the Better Future: A Matter of Conscious Choosing,* New Business Books, CA.

Seeman, T.E. and B. McEwen: 1996, 'Impact of Social Environment Characteristics on Neuroendocrinology', *Psychological. Medicine*, **58**, 459.

Simms, M: 2004, 'Catholic Insight on Workplace Human Rights and Corporate Humanism', In Miller, P.J. and R. Fossey (Eds.), *Mapping the Catholic Cultural Landscape*, Rowman & Littlefield, NY., 223-239.

Stackhouse, M., D. McMCann, S. Roels, and P. Williams: 1995, *On Moral Business: Classical and Contemporary Research for Ethics in Economic Life,* Eerdmans, MI.

'The Non-governmental Order: Will NGOs Democratise, or Merely Disrupt, Global Governance?': 1999, *The Economist* (December 11), 17.

Turner, L.: 1997, 'Bioethics, Public Health and Firearm-Related Violence: Missing Links Between Bioethics and Public Health', *Journal of Law, Medicine and Ethics*, **25**, No. 1, 42-48.

United Kingdom Strategy for Sustainable Development, definition as cited in Armstrong, M. and C. Bennett: 2001, *The Road to Sustainability: Business' First Steps*, The Conference Board, NY., 8.

United Nations Charter on Human Rights Office of Business and Human Rights: A Progress Report, Office of the High Commissioner for Human Rights, 2001.

Velasquez, M.: 1983, ' Why Corporations Are Not Responsible for Anything They Do', *Business and Professional Ethics Journal*, **2**, 1-18.

Werhane, P.: 1995, *Persons, Rights and Corporations*, Prentice-Hall, NJ.

Wilkinson, R.G.: 1986, *Class and Health,* Tavistock Publications. London.

World Bank: 2003, *World Development Report: Sustainable Development in a Dynamic World: Transforming Institutions, Growth and Quality of Life.*

Zarsky, L.: 1991, 'Trade Environment Linkages and Ecologically Sustainable Development', Report to Department of Arts, Sports, Environment, Tourism and Territories, Environmental Strategy Branch, Australia, October.

Chapter 2: CSE Illusion versus Reality

Illusion sersus Reality: Corporate Social Responsibility in the Global Economy

Gerald David Flint, Texas A&M, United States of America

Gregory R. Berry, Central Connecticut State, United States of America

Abstract: Corporate social responsibility has evolved from being of peripheral interest to practitioners and scholars to being an accepted mainstream field of study. CSR now has dedicated Divisions in the Academy of Management (SIM and ONE), dedicated Journals such as "Journal of Corporate Citizenship" and "Organization and Environment", and a constant stream of articles in other academic journals. The study of CSR has benefit for both corporations and society, and any field that attempts to enhance communities, society, or the common good must be lauded; however, this field has taken a path divorced from the overwhelming economic realities of global capitalism. An assumption that economic constraints and pressures have little effect on corporate decision-making and behavior seems to be common in the CSR literature. Too often we read of corporate decision-makers who undertake environmental or social behaviors because it is "the-right-thing-to-do" as though they were operating in a vacuum devoid of economic constraints. This paper argues that at least four economic realities and forces dominate all CSR decisions, regardless of the social patina of good intentions and social responsibility glossed over these decisions. These economic "realities" dominate and constrain all decisions regarding environmental, social, and political behavior, regardless of corporate desire or awareness. The study of CSR requires grounding in economic realities if the field is to have increased influence and power in developing a more sustainable global commons.

Introduction

Most members of North American society agree that apple pie is worthy of universal support, ignoring for the moment peripheral consequences such as the devastating effects of piecrust on cholesterol levels and health. Similarly, the value of corporate social responsibility (CSR) is also almost universally acclaimed as enhancing community and the well-being of both business and society. CSR is generally defined as discretionary corporate behaviour going beyond the demands of law and regulation and creating benefit for citizens or society generally (Buchholz, 1991). What could possibly be wrong with corporate policies that encourage corporate charity, or careful attention to environmental protection, or attempts to achieve sustainable development? As with apple pie resulting in increased cholesterol levels, however, there is also a dark side to CSR.

We need to look under the gloss of CSR to see the dark side. Two realities seem inescapable. First, corporations that spend *what-should-have-been* investor profit on social goods are simply dishonest; these monies do not belong to the corporation. Managers of public companies are rarely owners but are more often employees whose essential function is to maximize the long-term value of the owners' assets. Donating money to a children's playground is admirable, as long as it is your own money being donated. However, when XYZ Corporation donates part of an investor's dividend to that same playground, without the investor's permission, then under common understanding of property rights, XYZ Corporation has stolen from the investor. Therefore, CSR can be harmful to the corporate investor, and perhaps even encourages unethical conduct on the part of corporate executives and senior managers (Friedman, 1962).

Second, CSR often ignores the demands of competitive necessity. If XYZ Corporation spends funds on community playgrounds, nature habitats, or other so-called socially responsible ventures, these costs of undertaking CSR are passed along to the consumer via higher prices, unless diverted from investor dividends, as noted above. In a globally competitive world, in an extreme case, these added costs may be the difference between having a successful business or a failing business. CSR can diminish corporate financial success, thus damaging the corporation, the community, the employees of the corporation, and society.

Given that corporate executives are typically very astute, these *dark side* consequences of CSR must be obvious to them, yet CSR is still considered by many activists, politicians, and management theorists as proper behaviour for corporations regardless of the consequences. What is the real meaning of CSR? Is CSR perhaps just a drain on social capital? Is CSR perhaps just a collection of socially or politically correct policies, smacking of tokenism? Do corporations with commitments to CSR have a genuine concern in giving back to the community, or are these behaviours the equivalent of smoke and mirrors, masking the underlying economic agenda?

What is CSR?

CSR is founded on benevolence, going beyond the expectation of law and regulation to undertake discretionary behaviours. Adam Smith (1904) advocates that benevolence is not necessary to advance the public interest, and further, he notes that benevolence is often in short supply whereas self-interest is not. Smith would likely argue that CSR is completely irrelevant, and that rational, calculating self-interest is all that is required for a firm to worry about its reputation for honesty, or honouring agreements, or respecting the community. The rational firm considers short-term financial sacrifices today for the sake of gains tomorrow, or five years from now. The self-interested firm also makes a good neighbour. In Smith's and Friedman's world the patina of social responsibility is unneeded, and the self interested firm will still go beyond the demands of law and regulation in considering both social and political pressures.

At one end of the broad span of CSR lie corporate policies that any well-run company likely has in place. For example, not wasting resources and cutting down on pollution is beneficial for the firm, the natural environment, and the community that may otherwise be damaged by the negative externalities of corporate practice. At the other end of the range are large expenditures of time and resources on discretionary charitable activities or spending on environmental beautification projects far beyond what regulators demand. These activities may have an economic payback in terms of public relations or developing the perception of distinctive competencies, but the need to clothe these behaviours as CSR instead of just wise economic management seems disingenuous if not flat-out dishonest. Yet, some define CSR as encouraging corporate responsibilities beyond the parameters of short-term and firm-specific economic benefit (Buchholz, 1991), which brings us back to the two realities already discussed, namely that CSR is potentially harmful to both investors and to the very survival of the corporation.

Different stakeholders use different terminology in discussing CSR. CSR is shorthand for suggesting that the wise company acknowledges that profit is not everything (although this may not be true to investors), and profit should not be pursued relentlessly even at the expense of damage to the environment and infringements of the rights of workers and other stakeholders. Advocates of CSR frequently offer homilies about responsible behaviour being good business, or even quasi-economic arguments about responsible behaviour leading to improved societal environments and, therefore, to long-term business viability. A core aspect of the theory of CSR is that businesses need to take account of other interested parties if they expect long-term success. Businesses must satisfy their customers, get on with their suppliers, motivate their workers, and placate the community as a minimum if they expect sustainable profits. These different stakeholders are perhaps worthy of attention and will negatively exercise their influence if ignored, but *taking account of* is not the same as *being accountable to*.

Is Corporate Social Responsibility Related to Stakeholder Theory?

The challenge for corporate executives and others in running their businesses is balancing and attempting to satisfy demands from various stakeholders (Calton and Kurland, 1996; Harrison and Freeman, 1999; Mitchell, Agle and Wood, 1997). The classic definition of a stakeholder is "any group or individual who can affect or is affected by the achievement of the organization's objectives" (Freeman, 1984: 46). Primary corporate stakeholders are usually identified as the community, owners, employees, customers, and suppliers (Mitchell, Agle and Wood, 1997; Rowley, 1997; Wartick and Cochran, 1985; Logsdon, Wood and Benson, 2000), and are defined as those "without whose continuing participation the corporation cannot survive" (Clarkson, 1995: 107). Secondary stakeholders may include regulators, lobbyists, activist groups, the media, and many others. Some researchers also include society at large as a stakeholder (Carroll, 1991), including, specifically, the natural environment.

Stakeholder theory suggests that corporate bodies should protect their autonomy by not focusing exclusively on the profit demands of their stockholders (Clarkson, 1998). The stockholder is only one of the primary stakeholders. Stakeholder theory has a definite managerial focus and describes the relationship firms have with various stakeholders. It also recommends attitudes, structures and practices to meet the needs and expectations of all stakeholders (Donaldson and Preston, 1995). Thus, stakeholders are not only affected by corporate practice, but influence corporate practice. This fact is crucial because even non-economic stakeholders can influence the success or failure of corporate strategies. In summary, stakeholder theory encourages a broad social and political perspective on corporate behaviour (Pichardo, 1997).

Stakeholder management is complex, partly because the corporation does not control who its stakeholders are, and partly because even the most *aware* manager may have difficulty in paying attention to or satisfying the interests of multiple stakeholders (Berry, 2003). Firms can often manage their relationships with stakeholders, but can only rarely manage the stakeholders themselves (Andriof and Waddock, 2002). Stakeholder interests are fluid because social, cultural, and political environments are constantly changing (Davenport, 2000), and as context changes the relevant stakeholders and their demands change as well (Beaulieu and Pasquero, 2002). Fortunately, unanimous stakeholder endorsement of corporate behaviour is not required to achieve organizational effectiveness (Ashford and Gibbs, 1990; Elsbach and Sutton, 1992), so organizations can be selective regarding which stakeholders they attempt to satisfy (Ogden, 1999; Reich, 1998). Stakeholder theory is relevant to CSR because social issues are constructed by the organization in relationship with selected stakeholders (Beaulieu and Pasquero, 2002), so it is required that corporate responses are formulated in social, political, and economic terms. CSR is focused on social and political forces, at least in public discussion, but economic forces underlie both social and political influences. The paradox for many corporations is that they are compelled to satisfy an increasing number of social and political stakeholders, but survival is still dependent on satisfying economic stakeholders (Berry, 2004).

Because companies operate in a climate of public opinion, they must take into account how they are perceived if they expect sustainable success and profitability. Social and political forces often evolve into economic costs for the firm, so CSR can be viewed as a means of balancing the economic needs of the firm against external forces and demands, which may or may not be directly economic or competitive. A balance among economic, political, and social forces and behaviours is required if firms expect long-term success because, otherwise, company autonomy will be thwarted by ongoing government and regulatory constraints which usually evolve from ignored social or political forces. This could be considered a "mutuality" of practice and interests between business and society, where societal investment in infrastructure supports corporate health in exchange for employment and taxation opportunities (Waddock and Smith, 2000) and responsible corporate behaviour.

Is Environmental Management a Competitive Substitute for CSR?

Environmental management should be viewed as an important part of CSR because it is directly concerned with managing a firm's wider influence and effects on society (Andriof and Waddock, 2002), especially the firm's negative externalities of production. Regulatory systems and permitting processes evolve through negotiation and influence between government, lobbyists, political campaign contributors, corporations, and other stakeholders (Orssatto and Clegg, 1999). The corporation that improves its environmental performance may be undertaking CSR behaviours as part of a defensive stance to avoid fines or other economic costs resulting from regulatory violations. Voluntary environmental behaviour (the corporation choosing its own timelines and methods) sometimes sets standards that less proactive competitors are forced to achieve under regulated timelines and conditions, creating a competitive cost advantage for the proactive firms in some instances (Berry, 2000).

Environmental management can be viewed as little more than yet another strategy to create a competitive advantage. The core of this strategy is the belief that organizations can reduce costs by incorporating environmental concerns into the decision-making process (Welford, 1996). The direct benefits of pollution elimination through production process improvements, for example, include lower cost for pollution control equipment and personnel, improved community relationships, and, possibly, relief from government regulation. Other benefits may include improved product quality, improved materials efficiency, improved pressure-group relations and media coverage, reduced risk exposure (therefore lower insurance premiums and financing rates), and increased staff commitment (Bhargava and Welford, 1996). Adam Smith (1904) would approve of this self-interested behaviour, but he would not call it CSR. Efficiency in environmental spending and achieving required environmental performance for the lowest possible cost is a desirable goal for any prudent manager as greater efficiency translates into less waste which in turn results in more profit.

It may be obvious that corporate executives make economically constrained choices (Henriques and Sandorsky, 1999; Hrebeniak and Joyce, 1985; Marcus, 1988) in an attempt to satisfy their critical stakeholders, but wise executives also make efforts to mitigate anticipated future consequences of regulation or negative public opinion on the firm. In such instances, CSR is no more than prudent economic management being sold to the government and society under the guise of public concern and benevolence.

Is Government Necessary for CSR and Civil Society?

There is broad consensus in North American society that government is a necessary partner for business and society in developing stable, healthy market systems. There is vigorous debate across the political landscape regarding the extent of just how much government control and influence is *sufficient*, with the debate ranging from those who support unfettered corporate freedom, to those who support considerably more government control. An historical panorama of the development of business-government relationships during the 20th century has been presented well by Yergin and Stanislaw (2002). Friedman and Friedman (2002), Schumpeter (1976), and von Hayek (1994) among others argue for a free marketplace, while Olson (1971) provides a moderating view explaining why the free marketplace cannot always provide adequately for the needs of society. Olsen (1971) justifies the existence and role of government and its laws from a market failure perspective.

Regardless of one's position on the proper extent of government influence and control over the marketplace, consensus is possible regarding the necessity of at least some government and law. Government needs sufficient coercive power to establish and enforce the rules of the marketplace. Property rights must be defined and enforced. Public goods that will not be produced by private means must be supplied via the government, which coercively taxes the marketplace participants and directs resources toward the provision of the goods. Problematic negative and positive externalities arising from specific market transactions require compensation or remuneration through governmental redistribution of the resources surrounding those specific transactions. These and other governmental roles maintain the viability of the marketplace and promote efficient market outcomes by which participants have the potential to maximize their self-interests. Consequently, most market participants accept government influence. However, CSR goes beyond the requirements established by governments and beyond the minimum boundary of the law.

What Prompts CSR beyond the Boundary of Law?

Participants in the marketplace must meet government regulations, yet these standards only set a boundary condition that defines the minimum expectation. The law identifies what is forbidden and detrimental to efficient market operations, and encourages and rewards certain behaviours to improve conditions for the players within a market. Unless the consequences for ignoring these legally defined boundaries are salient they risk being ignored. The law is like a series of highway signs conveying pieces of information as the players move in relationship to the signs; yet, the process of driving on the highway is not entirely defined by those signs, nor are the signs guaranteed to be sufficiently important to a particular driver to demand attention, assuming they are visible in the first place. These signs are useful and necessary to the conduct of business in the marketplace, but there are at least four reasons why market participants seeking to act as good corporate citizens in society must look beyond the boundary of the law in order to achieve their goals. These actions are often *sold* as CSR efforts but are more realistically motivated by prudent economic management of market participants.

The first reason why corporations must look beyond the boundary of law is that the law only sets minimum standards for organizations. Legality should not be mistaken as the equivalent of societal expectations that are deemed to be fair, just, and ethical. Societal expectations change over time and are often at odds with laws established under different conditions. Laws may only focus on egregious circumstances, which vary from societal norms and may fail to address the subtle interpretations of actions and decisions by market participants. These may be adequate in some areas, but inadequate in others, or may not capture the complex nature of various circumstances within formalized statements and definitions. It is dangerous for market participants to assume that compliance with the law or regulation automatically captures socictal norms.

Recent developments in the tobacco industry provide an example of this first condition. Even though tobacco is a legal product, the industry has been subject to intense societal and political pressure to change its business methods. Although several illegal behaviours found via judicial cases have been exercised, the tobacco industry has been affected greatly by media campaigns challenging the industry's products and practices. Companies engaged in the industry are compelled to go beyond the boundary set by the law in order to respond to the societal and political pressures.

The second reason why corporations must look beyond the boundary of law is that market participants can craft and manipulate laws and the judicial system in ways that violate societal norms regarding concepts of fairness, justice, and ethicality. In essence, the boundary of the law or regulation can be moved in order to accommodate the self-interests of various players who can exert influence in the political system. Some corporations spend millions of dollars on lobbyists or politically directed activities in an obvious effort to do exactly this. It is possible that the law even promotes and rewards behaviours that are deemed unethical or against the broad public interest. In some cases, the law is not a boundary condition that prevents behaviour unacceptable in the market, but encourages or allows unacceptable behaviour in the market.

For an example of this second condition, consider how certain industries in the United States have successfully imposed extra costs upon consumers through manipulation of the law. This has been true in the agricultural sector of the U.S. economy for decades with particularly notable costs imposed upon the consumers of sugar, tobacco, corn, and wheat. This has also been true more recently during the Bush presidency in regard to the steel industry and its successful lobbying for protective tariffs (The Economist, 2002). The textile industry has also benefited from the Multi-Fiber Arrangement in the international market (Xu, 1997). These examples are based on the imposition of costs upon consumers through the law. There are few arguments from either a teleological or deontological perspective supporting the imposition of costs via the law upon a set of consumers in order to benefit producers. In these cases, the law is used as an instrument to blunt competition and open strategic directions to producers instead of serving as a boundary that governs market behaviours for the benefit of consumers. A related example may be found in environmental regulation, where legal levels of pollution far exceed pollution levels considered safe by community members or other interested stakeholders (Beamish, 2001). Many believe that government and industry share an interest in growth and development regardless of the negative externalities imposed on citizens or communities (Gould, 1994). If this is the case, what may be portrayed as CSR could actually be manoeuvring by firms to shift legal boundaries in pursuit of market advantages.

The third reason why corporations must look beyond the boundaries of law is because of ongoing market globalization. Legal boundaries that must be considered and understood by market participants are increasingly expanding, sometimes overlapping and conflicting, as they reflect the realities of conducting business across international borders. Also, there is no guarantee in some international markets that the legal boundaries (or lack of legal boundaries) of those markets encompass what the societal norms for those markets actually are, domestically or internationally. The societal norms in some foreign markets may be fundamentally different from a business' home market norms, and the laws in that foreign market may not adequately guide the business in its efforts to understand that fundamental difference. Consequently, what may be construed as CSR in these circumstances may actually be an attempt to harmonize conflicting stakeholder and governmental expectations across legal jurisdictions.

As an example of this third condition the Nike Company experienced ill effects on sales and reputation by not realizing this relationship between the law and the market. Nike was pilloried in the North American and European press for its acceptance of factory working conditions in developing nations that were far different than conditions in the United States. While conditions in the supplier factories utilized by Nike conformed to or surpassed local standards for safety, hours, and wages, the contrast between those local standards and U.S. standards allowed the company to be targeted by anti-globalization activists and others seeking to tarnish Nike's image in the U.S. market. In response, Nike has implemented several programs to monitor and respond to critical issues in a socially responsible manner (David, 2003).

The fourth reason why corporations must look beyond the boundaries of the law is because the law itself may become so complex and subject to interpretation that it becomes impossible for a company to be assured that its conduct is not in violation of the law. The United States tax code is an example of a body of laws that has become so complex that companies must regularly appeal for interpretations of the law in order to know whether or not their accounting methods and interpretations of what is taxable and non-taxable will be deemed acceptable to the U.S. Internal Revenue Service. Interpretations change over time, and what was accepted as legal under prior interpretation is sometimes considered illegal under the current interpretation. The failure of Enron was due, to some extent, to the exploitation of the various interpretations of accounting standards and the tax code that were acceptable in the 1990s in regard to the formation of special purpose entities and off-book accounting for those entities (Crawford and Fredericks, 2003). Companies must adjust their strategies and accounting standards to comply with new interpretations. Are companies liable for infractions of the tax code in the past, even though the practices were considered legal at the time of use? Consistently exceeding tax expectations may be little more than prudent management, yet is also an illustration of behaviour often *sold* as CSR. Similarly, the interpretation of environmental law often seems equally capricious, with different regions of the country interpreting EPA regulations in idiosyncratic ways, but again, the company seeking prudent economic management always exceeds current interpretation of the law or regulatory standard.

The future liability for the firm facing changing standards and laws is also a potential disaster regardless of CSR concerns. Although behaviours may be legal and meet regulatory standards today, at least in environment management, regulations typically become stricter as scientific knowledge and awareness increases. Non-proactive organizations may face huge liabilities as regulations become increasingly strict, and yesterday's legal behaviour evolves into today's lawsuit, as the asbestos industry is still discovering.

These four realities create serious problems and potential consequences for the corporation. Market participants must look beyond the law if they desire to fully conform to societal norms and operate as respected corporate citizens. The law outlines the minimum conditions for market transactions to conform to societal norms, but it is not a sufficient factor in fully achieving the norms of responsible corporate citizenship. In fact, for the reactive firm the law can actually provide signposts along the market highway that lead these firms into less than desirable business practice. Thus, prudent economic management should be understood as the dominating motivation for what is called CSR.

Is the Market Capable of Economic Self-regulation?

Market participants need to understand what the various stakeholders in a particular market actually value as the foundation of their operations, regardless of where they may operate. Absent the support of a coercive power that redirects resources toward a business, such as government bailouts of the airline industry for example, any business must provide and retain more value in a market than what it consumes, if it is to survive in the long term. Understanding the societal norms regarding fairness, justice, and ethicality is critical in the marketplace. A business that consistently and obviously flouts those societal norms will be perceived as either not presenting value to the market, or worse, to be removing value from the market. Competitors in a market where the government does not prevent or inhibit competition would seize the opportunity left available by such a failing business. Competitors would recognize that societal norms were being ignored and move to satisfy those norms in their operations, thus taking market share into their hands as consumers find more value in their alternative products and services. In short, the firm failing to meet societal norms over time would essentially take itself out of the marketplace.

The market is economically self-regulating in imposing conformity to effective corporate citizenship among firms that face competition. The self-regulating potential for the market increases when information about the conduct of business is readily available, as is increasingly the case given the information explosion of the past decade. Consumers who desire to know how products and services are created, in addition to the characteristics and quality of the products and services themselves, provide additional incentives to businesses to demonstrate their support for societal norms. The economic self-regulating nature of the market imposes conditions upon final products, services, and process operations of firms. Those conditions compel businesses to consider what societal values are and how to operate within those values. The law and the judicial system do not provide a full definition of those values.

What Business Conduct Defines CSR?

Because businesses are a part of the mix in which societal norms are realized, there is potential for the conduct of business to move those norms in certain directions to benefit the business. Corporations have well-documented abilities to influence public opinion or government agencies to their own advantage (Buttell, 1995; Yeager, 1987). The Enron debacle, for example, was at least in part caused by Enron's ability to influence and change the laws regarding energy deregulation. Therefore, the law is again highlighted as a less than sufficient means for businesses to determine where the social, political, and economic boundaries for market actions lie. If businesses can influence where the boundaries lie and law is a secondary outcome in society that attempts to reflect where the boundaries lie, business conduct may be moving boundaries faster than the law can respond through the institutions that serve to create and modify the law. Businesses with an ability to influence societal norms realize that the law may not respond quickly to their influence in society, and that reality may compel corporate leaders who profess concern with CSR to a greater degree of thoughtfulness and concern for the corporation regarding its behaviour. Uncertain future regulatory requirements may lead to CSR practices as the firm waits for the setting of definitive and final standards, especially as tomorrow's standard (with a change in government or regulatory rigor) might be easier than today's (Berry, 2000).

Wise managers recognize that social and political pressures translate into economic pressures and move to satisfy them. Although social and political pressures are just as real as economic pressures, they are more difficult to quantify. This haziness may allow greater corporate discretion in dealing with these pressures. Economic *realities* drive what is called CSR behaviour even though benevolent or socially and politically correct non-economic reasons may be given for these actions (Berry, 2004).

Corporations do more than required by law or regulation for economic reasons, yet they may *sell* these behaviours through public relations and spin. The honest firm admits to economic motives instead of claiming benevolent motives for CSR. The honest firm admits that CSR is merely a means to achieving and maintaining economic goals. It is an error to assume that profit seeking, as such, always fails to advance the public good, and that special efforts to give something back to society are always needed to redeem the company given its search for profit. Economic forces, including fear of future regulation, fear of financial liability for poor performance, and the search for competitive advantage drive most CSR policies and procedures (Berry 2004). CSR behaviours, although apparently beneficial to society, are often used as little more than marketing or public relations tools to assist the firm by providing politically and socially *correct* stories to use when explaining behaviours undertaken for a variety of reasons (Berry, 2000).

Is CSR a Necessary Response to Government Imperfections?

In a perfect world, proper guardians of the public interest are governments, which are accountable to all citizens. It is the job of elected politicians to set goals for regulators, deal with negative externalities, mediate among different interests, attend to the demands of social justice, provide public goods and collect the taxes to pay for them, establish collective priorities where that is necessary and appropriate, and organize resources accordingly. Managers, acting in their professional capacity ought not to concern themselves with the public good because they are not competent to do it, they lack the democratic credentials for it, and their day jobs should leave them no time to think about it.

However, given the failure of government, corporate citizenship that relies solely upon the definitions contained within a set of laws to guide judgments of what is fair, just, and ethical is a potential liability to the future performance of market participants. The law may be insufficient to define societal norms necessary to the prudent management of business. Public policy may be manipulated to allow less than desirable business behaviour. The law across international boundaries may be conflicting or exhibiting widely varying standards. Legal requirements or regulation may be overly complex and subject to evolving re-interpretation, thus creating uncertainty for the conduct of business. The conduct of business that relies upon finding and satisfying societal values may, in and of itself, be more reliable as a regulator of what is considered to be good corporate citizenship than the law's boundaries. The potential influence of some business conduct upon societal values and norms may require some businesses to more carefully consider their conduct in regard to good corporate citizenship because the law may be simply unable to adequately adjust to that influence in a timely manner.

The prudent management of firms thus responds to government imperfections with actions that are deemed to be CSR. Regardless of the motivations for those actions, the CSR label provides a means to categorize the attempts of firms to wisely and prudently maximize economic returns using actions that surpass the boundaries and imperatives of laws and regulations.

Conclusion

The ambiguous nature of CSR with its conflicting definitions and confused use of the CSR label is understandable. CSR is a fluid concept that covers responses to stakeholder pressures, strategic positioning in the market, compensating for government imperfections, adapting to changing societal norms, and a fundamental pursuit of profitability. Given the broad range of activities covered by the CSR label, one can question its usefulness. However, the CSR term is still not irrelevant because it suggests business actions that are not compelled by the coercive power of governments or direct competitive pressures. CSR indicates that a decision is being made to advance the interests of a firm in the context of stakeholder, societal, or competitive pressures that are not related to traditional market actions such as price, quality, service, or other aspects of direct market competition. One could argue that the CSR label is simply *spin* upon what is essentially a form of competition and should be dropped out of concern for honesty. But, one could also argue that using the CSR label prompts thought by managers regarding the broader social, political and economic pressures they face, prompting behaviour beyond what is legally prescribed. If the CSR label does indeed prompt managerial thought regarding what behaviours result in effective and profitable corporate citizenship, then one may accept its ambiguous definition and construct as a necessary, though sometimes perplexing aspect of its usefulness.

References

Andriof, J., and Waddock, S. 2002. Unfolding stakeholder engagement. In J. Andriof, S. Waddock, B. Husted, and S.S. Rahman (Eds.) *Unfolding Stakeholder Thinking: Theory, Responsibility, and Engagement*. Sheffield, UK: Greenleaf Publishing: 19-42.

Ashford, B.E., and Gibbs, B.W. 1990. The double-edge of organizational legitimation. *Organizational Science*, 1(2): 177-194.

Beamish, T.D. 2001. Environmental hazard and institutional betrayal. *Organization and Environment*, Vol. 14, No. 1: 5-33.

Beaulieu, S., and Pasquero, J. 2002. Reintroducing stakeholder dynamics in stakeholder thinking. In J. Andriof, S. Waddock, B. Husted, and S.S. Rahman (Eds.) *Unfolding Stakeholder Thinking: Theory, Responsibility, and Engagement*. Sheffield, UK: Greenleaf Publishing: 101-118.

Berry, G. R. 2000. Telling stories: Making sense of the environmental behaviour of chemical firms. *Journal of Management Inquiry*, Vol. 10 (1): 58 – 73.

Berry, G.R. 2003. Organizing against multinational corporate power in Cancer Alley: The activist community as primary stakeholder. *Organization and Environment*, Vol. 16 (1): 3-33.

Berry, G.R. 2004. Environmental management: The selling of corporate culture. *Journal of Corporate Citizenship*, Vol. 16 (Winter): 71-84.

Bhargava, S., and Welford, R. 1996. Corporate Strategy and the Environment: The Theory. In R. Welford (Ed.), *Corporate Environmental Management: Systems and Strategies*. p13-24. London, UK: Earthscan.

Buchholz, R.A. 1991. Corporate responsibility and the good society: From economics to ecology. *Business Horizons*, 34(4): 19-31.

Buttel, F.H. 1995. Environmental quality and the state: Some political-sociological observations on environmental regulation. *Research in Political Sociology*, 1: 167-188.

Calton, J.M. and Kurland, N.B. 1996. A theory of stakeholder enabling: Giving voice to an emerging postmodern praxis of organizational discourse. In D.MM. Boje, R.P. Gephart, Jr., and T.J. Thatchankary (eds.), *Postmodern management and organization theory*. Thousand Oaks, CA: Sage.

Carroll, A. B. 1991. The pyramid of corporate social responsibility: Toward the moral management of organizational stakeholders. *Business Horizons*, 34 (4): 39-48.

Clarkson, M. B. E. 1995. A stakeholder framework for analyzing and evaluating corporate social performance. *Academy of Management Review*, 20 (1): 92-117.

Clarkson, M. B. E. (ed.). 1998. *The Corporation and Its Stakeholders*. Toronto: University of Toronto Press.

Crawford, P.J., and Fredericks, E.H. 2003. Special purpose entities: Throwing the baby out with the bathwater? *Journal of Contemporary Business Practice*, Vol. 6 (2). http://gbr.pepperdine.edu/032/spe.html

Davenport, K. 2000. Corporate citizenship: A stakeholder approach for defining corporate social performance and identifying measures for assessing it. *Business and Society*, 39 (2): 210-219.

David, Fred R. 2003. *Strategic Management: Cases*. Upper Saddle River, NJ: Pearson Education, Inc.

Donaldson, T., and L. E. Preston. 1995. The stakeholder theory of the corporation: Concepts, evidence, and implications. *Academy of Management Review*, 20 (1): 65-91.

Elsbach, K.D., and Sutton, R.I. 1992. Acquiring organizational legitimacy through illegitimate actions: A marriage of institutional and impression management theories. *Academy of Management Journal*, 35: 699-738.

Freeman, R. 1984. *Stakeholder Management: A Stakeholder Approach*. New York: Basic Books.

Friedman, M. 1962. *Capitalism and Freedom*. Chicago: University of Chicago Press.

Gould, K.A. 1994. Legitimacy and growth in the balance: The role of the state in environmental remediation. *Industrial and Environmental Crisis Quarterly*, Vol. 8: 237-256.

Harrison, J.S., and Freeman, R.E. 1999. Stakeholders, social responsibility and performance: Empirical evidence and theoretical perspectives. *Academy of Management Journal*, 42(5): 479-487.

Henriques, I., and Sandorsky, P. 1999. The relationship between environmental commitment and managerial perceptions of stakeholder importance. *Academy of Management Journal*, 42(1): 87-99.

Hrebeniak, L., and Joyce, W. 1985. Organizational adaptation: Strategic choice and environmental determinism. *Administrative Science Quarterly*, 31: 336-349.

Logsden, J.M., Wood, D.J., and Benson, L.E. 2000. *Research in stakeholder theory: The Sloan Foundation minigrant project*. Toronto: The Clarkson Centre for Business Ethics.

Marcus, A. 1988. Responses to externally induced innovation: The effects on organizational performance. *Strategic Management Journal*, 9: 387-402.

Mitchell, R. K., Agle, B.R., and Wood, D.J. 1997. Toward a theory of stakeholder identification and salience: Defining the principle of who and what really counts. *Academy of Management Review*, 22(4): 853-886.

Ogden, S. 1999. Corporate performance and stakeholder management: Balancing shareholder and customer interests in the U.K. privatized water industry. *Academy of Management Journal*, 42 (5): 526-538.

Olson, Mancur. 1971. *The Logic of Collective Action: Public Goods and the Theory of Groups*. Cambridge, MA: Harvard University Press.

Orssatto, R.E., and Clegg, S.R. 1999. The political ecology of organizations: Toward a framework for analyzing business environment relationships. *Organization and Environment*, Vol. 12, No. 3: 263-279.

Pichardo, N.A. 1997. New social movements: A critical review. *Annual Review of Sociology*, Vol. 23: 411-430.

Reich, R.B. 1998. The new meaning of corporate social responsibility. *California Management Review*, 40(2): 8-17.

Rowley, T. I. 1997. Moving beyond dyadic ties: A network theory of stakeholder influences. *Academy of Management Review*, 22: 887-911.

Schumpeter, Joseph A. 1976. *Capitalism, Socialism and Democracy* (First published in 1942). London: Taylor & Francis Books, Ltd.

Smith, Adam. 1904. *An Inquiry into the Nature and Causes of the Wealth of Nations*, (First published in 1776). Fifth Edition, Cannan, E., Editor. London: Methuen and Co., Ltd.

The Economist. May 7, 2002. Anger over steel. http://www.economist.com/agenda/displayStory.cfm?story_id+1022220

von Hayek, Friedrich. 1994. *The Road to Serfdom* (First published in 1944). Chicago: The University of Chicago Press.

Waddock, S., and N. Smith. 2000. Relationships: The real challenge of corporate global citizenship. *Business and Society Review*, 105 (1): 47-62.

Wartick, S. L. and P. L. Cochran. 1985. The evolution of the corporate social performance model. *Academy of Management Review*, 4: 758-769.

Welford, R. 1996. Environmental issues and corporate environmental management. In R. Welford (Ed.), *Corporate Environmental Management: Systems and Strategies*. p 1-12. London, UK: Earthscan.

Xu, P. 1997. Effect of the multi-fiber arrangement trade restrictions on textile industry profit margins. *Contemporary Economic Policy*, Vol. 15 (3): 93-102.

Yeager, P. C. 1987. Structural bias in regulatory law enforcement: The case of the U.S. Environmental Protection Agency. *Social Problems*, 34: 330-344.

Yergin, Daniel and Stanislaw, Joseph. 2002. *The Commanding Heights*. NY: The Free Press.

Part II: Organizations and Corporate Social Responsibility—Overview

Chapters 3-7 make up Part 2 of the book, which focuses on organizations and corporate social responsibility. Chapter 3 looks at creating sustainability in organizations. Chapter 4 explores the role of corporate social responsibility strategy on success of multi-national organizations. Chapter 5 explores how human resource management and human capital management influence corporate social responsibility. Chapter 6 looks at executive perceptions of CSR. Chapter 7 looks at employee perceptions of CSR.

Chapter 3: Sustainability in Organizations

Creating Sustainability in Organisations: Beyond Being Green

Ling Wong, Macquarie University, NSW, AUSTRALIA

Gayle C Avery, Macquarie University, NSW, AUSTRALIA

Abstract: Sustainability in organisations is not just about addressing social responsibility or meeting triple bottom line criteria to maximise shareholders' short-term interests. This paper proposes that sustainability can only be created when business leaders transform the way they currently think, challenge economic myths, and adopt a systematic and holistic view. This will generate a philosophy of leadership that embraces a set of sustainable values and principles. Sustainable practices will become embedded in corporate strategies, balancing hard and soft goals for the long-term interests of multiple stakeholders. To execute such sustainable strategies well demands a culture of enrichment, trust, shared values, professionalism and collegiality, learning, innovation and communitarianism. Sustainability in organisations is created when all three components – leadership, corporate strategies and culture – reinforce each other for the long-term benefit of multiple stakeholders.

Introduction

Modern humans are challenged with world problems of poverty, ecological destruction, hunger, global warming and population growth. Ecological footprint analyses show that for all who are alive today to live a Western lifestyle, we would need four or five planet Earths. How did we end up in this state?

For years, scientists have claimed that people are living separately from nature. They do not see themselves linked to a bigger, ecologically- and socially-interconnected complex system. Instead Charles Darwin's idea of survival of the fittest applies. Humans exploit the Earth's resources (including each other) to produce things, all in the name of improving the quality of some people's lives via consumerism. As such they developed a set of economic practices that are not viable in the long term. Traditional economics is based on assumptions like: individual self-interest is the best criterion for the fair allocation of resources, the growth of the economy is infinite, and there is permanent access to the natural energy and resources required for economic activity (Stead and Stead, 1992). These old, unsustainable premises need to be re-examined and replaced if we want to continue to share the one Earth.

Humans often fail to think systemically about their lives being connected to nature. In the 1940's, biologist Ludwig von Bertalanffy identified that real systems are receptive to and affect each other in their environments, and can possess qualitatively new characteristics through emergence, providing continual evolution. Thus if one part is changed, the nature of the overall system is often changed as well.

Herman Daly (1991) asserted that an economy sits within a larger social system and ecosystem, using energy and materials from the environment. Following this argument, it is important to adopt the idea of communitarianism (Stead and Stead, 1994) in the economic framework. That means being as one with the larger society and ecosystem. People are now demanding that the environment be treated respectfully, and governments are legislating for environmental protection. Customers insist on safer products. In a talent-starved world, employees are seeking better treatment from their employers. The United Kingdom has included in the Companies Act 2006 (section 172) that directors must have regard to long-term consequences of their decisions, employees, community, environment and their reputation for high standards of business conduct. Other countries are also tightening corporate governance requirements to achieve similar ends.

Despite these social and political pressures, many business managers still resist the pressures to adopt the above new mindset for sustainability (Kearins, 2004). Some of the reasons are: no common definition or understanding of sustainability, sustainability is too expensive because changes have to be made in existing management systems, and managers making economic decisions do not ascribe financial values to human and environmental resources. It is therefore difficult to gauge the widely dispersed and unrecognised social and environmental benefits (and costs) compared with the economic ones (Bansal, 2002).

Nevertheless, some managers realise that they must turn towards environmentally-responsible business practices for the survival of their enterprise. At a macro level, some adopt a Rhineland leadership philosophy (Albert, 1992). Rhineland business, unlike its direct counterpart the Anglo/US neo-liberal approach, is based on the assumptions that all stakeholders' interests need to be balanced and optimised, the long-term view is more important than a short-term view, and business and society are interdependent (Avery, 2005). Rhineland principles lead business to practices like nurturing positive relationships internally and externally with multiple stakeholders; long-term thinking; valuing people; developing managers internally; trust and loyalty; team-based top management; high levels of innovation in products, services and processes; and pursuing social and environmental responsibilities. Geographical location and the existing business culture do not stop businesses from embracing sustainable Rhineland practices (Avery, 2005). Rhineland philosophy is found in firms all over the world and is associated with higher levels of sustainability. Adopting a sustainable leadership philosophy is first a matter of choice, then of changing mindsets, systems and cultures.

Although the Rhineland model may be considered an example of best practice, it does not mean everything will be fine when organisations decide to copy it. Best practice depends on the strategies, practices or variables used in a particular context at a given time. Hence it is subject to change and underpinned by continual improvement and learning. Rhineland leadership is sensitive to its context socially, politically, environmentally, economically, technologically, and legally. Establishing the range of possibilities as the benchmark should be the aim of any best practice and not merely copying what others are doing (Hoag and Cooper, 2006). This raises the question of whether a business based on Anglo/US practices can ever be sustainable.

Shifting to Rhineland leadership involves adopting new strategies, operating principles, structures, values, management and philosophies – new ecologically-sensitive paradigms. This paper reflects on myths such as the need for continual growth in economic wealth. Businesses can be sustainable by reframing the economic system using the concepts of communitarianism, Rhineland philosophy and systems theory. This enables the economy to function within the limits of the Earth while meeting the needs of the greater community. Therefore we discuss how organisations can take a holistic approach to sustainability that goes beyond the triple bottom line. It starts with organisations embracing the concept of sustainability in their strategy, leadership and culture. Then it concludes by showing how leadership needs to create a culture based around core values and trust, in order to support a sustainable corporate strategy.

Sustainability

Sustainability is frequently seen in the same light as being environmentally friendly or socially responsible. However in business, sustainability goes beyond that, beyond the so-called triple bottom line of social, financial and environmental performance. Changing organisations to be sustainable in the long run is not simply about putting ticks on an ISO14001 report. An organisation must exist with intent. That is, sustainability should be the intent of the entire existence of an enterprise. That intent is to add sustainable value to all stakeholders, not only making money for shareholders. It means accepting a systems view, being mindful of how all our daily decisions and actions affect each other and ultimately the delicate balance of ecological, social and economic systems – because we are all connected with the larger systems. For an organisation to embrace this idea, many of its activities that are not regarded as sustainable will be challenged and changed. The way people think and how they perceive the world are reflected in their behaviour. Unless people can change the way they think, nothing will alter in their behaviour towards the world. Let us look at some common myths.

The first myth to examine is that business is only about maximising shareholder value. Why do we think in dichotomies? Either it is good for business or good for society. Why can business not address the interests of other stakeholders such as communities, customers and employees? Surely a business has a meaningful intent for its existence? Doing something that makes a positive difference in society, having a socially-responsible goal and thus engaging in a systems view (Senge, 2007a) Yes, profit is vital but it does not say anything about the intent of the business, for profit is mere money, a form of exchange for something else. Managers make profits to exchange (to manage the business) for meeting social and environmental bottom lines. It is a means to an end but not an end in itself (Kiuchi, 2003).

A second change required in management thinking is to stop giving in to absurd behaviour like satisfying financial market expectations at the expense of long-term goals or relationships such as those with committed employees. Shareholders can trade their ownership anytime and have no commitment to the business at all. However, employees who are literally creating economic value and often have strong commitment to the business are frequently treated as dispensable (Mintzberg, Simons and Basu, 2002). Why?

Thirdly, why do people think that the CEO is more important than the factory worker? Value is now tied to positions, assuming that some people are more valued because of their positions. The CEO is more valued than the workers who also contribute to the business's success. Instead, leadership should be regarded as arising from teamwork and adopting a long-term view, with leaders being stewards and coaches rather than key decision-makers (Mintzberg et al., 2002).

A fourth error in thinking is breaking a problem into parts, thereby losing the essence of the entire problem and its deeper causes. Yet the challenges faced today are systemic, beginning with climate and social problems. Removing this mental barrier and thinking systemically lets people see things as interrelated and as a whole instead of just the parts (Senge, 1990a).

Fifthly, people often think too competitively and do not balance it with cooperation (Senge, 2007b). Instead of cooperating with people, we compete with them. Managers and departments compete with each other to show who knows more or is right, rather than collaborating and sharing knowledge. Ultimately, thinking competitively drives short-term actions with little regard for long-term, systemic consequences, resulting in 'system blindness'.

Finally, people typically think about changes only as a reaction to outside forces. When managers conceptualise management as problem solving, they are not creating any value that comes from within the organisation but from outside, the need to eradicate problems when they arise (Senge, 2007b). People need to think proactively, be sensitive to their surroundings and anticipate change. These changes come from within individuals and organisations. New thinking engages employees with the organisation and inspires them to create a new – sustainable – future.

Challenging these traditional ways of thinking provides more choice of action, including taking a holistic and systemic approach to sustainability in corporate strategy, leadership and culture.

Sustainability as a Corporate Strategy

With all the changes in demographics, climate and resource availability, most existing business models will soon be irrelevant. Environmental, social, ethical and governance factors are becoming more significant to financial performance. Businesses that merely comply with environmental, social, health and safety regulations will soon be left behind by their competitors. Businesses that meet these challenges head on with superior management are quickly gaining an edge over their competitors in the long term (Avery and Bergsteiner, 2011).

Sustainability in organisations is more than just doing 'good' in the social or environmental context as a public relations exercise. Some organisations make very conscious strategic decisions to incorporate sustainability into their strategy. Indeed adopting a systemic and holistic methodology in moulding the future of the entire organisation and planning how to get there is now part of corporate strategy. A sustainable course encompasses both hard goals like capturing market share and achieving financial goals, and soft goals like crafting a management culture that will establish values to set the tone of the business and guide decision making towards a sustainable future.

In addition, a sustainable business strategy will try to balance the three general objectives of economic prosperity, social responsibility and environmental stewardship for all its stakeholders and itself (Placet, Anderson and Fowler, 2005). From a systems perspective, these goals are interrelated and mutually reinforcing. Attending to the environmental challenges helps attain economic goals that, in turn, provide the means to achieve social responsibility and meet more environmental challenges. For instance, conducting international meetings using teleconferencing helps reduce carbon emissions from air travel and saves the cost of airfares. Such cost saving can now be applied to social responsibilities. Being seen as a socially-responsible employer enhances a firm's image as a good employer in the present talent war. This in turn makes it easier to raise capital as investors adopt social and environmental screens for their investment decisions. Hence, a virtuous cycle is created.

Developing sustainable strategies that use fewer resources and optimise both shareholder and stakeholder value as compared to conventional resource-intensive and profit-maximising (at all cost) strategies, requires sustainable leadership.

Sustainable Leadership

The only way to truly transform an organisation is to transform its leaders. Sustainable business demands sustainable leadership that will create sustainable cultures to embrace a sustainable strategy. Hence, leadership here means thinking and behaving as a team rather than as individuals (Bassett, 2005). Charismatic leaders may turn the organisation around temporarily but when these individuals leave, the organisation is threatened because success is linked to them as individuals. These talented leaders must align themselves with the organisational goals and work as a team.

Thus, sustainable leadership is also about distributed leadership (Hargreaves, 2005), extending leadership to others and not just relying on a select few.

Especially in this fast changing complex world, it is unwise to empower only a few leaders. This creates inflexibility and increases potential for mistakes and cover ups that will make the organisation vulnerable. In this knowledge-based world, tapping into everyone's knowledge helps the business adapt in unpredictable and demanding times. So distributed leadership allows other people to be empowered, able to initiate leadership whenever necessary, and act as a team towards achieving shared goals. Effective teams achieve synergy between the individuals.

Leadership succession challenges leaders to ensure that all the good they did in the organisation will continue and be further improved after they are gone. It is very unlike the trail of superficial improvements made by some heroic leaders that vanishes with them when they leave, because these improvements are not well embedded in the organisation. Or worse, these leaders leave behind some very negative consequences for the organisation to face.

As such, sustainable leaders understand systems thinking (Senge, 1990a) and how they are connected with others and the wider society that permits their organisations to exist in the first place. They know their actions affect others over the long term. Thus they query not only the economic, but the moral and social implications of their decisions. Sustainable leadership is about community and finding the shared intent. It has depth and meaning in its communication that transcends differences in gender, age, education and ethnicity. In addition, systems-thinking reflects a holistic approach, working with the entire system, addressing all its psychological, physical, mythical and spiritual aspects. Rather than just work-related leadership, sustainable leadership recognises and respects the whole person (work-life balance), likewise the whole organisation. It looks at issues in their entirety and not just portions of the whole. For instance, when the organisation recruits people, it does not just look at their skills to fit the jobs but also ensures that people have values that fit the culture of the company. Such a holistic approach enables a sustainable culture.

Further, sustainable leadership is mindful that situations can be paradoxical and ambiguous. So there is no need to demand certainty, predict results or control outcomes. Everyone is presented with the same uncertainty and nobody has the answer when entering the unknown. When things go wrong, there is no necessity to find a scapegoat for mistakes because it is all part of experimenting. It is all about continuous learning, reflecting, adjusting and sharing new knowledge with others.

With continuous learning, sustainable leadership is sensitive to the surroundings, gets constant feedback from it, adapts to it and is in constant evolution – continuous improvement. Listening to feedback is the impetus of creativity and innovation. Shell listened to feedback, adapted from being an oil producer to an energy producer, and rejuvenated its business. Businesses that are getting feedback not only from the economic marketplace, but also the social and environmental marketplaces, can innovate in new products and services.

Sustainable leadership is leading through creative tension (Senge, 1990b) by helping organisations visualise the future state (a sustainable future), and by honestly facing the present state. It is not just about eradicating current problems that are stopping organisations from achieving that future state. Such motivation to change is temporary since it disappears the moment the problems are gone.

Instead, creative tension generates motivation from within the organisation, its people wanting to head towards a future state, and act accordingly for the long haul. In this light, it is important that leadership establishes a shared vision from personal visions.

Sustainable Culture

For a business to be sustainable, leaders must nurture a culture that ensures sustainable strategies are well executed. Culture is the way things are done in an organisation, which gives it a unique identity and character. People need to respect an organisation as a living, social organism (Schneider, 2000) instead of as a machine. Organisations are made up of people with a mission. They exist for a purpose beyond their own self-interest.

A sustainable core culture promotes effective stakeholder engagement. Stakeholders include government, non-government organisations, regulators, local community, industry associations and groups, business partners, employees, investment community, media, suppliers, customers, and shareholders. The organisation understands that what defines it as sustainable is not only the big, but also the small, decisions and actions it takes that directly or indirectly support and affect various stakeholders over the long term. At the same time, it also provides stakeholders with opportunities to influence organisational decisions that affect their livelihood. Sustainable leadership creates a gamut of informal and formal stakeholder relationships and ways to identify and assess stakeholder concerns and needs. Also, it provides a platform to receive honest and open feedback about the organisation's performance, and what stakeholders expect from it. These relationships, based on trust, are mutually respecting, supportive and understanding. They help the organisation find and pursue opportunities for sustainable solutions. This contributes to learning, risk management and innovation, helping the organisation to recognise potential issues and opportunities to create unique products and services. This is a value-creating activity.

Therefore successful execution of a sustainable strategy requires values that guide people in the organisation to make decisions. It is vital that an organisation has shared values so that it can show what it stands for. Long-term survival relies on an organisation's connection with the larger systems of the environment, understanding the impact of all its actions, and awareness of working within the planet's limited resources (Stead and Stead, 1993). These values should include treating others with respect, behaving ethically, being trustworthy, and adopting a long-term perspective.

When organisations value true community, they free leaders from controlling people who then are likely to become more committed and self-managing (Sergiovanni, 1992). Viewing organisations as communities identifies values and beliefs that unite people in a common cause. No longer will people keep knowledge to themselves, but share knowledge and collaborate to improve the organisation as a whole. Managers no longer spend time watching over workers for mistakes, but find creative ways to guide their team towards achieving organisational goals. They become coaches, facilitators and acknowledgers. People feel more appreciated and more committed towards the vision they developed together, and more assured about trying out and sharing new ideas. These people are intrinsically motivated, and soon they become self-motivated and self-managing.

People in this culture display professionalism and collegiality, which are substitutes for leadership (Sergiovanni, 1992). The former is the dedication to be a role model, having a conscience to care for the whole person, and being best at one's work. The latter is sharing success with the team because the team efforts way exceed the total achievements of individual contributions, observing and critiquing each other's work for a positive outcome, and having healthy debate about intentions and goals. When people are professionals and behave collegially, there is less need for supervision. In fact these professionals are more concerned about peer reviews than a manager's view.

A culture of trust is essential in a sustainable organisation, especially in overcoming testing times. To develop organisational trust, people must be consistent in their actions over time. This encourages meaningful relationships with various stakeholders. When confronted with difficult times, these trusting relationships persevere, allowing the organisation to overcome tough challenges. Trust is needed to tell each other the reality of the situation and not make it all look rosy. In addition the organisation that respects "covenantal relationships" enhances trust (Caldwell and Karri, 2005). Employees know that they will not be retrenched when the organisation restructures because they believe it will either find them new positions in the new structure or train them for new roles. On the other hand, employers trust that employees are committed to the shared vision with an intrinsic motivation to achieve the vision; they will spend money training and developing committed employees. Loyalty is pledged from both sides over time.

This new culture is about sharing knowledge (Senge, 2007c), which is different from sharing information. The latter is an exchange of data but the former is about people developing a shared understanding of how things really are, how the organisation works, trusting that they can make mistakes in the system without punishment, learning together and making effective moves as a result. It is about building together as a team, learning and hence acting effectively. In the same vein, this fosters innovation where people are encouraged to experiment, relying on human ingenuity to explore new processes to do old and new things. New ideas are generated throughout the organisation from the factory floor and from various stakeholders. Innovation here is not merely reacting to radical and major changes, nor is it fickle. It is systemic. Innovation is used strategically to leverage shared knowledge and drive it incrementally throughout the entire organisation, not only in products and services, but in management and processes.

A sustainable culture honours people (Avery, 2005). Employees are not exploited, treated as organisational resources or reflected as an 'expense' in the financial statements. On the contrary, they are 'assets' to be nurtured and invested in. People are developed for growth, mentored and coached as future leaders, and their skills are continually honed to equip them for fast changing environments. In addition their welfare beyond work is also being looked into, ensuring life-work balance by providing child and elder care, subsidised medical care, counselling to help them cope with a modern, complicated life, financial planning for their retirement, and incentives to show appreciation for their contributions. When people realise they have valuable positions in both the present business and the future, they are more committed to stay and overcome difficult times with the business as a team.

Conclusion

Sustainability cannot be implemented using piecemeal methodology like sponsoring some community work just to get some boxes ticked or to satisfy the conventional triple bottom line. We have been confronted with systemic problems as a result of following myths for a long time. One of the most dominant myths concerns economic wealth. Since the Industrial Revolution, many have viewed organisations as machines, sitting in isolation from the larger life systems, operating in a closed economic loop of producing products and services for consumption – all in the name of improving our standard of living. Is it really? Our illusory drive for economic wealth has run down the Earth's limited resources and ignored the finely-balanced interdependent life systems. Times have changed and we need to view organisations differently and change our thinking about them. New thinking drives new actions. In other words, we need to think systemically about these systemic problems to derive systemic solutions.

Thus we need to attack the root causes and not the symptoms. That is, myths have to be challenged to make paradigm shifts, including viewing the world through changed fundamental values and assumptions. Such paradigm shifts are enabled by systems theory, communitarianism and Rhineland philosophy. These theoretical approaches assist in viewing human activity as linked to a bigger, ecologically- and socially-interrelated, complex system. Defining the essence of a business as sustainability – giving all stakeholders quality of life, building the kind of world that people want to live in and future generations to inherit, and understanding the impact our actions have on others – requires a systemic and holistic approach to corporate strategy, leadership and culture. Otherwise a business is likely to leave a large corporate footprint and be less sustainable.

This paper has argued for a sustainable model that requires business leaders to transform the way they think; adopt sustainable leadership practices; embrace a new philosophy, and set of values and principles; and lead with the conviction that sustainability should be enveloped within corporate strategy. That is, corporate strategy should balance hard and soft goals not only for shareholders, but for various stakeholders over the long-term. That strategy requires a sustainable culture to support it. It means building a culture of trust, shared values, learning, innovation, stakeholder engagement, leadership substitution (via professionalism and collegiality), and communitarianism. Ultimately organisations need to align their leadership, strategy and corporate culture sustainably in order to be effective.

For many organizations, this is a huge ask, but even if just one percent start to make the change now, other businesses could soon be inspired to do the same. A sustainable future awaits those who work towards it.

References

Albert, M. (1992). The Rhine model of capitalism: An investigation. *European Business Journal*, 4(3), 8-22.

Avery, G.C. (2005). *Leadership for sustainable futures: Achieving success in a competitive world.* UK: Edward Elgar.

Avery, G.C. and Bergsteiner, H. (2009). *Honeybees and locusts: The business case for sustainable leadership.* Forthcoming.

Bansal, P. (2002). The corporate challenges of sustainable development. *Academy of Management Executive,* 16(2), 122-131.

Bassett, P.F. (2005). Teaming for sustainable leadership. *Independent School*, 01459635, Winter 2005, 64(2), 1-3. Retrieved April 23rd, 2007, from Academic Search Premier Library Database.

Caldwell, C. and Karri, R. (2005). Organizational governance and ethical systems: A covenantal approach to building trust. *Journal of Business Ethics*, 58(1-3), 249-259.

Daly, H.E. (1991). *Steady-state economics.* (2nd ed.). Washington DC: Island Press.

Hargreaves, A. (2005). Sustainable leadership. *Independent School*, 01459635, Winter, 64(2), 1-5. Retrieved April 23rd, 2007, from Academic Search Premier Library Database.

Hoag, B. and Cooper, C.L. (2006). *Managing value-based organisations: It's not what you think.* UK: Edward Elgar.

Kearins, K. (2004). Making sense out of mixed meanings: Is sustainability a responsibility of business? *Chartered Accountants Journal,* 83(1), 62-63.

Kiuchi, T. (2003). Keynote address to GreenBuild 2003. Pittsburg.

Mintzberg, H., Simons, R. and Basu, K. (2002). Beyond selfishness. *MIT Sloan Management Review,* 44(1), 67-74.

Placet, M., Anderson, R. and Fowler, K.M. (2005). Strategies for sustainability. *Research – Technology Management,* 48(5), 32-41.

Schneider, W.E. (2000). Why good management ideas fail: The neglected power of organizational culture. *Strategy and Leadership*, 28(1), 24-29.

Senge, P.M. (1990a). *The fifth discipline.* New York: Doubleday.

Senge, P.M. (1990b). The leader's new work: Building learning organizations. *Sloan Management Review,* 32(1), 7-23.

Senge, P.M. (2007a). Making a better world. Accessed May 23rd, 2007 from http://www.solonline.org/res/kr/world.html.

Senge, P.M. (2007b). Personal transformation. Accessed May 23rd, 2007 from http://www.solonline.org/repository/download/transform.html?item_id=505852.

Senge, P.M. (2007c). Sharing knowledge. Accessed May 23rd, 2007 from http://www.solonline.org/res/kr/shareknow.html.

Sergiovanni, T.J. (1992). Why we should seek substitutes for leadership. *Educational Leadership,* 49(5), 41-45.

Stead, J.G. and Stead W.E. (1993). Implementing sustainability strategies: A matter of values. Paper presented at the meeting of the Society for the Advancement of Socio-Economics, 28th March, New York.

Stead, W.E. and Stead, J.G. (1992), *Management for a small planet: Strategic decision making and the environment.* Newbury Park, C.A.: Sage Publications Inc.

Stead, W.E. and Stead J.G. (1994). Can humankind change the economic myth? Paradigm shifts necessary for ecologically sustainable business. *Journal of Organisational Change Management,* 7(4), 15-31.

Chapter 4: Strategic CSR in Multinational Organizations

The Role of Corporate Social Responsibility Strategy on Success of Multi-National Organizations

Mohammad Esmael Ansari, University of Isfahan, Isfahan, Iran (Islamic Republic of)

Hadi Teimouri, University of Isfahan, Isfahan, Iran (Islamic Republic of)

Abstract: Business leaders agree that managing in times of turbulence and accelerating change challenges their traditional views of competitiveness and success factors needed for survival and profitability. Today's managers must deal with globalization of markets, increasing intensity of competition, rapid technological changes, a shift from an industrial economy to a knowledge, human capital and information based economy, demographic changes, environmental challenges, changing value systems and consumer preferences. The changes in society are forcing companies to consider the views of various interest groups in decision making. Building relationships with customers, suppliers, employees, communities and other stakeholders can become central to competitiveness and form the foundation for a new, progressive and people centered corporate strategy which attacks the sources – not the symptoms – of challenges facing business today. This brings us to the increased importance of corporate social responsibility. Corporate social responsibility (CSR) is a strategic decision whereby an organization undertakes an obligation to society in the form of sponsorship, commitment to local communities, attention to environmental issues and responsible advertising. Today, multi-national organizations face to different challenges such as, culture, regularity environment, non-government organizations (NGOs) and global standards. The major aim of this paper is to study CSR strategy and the role of its in success multi-national organizations. The research methodology is descriptive and for collecting theoretical aspects of the research scientific books and journals are used. The results of this paper indicate that CSR is a critical factor for success multi-national organizations. This paper is valuable for marketers in planning for strategic CSR and for academic researchers in further clarifying the boundaries of strategic CSR.

Introduction

Corporate social responsibility (CSR) is fundamentally an ethical concept. It involves changing notions of human welfare and emphasizes a concern about the social dimensions of business activity that have a direct concern with quality of life in the society. The concept provides a way for business to concern itself with social dimensions and pay some attention to its social impacts. The word ''responsibility'' implies that business organizations have some kind of obligation towards the society in which they function to deal with social problems and contribute more than just economic services.

The Strategic Advisory Group on CSR of International Organization for Standardization (ISO), describes it as ''a balanced approach for organizations to address economic, social and environmental issues in a way that aims to benefit people, community and society'' (ISO, 2002).

CSR, in its true sense, is hard work and must be seen in conjunction with the basic functioning of the company. It must radiate outwards to the society from within the core efficiencies of the firm in order to strengthen them in a not-too-long-run. CSR, thus, self-consciously raises the stakes for itself and in doing so sets new targets and challenges that eventually impact the industry as a whole(Dipanker,2003).

Globalization has resulted in the proliferation of new laws and regulations that direct business activities to address diverse social problems. The long-term impact of these social policies is a sea change in the ''rules of thumb'' by which business is expected to operate in harmony with social environment. The firm's external environment manifested in public policies and expectations is becoming a key factor in major strategic business decisions. In addition, change in social values and ideologies have tremendous implication for the role that business is expected to play in the society. Growing concern about the ethical dimensions by corporations has become a practice. In this scenario, it is no wonder that the attention of top management, Government and society are being directed towards corporate governance and corporate accountability (Hazarika, 1998).

History of Corporate Social Responsibility (CSR)

Society's Rising Expectations for Business

The notion that business has duties to society is firmly entrenched, although in the past several decades there has been a revolution in the way people view the relationship between business and society. Archie Carroll (1979) and other researchers believe that we should judge corporations not just on their economic success but also on non-economic criteria. Carroll (1979) proposed a popular four-part definition of CSR, suggesting that corporations have four responsibilities or "four faces" (Carroll, 2000) to fulfill to be good corporate citizens: economic, legal, ethical, and philanthropic.

Economic responsibilities. Ever since the industrial revolution, we have depended on business as a major economic institution for producing want-satisfying goods and services; providing jobs and fair pay for workers; seeking raw materials supplies; discovering new resources, technological improvements, and products; paying taxes for public needs; generating the investment capital necessary for economic growth; all while earning a profit for the owners and serving as an investment opportunity. Previously, if a firm did all of this while obeying the law, it was praised (Lantos, 2001).

Eighteenth-century Scottish philosopher Adam Smith, in The Wealth of Nations, provided us with a framework for modern business and its relationship to society. Smith proposed that capitalism, by encouraging the pursuit of gain and efficiency, works to create greater wealth than any other economic system, and maximizes liberty by allowing individuals freedom of choice in employment, purchases, and investments, thereby benefiting the common good. Endeavoring to beat one's rivals, and toiling to produce better work to earn the next promotion, if done ethically, will result in high personal development and therefore excellent use of one's time and talents and the firm's treasury (Johnson, 1990). The manager's role is to act as a fiduciary or trustee to a principal, the owners or shareholders, being their steward in effectively and efficiently managing the organization's assets.

Economic responsibility, then, is to be profitable for principals by delivering a good quality product at a fair price is due to customers. Novak (1996) more fully delineated a set of seven economic responsibilities. These are to: (1) satisfy customers with goods and services of real value, (2) earn a fair return on the funds entrusted to the corporation by its investors, (3) create new wealth, which can accrue to nonprofit institutions which own shares of publicly-held companies and help lift the poor out of poverty as their wages rise, (4) create new jobs, (5) defeat envy though generating upward mobility and giving people the sense that their economic conditions can improve, (6) promote innovation, and (7) diversify the economic interests of citizens so as to prevent the tyranny of the majority. Lantos call these duties economic CSR. Societal expectations in this realm have appeared to hold steady over the years (Lantos, 2001).

Legal responsibilities. Legal duties entail complying with the law and playing by the rules of the game. Laws regulating business conduct are passed because society does not always trust business to do what is right. However, laws have certain shortcomings to ensure responsible behavior: they are of limited scope (they can't cover every possible contingency); merely provide a floor or moral minimum for business conduct; are reactive, telling us what ought not to be done, rather than proactive, telling us what ought to be done; and might be followed involuntarily out of fear of punishment rather than voluntarily out of internal moral conviction (Lantos, 2001).

Ethical responsibilities. Ethical duties overcome the limitations of legal duties. They entail being moral, doing what is right, just, and fair; respecting peoples'' moral rights; and avoiding harm or social injury as well as preventing harm caused by others (Smith and Quelch, 1993). Ethical responsibilities those policies, institutions, decisions, or practices that are either expected (positive duties) or prohibited (negative duties) by members of society, although they are not necessarily codified into law (Carroll, 2001). They derive their source of authority from religious convictions, moral traditions, humane principles, and human rights commitments (Novak, 1996). Today, virtually all members of the business system agree, at least in theory (although, unfortunately, often not in practice) with this third set of "social responsibilities that Lantos call ethical duties ethical CSR.

Prior to the 1960s, business ethics was not a major concern of business people. Rather, it was left to theologians to discuss issues of fair wages, unfair labor practices, and the morality of capitalism. The Protestant work ethic taught people to work hard and be successful—this was the essence of business' social responsibility.

Beginning in the 1960s ethical issues in business were raised on an unprecedented scale. There was a heightened realization that repressive labor practices could be found at even some of the most admired corporations, unsafe products were being sold, the business system was taking a toll on the natural environment, society was not succeeding in elevating those most economically deprived, bribery was occurring on an international scale, and morality was being compromised in the pursuit of money and power. Liberal consumerist media portrayed business as evil, implying that almost any business activity is morally reprehensible. Consequently, we heard consumer outcries against insensitive and immoral business practices. As a reaction to the negative publicity, by the mid-1970s, the concept of raising corporate America's consciousness was in vogue in both corporate boardrooms and college classrooms. The idea was that enterprises should not single-mindedly pursue profit without regard to morality.

Thus, since the 1970s, society's expectations of business ethics have been climbing. Today's, productivity alone is no longer considered sufficient to morally justify a business organization. Also important is how wealth generation affects non-economic aspects of society, such as the welfare of employees, customers, and other members of the business system, as well as other outside groups and the natural environment (Lantos, 2001).

Altruistic responsibilities. Carroll's discretionary or philanthropic responsibility—"giving back" time and money in the forms of voluntary service, voluntary association, and voluntary giving—is where most of the controversy over the legitimacy of CSR lies. Over the past half century, business increasingly has been judged not just by its economic and its moral performance, but also by its social contributions. Henry Ford II identified this when he spoke at the Harvard Business School as far back as 1969: "The terms of the contract between industry and society are changing...Now we are being asked to serve a wider range of human values and to accept an obligation to members of the public with whom we have no commercial transactions" (Chewning et. al, 1990).

CSR actually has its roots in the thinking of early twentieth century theologians and religious thinkers, who suggested that certain religious principles could be applied to business activities. For example, Andrew Carnegie devised a classic twofold statement of corporate social responsibility based on religious thinking. First, was the charity principle, which required more fortunate individuals to assist less fortunate members of society. Second, was the stewardship principle, a biblical doctrine that requires businesses and wealthy individuals to see themselves as stewards or caretakers, not just of shareholders' financial resources, but also of society's economic resources, holding their property in trust for the benefit of society as a whole.

Thus, there was a concern for the macro-level outcome of business decisions in ways that went beyond the loyal agent's argument that a manager's duty is solely to loyally serve the employer by contributing to profit maximization. Now, it was suggested that stewardship of the corporation's resources somehow be melded with a view of stewardship of society's resources to more broadly serve society. Business was said to have stewardship responsibilities not just to shareholders, but also to so-called "stakeholders" (a.k.a. constituencies or publics), notably employees, customers, competitors, suppliers, distributors, the local community in which the enterprise operates, the general public, and the natural environment. When corporations make business decisions they have both short- and long-term effects on many sectors of society (Lantos, 2001).

During the latter half of twentieth century there arose the idea of the corporate social contract, which today underlies the CSR concept. Given the sometimes-adverse effects of business decision-making on society as well as corporate reliance upon society, the notion of an implied corporate social contract was conceived by social and economic theorists. This contract spells out society's expectations of business as well as (although much less discussed) business' expectations of society. The social contract theory of business is widely held today by both business ethicists and business decision-makers (Bowie, 1983).

The corporate social contract concerns a firm's indirect societal obligations and resembles the "social contract" between citizens and government traditionally discussed by philosophers who identified the reciprocal obligations of citizen and state. Originally, this social contract focused solely on economic responsibilities. Social progress and quality-of-life advancement were assumed to be a by-product of economic growth. Business' social responsibility was to maximize profits, subject to the constraints of the law. Private business had no accountability for the general conditions of life or the specific conditions in local communities (Anshen, 1988).

This new social contract postulated that social progress should weigh equally in the balance with economic progress. The idea that corporations as organizations have "social responsibility" and obligations tying them to a wider society became popular in the 1950s, and continued through the 1960s and 1970s, when American businesses rapidly gained in size and power (Davis, 1983). Several groups were responsible for this heightened social consciousness, including the feminist movement and those advocating for the mentally and physically challenged, for native people, and for minorities. Much of the public embraced the concerns of these groups because unfortunate events brought the realization that some special-interest groups were worth listening to, such as environmentalists, consumer advocates, and antiapartheid supporters.

Thus, it was suggested that business, as a social institution, should join with other social structures like the family, educational system, and religious institutions, to help enhance life and meet needs (Chewning et. al, 1990). Whereas in Adam Smith's model, property was owned by individuals who directly decided how it was to be used, the modern corporation is characterized by professional managers who make decisions on behalf of the stockholder owners, and these decisions affect tens of thousands of citizens (Miller and Ahrens, 1993). Moreover, corporations need the resources of society if they are to survive and thrive. Corporate taxes are supposedly not sufficient to pay for these resources, and so the corporation should, out of a duty of gratitude, assist in solving social problems (Bowie, 1995).Moreover, multinational corporations control a tremendous amount of economic and productive resources, such as technology, finances, and labor power on a scale that no adequate accounting of their duties should ignore (Lippke, 1996). Therefore, social contract theorists feel these resources should have some use beyond producing more brands of household cleaners for consumers and wealth for stockholders. The corporate social contract holds that business and society are equal partners, each enjoying a set of rights and having reciprocal responsibilities.

Benefits of CSR

Any company with ambitions regarding CSR clearly must display all the hallmarks of a learning organization. While the journey is invariably difficult, tangible rewards can make all the effort worthwhile (Strategic Direction, 2005). The payoff can include:

- **Enhanced reputation**: Bearing in mind almost two-thirds of UK adults allegedly mistrust business leaders, any boost to reputation can be worth its weight in gold.
- **Satisfaction and loyalty among employees when organizational values mirror their own.**
- **Innovation**: Evidence suggests that responsible companies are more creative. It can have significant long-term benefits if a company is able to introduce effective practices that also positively impact on society or the environment.
- **Greater prospect of attracting investment**: Investors are now looking beyond the figures towards those organizations noted for their responsible business practices. Analysts believe this trend will grow even more because investors have their own reputations to consider. Pressure from investors can also help bring other companies into line.
- **Interaction with a wider audience that increases knowledge and helps to improve risk management.**

- **Enhanced product lifecycles with better management of materials and waste combining to lower operational costs.**

Corporate Social Responsibility and Global Considerations

To address CSR strategy in a broader, global context, four key aspects are discussed: culture; regulatory environment; NGOs; and global standards (*Galbreath*, 2006).

Culture

Just as business firms development their own unique cultures - and strategies - in a home country, if they plan global expansion, they must operate within the context of national and even regional cultures of another country (Hofstede, 1980; 1983). According to Burton et.al, (2000), "Different cultures will emphasize different values; what is important to one culture at one time may not be important to another culture or even to the first culture at some time in the future. These values may affect both the role institutions assume within society and what society expects of those institutions."

Based on Burton et al., (2000) assessment, understanding the cultures of the countries and regions a firm is seeking to operate in is very important (cf. Schwartz, 1992; Maignan and Ferrell, 2003). By way of example, in India, ten-year olds working 12-hour days weaving rugs occurs. In Honduras, 15-year old girls working 80 hours per week producing sweaters occurs. In Bangladesh, incidents of nine-year olds working in shoe factories with imposed production quotas occurs (Quindlen, 1994). In many countries, such labor-related activities would not only be seen as appalling and quite contrary to culturally accepted norms of socially responsible behavior, but would also be in criminal violation of labor laws. However, the reality is in some countries the use of very young workers is a necessity as this keeps them off the street begging for survival or from committing criminal acts to obtain money (Greenfield, 2004). Research (e.g. Orpen, 1987; Burton et al., 2000) does show that individuals view CSR differently from country to country.

The above examples do raise a fundamental issue: should the culture of a particular region or nation or should the firm's own standards (in the home country) form the basis of CSR strategy in international locations? For example, if a firm adopts a shareholder strategy with respect to CSR in the home country, will the same approach translate into an acceptable strategy in a different country of operation? Thus, firms must address the issue of whether to adapt to the socially responsible norms of a national or regional culture (a "relativism" approach) or to impose an international standard of CSR (a "universalism" approach) regardless of the cultural norms of a specific country or region of operation (Smeltzer and Jennings, 1998; Carroll, 2004).

The reality is firms must apply ethical and moral standards to address cultural differences with respect to CSR (Robertson and Fadil, 1999). In some cases, firms might choose not to do business in a given country or region due to suspect norms of socially responsible behavior. In other cases, they might compromise and conduct CSR in a manner that it opposed to the policy set in the home base of operation. Even in other cases, firms might act to offer their CSR leadership in the home base to the foreign base of operation, setting the standard for domestic businesses operating in that community. By way of example, Sony recently announced that its environmental targets and policies will be standardized, implemented and enforced in all of its global locations. Lastly, understanding culture is important with respect to CSR as societal - if not stakeholder - concerns vary from country to country. For example, in Australia, Canada and China, environmental concerns take center-stage within society. In Indonesia, Turkey and the USA, improving education ranks highest among social concerns. Finally, in Brazil, Chile and South Africa, reducing poverty and homelessness are the most important social concerns (Environics International, 2002). Based on this information, while having a "universal" policy with respect to CSR globally may be an ideal in some areas (e.g. workers rights, the environment), firms who understand the intricacies of a national or regional culture are better equipped to address local concerns of social responsibility when and where necessary (e.g. through philanthropic giving or strategic partnerships).

Regulatory Environment

According to Carroll (1979, 2004), the regulatory environment, in the form of an enforceable legal framework, is a key component of CSR. In general, laws and regulations have been theorized as necessary in an economy as a response to inefficient or inequitable behavior (Posner, 1974). Indeed, a widely held view is that federal and state bodies impose laws where the marketplace has failed to ensure fair competition, safe products, fair and equitable working conditions and a clean and healthy environment.

Although firms are expected to operate within the overall regulatory framework of the land, since the 1970s the development of laws with respect to specific facets of social responsibility have been growing. For example, in the USA, laws have been implemented with respect to the environment (under the auspices of the Environmental Protection Agency, or EPA) and workplace safety standards (under the auspices of the Occupational Safety and Health Administration, or OSHA). Other laws are more global in nature.

In November, 1997, for example, 34 nations signed the OECD Convention on Combating Bribery of Foreign Public Officials in International Business Transactions. The convention now makes bribery of foreign public officials a criminal act on an extraterritorial basis. Although in many ways seen as something unnecessarily imposed on business by the government (Harrington, 1996), the regulatory environment under which a firm must operate in a given country is yet another area of consideration with respect to global CSR strategy. Here, firms are again faced with ethic decisions regarding home versus host country considerations. For example, if a firm adopts a reciprocal strategy with respect to CSR in the home country and implements environmental production standards that go beyond those required by law as part of that strategy, should the same policy be adopted in a host country of operation where environmental laws don't even exist.

Non-government Organizations (NGOs)

Historically, associations of private individuals (e.g. churches) have come together for public purposes, typically to provide services (e.g. education, health, welfare) in the community not available from the state, long before the establishment of democratic government and the concept of the welfare state (Novak, 1996). In more recent times, particularly since the 1950s, a new class of private "association" has been established which generally focuses directly on changing public policy. These local, regional and international non-governmental organizations, or NGOs, have grown to over 50,000 in number, almost double the number just 25 years ago, up from just over 1,000 in 1956 (Gordenker and Weiss, 1996; Smith, 1997).

A general definition of NGOs is "non-profit groups that combine resource mobilization, information provision and activism to advocate for changes in certain areas" (Spar and La Mure, 2003). NGOs are generally either ideas-based - human rights, education, equality, environmental sustainability, etc. - or identity-based - indigenous, female, homosexual and the like. However, these lines may be blurring with many NGOs integrating ideas - and identity-based causes (van Tuijl, 1999).

With respect to what NGOs actually do, there are three approaches to classification: operational; advisory; and advocacy. Operational NGOs act to provide social services such as education, health and disaster relief. Advisory NGOs are involved in providing information and consulting services, for example, to mutual funds focused on socially responsible investing (SRI). Advocacy NGOs are directly involved in lobbying governments and local, national and international organizations for changes and/or adoption of socially responsible policies for businesses. They may also file resolutions on behalf of shareholders to pressure businesses into acting more socially responsible. Although sometimes seen as questionable and unaccountable (Johns, 2001), NGOs are causing substantial changes in corporate management, strategy and governance (Doh and Teegen, 2003). Of particular interest is discerning the role and impact of NGOs in the host country to ascertain whether CSR policy set in the home country needs to be customized to the local environment.

Global Standards

Lastly, just as NGOs can add pressure to businesses to act on behalf of society in many different ways, global standards, many coming from NGOs themselves, are another source of institutional pressure. The majority of CSR-related global standards are voluntary in nature, asking firms to develop and implement policies and practices on various CSR issues (Neergaard and Pedersen, 2003). The standards help users to establish a systematic process that generates indicators, targets and reporting systems necessary for effective implementation and monitoring of various CSR programs and activities. In essence, global standards are instruments designed for corporate self-regulation (Waddock et al., 2002).

A variety of global standards have emerged over the years and the Business and Social Initiatives (BSI) database, established by the International Labor Office, now lists over 400 different standards, principles and codes of conduct

(Waddock et al., 2002). Some of the more recognized standards, however, include the ISO (International Standards Organization) 14000 and 14031 for the environment; Social Accountability (SA) 8000 for labor-related issues; the United Nations (UN) Declaration on Human Rights and the Environment; the Caux and Sullivan Principles for economic, social and political justice and general CSR; and the OECD (Organization for Economic Cooperation and Development) Guidelines for Multinational Enterprises for voluntary principles and standards with respect to CSR. With these and a host of other global standards covering every conceivable aspect of social responsibility, firms are faced with increasing pressure to strategically evaluate a cadre of external benchmarks as they establish CSR policy. Of course, strategic decisions here can become complicated when firms operate, or plan to operate, in multiple locations. Operating in multiple locations raises the issue of the choice of implementing a single, uniform policy worldwide with respect to CSR or whether to allow flexibility based on, for example, culture or the regulatory environment of a given country or region (Smeltzer and Jennings, 1998).

Discussion

When extending a CSR strategy from home to host countries, various aspects, such as local cultures, regulatory environments, NGOs and global standards, must all be taken into consideration (Figure 1). Given that local cultures tend to view CSR differently (Orpen, 1987; Burton et. al, (2000), firms must carefully examine the location of operation before transposing home to host CSR strategies. As with culture, regulatory environments also differ from country to country. However, some emerging regulations, such as the OECD convention

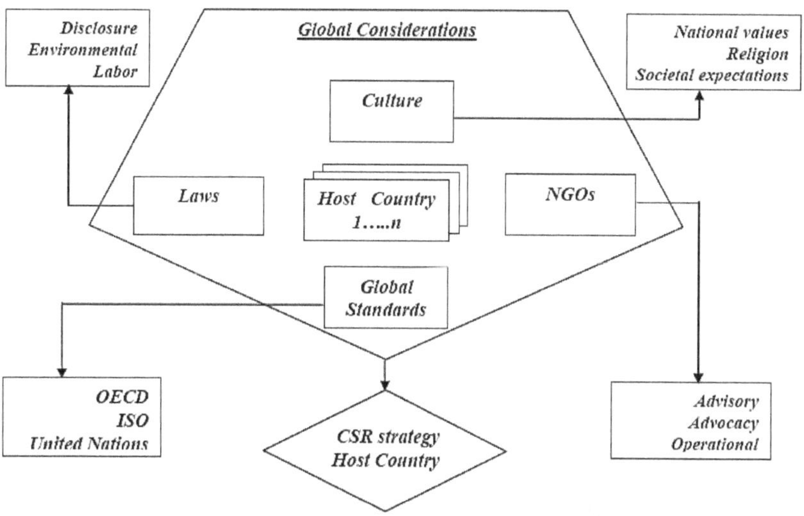

Figure 1: Considerations for CSR strategy in a global context (*Jeremy Galbreath*, 2006)

On bribery of foreign officials, are universal in nature. Thus, as with culture, a thorough examination of the regulatory environment is an important consideration with respect to global CSR strategies. As for NGOs, their influence continues to increase around the world and many countries have powerful NGOs that are specifically focused on issues of importance in the focal country. Thus, understanding the "who's who" of NGOs in any given country lends itself to informed decisions with respect to CSR strategies in that country. With respect to standards, global CSR standards such as the ISO 14000 and 14031 for the environment and the Social Accountability (SA) 8000 for labor-related issues are becoming important benchmarks for which to compare who is practicing CSR and who is not in the world. Thus, by adopting appropriate global CSR standards, firms are signaling their adherence to socially responsible practices in business, which is becoming an increasingly important means of competitive differentiation in a global economy (Waddock et. al, 2002).

Conclusion

In this paper corporate social responsibility (CSR) and its role in the success of multi-national organizations in term of global consideration such as culture, regulatory environment, non-government organizations (NGOs) and global standards has been studied.

Findings suggest that CSR is an area of corporate concern that can not be overlooked. In fact, CSR is argued to be essential to a firm's overall strategy. Furthermore, as globalization continues to broaden its reach, firms must increasingly acknowledge and assess their responsibilities on a global scale. Thus, managers should pay keen attention to the matters of CSR.

References

Anshen, M. (1988), "Changing the social contract: a role for business," in Callahan, J.C. (Ed), Ethical Issues in Professional Life, Oxford University Press, New York.

Bowie, N. (1995), "New directions in corporate social responsibility," in Hoffman, W. M., and Frederick, R.E. (Eds), Business Ethics: Readings and Cases in Corporate Morality, Third Edition, McGraw-Hill, New York.

Bowie, N.E. (1983), "Changing the rules," in Beachamp, T.L., and Bowie, N.E. (Eds), Ethical Theory and Business, Second Edition, Prentice-Hall, Inc., Englewood Cliffs, NJ.

Burton, B.K., Farh, J.-L. and Hegarty, W.H. (2000), "A cross-cultural comparison of corporate social responsibility orientation: Hong Kong vs United States students", Teaching Business Ethics, Vol. 4 No. 2, pp. 151-67.

Carroll, A.B. (2004), "Managing ethically with global stakeholders: a present and future challenge", Academy of Management Executive, Vol. 18 No. 2, pp. 114-20.

Carroll, A.B. (2000), "The four faces of corporate citizenship," in Business Ethics 00/01, Richardson, J.E. (Ed)., Dushkin/McGraw-Hill, Guilford, CT, pp. 187-191.

Carroll, A.B. (1979), "A three-dimensional conceptual model of corporate performance", Academy of Management Review, Vol. 4 No. 4, pp. 497-505.

Chewning, R.C., Eby, J.W., and Roels, S. J. (1990), Business Through the Eyes of Faith, Harper & Row, San Francisco.

Davis, K. (1983), "An expanded view of the social responsibility of business," in Beachamp, T.L., and Bowie, N.E.(Eds), Ethical Theory and Business, Second Edition, Prentice-Hall, Inc., Englewood Cliffs, N.J.

Dipankar, G. (2003), ''Profits & ethics – why CSR makes business sense'', The Times of India, Vol. 25, p. 12.

Doh, J.P. and Teegen, H. (2003), Globalization and NGOs: Transforming Business, Governments, and Society, Praeger, Westport, CT.

Environics International (1999), The Millennium Poll on Corporate Social Responsibility: Executive Brief, Environics International, Toronto.

Gordenker, L. and Weiss, T.G. (1996), "Pluralizing global governance: analytical approaches and dimensions", in Weiss, T.G. and Gordenker, L. (Eds), NGOs, the UN & Global Governance, Rienner Publishers, London.

Galbreath, J.(2006), *Corporate social responsibility strategy: strategic options, global considerations*, Corporate Governance. Bradford, Vol. 6, Iss. 2, pg. 175, 13 pgs.

Harrington, L.K. (1996), "Ethics and public policy analysis: stakeholders' interests and regulatory policy", Journal of Business Ethics, Vol. 15 No. 4, pp. 373-82.

Hazarika, A. (Ed.) (1998), Corporate Social Responsibility and the Oil Industry: Global Experiences, Tata McGraw-Hill Publications, New Delhi.

Hofstede, G. (1983), "Dimensions of national culture in fifty countries and three regions", in Deregowski, J.D., Dziurawiec, S. and Annios, R.C. (Eds), Explications in Cross-cultural Psychology, Swets and Zeitlinger, Lisse.

Hofstede, G. (1980), Culture's Consequences: International Differences in Work-related Values, Sage. Beverly Hills, CA.

ISO (2002), Strategic advisory group on corporate social responsibility: preliminary working definition of organizational social responsibility, ISO/TBM AGCSR N4, International Organization for Standardization, Geneva.

Johns, G. (2001), "Protocols with NGOs: the need to know", IPA Backgrounder, Vol. 13 No. 1, pp. 1-16.

Johnson, T.S. (1990), "How the notion of a calling manifests itself in the world of business: one viewpoint," America, Vol. 162 No. 5, February 10, pp. 117-120.

Lantos, G.P.(2001), The Boundaries of strategic corporate social responsibility, Journal of Consumer Marketing, Vol.18, No.18, pp.595-630.

Lippke, R. L. (1996), "Setting the terms of the business responsibility debate," in Ethics in the Workplace: Selected Readings in Business Ethics, Larmer, R.A. (Ed), West Publishing Company, Minneapolis/St.Paul, MN.

Lippke, R. L. (1996), "Setting the terms of the business responsibility debate," in Ethics in the Workplace: Selected Readings in Business Ethics, Larmer, R.A. (Ed), West Publishing Company, Minneapolis/St.Paul, MN.

Maignan, I. and Ferrell, O.C. (2003), "Nature of corporate responsibilities: perspectives from American, French, and German consumers", Journal of Business Research, Vol. 56 No. 1, pp. 55-67.

Miller, F.D., and Ahrens, J. (1993), "The social responsibility of corporations," in White, T.I. (Ed), Business Ethics: A Philosophical Reader, Prentice Hall, Upper Saddle River, NJ, pp. 187-204.

Novak, M. (1996), Business as a Calling: Work and the Examined Life, The Free Press, New-York.

Neergaard, P. and Pedersen, E.R. (2003), "Corporate social behavior: between the rules of the game and the law of the jungle", Journal of Corporate Citizenship, Vol. 12, Winter, pp. 43-57.

Orpen, C. (1987), "The attitudes of United States and South African managers to corporate social responsibility", Journal Business Ethics, Vol. 6 No. 2, pp. 89-96.

Posner, R.A. (1974), "Theories of economic regulation", The Bell Journal of Economic and Management Science, Vol. 5 No. 2, pp. 335-58.

Quindlen, A. (1994), "Out of the hands of babes", New York Times, November 23, p. A15.

Robertson, C. and Fadil, PA. (1999), "Ethical decision making in multinational organizations: a culture-based model", Journal of Business Ethics, Vol. 19 No. 4, pp. 385-92.

Schwartz, S.H. (1992), "Universels in the content and structure of values: theoretical advances and empirical tests in 20 countries", in Zanna, MP. (Ed.), Advances in Experimental Social Psychology, Academic Press, San Diego, CA.

Smeltzer, LR. and Jennings, M.M. (1998), "Why an international code of business ethics would be good for business", Journal of Business Ethics, Vol. 17 No. 1, pp. 57-66.

Smith, J. (1997), "Characteristics of the modern transnational social movement sector", in Smith, J., Chatfield, C. and Pagnucco, P. (Eds), Transnational Social Movements and Global Politics: Solidarity Beyond the State, Syracuse University Press, Syracuse, NY.

Smith, N.C., and Quelch, J.A. (1993), Ethics in Marketing, Irwin, Homewood, IL.

Spar, D.L. and La Mure, LT. (2003), "The power of activism: assessing the impact of NGOs on global business", California Management Review, Vol. 45 No. 3, pp. 78-101.

Strategic Direction. (2005), Vol. 21, No. 7, pp. 24-28, Emerald Group Publishing Limited, ISSN 0258-0543.

van Tuijl, P. (1999), "NGOs and human rights: sources of justices and democracy", Journal of International Affairs, Vol. 52 No. 2, pp. 493-512.

Waddock, S.A., Bodwell, C. and Graves, S.B. (2002), "Responsibility: the new business imperative", Academy of Management Executive, Vol. 16 No. 2, pp. 132-48.

Chapter 5: HR Influence on CSR

How Human Resource Management and Human Capital Management Influence Corporate Social Responsibility (CSR)

Johanna Maksimainen, University of Jyväskylä, Finland

Pertti Saariluoma, University of Jyväskylä, Finland

Abstract: Corporate social responsibility (CSR) is a vital issue for corporations today. Values that CSR includes, guide many essential management choices and also create, in many respects, the cor-porate public image. The results of our previous analyses indicate that respondents in higher organizational level consider Corporate Social Responsibility (CSR) to be a more important factor in their work than do the employees in lower levels. The results suggest there is a communication gap in the organizations with respect to CSR knowledge. In order to understand better the nature of this gap, we investigated the relation of two management paradigms, human resource management (HRM) and human capital management (HCM), to CSR. Our results illustrate that there is a strong association between the two and CSR. However, it is also evident that the two managing approaches have somewhat different focuses. While HRM concentrates on external and organizational aspects of management, HCM emphasizes internal employee relations. This means that the two management approaches are not contradictory but can support each other in improving CSR in organizations.

Introduction

Corporate social responsibility is an important issue for any business organization. From the psychological point of view, corporate social responsibility is represented in the minds of employees in one way or another. Depending on how employees see and experience corporate social responsibility issues, corporations take care of their duties. There are simply no corporate social responsibilities outside the minds of people in corporations, and therefore we have to investigate these webs of knowledge, concepts, attitudes and practices concerning CSR to understand this vital phenomenon. For these reasons, mental representations of CSR within companies form an important problem and offer new possibilities to consider the phenomena relevant in investigating this vital organizational issue.

Traditionally, variations in CSR's conceptualizations have flourished. Swanson and Niehoff (2001) developed a model of business citizenship, distinguishing between employee citizenship behavior and corporate citizenship responsibilities. A model of corporate citizenship that contains strategic philosophy, outcomes and social responsibilities was invented by McAlister et al. (2003). The World Economic Forum (2003) structured some key corporate citizenship issues, such as ethics, people, environment, contribution to development and corporate governance, in their model. In Quazis' and O'Briens' (2000) two-dimensional model of CSR, narrow and wide responsibilities and costs and benefits of CSR actions are distinguished. Matten and Crane (2005) separated social rights, civil rights and political rights in their conceptualization of corporate citizenship. Social and ethical commitments are stressed in the model Meehan et al. (2006). One prominent example of the CSR model is Carroll's pyramid that consists of economic, legal, ethical and philanthropic responsibilities (Carroll 1991). However, CSR activities revolve around three dimensions: environmental, economical, and social responsibilities (see Fig 1).

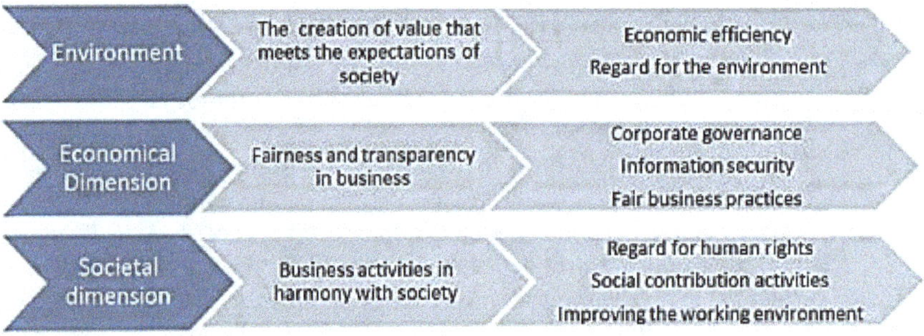

Fig. 1: Three Foundational Dimensions of CSR

CSR reflects a certain set of organizational values, which often are related to social, environmental and economic issues and to stakeholder relationships (e.g. Gao & Zhang 2006; Marrewijk 2003). In literature, CSR and other values are usually supposed, explicitly or implicitly, to be represented by management (e.g. Pedersen 2006, 2009; Quazi 2003). For example, a relationship amongst top managers' tenure, functional background, and CSR can be found (Thomas & Simerly 1994), and correlations have been identified between the attitudes towards CSR and managers' demographics (Quazi 2003). Evidently, perceptions of organizational values guide the executives actions, which, as expected, also form the behaviour and actions in other organizational levels. However, support by the management is a precondition for organizational actions (e.g. Baines et al. 2006; Epstein 2008; Jenkins 2006).

Our previous study has shown that valuation of CSR is strongly dependent of individuals' position in the organization: the higher the respondents' position in the organization, the higher CSR is valuated (Maksimainen, Saariluoma & Jokivuori 2009). Social responsibility should be seen as a cultural and mental representation in the minds of employees (Harrison & Boyle 2006), and therefore it is logical to consider the internalization of CSR in corporations, how CRS is understood, how it is fleshed out in actions and decision and how it could be manifested more effectively in employer-employee relations. For this, we have to think about the ways traditional personnel management paradigms can foster the internalization of CSR concepts in everyday life of an organization.

Today, corporate employer relations are based either on paradigms of Human Resource Management (HRM) or on those of Human Capital Management (HCM) (e.g. Armstrong 2006; Legge 2004; Barnett 2000). Based on literature (e.g. Barrett 2000; Collins & Porras 1994; Kleiman 1997; Marrewijk & Werre 2003; Marrewijk & Hardjono 2003; Marrewijk & Timmers 2003), HCM is a value-driven personnel management approach, aspiring to build up employees' commitment and motivation. Its orientation is not along strictly functional objectives, but focuses on the practice of the relevant values. HCM should not be seen as opposite to more performance driven and functionally orientated HRM, but as a supplement that focuses on the alignment between subjective and collective, incorporating additional values into HRM. Some of the most basic differences between HCM and HRM are shown in Table 1.

Human Capital Management	**Human Resource Management**
Interactive communication, dialogue	Communication
Individualized tasks and responsibilities	Individualized tasks
Personal development	Multitasking
Professional discussions about outputs	Optimal outputs
Personal competencies and values	Personal competencies
Alignment	Attraction

Table 1: Some Main Attributes of HCM and HRM

Considering the employee-organization relation (e.g. Tsui et al. 1997; Eisenberger et al. 2004), a major problem with HRM can be pointed out: the unfeasible paradigm, wherein the human resources can be managed and controlled (e.g. Armstrong 2006; Legge 2004; Ulrich 1996). Even if adjustments have been made within HRM as a reaction to the development of increasing number of high quality jobs and to the increase in the number of independent employees, the old paradigm has not been disqualified. The assumption that people can be controlled remains. Therefore, we might think that HRM is losing its affiliation with current developments in industrialized societies.

From our point of view, the differences between HCM and HRC can be found in the way employees mentally represent these concepts and related practices.

The respondents have their mental representations of organizations and of HRM as well as HCM. A way of looking at these two issues is to pay attention to how people represent these organization matters (Barnett, Jeremier & Lafferty 2006; Rindova 1999; Senge 1990). From our point of view, the critical issue is the contents of mental representations, or mental contents (Saariluoma 1990, 2003). Here we assume that there is some underlying difference between HRM and HCM. Our main questions are: how do these two perspectives differ in their information contents in the minds of respondents and what will the consequences of these differences to CSR management be?

Empirical Study and Analysis

Objective

The objective of this study is to examine the content of mental representations regarding two different people management approaches, HRM and HCM, and their effect to the valuation of CSR.

Arguments and Hypothesis

In this article, the basic observation, based on earlier study, is that the essence of CSR is not fully internalized in corporation practices (Maksimainen, Saariluoma & Jokivuori 2009). That can be achieved, however, by using appropriate CSR management methods. The hypothesis is that value orientation that emphasizes HCM predicts higher CSR valuation and that the HCM approach advances the adoption of CSR more effectively than the HRM approach does. The argument is that in new organization cultures where CSR is strongly advocated a paradigm shift from HRM towards HCM is required in order to promote the internalization of CSR within organizations.

Scope and Methodology

In the empirical research, the values that are considered to be important as guiding principles in work were studied. The survey was sent to randomly selected companies in the engineering field through Finnish Federation of Design and Consulting Agency, which is the employee union in the field. The only criterion for selecting participants was that the participating company's domain was engineering. The surveys were delivered by the companies over their intranet to the personnel concerned, designers, personnel in middle management and CEO's. The size of the sample was 118 respondents.

The empirical study was carried out as an Internet survey in which a structured questionnaire was used. The questionnaire, based on previous value research, was formulated for measuring values prevalent within the groups of people. Schwartz and Bilsky (1987, 1990), for example, stress the profound nature and universal character of values. Thus, also in the questionnaire, each value claim represents a certain value or value set considered to be universal. The collected quantitative data was organized and analyzed using statistical methods. In the survey, there were two patterns of value questions for gathering data about respondents' own work-related values and organizational values. In this study, only a question pattern concerning organizational values is used.

Analysis and Results

Analyses were conducted on the collected data in order to find out relations between variables HRM, HCM, and CSR and the degree of confidence for them. To get an idea about how different management approaches affect the valuation of CSR within organizations, the following qualitative analyses were conducted.

The variables representing HRM, HCM and CSR were operationalized as value-bundles. As a basis for operationalization, factor analysis (Maximum Likelihood with Varimax rotation) was used. The relations between the variables, indicating value dimensions HRM, HCM and CSR, were studied using the linear regression analysis. With the help of such statistical method, a situation can be modelled where the dependent variable (CSR) depends linearly on independent variables HRM and HCM. Thus it is possible to examine the causal relations between variables.

In this study, the human management approaches HRM and HCM are elaborated as value dimensions that differ in their focus. HRM is more performance-driven, whereas in HCM the interaction values are emphasized. These approaches should not be seen as exclusive management methods; we suggest that implementation of HCM-oriented practices in human management would strengthen employer-employee communication advances in the internalization of CSR.

Factor Analysis

A factor analysis provides, as a result, three factors corresponding to significant values (see Table 2): *HRM* (mean = 6.2), *HCM* (mean = 6.8) and *CSR* (mean = 5.6). Each factor represents a bundle of value attributes. The three factors represent the corporate level, indicating (to?) the values that are expected to be guiding principles in work from the viewpoint of the employer. The first factor, *HRM,* includes the values of customer orientation, long-term customer relations, support services, innovativeness, continuous product development, usability of products, quality of products, and regeneration. The second factor, *HCM,* includes the values of up-to-date production devices, solidarity of personnel, commitment of personnel, and effectiveness of management. The third factor is *CSR* and includes the values of CSR and environmental consciousness. For all the factors the mean was relatively high. This was presumable due to the nature of the questions. Within the factors, a whole nine-point scale was used.

The first factor expresses the most important attributes of HRM and represents the organization's external dimension and the relations between the organization and its stakeholders. The second factor defines the attributes of HCM in respondents' mental representations. According to the results HCM represents the organization's internal dimension, and social relations of the personnel. The third factor, CSR, suggests that environmental awareness is strongly attached to respondents' considerations of CSR. Of these factors, HCM is estimated to be the most important (mean = 6.8). This means that in engineering professions, solidarity and commitment of personnel, efficient management and working tools are held in high importance.

	Factor		
	1	2	3
CV continuous product development	,783		
CV usability of products	,713		
CV innovativeness	,711		
CV regeneration	,701		
CV customer orientation	,693		
CV long-term customer relations	,672		
CV product support services	,623		
CV quality of products	,606		
CV commitment of personnel		,826	
CV solidarity of personnel		,825	
CV up-to-date tools		,566	
CV effectivity of management		,556	
CV economical production process			
CV environmental awareness			,797
CV CSR			,634
Extraction Method: Maximum Likelihood. Rotation Method: Varimax with Kaiser Normalization.			
Rotation converged in 6 iterations. The cutpoint was 0,5.			

Table 2: The Three Main Factors Concerning Connections between HRM, HCM and CSR

Kaiser-Meyer-Olkin Measure of Sampling Adequacy.		,898
Bartlett's Test of Sphericity	Approx. Chi-Square	1112,734
	df	105
	Sig.	,000

Table 3: KMO and Bartlett's Test

We made follow-up analysis using first KMO and the Bartlett's test to study the problems caused by our relatively small samples size of 118 respondents. These tests can be used to investigate how stable our solution is (Field 2005).The KMO test gives .898 (>0,6) as a result, which means that data is acceptable for factor analysis. The Bartlett's test (.000) shows that the assumption of the diagonality of correlation matrix is improbable (see Table 3). Therefore, we do not see any serious risks in our interpretation.

Next the relations between the factors are studied. It is assumed that the factors have positive correlations between eachothers. Table 4 below shows bivariated correlations.

		HRM	HCM	CSR
	Pearson Correlation	1	,613(**)	,602(**)
HRM	**Sig. (2-tailed)**		,000	,000
	N	118	118	118
HCM	**Pearson Correlation**	,613(**)	1	,673(**)
	Sig. (2-tailed)	,000		,000
	N	118	118	118
CSR	**Pearson Correlation**	,602(**)	,673(**)	1
	Sig. (2-tailed)	,000	,000	
	N	118	118	118

Table 4: Correlation Matrix

There are two ways to interpret the degree of relationships indicated by the correlations' coefficients of interest. The first is to judge whether or not the variables are significantly related. Because the significance value listed for correlation is .05 or less, it can be assumed the correlation is not a chance result or a random sampling error. Therefore, the correlation is real one and can be generalised from the sample to the overall population. It can be concluded that variables (i.e. respondents' valuations) are not independent. This means, for instance, that having high scores in CSR while having low scores in HRM and HCM is not likely.

Although all the ten correlations are statistically significant ($p<.05$), r-values vary in range .524 (the weakest) and .725 (the strongest). The correlation was very strong between HCM and CSR ($r = .673$, $p = .000$). The weakest correlation was obtained between variables CSR and HRM ($r = .602$, $p = .000$). All in all, the correlation matrix shows that indicators have strong positive correlations.

By using factor analysis, value-dimensions can be created. Here, based on the factor analysis, the mean estimated sum variables HRM and HCM were created. For both variables, the alpha values were high (Table 5). The range of each sum variable is from 1 to 9. The third factor, CSR, includes the value 'environmental consciousness', but it was dropped out in the subsequent regression analysis in order to measure, more specifically, only CSR.

Cronbach's Alpha	N of Items
HRM ,916	8
HCM ,860	4

Table 5: Reliability Statistics

Linear Regression Analysis

Linear regression analysis was conducted in order to examine whether HRM or HCM have effect on the valuation of CSR. HRM and HCM are treated as independent variables in the model. In linear regression analysis, the basic assumption is that there is a linear relation between dependent and independent variables.

In Table 6, the means for each variable are shown. The HRM value orientation got the highest mean (6.8). The means for the HCM (6.2) value orientation and CSR (5.1) were relatively close to each other, but distinctly lower than they were for HRMs.

	Mean	Std. Deviation	N
CV CSR	5,08	2,317	118
HRM	6,8125	1,34706	118
HCM	6,1589	1,74455	118

Table 6: Descriptive Statistics

Model	R	R Square	Adjusted R Square	Std. Error of the Estimate	Change Statistics				
					R Square Change	F Change	f1	df2	Sig. F Change
1	,670[a]	,449	,439	1,736	,449	46,790		115	,000
a. Predictors: (Constant), HCM, HRM									
b. Dependent Variable: CV CSR									

Table 7: Model Summary[b]

In the output (Table 7), the R^2 value is .449, meaning that both independent variables, HRM and HCM, together explain 45% of the variable CSR variation. The explanatory rate this high can be perceived retentive.

Model		Sum of Squares	df	Mean Square	F	Sig.
1	Regression	281,896	2	140,948	46,790	,000[a]
	Residual	346,418	115	3,012		
	Total	628,314	117			
a. Predictors: (Constant), HCM, HRM						
b. Dependent Variable: CV CSR						

Table 8: ANOVA[b]

F-test (Table 8) indicates whether the independent variables are able to explicate the variation of dependent variable. F-value (F (2.115) = 46.80, p< .000) describes the collaborative effect of the variables HRM and HCM to the CSR variance.

Model		Unstandardized Coefficients		Standardized Coefficients	t	Sig.	Correlations		
		B	Std. Error	Beta			Zero-order	Partial	Part
	(Constant)	-1,673	,832		-2,012	,047			
	HRM	,373	,151	,217	2,470	,015	,532	,224	,171
	HCM	,684	,116	,515	5,871	,000	,648	,480	,406
a. Dependent Variable: CV CSR									

Table 9: Coefficients[a]

Table 9 shows the regression coefficients and the statistical significance levels of the variables HCM and HRM (p<.001). The reciprocal relative effect strength of variables can be examined more closely by using the information in the Standardized Coefficients Beta column. By standardizing the variables, the coefficients have been modified to make them comparable with each other. Standardized coefficients indicate how many standardized dispersion units the dependent variable (CSR) changes when its dispersion increases by one unit. However, our interest here is to examine the effect of independent variables separately. Therefore, the focus is on values in partial correlations. The value .224 indicates that the HRM orientation explains 5% of the variance in CSR valuation. Partial correlation value for HCM is .480, meaning that the HCM orientation explains 23% of the variance. This means that both the HRM and the HCM orientation predict higher valuation of CSR, but the effect of HCM is significantly stronger.

In the following tables, the effects of values that HRM (Table 10) and HCM (Table 11) include, are examined.

Model	Unstandardized Coefficients		Standardized Coefficients	t	Sig	Correlations		
	B	Std. Error	Beta			Zero-order	Partial	Part
(Constant)	,245	1,174		,209	,835			
CV customer orientation	,020	,201	,013	,101	,919	,395	,010	,008
CV long-term customer relations	-,092	,202	-,052	-,453	,652	,337	-,043	-,035
CV product support services	-,036	,147	-,024	-,244	,808	,263	-,023	-,019
CV innovativeness	,376	,168	,300	2,241	,027	,500	**,210**	,173
CV continuous product development	-,196	,172	-,161	-1,140	,257	,410	-,109	-,088
CV usability of products	,045	,175	,032	,258	,797	,440	,025	,020
CV quality of products	,271	,155	,208	1,749	,083	,476	,165	,135
CV regeneration	,379	,154	,322	2,469	,015	,529	**,230**	,191
a. Dependent Variable: CV CSR								

Table 10: Coefficients[a]

Table 10 presents the values that the variable HRM includes. According to these results, the effects of innovativeness (4.4%) and regeneration (5.3%) on the CSR variance are the strongest. On the other hand, the valuation of customer orientation (0.1%), long-term customer relations (0.2%), product support services (0.05%), continuous product development (1.2%), usability of products (0.6%) and quality of products (2.7%) have very little effect to the CSR variance.

Model	Unstandardized Coefficients		Standardized Coefficients	t	Sig.	Correlations		
	B	Std. Error	Beta			Zero-order	Partial	Part
(Constant)	-,352	,634		-,555	,580			
CV up-to-date tools	,244	,115	,195	2,125	,036	,514	**,196**	,149
CV solidarity of personnel	,162	,116	,162	1,405	,163	,533	,131	,099
CV commitment of personnel	,065	,133	,059	,489	,626	,528	,046	,034
CV effectiveness of management	,427	,104	,377	4,121	,000	,603	**,361**	,289
a. Dependent Variable: CV CSR								

Table 11: Coefficients[a]

Table 11 shows the effects of the values that are included in the HCM variable. Effectiveness of management explains up to 13.6% of the CSR variance and also the values of up-to-date tools (3.8%) and solidarity of personnel (1.7%) have a certain impact. However, the effect of commitment of personnel is minor (0.2%).

The results in Tables 10 and 11 demonstrate the effects of different management approaches to CSR. The HRM approach emphasizes organizations' external processes, while HCM is related to internal processes. In summary, according to the results it seems that in the HRM orientated management approach, organizations' openness to innovativeness and regeneration have a positive effect on CSR internalization and organizations' external social responsibilities within employees. Efficacy of management, by advancing CSR in organizations' internal responsibilities, has a major role in the HCM orientated approach.

Discussion

As mentioned in the introduction, it is important to focus on the mental representation prevalent in organizational culture and on individual employees if we wish to understand how people think about corporate social responsibility. From our point of view, the key issue here is the information contents of prevailing cultural and individual mental representations. This can be referred to as mental contents and the way of thinking corresponding to it as content-based psychology (Saariluoma 2003, Saariluoma and Maarttola 2003, Saariluoma and Nevala 2006). In concrete terms, this means that we have to consider the differences in mental contents of the people in different cultural groups of their organization because these differences are essentially differences in their mental contents.

If we consider the outcome of the factor analysis, it is evident that factor 1, HRM, entails traditional business values such as customer orientation, long-term customer relations, support services, innovativeness, continuous product development, usability of products, quality of products, and regeneration. This is obviously the traditional HRM way of looking human relations in a corporate setting. The corporation is seen externally as a social unit effectively serving its customers.

The second factor opens an alternative way to consider HR processes in corporations. Factor 2, HCM, emphasizes up-to-date production devices, solidarity of personnel, commitment of personnel, and effectiveness of management. This is evidently an internal perspective to the organization. All the attributes emphasize the internal life within the corporation. This means that, in relation to the corporation, the second factor offers a perspective that is different from that of the first factor.

In terms of mental contents, the outcome is very straightforward. Respondents form two different types of models of their company. They either conceptualize the system from the outside and in terms of external and performance-oriented perspective or internal and employee relations perspective. Both models are linked with very different systems of concepts and values, and therefore they provide two different views to one and the same company.

It is important here to pay attention to the fact that objectively the two models are not contradictory but, rather, complementary. The external efficiency of a corporation does not mean that it is internally inefficient. The high correlation between the two factors implies also that the two perspectives should be seen mutually reinforcing rather than contradictory. This means that a good internal process supports an effective external processes or/and vice versa. However, one can hardly look at a company from the two perspectives at the same time any more than one can view the buildings of a company simultaneously inside and outside. The mental representations are thus psychologically incompatible.

The contents of human mental representations are always systems of integrated elements such as concepts, assumed facts and values (Saariluoma 1995, 2001). By investigating the attributes of the factors we can explicate more about the contents of the two types of mental models. Whereas the external model has the attributes of customer orientation, long-term customer relations, product support services, innovativeness, continuous product development, usability and quality of products, and regeneration, the internal model has the attributes of modern tools, solidarity and commitment of personnel as well as efficacy of management.

When subjected to a more detailed analysis, the CSR factor seems to be in a closer association with the internal than with the external process in organizations. Of course, there are several explanations for the result. It may be that the respondents who are more oriented towards HCM-type thinking also regard CSR and the relevant values important, but it may also be that the internal process is indeed more important for developing CSR than the external process is. It seems also logical that both of the interpretations have certain significance.

This means that advancing CSR is an internal process, and people who have this focus on the company are also more sensitive to the internal issue.

Presumably, the most interesting contribution of this research to management thinking is that HRM and HCM provide us with two different perspectives to organization. Respondents apparently see concepts of HRM as the external perspective to organization and HCM as the internal perspective to contents. This result is somewhat different from what the table presented in the introduction shows. This outcome implies that the two approaches are complementary. Nevertheless, it is interesting to see that the respondents with a high appreciation of the internal and organizational perspective (HCM) seem to be more aware of the importance of CSR.

Discourses may seem quite futile when one of the disputants emphasizes internal and the other one external perspective. The two perspectives both are important in developing corporate management. They are also linked, and if one of them does not work properly, it is very probable that the other one will also suffer. This is why it is important to understand the interplay of concepts, values and mental models in building harmonious organizations.

The paper as a whole illustrates one way of investigating how companies are mentally represented. People who belong to a certain company have quite a lot of knowledge of it. A part of that knowledge may be quite irrelevant, such as where to get coffee in the building, but much of it is highly relevant for the way the company operates. The HRM/HCM/CSR concepts are part of the representation. They are complex knowledge systems in the minds of the employees. They entail concepts, facts and values. These are elements for systems of integrated mental contents. They have a complex structure, but the different models close each other as they have different contents and focuses. However, on a higher level they may complement each other. More work should be done to reveal and explicate the contents of various systems of corporate mental models.

References

Armstrong, M. (2006). A Handbook of Human Resource Management Practice (10th ed.). London: Kogan Page.

Baines, T., Lightfoot, H., Williams, G.M. & Greenough, R. (2006). State-of-the-art in Lean Design Engineering: A Literature Review on White Collar Lean, in *Journal of Engineering Manufacture*, Vol. 220, No 9, 1539-1547.

Barnett, M.L., Jeremier, J. & Lafferty, B. (2006). Corporate Reputation: The Definitional Landscape , in *Corporate Reputation Review*, Vol. 9, 26 – 38.

Barrett, R. (2000). Building a Value-Driven Organisation. Woburn: Butterworth Heinemann.

Carroll, A.B. (1991). "The Pyramid of Corporate Social Responsibility: Toward a moral Management of Organizational Stakeholders", in *Business Horizons*, Vol. 34, No. 4, 39-48.

Collins, J.C. & Porras, J.J. (1994). Built to Last. New York: Harper Business.

Eisenberger, R., Jones, J.R., Aselage, J. & Sucharski, I.L. (2004). Perceived Organizational Support, in J.Coyle-Shapiro, L.M. Shore, M.S. Taylor & L.E. Tetrick (eds) *The Employment Relationship – Examining Psychological and Contextual Perspectives.* Oxford: Oxford University Press.

Epstein, M.J. (2008). Making Sustainability Work. Greenleaf Publishing Limited, Sheffield.

Field, A. (2005). Discovering statistics using SPSS. London: Sage.

Gao, S.S. & Zhang, J.J. (2006). "Stakeholder Engagement, Social Auditing and Corporate Sustainability", in *Business Process Management Journal*, Vol. 12, No. 6, 722-740.

Harrison, J. & Boyle, E. (2006). "Falling into Capability Learning Traps: The Role of the Firms' Predominant Managerial Mental Models", in *Management Decision*, Vol. 44, No 1, 31-43.

Jenkins, H. (2006). "Small Business Champions for Corporate Social Responsibility", in *Journal of Business Ethics*, Vol. 67, No. 3, 241-256.

Kleiman, L.S. (1997). Human Resource Management – A Tool for Competitive Advantage. Minneapolis: West Publishing Company.

Legge, K. (2004). Human Resource Management: Rhetorics and Realities (Anniversary ed.). Basingstoke: Palgrave Macmillan.

Maksimainen, J., Saariluoma, P. & Jokivuori, P. (2009). "Corporate Social Responsibility and Values in Innovation Management," *Proceedings of World Academy of Science, Engineering and Technology*, Vol. 41, 557-561.

Marrewijk, M. (2003). Concepts and Definitions of CSR and Corporate Sustainability: Between Agency and Communion, in *Journal of Business Ethics*, Vol. 44, No. 2-3, 95-105.

Marrewijk, M. & Hardjono, T.W. (2003). "The European Corporate Sustainability Framework from Managing Complexity and Corporate Transition", *Journal of Business Ethics*, Vol. 44, No. 2-3, 121-132.

Marrewijk, M. & Timmers, J. (2003). ''Human Capital Management'', *Journal of Business Ethics*, Vol. 44, No. 2-3, 171-184.

Marrewijk, M. & Werre, M. (2003). "Multiple Levels of Corporate Sustainability", in *Journal of Business Ethics*, Vol. 44, No. 2-3, 107-119.

Matten, D. & Crane, A. (2005). "Corporate Citizenship: Toward an Extended Theoretical Conceptualization", *Academy of Management Review*, Vol. 30, No. 1, 166-179.

McAlister, D.T., Ferrell, O.C. & Ferrell, L. (2003). Business and Society: A Strategic Approach to Corporate Citizenship. Boston: Houghton Mifflin Company.

Meehan, J., Meehan, K. & Richards, A. (2006). "Corporate Social Responsibility: the 3C-SR Model", *International Journal of Social Economics*, Vol. 33, No 5/6, 386-398.

Pedersen, E.R. (2006). "Making Corporate Social Responsibility (CSR) Operable: How Companies Translate Stakeholder Dialogue into Practice", *Business and Society Review*, Vol. 111, No. 2, 137-163.

Pedersen, E.R. (2009). "Modelling CSR: How Managers Understand the Responsibilities of Business Towards Society", *Journal of Business Ethics*, Vol. 91, 155-166.

Quazi, A.M. (2003). "Identifying the Determinants of Corporate Managers' Perceived Social Obligations", *Management Decision*, Vol. 41, No. 9, 822-831.

Quazi, A.M. & O'Brien D. (2000). "An Empirical Test of a Cross-National Model of Corporate Social Responsibility", *Journal of Business Ethics*, Vol. 25, 33-51.

Rindova, V. P. (1999). "What corporate board have to do with strategy", *Journal of Management Studies*, Vol. 36, 953-975.

Saariluoma, P: (1990). "Apperception and restructuring in chess players' problem solving", in K J Gilhooly, MTG Keane, RH Logie & G Erdos (eds.), *Lines of thought: Reflections on the Psychology of Thinking*. London: Wiley. 41-57.

Saariluoma, P. (2003). "Apperception, content-based psychology and design", in U. Lindeman (ed.), *Human behavious in design* Berlin: Springer. 72-78.

Saariluoma, P. & Maarttola, I. (2003). "Errors and functional reasons in architectural design", *Journal of Architectural and Planning Research*, Vol. 20, 344-354.

Saariluoma, P. & Nevala, K. (2006). "The focus of content-based approach to design engineering", in V. Vanek & S. Hosnedl (eds.), *Aeds Workshop proceedings* Pilsen: University of Western Boemia. 105-110.

Schwartz, S.H. & Bilsky, W. (1990). "Toward a theory of the universal content and structure of values: Extensions and cross-cultural replications," *Journal of Personality and Social Psychology*, Vol. 58, 878-891.

Schwartz, S. & Bilsky, W. (1987). "Toward a universal psychological structure of human values," *Journal of Personality and Social Psychology*, Vol. 53, 550-562.

Senge, P.M. (1990). The Fifth Discipline – The Art and Practice of the Learning Organization. New York: Doubleday.

Tsui, A.S., Pearce, J.L., Porter, L.W. & Tripoli, A.M. (1997). Alternative Approaches to the Employee-Organization Relationship: Does Investment in Employees Pay Off? *Academy of Management Journal*, Vol. 40, No 5, 1089-1121.

Swanson, D. & Niehoff, B.P. (2001). "Business Citizenship Outside and Inside Organisations", in J. Andriof & M. McIntosh (eds.), *Perspectives on Corporate Citizenship*. Sheffield: Greenleaf Publishing Ltd., 104-116.

Ulrich, D. (1996). Human Resource Champions. The next agenda for adding value and delivering results. Boston, Mass.: Harvard Business School Press.

Chapter 6: Executive Perceptions of CSR

Executive Perceptions of Corporate Social and Environmental Disclosure: Evidence from a Developing Country

Hadrian G. Djajadikerta, Edith Cowan University, WA, Australia

Terri Trireksani, Murdoch University, WA, Australia

Abstract: In the last four decades, the practice of corporate social and environmental disclosure (CSED) has been increasing in popularity and acceptance among business entities, scholars and practitioners. However, it has been found that the practice of CSED in developing countries is still very limited. This paper conducts in-depth semi-structured interviews to seek perceptions of Indonesian executives about CSED through the lens of stakeholder and legitimacy theories. Evidence from the interviews offers some indications about the level of managerial understanding regarding CSED, the motivations for CSED, and the preferred means for disclosure. The paper reflects on the managerial implications of the findings for future practices.

Introduction

In the last four decades, there has been a growing body of literature that focuses on the extent of corporate social and environmental disclosure (CSED). This practice of disclosure speaks about the issue of corporate social responsibility (CSR). The majority of these studies have been carried out in the context of developed countries, such as those in Australia, Canada, Japan, Singapore, the UK, the USA, or New Zealand (e.g. Brown and Deegan, 1998; Deegan and Rankin, 1996; Deegan, Rankin and Tobin, 2002; Fukukawa and Moon, 2004; Gray, Kouhy and Lavers, 1995; Raar, 2002; Ramasamy and Hung, 2004; Snider, Hill and Martin, 2003; Thomson and Bebbington, 2005; Tilt, 1994; van Staden and Hooks, 2007).

CSED studies in the context of developing countries so far have been rather limited. However, the existing literature which includes such studies conducted in

Bangladesh, Indonesia, or Thailand, suggests that despite a trend of increasing amounts of CSED in the developing countries, the overall extent of the disclosure is still low (e.g. Belal, 2001; Chappel and Moon, 2005; Djajadikerta and Trireksani, 2012; Gunawan, Djajadikerta and Smith, 2009; Imam, 2000; Ratanajongkol, Davey and Low, 2006). This has led to a question of perceptions of company executives in developing countries regarding CSED. This study tries to explore this issue by conducting in-depth semi-structured interviews with Indonesian executives about CSED, and analyzing the findings through the lens of stakeholder and legitimacy perspectives.

The Indonesian Context

Indonesia is the world's fourth most populous country with an estimated population of around 237 million people. With its area of 1.9 million square kilometres, dozens of existing ethnic groups, and hundreds of different local dialects (United Nation, n.d.), Indonesia clearly has an extremely diverse culture and a complex social and geographical environment. Simultaneously, the country has a quite huge gap across groups of people and its regions, with reference to economic and social status, natural resources, and technological infrastructure (Djanali, n.d.).

Since the 1997 economic crisis, the country has seriously needed foreign direct investment. However, investors and lenders have been slow to return to Indonesia. Actually, there have been some promising signs of economic recovery in Indonesia, as mentioned in the Morgan Stanley's recent Indonesian report, "*As markets start to look towards the 2010 macro recovery, strong domestic demand economies will likely be key investment themes.*" However, at the same time some analysts have cautioned against this development and stated that "*Indonesia has made little progress against reducing poverty in recent years, its infrastructure is crumbling and its legal system is still very weak*" ("Economists split on Jakarta's komodo power", 2009).

The other factors that attract foreign direct investment are corporate transparency and the extent of CSED (e.g. Donaldson, 2005; Goyal, 2006). These are the two factors that Indonesian companies still lack (Djajadikerta and Trireksani, 2012; Greenlees, 2005; Gunawan et al., 2009). CSED is important for companies to create a positive image and gain public credibility (Leonard and McAdam, 2003; Ratanajongkol et al., 2006; Thompson and Zakaria, 2004). Djajadikerta and Trireksani (2012), in their analysis of website reporting made by 110 Indonesian listed companies, found that the extent of CSED made by Indonesian listed companies on their corporate websites is low. This is consistent with that reported by Chappel and Moon (2005), in which they analyzed the website reporting made by the top 50 Indonesian companies with the highest operating revenue. These findings are also consistent with the findings of Gunawan et al. (2009), in their study of CSED made by the Indonesian listed companies in their annual reports, in which they found that the amount of CSED was limited. Overall, these empirical findings point toward a rather worrying state for Indonesian companies and the country in general. The characteristic facts about the Indonesian situation, especially its social and economic situation, have suggested a need for Indonesian companies to improve their corporate transparency and provide an adequate amount of CSED. However, in practice the extent of CSED made by Indonesian companies is still low. This has led to a need for exploring Indonesian executives' perceptions regarding CSED.

According to political economy theory, business activities occur in an integrated social, political and economic framework (e.g. Gray, Owen and Adams, 1996). One part of the theory puts emphasis on inequality, structural conflict, and the role of the nation, which leads to rules for mandatory disclosure. This is commonly known as classical political economy theory. The other part of the theory recognizes the interactions between groups, in which companies are formed by the stakeholders and the environment in which they operate in. This is commonly known as bourgeois political economy theory. Within the bourgeois political economy structure, there are two known perspectives, stakeholder and legitimacy perspectives, which respectively focus on the issues of stakeholders and the social environment. Stakeholder perspective represents a concept wherein companies incorporate social and environmental concern within their business operations and their relations with the stakeholders (e.g. Roberts, 1992; Wilson, 2001). Legitimacy perspective focuses on the companies' efforts to attain societal recognition of the adequacy of their social behavior (e.g. Deegan, 2002; Nasi, Nasi, Phillips, and Zyglidopoulos, 1997). The existing literature on CSED has shown the application of both stakeholder and legitimacy perspectives, and has provided evidence from both perspectives in explaining the practice of CSED (e.g. Brown and Deegan, 1998; Deegan et al., 2002; Delmas and Toffel, 2004; Donaldson and Preston, 1995; Mitchell, Agle, and Wood, 1997; Wilmhurst and Frost, 2000).

Accounting systems in Indonesia are regulated by the Indonesian Institute of Accountants (IAI). The IAI has developed a Statement of Financial Accounting Standards as a guideline for companies in preparing their financial statements (IAIGlobal, n.d.). There has been no specific requirement for CSED within this Statement of Financial Accounting Standards. It is quite apparent from the previous discussion that companies in Indonesia are formed by the stakeholders and the social and economic environment where they operate in, and with regard to the practice of CSED, they are not clearly bound by rules for mandatory disclosure. This strongly suggests that both the stakeholder and legitimacy perspectives shape the corporate social and environmental practices and their disclosure in Indonesia.

Research Method

This study conducted in-depth semi-structured interviews with seven executives of Indonesian middle and large size companies. The primary objective of the interviews was to obtain executive perspectives concerning managerial understanding on the subject of CSED, the motivations for CSED, and the preferred means for disclosure. The findings from the interviews were subsequently analyzed through the lens of stakeholder and legitimacy perspectives.

In general, industry groups can be categorized as sensitive and non-sensitive industries. The sensitive industries are those which are perceived as more socially and environmentally damaging than those which operate in socially and environmentally non-sensitive industries (Deegan and Gordon, 1996). In the Indonesian context, there are eight industry groups that are categorized as sensitive, and five industry groups that are categorized as non-sensitive based on the Indonesian Capital Market sector categories (e.g. Djajadikerta and Trireksani, 2012). The industry groups that are classified as sensitive include groups of agriculture, mining, basic industry and chemicals, miscellaneous industries, consumer goods industries, property and building constructions, infrastructure and utilities, and trade and services. The industry groups that are classified as non-sensitive include groups of finance companies, advertising and media, computer and services, investment companies, and other provider and broadcasting companies. This study tried to obtain perceptions from executives in both sensitive and non-sensitive industry groups, and therefore, conducted seven separate interviews with five executives from sensitive companies and two executives from non-sensitive companies. The interviewees' positions in the companies ranged from the regional manager to the CEO, and the interviews ranged from one hour to two hours in duration.

The Interviews and the Findings

The Interviews

Each interview started with an explanation of the purpose of the interview. It was emphasized that the study expected to obtain honest opinions from the interviewees, and therefore it was ensured that the anonymity of the interviewees would be guaranteed, and there would not be any interviewees' details mentioned in any parts of the paper. This then led to the interview, in which the following wide-ranging open-ended questions were used as guideline for the follow-on discussion.

- *Have you come upon CSED in your working life?*
- *Could you please describe your understanding regarding CSED?*
- *Does your company engage in CSED?*
- *What motivates your company to engage (or not to engage) in CSED?*
- *Could you please discuss your company's experience in the CSED engagement?*
- *Where does your company disclose its social and environmental information?*

The order in which the questions were asked varied and the wording of the questions were sometimes adjusted so as to maintain the flow of the discussion. Additional questions relevant to the main questions were sometimes asked to elaborate or to clarify the interviewees' points of view.

The Findings

Managerial Understanding Regarding CSED

The first finding from the interview suggests that the Indonesian executives in this study have quite a considerable understanding regarding the general concept of CSED. Although the answers that were received varied with regard to the way these executives described the CSED concept, contentwise there was no significant difference in their answers. There was also no significant difference between the answers from the executives from the 'sensitive' industry groups and those from the 'non-sensitive' industry groups. As an example, one executive from one of the 'sensitive' companies said, "*I believe [CSED] is a way for us to communicate our company's vision regarding corporate social responsibility (CSR), and our company's plan and actions in relation to the CSR, to our stakeholders.*" One executive from the 'non-sensitive' companies answered, "*CSED for us is an integral part of our company's overall corporate disclosure, in which we basically provide a report regarding our CSR activities.*"

This finding indicates that the executives in this study perceive CSED as an instrument to communicate social and environmental concern within their business operations to their stakeholders, and therefore, indicates some strong support for the stakeholder perspective in influencing the executives' opinions regarding CSED. In practice, this finding also indicates that although the practice of CSED in Indonesia is still at an infant stage (Djajadikerta and Trireksani, 2012; Gunawan et al., 2009; Chappel and Moon, 2005), it seems that the message of CSED has been heard and understood by the executives. This led to the next question of the motivations for CSED.

In two interviews, soon after the first three main questions were asked, the executives showed their company's CSR reports to the interviewer. Both of these executives were from 'sensitive' companies. Hence, for these two interviews, the succeeding questions practically focused on the matters that were reported in the CSR reports and by doing these the interviewer was able to collect significant responses regarding the companies' motivations for CSED and their preferred means for the disclosure. While the other five companies did not have separate CSR reports, one other executive from a 'sensitive' company and both executives from the 'non-sensitive' companies showed the interviewer their CSED in their annual reports. Accordingly, the follow-on discussions were centered on the issues described in the reports. The remaining two executives did not provide the interviewer with any report, and hence the interviews relied on the verbal discussion with the executives.

The Motivations for CSED

While it was initially expected that the executives' motivations for disclosure varied, the findings from the interviews suggested otherwise. All of the executives in the study had a similar opinion that CSED was important to show to the public the level of their CSR practices. They felt that their companies needed to do this since the public expected them to perform socially and environmentally responsible. Therefore, CSED was a necessary tool for reporting and gaining recognition from the public. For example, one of the executives from the 'sensitive' industry group said, "*We have to show the public that we are a responsible company. Running a business in this country is not easy since we have quite huge social, educational, and especially economic gaps between those who can do business like us and those who are common people. Therefore, the issue of us helping them, the common people, is very important to be informed to the public.*"

Another executive from the 'sensitive' industry group said, "We built our company in this area, which is surrounded by people's houses. Most of these people are poor. It is obvious for us that we should provide assistance as much as possible to these people and show the public that we have done our part in assisting the community surrounding us. Otherwise, we won't be sustainable. Most of these people are good hard-working people anyway, so we are happy if could somehow help them. The thing that we sometimes confuse is the amount that we should set aside for this assistance. This is not a normal business expense, but this is needed, and sometimes we are not sure how we should calculate it in our budget."

The answers received from the executives from the 'non-sensitive' industry group were in substance similar. One of them, for example, said, "*It is true that our business does not directly affect the social and environmental aspects of the community. However, we feel that we do business with the society and without the society we will not exist. Therefore, we feel that we are obligated to give some back to the society. For us, it is not a bad thing anyway. Surely we spend some money for this, but we spend a lot more in our advertising and promotion. So we don't think that providing assistance in the forms of, for example, scholarships or donation, is a big deal for us.*"

These findings indicate some strong support for the legitimacy perspective in influencing the executives' motivation for CSED, and suggest that the main reason for their CSED practices is to attain societal recognition of the adequacy of their social behavior. A couple executives mentioned that their companies disclosed their corporate social and environmental information not only to attain societal recognition from the public, but also to follow the regulations. It was not clear which regulations that they referred to since they did not want to elaborate further when a follow-up question was asked, but at least these comments provided a small indication of the influence of the classical political economy perspective relating to mandatory disclosure.

The Preferred Means for Disclosure

The findings from the interviews show that the preferred means for disclosure vary among the executives in the study. The two executives that provided their companies' CSR reports were in agreement that the best means for their companies' CSED was the CSR report. They both expressed their interests and mentioned their future plan to also include major parts of their CSED on their websites. At the time of the interview, they said that their companies had included some general information regarding their CSED on their websites, but they were not yet convinced of the benefits and the efficacy of a detailed website reporting.

The three executives that showed their companies' CSED in the companies' annual reports had different opinions regarding the means for disclosure. Two of them said that for them the annual report was the best means for their companies' CSED. They both thought that the website could be useful in providing CSED to wider audiences, but they had not yet explored that option. One of these two executives also expressed his interest in preparing a separate CSR report, but the other one simply thought that a CSR report was not needed. This is what he said, "*Honestly speaking I am not sure why a CSR report is needed. I know that some other companies prepare this kind of report, and I am always asked myself 'what things that they include in their reports?', 'are there really many things that they have done?' For me, that practice is rather questionable.*" The remaining one executive could not really decide which was his preferred means for disclosure. He simply said that he still needed to familiarize himself with the CSED practice and its benefits.

The two executives that did not provide the interviewer with any report interestingly provided quite comprehensive answers regarding their preferred means for disclosure. One of them described that for him combined annual report and website reporting was the best means for CSED. He focused on a broad point of view of stakeholders which might consist of both the 'traditional community' who like traditional means of reporting such as the annual reports, and the more 'tech-savvy community' who might like contemporary means of reporting such as the websites. With reference to the CSR report, he was indifferent. The other executive described his preferred means for CSED in the forms of a detailed CSR report and brief descriptions in both the annual report and the website. He argued that a CSR report symbolized the seriousness of a company's CSR policies and actions, and, therefore, should be the method for disclosure used by any company that practiced their CSR.

These inconclusive executive perceptions regarding the preferred means for CSED confirm the previous suggestions made by Djajadikerta and Trireksani (2012) and Gunawan et al. (2009) that Indonesian executives are still uncertain about how and where they should disclose their CSED, and they are still looking for suitable media for their CSED. Consequently, this situation in some way contributes to the low CSED extent in Indonesia.

Conclusions

The findings of this study suggest that Indonesian executives have quite a considerable understanding regarding the general concept of CSED, and the findings also indicate the influence of the stakeholder perspective on the executives' opinions regarding CSED. Regarding the motivation for CSED, the study finds some indication that the main reason for their CSED practices is to attain societal recognition of the adequacy of their social behavior. This provides some support for the legitimacy perspective as an influencing structure for the executives' motivations for CSED.

It is also found that the executives' perceptions regarding the important activities within the CSR framework lean to focus more on social activities rather than environmental activities. Most of the executives tended to mention about their efforts to provide assistance for the less fortunate people, for example in the forms of donation or scholarships, but rarely mentioned their environmentally related activities. This may provide some stronger evidence for the influence of the legitimacy perspective in motivating the companies' CSR practices since the effects of social assistance are more direct and more visible than environmental efforts, and hence can better increase the chance for the companies to attain societal recognition.

Finally, the findings of this study show that the executives in this study have different perceptions regarding the preferred means for disclosure. This has provided some stronger evidence to support the previous suggestions made by Djajadikerta and Trireksani (2012) and Gunawan et al. (2009) that Indonesian executives are still uncertain about the preferred media for their companies' CSED.

References

Belal, A. R. (2001), "A study of corporate social disclosure in Bangladesh", *Managerial Auditing Journal,* Vol. 16, No. 5, pp. 274-289.

Brown, N. and Deegan, C. (1998), "The public disclosure of environmental performance information – a dual test of media agenda setting theory and legitimacy theory", *Accounting and Business Research,* Vol. 29, No. 1, pp. 21-41.

Chapple, W. and Moon, J. (2005), "Corporate Social Responsibility (CSR) in Asia: A Seven Country Study of CSR Web Site Reporting", *Business and Society,* Vol. 44, No. 4, pp. 415-442.

Deegan, C. (2002), *Australian Financial Accounting,* McGraw-Hill, Roseville NSW.

Deegan, C. and Gordon, B. (1996), "A study of the environmental disclosure practices of Australian companies", *Accounting and Business Research,* Vol. 26, No. 3, pp. 187-199.

Deegan, C. and Rankin, M. (1996), "Do Australian companies report environmental news objectively? An analysis of environmental disclosures by firms prosecuted successfully by the environmental protection authority", *Accounting, Auditing and Accountability Journal,* Vol. 9, No. 2, pp. 50-67.

Deegan, C., Rankin, M. and Tobin, J. (2002), "An examination of the corporate social and environmental disclosures of BHP from 1983-1997: A test of legitimacy theory", *Accounting, Auditing and Accountability Journal,* Vol. 15, No. 3, pp. 312-343.

Delmas, M. and Toffel, M. W. (2004), "Stakeholders and environmental management practices: An institutional framework", *Business Strategy and the Environment,* Vol. 13, No. 4, pp. 209-222.

Djajadikerta, H.G. and Trireksani, T. (2012), "Corporate social and environmental disclosure by Indonesian listed companies on their corporate websites", *Journal of Applied Accounting Research,* Vol. 13, No. 1, pp. 21-36.

Djanali, S. (n.d.). Current update of Indonesia higher education. Obtained through the Internet:

http://www.rihed.seameo.org/NewsandEvents/current%20update/pindonesia.pdf, [accessed 8/8/2007].

Donaldson, T. and Preston, L. (1995), "The stakeholder theory of the corporation: Concepts, Evidence, and Implications", *Academy of Management Journal,* Vol. 20, No. 1, pp. 65-92.

Economists split on Jakarta's komodo power. (2009, September 10). *Financial Times,* p. 5.

Fukukawa, K. and Moon, J. (2004), "A Japanese model of corporate social responsibility", *The Journal of Corporate Citizenship*, Vol. 16, pp. 45-59.

Gray, R., Kouhy, R. and Lavers, S. (1995), "Corporate social and environmental reporting: A review of the literature and a longitudinal study of UK disclosure", *Accounting, Auditing and Accountability Journal,* Vol. 8, No. 2, pp. 47-77.

Gray, R., Owen, D. and Adams, C. (1996), *Accounting and Accountability: Changes and challenges in corporate social and environmental reporting*, Prentice Hall, London.

Greenlees, D. (2005). "Young Indonesian executives fight a business culture of corruption", *International Herald Tribune*, 9 November, Obtained through the Internet: *http://www.iht.com/articles/2005/11/08/business/rupiah.php*, [accessed 8/8/2008].

Gunawan, J, Djajadikerta, H.G. and Smith, M. (2009), "An examination of corporate social disclosures in the annual reports of Indonesian listed companies", *Asia Pacific Centre for Environmental Accountability Journal*, Vol. 15, No. 1, pp.13-36.

IAIGlobal (n.d.). Obtained through the Internet: *http://www.iaiglobal.or.id/*, [accessed 8/8/2008].

Imam, S. (2000), "Corporate social performance reporting in Bangladesh", *Managerial Auditing Journal*, Vol. 15, No. 3, pp. 133 – 141.

Leonard, D. and McAdam, R. (2003), "Corporate social responsibility", *Quality Progress,* Vol. 36, No. 10, 27-32.

Mitchell, R., Agle, B.R. and Wood, D. J. (1997), "Toward a theory of stakeholder identification and salience: Defining the principle of who and what really counts", *Academy of Management Review,* Vol. 22, No. 4, pp. 853-886.

Nasi, J., Nasi, S., Phillips, N. and Zyglidopoulos, S. (1997), "The evolution of corporate social responsiveness: An exploratory study of Finnish and Canadian forestry companies", *Business and Society*, Vol. 36, pp. 296 – 321.

Raar, J. (2002), "Environmental initiative: Towards triple bottom line reporting", *Corporate Communications: An International Journal,* Vol. 7, No. 3, pp. 169-183.

Ramasamy, B. and Hung, W. T. (2004), "A comparative analysis of corporate social responsibility awareness", *The Journal of Corporate Citizenship,* Vol. 13, pp. 109-123.

Ratanajongkol, S., Davey, H. and Low, M. (2006), "Corporate social reporting in Thailand; The news is all good and increasing", *Qualitative Research in Accounting and Management,* Vol. 3, No. 1, pp. 67-83.

Snider, J., Hill, P. R. and Martin, D. (2003), "Corporate social responsibility in the 21st Century: A view from the world's most successful firms", *Journal of Business Ethics,* Vol. 48, No. 2, pp. 175-187.

Thompson, P. and Zakaria, Z. (2004), "Corporate social responsibility reporting in Malaysia: Progress and prospects", *The Journal of Corporate Citizenship,* Vol. 13, pp. 125-136.

Thomson, I. and Bebbington, J. (2005), "Social and environmental reporting in the UK: a pedagogic evaluation", *Critical Perspectives on Accounting,* Vol. 16, pp. 507–533.

Tilt, C. A. (1994), "The influence of external pressure groups on corporate social disclosure: Some empirical evidence", *Accounting, Auditing and Accountability Journal,* Vol. 7, No. 4, pp. 47-72.

United Nation (n.d.). Population, latest available census and estimates (2006 - 2007). . Obtained through the Internet: *http://unstats.un.org/unsd/demographic/products/vitstats/serATab2.pdf,* [accessed 8/6/2009].

van Staden, C.J. and Hooks, J. (2007), "A comprehensive comparison of corporate environmental reporting and responsiveness", *British Accounting Review,* Vol. 39, pp. 197-210.

Wilmhurst, T.D. and Frost, G.R. (2000), "Corporate environmental reporting: A test of legitimacy theory", *Accounting, Auditing and Accountability Journal,* Vol. 13, No. 1, pp. 10-26.

Chapter 7: Employee Perceptions of CSR

Critical Factors for Boosting CSR Participation

Brynn Harrington, Northwestern University, IL, USA

Gail Ann Berger, Northwestern University, IL, USA

Mindy Douthit, Northwestern University, IL, USA

Abstract: Corporate Social Responsibility (CSR) initiatives impact a number of key stakeholder groups, including customers, shareholders, governmental organizations, and employees. Businesses should design CSR strategies to meet stakeholder needs. In this paper, we focus on the individual employee. Employees are a particularly important audience for CSR strategies and initiatives because they are often active participants in their employers' CSR efforts. Corporations seek to involve employees in CSR programs in order to bolster the strength of their efforts, tie CSR initiatives to financial results, and position themselves as responsible and desirable employers. Likewise, actively engaged employees benefit from participation through increased job satisfaction, pride, learning, and in some cases, social and environmental responsibility that translates into their personal lives. Because of the pivotal role of employees in the success of CSR initiatives, it is critical that employers understand how to best communicate and position their plans to their diverse employee populations. Using survey findings gathered from 139 non-executive-level employees at a global chemical company we sought to understand how 1) independent versus interdependent self-construal and 2) strategic versus moral motivation impact the employees' a) perception of the firm's CSR efforts/practices and b) willingness to participate in/contribute to CSR efforts. We found that independent self-construal and strategic motivation had the greatest positive impact on CSR perception and participation. There was no conclusive evidence of a significant interaction between self-construal and motivation.

In recent decades, corporate social responsibility (CSR) has become an increasingly visible and important issue at corporate decision-making tables, in employees' day-to-day work operations, and in the media limelight. Global leaders, such as Ban Ki-moon, Secretary General of the United Nations, are calling for businesses to become actively involved in the most pressing issues facing our global society today: "we need business to give practical meaning and reach to the values and principles that connect cultures and people everywhere" (United Nations Website, 2008). Businesses, recognizing the strategic and moral value of acting and reacting responsibly, have heard the cry and responded, often with robust CSR offerings.

As companies become increasingly global, and receive more internal and external pressure to develop sustainable business practices and practice strong corporate citizenship, it is critical that they understand the impact of CSR decisions from an individual employee, organizational, national, and international perspective. CSR initiatives impact a number of key stakeholder groups, including customers, shareholders, governmental organizations, and employees; and it is the responsibility of businesses to design CSR strategies to meet stakeholder needs. In this paper, we focus on one stakeholder – the individual employee – as we examine the relationship between the individual employee and CSR. Specifically, we seek to understand how 1) one's self-construal and 2) whether or not a CSR initiative is positioned from a strategic or moral perspective impacts a) the individual's perception of the firm's CSR efforts/practices and b) the individual's stated willingness to participate in and contribute to CSR efforts.

Employees are a particularly important audience for CSR strategies and initiatives because they are often active participants in their employers' CSR efforts. At their best, employees are the face, the arbiters, and the champions of CSR programs. Corporations seek to involve employees in CSR programs in order to bolster the strength of their efforts, tie CSR initiatives to financial results, and position themselves as responsible and desirable employers. Likewise, actively engaged employees can benefit from participation through increased job satisfaction, pride, learning, and in some cases, social and environmental responsibility that translates into their personal lives. For example, Perez, Amichai-Hamburger and Shterental (2009) found that environmental certification at an organization was positively correlated with employees' personal environmental commitment as well as their organizational citizenship behavior.

Because of the pivotal role of employees in the success of CSR initiatives, it is critical that employers understand how to best communicate and position their plans to their diverse employee populations. The results of this study may help inform companies how to develop and position CSR strategy with various cultural groups and workgroups/job functions in mind.

Corporate Social Responsibility (CSR)

As the field of CSR has evolved, so too has the way researchers, business leaders and the public define the concept and practice. In fact, Dahlsrud (2008) surveyed 37 definitions of CSR in an attempt to understand how CSR is both defined and construed in a social context. Many of the definitions cited in the research highlight the obligation of businesses to act in ways that benefit society (e.g. Kok,

2001), while other definitions focus on the integration of CSR with business strategy (e.g. Davis, 1973).

Although unanimous agreement about the definition of CSR might still not exist, Basu & Palazzo (2008) suggest that the focus of CSR research is shifting from understanding "why" and "what," to "how" to best adopt strategies and processes that support CSR decisions within organizations. This supports a case for conducting research focused on identifying practical, tactical ways to implement CSR. The study described in this paper is designed to fall into this emerging body of research by helping employers develop and communicate their CSR strategies effectively to their diverse employee audiences. Specifically, the results of this research may help employers position their CSR initiatives in way that will elicit positive perceptions of and increased participation in CSR initiatives.

CSR and the Individual Employee

As previously discussed, there is a large volume of existing research about various elements of CSR planning and implementation. Aguilera, Rupp, Williams, and Ganapathi (2007) provide an excellent overview of the theoretical framework of CSR in their multilevel study of the micro/individual, meso/organizational, macro/country, and supra/transnational levels of CSR practice. Their paper notes a significant gap in the literature with regard to CSR and the individual employee, suggesting that additional "micro/employee-level research [is needed] to test linkages between employee perceptions of CSR and such outcomes as participation in CSR efforts, as well as commitment to and performance in both CSR and the employee's job in general" (p. 855).

The value of this individual-level research is prompting the questions and hypotheses outlined within this study. The individual employee level of analysis is particularly important with respect to CSR implementation issues, as employees are often the key drivers in the success or failure of a CSR initiative. According to a review by Fenwick and Bierema (2008), "employee misunderstanding and even resistance to CSR, varying meanings and priorities of CSR are cited as key CSR implementation issues" (p. 32). Howard-Greenville and Hoffman (2003) reinforce the importance of individual communication in their study, in which they report that "too often, social initiatives falter because their proponents take for granted that the value of their programs is apparent to others [or] they fail to adapt the business metrics and language that are employed by other parts of the organization in communicating that value…" (p. 70). Thus research in this area continues to offer great promise to corporate leaders.

CSR and Perception/Participation

While a large portion of the literature has focused on CSR performance, a moderate amount of research studies highlight the importance of strong and positive employee perception of an employer's CSR strategy, both domestically and globally. Aguilera et. al. (2007) report their finding that "employees' perceptions of a firm's social policies will impact their willingness to participate in, contribute to, and initiate social change initiatives" (p. 840). Ramus and Steger (2000) reported a similar finding with respect to environmental practices. Their study concluded that when employees perceive their employing organizations to be strongly committed to environmental protection, they are more likely to generate ideas for making the firm's practices more environmentally friendly. Employee perception of CSR is also important with respect to organizational commitment, as found by Peterson (2004), who hypothesized that "[an employee's] ethical measure of corporate citizenship will be a stronger predictor of organizational commitment than economic, legal, and discretionary measures" (p. 303).

On a global scale, employee perception of CSR is important when considering the execution of and communication about CSR initiatives being implemented by multi-nationals. Corporate CSR strategies and explicit versus implicit communications about CSR activities vary greatly from country to country and culture to culture (Matten & Moon, 2008). Particularly for large, multi-national companies, it is important to understand employee perceptions of CSR in the various countries where they have operations, significant consumer bases, or have left a footprint in the past. A strong, well-thought-out, and culturally relative CSR strategy could help to bridge national cultures and unify a company's corporate culture. According to Aguilera et. al. (2007), "CSR standards can play a valuable mediating role in diverse cultures between universal ethical principles and local norms" (p. 856).

Self-Construal: Independent versus Interdependent

Self-construal refers to an individual's sense of self in relation to others. Two primary types of self-construal have been identified: the independent and the interdependent (Markus, 1991). According to Markus (1991), people with independent self-construals see the self as stable and separate from its interpersonal context, valuing self-promotion, autonomy, assertiveness, and uniqueness; while people with interdependent self-construals see the self as more flexible and intertwined with the social context, valuing the maintenance of group harmony and fitting in. When thinking about themselves, people with an individual self-construal will refer to their own abilities, attributes, characteristics or ambitions rather than referring to the thoughts, beliefs, or abilities of others; while people with an interdependent self-construal will derive self-enhancement from perceptions and emotions that remind them of their connectedness with others.

In the literature, self-construal is highly relevant in discussions about collectivist cultures (e.g., Asian and Hispanic cultures) versus individualistic cultures (e.g., Western Europe, the US), as interdependence is likely to align more closely with the former, and independence is likely to align more closely with the latter. In a global economy where a "one-size-fits-all approach to CSR may not work" ("Going Global," 2008, p. 20), understanding how employees see themselves in relation to the world around them is an important component of understanding how they may react to their employer's positioning of its CSR strategy and tactics. Shaped by cultural beliefs and believed to impact cognition, emotion, and motivation, self-construal is relevant to understanding the relationship between the individual and CSR perception and participation.

In this research study, the role of self-construal will be evaluated with respect to perception of the firm's CSR efforts and stated willingness to participate in CSR efforts. In a related study Arnocky, Stoink, & DeCicco (2007) looked at how self-construal relates to environmental concern, and found that self-construal was directly related to environmental concern, cooperation, and behavior, and that the stronger one's independent self-construal was, the more egoistic or self-directed the person's environmental concern. These findings indicate that self-construal is a worthwhile variable to consider when measuring environmental consciousness; a conclusion that helps inform our research about self-construal and CSR perception and participation.

We anticipate that a clearer understanding of how independent versus interdependent self-construal impact perceptions of and participation in CSR efforts will help companies tailor their communication about CSR to employees with varying self-construals and different cultural backgrounds. Since individuals with an interdependent self-construal see themselves as flexible and intertwined with their social context; they value maintaining group harmony and fitting in; and they derive self-enhancement from perceptions and emotions that remind them of their connectedness with others (Markus, 1991). CSR, regardless of the definition used, is marked by a company operating within a broader, more connected business, national, and global context. Therefore, the connected nature of interdependent self-construal seems to be much more closely aligned with the goals and outcomes of CSR programs. Therefore, we hypothesize:

> Hypothesis 1: Employees primed with an interdependent self-construal will have better perceptions of and participation in CSR efforts than those primed with an independent self-construal.

Positioning: Strategic Initiative versus Moral Initiative

Corporations are generally strategically/extrinsically motivated to implement CSR initiatives; a finding marked by a number of studies that have shown the financial rewards of CSR. Specifically, CSR has been shown to be rewarding via improvement in the company's reputation in the consumer market (Fombrun & Shanley, 1990); stronger employee commitment and higher profitability and productivity (R.L. Sims, 1997); and increased market value (Mackey, Mackey, & Barney, 2007). Aguilera et. al. (2007) compare employee and employer motives, suggesting that while employees will place the most pressure on companies to engage in CSR when their morality-based motives are especially strong; at the organizational level, CSR pressure will be strongest when instrumental needs are high among "corporate insiders." Although companies will always be strategically motivated, their employees need not share this alignment and may be more motivated by moral contribution.

According to Locke & Latham (2004), "the concept of motivation refers to internal factors that impel action and to external factors that can act as inducements to action" (p. 388). With respect to CSR perception and participation, both internal and external motivational factors impact individual employees. Thus it might be advantageous for companies to consider both moral and strategic factors when they position CSR initiatives. A number of authors consider similar frameworks for positioning of initiatives. For example, Berger, Cunningham, & Drumwright (2007) refer to positioning as stemming from either a business case model, social values-led model, or syncretic stewardship model. Similarly, Aguilera et. al. (2007) argue that employees have three main motives for pressuring firms to engage in CSR: instrumental (self-interest driven), relational (concerned with relationships among group members), and moral (concerned with ethical standards and moral principles).

CSR motivations were studied with respect to performance by Graafland and van de Nan (2006). In their study management-level employees at Dutch firms were asked to rate their agreement/disagreement with two propositions on a five-point scale. Their responses were compared with the analysis of the CSR performance of 111 Dutch firms, utilizing 22 measures of CSR performance. The authors defined a positive strategic view of CSR as implying that "companies believe there exists a win-win relationship between CSR and the financial success of the company" (p. 111); and they defined a positive moral view of CSR as implying that "the business culture upholds certain business principles according to which CSR is perceived as the moral duty of the firm" (p. 111). They found that the moral (intrinsic) motive was correlated with stronger CSR performance than the strategic (extrinsic) motive.

Our research will differ from Graafland and van de Nan's (2006) work in four important respects: 1) we seek to understand the perceptions of non-manager-level employees (no managers will be included); 2) we will be manipulating positioning of the CSR initiative; 3) we will examine the impact of positioning on individual employee perception and participation, rather than the firm level performance; and 4) we are introducing a second independent variable (self-construal). We anticipate that this study design will provide a unique perspective on the question of organizational positioning of CSR on employee perceptions and motivation to participate in CSR.

Strategic versus moral motivation of the individual employee will not always be aligned with the outcomes of the firm's CSR efforts. Understanding employee motivation and how it relates to company outcomes is a key component of designing and delivering (i.e. positioning) a strong CSR strategy – a point made clearly by Collier and Esteban (2007): "the effective delivery of corporate social and environmental responsibility initiatives is dependent on employee responsiveness....and in order for employees to be effective, they must be motivated and committed" (p. 22). Existing research points to a stronger connection between moral positioning of CSR initiatives and CSR involvement than strategic positioning. Thus consistent with existing research we hypothesize:

> Hypothesis 2: Employees presented with a moral positioning of a CSR initiative will be more likely to have strong perceptions of and participation in CSR efforts than those presented with strategic positioning of the initiative.

Research Methods

Sample and Procedures

The study was conducted at a global chemical company with an existing CSR strategy. An online survey was distributed to 500 non-executive-level, U.S.-based employees at the company. The survey included questions about the subject's perception of and likelihood to participate in corporate social responsibility (CSR) initiatives, both generally and with respect to specific strategically and morally positioned outcomes. All survey questions were assessed based on a 6-point Likert scale. The survey yielded a total of 163 respondents (33% response rate). Of these 163 respondents, 24 were excluded from the final results because they failed to respond to one or more survey questions, leaving a final sample of 139 respondents (28%), who were distributed among the four conditions as outlined in Figure 1.

	Positioning		
Self-Construal	*Moral*	*Strategic*	*Total*
Independent	36	31	67
Interdependent	30	42	72
Total	66	73	139

Figure 1: Distribution of Subjects Across Treatments

Participants took an online survey onsite at their host company. The survey was sent out via email on the joint behalf of the Director of Sustainability and Director of Corporate Citizenship. Employees were given two weeks to complete the survey; one reminder email was sent at the conclusion of the first week. To ensure that employees did not discuss their primes and/or scenarios, they were asked to commit to confidentiality following survey completion. The target number of respondents was achieved at the end of the two-week period, at which point data collection was discontinued as planned.

Study Design

The 2x2 experimental study design was conducted utilizing an online survey with the following components. First, participants were primed for independent or interdependent self-construal. Numerous studies have evaluated self-construal through priming, and found that priming within a culture should usually create differences seen in cross-culture comparisons. By holding culture constant while varying self-construal, it is possible to utilize self-construal to understand interactions in the social world (Gardner & Gabriel, 1999). The sample was randomly distributed between the two primes. Self-construal was primed using instructions based on Ybarra and Trafimow's (1998) research. One group (interdependent) was asked to list five attributes they had in common with their colleagues, and the other group (independent) was asked to list five attributes that distinguished them from their colleagues.

Participants were then presented with one of the following two scenarios designed to segment them by strategic/external versus moral/intrinsic positioning of the initiative enabling us to test the second independent variable. The use of two controlled scenarios has been proven effective in segmenting groups to evaluate motivation (Graafland & van de Ven, 2006).

The ***strategic scenario*** was as follows:

> In 2005, a company launched a corporate social responsibility (CSR) initiative called "Blue Skies 2010." The initiative was designed to reduce the company's manufacturing facility energy usage by 20% by the year 2010. Today, halfway through the initiative's implementation period, the firm is reporting the following results:
>
> - 2007 energy usage was 11% lower than 2005 usage
> - Changes in the manufacturing process, which were implemented to reduce energy usage, have reduced manufacturing costs by 5%, which increased net profit margins in 2006 and 2007
> - Company's stock price hit an all-time high in 2007
> - A consumer survey showed less price sensitivity due to the Company's "Blue Skies 2010" initiative, allowing the company to increase prices by an additional 3% in 2007, thereby increasing the company's profits

The ***moral scenario*** was as follows:

> In 2005, a company launched a corporate social responsibility (CSR) initiative called "Blue Skies 2010." The initiative was designed to reduce the company's manufacturing facility energy usage by 20% by the year 2010. Today, halfway through the initiative's implementation period, the firm is reporting the following results:
>
> - 2007 energy usage was 11% lower than 2005 usage
> - As part of the "Blue Skies 2010" program, the company offset the difference between its progress and its 20% goal by purchasing wind and solar power credits in 2005, 2006 and 2007, thereby supporting the emerging clean energy industry.
> - The United Nations highlighted the company's innovative program in its recent review of environmental responsibility
> - In 2007, for the first time ever, the company was included in a list of the "Top 100 Most Environmentally Conscious Companies"

After reading the scenario, participants answered a 15-question (plus sub-questions) online survey probing about the scenario, employee perception of CSR, and employee participation in CSR efforts.

Results and Analysis

The final participants represented diverse demographics. The largest segments in each demographic category included men (72%), 10+ years employed at the company (60%), ages 41-50 years (36%), and 4-year college degree completed (40%). Complete demographic information is included in Figure 2 below.

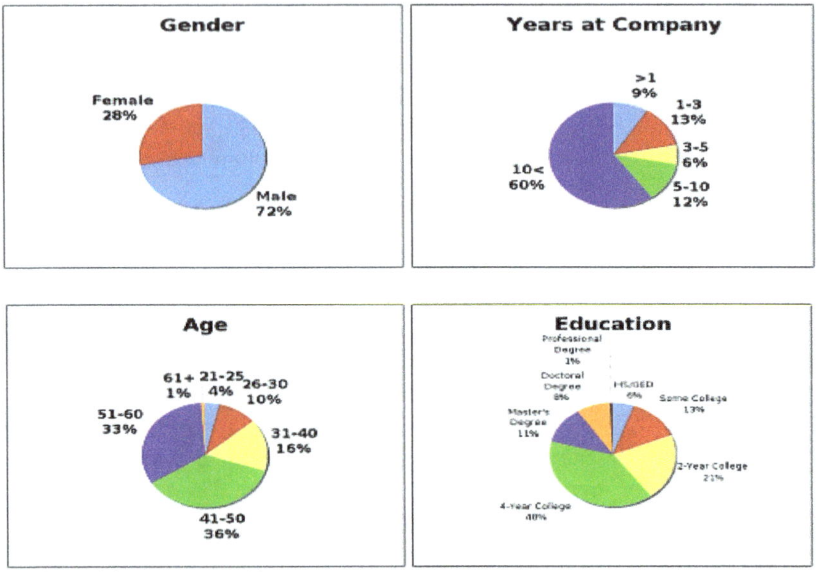

Figure 2: Participant Demographics

CSR Perception & Participation

To assess participants' overall perception of the importance of CSR programs they were asked, "How important do you believe it is for a company to have an explicit Corporate Social Responsibility (CSR) program?" Responses were recorded on 6 point scale where 1=not at all important, 2=not important, 3=of little importance, 4=marginally important, 5=important and 6=very important. The average across all conditions was 4.85 and the majority (75%) of survey respondents thought it was 'important' or 'very important' for an organization to have an explicit CSR strategy. Employee participation was measured by asking, "How likely are you to actively participate in a corporate activity or initiative related to corporate social responsibility within the next year?" The 6 point scale used included 1=will not participate, 2=very unlikely to participate, 3=unlikely to participate, 4=likely to participate, 5=very likely to participate and 6=definitely will participate. The average across all conditions was 4.14 and the majority of respondents (79%) stated that they were 'likely', 'very likely' or 'definitely will' participate in a CSR initiative within the next year.

Self-Construal and Perception & Participation in CSR

Hypothesis 1 predicted that employees primed with an interdependent self-construal will have better perceptions of CSR and will be more likely to participate in CSR efforts than those primed with an independent self-construal. Figure 23 displays that there is a slight difference in the means of CSR Perception between the two groups. The average response of those respondents who were primed with the independent self-construal was 4.97 whereas the average for those primed with the interdependent self-construal condition was 4.74. This slight difference in means is not significant (t=1.309, p=.193). However, it is worth noting that the perception of CSR is more positive for the independent group, not the interdependent group, as was hypothesized. Given this difference is not significant, we cannot draw any conclusions from this finding, but it is worth noting.

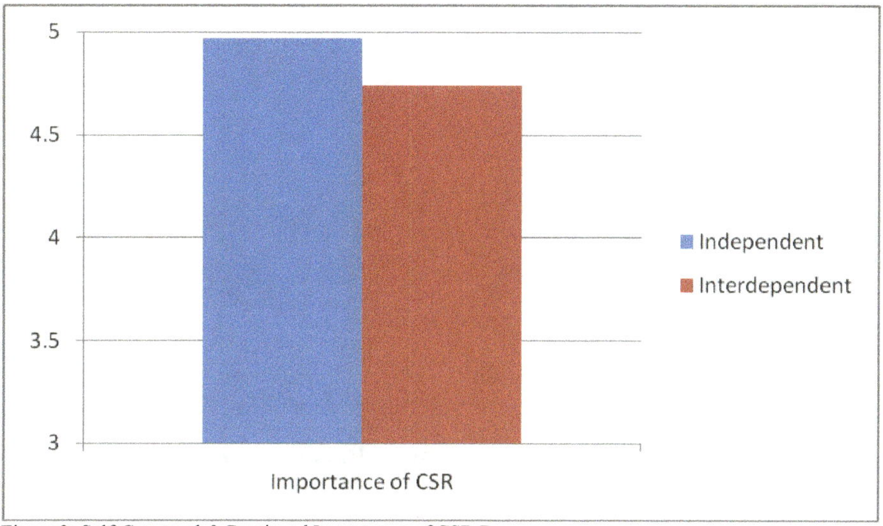

Figure 3: Self-Construal & Percieved Importance of CSR Programs

When the respondents were asked to indicate their likelihood to participate in a CSR initiative, the average response for those primed in the independent self-construal condition was 4.39 and the average for those given the interdependent prime was 3.90 (see Figure 4). This difference in means is significant (t=2.77, p<.01). However, it is the *independent* primed group that has a higher average likelihood to participate. Once again, this is in opposition with hypothesis 1. We expected the *interdependent* group to be those who, on average, would be more likely to participate in a CSR initiative within the next year.

Therefore, hypothesis 1 was not supported by the results. In fact, the exact opposite proved to be true for participation and there was indication that this same effect might exist for perception as well.

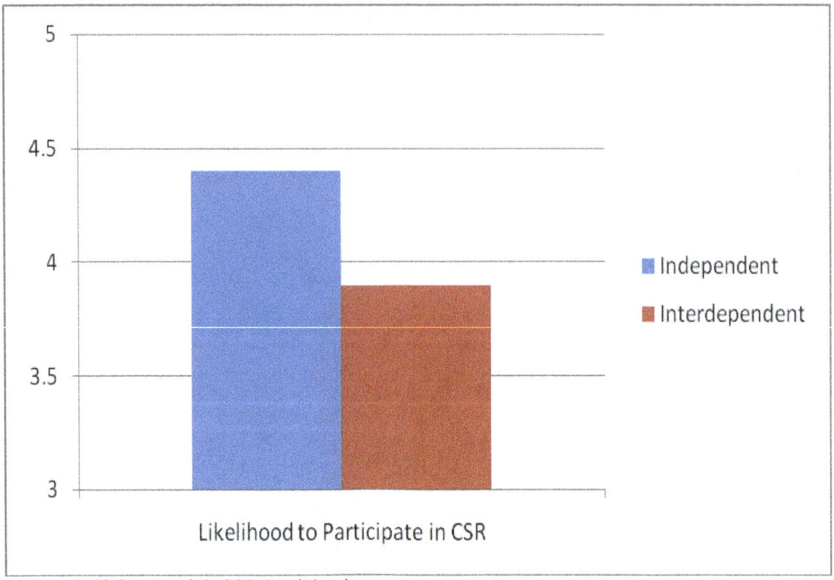

Figure 4: Self-Construal & CSR Participation

Positioning and Perception & Particpation in CSR

Hypothesis 2 predicted that employees presented with a moral positioning of a CSR initiative will be more likely to have strong perceptions of and participation in CSR efforts than those presented with strategic positioning of the initiative. However, when we compare the average values of CSR perception, we see that it is the employees who were presented with the strategic positioning who tend to evaluate CSR initiatives as more important (mean=5.0) than the employees who were given the moral positioning (mean=4.68). This slight difference in means (t=1.78, p<.10) is again in the opposite direction of our hypothesis. The group presented with the strategic scenario thought it was more important for a company to implement a CSR program than did the group presented with the moral benefits of CSR.

When we look at how respondents indicated their likelihood to participate in a CSR initiative, the positioning (moral versus strategic) did not have an effect. The two groups had the same average response (mean=4.13 for both groups) when asked if they were likely to participate in a CSR initiative in the next year.

Thus, hypothesis 2 was also not supported by the results. Again, initial evidence suggests that the opposite proved to be true, as there was more positive perception among the group presented with the strategic scenario versus the moral scenario.

Self-Construal, Positioning & CSR

In order to explore these effects in greater detail, we conducted a Univariate Analysis of Variance to test for both main effects with our independent variables of self-construal and positioning, as well asan interaction effect among these variables. Table 1 shows these results for our dependent variable of CSR perception, as measured by rated importance.

Source	Type III Sum of Squares	Df	Mean Square	F	Sig.
Corrected Model	6.257[a]	3	2.086	1.908	.131
Intercept	3210.236	1	3210.236	2936.779	.000
SelfConstrual	2.558	1	2.558	2.340	.128
Positioning	4.257	1	4.257	3.894	.051
SelfConstrual * Positioning	.134	1	.134	.123	.727
Error	147.570	135	1.093		
Total	3422.000	139			
Corrected Total	153.827	138			

a. R Squared = .041 (Adjusted R Squared = .019)

Table 1: Perceived Importance of CSR

As was indicated in the discussion above, there is a main effect for positioning (F=3.894, p=.05), but no main effect for self-construal (F=2.34, p=.13) nor an interaction between these two variables (F=.123, p=.727). Thus, employees' perceptions of CSR do not seem to be affected by self-construal, but positioning of the initiative does matter.

Now, turning to Table 2, we see that when we look at participation as the outcome variable, self-construal matters, but positioning does not. There is a significant main effect for self-construal (F=8.076, p=.005), but there is no main effect for positioning (F=.094, p=.759) nor an interaction between the variables (F=1.783, p=.184).

Source	Type III Sum of Squares	Df	Mean Square	F	Sig.
Corrected Model	10.201[a]	3	3.400	3.183	.026
Intercept	2328.922	1	2328.922	2180.303	.000
Self-Construal	8.626	1	8.626	8.076	.005
Positioning	.101	1	.101	.094	.759
Self-Construal * Positioning	1.904	1	1.904	1.783	.184
Error	144.202	135	1.068		
Total	2533.000	139			
Corrected Total	154.403	138			

a. R Squared = .066 (Adjusted R Squared = .045)

Table 2: Likelihood to Participate in CSR

Discussion

The results of the current study are inconsistent with the proposed hypotheses, however, they do point to alternative conclusions about the relationship between each of the independent variables (self-construal and positioning) and employee perception of CSR. More specifically, this study demonstrated that respondents with an independent self-construal and respondents with strategic positioning had stronger perceptions of CSR than respondents with an interdependent self-construal and those with a moral positioning.

Reviewing first the self-construal results, all of the main effects point to a stronger relationship between an independent self-construal and CSR perception than an interdependent self-construal and CSR (the opposite effect was hypothesized). Limited research has been conducted on the relationship between self-construal and CSR perception, and therefore, the original hypothesis was derived from similarities between the characteristics of interdependent individuals (flexible and intertwined with their social context) and the underlying philosophy of CSR (company operating within a broader, more connected business, national, and global context). The current study, however, indicates that the relationship between CSR and self-construal is a highly complex interaction that is worthy of directed study.

In an attempt to understand why the hypothesis proved to be false, limited research findings do reveal consistency between the current data and past results. Specifically, in their study about self-construal and environmental concern, Arnocky, Stoink, & DeCicco, (2007), found that the stronger one's independent self-construal was, the more egoistic or self-directed their environmental concern was. Similarly, in our study the likelihood of participation showed a main effect, indicating that the decision to participate in CSR may be more strongly related to one's time and interests than one's inherent desire to help other people.

The finding that an independent self-construal results in a more positive perception of CSR is relevant to companies that are trying to engage their employees to support and/or participate in CSR initiatives. This research indicates that employees view CSR initiatives as a way to satisfy their own personal interests within the workplace and broaden their careers, not so much for the good of the world, as for the betterment of themselves. It therefore could be reasoned that benefits of CSR participation should be presented in a way that helps individuals see how they themselves relate to the initiative, not merely how the initiative helps their broader corporate, local, or global community.

Next, reviewing the positioning results, across both conditions (moral and strategic), participants found the scenarios that they read to reflect effective initiatives. However, employees presented with the strategic scenario were more supportive of CSR initiatives than those presented with the moral scenario, and respondents in the strategic condition showed a higher likelihood of participation in CSR programs. These findings are inconsistent with the original hypothesis and the majority of past research studies; however, limited research aids in the understanding of these conclusions. A review study conducted by Aguilera et al (2007) indicated that while companies will always be strategically motivated, employees will place the most pressure on companies to engage in CSR when their [the employees'] morality-based motives are especially strong. This is reflected in the current study, demonstrated by the finding that the employees who were presented with the strategically-oriented scenario showed strong moral motivation to implement CSR. The scenario, the marker of the organization's success, may have strengthened employees' support of CSR in general. Experiencing an overall positive view of CSR, the subjects may have then focused on the moral benefits, hoping to ensure that the moral benefits would receive equal attention from company leadership. If true, these results could lead one to speculate that when a company's CSR efforts are successful in a strategic/financial sense, it is equally or more important to translate these benefits into moral, value-driven outcomes for employees and their communities.

Lastly, there was no conclusive evidence that there was a significant interaction between self-construal and positioning. While the individuals in the independent self-construal and strategic positioning condition showed the strongest perception of CSR, those with the independent self-construal and moral positioning showed the strongest likelihood to participate in CSR initiatives. This could be interpreted to indicate that in order for individuals to move from supporting to participating in a CSR initiative, the moral factors are of the greatest importance.

Failure to observe significant interaction effects was not completely unexpected because there was clearly minimal prior evidence to support the interaction between these two variables. One explanation for these results may be that both of the independent variables impact different types of decision-making, which do not intersect. Aguilera et al (2007) argue that the main motives employees have for pressuring firms to engage in CSR include: instrumental (self-interest driven), relational (concerned with relationships among group members), and moral (concerned with ethical standards and moral principles). It could be that these motives are too different, and too strong, to interact with any significance.

Implications for Future Research

Building upon this study, it would be interesting to research which moral outcomes of CSR are most important to a strategically-oriented subject pool, which could help companies better understand how to position the broader impact of their CSR efforts. For example, such information could help companies decide how to design CSR initiatives and/or talk about these initiatives to better engage their employees, better attract new customers and engage existing ones, and how to communicate their CSR efforts and achievements to the public at large. Moreover it would be interesting to investigate if positioning of CSR initiatives should vary depending on the industry and size of the company.

Additionally, methodologically, as noted above, the positioning prime may have been interpreted as the company's strategic versus moral success, which is not the same as the survey participant's personal motivation. Therefore, one could conduct a comparable study, but instead of using a prime, present subjects with two scenarios (one morally-grounded and one strategically-grounded) and ask subjects to assess the success of each. This data point could then be used to determine each subject's personal motivation, which could define the condition in the study.

With regard to future research directions, the findings of this study point to a possible relationship between job fit/career success and an employer's CSR initiatives. Pursuing this relationship could help companies better integrate all jobs (not just sustainability-focused jobs) with sustainability efforts. Lastly, future researchers interested in the topic may want to consider examining the interaction of other variables (e.g., time, education about initiatives, organizational commitment) with either self-construal or positioning. Together, this study and future research about CSR perception, have the potential to impact corporate decision-making and possibly, employee retention, engagement, and fulfillment.

Conclusion

We live in a world in which business and social ventures are becoming increasingly intertwined. Responsible and sustainable business practices are no longer just acts of altruism, rather they are mechanisms to improve the bottom line for companies in a multitude of sectors. This is great news for organizations in terms of operations, image, and in a more philosophical sense, fulfillment. However, without the support of employees, many CSR initiatives fizzle out or fall flat. Employees are central to the success of CSR initiatives, and likewise, CSR is often an important factor in employee recruitment, retention, and satisfaction.

The results of this study demonstrate that respondents with an independent self-construal and respondents with strategic positioning have stronger perceptions of CSR than respondents with an interdependent self-construal and those with a moral positioning. It was difficult, however, to draw conclusions about the interactive effects between the two independent variables. The findings in this paper should help both company leadership better understand employee perspectives, and future researchers explore the relationship between CSR and employee perception/behavior more deeply. With additional information about how CSR strategies impact individual employees, organizations will be better equipped to utilize CSR to drive business decisions and corporate culture while meeting the diverse needs of a global workforce and the growing needs of a changing world.

REFERENCES

Aguilera, R. V., Rupp, D. E., Williams, C. A., & Ganapathi, J. (2007). Putting the S Back in Corporate Social Responsibility: A Multilevel Theory of Social Change in Organizations. *Academy of Management Review, 32*(3): 836-863.

Arnocky, S., Stroink, M., & DeCicco, T. (2007). Self-construal predicts environmental concern, cooperation, and conservation. Journal of Environmental Psychology, 27(4): 255-264.

Basu, K., & Palazzo, G. (2008). Corporate Social Responsibility: A Process Model of Sensemaking. Academy of Management Review, 33(1): 122-136.

Berger, I. E., Cunningham, P., & Drumwright, M. E. (2007, Summer2007). Mainstreaming Corporate Social Responsibility: Developing Markets for Virtue. California Management Review, 49(4), 132-157.

Collier, J., & Esteban, R. (2007). Corporate social responsibility and employee commitment. Business Ethics: A European Review, 16(1), 19-33.

Dahlsrud, A. (2008). How corporate social responsibility is defined: an analysis of 37 definitions. Corporate Social Responsibility and Environmental Management, 15(1), 1-13.

Davis, K. (1973). The case for and against business assumption of social responsibilities. Academy of Management Review, 16, 312-323.

Fenwick, T., & Bierema, L. (2008). Corporate social responsibility: issues for human resource development professionals. International Journal of Training & Development, 12(1), 24-35.

Fombrun, C., & Shanley, M. (1990). What's in a name? Reputation Building and Corporate Strategy. Academy of Management Journal, 33(2), 233-258.

Gardner, W. L., & Gabriel, S. (1999). `I' value freedom, but `we' value relationships: Self-construal priming mirrors cultural. Psychological Science, 10(4), 321.

Going Global. (2008, 1/19/08). The Economist, 386, 20-21.

Graafland, J., & van de Ven, B. (2006, Summer2006). Strategic and Moral Motivation for Corporate Social Responsibility. Journal of Corporate Citizenship(22), 111-123.

Howard-Grenville, J. A., & Hoffman, A. J. (2003). The importance of cultural framing to the success of social initiatives in business. Academy of Management Executive, 17(2), 70-84.

Kok, P., T.V.D. Weile, R. Mckenna, A. Brown. (2001). A Corporate Social Responsibility Audit within a Quality Management Framework. Journal of Business Ethics, 31, 285-297.

Locke, E. A., & Latham, G. P. (2004). What should we do about motivation theory? Six recommendations for the twenty-first century. Academy of Management Review, 29(3), 388-403.

Mackey, A., Mackey, T. B., & Barney, J. B. (2007). Corporate social responsibility and firm performance: Investor preferences and corporate strategies. Academy of Management Review, 32(3), 817-835.

Markus, H. R. a. K., S. (1991). Culture and the self: Implications for cognition, emotion, and motivation. Psychological Review, 98, 224-253.

Matten, D., & Moon, J. (2008). "Implicit" and "explicit" CSR: A conceptual framework for a comparative understanding of corporate social responsibility. Academy of Management Review, 33(2), 404-424.

Perez, O., Amichai-Hamburger, Y., & Shterental, T. (2009). The Dynamic of Corporate Self-Regulation: ISO 14001, Environmental Commitment, and Organizational Citizenship Behavior.Citation. Law & Society Review, 43(3), 593-630.

Peterson, D. K. (2004). The Relationship Between Perceptions of Corporate Citizenship and Organizational Commitment. Business and Society, 43(3), 296.

R.L. Sims, T. L. K. (1997). Ethical Work Climate as a Factor in the Development of Person-Organization Fit. Journal of Business Ethics, 16, 1095-1105.

Ramus, C. A., Steger, U. (2000). The roles of supervisory support behaviors and environmental policy in employee "ecoincentives" at leading-edge European companies. Academy of Management Journal, 43, 605-626.

United Nations. (2008). Message posted to http://www.unglobalcompact.org.

Vogel, D. (2005). The Market for Virtue: The Potential Limits of Corporate Social Responsibility. Washington, D.C.: Brookings Institution Press.

Ybarra, O. & Trafimow, D. (1998). How priming the private self or collective self affects the relative weights of attitudes and subjective norms. Personality and Social Psychology Bulletin, 24(4), 362-370.

Part III: Corporate Social Responsibility and Economic Development

Chapters 8-10 make up Part 3 of the book, which focuses on corporate social responsibility and economic development. Chapter 8 explores the role of CSR in development. Chapter 9 explores the interaction between multinational companies and development countries. Chapter 10 looks at cooperation between the government and business in CSR development efforts.

Chapter 8: CSR and Development

Corporate Social Responsibility and Development: Can CSR Replace Development Aid?

Jan Boon, University of Ottawa, Ontario, Canada

Abstract: The CSR movement is helping address negative consequences of globalization. The proportion of participating businesses is low, and power relationships between actors are skewed towards business, posing a risk of regulatory capture of governments and NGOs by business. The current CSR paradigm does not address systemic world power structure issues. Its instrumentalist orientation limits its ability to address problems with complex root causes. The application of CSR in development faces additional challenges: the incompatibility of the CSR business case with CSR as a development tool; the power asymmetry between corporations, and governments and communities in developing countries; lack of capacity; cultural differences; and poor alignment of CSR and development strategies. Many companies are working on internal CSR issues, and few impact studies have moved beyond the business case. Governments and international governance institutions could enhance CSR's contribution to development through policies linked to these challenges, guide an integrated approach to aligning CSR development initiatives with overall development strategies, and institute a balanced mix of incentives and sanctions. A robust regulatory environment, intense debate and mutual scrutiny of the actors, and continued learning by all would help CSR realize its potential. Global factors affecting future directions of CSR include changing world power structures, demographics, and climate. These could have a profound effect on CSR battle strategies and tactics of all players. Will the paradigm shift away from neo-liberalism? In which direction? Will it alleviate the plight of the poor or will it worsen it? Will the emerging trend of linking CSR to climate change issues continue? All actors have a responsibility to be aware of the challenges and to ensure that their perspectives are heard and taken into account. They should prepare for a long "power interregnum".

Introduction

Corporate Social Responsibility (CSR) continues to receive widespread attention and is touching communities, academics, governments, international institutions, trade associations, churches and other civil society organizations, investors and corporations alike. In the extractive industries sector, properly addressing CSR issues is now considered to be a survival issue (Prospectors and Developers Association of Canada, 2007). The rhetoric of CSR implied in the term itself and used in many of the documents produced by industry associations and individual corporations (e.g. Holme and Watts, 2000) is raising considerable expectations.

CSR and Development

Broadly accepted overall development goals include elimination of poverty, equitable access to resources, empowerment of individuals and communities, and a clean environment. Potential contributions by business to development should be measured against such goals, of which the United Nations Millennium Development Goals (2000) are an example. However, the relative roles of the state and private companies in development are a controversial issue in development research (Martinussen, 1997: 32-33).

Private sector investment drives economic growth and development, and CSR commits corporations to incorporate 'beyond the law' activities related to corporate governance and ethics and a host of other subjects (On Common Ground Consultants, 2007: 2), many of which can be related to development goals. CSR recognizes that corporations have economic, social, environmental and human rights responsibilities to society that go beyond their duties to shareholders, and that includs the CSR policies and practices that meet these responsibilities. Many corporations now prefer to use the term "sustainability"rather than CSR, and more recently "Shared Value Creation" is coming en vogue. "The concept of shared value can be defined as policies and operating practices that enhance the competitiveness of a company while simultaneously advancing the economic and social conditions in the communities in which it operates. Shared value creation focuses on identifying and expanding the connections between societal and economic progress (Porter and Kramer, 2011: 66).

Drivers of CSR

Globalization has weakened the capacity of nation states to establish and enforce regulations that ensure fair competition, respect for human rights, just distribution of wealth, control of criminal economic activity and protection of the natural environment. At the same time, wealth is increasingly being concentrated in corporations that now have a strong capacity to choose and shape their regulatory environments. Developing nation governments are revising their regulations to attract economic activity and direct investment, in a regulatory 'race to the bottom' (Graham and Woods, 2006: 869).

The growth of CSR over the past few decades was spurred by Non-Government Organizations (NGO) and civil society reaction to the vastly increased power of TNCs accompanying globalization and its associated neo-liberal policies (Eade, 2005: 249,250; Bendell, 2005: 368; Fridell, 2007; Saul, 2005: 152-156). The Internet provided a very powerful tool for exerting public pressure. Also, the corporate sector has realized that "ethical business is good business" (Industry Canada, 2006: 7) and governments are actively encouraging businesses to embrace CSR (e.g. National Roundtables on Corporate Social Responsibility and the Canadian Extractive Industry Advisory Group, 2007; Federal Interdepartmental National Roundtable Steering Committee, 2006). The Advisory Group of the National Roundtables on CSR in the Canadian Extractive Industry Abroad, composed of members from industry, the NGO sector, investors and academia, produced a hard-won consensus report containing recommendations that include the establishment of a Canadian CSR framework with Canadian standards; reporting against the Canadian standards in an internationally recognized format; links to income tax incentives, stock exchange listing requirements and institutional investor social, environmental and governance disclosure requirements; and the establishment of an independent ombudsman and a tripartite compliance review committee (National Roundtables on Corporate Social Responsibility and the Canadian Extractive Industry Advisory Group, 2007; Drohan, 2010).The government, after two years of deliberation, announced a CSR policy that was considerable weaker than the recommendations of the Advisory Group (Department of Foreign Affairs and International Trade, 2009). This led to private member's Bill C-300 that contained some of the recommendations mentioned above. It was defeated by a few votes. Recently the Congress of Peru unanimously approved a bill on prior consultation that gives indigenous and original peoples of the country the right to pronounce themselves on possible extractive industry projects (Anonymous, 2011: 30). Cragg (2005: 2) views corporate self-regulation as one option for filling the regulatory vacuum resulting from globalization. CSR is being advocated by policy makers as an alternative to the public delivery of development (Frynas, 2005: 582). Szablowski (2007: 72) comments that "…Together, certification institutions [associated with the CSR codes] and the [de facto] regulatory efforts of civil society de-certifiers [through their campaigns] are interlocking parts of a single legal mechanism. Szablowski applies the term "legal" to both formal and informal frameworks. This legal mechanism is itself an expression of the balancing powers of the actors.

Development and CSR

The "orthodox" approach to CSR fits within the neo-classical economics paradigm, leading to development limitations (Blowfield and Frynas, 2005: 503; Garvey and Newell, 2005: 401; Prieto-Carrón et al., 2006). Garvey and Newell (2005: 391) see struggles for corporate accountability (their preferred term) as "contests of power between actors with competing agendas and very different capabilities". Newell (2005: 556) is concerned that "orthodox" CSR overlooks the importance and inevitability of conflict and that it vastly underestimates the importance of power and resistance to the achievement of development outcomes. Already at the beginning of the 20th century the German sociologist Georg Simmel believed that conflict is inseparable from social life, and an essential instigator of change and development. He saw conflict and order as two sides of the same coin (Coser, 1965: 12). Van der Putten (2005) discusses the effect of societal demands on business behaviour in developing countries and about the conditions under which Western-based firms can make a positive contribution to local communities in developing countries. CSR theories that are particularly relevant to development include those that address the integration of social demands into business activities, and those that relate to the social power of business and its responsibility to play a positive role (Garriga and Melé, 2004: 52). Boele et al (2001b: 124) assign various tiers of company achievement related to development: the traditional notion of 'license to operate'; an ability to move beyond a compliance-based approach to recognize and internalize societal expectations; the competence required to navigate uncertainty, maximize opportunity and engage effectively with external stakeholders on issues and concerns; and an ability to transcend instrumental reasoning. Other authors (Blowfield and Frynas, 2005: 512; Blowfield, 2005: 520; Bakan, 2005: 161) suggest that CSR theory should broaden its approach to include factors such as the world economic structures and events that cause poverty. Sagebien and Lindsay see CSR as part of a Social and Environmental Governance Ecosystem (SEVGE), a view that "can provide finer-grained understanding of the complex dynamics surroundingCSR and development issues. The diagram shown in Figure 1 is based on their Figure 1.2 (Sagebien and Lindsay, 2011: 13, 26). The lines connecting the boxes represent possible bilateral relations. For the 11 actors shown there are 11!/(2!x9!) = 55 possible bilateral relationships. For trilateral relationships the mathematical possibilities are even more numerous: 11!/(3!x8!) = 165. However, usually only a fraction of these is realized at any one time.

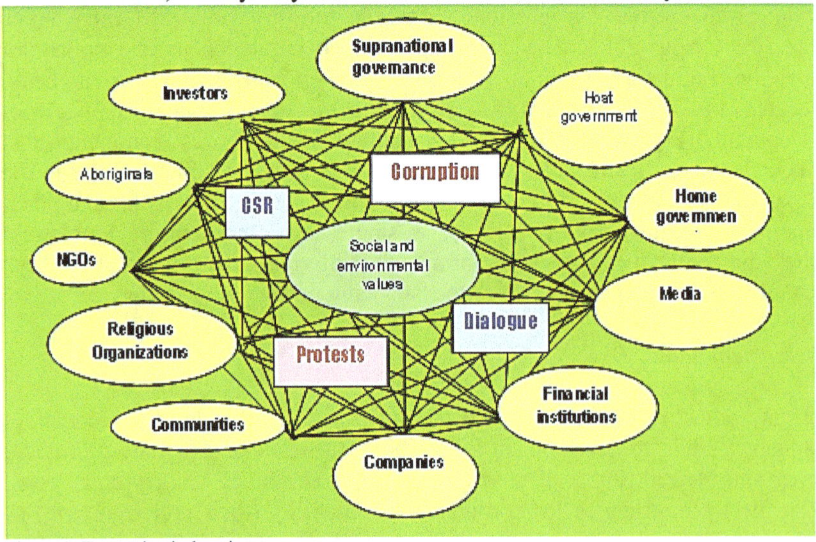

Figure 1. Extractive industries ecosystem

Stiglitz (2006: 105) argues changing the unfair rules that presently govern globalization would create development gains that dwarf those of official development assistance and corporate social responsibility combined.

There is little doubt that governments will continue to rely on the private sector for a contribution to development. The amount of Foreign Direct Investment (FDI) in developing nations far exceeds total official development assistance (Jenkins, 2005: 529). Globalization has "hollowed out" the state and its limited resources make it impossible to keep an eye on every process even at the best of times. Much of the state's effort is now directed towards an ongoing process of negotiation and consensus building between stakeholders. It is in the state's interest for corporations to 'take ownership' (Arthurs, 2005: 195, 203). This is especially the case in weak states with limited freedom of regulatory action because of the current global economic ordering, and that often lack capacity, resources and political will (Szablowski, 2007: 27-60).

Voluntary CSR Codes

Voluntary CSR codes help corporations find their way through a field that can be treacherous to navigate. They increase consistency, and help level the playing field by codifying public expectations (Cragg, 2005: 43), being somewhat comparable to the rules that govern markets (Cragg, 2005: 30). Nuñez (2003) provided a thorough overview of global and Latin American regional and national CSR initiatives embodied in (then available) codes, indexes, or technical norms and standards. All mention accountability, transparency, environment, labour standards, and human rights. The role of government is mentioned in many but not all, as are corporate governance, corruption and bribery. As the codes are intended to regulate corporate behaviour they naturally focus on the corporation. They don't specifically include development aspects of CSR, a potentially significant barrier to the effectiveness of CSR as a development tool (Simons, 2005: 99).

Actors

Major actors include corporations, NGOs, local and national governments, international institutions, communities, and investors.

Corporations

Corporations are *de facto* parts of our lives. All are driven by the need to be globally competitive. Interdependent factors influencing their approach to CSR and development include their mission, organizational structure, corporate culture, size, and industrial sector. The senior management team has a major influence on how organizations approach CSR. The length of the chain-of-command, individual managers' span of control, and definition of organizational units affect the nature of CSR initiatives in development and their ease of implementation.

Modern manufacturing corporations are often set up as loose networks of units that are constantly being assembled and disbanded as product markets wax and wane (Sennett, 1998). This and their long often globally intertwined supply chains present unique challenges to the task of inculcating a CSR culture and ensuring adherence to CSR policies across the organization.

Extractive industries have an impact on the land, occur often in remote locations, and exploit a resource that belongs to the host nation. Local political power relationships surrounding the benefits to be gained from extraction of the resource further complicate matters. The finite lifetime of a mining project and transition into "post-mine" life can present a significant community challenge, as can environmental protection into the future. Therefore, extractive industries have a strong impact on development issues and it is not surprising that CSR has become a survival issue for this sector.

Current corporate culture is not well suited to development. Bakan (2004: 57, 94, 151) mentions lack of empathy and of social tendencies, and Saul (1993: 22) believes that corporate managers are amoral technocrats. The managerial/engineering mindset focuses on quantitative, measurable results. Problems are there to be solved, through a linear series of steps. Meeting targets and deadlines is all-important, as is lowering costs. While these attributes are necessary for a company to achieve its business goals, they are often not helpful in dealing with CSR issues. For example, companies often do not take the time to build bridges with communities, with negative consequences for development projects (Frynas, 2005: 592). While much of the emphasis in the literature has been on large TNCs, there are millions of Small and Medium-sized Enterprises (SMEs) with fewer resources to dedicate to CSR. Most private-sector activity in any economy is small and domestic, and local businesses are just as prone to corporate misdemeanour as TNCs (Sayer, 2005:259). On the other hand, their good fit with the local culture means that any CSR development initiatives can be more easily targeted and implemented. The author recently became aware of a small company in the extractive sector that had drawn on its relationship building core competency to fully incorporate an effective home-grown CSR approach into its operations. However, they are more vulnerable to policy and economic changes than large TNCs.

The business case for CSR

Factors supporting the business case include: improved risk and reputation management; enhanced ability to recruit and retain staff; improved market positioning; enhanced operational efficiencies and cost savings; and better supply chain relations (Frynas, 2005: 586; Industry Canada, 2006:7-9; Graham and Woods, 2006: 870; Blowfield and Frynas, 2005: 511; Boele et al., 2001b: 125; Dashwood, 2005: 991). Kowske et al. (2011) reported on a recent survey of companies that showed "...a profound relationship between high scores on corporate responsibility and impressive gains in employee opinion, customer service and financial merits. Most of these are "instrumental"; i.e. they focus on business operational considerations rather than intrinsic values. However, some companies' commitment to CSR is based on intrinsic values (Dashwood, 2005: 993; Boele et al., 2001b: 132). Whatever its motivations, the business sector has become involved in CSR in a big way, developing guidelines, lobbying governments and in general influencing the agenda as an active player (Utting, 2005). Whether it will evolve from a business case approach to a values-based approach to CSR remains to be seen.

Corporate challenges

CSR expectations and problems are often ill defined; the road to success is long and may seem like a maze. This does not fit well with the instrumental control culture of modern corporations. Managers may discover the hard way that their "CSR paradigm" has critical gaps and while their mindset calls for "stakeholder management", reality calls for "stakeholder engagement" (Blowfield and Frynas, 2005: 507). For corporate CSR initiatives to be effective, the corresponding value system needs to permeate the organization at all levels (Varley, 2006). This is quite a complex task that can be compounded by geographical distance and cultural differences between the components of far-flung organizations

External challenges include the "free rider syndrome" in which competitors benefit from the positive spin-offs of successful CSR initiatives without having had to invest. Kolk and van Tulder (2006: 791) argue that when penalties or incentives are present, companies become active in CSR only if others do too, which they term "conditional morality." Without penalties or incentives, the likelihood of the sector adopting CSR practices is low. However, the author of this chapter believes that since 2006 interest in CSR has been increasing and is gradually becoming part of the industry discourse. As such it may become part of the "phantom community" against which corporations measure themselves (Athens, 2010: 113) Also, the ecosystems approach proposed by Sagebien and Lindsay (2011) provides a holistic framework that shows the importance of mutual awareness and cooperation.

Odell and Silva (2006) identified social context, governance, militarization/impunity and NGO behaviour as challenging domains for mineral exploration companies. Senior managers of Canadian junior mineral exploration companies listed as concerns: host governments (poor governance); rogue NGOs; community expectations; problems between communities; corruption; cultural differences; lack of skills; internal communication issues; and the risk of a single person ruining an entire project through unsuitable behaviour (Boon, 2007).

NGOs

NGOs act as both "watchdogs" of corporations and as operators of CSR initiatives in joint ventures with or under contract to corporations (Garvey and Newell, 2005: 398). Many NGOs advocate mandatory disclosure requirements imposed by states to "level the playing field" for companies, expose free riders and allow suing for misstatements (Graham and Woods, 2006: 877). Also, international standards create international expectations that help mobilize civil society if they are not met (Graham and Woods, 2006:881). Within sectors, NGOs set the "floor" of CSR performance, whereas competitor behaviour sets the "ceiling". Because of conditional morality a by sector approach may be more effective in deriving development benefits from TNCs than a focus on individual companies (Kolk and van Tulder, 2006: 798).

Accountability of NGOs

Ite (2005: 926) advocates independent reviews of initiatives and actions by governments, NGOs and corporations alike and supports a multi-stakeholder and partnership approach to social issues management within the general framework of CSR. This should ensure that the major stakeholders, including NGOs, in the development process are clearly identified and their roles, responsibilities and obligations are well articulated. NGOs need to become more accountable and to involve stakeholders more effectively in the design of strategies and activities (Odell and Silva, 2006: 4; Jones, 2007: 40; McAleer and McElhinney, 2006; Bendell, 2006: 362).

Governments

Governments of developed nations affect CSR through their influence in international bodies and on the foreign activities of companies headquartered in their countries. They can influence "home" activities of such companies through regulation or the threat of regulation. Australia, Norway and Great Britain are investing in awareness campaigns and education on CSR and the Norwegian Government Pension Fund has instituted a mechanism to deal with complaints related to CSR, and to screen investments against CSR criteria. The ethical guidelines for the Norwegian Government Pension Fund Global are promoted through exercise of ownership rights; exclusion of companies; and observation of companies. "The exercise of ownership rights is Norges Bank's responsibility. The bank's Executive Board has adopted a set of principles governing this work. The Ministry of Finance decides on placing a company on the observation list and exclusions of companies. The government has appointed a Council on Ethics which makes recommendations to the Ministry. The Ministry then issues instructions regarding exclusions to Norges Bank, so that divestments can happen before any announcements are made." (Norges Bank Investment Management, 2011)

Governments of developing countries have less power, because they lack resources, skills and experience to stand up to multinationals with deep pockets. They may be able to rely on NGOs and civil society to expose non-adherence to regulations and voluntary, exerting "shaming power" as proxies. Many governments, especially in developing nations, face bribery and corruption problems. CSR codes such as the Extractive Industries Transparency Initiative (EITI, 2005) and the OECD Guidelines for Multinational Corporations (Organization for Economic Cooperation and Development, 2000) contain clauses aimed at reducing the incidence of such situations.

Pressure to deregulate has left many countries with a weak framework for ensuring the development of their societies (Graham and Woods, 2006: 869). This can leave local communities unprotected by their own government. When combined with corruption, poor management and inappropriate use of resource rent, this has led to a "resource curse" in countries like Nigeria, where extreme poverty continues to co-exist with high resource revenues (Ite, 2005: 915; Boele et al. 2001a).

The enforcement and accessibility of a legal framework is a key factor influencing CSR development initiatives. National and local governments often are poorly prepared for effective co-operation in development programs with communities and corporations, a cause of great frustration to both (International Development Research Centre, 2003: 7). State dependence upon loans from institutions such as the World Bank or the IMF, whose loan conditionalities require export-led industrialization, often provides incentives to promote industrial expansion at the expense of social and environmental safeguards (Garvey and Newell, 2006: 394).

Boon (2011) suggests that the roles of government can be categorized into two main groups: direct involvement and accompaniment. The former includes setting a vision and goals for the role of business, human rights issues, establishing a context and boundaries for CSR and market rules (e.g. linking export credits to CSR performance). The latter includes facilitation, capacity building, coordination and conflict management strategies.

Communities

Income, age, gender, occupation, religion, education level, and part of town, dialect, and other factors internally differentiate communities. Corporations need to determine which differences within communities are significant. The internal dynamics of a community can be quite complex (Garvey and Newell, 2005: 400) and influence the conversion of individual choices into community choices (Martinussen, 1997: 244). The sphere of influence of a corporation often extends beyond the community located closest to its operations (Frynas, 2005: 593). Also, communities located close together can have completely different attitudes and value systems which may lead one community to support a planned corporate development while another community only a few kilometers away may be opposed to it (Instituto de Estudios Indígenas, 2005). De Echave et al. (2008) listed as community characteristics: culture, values and identity; historical "set-up"; national and local politics; capacity to organize and mobilize; perceptions of mining; local communications media; lack of capacity and resources; and power asymmetry with corporations (237-256). They identified the following as basic themes of conflicts: identity and respect; (e.g. way of life, social significance of land, relational expectations); defence of autonomy; risk perception; environment (water, soil, air); high expectations (employment and other benefits); competition for resources (water, land); development models; history; mining legacy issues; distribution of economic benefits; and existence of multiple hidden agendas (271-288).

Corporations occupy and affect a significant part of the physical environment with their machines, buildings and other infrastructure. Their economic weight, employment practices, work organization and hierarchies, and value system inevitably influence the social structures, values, worldview and attitudes of the communities in which they operate. At the same time, the community influences the operational decisions of the local branch of the corporation and thereby its internal culture. For example, a divided community that is a weak opponent may lead to an arrogant, non-consultative, sloppy local corporate culture whereas a well-organized community that stands up for itself will attenuate such tendencies (Garvey and Newell, 2005:401).

CSR is a political process involving power struggles (Garvey and Newell, 2005: 392) and its "battles" are most often related to community issues and fought on community territory. Such issues include adverse social effects, destruction of private property and agricultural land, conflicts over land, prostitution, and the spread of AIDS (Frynas, 2005: 595). Challenges faced by communities when negotiating with corporations include leadership, representation, unity, and decision-making processes. While the community ultimately has to make its own decisions, NGOs and unions can provide useful assistance (International Development Research Centre, 2003: 7), provided any questions about their own accountability are addressed. Garvey and Newell (2005: 401) observed that certain companies used perceived existence of conflicts of interest to derail the community's proposals resulting from such assistance. When judging the company's overtures, communities should beware of the tendency of some companies to focus on those people willing to co-operate and to pay no attention to those who object (Garvey and Newell, 2005: 400). Companies may just want to "buy peace" during critical initial project phases and social support initiatives may not be sustained once the critical project phases have been completed (Frynas, 2005: 585). While the negotiation agenda often is ostentatiously set jointly, the imbalance of power between community and company may still allow the latter to control the agenda and frame the issues in a way that neutralizes opposition (Garvey and Newell, 2005: 392). Some companies use expert knowledge to "snow" those with less education or less access to information (Garvey and Newell, 2005: 401. It may be advantageous to work with local universities or professional organizations to counter such tactics.

Once operations have started, it may be difficult for a community to call a company to account. A corporation can use its financial resources to fight sanctions the community wants to apply in many ways. Naturally, corporations construe their operations to be an intrinsic benefit to the community, and can be quite persuasive in arguing that the downsides of their operation are a worthwhile trade-off to make. Communities may be able to obtain leverage through consumer pressure, shareholder pressure, and influential NGOs in the company's home country (Garvey and Newell, 2005: 397).

Communities often lack government support that may instead be given to more powerful groups or constituencies (Garvey and Newell, 2005: 393).

Investors and Financiers

Ethical investing has grown in importance and many institutional investors have developed or are developing social and ethical criteria that have to be met by corporations in which they are willing to invest. A number of large banks have agreed to the Equator Principles that set out the social, environmental and ethical considerations they will take into account when making project financing decisions (Equator Principles, 2006). These principles are similar to the International Finance Corporation Performance Standards (International Finance Corporation, 2006b). While investors do not tend to play an active role "on the ground" they can provide communities with leverage. Sullivan (2011) reported that investors pay attention to breadth of reporting, and greenhouse gas emissions, while paying less attention to social reporting. At least investors are paying some attention to non-financial information. Unfortunately, they do not appear to much attention to data quality.

Progress

CSR has now been in the spotlight for over a decade, and interest in it continues to grow. Is the effort leading to progress on the development continuum?

It is appropriate to measure progress against the United Nations Millennium Development Goals (MDG) (United Nations, 2000). Corporations are engines of economic growth and one would expect them to be able to contribute to goal (i): eradication of extreme poverty and hunger, and to make subsidiary contributions to other goals as needed to support reaching this goal. Economic growth has often not reduced extreme poverty and hunger. CSR could make a difference in the area of "economic development for communities" defined as (AccountAbility and BSR, 2003: 13):

> "... a process by which communities can initiate and grown their own solutions to their common economic problems and thereby build long-term community capacity and foster the integration of economic, social and environmental objectives."

AccountAbility and BSR (2003: 6) argue that, when judging the CSR development success of TNCs, society will focus on economic impacts because economic choices result in social and environmental outcomes. Business activities that have an economic impact include: siting and management of facilities; employment; product and service development, use and delivery; sourcing and procurement; financial investments and fiscal contributions; and philanthropy and community investment (AccountAbility and BSR, 2003: 7). Each of these offers opportunities for choices that can further CSR development objectives.

Moving Forward

In an idealized conceptual model a community puts together a development strategy and a corresponding governance structure; tools; infrastructure projects; and stakeholder networks; resulting in *community readiness, community economic development, and achievement of MDG (i)* as its short-term, medium-term, and long-term target outcomes, respectively. A conceptual model for a company's contribution to MDG (i) involves work on culture change and codes and standards leading to a corporate CSR strategy and associated management systems to achieve *internal readiness* as its first short-term target outcome. Once internally ready, the company engages the community and other stakeholders, selects the economic activity domains on which it wants to focus, and jointly with the stakeholders designs an economic impact strategy and associated measures and indicators. Now being *externally ready* (its second short-term target outcome), it can successfully contribute to the community's medium-term target outcome:

economic development. For the company and the community models to align, company actions have to be planned with the community time frame in mind. Development is a complex process that is not really amenable to linear "cause and effect" thinking. The most successful development programs devolve power and responsibility to endogenous actors (Earl et al., 2003). However, this kind of thinking is not yet part of the business culture, and most reporting of CSR results follows patterns similar to those proposed by initiatives such as the Global Reporting Initiative (2002), Extractive Industries Transparency Initiative (EITI, 2005), ISO 14000 series (2007), AccountAbility 1000 (2007).

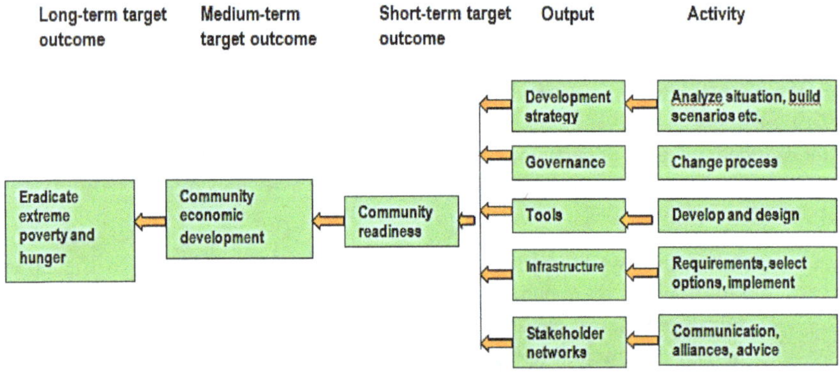

Figure 2. Conceptual logic model for Millennium Development Goal achievement through communities. (Note that the feedback loops linking outcomes back to activities are not shown for clarity.)

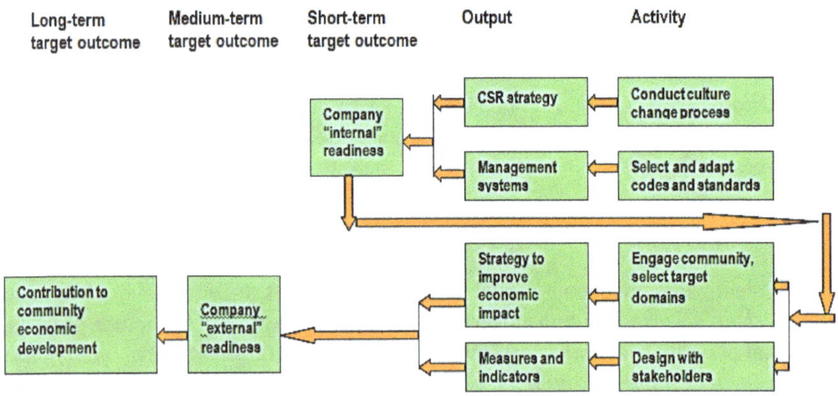

Figure 3. Conceptual logic model for achieving company contributions to community economic development (contains elements from the process summary shown by AccountAbility and BSR, 2003, p. 9). Note that the feedback loops linking outcomes back to activities are not shown for clarity.

Research Findings

Most CSR research and analysis has focused more on company aspects of CSR than on development outcomes (EU 2007b, conference brochure; Blowfield and Frynas, 2005: 506; Prieto-Carron et al., 2006: 981; Blowfield, 2007:519). Despite claims on company and NGO websites, it is difficult to ascertain actual developmental results. Much more is known about the business case and company attitudes, awareness and practices than about how CSR affects developing countries (Blowfield, 2007: 519). An Internet search conducted by the author in January 2012 confirmed that this is still very much the case. This may be because of the difficulty of unambiguously measuring CSR and attributing outcomes for communities, and data quality and availability varies across the globe. Companies are much better at reporting and measuring environmental than social results, and economic (not financial) reporting is in its infancy (Blowfield, 2007:686). Campbell (2005) and AccountAbility and BSR (2003) both outline possible approaches to economic development reporting.

The application of Nelson et al.'s (2005) CSR impact assessment methodology to workers in the South African wine industry is showing encouraging preliminary results, with respect to both the effect of the codes and the methodology. León Castro's (2001: 12, 24) approach to community development policies of mining companies in Latin America was used to review community development activities by mining companies and other natural resources companies in Chile, Colombia, and Peru (International Development Research Centre, 2003). Findings include: local governments and communities have become important pressure groups; the Sustainable Development Model ubiquitous in mining industry promotional material rarely translates into practice; paternalistic assistance practices are gradually being eliminated; state and local economic agents lack capacity for linking with the mining industry in development programs; and differences in culture and interests between the actors need to be taken into account. The companies involved in the case studies, while engaging the communities out of necessity, were often not internally ready. Odell and Silva (2006) report that the community engagement process is consuming most of the companies' attention. They also note that extreme poverty aggravates conflict because people fear that a mine can negatively impact their already difficult lives. They may push for benefits that are not in the company's domain of responsibility, and Odell and Silva (2006: 4) suggest that careful social assessment of sites be carried out in conjunction with the initial geological assessment to recognize situations that are beyond company social and technical capacity. The Rhetoric and Reality (RARE) project (European Union, 2007a) looked at improvement of company CSR practices and attainment of company social/environmental goals. Interestingly, many companies considered CSR as a means to improve compliance with non-voluntary regulation. Most were at an early stage, with even forerunner companies not systematically assessing their CSR performance and impact. However, CSR was found to have made a valuable contribution in many areas and helped fill gaps and complement other existing instruments. EU policy mixes need to recognize that the potential for CSR impact on sustainability is sector and issue specific. The strongest contributions to EU sustainability policy occurred in areas not yet densely regulated; where companies perceive a strong business case; when changes required by CSR relate to production/organization rather than products; and when the target impact is within the company's immediate sphere of influence. For CSR to contribute to EU sustainability goals strong binding social and environmental policies remain essential both to promote sustainability and to create a level playing field among companies. While rhetoric is stronger than reality, reality is strong enough to allow some rhetoric. The conclusions of the RARE study contain important lessons for CSR applied to development.

Critiques of Business Approaches to CSR and Development

With respect to philosophical underpinnings, many authors consider the CSR agenda to be set by business determining what is ethical behaviour and what is not (Blowfield and Frynas, 2005: 512, 513; Blowfield, 2005: 521, 523; Newell, 2005: 541; Sayer, 2005: 261; Prieto-Carrón et al., 2006: 980, 986). Prieto-Carrón et al. warn of the risk of unwitting "institutional capture" of governments and NGOs by business. Utting (2007: 701) finds CSR to be weak on rights, empowerment, and redistribution, and much stronger on social protection. In this respect, the recent report of John Ruggie, the Special Representative to the Secretary General of the UN on human rights and transnational corporations and other business enterprises: "Guiding Principles on Business and Human Rights: Implementing the United Nations "Protect, Respect and Remedy"Framework" may have a significant impact. It has been widely hailed by business, governments and civil society. The Guiding Principles highlight what steps States should *take* to foster business respect forhuman rights; provide a blueprint for companies to know and show that they respect human rights, and reduce the risk of causing or contributing to human rights harm; and constitute a set of benchmarks for stakeholders to assess business respect for human rights.

In terms of alignment with development, Blowfield and Frynas (2005: 512) argue that CSR standards for workers' rights and for natural resources management do not adequately address important development issues. Blowfield (2005: 517) believes that issues not addressed by CSR will not be addressed in any other way, because regulators assume that "the waterfront is covered" and he questions business' ability to redefine its practices in the interests of the poor and the marginalized (2005: 518). Sayer (2005: 261) believes that the mismatch between business interests and local interests leaves important gaps in CSR development coverage. These and earlier observations support Newell and Frynas' (2007: 670) contention that the logic of CSR as a business tool conflicts with the logic of CSR as a development tool. For CSR to have a development impact, the priorities of the poor should be put first, which would change CSR content and process of (Newell and Frynas, 2007, 670).

There are gaps between stated intentions of business leaders and their actions in the development area (Frynas, 2005: 585; Hilson and Haselip, 2004: 42; Dhanarajan, 2005: 532) Companies far down the supply chain are often located in developing countries, and Prieto-Carrón et al. (2006: 984) accuse retailers (particularly supermarkets and brand companies) of using their consolidated power to push the risks and costs of business down the supply chain. Kolk and van Tulder (2006) conclude that published poverty policies of a number of "CSR forerunner" TNCs do not address a significant number of development issues.

The incompatibility between company goals and long-term development means that CSR cannot replace development (Frynas, 2005: 593). Constraints on the achievement of developmental objectives by companies include: country- and context-specific issues (e.g. work in war zones); failure to involve the intended beneficiaries of CSR development initiatives; lack of human resources; social attitudes of company staff and focus on technical/managerial solutions; and failure to integrate CSR initiatives into a larger development plan (Frynas, 2005: 588). The RARE study found that the executives of global majors, while committed to CSR, are hardly able to control their vast companies (European Union, 2007b). Jenkins and Yakovleva (2006) found much room for improvement in CSR disclosure practices in the mining industry.

Conclusions

While the reasons for the blossoming of CSR may be associated less with the moral high ground than with hard-nosed calculations of risk and benefits, the movement is helping address some of the negative consequences of globalization on development. It has led to a positive change in attitudes, knowledge, and practices. There is much rhetoric, only some of it justified by reality, and there is much room for improvement. The proportion of businesses that are actively participating is still relatively low, and power relationships between the actors are skewed towards business. The latter poses the risk of regulatory capture of governments and NGOs. The current CSR paradigm does not address systemic issues related to the world's power structure such as injustices in the world trade rules. Also, its strong instrumentalist orientation limits its ability to address problems with deep complex root causes. Most studies of the impact of CSR have stayed close to the business case and many less have been published on CSR development outcomes.

Conditions that would help CSR realize its potential include a robust regulatory environment with incentives and credible sanctions, dynamic conditions that promote intense debate and mutual scrutiny of the actors, and continued learning by all. A sector-by-sector approach is more likely to be successful than a focus on individual enterprises. More studies of the impact of CSR beyond the business case need to be undertaken. There is an opportunity for governments and international governance bodies to design and implement corresponding policies and thereby catalyze CSR's positive contribution to society. CSR is not a 'silver bullet': it is one tool among others.

Global factors that will almost certainly affect future directions of CSR include changing world power structures, demographics, and climate. The increasing economic strength of countries such as Brazil, Russia, India, and China coupled with the declining fertility rates and ageing populations in the present "Western hegemonic bloc" are already shifting the world balance of power. This could have a profound effect on CSR battle strategies and tactics of all players. Will the continued rise of China, India and Brazil lead to a paradigm shift away from neo-liberalism and, if so, in which direction? Will it alleviate the plight of the poor or will it worsen it (as some of the recent industry human rights abuses discovered in China might suggest)? Will the emerging trend of viewing CSR as a vehicle through which to affect corporate behaviour on climate change issues continue? It is impossible to predict how CSR will play out, however, all actors have a responsibility to take the high road, be aware and ensure that their perspectives are heard and taken into account. They should prepare for a long power interregnum.

References

Note: where a page number is not provided in a citation (in the text of the paper), either the concept expressed summarizes multiple parts or the entire reference, or the document to which the citation refers was not accessible at the time of writing for logistical reasons.

AccountAbility 1000 www.accountability.org.uk. Accessed July 2007.

AccountAbility and Business for Social Responsibility, with Brody Weiser Burns. (2003). *Business and Economic Development – The Impact of Corporate Responsibility Standards and Practices. Insights from Recent Experiences.* London and San Francisco: AccountAbility and Business for Social Responsibility.

Anonymous (2011) *Ley de Consulta Previa*, Proveedor Minero, 5(22), Agosto-Setiembre, 30.

Arthurs, H.W. (2005). *Private Ordering and Workers' Rights in the Global Economy: Corporate Codes of Conduct as a Regime of Labour Market Regulation.* In: Cragg, W. (editor). Ethics Codes, Corporations and the Challenge of Globalization. Cheltenham (U.K.): Edward Elgar.

Athens, L. (2010) *Naturalistic Enquiry in Theory and Practice,* Journal of Contemporary Ethnography 39(1) 87-125

Bakan, J. (2004).The Corporation – *The Pathological Pursuit of Profit and Power.* Toronto: Penguin Canada.

Bendell, J. (2005). *In whose name? The accountability of corporate social responsibility*. Development in Practice, 15(3-4): 362 – 374

Blowfield. M. (2005). *Corporate Social Responsibility: Reinventing the Meaning of Development?* International Affairs 81(3): 515-524.

Blowfield, M. (2007). *Reasons to be Cheerful? What we know about CSR's impact.* Third World Quarterly 28(4): 683-695

Blowfield, M. and Frynas, J.G. (2005). *Setting new agendas: critical perspectives on Corporate Social Responsibility in the developing world.* International Affairs 81(3): 499-513.

Boele, R., Fabig, H. and Wheeler, D. (2001a). *Shell, Nigeria and the Ogoni. A Study in Unsustainable Development: I. The Story of Shell, Nigeria and the Ogoni People – Environment, Economy, Relationships: Conflicts and Prospects for Resolution.* Sustainable Development 9: 74-86.

Boele, R., Fabig, H. and Wheeler, D. (2001b). *Shell, Nigeria and the Ogoni. A Study in Unsustainable Development: II. Corporate Social Responsibility and 'Stakeholder Management' versus a Rights-Based Approach to Sustainable Development.* Sustainable Development 9: 121-135.

Boon, J, (2007). Personal communication with companies during the March 2007 Prospectors and Developers Association of Canada Annual Convention.

Boon, J. (2011) *The Role of Governments in CSR*. In: Governance Ecosystems – CSR in the Latin American Mining Sector. Houndmills, Basingstoke, Hampshire: Palgrave Macmillan 64-83

Campbell, H. (2005). *Business economic impacts: The new frontier for corporate accountability,* Development in Practice, 15: 413-421.

Coser, L. (1965). *Georg Simmel.* Englewood Cliffs, New Jersey: Prentice Hall.

Cragg, W. (2005). *Ethics, Globalization and the Phenomenon of Self-Regulation: An Introduction*. In: Cragg, W. (editor). Ethics Codes, Corporations and the Challenge of Globalization. Cheltenham (U.K.): Edward Elgar: 1-17.

Dashwood, H.S. (2005). *Canadian Mining Companies and the shaping of global norms of corporate social responsibility.* International Journal, 64(4): 977-998.

De Echave, J., Díez, A., Huber, L., Revesz, B., Ricard, X. y Tanaka, M. (2008), *Minería y Conflicto Social*, Lima: Instituto de Estudios Peruanos.

Dhanarajan, S. (2005). *Managing ethical standards: When rhetoric meets reality*. Development in Practice, 15(3-4): 529-538.

Eade, D. (2005).*Editorial*. Development in Practice, 15(3-4): 249 – 250.

Earl, S., Carden, F. and Smutylo, T. (2001). *OUTCOME MAPPING Building Learning and Reflection into Development Programs*. Ottawa: International Development Research Centre.

EITI (2005). *Extractive Industries Transparency Initiative Sourcebook*. www.eitransparency.org. Accessed July 2007.

Equator Principles (2006). *The " Equator Principles", a financial industry benchmark for determining, assessing, and managing social & environmental risks in project financing.* www.equator-principles.com. Accessed August 2007.

European Union. (2007a) *Rhetoric and Realities: Analysing Corporate Social Responsibility in Europe (RARE)*. A European Research Project Funded within the EU 6th Framework Programme. http://www.rare-eu.net. Accessed August 2007

European Union. (2007b). CSR Conference*: "Rhetoric and Realities – Corporate Social Responsibility in Europe*". Brussels, June 27, 2007.

Federal Interdepartmental National Roundtable Steering Committee. (2006). *National Roundtables on Corporate Social Responsibility and the Canadian Extractive Sector in Developing Countries – Discussion Paper.* Ottawa: Department of Foreign Affairs and International Trade.

Fridell, G. (2007). *Fair Trade Coffee: the prospects and pitfalls of market-driven social justice.* Toronto: University of Toronto Press.

Frynas, J. G. (2005). *The False Developmental Promise of CSR: Evidence from Multinational Oil Companies.* International Affairs 81(3), 581-598.

Garriga, E and Melé, D. (2004). *Corporate Social Responsibility Theories: Mapping the Territory*. Journal of Business Ethics, 53(1-2): 51-71.

Garvey, N. and Newell, P. (2005). *Corporate Accountability to the Poor? Assessing the Effectiveness of Community-based Strategies.* Development in Practice, 15(3-4): 389-404.

Global Compact (2000) www.unglobalcompact.org. Accessed July 2007.

Global Reporting Initiative. (2002). Sustainability Reporting Guidelines. www.globalreporting.org. Accessed July 2007.

Graham, D. and Woods, N. (2006). *Making Corporate Self-Regulation Effective in Developing Countries.* World Development 34(5): 868-883.

Hilson, G and Haselip, J. (2004). *The Environmental and Socioeconomic Performance of Multinational Mining Companies in the Developing World.* Minerals and Energy, 3: 25-47.

Holme, R. and Watts, P. (2000). *Corporate social responsibility: making good business sense.* Conche-Geneva, World Business Council for Sustainable Development. http://www.wbcsd.ch/b. Accessed July 2007.

Industry Canada. (2006). *Corporate Social Responsibility – An Implementation Guide for Canadian Business.* Ottawa: Multimedia and Editorial Services Section, Communications and Marketing Branch.

Instituto de Estudios Indígenas, Universidad de la Frontera. (2005). Proyecto No. 050317-044 : *Grupos Étnicos y Minería en Pequeña Escala (MPE) en América Latina y el Caribe, Análisis de Experiencias en Chile* – Informe Final de Proyecto. Ottawa: IEI report to International Development Research Centre.

International Development Research Centre. (2003). *Mining Companies and Local Development – Latin America: Chile, Colombia and Peru. Executive Summary*. Ottawa: International Development Research Centre/Mining Policy Research Initiative.

International Finance Corporation (IFC). (2006a). *International Finance Corporation's Policy on Social and Environmental Sustainability.* www.ifc.org/ifcext/enviro.nsf/Content/SustainabilityPolicy. Accessed July 2007.

ISO 14000 www.iso14000-iso14001-environmental-management.com/. Accessed July 2007.

Ite, U. (2005). *Poverty reduction in resource-rich developing countries: what have multinational corporations got to do with it?* Journal of International Development 17(7): 913-929.

Jenkins, R. (2005). *Globalization, Corporate Social Responsibility and poverty.* International Affairs 81(3): 525-540.

Jenkins, H. and Yakovleva, N. (2006). *Corporate social responsibility in the mining industry: Exploring trends in social and environmental disclosure*. Journal of Cleaner Production 14: 271-284.

Jones, N. (2007). *Campaigners scrutinized but unrepentant.* Ethical Corporation Magazine, June 2007, 40-41.

Kolk, A, and van Tulder, R. (2006). *Poverty Alleviation as Business Strategy? Evaluating commitments of Frontrunner Multinational Corporations.* World Development 34(5): 789-801.

Kowske, B., Hermann, A. and D'Mello, S. (2011). *Assessing Corporate Responsibility; Is it Good for Business?* Kenexa High Performance Institute white paper. http://www.kenexa.com/

León Castro, C. (2001). *Políticas de Desarrollo Comunitario de Empresas Mineras y de Extracción de Recursos Naturales en América Latina y el Caribe – Términos de Referencia sobre Aspectos Políticos y de*

Gobernabilidad. Ottawa: International Development Research Centre/Mining Policy Research Initiative.

Martinussen, J. (1997, Fifth Impression 2005). *Society, State & Market - A Guide to Competing Theories of Development.* Halifax: Fernwood Publishing.

McAleer, P. and McElhinney, A. (2006). *Mine your own business.* http://www.mineyourownbusiness.org. Viewed March 2007.

National Roundtables on Corporate Social Responsibility and the Canadian Extractive Industry Advisory Group. (2007). *Corporate Social Responsibility (CSR) and the Canadian Extractive Industry in Developing Countries. Advisory Group Report.* Toronto: Prospectors and Developers Association of Canada, http://www.pdac.ca/. Accessed August 2007.

Newell, P. (2005). *Citizenship, accountability and community: the limits of the CSR agenda.* International Affairs 81(3): 541-557.

Newell, P. and Frynas, J.G. (2007). *Beyond CSR? Business, Poverty and Social Justice: an Introduction.* Third World Quarterly 28(4): 669-681

Norges Bank Investment Management (2011). *Ethical Guidelines* http://www.nbim.no/en/About-us/Government-Pension-Fund-Global/ethical-guidelines/ Accessed January 2012.

Nuñez, G. (2003). *La responsabilidad social corporativa en un marco de desarrollo sostenible.* Comisión Ecconómica Para Latino-America (CEPAL), Serie Medio Ambiente y Desarrollo No. 72.

Odell, C. and Silva, A. C. (2006). *Mining Exploration, Corporate Social Responsibility and Human Rights: Untangling the Facts, Seeking Solutions*. Submission to the National Roundtables on Corporate Social Responsibility, November 14, Montreal, Canada. Ottawa: http://geo.international.gc.ca/cip-pic/current_discussions/csr-roundtables-en.asp. Accessed December 2007.

On Common Ground Consultants. (2007). *Corporate Social Responsibility and Mineral Exploration.* Background notes for Prospectors and Developers Association Short Course: From Theory to Practice: Corporate social responsibility and sustainable development in mineral exploration. Toronto: PDAC.

Organization for Economic Cooperation and Development. (2000). *The OECD Guidelines for Multinational Enterprises.. REVISION 2000.* www.oecd.org/dataoecd/56/36/1922428.pdf. Accessed July 200, Harvard Business Review Magazine7.

Porter, M. E. and Kramer, M. R. (2011), *Creating Shared Value*, Harvard Business Review, 89(1/2): 62-77

Prieto-Carrón, M, Lund-Thomsen, P., and. Chan A. (2006). *Critical perspectives on CSR and development: what we know, what we don't know, and what we need to know.* International Affairs 82(5): 977-87.

Prospectors and Developers Association of Canada. (2007). *Sustainable Development and Corporate social responsibility – Tools, codes and standards for the mineral exploration industry.* Toronto. http://www.pdac.ca. Accessed December 2007.

Ruggie, J. (2011). *Guiding Prnciples on Human Rights: Implementing the United Nations "Protect, Respect and Remedy" Framework.* United Nations Report A/HRC/17/31, http://www.ohchr.org/Documents/Issues/Business/A-HRC-17-31_AEV.pdf. Accessed January 2012.

Sagebien, J. and Lindsay, N.M. (2011). *Systemic Causes, Systemic Solutions.* In: Governance Ecosystems – CSR in the Latin American Mining Sector. Houndmills, Basingstoke, Hampshire: Palgrave Macmillan 12-30

Saul, J.R. (1993). *Voltaire's Bastards – The Dictatorship of Reason in the West.* Toronto: Penguin Books

Saul, J. R. (2005). *The Collapse of Globalization and the Reinvention of the World.* Toronto: Viking Canada.

Sayer, J. (2005). *Do more good, do less harm: development and the private sector.* Development in Practice 15: 251 – 268.

Sennett, R. (1998). *The Corrosion of Character – The Personal Consequences of Work in the New Capitalism.* New York and London: W.W. Norton & Company.

Simons, P. (2005). *Corporate Voluntarism and Human Rights: The Adequacy and Effectiveness of Voluntary Self-Regulation Regimes.* In: Cragg, W. (editor). Ethics Codes, Corporations and the Challenge of Globalization. Cheltenham (U.K.): Edward Elgar: 75-111

Stiglitz, J.E. (2006). *Making Globalization Work.* New York: W.W. Norton & Co. Inc.

Sullivan, R. (2011). Are Investors Really Interested in CR data? http://www.ethicalcorp.com/communications-reporting/are-investors-really-interested-cr-data. Accessed January 2012

Szablowski, D. (2007). *Transnational Law and Local Struggles –Mining Communities and the World Bank.* Oxford and Portland. Oregon: Hart Publishing

United Nations (2000). *The Millennium Development Goals.* http://www.un.org/millenniumgoals/ Accessed June 2008.

Utting, P. (2005). *Corporate Responsibility and the Movement of Business.* Development in Practice 15(3-4): 375-388.

Utting, P. (2007). *CSR and Equality.* Third World Quarterly 28(4): 697-712.

Van der Putten, F.P. (2005). *A Research Agenda for International Corporate Social Responsibility.* Nyenrode Research Group Research Report No. 05-09. http://www.nyenrode.nl/research/publication. Accessed August 2007

Varley, J. (Chairman, Barclays Bank). *Presentation given at Ethical Corporation Europe Summit 2006.* Ethical Corporation Conference Summaries. London. http://www.ethicalcorp.com. Accessed August 2007.

Chapter 9: CSR Considerations of Multinational Companies in Development Countries

Corporate Social Responsibility: Interaction between Multinational Companies and Development Countries

Naci Polat, Dumlupinar University, Turkey

Abstract: Since the second half of the 20th century a long discussion on corporate social responsibility (CSR) has been taking place. In 1953, Bowen (1953) wrote Social Responsibilities of the Businessman. Since then, there has been a shift in terminology from the social responsibility of business to CSR. Additionally, this area has grown significantly and today contains variety of theories, approaches and terminologies. As the starting point for a proper classification, I assume as hypothesis that the most relevant CSR theories and related approaches are focused on one of the following aspects of social reality: economics, politics, social integration and ethics. The inspiration for this hypothesis is rooted in four aspects that, according to Parsons (1961), can be observed in any social system: adaptation to the environment (related to resources and economics), goal attainment (related to politics), social integration and pattern maintenance or latency (related to culture and values).

Summary

This paper builds on Corporate Social Responsibility (CSR). Questions about CSR, social standards, profit maximization and social change relationship will firstly be examined. The historical dimension of CSR, theories about CSR, common works of corporates and Non- Governmental Organizations (examples from Turkey) are described and future questions and possible answers will be investigated.

Questions

a) How does the process of establishing absolute (also 'international' or 'universal') standards for social and environmental issues – supposedly related to the objectives and values of developing societies – affect business behaviour?
b) Under which conditions can profit maximisation by Western firms lead to responsible business behaviour in developing countries, and under which conditions does such behaviour contribute to profit maximisation?
c) What is the relevance of societal demands on business behaviour related to developing countries, and what is the legitimacy of these demands?
d) Under which conditions can Western-based businesses make a positive contribution to local communities in developing countries?

Research Level

Since the second half of the 20th century a long discussion on corporate social responsibility (CSR) has been taking place. In 1953, Bowen (1953) wrote 'Social Responsibilities of the Businessman'. Since then, there has been a shift in terminology from the social responsibility of business to CSR. Additionally, this area has grown significantly and today contains variety of theories, approaches and terminologies.

As the starting point for a proper classification, I assume as hypothesis that the most relevant CSR theories and related approaches are focused on one of the following aspects of social reality: economics, politics, social integration and ethics. The inspiration for this hypothesis is rooted in four aspects that, according to Parsons (1961), can be observed in any social system: adaptation to the environment (related to resources and economics), goal attainment (related to politics), social integration and pattern maintenance or latency (related to culture and values).This hypothesis permits us to classify these theories in four groups:

1. The first group in which it is assumed that the corporation is an instrument for wealth creation and that this is its sole social responsibility. Only the economic aspect of the interactions between business and society is considered. So any supposed social activity is accepted if, and only if, it is consistent with wealth creation. This group of theories could be call instrumental theories because they understand CSR as a mere means to the end of profits.
2. The second group in which the social power of corporation is emphasized, specifically in its relationship with society and its responsibility in the political arena associated with this power. This leads the corporation to accept social duties and rights or participate in certain social cooperation. We will call this group as political theories.
3. The third group includes theories which consider that business ought to integrate social demands. They usually argue that business depends on society for its continuity and growthand even for the existence of business itself. We can term this group integrative theories.

4. The fourth group of theories focus on the ethical requirements that cement the relationship between business and society. They are based on principles that express the right thing to do or the necessity to achieve a good society.

Theories

Instrumental Theories

Representative of this approach is the well-known Friedman view that ''the only one responsibility of business towards society is the maximization of profits to the shareholders within the legal framework and the ethical custom of the country'' (1970).

Three main groups of instrumental theories can be identified, depending on the economic objective proposed.

- In the first group the objective is the maximization of shareholder value, measured by the share price. Frequently, this leads to a short-term profits orientation.
- The second group of theories focuses on the strategic goal of achieving competitive advantages, which would produce long-term profits. In both cases, CSR is only a question of enlightened self-interest (Keim, 1978) since CSRs are a mere instrument for profits.
- The third is related to cause-related marketing and is very closed to the second.

Table 1: Instrumental Theories

Type of Theories	Approaches	Short Description	Key References
Instrumental Theories (Achieving Economic Targets with Social Activities)	Maximization of Shareholder Value	Long Term Value Maximization	Friedman (1970), Jensen (2002)
	Strategies for Competitive Advantages	-Social investments in a competitive context -Strategies based on the natural resource view of the firm and the dynamic capabilities of the firm -Strategies for the bottom of the economic pyramid	Porter and Kramer (2002) Hart (1995) Prahalad (2002)
	Cause-related Marketing	Altruistic activities socially recognized used as an instrument of marketing	Varadarjan and Menon (1988)

Political Theories

A group of CSR theories and approaches focus on interactions and connections between business and society and on the power and position of business and its inherent responsibility. They include both political considerations and political analysis in the CSR debate. Although there are a variety of approaches, two major theories can be distinguished: Corporate Constitutionalism and Corporate Citizenship.

Table 2: Political Theories

Type of Theories	**Approaches**	**Short Description**	**Key References**
Political Theories (focusing on a responsible use of business power in the political arena)	Corporate Constitutionalism	Social responsibilities of businesses arise from the amount of social power that they have	Davis (1960, 1967)
	Integrative Social Contract Theory	Assumes that a social contract between business and society exists	Donaldson (1982)
	Corporate (or business) Citizenship	The firm is understood as being like a citizen with certain involvement in the community	Andriof and McIntosh (2001)

Integrative Theories

This group of theories looks at how business integrates social demands, arguing that business depends on society for its existence, continuity and growth. Social demands are generally considered to be the way in which society interacts with business and gives it a certain legitimacy and prestige. As a consequence, corporate management should take into account social demands, and integrate them in such a way that the business operates in accordance with social values.

Table 3: Integrative Theories

Type of Theories	Approaches	Short Description	Key References
Integrative Theories (focusing on the integration of social demands)	Issues Management	Corporate processes of response to those social and political issues which may impact significantly upon it	Sethi (1975), Ackerman (1973), Jones (1980), Vogel (1986), Wartick and Mahon (1994)
	Public Responsibility	Law and the existing public policy process are taken as a reference for social performance	Preston and Post (1975, 1981)
	Stakeholder Management	Balances the interests of the stakeholders of the firm	Agle and Mitchell (1999)
	Corporate Social Performance	Searches for social legitimacy and processes to give appropriate responses to social issues	Carroll (1979), Wartick and Cochran (1985)

Ethical Theories

There is a fourth group of theories or approaches focus on the ethical requirements that cement the relationship between business and society. They are based on principles that express the right thing to do or the necessity to achieve a good society.

Table 4: Ethical Theories

Type of Theories	Approaches	Short Description	Key References
Ethical Theories (focusing on the right thing to achieve a good society)	Stakeholder Normative Theory	Considers fiduciary duties towards stakeholders of the firm. Its application requires reference to some moral theory (Kantian, Utilitarianism, theories of justice, etc.)	Freeman (1984, 1994), Donaldson (1982)
	Universal Rights	Frameworks based on human rights, labor rights and respect for the environment	The Global Sullivan Principles (1999), UN Global Compact (1999)
	Sustainable Development	Aimed at achieving human development considering present and future generations	World Commission on Environment and Development (Brutland Report) (1987)
	The Common Good	Oriented towards the common good of society	Alford and Naughton (2002), Mele and Garriga (2002)

Some Social Responsibility Projects and Effects in Turkey

Firms	Result-Oriented Corporate Social Responsibility Projects (Infomag, 2004)	Source
ARÇELİK	Project:'Standing United for Education Programm' Objective: 'Equal opportunity in education'	www. arcelik.com.tr
DOĞAN Media Holding	Project: 'Father, please send me to the school' Objective: To help young girls to be sent to the school	www. dmg. com.tr
Eczacıbaşı	Project: Education expenses of young artists are paid by the company Objective: Helping for talented artists who needs economic help	www. eczacıbasi. com.tr
Turkcell	Project: 'Contemporary Girls of Modern Turkey ' Objective: 8300 young girls education expenses are paid by the company Project: 'Free Sport Schools' Objective: 20.000 youngs went to Sport Schools free of charge with the help of company	www.turkcell.com.tr

Expected Results and Objectives

Expected Future Researches about CSR in Turkey and in the Western World

Turkey

- CSR is a new concept for Turkey. Companies will need to pay attention to this subject in the next 4-5 years. Concerning social responsibility, the consciousness and expectations of society is rising continuously.
- Society expects companies to transmit information about CSR by using communication channels.
- Contribution of companies to the projects driven by social sensivity improves the prestige of companies.

Western World

- Developed countries proceeded long way concerning CSR. They regard it as a long term concept.
- Not only the financial performance is determining factor but also sustainability is very important.
- They win confidence of the society through long term CSR projects
- Mechanisms has been intermingled.

Expected Objectives:

Although the academic researches on CSR goes back to long years, as this subject is in the scope of many science fields, there has been no common definition for it so far. In the near future, assuming that the relationships between society and companies will move to different platforms, we estimate that the studies related to CSR will proliferate. Increasing studies will result in the shift of the relationships and cooperation of scientists studying CSR to more concrete areas.

On the other hand, economic imbalances between developed and developing countries, revealed by globalisation all over the world, will necessitate the global and local companies to sacrifice in their decisions for the favor of below two points.

- Companies will undertake the mission of strengthing their potential customers with low buying power, economicaly and socially.
- Companies will apply the costumer winning methods which is personalized and not has been used so far.

Against the possibility of these two proposal to come into life, there is a need to rethink about CSR. The efficiency of forthcoming academic studies will only be possible through reliefing social science discipline which has the interdiciplinary research power and ability to make publication by ending research inconveniences and the supports given by other disciplines. The development of a theory which covers and goes beyond of the other theories in different categories might be possible only in this way.

References

Ackerman, R. W.: 1973, 'How Companies Respond to Social Demands', Harvard University Review 51(4), 88–98.

Ackerman, R. and R. Bauer: 1976, Corporate Social Responsiveness (Reston, Virginia).

Agle, B. and R. K. Mitchell: 1999, 'Who Matters to CEOs? An Investigation of Stakeholder Attributes and Salience, Corporate Performance, and CEO Values', The Academy of Management Journal, 42(5).

Alford, H.J. and M. J. Naughton: 2002, Managing As If Faith Mattered (University of Notre Dame Press).

Altman, B. W. and D. Vidaver-Cohen: 2000, 'Corporate Citizenship in the New Millennium: Foundation for an Architecture of Excellence', Business and Society Review 105(1), 145–169.

Andriof, J. and M. Mc Intosh: 2000, Perspective on Corporate Citizenship (Greenleaf Publications).

Avrupa Birliği: 2006, Kurumsal Sosyal Sorumluluk (http://ec.europa.eu/enterprise/csr/campaign/documentation/download/guide_tr.pdf)

Berkman, Ü.: 1999, 'Sosyal Sorumluluk, İş Ahlakı Gelişimi ve Yakın Geleceği' (www.kho.edu.tr/yayinlar/bilimdergisi/doc/1999-2/bilder5.doc).
Bowen, H. R.: 1953, Social Responsibilities of the Businessman (Harper & Row, New York).
Brummer, J.: 1991, Corporate Responsibility and Legitimacy (Greenwood Press, New York).
Burke, L. and J. M. Logsdon: 1996, 'How Corporate Social Responsibility Pays Off', Long Range Planning 29(4), 495–503.
Business Social Responsibility: 2006, Corporate Social Responsibility (www.bsr.org/Meta/about/bsrdetails.cfm).
Carroll, A. B.: 1979, 'A Three-Dimensional Conceptual Model of Corporate Performance', Academy of Management Review 4(4), 497–505.
Carroll, A. B.: 1999, 'Corporate Social Responsibility. Evolution of Definitional Construct', Business and Society 38(3), 268–295.
Cassel, D.: 2001, 'Human Rights Business Responsibilities in the Global Marketplace', Business Ethics Quarterly 11(2), 261–274.
Davis, K.: 1960, 'Can Business Afford to Ignore Corporate Social Responsibilities?', California ManagementReview 2, 70–76.
Davis, K.: 1973, 'The Case For and Against Business Assumption of Social Responsibilities', Academy of Management Journal 16, 312–322.
Donaldson, T.: 1982, Corporations and Morality (Prentice- Hall, Englewood Cliff, NJ).
Donnelly, J.: 1985, The Concept of Human Rights (Croom Helm, London).
Frederick, W. C.: 1987, 'Theories of Corporate Social Performance', in S. P. Sethi and C. M. Flabe (ed.), Business and Society: Dimensions of Conflict and Cooperation (Lexington Books, New York), pp. 142–161.
Emshoff, J. R. and R. E. Freeman: 1978, 'Stakeholder Management',Working Paper from theWharton Applied Research Center (July). Quoted by Sturdivant (1979).
Frederick, W. C.: 1998, 'Moving to CSR4', Business and Society 37(1), 40–60.
Freeman, R. E.: 1984, Strategic Management: A Stakeholder Approach (Pitman, Boston).
Friedman, M.: 1970, 'The Social Responsibility of Business is to Increase its Profits', New York Times Magazine, September 13th, 32–33, 122, 126.
Global Sullivan Principles: 1999, (http://www.thesullivanfoundation.org/gsp/default.asp).
Griffin, J. J.: 2000, 'Corporate Social Performance: Research Directions for the 21st Century', Business and Society 39(4), 479–493.
Hart, S. L.: 1995, 'A Natural-Resource-Based View of the Firm', Academy of Management Review 20(4), 986–1012.
Heald, M.: 1988, The Social Responsibilities of Business: Company and Community, 1900–1960 (Transaction Books, New Brunswick).
Infomag: 2004, Şirketler Sosyal Sorumluluk Kuyruğunda (www.infomag.com.tr/v2/content/10422).
Jensen, M. C.: 2002, 'Value Maximization, Stakeholder Theory, and the Corporate Objective Function', Business Ethics Quarterly 12(2), 235–256.

Jones, T. M.: 1980, 'Corporate Social Responsibility Revisited, Redefined', California Management Review 22(2), 59–67.

Jonker, J. J. Cramer and A. van der Heijden: 2003, 'Developing Meaning in Action; (Re)constructing the process of embedding Corporate Social Responsibility (CSR) in Companies', 16, 1-28.

Keim G. D.: 1978, Corporate Social Responsibility: An Assessment of the Enlightened Self-Interest Model. Academy of Management Review, 32–39

Mele, D., Garriga E.: 2004, Corporate Social Responsibility Theories: Mapping the Territory, Journal of Business Ethics 53: 51-71.

PerYön: 2006, 'Kurumsal Yurttaşlık' Dönemi, 2 (www.peryon.org.tr/default.asp).

Porter, M. E. and M. R. Kramer: 2002, 'The Competitive Advantage of Corporate Philanthropy', Harvard Business Review 80(12), 56–69.

Prahalad, C. K.: 2002, 'Strategies for the Bottom of theEconomic Pyramid: India as a Source of Innovation', Reflections: The SOL Journal 3(4), 6–18.

Preston, L. E. and J. E. Post: 1981, 'Private Management and Public Policy', California Management Review 23(3), 56–63.

Sethi, S. P.: 1975, 'Dimensions of Corporate Social Performance: An Analytical Framework', California Management Review 17(3), 58–65.

Smith, W. and M. Higgins: 2000, 'Cause-Related Marketing: Ethics and the Ecstatic', Business and Society 39(3), 304–322.

Varadarajan, P. and A. Menon: 1988, 'Cause-Related Marketing: A Coalignment of Marketing Strategy and Corporate Philanthropy', Journal of Marketing 52 (3), 58-74.

Vogel, D.: 1986, 'The Study of Social Issues in Management: A Critical Appraisal', California Management Review 28(2), 142–152.

Wartick, S. L. and R. E. Rude: 1986, 'Issues Management: Corporate Fad or Corporate Function?', California Management Review 29(1), 124–132.

World Bank: 2006, Corporate Social Responsibility (www.worldbank.org/developmentcommunications/csr).

World Commission on Environment and Development :1987, BrutlandReport (http://www.un-documents.net/wced-ocf.htm).

United Nations: 2008, United Nations Global Pact (http://www.unglobalcompact.org).

Chapter 10: Socially Responsible Cooperation between the Government and Business

Social Responsibility—Mapping the Cooperation between the Government and Business Where the Idealist Meets the Pragmatist

Leon Zurawicki, University of Massachusetts-Boston, United States of America

Mohsin Habib

Abstract: The theme of this paper is to explore where and how the governments' and corporate responsibility should interplay. The main focus is to address the poverty as the greatest obstacle to development. Our goal is to highlight the concepts of the dialogue and cooperation between the government and business, less so the practicalities thereof. The following issues will be addressed: Clarity of positions and expectations; Parity and reciprocity. In terms of singling out the most burning issues the focus will be on: 1. Marketing the products and services to the poor — issues of concerns and best practices. It is a good challenge for capitalism but still potentially a profitable proposition. 2. Responses to economic and financial crises — the plague causing havoc and undermining development. In conclusion, it is posited that the development goals need to be "localized" and adapted to socio-economic environment of individual countries. In addition, rather than advocating a set of rigid standards, the "best practices" approach by business can produce desired results.

Introduction

Poverty is a disgrace to humanity, especially if viewed in the context of huge inequalities of the standard of living between and within the countries. To reduce the poverty is a noble task and the key to sustainable development. The problem has never been so severe before and the political pressure is very high. Governments alone cannot resolve the problem through own economic and income re-distribution policies. At the same time, the corporate world has become more sensitive to the issues of social responsibility in general and the concerns of the poor in particular (see WBCSD, 2004). For example, the pharmaceutical companies consented, albeit not without pressure, to quote reduced prices for critical medications in developing countries even if it reduces profits overall. There is obviously much more to do when we realize that altogether 4 billion people on earth starve on less than $2 per day (Kim Hak-Su, 2004), with all the dire consequences in terms of the quality and longevity of life[1].

The sheer economic growth, even if very fast, does not necessarily reduce poverty. While it appears to generate improvements at the very bottom of the pyramid of the populous countries in Asia--the percentage of the population living on less than $1 per day (Kim Hak-Su, 2004) is decreasing-- analogous results were not confirmed for the slightly less deprived people in Latin America (Szekely & Attanasio, 2001; Bourguignon, 2001). No changes were observed in sub-Saharan Africa (UNMP, 2005), either.

The government of the country is the most powerful actor for generating and distributing the tax income. But it still needs an ally in order to fulfill its poverty-reduction mission. Except for a few countries, the states today do not get involved in the bulk of economic activities and the wealth is created foremost through the private business sector. Thus, a concerted effort involving the government, private businesses, non-governmental organizations (NGOs) and trade unions can only prove beneficial.

The concept of Corporate Social Responsibility (CSR) has evolved during the past 40 years with respect to the society's expectations of the role of business and its eagerness to go beyond the strict compliance with the laws (Schwartz and Carroll, 2003). It appears that the willingness to develop a desirable image of a good corporate citizen (with all of its beneficial implications) becomes the main driver of the CSR (UNDP/BC/CII/PwC, 2002). If so, such an approach reflects clever brand marketing. Whether the corporate world is going to adopt a more deontological approach to CSR and transplant the social values in the private business, remains however to be seen (De George, 1999).

While there exist many important areas of CSR such as good governance, fair employment practices, harmonious growth and protection of natural environment, it is the reduction of poverty—especially in its extreme form—which emerges in our view as the paramount imperative.

Today, many executives start considering the planet's poor as a part of their company's growth strategy. They realize that stepping up their company's

---

[1] According to World Health Organization survey, Nigeria and China had a much lower incidence of mental disorders than was the case of developed countries. This suggests that unhappiness is not necessarily linked to poverty. See: Prevalence, Severity, and Unmet Need for Treatment of Mental Disorders in the World Health Organization World Mental Health Surveys JAMA. 2004;291:2581-2590.

presence in developing countries by 'doing business with the poor' will be crucial to their long-term competitiveness and success.

One can posit that discovering the world's poor is a function of the internationalization path of a company. Large multinational corporations (MNCs) have traditionally been selling in the vast and rich national markets and did not need to consider the countries and regions marked by poverty. If anything, these areas served as the location for the asset-searching investment: natural resources and cheap labor. However, in the present stage of globalization and increased international competition, that perspective is also changing. At the end of January 2005, some distinguished speakers at the Davos World Economic Forum such as Jacques Chirac, Tony Blair, and Bill Gates clearly focused on global poverty (WEF, 2005). More importantly, for the first time in the history of the prestigious meeting where the majority of the participants represented the top brass of the largest MNCs, poverty was voted the number one global priority issue to be addressed.

In this paper, we explore where and how the government and corporate responsibilities should interplay. The goal is to conceptually highlight the key areas of possible cooperation between the government and the business, less so the practicalities thereof. The two principles we want to emphasize will be (a) the clarity of positions and expectations and (b) the parity and reciprocity between the two parties.

In terms of singling out the most burning issues the spotlight will be on:

1. Marketing the products and services to the poor. The concept is a challenge for capitalism but still potentially a profitable proposition.
2. The poor as suppliers.
3. The poor as employees.
4.

The first aspect will be treated here from a marketing standpoint, while the second and the third call for a managerial perspective.

The Poor as Consumers

Studies in consumer behavior typically focus on the households who live above the poverty line and enjoy the luxury of a considerable choice in buying. Much less attention has been paid to the "have-not's". (Shultz, 2001). As a result, there are very few studies addressing the spending pattern at the stage of deprivation. This is the result of the "Western" thinking about consumption with the emphasis on stimulating new needs as opposed to satisfying the essential ones. Hence, the sophistication and the purchasing power of the affluent consumers is the main driver of the marketing policies of the corporations headquartered in the developed countries. From the social standpoint this targeting focus seems controversial as even in the richest countries of the world, some members of the society endure unacceptably low living standards. However, Western MNCs extend such strategies globally to less developed and very poor markets. In case of extremely destitute countries (e.g. parts of Africa), the MNCs limit their operations to the minimum.

Hence, the advanced theory of marketing focuses on the ever changing whims of the well-to-do households. This approach may be even re-enforced by the very competitive nature of business environment and the volume of discretionary spending income in the industrialized countries. Yet, at the same time such an attitude contradicts the fundamental principle of marketing: satisfaction of the varying needs of different market segments. The sheer huge number of the households with extremely low income reflects substantial virtual demand at least for bare necessities (Pralahad, and Hammond. 2002). Certainly, the demand for staple products is there. However, meeting this demand requires a significant change in companies' approach. In some cases, the companies may have to make the consumers aware of the "hidden" needs first (e.g. safe, treated water for drinking and other household purposes) before offering them the necessary products.

Designing the Right Products

Typically, the value orientation by the poor is more focused on price as opposed to quality of the whole spectrum of products and services. It follows that the quality-price relationship is shaped differently in the minds of the "have-not's" in contrast to the more affluent buyers. It is after all, the poor consumers who nourish the market for imitations, counterfeit or look-alike products. Notwithstanding the fight against piracy launched by the MNCs, the above phenomenon simply indicates the pent-up demand and the existing opportunities.

To exploit them, the international product line managers need to follow a strategy different from the present one. The offer addressed to the poor customers (in poor countries) needs to center on the usefulness and affordability of the essential products and services. Furthermore, the appropriate product design needs to be accompanied by greater emphasis on consumer education. The enhanced marketing effort directed to poor consumers should educate how to use the products sparingly and efficiently, how to extend the durability, and even how to "perform-it-yourself" such functions as maintenance and service. This would reflect the emphasis on frugal consumption, something which is not very dear to Western marketers who actually promote higher consumption and ultimately waste (either in terms of volume or the ever more complex, pricier products). At the same time, the psychological need espoused by the poor consumers who do not wish to be confined to secondary categories of products and services, deserves attention. By extending their brand names to well-designed and well-built basic products, the icons of global business gain the opportunity to increase the satisfaction of the poor customers. Will they do this? It poses a big challenge for the boardrooms which may fear "diluting" the brand. Equally important is the competence gap. Even when the Western companies are willing to target the poor in the developing countries, they often lack market intelligence and/or distribution channels. The preponderant point is to learn more.

Thus, in marketing terms the key issues to consider are:

- Do we understand the real needs of the poor consumers as they pertain to our type of offerings? How do we identify prospective poor customers? Do we need to segment them?
- Do we have the right products/services to offer?
- How do we ensure that there is sufficient demand for our products/services to make our new offering venture economically viable?
- How do we help our customers to afford our products?
- How do we reach our customers?
- How do we collect revenues?
- How can we best design our supply chain?

One way to learn is through tapping into local networks and local knowledge. This will hopefully reveal to what extent catering to the poor requires a revision of the typical Western approach which emphasizes the importance of the brand and the new ever more sophisticated offerings. If the poor are, by definition, more rational and intrinsic value-oriented consumers, then another emerging challenge is how to convey the relevant information and experience to mostly illiterate audience. This adds another dimension to the list of questions above: How do we prepare and implement the communication strategy? Is it ethical to lure the poor with exaggerated claims? Otherwise, how does one handle the task if no independent product tests run by the third party are available?

To comprehensively comment on the issues just evoked warrants writing another paper. Here we only wish to point to strategic options. In a simple framework, stripping down the "deluxe" versions of existing products of the less essential features is one option. This kind of strategy could produce "people's computer" as much as "people's car." The process can be possibly extended to items like footwear or food supplements. Ironically, some dietary mixes developed to help lose excess weight can be reformulated to assist malnourished. However, in considering this option, its limitations need to be identified as the products to be downsized were originally created with a different purpose in mind.

A big question for the big army of extremely poor is how to cope with more pressing needs before dreaming of a refrigerator, air-conditioner or a computer. Efficient nutritional items and inexpensive suitable housing is certainly a greater priority. To an extent, it presents the challenges which the Western companies had little interest in. The conceptual and technological resources exist, however, and the inspiration may come from various sources. Military, for one, can be named. The problem with that approach is the cost-economic return equation. The specific consumer preferences are hardly known -- who should define them is not clear. In view thereof, the sales prospects although potentially huge if the sheer number of prospective buyers is considered, are doubtful. The struggle which Procter and Gamble endured with its nutritional mixes in several countries (WBCSD, 2004) well illustrates the point.

On a different note, the global trade in pre-owned goods -- clothing and household appliances -- often discarded at an additional cost in the developed countries represents another avenue to help the poor satisfy their needs. However, in 1999, documented export sales of worn clothing from the U.S. reached only $217 million, a miniscule figure compared to the needs of the have-not's (Green, 2001). Indeed, it is a shame that in 2006, 59.6 million computers and televisions would be designated for disposal in the US alone (Erle, 2004) when the needy are deprived of using them. Not to mention millions of toys discarded each year in the Western world. Whether this is the area of activity suitable for established multinationals, typically involved in marketing of **new** products, is open for discussion. Accordingly, interesting recycling cum exporting projects in partnership with the waste management authorities in industrialized countries could become viable.

In sum, the viable solutions boil down to 3 mutually non-exclusive suggestions:

1. Drop the prices quoted in the developing countries to the rock-bottom level.
2. Simplify and "cheapify" what you already have.
3. Design from scratch specific offerings geared to the poor.

Stretching the Purchasing Power

Allowing the poor to manage and stretch their limited budgets is yet another challenge to boost the sales and cater to the worse-off customers. Naturally, the banking industry has a primary role to play. However, before getting into the credit facilitation issues, there are strategies to pursue more vigorously by the marketers themselves. Selling in smaller chunks is crucial to ensuring affordability. With some products, this is a straightforward physical process of dividing the product into smaller subunits. Using smaller packaging alleviates the burden of a one-time expense and establishes a "pay-as you consume"[2] system. To that effect, frequent and small orders of products made available through a streamlined and direct distribution system in poor neighborhoods can be effective. Although companies lose economies of scale benefits in this process, with respect to poor customers it may be more than compensated through consistent and long-term repeat sales (WBCSD, 2004). This strategy (involving both manufacturing and retailing) can apply to items like food products, toiletries, cosmetics, and even medications. Some other products, however, cannot be physically sub-divided and more creative thinking is required in coping with selling them.

Regarding services, prepayment for ongoing deliveries in small installments (through tokens, prepaid cards or similar mechanisms) can reduce the credit risk and the burden of one large lump sum charges[3]. In addition, successful experiments including incentives to encourage payments (e.g., a discount on the next bill for payment in due time) have been implemented in some countries. Further, viability of a collective billing arrangement allowing the community to

---

[2] For example, it is not uncommon to see cigarettes sold in some countries in packs of 5 or even per one by the street vendors.

[3] This concept has been successfully implemented by the South African utility company – Eskom.

make a joint investment and decide how to split the costs among the members could be tested.

While the financial institutions typically take responsibility for providing and facilitating credit, it does not preclude the suppliers of other products and services from offering the same. Especially, the leasing option appears suitable for the customers with poor or no credit history. This could even be more practical since in the case of payment delinquency the re-possessed goods are more easily marketable by the original manufacturer or the retailer than by the provider of the financial credit. Such approach may prove suitable not only with poor consumers in mind but, even more so, when targeting the poor as business partners. Overwhelmingly, the poor of the world live in the countryside and their subsistence depends on farming. Thus, promoting and organizing users' cooperatives and equipment-rental centers (e.g. for agricultural machines) would make business sense. Through the design and mass marketing of low-cost capital equipment in the agricultural sector (e.g. micro-irrigation pump), companies in developing countries have already been able to help the poor grow high value fruits and vegetables and eventually gain access to purchasing power (WBCSD, 2004).

Micro-financing and Warranties

Extending loans to customers with hardly any collateral and a miniscule income which cannot generate any savings poses a tremendous challenge to the credit institutions prospecting the poor. The key issue is to secure payment guarantees in case of default by the primary borrower. Through involvement of the family and other local community members the problem can be alleviated. As an example, the cement company, Cemex, in collaboration with Ashoka (an NGO specializing in social entrepreneurship) has organized people in small groups in poor Mexican neighborhoods to save money which then can be used to buy building materials and expertise to improve their living conditions. Such company efforts are extremely helpful for the individuals in the group because they permit to save at lower cost and make faster improvements to their dwellings. Again, in the matter of financing as much as with respect to marketing activities, the question of low profitability emerges. But again this is why (no matter how difficult) it behooves business companies to review the targeted rates of return when selling to the destitute customers. However, attracting those new customers is not just a question of philanthropy but eventually a good strategy -- the poor do not need to stay poor all their lives.[4]

The Poor as Entrepreneurs and Business Partners

A primary question which comes to mind: are the poor in developing countries more risk-takers as entrepreneurs compared to their richer counterpart? Intuitively, we would say "yes" as absorbing a high risk could be the only way out of poverty.

[4] Think of how credit card companies go after students of law or medicine who only offer a promise of being well to do one day

Also, in most underdeveloped countries the bulk of the population at large and the majority of entrepreneurs in particular are very young which further encourages bold business attitude. It is amazing how supporting entrepreneurship can be accomplished by providing funds which from the Western perspective are very small, say $50. Yet, this money can buy a small market stall or a basic means of transportation, a rickshaw or a bicycle.[5] In India, the rickshaw would allow a poor rural family to retain 50 percent of the profits from the wheat that would have gone to pay another transporter (Khosla, 2004). Lending to small groups in the same community creates a strong social pressure against failure to pay. It is embarrassing to default, and if one person does, the others have to make up for it. At the same time, the Western standards have to be modified. The "usurious" interest rates of 20 to 30 percent are still less taxing relative to the local money lenders who charge 5 to 10 percent per day.

How to streamline the entrepreneurial activity? One area is production and a way the large corporations (local and foreign) can take the entrepreneurs under their wings is through subcontracting. Specifying what supplies are desirable—crops, medicinal plants, handicrafts—can assure outlets for otherwise misdirected energy. After all, how many African masks or woven hammocks can be sold at the roadside stalls to the visiting tourists? Yet, many of the local craftsmen do not know better how to use their talents[6]. In this context, the strategies and activities of companies like Pier 1 Imports or the Body Shop provide an inspiration. Lifting the shroud of anonymity from the poor suppliers should already prove helpful. Just like when the trading organizations and MNCs emphasize in the developed markets the "natural" character of the ingredients and/or provide the information about the poor communities who are the suppliers of the inputs/raw materials. Such efforts in turn help boost the sales.

Another form of assistance is to provide farmers with credits to buy yield-enhancing inputs. In other areas, similar effects can be obtained when supplying cabinet or purse hardware, attractive buttons etc. The resulting increased production and sales can help to repay the loan. Large, agriculture-based companies operating in developing countries like India have not only extended credits but also actively engaged in educating the farmers on how to use their products effectively.

Companies with dual roles of providing resources and knowledge (advice) can be a very attractive option for the poor entrepreneurs in the developing markets. As one author puts it, corporate responsibility must align organizational learning with societal issues to the point that such issues then turn into higher opportunities for both sides (Zadek, 2004). A shift in the managerial mindset is required for this to happen – a shift from the risk-based, reputational view of

---

[5] Critics had argued that lending money in very small increments would be uneconomical and would lead to even greater burdens for the poor. The success of the more than 6,000 institutions doing some form of microfinance today has proven this wrong. The Grameen Bank in Bangladesh is perhaps the best known case in point.

[6] Costa Rica offers an encouraging example of how traditional designs of woodcrafts and jewelry were supplemented by modern styles in tune with the preferences of the Western markets. This was accomplished through the joint effort of government and European marketers.

corporate responsibility to one focused on innovation and knowledge that will help realign the business model and the market according to the "emerging" societal concerns. The giant footwear and apparel company, Nike, has made significant strides to do exactly that. It has joined a group of companies, NGOs and labor organizations to explore how an alliance can help to deal with the challenges of developing programs for workers in transition in sourcing countries as well as establishing a framework to guide companies in re-adjusting supply chain in the post-MFA (Multi-Fiber Arrangement) world when all country-based garments quotas will be lifted for the all-important US market..

An important objective of the resource deployment of the companies is to improve access for the poor. The economically disadvantaged segment of the population lacks good distribution and communication links. Granting access is a pre-requisite for economic development and the companies involved in business with the poor must address this issue. In other words, it is not just the end product or service but the process through which they will be created and delivered that companies must participate in. This is where the entrepreneurial spirit of the poor business partners can be put to good use, especially when the small scale of undertaking (e.g. street or village vendors) does not require substantial investment. As discussed above, the nature of the poor consumers and their spending patterns require a different type of middlemen capable to distribute in small quantities and quickly attend to the local market needs. Lack of refrigeration compounds the issue regarding the food items. Hence, the opportunity for micro scale business-oriented salespeople operating on a door-to-door or similar basis becomes evident. For instance, a soft drink company such as Coca-Cola can offer not only its products but also the delivery means (manually pulled tri-cycles) to carry them in remote locations. In yet another example, Grameen Phone in Bangladesh and WorldTel Ltd. in India have introduced the concept of community telephone in rural areas operated by an entrepreneur (usually a woman) who charges a fee for the use of the telephone (Prahalad and Hart, 2002).

Poor as Employees

By providing new jobs, the companies create income opportunities for the poor. In this respect, it is crucial that there is sufficient job security. The importance of steady income as opposed to ad hoc employment cannot be overemphasized. In hiring and subsequent employment, companies have found success more often than not when they have included local community members in the decision process. For example, setting up assessment workshops monitored by community specialists and company human resources personnel for hiring new employees have been quite effective in the Australian diamond mines (WBCSD, 2004). The location of industrial activities in many developing areas determines access to a specific pool of the workforce (the lack of housing limits mobility). Hence, it is also in the best interest of the employer not only to keep workers satisfied but also to help improve their living conditions and enhance their qualifications as a way to reduce the absenteeism and increase productivity. Loyalty and commitment of the employees depend upon the quality of life they are provided with at work and at home. The respective needs can vary from area to area but at a minimum encompass the need for basic infrastructure (to help facilitate transportation to and from work), fair housing standards, access to electricity, clean water, primary health care, and basic education. Correspondingly, the interests of the communities from which the workers are recruited will also be better served. Developing the people and the infrastructure is an essential part of a company's overall strategy in developing countries. As noted by researchers (London and Hart, 2004; Sharma, Vredenburg and Westley, 1994; Prahalad and Hammond, 2002), this element of the MNC's strategy is critical for ultimate success because it helps develop local capacity for the long run by sharing resources across regional boundaries.

It is important to emphasize that one important way to overcome the credit and borrowing limitations witnessed by the poor is by having the employer guarantee the loans. After all, the employers do verify, provide and control the steady flow of income to employees.

Two other aspects deserve mentioning as well.

1. The use of corporate infrastructure to generate positive externalities benefiting not only own employees but communities at large. Examples include the use of the company clinics to voluntarily screen the public for HIV/AIDS and other illnesses. Further, continuing education need not only be geared towards own workforce but also training (while utilizing own centers) of the local youth in computer and other skills.
2. Involving own employees as volunteers to do the work for the community when implementing the corporate social policy projects. The latter trend also helps to address the psychological rift between those who have jobs and the unemployed within a particular commune or village. Adoption of such a "Robin Hood approach" enhances the embedded social capital (Coleman, 1994) and cohesion.

It is not accidental that some of the best practices in dealing with the poor were developed by the corporations deeply rooted in the underdeveloped countries (e.g. Tata Group in India). Some created original and demanding social responsibility standards in following the ideas of the charismatic business owners. In doing so, they proved that the Robert Owen's spirit was (and is) alive and well[7]. It is amazing, though that most of the corporations from the industrialized countries (foremost large Japanese companies) who have adopted "employment for life" and provide social protection for their workers at home, failed to export this model to other countries where they operate. One is then tempted to stipulate that what the parent companies practice on their home turf should as well be transferred to their subsidiaries abroad. The directives of some international organizations, for example OECD, clearly advocate this approach.

---

[7] Porter and Kramer, 2002, came with the modern-day version of same approach.

Recommendations for Renewing Company and Government Efforts

One of the main problems with intensifying social contributions of the corporations and helping the poor in particular is the lack of measures of economic impact. Since it is hard to assess the effectiveness, it is difficult to decide on how many resources to commit. Correspondingly, a practical judgment needs to be made: to what extent helping the poor is a business decision and to what degree it is the issue of conscience. The "feel good" factor can be an important driver but under strong competition and thin margins, capitalism imposes its rules. In that spirit, we recommend that:

1. Realistic expectations are established regarding what private companies can accomplish. However, plenty of room for creativity needs to be allowed. There are many little important things to be done before more ambitious (= more difficult to manage) tasks are undertaken. After all, the strength of the business lies in the creativity to promptly find efficient solutions to the emerging problems. For example, partnering with NGOs and allowing for "piggybacking" on companies' physical and technological infrastructure generates opportunities in the field of education, construction, transportation, and telecommunication. The knowledge and asset bases of the companies can be further utilized to coach potential local entrepreneurs on how to run a successful business. In the end, mentoring will ensure a good local partner for the long run and will increase the likelihood of societal acceptance for the international company.
2. Companies are advised to stick to the programs related to their core business operations -- efficient marketing of product and services and the harmonious co-existence with the communities where they manufacture. To illustrate, large multinational banks have always set up their bases in few major cities in the developing countries serving the rich. They can stick to their core skills but should think of extending their reach to the poor through innovative products and processes. Getting involved through some kind of micro-lending, for example, could be just the right solution for that context.
3. The role of the governments is well defined and diligently performed.

It is with respect to the last point that we offer the concluding remarks. An enabling environment is a prerequisite for business companies to do their share of good deeds. It means that at first clear social priorities need to be announced by the governments (national and local where applicable). This provides guidance for business companies which will act more in sync with the societal goals and earn the rewards they merit. Without the message of clear priorities, the companies might end up mimicking each other in pursuit of one idea: to ingratiate themselves with the government. Today, governments, communities, and civil society increasingly anticipate the companies to become involved with social issues. The expectations of corporate social responsibility translate into challenges for governments as well.

Guidance, responsible fiscal and tax policies, effective programs in the areas of public domain (education, health care), transparency, good governance and business-friendly environment, and efficient judicial system are all important aspects. Because of the elevated risk of some investments (for example, utilities), there is the additional need for government guarantees extended to private business operations.

1. Since it is first and foremost the role of the governments to promote the national development, the cooperation from business will be enhanced by governments' own "leading by example" approach. It is imperative that good governance, transparency, stability of government practices become a norm. How can one expect businesses to make a serious commitment to the government's cause if at the same time it is plagued by corruption, show-off projects, divisiveness or disregard of political process? What is more, overly complicated, ambiguous, biased policies followed by the government only invite opposition and cheating from business. And obviously, it is not just the central administration but the public sector agencies (central bank, utilities, social security, transportation sector, even police) as well who need to demonstrate leadership as frontrunners of caring about the poor -- whether at issue are social benefits for the employees or community at large. Needless to say, public sector represents a big part of GDP in many relevant countries (OECD, 2004b). Apart from the philanthropy-oriented private companies, many more private businesses are motivated by what is expected of them (Schwartz and Carroll, 2003). It might be hard to convince the private enterprises to undertake a relatively greater effort than their state-owned counterparts[8]. In addressing the issue of symbiotic behavior of businesses end governments, the latter should be advised to:
2. Use persuasion and incentives. They seem to work better than coercion.
3. Recognize the contribution businesses make to your economic and social development and reward good action.

Proper understanding of the above stipulations will facilitate spreading out of the "public-private" partnerships (PPPs). Such partnerships involving the business, the government, and the non-governmental organization (NGO) are a must since the challenges of poverty reduction in the developing world are so great that no one sector can "go it alone."

Helping the poor in the ambiguous profit-oriented context is a complex intellectual and practical challenge. Multiple parties may become involved and the process can require innovative solutions. The ideas presented here are just a starting point to an in-depth discussion of the problem and its possible answers.

References

Bourguignon, F. 2001. The Pace of Economic Growth and Poverty Reduction. Washington, DC, United States: World Bank. Mimeographed document.

[8] The argument can also apply to foreign investors vs. local companies.

Coleman, J., 1994. *Foundations of Social Theory*, Cambridge: Harvard University Press.

De George, R.T. 1999. Business Ethics. Upper Saddle River, NJ: Prentice Hall.

OECD. 2004a. Accelerating Pro-Poor Growth through Support for Private Sector Development. An Analytical Framework, Paris, 2004

OECD. 2004b. Guidelines on Corporate Governance of State-Owned Enterprises. Draft Text. http://www.oecd.org/dataoecd/33/31/34051587.pdf

Erle, B., 2004. Junked computers, environmental risks, Baltimore Sun, July 12, 2004

Green, S.L., 2001. Export of used equipment, clothing and vehicles including remanufactured automobile parts, Export America, April 2001 (April):14-15.

Kim Hak-Su, Equitable Growth Can Defeat Poverty, Economiquity, No.1, 2004, p.2

Khosla, V. 2004. Microlending: An Anti-Poverty Success Story, May 2004, http://www.gsb.stanford.edu/news/headlines/2004globalconf_khosla.shtml.

Porter, M.E. and M.R. Kramer. 2002. The Competitive Advantage of Corporate Philanthropy, Harvard Business Review, 2002 (December): 5-16.

Pralahad, C.K. and A. Hammond. 2002. Serving the World's Poor, Profitably, Harvard Business Review, 2002 (September): 4-11.

PWC, 2002. Uncertain Times, Abundant Opportunities. http://www.pwc.com/gx/eng/ins-sol/survey-rep/ceo/PwC_Global_CEO_Survey.pdf

Schwartz, M.S. and A.B.Carroll. 2003. Corporate Social Responsibility: A Three-Domain Approach, Business Ethics Quarterly, 13 (4): 503-530.

Sharma, S., Vredenburg, H., and Westley, F. 1994. Strategic bridging: a role for the multinational corporation in Third World development. Journal of Applied Behavioral Science, 30(4): 458-476.

Székely, M. and O. Attanasio (eds.). 2001. *Portrait of the Poor: An Asset-Based Approach*. Inter-American Development Bank (August 1, 2001) Baltimore: Johns Hopkins University Press.

Tata Steel. 2003. Corporate Sustainability Report 2002-2003. http://www.tatasteel.com/corporatesustainability/pdfs/csr6.pdf.

UNDP/BC/CII/PwC. 2002. Corporate Social Responsibility Survey 2002-India. New Delhi. 48 pages.

UNMP.2005. Investing in Development. A Practical Plan to Achieve the Millennium Development Goals, http://unmp.forumone.com/eng_full_report

WBCSD. 2004. Doing business with the poor - a field guide. Geneva: World Business Council for Sustainable Development. 73 pages.

WEF. 2005. http://www.weforum.org

Zadek, S. 2004. The Path to Corporate Responsibility. (Best Practice) Harvard Business Review, December.[9]

[9] [i] According to World Health Organization survey, Nigeria and China had a much lower incidence of mental disorders than was the case of developed countries. This suggests that unhappiness is not necessarily linked to poverty. See: Prevalence, Severity, and Unmet

Need for Treatment of Mental Disorders in the World Health Organization World Mental Health Surveys JAMA. 2004;291:2581-2590.

[ii] For example, it is not uncommon to see cigarettes sold in some countries in packs of 5 or even per one by the street vendors.

[iii] This concept has been successfully implemented by the South African utility company – Eskom.

[iv] Credit card to law and medicine students

[v] Critics had argued that lending money in very small increments would be uneconomical and would lead to even greater burdens for the poor. The success of the more than 6,000 institutions doing some form of microfinance today has proven this wrong. The Grameen Bank in Bangladesh is perhaps the best known case in point.

[vi] Costa Rica offers an encouraging example of how traditional designs of woodcrafts and jewelry were supplemented by modern styles in tune with the preferences of the Western markets. This was accomplished through the joint effort of government and European marketers.

[vii]Porter and Kramer, 2002, came with the modern-day version of same approach.

[viii]The argument can also apply to foreign investors vs. local companies.

Part IV: Corporate Social Responsibility and Sustainable Development—Overview

Chapters 11 and 12 make of Part 4 of the book, which focuses on corporate social responsibility and sustainable development. Chapter 11 explores targeting demand instead of supply when looking at the economics of sustainability. Chapter 12 looks at the role of CSR assurance reporting.

Chapter 11: Economics and Sustainability

Economics and Sustainability: Targeting Demand Instead of Supply

Abbas Ameli-Renani, University of Cambridge, Cambridgeshire, UK

Abstract: Left to themselves, multi-national corporations (MNCs) seek to first and foremost profit- maximise. Every other act carried out by MNCs is merely a means to an end, which is profit maximisation. Consumers on the other hand have a more profound purpose to their being. They seek to maximise their satisfaction of life; and this satisfaction is not just maximised by material concepts such as money and wealth, but in many cases so much more by non-material aspects of life such as the urge to live in a clean and non-polluted atmosphere, to live a healthy and educated life and to ensure a suitable living environment for the future of their children and grandchildren. Whilst the occasional clash and conflict of private and public costs and private and public benefits means that relying upon consumers' decisions alone can be problematic, contemporary signs show that consumers are becoming increasingly conscious about what they consume. Not only do they care more about what directly affects their own health, especially about what they eat, they are also demanding their suppliers to be more ethical in what they produce and how they produce it. Suppliers have responded in more ways than one. Instead of focusing on government-imposed rules and regulations on the supply-side to enforce the sustainability of all that surrounds us, we should direct our attention at increasing consumer awareness and ensuring that consumers are well-informed of what is in their long-term best interest. This requires government attention and also a more active civil society. Initiatives already in place such as Corporate Social Responsibility (CSR) which are now being taken up by many MNCs are a direct result of increased consumer awareness and consumer demand for a more ethical economic activity. Influencing demand through directing consumer choice is a better option than influencing supply through government intervention, which may very well end up in government failure. We can still maintain sustainability by relying upon the basic rules of supply and demand.

Introduction

The purpose of this paper is to suggest an alternative method to achieving sustainability in the 21st century. The concept of sustainability has for long appeared in various literatures and in differing contexts and has become a prominent area of study in recent years. In discussing sustainability, it is important to first, provide a definition and to determine the context in which it is to be discussed.

The *Oxford English Dictionary* defines 'sustainable' as something which is "capable of being borne or endured; supportable, bearable" or as something "capable of being upheld or defended; maintainable". To this end it suggests in economics terms that "an increase beyond limits of sustainability existing at any given time would lead only to reduced earnings and subsequent contraction of the quantity supplied".

Brown et. al. (1987) suggest several areas under which sustainability can be discussed. These areas include sustainable biological resource use, sustainable agriculture, sustainable carrying capacity[1], sustainable energy, sustainable society and economy and sustainable development. Although it is not in the scope of this paper to review and discuss the literature available on each of these fields of sustainability, these fields provide us with a feeling for the contexts under which sustainability has thus far been discussed.The sustainability context which I would like to adapt for this paper is sustainable development.

Sustainable development can be defined as a "development strategy which manages all assets- natural and human resources, as well as financial and physical assets- for increasing wealth and wellbeing" (Repetto 1985). Today, the notion of sustainability is becoming increasingly tied in with concerns about the environment. In the *Environmental Requirements of the World Bank,* the World Bank states "sustainable economic development depends on sound environmental management" (1985).

The increasing attention to the concept of sustainability comes in part, from the increasing concern about the environment and what has become evident as a tip-toeing global economy towards non-sustainability. In recent years the Stern Review of the Economics of Climate Change (Stern 2007) has provided us with fresh insight about the interlinked relationship between the environment and the economy. The review claimed that if no action is taken on emissions, there is more than a 75% chance of global temperatures rising between two and three degrees Celsius over the next 50 years. Meanwhile, the review estimated a 50% chance that average global temperatures could increase by five degrees Celsius. On the economics-side, the review suggested that a two to three degrees Celsius rise in temperatures could reduce global economic output by 3%. If temperatures rise by five degrees Celsius, up to 10% of global output could be lost. The Stern Review also proposed a number of public policy initiatives in an attempt to halt

---

[1] Carrying capacity is defined as the "number of people that a given amount of land can support" (WRI/IIED 1986).

the current trend towards global warming. This paper does not intend to discuss the merits and demerits of Stern's findings, nor his alternative public policy suggestions. As Dasgupta (2007) suggests, "Disagreements over the desirability of alternative public policies arise when people don't agree on facts (e.g., the economic effects of a doubling of carbon concentration in the atmosphere) or when they don't agree on values (e.g., the way our well-being ought to be balanced against the well-being of all those future thems). Usually, of course, both facts and values are subject to dispute." However, the Stern review provides us with an idea of what the world could potentially be facing and helps us emphasise the importance of finding the correct remedy. In economics, the main concern that exists with the issue of climate change is that it threatens sustainable development. To this end, environmental policies, from an economist's point of view, need to work towards enhancing the prospects of sustainable development.

In recent years, the most significant public policy aimed at curbing greenhouse gas emission has come as a result of the implementation of the Kyoto protocol. When put in effect in February 2005, the Kyoto protocol obliged its signatories to reduce total greenhouse gas emissions by an average 5.2% compared with 1990 levels between 2008 to 2012. Whilst many (mostly developed) countries have since adapted variations to the Kyoto protocol- mainly setting themselves higher targets for cutting carbon emissions- the Kyoto treaty is widely considered to have laid the stepping stone towards implementing widespread government policies to halt the growth of carbon emissions.

In this paper I will discuss the limits of the Kyoto protocol and its likes, as measures which seek to influence supply, and I will suggest looking at an alternative method of ensuring sustainable development by looking to influence demand. My suggestions will be based on evidence gathered from different papers assessing the significance of Corporate Social Responsibility. Yet, this paper remains unique in recommending the expansion of CSR and its demand-side effects as a means of ensuring sustainable development. Having said that, this paper only serves to initiate a discussion on this matter and leaves much room for further in-depth analysis and study of possible demand-side alternatives in achieving sustainable development.

The Limits of Targeting Supply

In the past decade there have been serious efforts to implement policy aimed at reducing carbon emissions. Various emission targets have been set by individual governments, but the most internationally widespread commitment to cutting carbon emissions has come through the ratification of the Kyoto protocol. As of October 2008 182 countries had signed and ratified the Kyoto protocol (United Nations Framework Convention on Climate Change 2008). Many signatories, such as the UK, have set themselves targets which go beyond the requirements of the protocol. For the purpose of this paper, I shall discuss only the Kyoto protocol as an example of policy aimed at reducing carbon emissions through influencing supply. The international context in which Kyoto is implemented makes it a suitable case study.

As a means towards meeting the emissions targets, the Kyoto protocol introduced three mechanisms. A direct implication of these mechanisms has been the creation of what has come to be known as the "carbon market". The first of the three mechanisms is the emissions trading mechanism. Under the Kyoto protocol, this mechanism allows parties with commitments to the protocol that have emission units to spare to sell the excess capacity to countries that are over their targets. An implication of this mechanism has been the introduction of a new commodity to the market- greenhouse gas emissions (UNFCCC 2008).

The second mechanism is the Clean Development Mechanism (CDM). This mechanism allows countries with emission-reduction or emission-limitation commitments under the Kyoto protocol (Annex B Party[2]) to implement emission-reducing projects in developing countries. Implementing such projects would earn saleable certified emission reduction credits which can be counted towards meeting Kyoto targets (UNFCCC).

The third mechanism is the Joint Implementation mechanism which allows Annex B countries to earn emission reductions units from an emission-reduction or emission removal project in another Annex B Party, which can also be counted towards meeting Kyoto targets (UNFCCC).

The Kyoto protocol should be praised as a stepping stone towards an international attempt at curbing greenhouse gas emissions. For the first time, it provided a legally-binding frame-work for countries to work towards achieving sustainable development. However, it is important to understand its limitations and areas of the protocol which are a cause for concern.

A particular criticism of the Kyoto protocol has been aimed at the regulatory aspects, or lack thereof, of the program. Bachram (2004) notes that "while many hundreds of millions of dollars are being invested in setting up emissions trading schemes all over the world (the UK government alone spent £215 million on its trial trading scheme), virtually no resources are being channelled into their regulation." Bachram states that such an imbalance may lead to an emissions market which is dangerously reliant upon the integrity of corporations to file accurate reports of emissions levels, and reductions. She gives an example of corporations such as PricewaterhouseCoopers which act as both accountants and consultants to polluting firms and are also verifiers of emission reduction projects.

Najam et. al. (2003) discuss the often incompatible interests of developing and developed countries under the Kyoto protocol. They note that the challenges to the Kyoto protocol emerge from the fact that the concerns of developing countries, which have always been marginal to the thrust of the UNFCCC, have in recent years become even more marginalised in recent conferences of parties. Najam et. al. argue that this has come about as the focus has had to be diverted to get reluctant northern countries (those listed in Annex 1[3]) to accede to the Kyoto protocol. They state that "as the industrialised countries dragged their feet, the concerns of the developing nations have largely been lost in the dust." Najam et. al. also suggest that the Kyoto protocol is inequitable in its nature and fails to implement fairness between its member states. They claim "even though the European Union has chosen a framework of burden sharing amongst its own

[2] Annex B countries include mainly industrialised countries and a number of Eastern European countries.

[3] These are industrialised countries.

members on the argument of equity and fairness, the Kyoto regime as a whole is devoid of a basis in equity and emanates, instead, from the basis of stated willingness and political expediency."

On a similar line of argument, Nordhaus & Boyer (1999) argue that while the environmental damages from climate change do not differ markedly among the different Kyoto Protocol variants, the costs of implementation vary enormously. They suggest that "the cost of the no-trade variant of the Kyoto Protocol is about 9 times the cost of the global-trade variant." Meanwhile, Nordhaus and Boyer note that most of the gains from trade come from including non-OECD countries such as Russia, China and India. Moreover, Nordhaus & Boyer criticize the Kyoto protocol on a cost-benefit analysis basis suggesting the costs of an efficiently designed Kyoto protocol ranges from $0.8 to $1.5 trillion in discounted costs, while the benefits of the emissions reduction from the Kyoto protocol are around $0.12 trillion.

Recent UN data shows promising, yet alarming signs of how well the Kyoto protocol has worked in the international context. National greenhouse gas inventory data for the period 1990-2006 (UNFCCC 2008) shows that emissions by the 40 industrialised nations that agreed binding cuts in pollution are down 5% on 1990 levels. That suggests the target set by Kyoto has been met. However, this drop is not necessarily a direct result of changing climate policies of the industrialised nations. The bulk of the decline has come through the collapse of the Soviet Union and the subsequent economic decline in eastern European countries in the 1990s. Without these nations, with so-called "economies in transition", greenhouse gas emissions have actually grown by 10% since 1990. These figures put a serious question mark on the impact of the Kyoto protocol. Moreover, the UNFCCC report shows 20 industrialised countries are lagging behind their Kyoto target.

Targeting Demand

The Kyoto protocol is an example of supply-side policy initiatives aimed at curbing greenhouse gas emissions and by doing that striving towards achieving greater sustainable development. As we have discussed, there are limitations with how successful such a policy initiative could be and reviews of the impact of the Kyoto protocol are further cause for concern over the practicality of such measures. This paper intends to emphasise the importance of demand-side policies as means by which sustainable development could be achieved through free-market mechanisms.

Recent decades have been witness to an unprecedented growth in mass media and the ability of people to get their hands on information from any part of the world with significant ease and pace. We are indeed living in "the information age" (Castells 1996). This information age provides us with a magnificent opportunity in many aspects. We should look to the tools and facilities provided to us by this age as ones which supply us with cost-effective methods of targeting the problems facing 21st century society.

With widespread media communications and the effective flow of information consumers are more aware than ever of the kind of products they consume. Consumers today hold greater awareness of how their suppliers perform on a social level, whether their business is damaging to the environment, to human rights and civil liberties, and many other social factors which go beyond the day to day expenditure-minimising concern of consumers. In this paper, I would like to discuss the concept of Corporate Social Responsibility as an example of how consumer expectations can be used to influence how businesses perform.

Significant social legislation in the early 1970s in the US led to the creation of institutions such as the Environmental Protection agency (EPA), the Equal Employment Opportunity Commission (EEOC), the Occupational Safety and Health Administration (OSHA), and the Consumer Product Safety Commission (CPSC). The creation of such institutions "established that national public policy now officially recognised the environment, employees, and consumers to be significant and legitimate stakeholders of business" (Carrol 1991).

Most literature on CSR tends to distinguish between a firm's social responsibilities, and its mainstream economic responsibility of profit maximisation. The literature tends to suggest these two are not compatible, but that firms engage in such social responsibilities only to adhere to stakeholder expectations. Carrol (1991) states "social responsibility can only become reality if more managers become moral instead of amoral or immoral." Furthermore, counting ethical responsibilities as one of four corporate social responsibilities[4], he defines ethical responsibilities as those which "embody those standards, norms, or expectations that reflect a concern for what consumers, employees, shareholders and the community regard as fair, just, or in keeping with the respect or protection of stakeholders' moral rights.

Along the same lines of the definition offered by Carrol, Davis (1960) suggests that social responsibility refers to busines' "decisions and actions taken for reasons at least partially beyond the firm's economic or technical interest." McWilliams & Siegel (2001) define CSR as "actions that appear to further some social good, beyond the interests of the firm and that which is required by law."

In Capitalism and Freedom, Friedman (1962) states that in a free society "there is one and only one social responsibility of business- to use its resources and engage in activities designed to increase its profits so longs as it stays within the rules of the game, which is to say, engages in open and free competition without deception or fraud." In a later article entitled "The social responsibility of Business is to increase its profits" Friedman (1970) states that resources devoted to CSR would be more wisely spent, from a social perspective, on increasing firm efficiency. He notes that the sole responsibility of corporate executives is to ensure profit maximisation for their employers, i.e. the shareholders.

In this paper, I argue that Friedman is indeed correct in stating that the only responsibility of businesses is to increase profits, but that there needs not be a conflict between profit maximisation and adopting social responsibility with regards to ethical and philanthropic activities. This paper also offers a new approach towards the definition of CSR; one that differs from the definitions which suggest CSR goes beyond the profit maximisation objective of firms and is not part of the firm's economic or technical interest. This paper suggests that CSR can be viewed simply as a marketing campaign by firms aware of the

[4] The other three are Economics, Legal and Philanthropic responsibilities.

requirements of consumers for products which are not produced by ethically indifferent firms. Firms seek to first and foremost profit maximise. The implementation of any social responsibility is also within the aims of profit-maximisation. As McWilliams and Siegel have pointed out, CSR goes beyond the legal requirements of corporations. If there is no legal requirement, why would corporations implement CSR in the first place, unless it serves to maximise their profits? The increasing acceptance of CSR by multi-national corporations represents the realisation by firms that consumers require ethical products and it suggests that the benefits of adhering to CSR policies outweigh the costs of such programmes.

Webb et. al. (2001) assessed whether consumers expect companies to be socially responsible. They carried semi-structured interviews, using a sample size of 48 people. Their findings show that a "substantial, viable, and identifiable market segment exists that considers a company's level of social responsibility in its purchase and investment decisions." Webb et. al. suggest that manufacturers and retailers have an opportunity to appeal to this group while simultaneously meeting their business objectives and making a contribution to society.

Webb et. al.'s paper suggests that most of the respondents were positive toward business in general and toward socially responsible companies. Of those who were interviewed only a handful appeared completely disinterested or opposed. Webb et. al. state two reasons for the lack of "socially responsible consumer behaviour" (SRCB). Firstly, there is self-interest manifested in buying based on the traditional criteria of price, quality and convenience combined with the assumption that using CSR would compromise their choice on the criteria. Secondly, there seems to be a low level of knowledge and difficulty obtaining information on the social responsibility records of companies. There is little that can be done to provide a solution for the first problem. A segment of consumers shall always seek to minimise their expenditure whilst maintaining a suitable standard of living. But there is much that can be done about the second problem, and this is where the main policy suggestion of this paper comes in.

This paper suggests that governments should focus on influencing demand by increasing consumer awareness, either through education tools, encouraging non-governmental organisations, mobilising the civil society or any other method which would enhance consumer awareness of products they consume. The existence of CSR shows that consumer awareness matters and firms cannot ignore the wants of consumers. By focusing on demand, consumers can be given the task of ensuring sustainable development. Of course, this may not work as consumers, as economic agents, may seek to minimise expenditure and look for cheap rather than slightly more expensive ethically-produced goods. However, suitable communication and the transfer of information to consumers and creating transparency on what the consumers' current decisions could mean for future development could mean that consumers, even as economic agents, would allow for social factors to influence their decisions. The information age provides a great opportunity for educating and increasing consumer awareness more than ever before.

Webb et. al. state that consumers first need to become aware of a firm's level of social responsibility before CSR can impact their purchasing. They state that building awareness is arguably the major purpose behind cause-related marketing[5].

The 1999 Cone/Roper Cause Related Trends Report (Cone Communications Press Release 1999) is a five-year study of cause-related marketing. Since 1993 at least 80% of those surveyed have reported having a positive image of a firm that offered support to a cause they cared about. More importantly, given parity in price and quality, more than 66% of the respondents said they are likely to switch brands or retailers to those participating in cause related marketing.

Meanwhile a study by Waddock and Graves (1997) on the relationship between corporate social performance and corporate financial performance shows that financial performance also depends on good social performance. Their study concludes that "there is something about performing well in social arenas that may be simply linked to good managerial practice" and that firms may "do well by doing good".

Summary and Conclusion

These studies provide further evidence that we can, to an extent, rely upon decisions made by consumers to work towards ensuring sustainable development. By increasing consumer awareness and using government force on the demand side we ensure that economic decisions are being made in a free market by economic agents without the undue intervention of governments. Governments only need to ensure suitable channels are created through which information about corporations and their products are fed to consumers. With perfect information available, we can expect a high percentage of consumers to factor in ethical and environmental issues when deciding on what product to buy. In markets with environmentally conscious consumers, firms will have little option but to adhere to appropriate corporate social responsibility. This process has already begun, with many multi-national corporations adopting significant CSR measures. But as was pointed to earlier, one of the important factors behind the indifference of some consumers towards corporate social performance is their lack of knowledge. This is what needs to be targeted by governments.

Moreover, we have discussed in this paper the limitations of implementing supply side policies with the long term aim of achieving sustainable development. The Kyoto protocol is praise-worthy for initiating an important internationally recognised action plan aimed at reducing carbon emissions, but policies are required on the other side of the economic spectrum to complement, if not partially replace such policies.

This paper does not recommend abandoning supply-side policy efforts and replacing them completely with demand-side policies. Rather it seeks to suggest an alternative which has largely been looked over in both academic literature and in policy-making circles. Implementing supply side targets alongside ensuring environmentally conscious consumers who are aware of what they are demanding can provide the world with a better chance of avoiding what could truly be a global disaster if the environment is left to meet its demise.

---

[5] This is a subset of CSR defined by Varadarjan and Menon (1998) as company promoting that a percentage of sales will go to support a specific non-profit organisation or cause.

References

Bachram, H. (2004). Climate fraud and carbon colonialism: the new trade in greenhouse gases. *Capitalism Nature Socialism (After Jan 1, 2004).* 15 (4), 5-20.

Brown, B. J. (1987). *Global sustainability: Toward definition.* Madison, WI: Global Sustainability Project, Center for Human Systems, Institute for Environmental Studies, University of Wisconsin-Madison.

Carroll, A. B. (2001). *The Pyramid of Corporate Social Responsibility: Toward the Moral Management of Organizational Stakeholders.* Business Horizons.

Castells, M. (1996). *The rise of the network society.* Malden, Mass: Blackwell.

Cone Communications Press Release. 1999. (March 8), Boston, MA.

Dasgupta, P. (2007). Commentary: The Stern Review's Economics of Climate Change. *National Institute Economic Review.* 199 (1), 4-7.

Friedman, M. (1962). *Capitalism and freedom.* [Chicago]: University of Chicago Press.

Friedman, M. (1970). The social responsibility of business is to increase its profits. New York Times, September 13: 122-126.

Keith, D. (1960). *Can Business Afford to Ignore Social Responsibilities?* California Management Review, 2, 3, (1960): 70-76.

McWilliams, A., & Siegel, D. (2001). NOTE - Corporate Social Responsibility: A Theory of the Firm Perspective. *The Academy of Management Review.* 26 (1), 117.

Mohr, L. A., Webb, D. J., & Harris, K. E. (2001). Do Consumers Expect Companies To Be Socially Responsible? The Impact of Corporate Social Responsibility on Buying Behavior. *Journal of Consumer Affairs.* 35 (1), 45-72.

Najam, A., Huq, S., & Sokona, Y. (2003). Climate negotiations beyond Kyoto: developing countries concerns and interests. *CLIMATE POLICY.* 3 (3), 221-231.

Nordhaus, W. D., & Boyer, J. G. (1999). Requiem for Kyoto: An Economic Analysis of the Kyoto Protocol. *ENERGY JOURNAL -CAMBRIDGE MA THEN CLEVELAND OH-.* 20, 93-130.

Repetto, R. C. (1985). *The Global possible: Resources, development, and the new century.* New Haven: Yale University Press.

Sustainable (2008). In *Oxford English Dictionary.* Retrieved December 27th, 2008, from http://dictionary.oed.com

UNFCCC (2008). Kyoto Protocol Status of Ratification.

UNFCCC (2008). National Greenhouse gas inventory data for the period 1990-2006.

Varadarajan, P. Rajan and Anil Menon. 1988. Cause-Related Marketing: A Coalignment of Marketing Strategy and Corporate Philanthropy. *Journul c$Murketing, 52* (July):58-74.

Waddock, S. A., & Graves, S. B. (1997). The Corporate Social Performance -- Financial Performance Link. *Strategic Management Journal.* 18 (4), 303.

World Bank. 1985b. Environmental requirements of the World Bank. *Environmental Professional* 7:205- 212.

WRI/IIED (World Resources Institute and International Institute for Environment and Development). 1986. World resources 1986. Basic Books, New York.

Chapter 12: CSR Assurance Reporting

Is CSR Reporting Just Reputation Assurance or Is There More To It?

Cynthia Cann, The University of Scranton, United States of America

Natalya Parente Boock, University of Scranton, United States of America

Abstract: Many companies today have rallied to the call from society to align their business operations with environmental and social values. Toward that end, numerous companies have chosen to communicate, to their stakeholders, assurance of sustainability on their Web site through CSR, as verified by previous research. This study will attempt to determine whether or not companies that communicate on their Web site that they are good corporate citizens actually embed sustainability into their core business practices. To accomplish this task, the World Wide Web will be used as a medium to investigate a sample of the top Fortune Global 100 companies. The research will occur in stages. First, hypotheses will be developed. The researchers will use content analysis to examine whether the companies in the sample use their Web pages to present themselves in a socially responsible manner. The indicators employed will be similar to the indicators used in other content analyses from comparable studies. In the second stage, the researchers will look for a correlation between the list of companies determined in stage one that use CSR as a tool for sustainability assurance with the list of global companies on the Accountability Rating 2004. The Accountability Rating is a tool used to determine how well the Global 100 have embedded sustainability practices into their operations.

Introduction

As the public continues to demand good corporate citizenship from businesses, the standard of corporate social responsibility is becoming more and more a requirement for stakeholders to do business with a company. The results of a

2003 study by MORI [Market & Opinion Research International], the largest independently-owned market research company in Great Britain, identifies that 84% of those surveyed indicate that it is important or very important that the particular company show a high degree of social responsibility when forming a decision about buying a product or service. MORI has been conducting such research since 1998. Each year the proportion of respondents who indicate that an organization's social responsibility is important has risen (MORI 2005). In addition to the public, socially responsible investors (SRI), government agencies, employees, NGOs and the like are applying pressure for companies to provide full disclosure of their corporate citizenship (Harrison and Freeman 1999).

Annual reporting, either in the form of formal standalone reports or embedded reports, has become an acceptable method for businesses to use to communicate their level of sustainability/CSR (S/CSR) to all stakeholders (Idowu and Towler 2004). A study performed by Esrock and Leichty (1998), indicates that 80% of the Fortune 500 companies address CSR on their websites. These companies use their websites to communicate corporate citizenship to their stakeholders.

This study examines a sample of 100 of the Fortune Global 500 companies to determine if the companies are communicating about S/CSR on the company's website. Each company's website is then studied to ascertain if the particular company is embedding S/CSR practices into operations. Finally, in order to update the study done by Esrock and Leichty (1998), the list of companies determined to embed CSR into their operations is compared to the list of companies purported to be good corporate citizens according to the Accountability Rating® 2004 Report.

Background and Theory

Sustainability/CSR Reporting

In business, sustainability is about doing well while at the same time meeting and integrating the environmental, economic and social needs of all stakeholders without compromising the ability of future generations to meet their needs. Corporations are no longer evaluated in terms of financial performance alone, but also on the basis of a new triple bottom line of financial, social and environmental performance. In this new business environment, a company's reputation has become one of its most valuable assets, and corporate social responsibility has become one of the key components of a company's reputation (Stewart 2003).

Corporate Social Responsibility (CSR) is defined in much the same way as sustainability (Hockerts and Moir 2004). As Maignan and Ferrel (2004) point out, CSR has been conceptualized in many ways, but almost all involve environmental practices, ethics management, service to others, and a sense of accountability to various stakeholder groups. Esrock and Leichty (1998) report that the general public sees CSR as "(1) maintaining fair and honest business practices, (2) maintaining product safety and reliability, (3) taking care of employees, and (4) improving environmental record" (306).

Sustainability reporting is all about finding out how a company is doing at performing economically while staying in balance with nature and society. Although this type of reporting goes by a variety of different names such as "sustainability", "CSR", "environmental, health, and safety" or "corporate citizenship", the main purpose is to make information available to a variety of publics on how the company is discharging its obligations (GreenBiz.com 2004). As it becomes more apparent that the public is reading these reports (Global Initiative 2004), organizations are seizing the opportunity to use this venue to present company achievements and activities to all stakeholders.

Based on the literature, there are a variety of different reasons why organizations employ CSR. According to Swanson (1995), there are three primary factors that motivate companies toward CSR: as a method to enhance performance, to comply with expectations of stakeholders and because CSR is an important reflection of the values and norms of the company. In addition, Schaltegger et al (1996) suggest that another reason organizations communicate CSR is to pacify some external group. Hooghiemstra (2000) indicates that certain organizations use CSR as a public relations exercise to enhance their image and reputation by manipulating stakeholders' perceptions of the company. A study performed by Idowu and Towler (2004) finds that most companies today realize that there are major benefits in reporting how the company stands with regard to CSR. The big question appears to be whether firms work to satisfy stakeholder interests just to gain financial benefits or for more fundamental reasons (Donaldson and Preston 1995), or do they simply communicate CSR because it is the right thing to do? A recent study conducted of sustainability experts and practitioners in North America (9% from other regions) by InterPraxis (Anonymous 2004) finds that the motives for companies to report on their CSR/Sustainability performance are as follows:

- to enable stakeholders to judge performance
- to improve their public image
- to improve performance of the organization
- to identify risks and deal with them
- other
- to attract investment from SRI investors (2).

To synthesize, one might argue that the main reason why organizations employ CSR is to establish or maintain organizational legitimacy.

Organizational Legitimacy

As indicated above, stakeholders are pushing organizations harder than ever to defend that they are acceptable by the norms of today's society. In response, many companies are trying to establish, maintain or regain legitimacy.

According to Suchman (1995), "Legitimacy is a generalized perception or assumption that the actions of an entity are desirable, proper, or appropriate within some socially constructed system of norms, values, beliefs, and definitions." Two types of legitimacy appear relevant to CSR reporting.

The first, structural legitimacy is attained by putting into place proper structures and symbols that stakeholders perceive as important to a legitimate firm (Suchman 1995). As an example, providing information about the company's CSR on the company website. In the case of moral legitimacy, legitimacy is established based on whether or not an activity is the "right thing to do" (Suchman 1995). Therefore, because it is considered the right thing to provide transparent, available information on the economic, environmental and social activities of the firm, a firm is legitimized because it provides a CSR. At the same time, Massey (2001) advocates that, "legitimacy is managed successfully when organizational actions are perceived as being consistent with stakeholder expectations" (2). This brings us back to the idea that stakeholders expect transparent reporting from organizations today on economic, environmental and social issues. Therefore, one way to achieve expected reporting is to communicate to stakeholders via the company's website.

Web Based Sustainability/CSR Reporting

In order to get the information out to stakeholders for evaluation of performance and to improve public image, many companies are using the World Wide Web as the most viable method available. As indicated by Esrock and Leichty (1998), the Internet and the World Wide Web provide a very practical means for public relations. They make information quick and easy to disseminate, quick and easy to access, and quick and easy for the public to give feedback. Companies are now encouraged by their stakeholders to provide full disclosure: reports that not only emphasize successes but that also include information on failures (Anonymous 2004, Sjoberg 2003). The Internet has made sustainability reporting a much more open and transparent process. Also, Investment Relations Officers see good reporting on social and environmental performance, and improved disclosure as important for Socially Responsible Investors (SRIs) (Hockerts and Moir 2004). Therefore, to address these issues of accountability and public relations, many companies are making Sustainability Reports available on line. Some are even communicating through web-based reports exclusively.

Hypotheses

A study conducted by Maignan and Ralston (2002), examines the websites of 400 companies located in the U.S. and Europe to appraise: "(1) the extent to which businesses attempt to display the image of a socially responsible firm, and (2) the nature of the motivations, processes, and issues discussed to convey the image of good corporate citizenship" (497). Our study follows a similar path. This study also investigates the extent to which businesses attempt to communicate CSR on their websites. However, the investigation moves in another direction. In order to attempt to answer the question: is CSR reporting just reputation assurance or is there more to it?, this study examines whether or not companies that communicate a commitment to CSR actually embed CSR into their operations, and are considered good corporate citizens according to the Accountability Rating®. We begin with the fact that all of the Fortune Global 100 companies samples have web pages.

- H1: All of the Fortune Global 100 Companies studied communicate some level of CSR on the company website.
- H2: Companies that communicate some level of CSR on the company website, will embed the practice of CSR into operations.
- H3: Companies that embed the practice of Sustainability/CSR into operations will be rated as good corporate citizens according to the Accountability Rating® 2004 Report.

Method

Because of the increasing trend for businesses to provide information on CSR through the Internet, company websites have been selected as the best medium to use to investigate whether or not companies practice CSR in word and deed.

To test hypotheses 1 and 2, a content analysis of the websites of a sample of 100 of the Fortune Global 500 companies is performed. The Fortune Global 100 represents a sample of the largest companies in the world from a variety of industries. Since there is no single indicator of a good corporate citizen, the websites are judged based on thirteen S/CSR categories. Below is a description of the items used to measure if a company is portrayed as socially responsibility. If the company's website meets the criterion for a particular category, a one is awarded; otherwise a zero is assigned. To receive a one, the website has to have a substantial amount of information about the topic. It is not sufficient just to mention the environment or mention employee relations, but rather the site has to describe what the company does for the environment or employees.

In the second phase, Hypothesis 3 is tested. The list of companies determined in the first phase that communicate some level of CSR, is compared with the list of Fortune Global 100 companies in the Accountability Rating® 2004 report, thereby providing insight into whether or not a company is practicing CSR in word and deed.

The Accountability Rating® is the first global index that evaluates how well the world's 100 largest companies account for their impact on society and the environment (Report 2004).

Measures and Data Coding

As mentioned above, the key elements of CSR are reported to be implementing fair and honest business practices, maintaining product safety and reliability, taking care of employees and improving environmental performance (Esrock and Leichty 1998). *Business Ethics* (2005) uses seven stakeholder groups for the annual ranking of the Best Corporate Citizens. They include shareholders, the community, minorities and women, employees, environmental groups, non-US stakeholders, and customers. A combination of items from these two sources plus a few original items form the thirteen categories used to test the hypotheses. Each company website is checked for either the presence or absence of the content areas.

Social Responsibility Link. The website receives a one in this field if a link exists that is exclusively devoted to the overall theme of social responsibility. There is also a subset of this category, called layers based on how many "layers" deep this link is.

Maintaining fair and honest business practices. If the website provides information that shows how the company actively addresses this issue: e.g. an active ethics committees or an employee hotline to report misdeeds, a one is awarded.

Maintaining product safety and reliability. Once again, in order to receive a one in this category, information has to be available on the company website that shows how the company actively addresses this issue such as identifying safety checks or instituting educational programs about the dangers of their product.

Employee relations. If a company conveys a commitment to employees by establishing work/life programs, extraordinary benefits or support groups, the company receives a one in that category.

Environmental performance. To receive a one in this category, a company had to communicate a commitment to the environment. Evidence of that commitment can be displayed through information on programs that reduce emissions or other types of pollution or waste, products designed with the environment in mind, and/or donations or involvement with environmental organizations.

Community relations. To receive a one in this category, a company has to communicate involvement in the local community: e.g. participating in local community service organizations or employee volunteerism in local organizations.

Diversity. In order to receive a one in this category, it is necessary for the company to provide evidence of diversity programs, scholarships for minorities, supporting minority charities, having a supplier diversity program, etc.

Donating to charities. If evidence of philanthropy to good causes is present on the website, the company receives a one in that category.

Education. Many corporations choose to use their resources to support educational opportunities through scholarships or by sponsoring/volunteering for educational organizations or events. If this is communicated on the company website, the company receives a one in that category.

Gift Matching. If evidence of this type of specific program in which the company can demonstrate support for both the employee and an organization at the same time exists on the website, the company receives a one in that category.

Social responsibility or sustainability report. If a company provides a formal Sustainability/CSR Report on the website, the company receives a one for that category.

Corporate foundation or fund. If evidence of a foundation or fund for social responsibility exists on the company website, the company receives a one for that item.

Analysis

Content analysis was used to systematically sift through the rhetoric on the websites. As mentioned above, for most categories, it is not sufficient that only a specific term is invoked. The judges look for more in-depth proof that an activity or program or tangible benefit is involved before a company receives a one for that category.

Three judges independently reviewed the websites. Reliability is calculated by using Cohen's Kappa (Stemler 2001). The strength of agreement between the three raters is 68%. According to Landis & Koch (1977, 165), this suggests that there is substantial agreement between the judges.

Results

Hypothesis 1

All of the companies on the Fortune Global 100 list have Websites and all of the Fortune Global 100 companies except three communicate some level of information about CSR on the company website.

Hypothesis 2

A ranked list of the companies that communicate CSR on the company website and portray themselves as socially responsible is provided in Table 1. The list is ranked from best performance to worst performance. The companies are arranged in order, by the total number of points they received. If there is a tie, it is broken by the number of clicks that it took to find the social responsibility link (layers). The score for companies that do communicate some level of information about CSR ranges from a high of 12 to a low of 1. Of the 100 companies, 31% have a total score of 10 or greater; 44% have a score that ranges from 6 to 9; and 25% have a total score that ranges from 0 to 5.

Of the company websites studied, 82 percent had some type of link that led to information solely about social responsibility. Of these, 50 had the link directly on their homepage. Information about fair and honest business practices was evident on 31 percent of websites. Philanthropy, or donations to charities, came up most often on company websites with 89 percent of the companies reporting their philanthropic activities. Diversity issues were prominent on 65 percent of the websites. 72 percent of the companies included community activities and relations on their corporate website. Education was also a commonly reported element of social responsibility with 74 percent of the companies acknowledging their support of education. The environment was discussed on 80 percent of the websites. 68 percent of the companies have established a corporate foundation or fund that they present on their website. 42 percent of the companies have a gift-matching program for their employees. 46 percent of the companies had information about employee relations on their website. 50 percent of the Fortune Global 100 corporations have a social responsibility or sustainability report available on their website. Only 45 percent included information about product safety and reliability. This information is summarized in Table 1.

Table 1: Percentage of Companies that Received a One in the Categories Listed Below

Category[1]	Percent
Sustainability/CSR link	82
Fair and honest business practices	31
Grant matching	42
Product Safety and Reliability	45
Taking care of employees	46
Sustainability/CSR Report	50
Diversity	65
Establishing foundations or funds	68
Communities	72
Education	74
Environment	80
Donations to charities	89

The companies who performed the best in this study were Unilever, BP, Citigroup and Ford Motor. These companies received a total of twelve points or a one for all of the categories. They also received a higher rating because their social responsibility link was on the company's home page. Verizon Communications and Procter & Gamble also had a score of 12. However, it took two clicks to get to Verizon's social responsibility page and three to get to Procter & Gamble's. The top five companies represent a broad range of industries. All of the best CSR companies are in different sectors.

Nissho Iwai, Sumitomo Life Insurance and Berkshire Hathaway all received zeros. They did not address any social responsibility issues on their websites. AmerisourceBergen, Sinopec and Costco Wholesale each only had a score of one and neither had links for social responsibility. Two out of the three worst companies (those who received zeros), Sumitomo Life Insurance and Berkshire Hathaway, are in the same sector - financial services.

Hypothesis 3

Table 2: Comparison of Fortune Global 100 Companies Communicate Sustainability/CSR vs. Embed Sustainability/CSR

[1] *Source:* Research data base for this study.

Company Name[2]	Sustainability /CSR Ranking	Accountability Rating®	Sector	Region
BP	1	1	OC	Europe
Unilever	1	4	CP	Europe
Ford	1	23	A	Nth
Citigroup	1	29	FS	Europe
Verizon	5	7	UT	Nth
P & G	6	21	CP	Nth
Carrefor	7	5	M	Europe
Mitsubishi	7	11	T	Asia
Total	7	14	OC	Europe
Daimler	7	15	A	Europe
Nestle´	7	19	CP	Europe
Aviva	7	20	FS	Europe
HSBC	7	45	FS	Europe
Hewlett-	14	8	CE	Nth
Vodafone	14	9	UT	Europe
IBM	14	52	CE	Nth
Tokyo	17	6	UT	Asia
ENI	17	13	OC	Europe
BMW	17	16	A	Europe
EDF	17	22	UT	Europe
Toshiba	17	24	CE	Euorpe
Chevron	17	27	OC	Nth
Hyundai	17	31	A	Asia
Royal	17	38	M	Europe
GE	17	48	CE	Nth

A comparison of the rating of the Fortune Global 100 companies listed in the Accountability Rating® 2004 Report with our rating of the best CSR performers among the Fortune Global 100 companies indicates that the majority of companies investigated communicate CSR on the company website, but do not embed the practice of CSR into operations - at least not as much as the rhetoric on the website might suggest. As an example, Ford Motor Company is tied for

[2] *Source:* Accountability Rating® 2004 Report, Encoding Accountability, http://www.accountability.org.uk/uploadstore/cms/docs/AR_Execsumm.pdf March 5, 2005; Research data base for this study.

number one in our study of companies that portray themselves as socially responsible on their websites. However, Ford is only ranked 23rd on the Accountability Rating® index. IBM is tied for 14th place in our study, but is ranked 52 out of 100 companies on the Accountability Rating® index. See Table 2.

Discussion and Implications

Of the company websites studied, 82 % had some type of link that led to information solely about social responsibility and 50 % had a direct link to this information on the company's home page. Research performed by Esrock and Leichty (1998) reports only 27% of the Websites studied had some type of direct link on the home page to social responsibility materials. This evidence clearly indicates that more companies are now providing direct links to information on S/CSR. The increase in the number of direct links suggests that companies are feeling the pressure by stakeholders to be more transparent and to communicate more about these issues.

As mentioned above, the majority of companies investigated communicate S/CSR on the company website. However, according to the comparison with the Accountability Rating® 2004 Report, these same companies do not embed the practice of S/CSR into operations, at least as much as the rhetoric on the website indicates. This reinforces that a large percentage of companies may be communicating information about S/CSR on their website to gain legitimacy by pleasing external stakeholders, or to enhance their reputation and image, as suggested in the literature (Schaltegger et al 1996, Hooghiemstra 2000).

It should be noted that the opposite situation is also evident. Toyota is ranked 56th in our study and 7th by Accountability Rating® Report, while Suez is ranked in second place by Accountability Rating®, but 46th in our study. The indication here is that companies who are embedding S/CSR in their operations are not communicating that effort on their websites even though most companies today realize that there is major benefit to reporting how the company stands with regard to S/CSR (Idowu and Towler 2004).

The Fortune 100 is broken down into 8 sectors with a varying number of companies in each sector. To get an overall average score for each sector, we added up all the points that the individual companies in each sector received and divided that total by the number of companies in that sector. The consumer products sector (n = 5) had the highest average score of 10.6. This may be because this sector has a direct relationship with their customers, whereas a sector such as oil & chemicals is more distant from their stakeholders. The oil & chemicals sector (n=10) and the trading sector (n=10) had the lowest average scores of 6.8 and 5.5 respectively. The ratings are summarized in Table 3.

Table 3: Number of Companies in Each Fortune Global 500 Sector

Number of companies[3]	Sector	Average
5	consumer products	10.60
12	computer & electronics	8.42
12	automotives	7.83
16	utilities & telecoms	7.63
9	merchandising	7.33
26	financial services	7.12
10	oil & chemicals	6.80
10	trading	5.50

Limitations and Future Research Issues

Limitations

The results of this study should be interpreted with caution, keeping in mind some main limitations of the research. First, one major limitation is that these results are only a snapshot in time. Companies change their Websites on a regular basis and we have only captured information as of one particular date. Technology, globalization, a rising concern for ethics and values and the changing role of government will continue to push companies and managers to revise and reinvent their businesses and to continue to communicate more and more information. In addition, it should be noted that only three judges were used to perform the content analysis. The reliability is 68 percent. A future study should involve more, better trained judges, in order to achieve a higher degree of reliability.

The study is also limited by the number and type of companies that were used for the sample. The Fortune Global 100 companies are the largest and most successful businesses in the world. Therefore, results cannot be generalized to organizations outside of this unique population. Third, the study is limited because the categories that were chosen to represent CSR may not completely embody the concept. No statistical analysis was performed to determine this. In addition, the degree to which the categories represented S/CSR is not identified because only the presence or absence of information was noted. The company either received a check or it did not. So, while some companies may have had ten pages about the environment and others only two pages, they both received only one check. The use of layers was implemented to try to provide some quantification to this aspect of the study.

[3] *Source:* Fortune, The 2004 Fortune Global 500, http://www.fortune.com/fortune/global500, March 12, 2005; Research data base for this study.

Future Research

Technology is at the heart of this study. As companies increasingly use the Internet as a medium to communicate to stakeholders about S/CSR, new research methods to capture a more longitudinal look at these practices may be in order. In addition to innovative methods to measure communication on the Internet, a new approach to gathering information on the subject would provide more in-depth information. As indicated above, one of the main limitations of the study is that the categories that were chosen to represent S/CSR may not completely embody the concept. More research or perhaps a meta-analysis into what does constitute S/CSR is needed. As stakeholders continue to raise S/CSR expectations for the companies that they do business with, understanding the true reasons for S/CSR reporting will become even more important.

The next logical step in this research study is to add one more hypothesis to test the relationship between companies that do embed S/CSR into their operations and financial performance. A better understanding of this relationship may attract even more companies to communicate and practice S/CSR.

Conclusion

In conclusion, this study did accomplish what it set out to achieve. All of the Fortune Global 100 companies except three communicate some level of information about Sustainability/CSR on the company website. Of the 100 companies, 31% have a total score of 10 or greater; 44% have a score that ranges from 6 to 9; and 25% have a total score that ranges from 0 to 5. These results suggest that approximately 75% of the companies surveyed communicate that they are socially responsible on the company website. The comparison performed between the total score that the companies received in our study with the ranked list from the Accountability Rating® Report indicates that these same companies do not necessarily embed the practice of S/CSR into operations, at least as much as the rhetoric on the website indicates. This reinforces that a large percentage of companies may only be communicating information about S/CSR on their website to please external stakeholders or to enhance their reputation and image, as suggested in the literature (Schaltegger et al 1996, Hooghiemstra 2000).

References

Accountability Rating® 2004 Report, Encoding Accountability, http://www.accountability.org.uk/uploadstore/cms/docs/AR_Execsumm.pdf, March 5, 2005.

Anonymous (2004), "More than Good, CSR Demands the Bad and the Ugly, Too," *PR News*, Aug 16, 60 (33): 1.

Business Ethics, "Corporate Social Responsibility Report 2004, Business Ethics Magazine, http://www.business-ethics.com/100best.html, February 20, 2005.

Corporate Social Responsibility Report 2004 *Business Ethics,* http://www.business-ethics.com/100best.htm, February 20, 2005.

Donaldson, T. and L. E. Preston (1995), "The stakeholder theory of the corporation: Concepts, evidence and implications," *Academy of Management Review*, 20:65-91.

Esrock, Stuart L. and Greg B. Leichty (1998), "Social Responsibility and Corporate Web Pages: Self-Presentation or Agenda-Setting?" *Public Relations Review*, 24 (3): 305-19.

Fortune, The 2004 Fortune Global 500, http://www.fortune.com/fortune/fortune500?promoid=cnnmoney, March 12, 2005.

Global Initiative, "Guess What? People Do Read CSR Reports," http://www.via3.net/pooled/articles/BF_NEWSART/view.asp?Q=BF_NEWSART_98995, February 24, 2005.

GreenBiz.com, "The Big Picture," Corporate Reporting, GreenBiz.com, http://www.greenbiz.com/toolbox/essentials-third.cfm?LinkADVID=25026, February 23, 2005.

Harrison, Jeffrey S. and R. Edward Freeman (1999), "Stakeholders, social responsibility, and performance: Empirical evidence and theoretical perspectives," *Academy of Management Journal*, 42 (5): 479-486.

Hockerts, Kai and Lance Moir (2004), "Communicating Corporate Responsibility to Investors: The Changing Role of the Investor Relations Function," *Journal of Business Ethics,* 53 (1): 85.

Hooghiemstra, Reggy (2000), "Corporate Communication and Impression Management-New Perspectives Why Companies Engage in Corporate Social Reporting," *Journal of Business Ethics*, 27: 55-68.

Idowu, Samuel O. and Brian A. Towler (2004), "A comparative study of the contents of corporate social responsibility reports of UK companies," *Management of Environmental Quality*, 15 (4): 420-437.

Landis, J.R. and Koch, G.G. (1977), "The Measurement of Observer Agreement for

Lewis, Stewart (2004), "Reputation and Corporate Responsibility," *Journal of* Categorical Data," *Biometrics*, 33: 159-174. *Communication Management*, 7 (4): 356 - 365.

Maignan, Isabelle and O.C. Ferrell (2004), "Corporate Social Responsibility and Marketing: An integrative Framework," *Journal of the Academy of Marketing Science*, 32 (1): 3-19.

Maignan, Isabelle and Ralston, David A. (2002), "Corporate social responsibility in Europe and the U.S.: Insights from businesses' self-presentations," *Journal of International Business Studies*, 33 (3): 497-515.

MORI, "The Public's View of Corporate Responsibility 2003," Http://www.mori.com/csr/database.shtml, August 2005.

Massey, Joseph Eric (2001), "Managing Organizational Legitimacy: Communication Strategies for Organizations in Crisis," *Journal of Business Communication*, 38 (2): 153-82.

Schaltegger, S., Muller, K. and Hindrichsen, H. *Corporate Environmental Accounting*, Chinchester: John Wiley & Sons, 1996.

Sjoberg, Goran E. (2003), "Next challenge for communication management: CSR—a joint task for academe and practitioners," *Journal of Communication Management*, 7 (3): 191-193.

Stemler, Steve (2001), "An Overview of Content Analysis," *Practical Assessment, Research & Evaluation*, 7 (17), http://PAREonline.net/getvn.asp?v=7&n=17, February 20, 2005.

Stewart, Lewis (2003), "Reputation and corporate responsibility," *Journal of Communication Management*, 7 (4): 356-365.

Suchman, M.D. (1995), "Managing Legitimacy: Strategic and Institutional Approaches," *Academy of Management Journal*, 20 (3): 571-610.

Swanson, Diane L. (1995), "Addressing a Theoretical Problem by Reorienting the Corporate Social Performance Model," *Academy of Management Review*, 20 (1): 43-64.

Part V: Corporate Social Responsibility and Environmental Sustainability

Chapters 13 and 14 make up Part 5 of the book, which focuses on corporate social responsibility and environmental sustainability. Chapter 13 examines the role of interorganizational alliances in environmental sustainability. Chapter 14 looks at corporate greening initiatives.

Chapter 13: Interorganizational Environmental Sustainability

The Role of Interorganizational Alliances in Environmental Sustainability

Paul Ziek, Pace University, New York, USA

Abstract: In an attempt to combat the criticisms surrounding Corporate Social Responsibility (CSR), corporations are forming and maintaining interorganizational collective action alliances. These alliances include both private-public (business forms a coalition with non-governmental organizations) and private-private (federations consisting of only private enterprise) alliances. A great deal of popular and academic attention has been given to private-public unions where private-private collective action alliances are often overlooked. To begin to fill this void, this article examines the formation and maintenance of private-private interorganizational collective action alliances that focus on systemic social issues that constitute today's foundation of CSR and most particularly environmental sustainability. The World Business Council for Sustainable Development (WBCSD) serves as an example of interorganizational collective action alliances. The article is positioned with the theoretical perspective of public goods theory and social network theory. Moreover, because the issues at hand are systemic and require from those involved enormous interest, dedication, information sharing and resource allocation, the article focuses on interorganizational trust and cooperation within these modern alliances. The major contribution is a series of propositions concerning trust and cooperation among alliance members.

Introduction

The most widely accepted definition of Corporate Social Responsibility (CSR) states that profit driven enterprises are accountable to a wide range of actors with an interest or "stake" in the firm (Argandona, 1998). Although the concept of CSR has been around since the 1930s (Carroll, 1999), a series of business changes and scandals that occurred in the early 1990s has made the adoption of

CSR a business imperative (Vogel, 2005). Since this time, countless organizations have voluntarily worked toward improving labor practices, enacting community outreach, initiating corporate philanthropy, improving accounting standards and strengthening environmental behaviors. Yet even with the increased corporate acceptance of the "notion that companies are responsible not just to their shareholders, but also to other stakeholders (workers, suppliers, environmentalists, communities, etc.)" (Doh & Guay, 2006, p. 54), there is still a great deal of public, media and academic skepticism concerning CSR (see Kuhn & Deetz, 2008).

The list of criticisms that surround CSR range from questionable social reporting techniques (Chatterji & Levin, 2005) to the opinion that the business and society relationship is institutionalized and involves readily identifiable players engaging in predictable patterns of interaction (Ruggie, 2004). In an attempt to combat the criticisms surrounding CSR, corporations have invented and reinvented new strategies and instruments for CSR communication (Aakhus & Ziek, 2009; Ziek, 2009). One of these strategies is the formation and maintenance of interorganizational collective action alliances. These strategic alliances are networks of organizations (Gulati, 1998) that enable participating firms to adopt a substantial material and symbolic level proactive approach (Livesey, 1999) toward systemic social issues. A prime example of private-public alliances are those popularly known as green alliances (Hartman & Stafford, 1997, 1998; Stafford & Hartman, 1996) where business forms a coalition with non-governmental organizations dedicated to environmental management and sustainability. For instance, the Forest Stewardship Council is a green alliance where both private enterprise and non-profit organizations work together for responsible management of the worlds' forests (Stafford & Hartman, 1996). Other alliances include World Business Council for Sustainable Development, Business and Biodiversity Council, Global Business Coalition on HIV/AIDS, Tuberculosis and Malaria (GBC) and the World Banks Institute. In these instances, for example, private enterprise alone constructs collaborative interorganizational relationships for collective action. Although both private-public and private-private alliances have become mainstays in the corporate arena and the focus of discussion in the popular press, in terms of academic literature, private-public alliances are widely studied (Arts, 2002; Livesey, 1999) where as private-private alliances are often overlooked.

To address these issues, this article examines the formation and maintenance of private-private interorganizational collective action alliances that focus on systemic social issues that constitute today's Corporate Social Responsibility. This article relies upon public goods and social network theoretical frameworks. And because the issues at hand are systemic and the probability of obtaining the collective good (Oliver, Marwell & Teixeira, 1985) requires enormous interest, dedication, information sharing and resource allocation, the article focuses on interorganizational trust and cooperation within the formation and maintenance of these alliances. The major contribution of this paper is a series of propositions concerning trust and cooperation among alliance members.

Public Goods Theory

According to Crane (1998), many theoretical perspectives have been used to study green alliances such as resource-based theory of the firm, social exchange theory, stakeholder theory, relationship marketing theory, and the theory of industrial exchange. However to date, public goods theory has not been utilized to explain CSR related interorganizational relationships. But in a recent call to action, Bimber, Flanagin, and Stohl (2005) implore scholars not only to ask if contemporary action fits the current theoretical model "but also whether the theoretical ideal fits the rich array of collective actions now present in public life" (p. 366). Essentially, public goods theory lends itself well to variation and will serve as a solid theoretical basis from which to begin an exploration of these evolutionary alliances between private corporations.

Samuleson (1954) originally conceptualized public goods theory as collective action that results in physical or tangible products such bridges or national defense. Samuleson proposed that public goods are provided for each person to enjoy or not, and that one individual's consumption does not lead to the diminishment from any other individual's consumption of the good. In other words, public goods exhibit impossibility of exclusion and are 'joint' in supply (i.e., Marwell & Oliver, 1993). Samuleson's seminal model has become a central theory of social science research and has been employed in a great array of diverse phenomena (Bimber et al., 2005).

Olson (1965) extended public goods theory into the realm of political science to explain why some groups have a larger influence on policy. But more importantly, Olson described the concepts of free riding and group size which have become two critical and highly debated aspects of public goods theory. According to Olson, the problem of free riding is when individual actors involved in the collective choose to let others pay for the cost of the goods. In relation to free riding, Olson was the first theorist to propose that success is a function of group size. As Olson maintained, large groups are more likely to fail because individuals will free ride where small groups will succeed because there are limited actors contributing to the outcome.

Chamberlin (1974) was also concerned with the relationship between group size and the amount of good provided as he believes Olson did not effectively develop this point. Working from Olson's analysis of public goods theory, Chamberlain made the distinction between inclusive and exclusive public goods and how these dynamics explain the possibility of action by larger groups. As Chamberlin indicated, there is no reason to propose that the good provided by a large group will have little empirical importance as opposed to the good provided by a small group. In other words, Chamberlin argued that the outcome of collective action is likely to be a function of the relative strengths of the group.

Moving back to the world of economics, Oliver et al. (1985) devised a mathematical approach to collective action for public goods and describes the difference between accelerated and decelerated functions. According to Oliver et al., a decelerated function is illustrated as "the first few units of resources contributed having the biggest effect on the collective good, and subsequent contributions having less" (p. 526). An accelerated function, on the other hand, is defined by increasing returns, or "successive contributions generative progressively larger payoffs, each contribution makes the next one more likely" (p. 526).

These early and influential works on collective action are all focused on physical public goods. Spurred by a new array of collective actions, both Connolly and Thorn (1990) and Markus (1990) are the first attempts at applying public goods theory to interactive communication systems. Although the emphasis is different, both Connolly and Thorn and Markus demonstrated "the power of public goods thinking for the analysis of organizational communication issues" (Connolly & Thorn, 1990, p. 231). Connolly and Thorn explored how discretionary databases can be considered organizational public goods and they developed predictions on who will contribute and benefit from the information shared. Using critical mass theory, Markus described a communication discipline that focuses on the public good of universal access to interactive communication systems.

The importance of Connelly and Thorn (1990) and Markus' (1990) work is not only their focus on communications systems, but the fact that they contend that the public good is actually the information and communication functions that the systems provide. Based on this premsis, Fulk, Flanagin, Kalman, Monge and Ryan (1996) developed a useful theory about interactive communication public goods. In doing so, Fulk et al. provided an in-depth explanation of two features that distinguish communication and information public goods from traditional public goods. According to Fulk et al., communication and information public goods consist of connectivity, where all members are linked to one another, and communality, where members jointly hold a single body of information. Fulk et al. also pointed out that information sharing can also lead to the production of something new or tangible.

Using a network perspective, Monge, Fulk, Kalman, Flanagin, Parmassa, and Rumsey (1998) specifically discussed the production and maintenance of alliance based-interorganizational communication and information systems public goods. Monge et al. explained that there are other crucial factors to collective action such as characteristics of the participants (interest, costs, and resources contributed), characteristics of the group and the action process (how coordinated action grows through communication). However, the main contribution of Monge et al.'s article is the interplay between these characteristics and the constitution of interorganizational networks.

Recent iterations of public goods theory have included the work of Flanagin, Monge & Fulk (2001), Bimber et al. (2005) and Flanagin, Stohl and Bimber (2006). According to Flanagin et al. (2001), the formation of alliances for collective action is a complex task that includes idea generation, soliciting cooperation, securing contributions and negotiating structural arrangements. Flanagin et al. (2001) also asserted that the formative investments made by individual organizational representatives, such as the CEO, relate to network or alliance centrality. Bimber et al. reframed collective action as a set of communication processes involving crossing boundaries and placed a great deal of emphasis on how advanced communication and information tools are prompting a reassessment of successful contemporary collective action. Communication is also of primary interest to Flanagin et al. (2006), as they maintained that taking a communicative perspective allows "new ways to integrate and reconcile insights across traditional theories" (p. 33).

As can be seen from the vast literature on public goods, there is no "one size fits all" theory of collective action (Marwell & Oliver, 1993). Thus, public goods can certainly be used as a theoretical framework to help better understand how private company interorganizational alliances are created and maintained to solve systemic social issues. Indeed, the Business and Biodiversity Council, Global Business Coalition on HIV/AIDS, Tuberculosis and Malaria (GBC) and World Banks Institute are indeed new forms of collective action for public goods. These alliances produce both physical and intangible public goods and adhere to the qualities of jointness of supply, impossibility of exclusion, connectivity and communality.

Reference Points for Collective Action CSR Alliances

Before describing the particulars of why these alliances are public goods, it is prudent to begin with an example such as the World Business Council for Sustainable Development (WBCSD). This brief description will serve as a reference point for the application of public goods theory to private enterprise CSR collective action alliances. Formed when the Business Council for Sustainable Development (BCSD) in Geneva and the World Industry Council for the Environment (WICE), an International Chamber of Commerce (ICC) initiative joined forces in 1995 (Daboub & Calton, 2002), the WBCSD deals exclusively with business and sustainable development (www.wbcsd.org). Moreover, the alliance is created for companies to explore sustainable development and share knowledge concerning the systematic social issue of global warming (www.wbcsd.org). The WBCSD consists of over 150 international companies from 35 countries and more than 20 major industrial sectors (www.wbcsd.org; Daboub & Calton, 2002). And as Daboub and Calton (2002) explain, the WBCSD understands that corporate social responsibility has become an institutionalized element in the debate about what civil society expects from business; and it their mission to find new solutions for sustainable development to satisfy the need of both business and society.

On one hand, private enterprise CSR collective action alliances such as the WBCSD take a two-fold approach toward physical social public goods such as clean air and sustainable energy. First, individual members develop operational goals that adhere to the mission of the alliance and second, members work collectively toward the social public good. For example, the WBCSD views using sustainable energy as opposed to natural resources for building operations as a primary area of focus and has established The WBCSD on Energy Efficient Buildings – a project dedicated to "producing a roadmap for reaching energy self-sufficiency in buildings by 2050" (www.wbscd.org). Thus, member organizations not only build and maintain LEED certified buildings for their own use and operation, but also contribute to the overall public good which is clean air on a global level. In other words, the physical return (Oliver et al., 1985) of interorganizational collective action is sustainable energy and clear air for public consumption. As a result, consumption of clean air and reduced emission by one individual or organization does not limit the consumption of others and members of the public good, including society, cannot be excluded from using the return.

On the other hand, these alliances also develop intangible social public goods. Echoing Fulk's et al. (1996) contention that recent technological advancements have expanded the possibilities for collective action, private enterprise CSR interorganizational alliances certain rely on communication and information systems to create and maintain the union as well as share information pertaining to the social issue of interest. However, the intangible public good is not necessarily related to the development of proprietary communication and information systems, but more the information shared. When describing inter-organizational relationships, Bensaou and Venkatraman (1995) explain that IT-mediated mechanisms used range from simple to integrated platforms. Therefore, these alliances act much like virtual teams and rely on everything from e-mail, chat and asymmetric or interactive databases to on-line collaborative deliberation technologies (deMoor & Aakhus, 2006). But what is more important than the technologies used or developed specifically for the alliance, is that private CSR interorganizational alliances have both connectivity (organizations have the ability to reach other members, Monge et al., 1998) and communality (shared information, Monge et al.).

As Oliver et al. (1985) insists, "by definition any public good involves a 'free-rider problem'" (p. 547). And of course in this instance, benefiting from the effort of others (Marwell & Oliver, 1993), can still be a major problem. In particular, free riding bestows important organizational benefits beyond alliance outcomes and returns, most notable those associated with public relations such as increased visibility of CSR initiatives. Organizations can use their membership in the network to further reputation management, media relations, strategic communication and relationship management (Taylor & Doerfel, 2005) without necessarily contributing to the collective action. Yet too much free riding can and will eventually hamper the reach of these alliances and consequently their returns. As Porter and Kramer (2003) assert, if the social change to be achieved is the focus and not the publicity to be gained, the potential for collective action will expand.

Trust and Cooperation within Alliances

Beyond simply defining private enterprise CSR alliances as public goods, the goal of this article is to gain insight into the evolution of action (Gulati, 1998). Making this approach difficult is that the resulting social public goods, such as clean air or increased sustainability, require long-term commitments from interested and resourceful organizations. According to Malone and Klein (2007), to solve the most pressing and important problems facing humanity, a collective intelligence is required that includes the work of thousands of individuals. This is not an easy task considering that many of these firms operate within a competitive-cooperative realm (Doerfel, 1999) where sharing information could be considered a strategic liability. In addition, the reputation of the networked firms is contingent upon the action, behavior and alliance participation of others (Massey, 2001). Thus organizations involved in the alliance must trust and cooperate with one another. And although studies have demonstrated the importance of trust and cooperation in many types of networks (Doerfel, 2008), these concepts have not been used to describe green alliances yet alone their private-private counterparts.

Trust (Wakabayashi, 2003) and cooperation (Doerfel, 1999) are significant constructs within interorganizational relationships and interfirm networks. But because many researchers consider trust and cooperation interconnected, a brief description of the constructs is required. Due to different forms of trust (Rousseau, Sitkin, Burt & Cohn, 1998), definitions of the concept vary greatly[1], particularly as it relates to interorganizational alliances where enormous amounts of human and resource capital are required. Even though trust is ambiguous, it is nonetheless a critical criterion in networks, particularly those rich in information (Burt, 1992). Trust in the context of this paper means the belief in and the willingness to depend on another party (McKnight, Cummings & Chervany, 1998). Correspondingly, cooperation has been widely debated within academic literature (Smith, Carroll & Ashford, 1995; Williams, 2005). Consequently, within the context of this paper, Deorfel's (1999) definition of cooperation where organizations work together to achieve common goals has been adopted.

Social Network Theory

Alliances do not exist in a vacuum but rather are embedded in the social fabric that occurs between firms (Medlin, Aurifeille & Quester, 2005). Communication is the basis of collective action (Markus, 1990; Marwell & Oliver, 1993; Flanagin et al., 2006) and therefore these public goods are truly social networks, or a collection of organizations that are created out of a web of relations (Monge & Contractor, 2001). To explore the structure of the network and how it impacts collective action, social network analysis is an important framework with which to define "the IOC processes that facilitate such collaborative endeavors and result in collective advantages (public goods)" (Doerfel, 2008). Accordingly, it becomes significant to understand how network structure impacts trust and cooperation among alliance firms.

Many diverse theories have incorporated social network theory and analysis (see Kilduff & Tsai, 2003) including public goods (Monge et al., 1998; Marwell & Oliver, 1993) because as Doerfel (2008) explains, "social network analysis is a way to identify an overall system structure and within that context, the nature of individual organization's roles within it." Although there are a plethora of approaches to studying networks of organizations, Monge and Eisenberg (1987) suggest focusing on two major topics: the kinds of linkages and degree to which organizations are linked to one another through network positions and centrality.

According to Monge and Eisenberg (1987), external organizational linkages are "communicative (in that they almost always involve information exchange)" (p. 313). The content of linkages, or the nature of what flows between

[1] Monge et al. (1998) describes trust as the expectation that members of an alliance will protect the interests of contributors and the information shared. Where as Ring and Van de Ven (1994), employ a more restrictive definition of trust that emphasizes faith in the moral integrity or goodwill of others.

organizations, includes production, innovation and maintenance messages (Monge & Eisenberg, 1987). Among the measurements used to determine network position, are those of density (Kilduff & Tsai, 2003) and centrality (Doerfel & Barnett, 2003). Density measures the level of linkages among points in a network (Scott, 2003) or "the ratio of actual to potential contacts in a network" (Monge & Eisenberg, 1987, p. 317). Similarly, centrality refers to the extent to which organizations are linked to one another (Doerfel & Barnett, 2003) and includes 3 metrics: degree, betweeness and closeness. Following Krackhardt (1992), this paper is restricted to degree and betweeness centrality. Degree centrality is defined as the direct connection between organizations (Monge & Eisenberg, 1987) and betweeness is when an organization "falls between" others (Doerfel & Barnett, 2003). The remainder of this section is dedicated to setting forth a series of propositions about trust and cooperation between alliance members. These propositions are theoretically grounded by earlier works on public goods while at the same time adapted to meet the emerging needs of CSR alliances.

Linkages

Interorganizational linkages, or the social ties (Kilduff & Tasi, 2003) that bind alliance members, are both information sharing vehicles and constitutive. Private enterprise CSR interorganizational alliances are involved in knowledge-intensive work (Cross, Parker, Prusak & Borgatti, 2001) where the social ties no doubt provide key information and resources (Doerfel, Lai, Kolling, Keeler and Barbu, 2008) so that members can act toward the public good. However at the same time, communication between alliance organizations is constitutive, not just an expressive medium (Putnam & Krone, 2006). In other words, social relationships sustain the mechanism that consequently brings about the public good. Because the systemic social issues at the heart of these alliances can not be solved by one company or within one swift act, frequent exchange (Wakabayashi, 2003) of high quality information (Monge et al., 1998) is required for collective action returns. Proposition 1 illustrates how the returns of an alliance are connected to the frequency, quality and strength of communication within the network.

- Proposition 1A: Returns will be correlated with frequency and quality of communication and information exchange.

- Proposition 1B: The strength of the network, not the size of the network, will be correlated to the production and maintenance of the alliance.

- Proposition 1D: Free riding will occur through strategic interaction where organizations do not invest in the alliance but look to further external stakeholder perceptions.

Most all literature on interorganizational cooperation states that trust is an integral aspect and thus interconnected with organizations working together (Ring & Van de Ven, 1994). According to Gulati (1995), an important step in interfirm cooperative research is to identify, measure and assess the role of trust in the alliance's formation, governance and success. As defined by Smith et al., (1995), there are two types of cooperative relationships: informal includes arrangements where behavioral norms determine the contributions and formal cooperative relationships which are defined by contractual obligations. Proposition 2 illustrates the relationship between trust and cooperation within alliances and Proposition 3 deals with how the composition of the alliance will impact trust and cooperation.

- Proposition 2A: Trust will be correlated to cooperation.
- Proposition 2B: Trust and cooperation will be a function of the quality and frequency of information shared between alliance members.
- Proposition 3A: If the alliance is composed of groups that share homogeneous interests in the social public good, free riding will be low and trust and cooperation will not be related to the type of network structure.
- Proposition 3B: If the alliance is composed of groups that share heterogeneous interests in the social public good, free riding will be high and trust and cooperation will be related to the type of network structure.

Density

Weick (1979) famously describes organizing by explaining that "the current state of any system is the result away from some original state" (p. 120). Considering that formation and maintenance of alliances vary because organizational relationships emerge, evolve, grow and dissolve over time (Ring & Van de Ven, 1994), there will be differences between initial (McKnight et al., 1998) and sustained or long-term mutual (Sydow, 1998) trust. Proposition 4 illustrates the construct of trust within social public goods by using the measurement of network density. As Burt (1992) explains, in dense networks "each relationship puts players in contact with the same people treated through other relationships" (p. 21).

- Proposition 4A: In accelerated social public goods, density will be high during formation and decrease as time elapses.
- Proposition 4B: In accelerated social public goods, trust will be high during formation and decrease as maintenance occurs.
- Proposition 4C: In decelerated social public goods, density will be low during formation and increase as time elapses.
- Proposition 4D: In decelerated social public goods, trust will be low during formation and increase during maintenance.

Centrality

Another widely used network measurement that can be applied in this instance is centrality. According to Gulati and Gargiulo (1999), centrality is a direct function of the organizations involvement in strategic alliances. However when examining private social collective action alliances, organizational position will be contingent on a variety of factors that define involvement such as interest and resource allocation, time of entry and length of membership. In other words, there will be variation within the community of organizational actors (Markus, 1990) and this will subsequently impact cooperation among members.

As Krackhardt (1992) explains, degree centrality is the simplest form of centrality but it does provide a substantial basis which to determine network positions of organizations. According to Markus (1990), "interests are the values different individuals place on the public good; resources are what individuals must contribute to achieve it" (p. 201). Resources contribution includes effort, reputation, and human (Connolly & Thorn, 1990). In addition, differences in the timing and amount of resources contributed will consequently impact the organization's position within the network. Organizations that dedicate high levels of resources tend to be central in a network (Flanagin et al., 2001) and more collaborative (Taylor & Doerfel, 2005). Yet, when discussing public goods, Oliver and Marwell (1993) explains that there is a difference in interest and resource heterogeneity and this subsequently effects collective action. Proposition 5 illustrates with the relationship between the interests of alliance members and the structure of the network.

- Proposition 5A: Organizations with interest heterogeneity will be less collaborative and have low degree centrality.

- Proposition 5B: Organizations with interest homogeneity will be more collaborative and have high degree centrality.

- Proposition 5C: Organizations that dedicate resources heterogeneously will have low degree centrality and receive low cooperation from alliance members.

- Proposition 5D: Organizations that dedicate resources homogeneously will have high degree centrality and receive high cooperation from alliance members.

- Proposition 5E: Free riding will be a function of interest and resource dedication.

Doerfel and Taylor (2005) also explain that early entrants become important and influential in their networks. These network creators control the flow of information and resources (see also Flangin et al., 2001; Doerfel & Taylor, 2003). According to Scott (2003), betweeness is a complex measure but conceptually, organizations that fill structural holes (Burt, 1992) or have high betweeness centrality "act as gatekeeper for information that flows through the network"

(Krackhardt, 1992, p. 91). Based on this approach, it would be reasonable to conclude that network founders would play the role of broker and as a result have high betweeness centrality and receive high cooperation. However, jointly holding a single body of information and maintaining this store of information (Fulk et al., 1996) is a critical aspect in collective action for systematic social public goods. Accordingly, Proposition 6 examines the content of the information that the gatekeeper shares with other members and how this is related to the position within the network.

- Proposition 6: Cooperation is a function of alliance entry, moderated by the extent of resources shared (collective symbols, texts and sagas that represent communality).

Private enterprise social collective action alliances are not zero-sum games but intricate coalitions that are based on "a long-term perspective on the relationships of all the participants" (Meier, 1995, p. 146). And like many reviews of interorganizational networks, the above does not provide an unequivocal picture between structure and trust and cooperation. However, it does begin a discussion that follows the contention made by Flanagin et al. (2006) that understanding contemporary collective action "requires recognizing how people are interacting and what opportunities are afforded them, along with examining what organization and structure fit their behavior and help facilitate collective actions" (p. 30).

Discussion and Conclusion

Public goods theory has served as the theoretical underpinnings for a vast amount of social science research. From Samuleson's (1954) influential work that introduced jointness of supply and impossibility of exclusion, to Monge's et al. (1998) inclusion of communality and connectivity, public goods theory has enabled theorists and researchers to examine many diverse social phenomenon. This article has followed the seminal work these academics and applied public goods theory to the behavior of competing organizations during their attempt at collective action. The goal is to provide a deeper understanding of private enterprises that form alliances for systemic social collective action. These alliances are networks of organizations that create tangible and intangible public goods as well as exhibit the qualities of traditional and non-traditional action alliances.

What drives this paper is the simple contention that communication is the basis for collective action (Marwell & Oliver, 1985; Markus, 1990; Flanagin et al., 2006). Social ties between actors (organizations in this case) are vital to collective action (Marwell & Oliver, 1993) as they provide access to information. But considering that these alliances operate in competitive-cooperative environments (Doerfel, 1999), organizations are in a quandary because to resolve systemic social issues it takes great dedication of time, energy and resources. This means then trust and cooperation become crucial interorganizational issues. Therefore both trust and cooperation play important roles in alliances. Moreover, with the possible future increase in the formation of private enterprise CSR collective action alliances, Smith's et al. (1995) statement that "there is evidence that its role (cooperation) will become even more important in the future" (p. 9) is certainly correct.

The use of social network analysis here has also provided unique insights into the evolution these alliances "where strategic action and social structure are closely intertwined (Gulati, 1998, p. 297). Even though density and centrality are used to describe the "communication links in a network and thus represents how information flows among organizations" (Doerfel & Taylor, 2005, p. 379), one important factor stands out: research must not simply consider the availability or connection among organizations but the quality of the tie. As Uzzi (1997) maintains, an actor's ability to access the opportunities of a contact or network strategically depends on the quality of the relationship and the information shared. To achieve returns, social collective action must be the function of a densely constructed network of organizations that share high quality information about the public good. As always, free riding is certainly an issue within these alliances as organizations that do not invest in the action can still benefit through positive publicity.

In conclusion, this article is an attempt to shed some light on a subject of great importance because as the significance of CSR grows, so too does the act of forming social collective action alliances. According to Krathwohl (1998), "when a study contributes to explanations or significant ideas . . . it multiplies its impact" (p. 84). Although this article only considers trust and cooperation among organizational alliance members and not realization of goals and completion of public goods, if nothing else, it reveals that CSR alliances are a subject that needs and deserves further research.

References

Aakhus, M., & Ziek, P. (2009). *The role of instruments for communicating corporate social responsibility*. Proceedings of the National Communication Association, Chicago, IL.

Argandona, A. (1998). "The Stakeholder Theory and the Common Good", Journal of Business Ethics, Vol. 17 No. 9-10, pp. 1093-1120.

Arts, B.J.M. (2002). "'Green Alliances' of Business and NGOs. New Styles of Self-Regulation or 'Dead-End Roads'?", Corporate Social Responsibility and Environmental Management Vol. 9 No. 1, pp. 26-36.

Bennett, W.L. (2003). "Communicating Global Activism", Information, Communication and Society Vol. 6 No. 2, pp. 143-168.

Bensaou, M, & Venkatraman, N. (1995). "Configurations of interorganizational relationships: a comparison between US and Japanese automakers", Management Science, Vol. 41 No. 9, pp. 1471-92.

Bimber, B., Flanagin, AJ., & Stohl, C. (2005). "Reconceptualizing collective action in the contemporary media environment", Communication Theory, Vo. 15 No. 4, pp. 365-388.

Burt, R. S. (1992). "The social structure of competition. In *Structural holes*. Cambridge, MA: Harvard University Press", in Cross, R., Parker, A. and Sasson, L. (Eds.), Networks in the Knowledge Economy, Oxford University Press, London, pp. 13-56.

Carroll, A. B. (1999). "Corporate Social Responsibility. Evolution of a Definitional Construct", Business & Society, Vol. 38 No. 3, pp. 268-295.

Chamberlin, J. (1974). "Provision of Collective Goods As a Function of Group Size", The American Political Science Review, Vol. 68 No. 2, pp. 707-716.

Chatterji, A. & Levine, D. (2006). "Breaking Down the Wall of Codes: Evaluating Non-Financial Performance Measurement", California Management Review, Vol. 48 No. 2, pp. 29-51.

Connolly, T. & Thorn, B.K. (1990). "Discretionary Databases: Theory, Data, and Implications", in Fulk, J. and Steinfeld, C. (Eds.), Organizations and Communication Technology, Sage, Newbury Park, pp. 219-233.

Crane, A. (1998), "'Exploring Green Alliances'", Journal of Marketing Management, Vol. 14 No. 6, pp. 559-579.

Cross, R., Parker, A., Prusak, L., & Borgatti, S. (2001). "Knowing what we know: Supporting knowledge creation and sharing in social networks", In Cross, R., Parker, A. & Sasson, L. (Eds.), Networks in the Knowledge Economy, Oxford University Press, New York, pp. 208-234.

Daboub, A.J. & Calton, J.M. (2002). "Stakeholder Learning Dialogues: How to Preserve Ethical Responsibility in Networks", Journal of Business Ethics, Vol. 41 No. 1-2, pp. 85-98.

deMoor, A. & Aakhus, M. (2006). "Argumentation support: from technologies to tools", Communications of the ACM, Vol. 49 No. 3, pp. 93-98.

Doerfel, M. L. (1999). "Inter organizational networks: The convergence of cooperative competitors", Communication Research Reports, Vol. 16, pp. 175-184.

Doerfel, M. L. (2008). Interorganizational communication. In Donsbach (Ed.) *The international encyclopedia of communication.* Blackwell Publishing.

Doerfel, M.L., & Barnett, G.A. (1999), "A semantic network analysis of the international communication association", Human Communication Research, Vol. 25 No. 4, pp. 589-603.

Doerfel, M.L., Lai, C., Kolling, A.J., Keeler, T.L. & Barbu, D. (2008). "Post Katrina New Orleans Interorganizational Networks, Paper presented at the annual ICA meetings in Montreal, May.

Doerfel, M. L., & Taylor, M. (2004). "Network dynamics of inter organizational cooperation: The Croatian civil society movement", Communication Monographs, Vol. 71 No. 4, pp. 373-394.

Doh, J.P. & Guay, T. R. (2006). "Corporate Social Responsibility, Public Policy, and NGO Activism in Europe and the United States: An Institutional-Stakeholder Perspective", Journal of Management Studies, Vol. 43 No. 1, pp. 48-73.

Flanagin, A. J., Monge, P. R., & Fulk, J. (2001). "The value of formative investment in organizational federations", Human Communication Research, Vol. 27 No. 1, pp. 69-93.

Flanagin, A. J., Stohl, C., & Bimber, B. (2006). "Modeling the structure of collective action", Communication Monographs, Vol. 73 No. 1, pp. 29-54.

Fulk, J., Flanagin, A.J., Kalman, M.E., Monge, P.R. & Ryan, T. (1996). "Connective and Communal Public Goods in Interactive Communication Systems", Communication Theory, Vol. 6 No. 1, pp. 60-87.

Gulati, R. (1995). "Does Familiarity Breed Trust? The Implications of Repeated Ties For Contractual Choice in Alliances", Academy of Management Journal, Vol. 38 No. 1, pp. 85-112.

Gulati, R. (1998). "Alliances and Networks", Strategic Management Journal, Vol. 19 No. 4, pp. 293-317.

Gulati, R. & Gargiulo, M. (1999). "Where Do Interorganizational Networks Come From?", American Journal of Sociology, Vol. 104 No. 5, pp. 1429-93.

Hartman, C. L. & Stafford, E.R. (1997). "Green Alliances: Building New Business with Environmental Groups", Long Range Planning, Vol. 30, pp. 184-196.

Hartman, C. L. & Stafford, E.R. (1998). "Crafting Enviropreneurial Value Chain Strategies Through Green Alliances", Business Horizons, Vol. 41, pp. 62-72.

Kilduff, M., & Tsai, W. (2003). "Social networks and organizations", Sage, London.

Krackhardt, D. (1992). "The strength of strong ties: The importance of *philos* in organizations", In Cross, R., Parker, A., & Sasson, L. (Eds.), Networks in the Knowledge Economy, Oxford University Press, London, pp. 82-108.

Krathwhohl, D.R. (1998). "Methods of Educational and Social Science Research. An Integrated Approach (2nd ed.)", Waveland Press, Inc, Lake Grove.

Livesey, S.M. (1999). "McDonald's and the Environmental Defense Fund: A Case Study of a Green Alliance", Journal of Business Communication, Vol. 36 No. 1, pp. 5-39.

Malone, T. & Klein, M. (2007). "Harnessing Collective Intelligence to Address Global Climate Change", Innovations: Technology, Governance, Globalization, Vol. 2 No. 4, pp. 15-26.

Markus, M.L. (1990). "Toward a 'Critical Mass' Theory of Interactive Media", in Fulk, J. and Steinfeld, C. (Eds.), Organizations and Communication Technology, Sage, Thousand Oaks, pp. 194-218.

Massey, J.E. (2001). "Managing Organizational Legitimacy: Communication Strategies for Organizations in Crisis, Journal of Business Communication, Vol. 38 No. 2, pp. 153-182.

Marwell, G. & Oliver, P. (1993). "The Critical Mass in Collective Action: a Micro-Social Theory", Cambridge University Press, Cambridge.

Meier, J. (1995). "The importance of relationship management in establishing successful interorganizational systems", Journal of Strategic Information Systems, Vol. 4 No. 2, pp. 135-148.

Medlin, C.J., Aurifeille, J. & Quester, P.G. (2005). "A collaborative interest model of relational coordination and empirical results", Journal of Business Research, Vol. 52 No. 2, pp. 214-222.

Monge, P.R. & Contractor, N.S. (2001). "Emergence of Communication Networks", in Jablin, F.M. & Putnam, L.L. (Eds.), The New Handbook of Organizational Communication. Advances in Theory, Research and Methods, Sage, Thousand Oaks, pp. 440-502.

Monge, P. R. & Eisenberg, E.M. (1987). "Emergent Communication Networks", in Jablin, F.M., Putnam, L.L., Roberts, L. & Porter, L.W. (Eds.), Handbook of organizational communication, Sage, Newbury Park, pp. 304 – 342.

Monge, P. R., Fulk, J., Kalman, M. E., Flanagin, A. J., Parmassa, C., & Rumsey, S. (1998). "Production of collective action in alliance-based interorganizational communication and information systems", Organization Science, Vol. 9, pp. 411-433.

Oliver, P., Marwell, G. & Teixeira, R. (1985). "A Theory of the Critical Mass. I. Interdependence, Group Heterogeneity, and the Production of Collective Action", The American Journal of Sociology, Vol. 91 No. 3, pp. 522-556.

Olson, M. (1965). "The Logic of Collective Action", Harvard University Press, Cambridge, MA.

Porter, M.E. & Kramer, M.R. (2003). "The Competitive Advantage of Corporate Philanthropy", in Harvard Business Review on Corporate Responsibility, Harvard Business School Publishing Boston, MA, pp. 27-63.

Putnam, L.L. & Krone, K.J. (2006). "Editor's Introduction", in Putnam, L.L. & Krone, K.J. (Eds.), Organizational Communication. History and Theoretical Perspective, Sage, Thousand Oaks, pp. xxiii-xliii.

Ring, P.S. & Van de Ven (1994). "Developmental Processes of Cooperative Interorganizational Relatonships", Academy of Management Review, Vol. 19 No. 1, pp. 90-118.

Rousseau, D. M., Sitkin, S.B., Burt, R.S. and Cohn, C. (1998). "Not So Different after All: a Cross-discipline View of Trust", Academy of Management Review, Vol. 23 No. 3, pp. 393-404.

Ruggie, J.I. (2004). "Reconstituting the Global Public Domain – Issues, Actors, and Practices", European Journal of International Relations, Vol. 10 No. 4, pp. 499-531.

Samuelson, P. A. (1954). "The Pure Theory of Public Expenditure", Review of Economics and Statistics, Vol. 36, pp. 387-389.

Samuelson, P. A. (1955). "Diagrammatic Exposition of a Theory of Public Expenditure", Review of Economics and Statistics, Vol. 37, pp. 350-356.

Samuleson, P.A. (1958). "Aspects of Public Expenditure Theories", The Review of Economics and Statistics, Vol. 40, pp. 332-338.

Scott, J. (2000). "Social network analysis: A handbook (2nd ed.), Sage, London.

Smith, KG., Carroll, S.J. & Ashford, S.J. (1995). "Intra- and Inter- organizational Cooperation: Toward a Research Agenda", Academy of Management Journal, Vol. 38 No. 1, pp. 7-23.

Stafford, E. R. & Hartman, C.L. (1996). "Green Alliances: Strategic Relations Between Businesses and Environmental Groups", Business Horizons, Vol. 39, pp. 50-59.

Sydow, J. (1998). "Understanding the Constitution of Interorganizational Trust", in Lane, C. & Bachmann, R., Trust Within and Between Organizations.

Conceptual Issues and Empirical Application, Oxford University Press, London, pp. 31-64.

Taylor, M., & Doerfel, M. L. (2005). "Another dimension to explicating relationships : Network theory and method to measure inter-organizational linkages", Public Relations Review, Vol. 31 No. 1, pp. 121-129.

Taylor, M ., & Doerfel, M. L. (2003). "Building inter-organizational relationships that build nations", Human Communication Research, Vol. 29 No. 2, pp. 153-181.

Uzzi, B. (1997). Social Structure and Competition in Interfirm Networks: The Paradox of Embeddedness. *Administrative Science Quarterly*, 42(1), 35-67.

Wakabayashi, N. (2003). "Relational Trust and Embeddedness in Interorganizational Networks: An Analysis of Quality Control Manager Networks in Japanese Buyer-Supplier Relations", Retrieved April 29, 2010 from http://repository.kulib.kyoto-u.ac.jp/dspace/bitstream/2433/37949/1/71.pdf

Weick, K.E. (1979). "The Social Psychology of Organizing (2nd ed.), McGraw-Hill, Inc, New York.

World Business Council for Sustainable Development. Retrieved on April 31, 2008 from http://www.wbcsd.org/templates/TemplateWBCSD5/layout.asp?MenuID=1

Ziek, P. (2009). Making Sense of CSR Communication. *Corporate Social Responsibility and Environmental Management*, 16(3), 137-145.

Chapter 14: Corporate Greening

Reflections on "Corporate Greening": A Proposed Model for Organizational Change

Jennifer Davis, Consultant, Stratos Inc. Ottawa

Sharon Leiba O'Sullivan, Telfer School of Management, University of Ottawa

Rumaisa Shaukat, Telfer School of Management, University of Ottawa

Abstract: Is the emergence of social and environmental performance as dominant themes in the current business context an indication that society is beginning to challenge the myth of unlimited wealth? Perhaps. However, more often than not, both are treated as, and are perceived by customers to be, little more than public relations tools in the promotion of brand[1]*. This perception reflects the reality that companies are struggling with how to operationalize the concepts of social and environmental responsibility, while maintaining a fair return to shareholders*[2]*. The struggle arises because in this area, real change requires thinking about organizational purpose in ways that challenge deeply rooted values. In fact, it involves instilling and managing a change in the innate organizational culture. As such, this paper will view the operationalization of social environmental performance through the lens of the change management literature. The process by which change occurs, as well the factors which drive or impede green change in particular will serve as the framework for this paper. This paper draws extensively on archival documents that illustrate different traditions for addressing "corporate greening". The proposed discussion provides a*

[1] Porter & Kramer, 2006 & SustainAbility, 2000
[2] Sarkis et al, 2006

foundation for further theory based empirical investigations, and offers practical suggestions for improving social and environmental performance.

Introduction

By definition, a myth "reflects the underlying paradigm that guides the thoughts and actions of the people of a particular culture"[3]. Using this definition, few would disagree that the drive to generate economic wealth is today's greatest and most powerful guide. However, some argue that the pursuit of unlimited wealth is a faulty paradigm, one that ignores the well-known scientific principle that humans and their creations are part of a planet that is intimately interconnected and that operates at rates much, much, slower than that of human economic progression[4]. As such, we are ultimately confined by the planet's ability to absorb our impacts. In fact, in his 2008 publication, "Common Wealth – Economics for a Crowded Planet", the well-respected economist and Director of Columbia University's Earth Institute[5], Jeffrey Sachs directly addresses this limitation. He states that the "world's current ecological, demographic, and economic trajectory is unsustainable, meaning that if we continue with business as usual we will hit social and ecological crises with calamitous results"[6]. Consequently, at a time when more than 50% of the world's top 100 economies are corporations[7], the impact of business on the trajectory of the planet cannot be understated.

Increasingly, albeit slowly, organizations are becoming aware that the choices they make with regard to products, processes and services do not only have economic implications. These choices also have profound social and environmental consequences[8] that will impact their ability to survive in the long-term. Specifically, businesses need sustainable access to resources with which to make their products, they need access to employees who are healthy and happy and ready to contribute, and they need customers who are well off and healthy to buy their products[9]. In fact, "businesses that pursue their ends at the expense of society in which they operate will find success to be illusory and ultimately temporary"[10]. Is the emergence of social and environmental performance as dominant themes in the current business context an indication that society is beginning to challenge the myth of unlimited wealth? Perhaps. However, more often than not, both are treated as, and are perceived by customers to be, little more than public relations tools in the promotion of brand[11].

---

[3] Stead & Stead, 1994, pg 15
[4] Stead & Stead, 1994
[5] http://www.earthinstitute.columbia.edu/sections/view/9
[6] Sachs, 2008, pg 5
[7] Anderson & Cavanagh, 2000
[8] Sarkis et al, 2006; referencing Day and Arnold, 1998
[9] Porter & Kramer, 2006
[10] Porter & Kramer, 2006, pg 83
[11] Porter & Kramer, 2006 & SustainAbility, 2000

This perception reflects the reality that companies are struggling with how to operationalize the concepts of social and environmental responsibility, while maintaining a fair return to shareholders[12]. The struggle arises because in this area, real change requires thinking about organizational purpose in ways that challenge deeply rooted values. In fact, it involves instilling and managing a change in the innate organizational culture. As such, this paper will view the operalization of these concepts through the lens of change management. The world around us is constantly changing, and to be effective in it our organizations must change too (Jager, 2001). Change management is "widely recognized as one of the most critical and challenging responsibilities of organizational leadership" [13] because change efforts that involve big picture issues such as mission, strategy, culture and leadership[14] fail more often than not[15]. As such, it is important for any agent of change to understand the process by which it occurs as well as the factors which drive or impede it. These issues, and their relationship to the improvement of corporate social and environmental performance, provide the framework for this literature review. Considering the importance of corporate greening, this paper aims at deepening the understanding of this concept through a theoretical exposition.

The literature in this area is rife with terminology that overlaps conceptually (E.g., Branch, 2003; Lyon, 2004; Vos, 2003). Examples include: sustainability, sustainable development, corporate responsibility, business responsibility, corporate citizenship, social responsibility, corporate stewardship, corporate environmental responsibility and corporate social responsibility (a list which is by no means complete). Given this, though it is important not to dwell too long on semantics, it is useful to provide a common understanding of the two most relevant terms (sustainability & corporate social responsibility), and define how they will be used in this paper.

Sustainability & Sustainable Development

The term sustainability is often criticized as being able to mean anything to anyone[16], however, the most commonly used definition is likely that of the United Nations' Brundtland Report entitled "Our Common Future" which defines sustainable development as "development that meets the needs of the present without compromising the ability of future generations to meet their own needs.[17]" While this definition has relevance for business in countless ways, several of the most immediate requirements include:

- "an economic system that is able to generate surpluses and technical knowledge on a self-reliant and sustained basis"

[12] Sarkis et al, 2006
[13] Branch, 2003, pg 2
[14] Branch, 2003
[15] Miles, 2008 - MBA 5237 Change Management Slides, lecture 1
[16] Porter & Kramer, 2006
[17] UN, 1997, pg unknown (online document)

- "a production system that respects the obligation to preserve the ecological base for development"
- "an international system that fosters sustainable patterns of trade and finance" and
- "an administrative system that is flexible and has the capacity for self-correction"[18]

Conceptually, the term can be viewed as having three components: socio-political sustainability (social equity), economic sustainability (economic development) and environmental sustainability (environmental integrity), and success in any one area is interconnected with success in the others[19].

Figure 1: Sustainable development spheres[20]

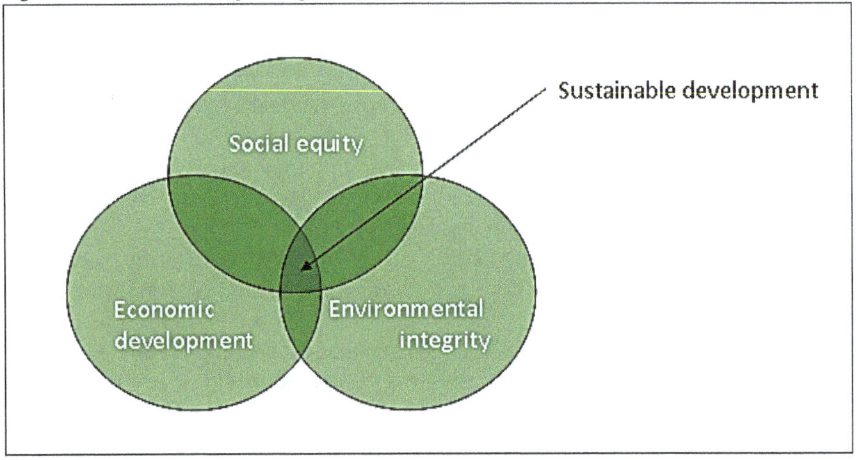

Corporate Social Responsibility

Corporate social responsibility (CSR) is "the broad concept that businesses are more than just profit seeking entities and, therefore, also have an obligation to benefit society"[21] (Gancerlli, 1995). In modern parlance, and the way in which the term is used within this paper, a company's CSR policy (and actions), reflect the way in which it views and reacts to the concept of sustainable development. The following quotation illustrates how CSR operationalizes the sustainability concept:

> "CSR is about businesses and other organizations going beyond legal obligations to manage the impact they have on the environment and society. In particular, this could include how organizations interact with their employees, suppliers, customers and the communities in which they

[18] UN, 1997, pg unknown (online document)
[19] Bansal, 2001
[20] Developed from Bansal, 2001
[21] Werther & Chandler, 2006

> operate, as well as the extent to which they attempt to protect the environment."[22]

When the word "strategic" is incorporated into the term, the definition evolves into the idea that "CSR should be integrated into the firm's strategic perspective and operations because of the long-term benefit this brings to the organization[23]". At a time when market strength is significantly derived from brand image, and corporations increasingly have to respond to public criticism about the way in which they exploit the world, CSR has emerged as a regulatory framework to aid in the management of this image[24] (Holland, 2003). *"If companies...analyzed their prospects for social responsibility using the same framework that guides their core business choices, they would discover that CSR can become much more than a cost, a constraint, or a charitable deed, [it is] a source of opportunity, innovation and competitive advantage". (Porter & Kramer, 2006)*

Corporate Greening: How Can CSR Designed to Achieve Sustainability?

To provide consistency and clarity, throughout this paper the term "corporate greening" will be used to denote the process by which an organization implements CSR with the objective of achieving sustainability. Occasionally, this will also be referred to as green change, or when used as a verb – greening. The use of a term that is biased toward the environmental is not accidental. Given the predictions of Jeffrey Sachs and his contemporaries, it is clear that particular focus must be placed on increasing the environmental performance of businesses of all shapes and sizes, because environmental performance inevitably has a profound impact on the social dimension, particularly in lesser developed countries. The goal of change management is to "create an organization whose structure, processes, people and culture, are tailored appropriately for its current mission"[25]. In the case of corporate greening, this mission requires becoming an organization that prioritizes not only economic, but also social and environmental performance.

Characteristics of the Green Corporation

While there is much literature describing the characteristics of a green culture, several broad themes present themselves. The findings have been compiled and are presented in Table 1.

---

[22] Werther & Chandler, 2006, pg 6, referencing Ruth Lea. 2002. Corporate Social Responsibility: IOD member Opinion Survey. The Institute of Directors, UK, November, 2002, p. 10. Referenced from

[23] Werther & Chandler, 2006, pg 6

[24] Sahlin-Andersson, 2006

[25] Branch, 2003, pg 2

Table 1: Characteristics of Green Culture

Cultural aspects[26]	
Values: "the key aspects of an individual or group belief system that are acknowledged as being important".	Balancing and reporting of economic, social and environmental priorities[27]. The exchange of a short-term perspective with an intergenerational time-frame[28]. Critical analysis of values and assumptions and cultivation of double-loop learning.
Attitudes: "positions adopted by individuals in relation to external events".	Green considerations should be incorporated throughout the supply chain[29]. Stakeholders can make valuable contributions to the development of the green corporation.
Perceptions: " an interpretation of reality".	Green change is possible and is supported
Behaviour: "what people do and the way in which they do it"	Integration of green considerations into governing principles, values, mission statement[30] and decision -making[31]. Sharing of knowledge throughout the entire organizations, both horizontally and vertically. Movement away from re-active strategies to the pro-active, anticipatory and innovative[32]. Collaboration and relationship building with other organizations, public institutions, NGOs, stakeholder groups [33]. Strong focus on linking desired behaviours to rewards and recognition[34]. Increasing budget for and availability of training and learning opportunities.
Competencies: "Ability to perform a task requiring a combination of knowledge, experience and skill /capacity"	Triple bottom line reporting / full cost accounting. Stakeholder analysis. Cultivation of problem solving and experimentation[35].

To understand the process by which this transformation occurs, a general outline of the change process is presented below, followed by descriptions of two broad

---

[26] Lyon, 2000, pg 135

[27] *Azzone & Noci, 1998; Bansal, 2001*

[28] Harris & Crane, 2002; referencing W*elford, 1995*

[29] Harris & Crane, 2002; referencing *Shrivastava, 1995*

[30] Bansal, 2001

[31] Harris & Crane, 2002; Benn et al, 2006; Azzone & Noci, 1998

[32] *Azzone & Noci, 1998*

[33] Benn et al, 2006; Lyon, 2000; Azzone & Noci, 1998

[34] Lyon, 2000

[35] Lyon, 2000

categories of change: evolutionary and revolutionary. Subsequently, the phases in the corporate greening process, a discussion of the aspects of green culture, and the conditions necessary for green change are presented.

Change Management Process

Most of the change management studies are primarily based upon Lewin (1951) who argued that the process of change involved three basic phases: unfreezing, changing, and refreezing. Unfreezing begins when a need is felt for some sort of revolution or adjustment within an organization. Change occurs when a real adjustment or revolution is actually implemented. Refreezing occurs after the new initiative becomes part of an organization. What is useful about this framework is that it gives rise to thinking about a practical and procedural approach to the change implementation process. Lewin basically advised that in order to implement change first unfreeze the target group by preparing it for the change. Next implement the change affecting that target group. Finally re-freeze the target group with the change in place. Lewin's (1951) three phrases of change: unfreeze, change and refreeze[36] remain the basis and starting point for most of the scholarly thinking about change. Detailed explanation of this model is presented in the ensuing section.

Phase 1: Unfreezing the organization. The first phase in the change process involves overcoming inertia, also called resistance to change (discussed in-depth in the section: Barriers to corporate greening). This is done by deconstructing the organizational mindset and individual defence mechanisms, which act as barriers to change. In order for this to occur, individuals must become dissatisfied with the current situation. Moreover, this dissatisfaction must be connected to something about which the individual feels strongly; otherwise the motivation to change, however great the dissatisfaction, will not be enough to overcome the barriers[37].

Often, even if the individual is motivated to change, anxiety develops because this phase involves the acceptance that something is wrong, that there is a failure. The feeling of failure is associated with a loss of identity, of ego, and this causes great anxiety for most individuals. Dealing with this anxiety is fundamental to successful change[38], in that the "key to effective change management…[is] the ability to balance the amount of threat produced …with enough…safety to allow the change target to accept the information, feel the…anxiety…and become motivated to change".[39]

Phase 2: Change and the concept of single- and double-loop learning. Change itself occurs in phase two, a phase characterized by confusion, transition

[36] Schein, n.d.; referencing Kurt Lewin's change model
[37] Schein, n.d
[38] Schein, n.d.
[39] Schein, n.d., pg2

and learning. It is in this phase where old processes and procedures are challenged and great uncertainty exists around what the final outcome will be.[40]

A related concept of critical importance to this stage, and in fact the entire change process, is that of single- and double-loop learning (SLL, DLL). This concept is grounded in the belief that all actions have consequences, either intended or unintended. It is how individuals, and in fact organizations, react to a mismatch between intended and actual consequences that leads to one type of learning or the other.[41] For example, when a mismatch as described above occurs, an individual might simply try something different in order to achieve the intended outcome. However, this action does not involve questioning why the mismatch occurred, therefore allowing the individual or the organization to carry on with their present set of policies and objectives. The result of this behaviour is SLL. Conversely, DLL involves questioning the reason for the mismatch, including the values and assumptions underlying the action.[42] DLL, also called higher order learning, involves the development of different interpretations of events[43] and may change the governing values, norms, policies and objectives of an organization[44]. Because the process of corporate greening involves challenging deeply held beliefs and values, for change to occur, companies seeking green change must increase their capacity for double-loop learning.

Phase 3: Re-freezing. The final stage involves freezing the organization by confirming the new mindset, such that the changes become ingrained. Called crystallizing the mindset, the comfort level of individuals within the organization, often severely strained during phase two, returns to normal levels.[45]

Figure 2: A general process of change (Based on Lewin, 1951)

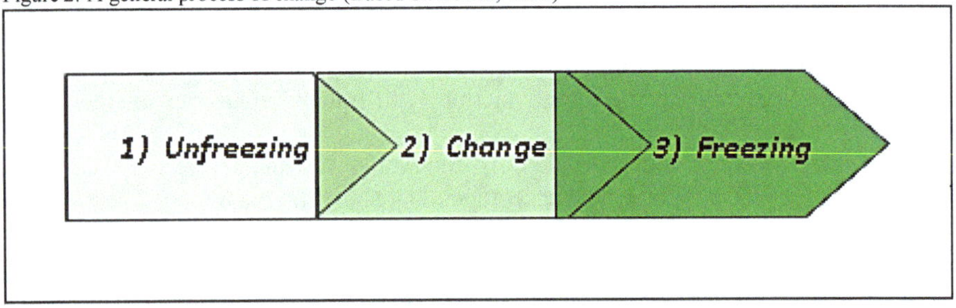

Types and Sources of Change

Two types of changes have been widely discussed in the literature. The first type is evolutionary or first-order changes. These changes are narrow and incremental in scope; it only alters small-scale problematic aspects for immediate

[40] Schein, n.d.
[41] Smith, 2001
[42] Smith, 2001
[43] Sharma & Vredenburg, 1998; referencing Fiol, 1994
[44] Smith, 2001
[45] Schein, n.d.

improvements but keeps the operations within the general working framework of the organization (Blumenthal & Haspeslagh, 1994; Goldstein, 1988; **Johnson-Carmer,** Cross, & Yan, **2003;** Mezias & Glynn, 1993). Examples include improvements to product or process design, delivery or quality. As such, it may not require attention of entire organization, or this involvement may be phased in gradually[46].

The second type is revolutionary or second-order changes. These types of changes are radical transformations that intend to bring changes in the core framework of the organizations (Blumenthal & Haspeslagh, 1994; Goldstein, 1988; **Kreitner, 1992).** Examples of revolutionary change include the de-regulation of a market, the determination of a material as carcinogenic, or the bankruptcy of a sole supplier. Revolutions of this sort generally require modification to an organization's mission and strategy. Furthermore, such change has ramifications for the entire organization, and as such, its management must involve all members of the organization. If such management is done poorly, transition to a healthy steady state can be hampered by resistance on the part of the organization's employees.[47]

Broadly speaking, the change process described in the previous section either occurs incrementally or radically. Organizations can exist in a steady state for significant periods of time, during which they experience change, but of a gradual, incremental nature. This steady state is periodically interrupted by crises, which thrust the organization into a state of extreme flux, or revolution. Generally, this period is followed by another steady state.[48] Organizational change is anticipated or triggered because of different changing circumstances; an organization might introduce a change because of the forces affecting its environment. These forces might be either external or internal. External forces come from out of the organizational boundaries beyond the organization's control (Francesco & Gold, 1998), which are obstinate in nature such as political and social pressures, economic conditions, market demands and so on. Internal forces for change come from inside the organization and may be slight, such as group relations, motivation level, morale, internal efficiency, competency level, internal conflict, organizational culture and so forth. Internal forces for change come from both human resource problems and managerial behavior or decisions (Shaukat, 2004).

A crisis that provides the impetus for revolutionary (radical) change may be internal, as when systems or processes become mis-aligned, or may be external, resulting from changes to the environment[49]. (In this context environmental change refers to changes in technology, markets, resources, societal expectations, suppliers and government regulations[50]). As will be further elaborated in the next section, green change can at times be evolutionary and at others revolutionary. However, what is important to note here is that it can no longer be exclusively

---

[46] *Burke, 2002, Chapter 4, Notes by Sharon O'Sullivan*
[47] *Burke, 2002, Chapter 4, Notes by Sharon O'Sullivan*
[48] Burke, *2002, Chapter 4, Notes by Sharon O'Sullivan*
[49] *Burke, 2002, Chapter 4, Notes by Sharon O'Sullivan*
[50] Miles, 2008. MBA 5237 Change Management Slides, Lecture 3 - Congruence model: Elements of an open system & Suarez & Oliva, 2005.

reactive. Green performance is now a continually evolving target and marginal modifications are no longer enough to meet even basic expectations[51].

Phases of Corporate Greening

Table 2: Phases in the development of the green corporation[52]

Phase	Social Perspective	Environmental Perspective
Stage One: Rejection	Employees and subcontractors exploited. Community concerns are rejected outright.	The environment is regarded as a free good to be exploited.
Stage Two: Non-Responsiveness	Financial and technological factors exclude broader social concerns.	Ecological factors are excluded from decision-making.
Stage Three: Compliance	The emphasis is on compliance with legal requirements in industrial relations and safety.	Ecological issues unlikely to attract strong litigation or strong community action are ignored.
Stage Four: Efficiency	Technical and supervisory training augmented with interpersonal skills training. Community projects and HR value-adding strategies are pursued only when a cost benefit to the company is obvious.	Environmental issues are ignored if they are not seen as generating avoidable costs or increasing inefficiencies. Sales of by-products are encourages.
Stage Five: Strategic Pro-Activity	Intellectual and social capital is used to develop strategic advantage through innovation in products/services.	Proactive environmental strategies such as product and process redesign are seen as a source of competitive advantage.
Stage Six: The Green Corporation	Key goals both inside and outside the firm are the pursuit of equity and human welfare and potential.	The firm works with society towards ecological renewal and positive sustainability policies.

The literature suggests several ways in which green change can be categorized, most of which are surprisingly consistent given the variation in terminology. However, the phased progression presented in
Table 2 is most useful because it describes both the social and environmental requirements of each category, illustrating how they are developed in a related manner along the path to the green corporation[53]. Corporations can move slowly from phase to phase, as in the case of evolutionary change. However significant

[51] Azzone & Noci, 1998

[52] Benn et al, 2006

[53] Benn et al, 2006, pg 156

shifts from one phase to the next, or the skipping of phases, may occur due to triggers such as changes in senior management, stakeholder pressure, changes to legislation or changes to markets[54]. In either case, such change is extremely complex because it involves the creation of new organizational elements, structures, processes and capabilities[55]. Given this complexity, such change must be closely managed.

Corporate Greening Must Include Revolutionary Cultural Change

The cultural change required for corporate greening is heavily weighted in learning, in that in order for companies to perform better environmentally and socially, they must engage in both single and double loop learning. Figure 3, illustrating the green organizational performance curve, has been adapted to show how the phases of corporate greening relate to the change management process of double loop learning.

The compliance phase can be characterized as one of adjustment, as green initiatives tend to be responsive to legislation and are reactive in nature. Processes and practices are modified as needed by the company, leading to a pattern of slow, evolutionary change. While organizations in this phase do tend to have environmental officers, their focus is often narrow and very technical in nature. In this phase, the learning is single loop, which does not lead to the critical examination.[56] While the efficiency phase is characterized by adaptation and anticipation, pro-activity and full transition into a green corporation requires significant innovation.

However, transition into any of these phases generally requires the push of a strong inciting force or crisis. As mentioned earlier, this could take the form of changes in senior management, stakeholder pressure, changes to legislation or changes to markets. By this point, double-loop learning is required so that the incorporation of sustainability values into the organization's core mission and vision can occur. This process of double loop learning not only leads to innovation around technologies, processes, specifications, inputs, and products, but learning and innovation build up the internal capabilities of the organization's employees. I t is this knowledge and the culture which fostered its development which translate into competitive advantage [57]. Structures and systems for reporting, internal and external communications and program evaluation must be developed to reinforce these objectives.[58]

As figure 3 shows, the complexity of the change increases significantly as corporations move past compliance, in that it requires changes to organizational culture[59], defined as "the product of the individual and group values, attitudes, perceptions, competencies and patterns of behaviours"[60]. Cultural change is

---

[54] Benn et al, 2006
[55] Post & Altman, 1994
[56] Post & Altman, 1994
[57] Sharma & Vredenburg, 1998
[58] Post & Altman, 1994
[59] Benn et al, 2006
[60] Lyon, 2000, pg 134

required because the "emergence of [green organizations]...is dependent upon the institutionalization of [new] beliefs and processes into the very fabric of [the] organizations[61], calling for an extreme change in management philosophy, and actions that go beyond technical fixes[62].

Figure 3: The Green Performance Curve

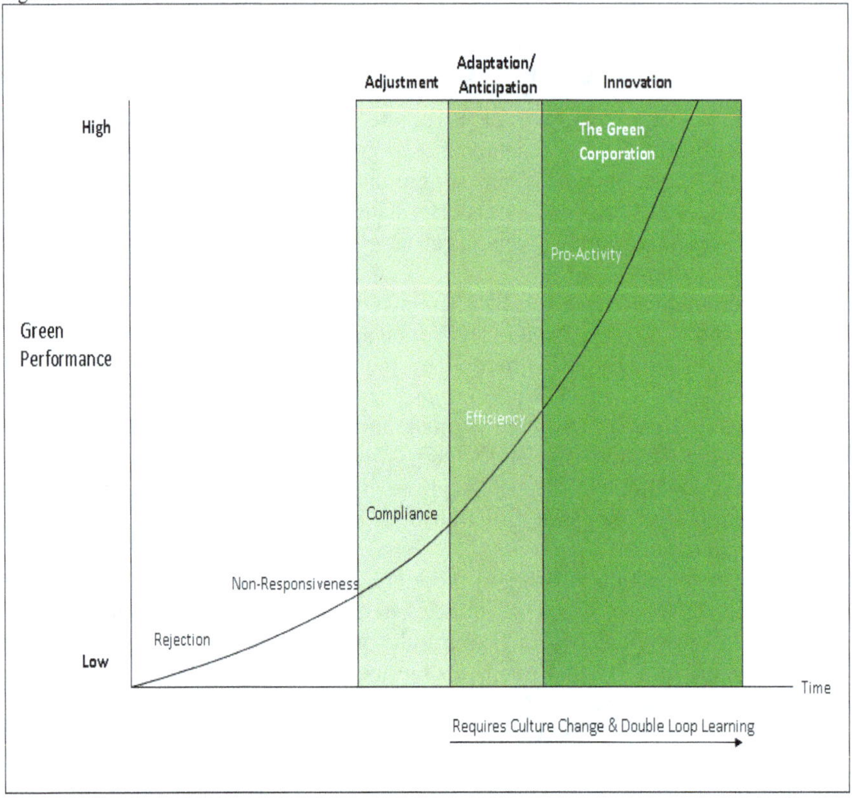

Furthermore, "continued improvement and delivery of commitments depends on buy-in not just from senior management...but from mangers and staff across the organization. This is only possible if there, is a [supportive] culture".[63] The importance of linking the aspects of this green culture to the corporate change strategy cannot be overemphasized. Only those organizations who set the tone at the highest levels and then build supportive and integrated structures and systems throughout, will realize the full benefit of the change initiative.

[61] Harris & Crane, 2002, pg 214; referencing *Purser, 1994, Jennings, and Zandgergen, 1995*

[62] Harris & Crane, 2002, pg 215, referencing *Stead and Stead, 1992, Davis, 1994; Shrivastava, 1995*

[63] Lyon, 2000, *pg133*

Conditions Necessary for "Unfreezing" into Green Change

As has been mentioned, for change to occur, the current organizational mindset must be unfrozen (i.e., deconstructed) and the barriers to change overcome. For this to happen, the forces driving the change must be stronger than those holding it back[64] (refer to Drivers of Corporate Greening

As the famous adage states: "the business of business is business". In the near future at least, this is likely to remain the case. As such, it is unlikely that arguments that do not directly impact a firm's bottom line will yield much more than compliance on the part of corporations. Most organizations have simply not yet advanced beyond the efficiency phase in the green performance curve.

For this reason, the following section will present the drivers for organizational greening from a pure business perspective. Specifically, arguments for how such initiatives can both increase a firm's revenues and cut its costs will be presented.

Figure 4). However, while initially the barriers might be stronger than the drivers, tools and techniques can help reduce their strength. If these facilitators are used appropriately, and the drivers are strong enough, change will occur. Furthermore, the more effectively the facilitators are used, the more rapid will be the change. These facilitators will be identified in the next section.

Drivers of Corporate Greening

As the famous adage states: "the business of business is business". In the near future at least, this is likely to remain the case. As such, it is unlikely that arguments that do not directly impact a firm's bottom line will yield much more than compliance on the part of corporations. Most organizations have simply not yet advanced beyond the efficiency phase in the green performance curve.

For this reason, the following section will present the drivers for organizational greening from a pure business perspective. Specifically, arguments for how such initiatives can both increase a firm's revenues and cut its costs will be presented.

---

[64] O'Sullivan, 2004; reference Lewin's force field model

Figure 4: Change as a function of the strength of its drivers, barriers and facilitators

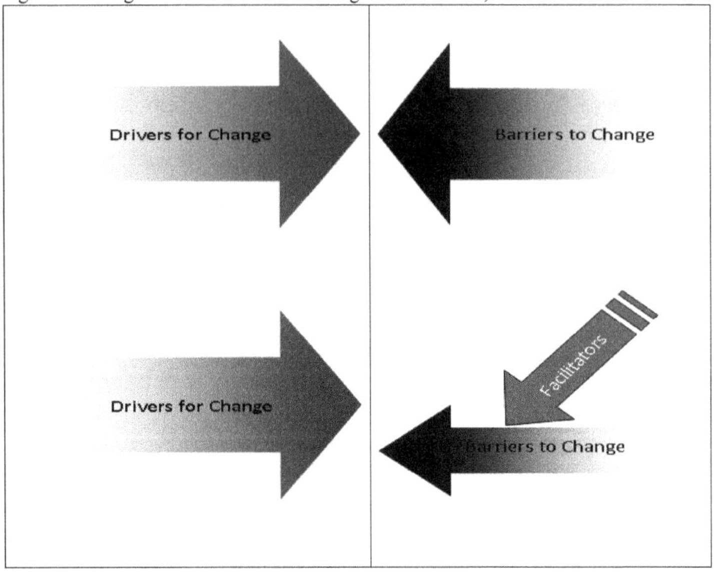

Revenue drivers

Share price growth

The link between good corporate citizenship and stock performance has been difficult to quantify, and this lack of quantification has historically been used by businesses to justify inaction around corporate greening. However, this position is no longer valid as recent studies positively correlate the relationship between corporate greening and financial performance.

Specifically, it is clear that green initiatives have a positive effect on long-term business performance as measured by share price. Moreover, the correlation between poor social and environmental performance and a reduction in share price is extremely strong[65]. The results of three studies on the relationship between green performance and stock price are presented below: A survey conducted by the Economist Intelligence Unit found that "companies with the highest share price growth over the past three years paid more attention to sustainability issues, while those with the worst performance tended to do less" [66]. Furthermore, the survey stated that "companies that rated their [green] efforts most highly…saw an annual profit increase of 16% and share price growth of 45%, whereas those that ranked themselves worst reported growth of 7% and 12% respectively".[67]

---

[65] SustainAbility, 2000

[66] Economist Intelligence Unit, 2008, pg 6

[67] Economist Intelligence Unit, 2008, pg 6

The Conference Board of Canada reviewed the share price of a number of sustainability funds and indices (Domini Social Equity Fund, EcoValue 21, Dow Jones Sustainability Group Index, Storebrand Scudder Environmental Value Fund, Jantzi Social Index, ethical Funds, Sustainable Value (Pension) fund) and found that overall, these instruments matched or over-performed their benchmarks. Additionally, the document reviewed 18 independent reports on sustainability which collectively point towards the fact that good sustainability practices leads towards positive share performance[68]. A meta-analysis of the existing studies that attempt to link corporate social and financial performance (52 studies, representing 38,878 observations – as of 2003) has shown that "corporate social performance is positively correlated with corporate financial performance".[69]

Green products as a revenue source

With regards to increasing revenues, it is often the area of green products that immediately comes to mind. Recently, there have been a number of standout examples including: Ben & Jerry's, Newman's Own, Patagonia, the Body shop, the Scott Bader Commonwealth, Tom's of Maine, Smith & Hawken and Seventh Generation. However, few companies have done as well as General Electric and their line of Eco-imagination products, which added US$12bn to their bottom line in 2006[70].

As will be discussed in further depth subsequently, there is some concern about the consumer's willingness to pay a premium for more environmentally friendly products. However, there is evidence that as a differentiator among equals, green products help capture market share when there is a minimal price difference [71]. Moreover, the population segment exerting pressure through purchasing choices is definitely growing[72]. Also, in the short-term, cause-related marketing, which links products to specific charitable causes [73], has a strong ability to attract customers and increase sales revenues. Finally, customers are more likely to remain committed to companies which strive to improve their green record[74].

Preserving and enhancing corporate reputation

Attracting and retaining customers through branding, reputation, customer service and other activities is a company's key revenue driver. Multiple studies now show that failure to enact efforts towards organizational greening exerts a clear negative effect on customer perception[75]. Specifically, negative information with

---

[68] CBC, 2003
[69] Orlizky et al, 2003
[70] Economist Intelligence Unit, 2008
[71] Economist Intelligence Unit, 2008
[72] Roper & Beard, 2006
[73] SustainAbility, 2000
[74] SustainAbility, 2000
[75] SustainAbility, 2000

regards to a firm's pollution, human rights and integrity record can inflict great damage. One well known example of the impact of such bad publicity is the case of Calgary-based Talisman Energy Inc and their investment in Sudan. Critics argued that Talisman payments to the Sudanese government were being used to fund civil war. As a result, Talisman's market capitalization decreased by 700 million and the Ontario Teachers' Pension Fund's sold all their investments[76]. (This particular example highlights the increasing power, especially in North America, of large institutional investors.)

Conversely, when in the late 1990's MacMillan Bloedel was faced with opposition to its clear cutting practices, they invested heavily in stakeholder consultations and new technologies, with the result that they not only cut costs by ten percent, but actually maintained yields and made the list of the Top Ten most respected companies in the world[77]. Finally, as a caveat to the above, it is extremely important to note that although corporate philanthropic activities are positively correlated to increases in customers and reputation. They do not reflect positively when they are perceived to be self-serving or used as a public-relations tool. Therefore, since to be effective as drivers of brand value and reputation, green activities must be reported, companies need to be very careful to promote concrete activities rather than public relations plugs.[78]

Cost drivers

Achieving operational efficiencies

Operational efficiency can be achieved by minimizing costs or maximizing resource productivity, i.e. generating the same number of units with fewer resources. Examples of such activities include waste reduction, recycling, reuse and waste diversion[79]. 3M and its Pollution Prevention Pays program is certainly one of the most well-known examples of operational efficiencies with regards to green performance. "Since 1975, 3M has initiated 4,700 projects that reduce pollution. From 1990 to 1999, the company reduced air emissions by 95 percent, volatile organic compounds by 85 percent, releases to water by 80 percent, the production of solid waste by 33 percent, and energy consumption by 25 percent"[80]. Since the program's inception in 1975, the global costs savings have neared 1 billion[81].

While investments in such programs have been criticized for costing more than they save, the proper use of investment analysis tools such as Net Present Value and Rate of Return contradict this criticism. Moreover, the results of such

[76] Bansal, 2001
[77] Bansal, 2001
[78] SustainAbility, 2000
[79] Sarkis et al, 2006
[80] Bansal, 2001, pg 49
[81] Kotsmith, n.d.

tools become even more positive when intangible factors such as reputational benefits are taken into consideration[82].

Maximizing human capital

In recent years, the bulk of a firm's assets have shifted from equipment and real estate towards human capital. As a result of this shift, companies are placing great emphasis on the attraction and retention of employees who can add to a firm's knowledge base. [83] Therefore, firms should pay attention to the factors which are linked to employee recruitment and retention. Among these factors are the greening of buildings[84], staff engagement in community initiatives, and corporate investment into the greening of its operation[85]. In fact, such initiatives can result in "lower employee absenteeism, reduced employee turnover, easier employee recruitment, and a generally positive corporate mood[86]".

Maintaining access to capital

Access to capital refers to a company's ability to acquire equity and debt capital. In regards to the former, equity can be accessed either through traditional financial markets, or through the growing socially responsible investing (SRI) markets. The majority of SRIs use an exclusionary process in the determination of the securities that make up a portfolio. Called negative screens, they serve to effectively eliminate certain companies on the basis of the activities in which they participate. Common exclusionary activities include tobacco, gambling, arms, alcohol, and nuclear power.

Conversely, some funds are using factors that serve to include companies in portfolios. Such funds focus on including companies that "support the environmental, economic and social practices that collectively constitute sustainable development[87]". It is understood that poor environmental performance can limit a firm's access to and increase the cost of equity capital in broader markets and restricted access in the SRI market, as a result of screening[88]. Moreover, as corporations are increasingly held legally responsible for environmental and social actions, resulting in financial penalties, corporations that do not attend to their environmental performance may find it increasingly difficult or costly to secure debt financing as well.

Decreasing legal costs associated with risk

In recent years, a company's risk profile has expanded beyond traditional boundaries. As has been indicated previously, poor environmental and social

---

[82] SustainAbility, 2000
[83] SustainAbility, 2000
[84] Roper & Beard, 2006
[85] SustainAbility, 2000
[86] Bansal, 2001, pg 50
[87] CBC, 2003, pg 1
[88] SustainAbility, 2000

performance poses risks for companies in terms of access to capital, financial penalties, and loss of reputation. Green initiatives can also lower legal risk by ensuring the firms are in compliance with statues, decreasing costs associated with fines and penalties, and lowering the cost of remediation and cleanup. Also, companies that are perceived to be enacting green change are more likely to be treated leniently by governments in the advent of an environmental accident[89].

Figure 5: Summary of drivers for corporate greening

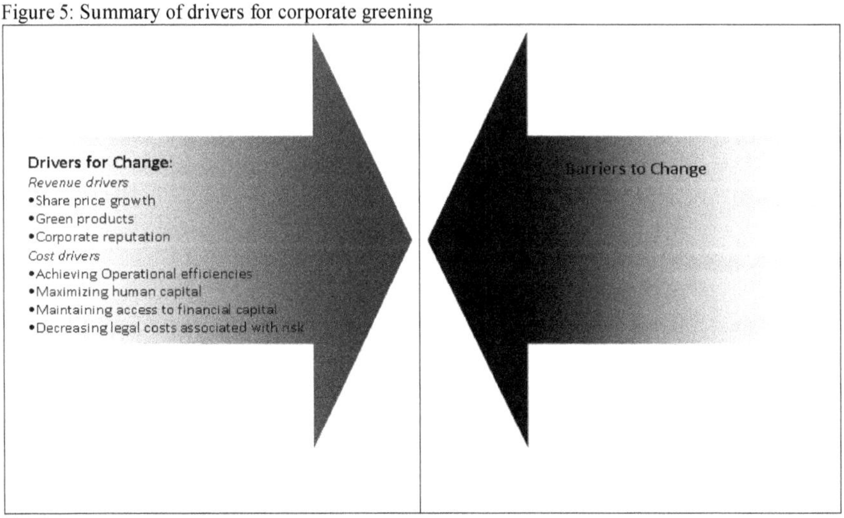

Barriers to Corporate Greening

Organization-wide change often goes against the entrenched ideals held dear by members in the organization, that is, the change may go against how members believe things should be done. Consequently, it usually provokes some kind of resistance, which may vary from hostility to more subtle forms of intransigence (Shaukat, 2004). Therefore much of the organizational change literature discusses needed changes in the culture of the organization, including changes in members' values and beliefs and in the way they enact these values and beliefs (e.g., Gancelli, 1995; Marshall et al., 2003; Ragsdell, 2000; Vallas, 2003; Zandler, 1950). The list of reasons why individuals might resist organizational change has grown since Zandler's initial six were first published in 1950.

For simplicity, barriers to change can be broadly categorized as external and internal. External barriers are those that affect the entire corporate community, or a sub-set as defined by a particular industry. These barriers are less accessible to direct intervention on the part of the change agent, and as such are difficult to challenge. This is not to say that nothing can be done to circumvent those barriers, simply that such barriers pose considerable difficulties. Internal barriers to change are often referred to as sources of resistance and occur when employees fail to support the change, either overtly or covertly. Such resistance can delay the

[89] Bansal, 2001

change process and often adds significantly to its cost[90]. However, these internal barriers are more accessible than external barriers to direct intervention. This division is not without its challenges however, because some barriers, though categorized as external could be challenged at a firm level, but due to internal resistance are not. It is useful to think of change barriers as a spectrum, as shown in Figure 6 , with the ability of the firm to affect the barrier as the scale.

Figure 6: The spectrum of change barriers

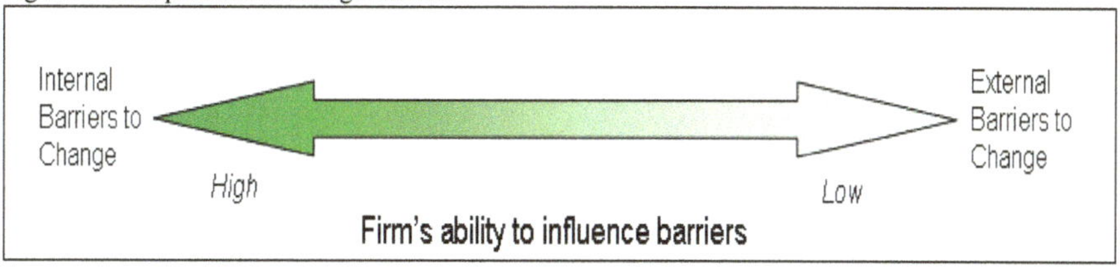

External Barriers

Measuring intangibles

One of the most challenging aspects for companies when considering and evaluating green initiatives is "the determination and allocation of [related] costs, tangible and intangible, across organizational activities and processes", as well as the assessment of the performances of those initiatives once in place[91]. The reason for this challenge is that for a number of the costs that affect green performance, there is no generally accepted market price. In fact, only recently have market-based economic theorists actually included natural resources into their formulas for production output[92]. Table 3 illustrates the range of cost categories, ordered based on their ease of measure and related ability to be integrated into a corporate cost assessment[93].

The difficulty of measuring green costs also translates into measuring their benefits. As a result, the use of traditional financial tools such as Net Present Value, Break-Even Analysis, and Payback Time, which require specific values for costs and benefits in order to make decisions with regards to investments, can prove challenging. This is further compounded by the fact that these tools require the use of a discount rate to calculate the present value of these future benefits and costs. Specifically, "the problem of fixing a discount rate faces difficulties when attempts are made to translate cultural value objectives and ecological metrics to a system of market prices [94]". Due to the difficulty of their measurement, the long term benefits of green initiatives often are outweighed by the short-term costs[95]. As a result, organizations either decide not to make

[90] del Val & Fuentes, 2003
[91] Sarkis et al, 2006, pg 753
[92] Stallworth, 1997
[93] Sarkis et al, 2006
[94] Roper and Beard, 2006, pg 95
[95] Steger & Ionescu-Somers, 2007

investments that will have substantial environmental or social benefits and / or decide to make investments that will have substantial environmental or social negative consequences.

Table 3: Various costs faced by organizations

	Type of cost	Examples
	Internal / private	
Easier to measure	Conventional	Capital equipment
		Materials
		Labour
		Utilities
	Hidden	Upfront
		Regulatory
		Voluntary
		Back-end
	Contingent	Future compliance
		Remediation
		Liability
	Relationship / image	Corporate image
		Supplier relationship
		Stockholder relationship
Harder to measure	*External / public*	
	Societal	Environmental degradation
		Non-legal damages to property and people

It is interesting to note that, as mentioned previously, the relationship between brand reputation and financial performance, one of the most positively correlated aspects of the business case[96], is also one of the most difficult for individual organizations to measure.

Managing the supply change

"The impossibility of having direct control over the whole product life cycle[97]" is cited as one of the largest challenges to implementing holistic green initiatives[98]. Businesses complain that though they are not directly responsible for the actions of the entire supply chain, they are held accountable for it nonetheless. This barrier is a specific challenge to the development of green products, eco-efficiency, and positive stakeholder relations.

96 Steger & Ionescu-Somers, 2007; SustainAbility, 2000
97 Azzone & Noci, 1998, pg 7
98 Economist Intelligence Unit, 2008

Lack of consistency and comprehensiveness of external reporting

Recent years have shown a growth in the number of publications that rank corporations according to their 'greenness'. Examples include Corporate Knights Top 50 Best Corporate Citizens and the Globe and Mail's Social Responsibility Ranking. This has been paralleled by growth in the number of SRIs including the Dow Jones Sustainability Index, the JANTZI Social index, and the FTSE4Good Index. In fact, in 2000 there were over 200 such investment tools[99]. However, business is not satisfied with the way in which they are being measured and judged because the criteria used vary widely. Also, even when similar criteria are used, they are inevitably weighted differently[100]. Firms complain that if they aim their sights at cracking one list or SRI, because of these differences, they will not be included in others.

Also, in the case of the rankings, the 'auditors' are often NGOs or other non-profit organizations. As a result, there is concern that they lack the resources with which to do an effective job. In fact, they often rely on data that is handy and inexpensive and businesses consider this to impact poorly on the process[101]. Finally, data collection methods tend to be surveys and self-reporting. There is a strong tendency for those who are already engaged in green activities to respond, creating biases in the data which make it less reliable[102].

Inadequacies of industry self-regulation

The question of the extent to which green principles should be formalized as regulations, and who should be responsible for their design and enforcement – industry or government[103], has plagued society since the advent of the green movement. "Internationally established regulations [have been] an important mechanism for placing [green] demands on companies[104]". Examples of such regulations include: "The OECD guidelines for multi-national enterprises" and the "UN Centre on Trans-national Corporations codes of conduct for trans-national companies"[105]. The adoption of these regulations was encouraged through the actions of state governments. However, since the late 1980s, due in part to the ramifications of globalization, international organizations have been bypassing states, and dealing directly with multi-national corporations. This has led to the development of new codes of conduct which involve the "voluntary collaboration of trans-national corporations in developing softer forms of self-regulation and self-monitoring"[106]. Such initiatives have been largely corporate driven and include significant leeway in terms of adoption of the principles.

---

99 Orlizky et al, 2003
100 Porter & Kramer, 2006
101 Porter & Kramer, 2006
102 Porter & Kramer, 2006
103 Sahlin-Andersson, 2006
104 Sahlin-Andersson, 2006, pg 597
105 Sahlin-Andersson, 2006
106 Sahlin-Andersson, 2006, pg 597

One example of such a voluntary industry code is that developed by the international mining industry. In response to the increasing environmental demands from investors and the general public, the mining industry formed a body called the International Council on Metal and Mining (ICMM) in 2001. In 2003, the council's board, composed of CEOs of the major mining companies, put forth a set of principles around sustainable development operations[107].

Though seemingly reflective of the intent and spirit of sustainability, these principles were met with significant public outcry because: the council and its board were completely dominated by the mining sector; there was no established mechanism for external stakeholder consultants; the principles were not easily quantifiable and therefore did not lend themselves to measurement, and finally, adherence to the principles was voluntary[108].

The outcry was apparently justified as in 2006, an independent study was published that analyzed the compliance of member companies with regards to this code. The study concluded that "the industry had substantially failed in meeting any of its objectives in terms of adequacy of principles, establishment and implementation of the framework, allocation of sufficient financial and human resources, and independent external monitoring for compliance verification"[109]. If any lesson can be learned from the ICMM example, it is that self-regulation, though good for businesses in terms of flexibility with regards to implementation, is not, under the circumstances outlined above, an effective mechanism for change. As such, more government regulation is certainly needed.

Failure of the government to legislate regulations

Surprisingly, businesses agree with the need for more legislation. Almost half of executives surveyed in an Economist Intelligence Unit initiative "believe that more government regulation is necessary if society wants to change the impact of business in social and environmental arena[110]". Furthermore, 62 percent said "uncertainty over government policy is making it difficult to plan strategies for corporate business sustainability"[111]. Overall, business agrees that if triple bottom line reporting (covered later in this review) is to be effective, more regulations are required[112]. Some businesses are going so far as to lobby the government for change. For example, in the US, an association of blue-chip companies called the "Climate Action Partnership" is lobbying for mandatory carbon emission caps[113]. The irony is that businesses, who normally push for market solutions are asking for regulation, while governments, who are normally proponents of regulations, tend to leave the solutions up to the market.[114]

---

[107] ICMM webpage: http://www.icmm.com/, accessed on June 16, 2008
[108] Prackash & Emelianova, 2006
[109] Prackash & Emelianova, 2006, pg 227
[110] Economist Intelligence Unit, 2008, pg 6
[111] Economist Intelligence Unit, 2008, pg 6
[112] Steger & Ionescu-Somers, 2007, pg 163
[113] Economist Intelligence Unit, 2008
[114] Porter & Karmer, 2006; Economist Intelligence Unit, 2008

Customer failure to pay green premium

Though there is a small and growing segment of the population interested in green issues, the majority of corporate stakeholders, including customers, are not knowledgeable of, nor are they forcing the issue with regards to, greener products[115]. In fact, only 10 – 15 percent of the executives in the Economist survey believe that a majority of their customers would pay a premium for greener goods[116]. The fact that public support of green initiatives is not believed to be backed by economic choices is a tough barrier to overcome.

Internal Barriers

Lack of understanding of what is meant by organizational greening

At the firm level, there is "considerable confusion regarding the definition and differences between various concepts and practices typically found within the green business discourse"[117]. It is argued that this confusion is a result of a lack of consistency in the literature's use of terminology. As mentioned in the introduction, terms such as charitable giving, strategic philanthropy, community involvement or cause-related marketing have been used in so many different ways as to become everything to everyone[118]. Even within organizations that are green oriented, there are differing interpretations as to what this orientation means (e.g. - the level to which stakeholders are managed, consulted or leveraged, as well as how aligned the orientation needs to be with regards to corporate and business strategy[119]). When a firm fails to clearly understand the nature of the goal they are trying to achieve, change will be slow and often unsuccessful.

Failure to prioritize green issues

It is perhaps this lack of knowledge and deep understanding of the issues that has led the topic to be viewed as a fad, or a trend – something that will in due time run its course, as so many others have done before[120]. When green issues are viewed through this lens, they will naturally be considered less important than the economic issues, even though they can clearly be shown to affect a firm's bottom line. Only when such issues get an equal seat at the table, with functions like procurement and finance, will large-scale change in this area be possible[121].

---

[115] Steger & Ionescu-Somers, 2007
[116] Economist Intelligence Unit, 2008
[117] Harris & Crane, 2002, pg 218
[118] Saunders, 2006
[119] Colbert & Kurucz, 2007
[120] Steger & Ionescu-Somers, 2007
[121] Economist Intelligence Unit, 2008

Failure to connect green policies and overall strategy

Within firms who are actively promoting some form of green activity, there often exists a gap between these activities and overall corporate strategy. This gap may be unintentional due to lack of knowledge, or it may be the result of the intentional use of the concept as a public relations ploy[122]. Either case proves problematic because it is only when these policies are directly connected to business strategy that the full benefits of green activities are realized[123]. The companies that do not make this link will be unable to make the changes necessary to move up the environmental performance curve.

Lack of capabilities in the identification and management of stakeholders

Organizations that consider implementing a green strategy must know how to both identify and manage their various stakeholders. However, it is unrealistic to expect companies to respond to all stakeholders and all stakeholder demands equally[124]. In fact it is not strategic for them to do so. As a result, questions such as "who are our stakeholders", "to what extent is it possible to draw the line between stakeholders and non-stakeholders", "what stakeholders do we take into account", "to what stakeholders are we willing to listen", have become challenging ones for organizations to answer[125]. These questions then relate directly to whether, and if so how, stakeholder demands should be formalized, and what the balance between these demands and the main corporate objective of profit earning should be[126]. Not having the internal capabilities to answer these questions strategically is a significant barrier to an organization's advancement along the green performance curve.

Deep rooted values

As noted in the introduction, the myth of unlimited wealth is pervasive in today's culture[127]. Individuals and corporations have long been seen to succeed by placing economic priorities above social and environmental ones. The drive to produce at an ever increasing pace is fundamental to the nature of business[128]. However, society is now realizing that this myth is causing long-term damage to society and the environment. The culture change required for organizational greening challenges some deeply rooted values. It is important to note that it is this challenging of deep rooted values that is considered by change practitioners to be the most powerful barrier to change[129].

---

[122] Porter & Kramer, 2006
[123] Porter & Kramer, 2006
[124] Vos, 2003
[125] Vos, 2003, pg 141
[126] Sahlin-Andersson, 2006
[127] Stead & Stead, 1994
[128] Stead & Stead, 1994
[129] del Val & Fuentes, 2003

Resistance to change and its sources

Change, whether it be green or not, is often a source of stress and anxiety for individuals, and when individuals experience stress or anxiety, they tend to resist the changes they perceive to be causing that anxiety. Therefore, being aware of and managing this resistance can be as important as managing the barriers with special reference to corporate greening. There are several factors that are quite common and prevalent, which help provide a solid basis to understanding the concept. Table 4 depicts the more prevalent factors mentioned in the resistance to change literature. In looking at reactions to change, it is too easy to trivialize potential reactions and cast aside individual doubts, worries and fears (Shaukat, 2004, P 1637). A change agent must understand that different people view proposed change differently, but must recognize that not all opposing behavior especially not that which is accomplished by concrete justification may be classified as resistance.

Table 4: Sources of resistance to change[130]

Category of resistance	Source of resistance
Resistance in the unfreezing phase	
Distorted perception, interpretation barriers and vague strategic priorities	Myopia – "inability to look into the future with clarity".
	Denial – "refusal to accept any information that is not expected or desired".
	Perpetuation of ideas – "tendency to go on with the present thoughts although the situation has changed".
	Implicit assumptions- "which are not discussed due to its implicit character and therefore distort reality".
	Communication barriers- "lead to information distortion or misinterpretations".
	Organizational silence – "limits the information flow with individuals who do not express their thoughts, meaning that decisions are made without all the necessary information".
Low motivation	Direct costs of change.
	Cannibalization costs – "change that brings success to a product but at the same time brings losses to others, so it requires some sort of sacrifice".
	Cross subsidy comforts – "the need for change is compensated through the high rents obtained without change with another different factors, so that there is no real motivation for change".
	Past failures – "leave a pessimistic image for future changes".

130 del Val & Fuentes, 2003, pgs 5 & 6

	Different interests among employees and management.
Lack of a creative response	Fast and complex environmental changes – "do not allow for proper situational analysis".
	Resignation – "tendency to believe that obstacles are inevitable".
	Inadequate strategic vision or lack of clear commitment of top management to changes.
Resistance in the implementation or change phase	
Political and cultural deadlocks	Implementation climate and relation between change values and organizational values.
	Departmental politics – resistance from departments that will suffer / need to sacrifice as a result of the change.
	Incommensurable beliefs – "strong and definitive disagreement among groups about the nature of the problem and its consequent alternative solutions".
	Deep rooted values, emotional loyalty.
	Forgetfulness of the social dimension of change.
Other sources	Leadership inaction.
	Embedded routines.
	Collective action problems – "specially dealing with the difficulty to decide who is going to move first or how to deal with free-riders".
	Capabilities gap.
	Cynicism.

Based on the selected literature (E.g., Dev Val, M. P, & Fuentes,, C. M. (2003; Piderit, 2000;), we can say that resistance has distinct diagnostic qualities that can be utilized as a means for increasing efficiency and productivity. If understood functionally, resistance can serve as a directing force towards collective efforts (Shaukat, 2004). In the context of this paper, our focus was to see the way resistance is being presented in literature irrespective of its positive or negative rationale.

Summary of barriers to green change

As illustrated above, the barriers to green change are varied, and can be broadly categorized as external and internal by their relative ability to be influenced by efforts to reduce their strength. Due to the fact that barriers internal to the organization are more accessible to direct influence, they should be considered a priority in the change management plan. This will help lessen the cost and duration of the change process, while helping the organization gain momentum along the green performance curve. This momentum can then be leveraged to challenge the external environment and its barriers to change.

Figure 7: Summary of barriers to corporate greening

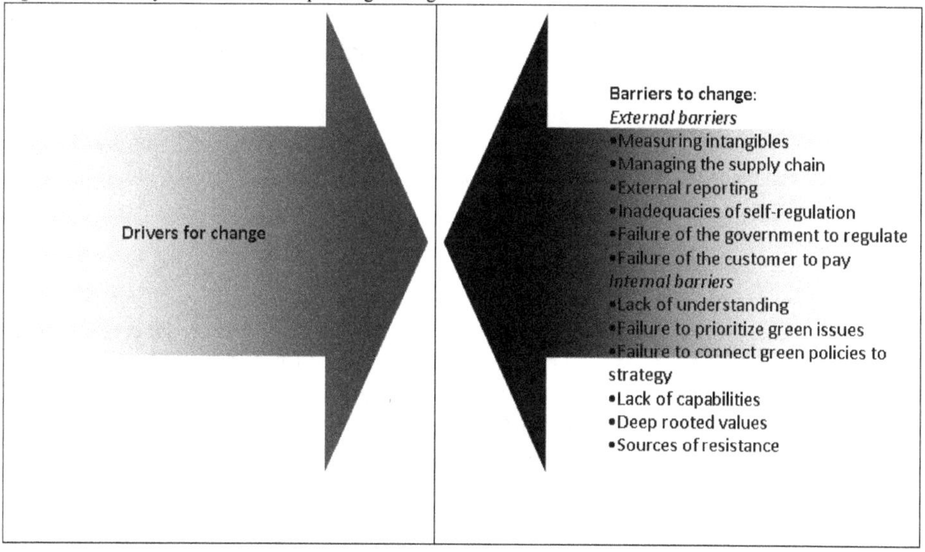

Overcoming the Barriers to Corporate Greening

In order for change to occur, the barriers to change must be overcome by the forces driving it. Therefore, if you can work to remove or weaken the forces of restraint, successful change is much more probable[131]. This is accomplished by leveraging change facilitators, as shown in figure 4. The concept of change facilitators is used broadly in this paper to mean all tools, techniques, or models that have been shown to aid the change process. While by no means comprehensive, the following set of facilitators represents those that are of most relevance to the process of corporate greening. Figure 10 which concludes this section, then illustrates which particular barriers to corporate greening is/are targeted by the facilitators discussed here

Documentation of values

When embarking on a plan to enact green change within the organization, it is important to formalize the desired values and principles within the corporate mission and vision [132]. A standard way in which corporations achieve this formalization is to establish six to ten principles which address issues pertaining to the environment, the economy and society, define these principles in terms of objectives, and then develop performance metrics with which to track organizational progress[133].

---

[131] Schein, n.d.
[132] Post & Altman, 1994
[133] Feltmate, 1997

The process by which these principles, objectives and metrics are established should be heavily weighted in employee engagement. This will set the tone for future involvement, show consistency between words and actions, and aid in the creation of a shared purpose and understanding, all general requirements for organizational change[134]. This formalization is also important because when it does not occur, positions within the company with regards to greening can often be often hostile and unsympathetic, and green initiatives will not receive the required priority, the result of which can be lack of any discernible change135.

Reporting

Reporting extends the documentation of values step further. It refers to the process by which companies select the social and environmental aspects on which to report, how to track performance of those aspects (metrics) and how to publish that performance externally. A spectrum of reporting options exist, with the least effective resembling "green glossies and newsletters" that have little, hard, quantifiable and comparable data[136]. Reports in the middle of the spectrum are often stand-alone reports, disconnected from overall corporate strategy.

At the other end of the spectrum are those companies who engage in Triple Bottom Line Reporting (TBLR). TBLR "captures the essence of sustainability by measuring the impact of an organization's activities on the world"[137]. When positive, the triple bottom line reflects a positive return to shareholders and well as a positive return to its social, human and environmental capital[138]. TBLR uses a tool called Environmental Cost Accounting, discussed below, which aids in the measuring of intangibles. The act of developing a corporate social responsibility report, while in and of itself is not enough to enact green change, can be a catalyst for change towards improved green performance. This is because the result of determining what to include and measure is an assessment of where the organization presently stands on the environmental performance curve (presented in Figure 3) and thus helps to illustrate the goals and objectives needed to move the company forward.[139]

The approach to developing a report generally involves the stages of analysis, discovery and implementation, stages which parallel the general process of change presented in Figure 2. During analysis, the organization conducts a self-assessment to determine their current state of sustainability performance. In the discovery stage, the company decides what information to present and how to present it (relies heavily on stakeholder analysis and benchmarking discussed later in this section). In implementation, the organization solicits feedback on their report and implements changes[140]. An excellent guide for creating a comprehensive report is that provided by the Global Reporting Initiative (GRI).

---

[134] Post & Altman, 1994, Branch, 2003
[135] Harris & Crane, 2002
[136] Herremans & Herschovis, 2006, pg 20
[137] Savitz & Weber, 2006, pg xiii
[138] Savitz & Weber, 2006
[139] *Adams & McNicholas, 2007, pg 386*
[140] *Herremans & Herschovis, 2006*

These guidelines "offer the most sophisticated and up-to-date approach to sustainability reporting, and thus provide a useful model for organizations that want to improve the quality of their environmental and sustainability reporting"[141].

The guide also suggests format and content for the report, prompting the organization to think about and formalize a number of the items already discussed in this report, including: vision, strategy, governance structure and management systems, and performance indicators[142]. When done correctly, "reporting helps push change inside the company" and can become an internal, self-driving mechanism"[143]. Once a company makes a decision to set and publish targets, it will strive to meet them. Furthermore, this publication of performance provides valuable and valid information to external reporting sources.

Environmental management systems (EMS)

Environmental management is "a series of actions taken by management [that] requires economic activities to be analyzed for their environmental impacts"[144]. When systemized, "EMS provides a structure that allows management the ability to better control the company's environmental impacts [145] and includes commitment and policy, planning, implementation, measurement and evaluation, and review and improvement"[146]. As illustrated in figure 8, it is a cyclical process in which strategy and policies are formulated, management processes are improved, environmental processes are improved, and stakeholders are taken into greater account. The input received from stakeholders then feeds back into organizational strategy and policies[147].

It is interesting to note that the development of EMS may parallel that of a system for Total Quality Management (TQM), in that the same factors or characteristics that bring success in the latter case, will also aid in implementing the former. As such, organizations who have implemented a TQM are uniquely well suited to integration of an environmental management system[148].

---

[141] Herremans & Herschovis, 2006, pg 22
[142] *Herremans & Herschovis, 2006*
[143] Herremans & Herschovis, 2006, pg 23
[144] *Holland, 2003, pg 225*
[145] Holland, 2003
[146] Daily & Huang, 2001, pg 1540; referencing Barnes, 1996
[147] Holland, 2003, pg 225
[148] Daily, pg 1540

Figure 8: The EMS cycle[149]

There are numerous EMS tools and guidelines from which to choose. Some examples include the European Eco-Management and Audit Scheme, ISO 14000, and EPA's environmental accounting project[150]. The most common of these tools is certainly the ISO 14000, a set of "guidelines [that] delineate the international standards for systems of environmental management [151]. EMS provides a framework from which to measure intangibles, and, due to its prevalence, helps provide consistency for external reporting mechanisms. The implementation of such a system forces an organization to gain a better understanding of green issues and encourages their prioritization, communication, and connection to strategy.

Environmental Cost Accounting

Connected to both reporting and environmental management systems is a tool called environmental cost accounting (ECA). Dealing specifically with the establishment of appropriate measurement indicators and criteria to ensure that established environmental principles are acted upon[152], [ECA] tries to place an economic value on intangibles, which aids in the prioritization of green issues. Being able to assign economic value also helps to lessen the challenge of deep rooted values. This tool falls into the skills and expertise of management accounts and represents a specific area on which training should be focused in order to achieve maximum benefit.

Stakeholder identification, analysis and engagement

As mentioned previously, "a stakeholder in an organization is any group or individual who can affect or is affected by the achievement of the organization's objective" [153]. The concept of stakeholder and stakeholder consultations is

[149] Holland, 2003
[150] Holland, 2003
[151] Daily & Huang, 2001, pg 1540; referencing Begley, 1996
[152] Feltmate, 1997
[153] Vos, 2003, pg 143; referencing Freeman, 1984

growing with the concept of CSR as "to a certain extent, management of CSR has become stakeholder management"[154].

In order to answer the questions inherent to the engagement of stakeholders, an organization must identify these individuals and groups. A simple way of doing so is to make a list of all the actors around an organization[155]. Organizations should aim to include employees from a variety of departments in the stakeholder consultation process. Not only does this help clarify green issues throughout the organization, but interacting with stakeholders helps employees understand the other side of green issues, working to lessen the impact of deep rooted values.

However, this does not help organizations determine which of the many competing stakeholder interests should take priority. One tool to help answer this question is the division, by management, of stakeholders into qualitative classes, as shown in

Figure 9. Once categorized, managers should give high priority to stakeholders with what are believed to be legitimate and urgent claims, and highest priority to those that also have the power to affect the organization and its activities[156]. Though basic, this tool helps organizations visualize their stakeholders and order them in terms of priority of action. In

Figure 9, stakeholder priority is as follows: 7; 6, 5, 4; 3, 2, 1; 8.

Figure 9: Qualitative classes of stakeholders

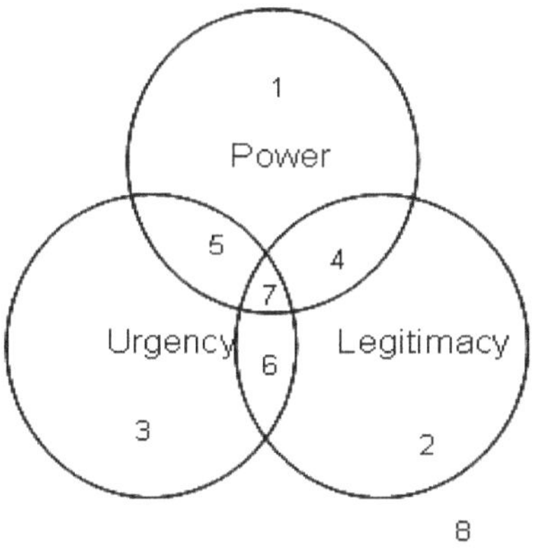

1	Dormant Stakeholder
2	Discretionary Stakeholder
3	Demanding Stakeholder
4	Dominant Stakeholder
5	Dangerous Stakeholder
6	Dependent Stakeholder
7	Definitive Stakeholder
8	Non-Stakeholders

[154] Vos, 2003, pg 141
[155] Vos, 2003, pg 143
[156] Vos, 2003

Benchmarking

Benchmarking is a process by which a company "compares current …processes to those used by leading organizations either within or outside the industry"[157]. The tool helps with the development of best practices with regards to report structures, measures and communication methodologies as well as helping to determine stakeholder expectations[158]. To successfully use the benchmarking tool, organizations must develop the capabilities to develop relationships with other (sometimes competing) organizations and use similar metrics to ease comparison.

Top management support

One of the most referenced facilitators in the literature related to green change (and indeed, to organizational change in general), is the involvement and commitment of top management. "Top management support can affect…success…by: promoting employee empowerment to affect changes, affecting organizational culture to support changes, instituting systems to promote desired behaviours such as rewards or incentive programs, provide training, and increase communication throughout the organization" [159]. Furthermore, top management plays an integral role in the formalization of sustainability principles, the balancing of green issues with economic issues, as well as facilitating cross-departmental sharing, learning and programmes[160].

One of the most crucial roles for management with regards to green change is to understand its own organization culture in order to effectively implement changes. As mentioned in the previous section, one of the main reasons that change efforts fail is that management fails to understand, or even ignores, the strength of assumptions and values that are integral to their employees' daily work routines[161]. In fact, without top management support, green change is likely to be limited to small, isolated initiatives within the organization.

Employee empowerment and engagement

Moving beyond compliance on the sustainability spectrum involves culture change, and such change cannot be enforced, only encouraged and allowed to evolve over time[162]. As such, though structural changes will likely be necessary to provide impetus to the change, only the enthusiasm and commitment of the workforce at all levels will allow for new ideas, solutions, and corrective action to be generated[163]. It is known that "the introduction of a new program will yield optimal results when employees are treated as major stakeholders in an

---

[157] Branch, 2003, pg 7
[158] Branch, 2003
[159] Daily & Huang, 2001, pg 1543; referencing Gupta and Sharma, 1996, Leitch et al., 1995
[160] *Azzone & Noci, 1998*
[161] Daily & Huang, 2001
[162] Benn et al, 2006
[163] Benn et al, 2006

organization[164]". After all, no matter how well thought out the corporate strategy and vision, it is the employees who operationalize these concepts.

The most effective way to achieve this motivation and enthusiasm is to both engage and empower employees. "Engaging employees involves the use of participative management in order to benefit from the full scope of their ideas and capacity…while empowering employees provides them with the ability and the responsibility to take active steps to identify problems and to deal effectively with them"[165]. Such processes will require the organization to become more horizontal in nature, as departments interact and authority and decision-making authority becoming decentralized[166].

While of course product design, manufacturing and other such departments are of vital importance in the empowerment and engagement process, human resources must not be overlooked. The involvement of this functional department in the process of green change is crucial in the management of cultural change through the development of new rewards and recognition programs, awareness raising courses, and internal communications[167].

Finally, of vital importance to empowerment and engagement is communication. It is essential that there be a constant flow of information both horizontally and vertically. It is also important that this flow be bi-directional (i.e. not only top-down). This is important so that all employees are aware of and understand environmental programs, initiatives and goals, and that they understand their role in each[168].

Training as was indicated in the previous section, the role of learning is of paramount importance in the process of cultural and green change, as is fostering an environment that reflects positively on inquiry, experimentation and divergent thinking [169]. In order to move the organization along the environmental performance curve, learning and training will be required in all departments, and budgets should be reflective of this requirement. While each organization and change agent are responsible for developing their own list of knowledge gaps and training requirements, some examples include: ecosystem health, pollutants and pollution preventions, stakeholder engagement and analysis, consensus-building, facilitation and new rewards programs.

Training should involve both new technical skills and softer skills such as team-building, benchmarking, brainstorming and consensus building[170]. Again, the human resources department should not be overlooked, and specific training with regards to building the new rewards system should be provided. The learning process should also be encouraged by providing opportunities for employees to interact with each other and with stakeholders in collective settings, the solicitation of ideas and questions, opportunities for feedback and for

---

[164] Daily & Huang, 2001, pg 1545, referencing Mohrman et al., 1996

[165] Daily & Huang, 2001, pg 1545; referencing Leitch et al. 1995, pg 72

[166] Daily & Huang, 2001

[167] Daily & Huang, 2001

[168] Daily & Huang, 2001

[169] Branch, 2003

[170] Daily & Huang, 2001

experimentation[171]. *Rewards and recognition* are crucial as well. If organizational rewards and recognition programs are not altered to reflect the new, shared, organizational vision and mission, then mixed messages are sent to employees, creating little incentive to change. Specifically, organizations that value environmental performance need to create a performance evaluation system that reflects this commitment[172]. Examples of components of such a system include: awards, public recognition (both internal and external), profit-sharing, raises, and benefits[173].

Teamwork

The individual contributions encouraged by employee empowerment and engagement are essential, but not sufficient. The contributions made by groups can be the difference between succeeding and failing at organizational greening[174]. One way to actualize this concept is through the use of green teams. Green teams are a collection of employees, usually from different departments, who are used to "generate ideas, enhance learning experiences, explore issues, identify conflict and focus action to enhance understanding about why, what, how, where and when to pursue the best practicable [green] options"[175]. For such teams to succeed there needs to be heavy emphasis on both informal and formal training, communication and the measuring of success.

Development of cooperative relationship with stakeholders

One of the characteristics of green organizations previously discussed was the ability of organizations to foster new relationships with external stakeholders and organizations. Specifically, when organizations work to build co-operative relationships with members of their supply chain, work with public institutions to have campaigns that affect customers' willingness to buy, and work with governments and industry associations to encourage effective regulatory processes, the organization no longer plays victim to the barriers to change on which it has limited control[176].

The facilitation tools shown in Figure 10 below are much more effective at reducing the strength of internal barriers, rather than external ones. However, as long as the strength of internal barriers is reduced and the organization becomes engaged in the process, the external barriers become easier to surmount.

---

[171] Fenwick, 2007
[172] Daily & Huang, 2001
[173] Daily & Huang, 2001; Post & Altman, 1994
[174] Daily & Huang, 2001
[175] Beard & Rees, 2000, pg1
[176] *Azzone & Noci, 1998*

Figure 10: Barriers to corporate greening and related facilitators

	External barriers					Internal Barriers						
FACILITATORS / **BARRIERS**	Measuring intangibles	Managing the supply chain	External reporting	Inadequacies of self-regulation	Failure of government to legislate	Failure of the customer to pay	Lack of understanding	Failure to prioritize green issues	Failure to connect green policies to strategy	Lack of capabilities	Deep rooted values	Other sources
Documentation							✓	✓	✓			✓
Reporting	✓		✓				✓	✓	✓			✓
EMS	✓		✓				✓	✓	✓			✓
ECA	✓		✓				✓	✓	✓	✓	✓	✓
Stakeholder analysis							✓				✓	✓
Benchmarking							✓			✓	✓	✓
Management support							✓	✓	✓	✓	✓	✓
Employee Engagement							✓	✓	✓	✓	✓	✓
Teamwork							✓	✓	✓	✓	✓	✓
Rewards & Recognition								✓	✓	✓	✓	✓
Training								✓	✓	✓	✓	✓
Cooperative relationships		✓	✓	✓	✓	✓	✓			✓	✓	✓

The Steps of Corporate Greening

While this information presented above is invaluable to understanding the process by which a corporation can become greener, the missing piece is explicit steps that prioritize the use of facilitators in order to make change happen. To respond to this, a well-respected set of steps[177] for organizational change will be presented, and will be adapted to the context of corporate greening. Figure 11 summarizes the steps for prioritization of activities in the organizational change process and links them to the general process of change outlined previously.

Figure 11: The steps of corporate change[178]

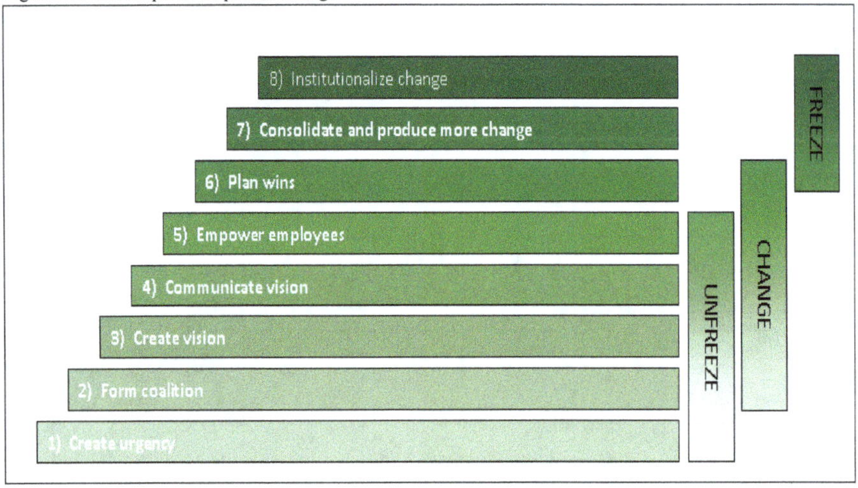

It is important to note that the "[successful] change process goes through a series of phases that, in total, usually require a considerable length of time. Skipping steps creates the illusion of speed and never produces a satisfying result"[179]. In fact, the more steps that are skipped, the more likely the change effort is going to fail[180]. The implications for the use of corporate greening facilitators within each organizational change step will be addressed further below.

Step 1: Establish a sense of urgency. The first step in the change process involves establishing where the organization stands with respect to the market and competitive realities, stakeholder issues using the stakeholder analysis facilitator, as well as identifying its current state of green performance using the benchmarking facilitator (refer to Figure 3). In this step, it is crucial to identify what failure to move along the green performance curve will mean to the organization with regards to the drivers of change, including lost revenue, cost savings and competitive advantage. Questions and answers to questions like "are there powerful stakeholders exerting influence on the organization?" and "Are

[177] Kotter, 2007
[178] Kotter, 2007
[179] Kotter, 2007, pg 59
[180] Kotter, 2007, pg 59

there impending legislative changes that will affect the industry?" should be asked and answered.

It is important to establish the sense that not changing organizational behaviour with regards to green performance might be more dangerous than making the change. As rule of thumb, the urgency is deemed to be high enough when about 75 percent of management has been convinced that business as usual is no longer acceptable[181]. Furthermore, failure to begin the facilitating process of employee engagement, or moving too quickly from this stage, can be detrimental to the process as the organization will not be convinced of the change and will as a result exert resistance to the effort.

Step 2: Form powerful guiding coalition (green team). Once the urgency has been established, a coalition should be formed to establish cooperative relationship to guide the change effort. This is important whether or not the organization is working with an external consultant to manage the process. The size of the group will vary depending on the size of the organization, but could be anywhere between five to 50 people. Though it is important that those involved in the coalition have enough power to lead the effort, and as such, the head of the organization should be involved, there also needs to be a good number of members outside the senior ranks. This team should also be cross-functional in nature, meaning that representatives from all product and functional divisions should participate.

Though important throughout the process, communication and the facilitation of management support, and teamwork are crucial in this phase, because the coalition, to be effective, will likely have to work outside the normal bounds of hierarchy and established protocol. If this breach is not seen to be supported, resistance will be high. The coalition should work to identify the tools and frameworks available to gather information and facilitate green change including use of facilitation tools such as GRI, ISO 140000, environmental management systems (EMS), cost accounting techniques (e.g., ECA), and benchmarking. Looking for and establishing cooperative relationships should begin in this stage and continue indefinitely. Also, a more in-depth stakeholder analysis should be conducted, as it will feed directly into the vision to be created in Step 3.

Finally, using the information gathered from these tools and frameworks, the green team should identify areas in which they require knowledge and seek out or organize the facilitation process of training in those areas. Cooperative relationships can play a significant role here as there are growing numbers of government programs providing funding and assistance, as well as NGOs willing to work with organizations in the process of corporate greening[182]. Learning and training should be continuous throughout the change process.

Step 3: Create a vision. Once the team is in place and some preliminary research done, it is time to create a vision that is "easy to communicate and appeals to

---

[181] Kotter, 2007

[182] Providing a list of such governmental programs or NGOs is beyond the scope of this paper, but is the next step in this change agent's research.

customers, stockholders, and employees"[183]. This vision will serve to clarify the direction to be taken by the organization and provides the lens through which plans should be viewed and assessed. Of integral importance is that this vision be connected to corporate strategy. Furthermore, short, medium and long-term objectives should be established.

Strategies to achieve the vision are also developed in this stage and have this represent the more expended use of the EMS cycle facilitators. However, the strategies need to be flexible enough to allow for contributions of those outside the guiding coalition. Examples of engagement might include town halls, department meetings, assigning members of the coalition with the responsibility for engaging other employees.

Step 4: Communicate the vision. Once the vision has been established, every possible avenue and opportunity to document and communicate the vision to employees, customers and stockholders should be used. Possible avenues for communication include (but are not limited to) conversations, performance appraisals, meetings, newsletters, webpage, emails, etc. It is integral that the vision be formally documented in as many places as possible and that the vision for change be able to be communicated to someone outside the coalition in less than five minutes. If this is not the case, the vision is not succinct or well-formed enough to be digestible. It is at this stage that the organization should begin the process of developing the facilitating process of a reporting mechanism to widen the scope of their external communications and provide an internal mechanism for formalizing short-term objectives.

Also, it is very important that the guiding coalition teach the desired behaviours by example. Bosses and members of the coalition who do not 'walk the talk' are large and often prohibitive barriers to change. Organizations tend to overestimate how well the vision has been communicated, often by a factor of about ten[184]. This must be kept in mind, because if the organization's stakeholders are not aligned with the vision, change will be slowed and will be more costly.

Step 5: Empower others to act on the vision. Employees need to be empowered to develop strategies to achieve the new vision, which may mean getting rid of systems and structures that undermine the vision or developing new ones that support it. It is during this empowerment phase that removing barriers to change becomes the most crucial. Therefore, the facilitating process of training and educational workshops should be provided and the rewards and recognition program altered to encourage behaviors in support of the new vision. Job categories might even need to be expanded or altered. Furthermore, employees should seize the opportunity to engage with stakeholders as much as possible, in order to benefit from ideas and to better understand and address stakeholder concerns.

Step 6: Plan for and create short-term wins. In order to maintain positive momentum with regards to the change, planning for and creating short-term opportunities for celebration is crucial. During step 3, creating a vision, short,

[183] Kotter, 2007, pg 63
[184] Kotter, 2007

medium and longer term goals should have been established, and when reviewed, progress should be celebrated. Following through on the rewards and recognition programs developed in support of the new vision is integral in this phase. Employees who contribute to the vision should be publicly (announcements, rewards, promotions) and privately (monetary, thank you by head of organization) rewarded. Failure to create short-term goals to meet and celebrate will cause the change process to lose momentum.

Step 7: Consolidate improvements and produce more change. The credibility gained through successful completion of the previous steps and through the use of short-term wins, will allow additional changes to systems, structures, and policies that have not been completely aligned with the new vision. After each short-term win, new goals and objectives should be established to continue the momentum. Furthermore, continued focus should be placed on the human resources, in the training, hiring, firing and promotion of individuals with skill sets and behavioural characteristics that support the vision.

Step 8: Institutionalize new approaches. This step occurs when the culture in support of the green vision is truly changed. There is no real end-point in the green performance spectrum, it is one of continual improvement and renewal. Change sticks when it becomes "the way we do things around here".[185]
For the change to become institutionalized, the links must be clearly drawn for stakeholders between the changes made and the improved performance. Too often management assumes that these links are clear. Furthermore, management must truly personify the new approach and methods. It is interesting to note that as is shown in figure 12, the institutionalizing (or freezing) of green change also involves the institutionalizing of the facilitators that serve to reduce the barriers to change, as they will have become integral components of green corporate culture.

Conclusion

Undoubtedly, corporate greening is a relevant topic for the organizational change literature and academic scholars should take it seriously to help organizations achieve the advantages of transformation. Though companies are realizing that their actions have implications that can affect their long-term survival, and that social pressure with regards to environmental and social performance is not likely to wane, they are struggling with how to operationalize these concepts in a meaningful way, while balancing expected return to shareholders[186].

---

[185] Kotter, 2007, pg 67
[186] Sarkis et al, 2006; referencing Day and Arnold, 1998

Figure 12: Use of facilitators in the steps to corporate greening

		Step 1	Step 2	Step 3	Step 4	Step 5	Step 6	Step 7	Step 8
Facilitators	**Steps to Greening ⇒**	**Create urgency**	**Form coalition**	**Create vision**	**Communication vision**	**Empower employees**	**Plan wins**	**Consolidate and produce more change**	**Institutionalize change**
Documentation		×	×		×	×	×	×	×
Reporting					×	×	×	×	×
EMS			×	×	×	×	×	×	×
ECA			×	×	×	×	×	×	×
Stakeholder Analysis		×	×			×			×
Benchmarking		×						×	×
Management Support			×	×	×	×	×	×	×
Employee Engagement		×	×	×	×	×	×	×	×
Teamwork			×	×	×	×	×	×	×
Rewards and Recognition						×	×	×	×
Training			×			×	×	×	×
Cooperative Relationships			×		×	×	×	×	×

Change management, the goal of which is to "create an organization whose structure, processes, people and culture, are tailored appropriately for its current mission"[187] is a valuable lens through which to view this operalization. An understanding of the literature in this area can help managers, and other agents of change, deal effectively with green change by understanding its nature, the process by which it occurs, and the lessons learned by others about implementing changes and "managing the behavioural, motivational, and performance dynamics that arise during the change process"[188]. Green change can occur both slowly and radically. However, in either case, it is characterized at some level by the unfreezing of the current organizational mindset, overcoming barriers to change, and 're'-freezing the new model. Companies can characterize their current green performance and identify direction, goals and objectives through the use of the green performance curve presented in Figure 3, the stages of which include rejection, non-responsiveness, compliance, efficiency, proactivity and the green corporation.

Tackling social and environmental issues requires the institutionalization of a new culture[189] whose key values, shown in Table 1, include balancing and reporting of economic, social and environmental priorities[190], the exchange of a short-term perspective with an intergenerational time-frame[191], the critical analysis of values and assumptions, and the cultivation of double-loop learning. It is this culture of learning and innovation which, when connected to corporate strategy, fosters the development of capabilities and resulting competitive advantage[192]. However, this cultural change will only occur if the drivers towards change are stronger than the forces impeding it. The drivers to green change are both revenue and cost driven, while its barriers can be internal or external.

There are numerous tools and techniques that can be used to facilitate the reduction in strength of these barriers, some of the most important of which include the commitment of top management, training, and employee empowerment. The development of a green reporting mechanism is also essential as it encourages the company to adopt key performance indicators and strive to meet published goals.

In conclusion, the authors would like to acknowledge that all studies have their limitations and this one is not an exception. It only investigates corporate greening through a limited number of research studies and the interpretation of text was by and large subjective. With regards to research design, the proposition of this analysis is that further research into organizational change needs to be empirical more than abstract and theoretical. It is expected that this area of research is ready for a shift to theory-based empirical investigations that test models and theories of organizational change with more sophisticated research designs and measurement strategies.

---

[187] Branch, 2003, pg 2
[188] Branch, 2003, pg 2
[189] Post & Altman, 1994
[190] *Azzone & Noci, 1998; Bansal, 2001*
[191] Harris & Crane, 2002; referencing W*elford, 1995*
[192] Sharma & Vredenburg, 1998

Implications for Further Research and Practice

This review revealed a number of key areas in which both further research and practical actions are required. Specifically, work needs to be done to reduce the strength of external barriers that prevent or slow the process of green change within organizations. First, there needs to be an integration of the approach by which companies manage total costs and benefits. There is a lack of consistency and competencies in this arena of corporate greening, and as such, valuable investment opportunities are being missed[193]. Second, there is a need for more cooperative relationships between government, corporations and civil society (including NGOs) in order to protect the environment. Collective action must be taken to educate consumers and encourage them to grow the market for green products by offering a price premium. Third, there is a need to educate business about institutions (NGOs, governmental, private, etc) available to serve as financial or informational resources for corporate greening in the local context. Fifth, additional research is required to better understand how industrial alliances and technology sharing arrangements (for example the Global Environmental Management Initiative[194]) can be leveraged to improve green performance[195]. Finally, governments need to raise the bar for green performance through increased regulations. However, in order to encourage innovation and the development of competitive advantage around green performance, governments should allow companies to determine how to meet these regulations[196].

It is this generation that faces the biggest challenges with regards to the environment, demography, poverty and global politics[197], and it is this generation that has the science, the political institutions, the willpower and the ability to change the direction in which these challenges are taking us. The demonization of business is not the answer. Society needs business. No government has yet to create a social program which can compete with the positive impacts of business in terms of "creating the jobs, health and innovation that improves standards of living and social conditions[198]". However, we can no longer afford to allow business to operate in a vacuum in which it is not responsible for its social and environmental by-products. Government, civil society and business must work together to lower the real and perceived barriers to change to ensure the sustainable development of our planet, economically, socially and environmentally.

References

Adams, C., McNicholas, P. (2007) Making a difference: Sustainability reporting, accountability and organisational change. *Accounting, Auditing &*

[193] Sarkis et al, 2006
[194] http://www.gemi.org/AboutGEMI.aspx
[195] Post & Altman, 1994
[196] Sharma & Vredenburg, 1998
[197] Sachs, 2008
[198] Porter & Kramer, 2006

Accountability Journal, 20(3), 382-402. Retrieved June 27, 2008, from ABI/INFORM Global database.

Anderson, S, Cavanagh, J. (2000) The world's 100 largest economic entities. Accessed at: http://www.corporations.org/system/top100.html, on August 6, 2008

Azzone, G., Noci, G. (1998) Seeing ecology and "green" innovations as a source of change. *Journal of Organizational Change Management*, 11(2), 94-111. Retrieved June 27, 2008, from ABI/INFORM Global database. (Document ID: 117542684).

Bansal, P. (2001) Sustainable development. *Ivey Business Journal*, 66(2), 47-52. Retrieved March 3, 2008, from ABI/INFORM Global database. (Document ID: 93931882)

Beard, C., Rees, S. (2000) Green teams and the management of environmental change in a UK County Council. *Environmental Management and Health*, 11(1), 27. Retrieved June 27, 2008, from ABI/INFORM Global database. (Document ID: 115729373).

Benn, S., Dunphy, D., Griffiths, A. (2006) Enabling change for corporate sustainability: an integrated perspective. *Australasian Journal of Environmental Management*, 13(3), 156-165. Retrieved July 5, 2008, from ABI/INFORM Global database.

Blumenthal, B., & Haspeslagh, P. "Towards a definition of corporate transformation". *Sloan Management Review,* 35(3), 1994: 101-106.

Branch, K. (2003) Chapter 4: Change Management. Accessed at http://www.au.af.mil/au/awc/awcgate/doe/benchmark/ch04.pdf on August 13, 2008

Burke, W. (2002) Organization Change: Theory and Practice. Thousand Oaks, CA: Sage Publications, Foundations for Organizational Science.

Colbert. B, Kurucz, E. (2007) Three Conceptions of Triple Bottom Line Business Sustainability and the Role for HRM. *Human Resource Planning*, 30(1), 21-29. Retrieved June 15, 2008, from ABI/INFORM Global database. (Document ID: 1261968171).

Daily, B., Huang, S. (2001) Achieving sustainability through attention to human resource factors in environmental management. International Journal of Operations & Production Management, 21(12), 1539-1552. Retrieved June 27, 2008, from ABI/IN

Del Val, MP., Fuentes, CM. (2003) Resistance to change: A literature review and empirical study. *Management Decision*, 41(1/2), 148-155. Retrieved July 15, 2008, from ABI/INFORM Global database. (Document ID: 328781791).

Economist Intelligence Unit (2008). Doing good - Business and the sustainability challenge. Accessed at http://www.atkearney.com/shared_res/pdf/SustainabilityWEBATKearney.pdf on May 15, 2008.

Feltmate, B. (1997) Making sustainable development a corporate reality. *CMA*, 71(2), 9-10+. Retrieved July 5, 2008, from ABI/INFORM Global database. (Document ID: 11320124).

Ferdig, M. (2007) Sustainability Leadership: Co-creating a Sustainable Future. *Journal of Change Management,* 7(1), 25. Retrieved July 5, 2008, from ABI/INFORM Global database. (Document ID: 1261872101).

Francesco, M. F., & Gold, B. A. "International organizational behavior: Text, Readings, Cases, and Skills". New Jersey: Prentice Hall, 1998.

Goldstein, J. "A Far-from-Equilibrium systems approach to resistance to change". *Organizational Dynamics,* 17(2), 1988: 16-26.

Grancelli, B. "Organizational Change: Towards a new East-West comparison". *Organization Studies,* 16(1), 1995: 1-25.

Harris, L., Crane, A. (2002) The greening of organizational culture: Management views on the depth, degree and diffusion of change. *Journal of Organizational Change Management,* 15(3), 214-234. Retrieved July 5, 2008, from ABI/INFORM Global data

Herremans, I., Herschovis, S. (2006) Sustainability Reporting: Creating an Internal Self-Driving Mechanism. *Environmental Quality Management,* 15(3), 19-29. Retrieved July 5, 2008, from ABI/INFORM Global database. (Document ID: 1012330961)

Holland, L. (2003) Can the principle of the ecological footprint be applied to measure the environmental sustainability of business? *Corporate Social - Responsibility and Environmental Management,* 10(4), 224-233. Retrieved July 5, 2008, from ABI/INFORM Global database.

Jager, P. D. "Resistance to Change: A new view of an old problem". *The Futurist,* 35(3), 2001: 24-27.

Johnson-Carmer, M. E., Cross, R. L., & Yan, A. "Sources of fidelity in purposive organizational change: lessons from a re-engineering case". *Journal of Management Studies,* 40(7), 2003: 1837-1870.

Johnson, D., Macy, G. (2001) Using environmental paradigms to understand and change an organization's response to stakeholders. *Journal of Organizational Change Management,* 14(4), 314-335. Retrieved July 5, 2008, from ABI/INFORM Global database

Kotsmigh. (n.d.) The Next Generation of Pollution Prevention Pays (3P) at 3M. Accessed at http://74.125.45.104/search?q=cache:wL5baZro8IJ:www.p2.org/summit 2004/documents/ Presentations/Kotsmith%2520James.ppt+3m+polluon +pays+savings&hl=en&ct=clnk&cd=1&gl=ca, on August 6, 2008

Kotter, J., Cohen, D. (2002). Creative ways to empower action to change the organization:Cases in point. *Journal of Organizational Excellence,* 22(1), 73-82. Retrieved June 27, 2008, from ABI/INFORM Global database. (Document ID: 25233604)

Kotter, J. (2007) Leading Change: Why Transformation Efforts Fail. *Harvard Business Review,* 85(1), 96-103. Retrieved July 5, 2008, from ABI/INFORM Global database. (Document ID: 1187037931).

Kreitner, R. *Management* (5th ed.). Boston: Houghton Mifflin, 1992.

L Etang, J (1995). Ethical corporate social responsibility: A framework for managers. *Journal of Business Ethics,* 14(2), 125. Retrieved June 27, 2008, from ABI/INFORM Global database. (Document ID: 4518405).

Lewin, K. "*Field theory in social sciences*". New York: Harper & Row, 1951.

Lyon, D. (2004) How can you help organizations change to meet the corporate responsibility agenda? *Corporate Social - Responsibility and Environmental Management*, 11(3), 133. Retrieved August 6, 2008, from ABI/INFORM Global database. (Document ID: 706443111).

Marshall et al. "Managing change in the culture of general practice: qualitative case studies in primary case trusts". *British Medical Journal,* 327,2003: 599-603.

Mezias, S. J. & Glynn, M. A. "The three facets of corporate renewal: institution, revolution, and evolution". *Strategic Management Journal*, 14(2), 1993: 77-101.

Miles, M. (2004) Strategies for Planned Organizational Change. *School of Management, University of Ottawa.*

Miles, M. (2008) Lecture Slides, MBA 5237: Change Management

Orlitzky, M., Schmidt, F., Rynes, S. (2003) Corporate social and Financial Performance: A Meta-analysis. *Organization Studies* 24(3): 403 - 441

O'Sullivan, S. (2004) Lecture notes MBA 6630S - Change Management.

Piderit, S. K. "Rethinking resistance and recognizing ambivalence: A multidimensional view of attitudes toward an organizational change". *Academy of Management Review,* 25(4), 2000: 783-794.

Porter, M., Kramer, M. (2006) Strategy & Society. The Link between competitive advantage and corporate social responsibility. *Harvard Business Review*, December. Retrieved May 22, 2008, from ABI/INFORM Global database

Post, J.E., Altman, B.W. (1994) Managing the environmental change process: Barriers and opportunities. *Journal of Organizational Change Management*, 7(4), 64. Retrieved July 5, 2008, from ABI/INFORM Global database. (Document ID: 704510).

Prackash, S., Emelianova, O. (2006). A failed strategy of using voluntary codes of conduct by the global mining industry. *Corporate Governance*, Vol 6, No 3, pp 226-238.

Ragsdell, G. "Engineering a paradigm shift? An holistic approach to organizational change management". *Journal of Organizational Change Management,* 13(2), 2000: 104-120.

Sachs, J.D. (2008) Common Wealth - Economics for a crowded planet. The Penguin Press, New York

Sahlin-Andersson, K. (2006) Corporate social responsibility: a trend and a movement, but of what and for what? *Corporate Governance*, 6(5), 595-608. Retrieved March 12, 2008, from ABI/INFORM Global database. (Document ID: 1150401531).

Sarkis, J., Meade, L., Presley, A. (2006) An activity based management methodology for evaluating business processes for environmental sustainability. *Business Process Management Journal*, 12(6), 751. Retrieved July 5, 2008, from ABI/INFORM

Saunders, R. (2006) How to get an ethical advantage. *Brand Strategy*, 32, December. Retrieved May 9, 2008 from ABI/INFORM Global database.

Savitz, A, Weber, K. 2006. The Triple Bottom Line. John Wiley & Sons, Inc. CA

Schein, n.d. Schein, E. (2008) Kurt Lewin's change theory in the field and the classroom. Accessed at http://www.a2zpsychology.com/articles/kurt_lewin's_change_theory.htm, on August 6, 2008

Sharma, S., Vredenburg, H. (1998) Proactive corporate environmental strategy and the development of competitively valuable organizational capabilities. *Strategic Management Journal* (1986-1998), 19(8), 729. Retrieved June 27, 2008, from ABI/INFOR

Shaukat, R. (2004). Resistance to change: An information processing perspective. *International Journal of Knowledge, Culture and Change Management, 4*, 1627-1646.

Smith, M.K., (2001). Chris Argyris: theories of action, double-loop learning and organizational learning, the encyclopaedia of informal education, www.infed.org/thinkers/argyris.htm. Last update: April 11,2008. Accessed on July 3, 2008

Stead, W. E., Stead, J. G. (1994) Can humankind change the economic myth? Paradigm shifts necessary for ecologically sustainable business. *Journal of Organizational Change Management*, 7(4), 15. Retrieved March 10, 2008, from ABI/INFORM Global database. (Document ID: 704504).

Steger, U., Ionescu-Somers, A., Salzmann, O. (2007) The economic foundations of corporate sustainability. *Corporate Governance*, 7(2), 162. Retrieved March 10, 2008, from ABI/INFORM Global database. (Document ID: 1342458111).

Strebel, Paul (1996). Why do employees resist change? Harvard Business Review, 74(3), 86. Retrieved July 5, 2008, from ABI/INFORM Global database. (Document ID: 9600241).

Suarez, F., Oliva, R. (2005). Environmental change and organizational transformation. *Industrial and Corporate Change*, 14(6), 1017-1041. Retrieved June 27, 2008, from ABI/INFORM Global database. (Document ID: 950902641).

SustainAbility. (2000). Buried treasure. Retrieved from www.sustainability.co.uk/programs/Business_case/default.asp, on August 13, 2008

United Nations. 1997. Our Common Future - Report of the World Commission on Environment and Development. Accessed at http://www.un-documents.net/wced-ocf.htm, May 28 08.

Vallas, S. P. "Why teamwork fails: obstacles to workplace change in four manufacturing plants". *American Sociological Review,* 68, 2003: 223-250.

Vos, J.F.J. (2003). Corporate social responsibility and the identification of stakeholders. *Corporate Social - Responsibility and Environmental Management*, 10(3), 141. Retrieved August6, 2008, from ABI/INFORM Global database. (Document ID: 389093861).

Werther, W.B. JR., Chandler, D. (2006) Strategic Corporate Social Responsibility - Stakeholders in a Global Environment. Thousand Oaks, CA: Sage Publications, Inc.

Yachnin, Ronald W. May 2003. "Executive Seminar on Linking Sustainable Development and Shareholder Value: Proceeding and Observations." The *Conference Board of Canada.* Accessed:

http://www.conferenceboard.ca/GCSR/research/sustainable_development.pdf on August 13, 2008

Zandler, A. (1950). "Resistance to change-its analysis and prevention". *Advanced Management,* 4(5), 9-11.

Part VI: What is Next for Corporate Social Responsibility? — Overview

Chapters 15 and 16 make up Part 6 of the book, which asks the question, "What is next for CSR?" Chapter 15 explores new directions in CSR. Chapter 16 explores the possibility of moving beyond CSR, to the democratic regulation of transnational corporations.

Chapter 15: New Directions for CSR

Will We Ever Learn?: The Costs of Profiteering and the Path toward a New Way

Leah Ritchie, Salem State College, MA, USA

Abstract: Business and society need each other. Communities need industry to provide economic stability and innovation, while corporations rely on society for infrastructure, and stability. In the early part of the 20th century, literature on corporate social responsibility (CSR) emphasized industry's social obligation to do no harm. It contained specific ethical imperatives that called for business to bear responsibility for the effects that their decisions had on society at large. By the end of World War II, corporations grew larger and more distant from the communities that they served. Competing discourses that questioned the importance of CSR also emerged at this time. In an attempt to remain relevant, CSR scholars shifted away from the normative approach and began publishing studies that demonstrated how CSR could positively affect financial and strategic performance of the firm. Business responded to this shift by applying CSR to maintain their customer base and to improve their financial and strategic performance. Although well-intentioned, the shift toward a performance-based model of CSR has had deleterious effects. It is argued here that this shift has significantly narrowed the field of CSR, and has diluted, if not eradicated, the do-no-harm standard in its most basic form. This paper traces the breakdown of the social compact between business and society, and provides a parallel view of the literature as it too departs from earlier socially-minded themes. Specific recommendations for recapturing a do-no-harm agenda is also discussed.

Introduction

Business and society need each other. Communities need industry to provide economic stability and innovation, while corporations rely on society for infrastructure and social capital. There was a time when the symbiotic nature of this relationship was commonly understood. According to Deetz (1995):

> Voluntary compliance with conceptions of social good and legitimate economic gain was generally considered to be both right and good business. If intrinsic moral feelings or long-term economic balance sheets did not lead to compliance, the fear of governmental intervention, force from potentially competitive institutions such as press, the church or the academy, or mobilization of stakeholders such as stockholders, labor groups or consumer groups would tend to bring leading officials into line (pp. 14).

In the early part of the 20th century, literature on corporate social responsibility (CSR) emphasized industry's social obligation to do no harm. It contained specific ethical imperatives that called for business to bear responsibility for the effects that their decisions had on society at large. In *Social Responsibilities of the Businessman*, Howard Bowen (1953) implored corporate leaders to make decisions and to take actions that were in line with societal values. He defined corporate social responsibility this way: "…it refers to the obligations of businessmen to pursue those policies, to make those decisions, or to follow those lines of action which are desirable in terms of the objectives and values of our society (pp. 215).

By the end of World War II, corporations grew larger and more distant from the communities that they served. Competing discourses that questioned the importance of CSR also emerged at this time. In an attempt to remain relevant, CSR scholars shifted away from the normative approach and began publishing studies that demonstrated how CSR could positively affect the financial and strategic performance of the firm. Many businesses responded to this shift by applying CSR to improve their corporate image, attract customers, and to improve financial outcomes.

Although well-intentioned, the scholarly shift toward a performance-based model of CSR has had deleterious effects. It is argued here that this shift has significantly muddied the field of CSR by adding several new definitions within an already splintered body of work, and it has diluted, if not eradicated, the do-no-harm standard that defined CSR when the concept was first developed over fifty years ago. The performance-based model has also inadvertently promoted a dualistic practice of CSR. Campbell (2007) wrote, "A firm may do a lot of public service work and contribute heavily to charities, but may systematically foul the environment, steal from its' employee pension fund, and discriminate against women in the work place (pp. 951).

Campbell (2007) also argued that a 'minimum behavioral standard' should be used to define CSR. He formed this definition by drawing on the work of comparative political economists who studied and wrote about the diminishing view toward the collective good (North, 1990; Ostrom, 1990; Streeck, 1997).

Campbell's definition has two dimensions: First, a corporation is socially responsible if it does not intentionally do anything that can harm multiple stakeholders. Second, if that harm does occur, intentional or otherwise, a company 'behaves' in a socially responsible way if it rectifies that harm when it is discovered. In light of the current world-wide economic crisis, and recent environmental disasters, it is argued here that CSR scholarship needs to develop a comprehensive agenda based on the "do no harm" or minimal behavioral standard definition (hereafter referred to as MBS) that Campbell proposes. In supporting this argument, the breakdown of the social compact between business and society, and a parallel view of the literature as it too departs from earlier socially-minded themes are discussed. Specific recommendations for recapturing a research agenda that addresses CSR as MBS are also discussed.

Corporate Social Responsibility: An Overview of the Field

Decades before Bowen laid out the central tenets of CSR, J. M. Clark (1930) warned of the potential outcomes of not holding business accountable for their decisions:

> We are coming to see that our everyday business dealings have more far-reaching effects than we have ever realized, and that the system of free contract is by itself quite inadequate to bring home the responsibility for these effects. We have begun to realize the many inappropriate values that are created and the many unpaid damages that are inflicted in the course of business exchanges (pp. 218).

Although rebuffed by business leaders of their time, early twentieth century scholars wrote consistently about the over-powering nature of corporate interests (i.e., Barnard, 1938; Clark, 1930; Kreps, 1940). Clark (1930) warned of what he termed "orthodox" economics, which he argued promoted unrestrained capitalism. He prescribed an "economics of responsibility" (pp. 29), that required business to understand and behave according to an implicit obligation to safeguard the public against the unwieldy power of industry, and to act on behalf of the public good.

During the next several decades, the field continued to grow, particularly in the 1960's within a context of anti-capitalist backlash. Growing concerns about the power of business led to a series of legislative initiatives including the Equal Pay Act (1963), the Truth in Lending Act (1969), the Clean Air Act (1970), and a host of consumer rights legislation that promised to change the face of industry and create a more equitable balance of power between business and society. At this time, a flurry of scholarly work and popular books were written in support of the 'do no harm' model (i.e., Blumberg, 1976; Cohn, 1970; Galbraith, 1967; Linowes, 1975).

Although a strong anti-corporate sentiment existed in the 1960's, proponents of social responsibility were not without their detractors. In 1962, Milton Friedman declared that social responsibility was not a concern of industry, "...there is one and only one social responsibility of business – to use its resources and engage in activities designed to increase its profits so long as it stays within the rules of the game, which is to say, engages in open and free competition, without deception or fraud" (p. 133). Competing discourses about the relevance of CSR left the field at a standstill, resulting in relatively few theoretical advances during the 1960's (Min-Dong and Lee, 2008).

A water-shed moment occurred in 1970 when the Center for Economic Development published a report entitled "*Social Responsibilities of Business Corporations*." In the report, Wallich and McGowan wrote a seminal article that discussed a new rationale that aligned CSR with stockholder interest. The "enlightened self-interest" perspective held that the concerns of business and society are not mutually exclusive, but in fact are mutually beneficial. The authors argued that because most stockholders own shares in many different companies, their interests are focused not just on quarterly returns, but on how corporate actions affected the economic environment as a whole. Davis (1973) made this argument more specific by describing the economic dangers of corporate irresponsibility. A disregard for community, he argued, could result in business essentially turning on itself. Others continued to write about enlightened self-interest in such a way as to reconcile competing economic and social concerns (i.e., Fitch 1976; Keim, 1978; Moyer, 1974).

By the mid 1970's many prescriptive studies emerged that described practical ways to implement CSR (i.e., Ackerman, 1973; Fitch 1976; Murray 1976), although the field still lacked a basic theoretical framework. Carroll (1979) addressed this problem by proposing a three dimensional model of CSR which included social responsibility, social responsiveness and social issues. One of the most important contributions of this article was that business and society were not represented separately in the model, but were integrated within one economic, legal, and ethical environment (Min-Dong & Lee, 2008). Freeman (1984) extended this model by developing the now well-known stakeholder model of the corporation. His article was significant in that it was the first time that customers, employees, and community interests were considered of equal importance to stockholders to the survival of the corporation. Others have applied and extended the stakeholder model (i.e., Clarkson, 1995; Jones 1995).

Despite these advances, by the 1990's, the field still lacked methods for clear and 'objective' measurement of those theories that framed the field (Wood and Jones, 1995). Studies that called for tighter connections between CSR models and strategic and financial outcomes emerged. It was primarily in response to this call, as well as growing pressure from the corporate sector to justify a CSR agenda, that the performance-based model emerged. This model investigated the effects of CSR on financial and strategic outcomes of the firm (i.e., Brancato, 1995; Gray 2000; McWilliams et al 2006; Paine 2003). Within this vein of research, the term "strategic philanthropy" was coined (Kanter 1999; Porter and Kramer, 2002). The performance-based model expanded significantly at this time, and still remains the primary stream within the CSR literature.

Currently, much of the literature assumes a blending of CSR and corporate financial performance. Even social activists now use financial arguments to market their ideas to multinational corporations. For example, in the past, environmentalists attempted to capture the attention of coal producers by showing them the impact that carbon emissions had on the atmosphere, land and water. Currently, the main argument used by activists is based on the potential cost savings that can result from lowering emissions and other pollutants (Vogel, 2005).

Business, Society, and the Minimum Behavioral Standard

The MBH is often dismissed by business and the academy as trite, moralistic and impractical. However, recent failures of corporations to comply with this standard, and the profound effects this failure has had on society, provide support for Campbell's assertion that MBH needs to be re-examined and supported.

Known as the decade of the corporate merger, the 1980's brought with it huge faceless corporations that were widely removed from customers and constituent communities. According to Former Secretary of Labor Robert Reich, as quoted in Deetz (1995), "...this was a purer form of capitalism practiced globally by managers who are more distant, more economically driven and in essence, more coldly rational in their decisions (pp. 13)."

It was also during the 1980's that executive salaries began to skyrocket. In 1965, CEO's in the U.S. earned 24 times more than average employees. By 1978, this ratio grew to 35 to one, and by 2005, the salary of an average CEO was 262 times that of an average worker (Michel, Bernstein and Sherholz, 2008). Also during the 1980's U.S. corporations began cutting employee "overhead" by implementing massive layoffs, moving operations overseas, replacing workers with computers, and hiring women and immigrants at lower wages. While technological advances allowed individual workers to be at their most productive in modern history, their wages remained stagnant (Wolfe, 2009).

Corporations dazzled stockholders with short-term financial results without concern for how layoffs and other cost-cutting measures affected employees and their communities. Financial managers were intensely focused on producing quarterly returns for their clients, rather than on maintaining and developing the intrinsic value of the corporation.

By 2003, economists and officials in Washington began to show concern about hyper-financial business practices. They worried that companies no longer seemed to care about creating long-term sustainable value, which would translate into staying power for the firm, its employees, the community, and the local economy. In 2003, former U.S. Securities and Exchange Commission (SEC) Chairman William H. Donaldson urged business leaders to move away from the "earnings per share" approach. In 2005, a joint symposium of the Center for Financial Marketing Integrity and the Business Roundtable Institute for Corporate Ethics concluded the following: "An obsession with meeting short-term expectations of varying constituencies too often hinders corporate managers and all types of investors from focusing on long-term value creation. The causes of this short-term fixation are multifaceted, which necessitates reforms that involve many stakeholders..." (pp. 3).

A report published by the Aspen Institute, a nonprofit organization for societal reform, also issued similar warnings:

> ...fund managers with a primary focus on short-term trading gains have little reason to care about long-term corporate performance or externalities, and so are unlikely to exercise a positive role in promoting

> corporate policies, including appropriate proxy voting and corporate governance policies that are beneficial and sustainable in the long-term. Risk-taking is an essential underpinning of our capitalist system, but the consequences to the corporation, and the economy, of high-risk strategies designed exclusively to produce high returns in the short-run is evident in recent market failures (2005, pp. 2).

In September 2008, some of the oldest banking institutions in the U.S. collapsed, necessitating an unprecedented government bailout of 700 billion. Financial markets descended in a crisis of global proportions, which created record foreclosures and joblessness. The housing crisis that ensued, now viewed as one of the triggers for the current recession, has had devastating effects on communities worldwide. The causes of the housing crisis have been widely discussed and are still under debate, so only a brief overview is provided here.

Early 2000 was record-setting in terms of the number of Americans who owned homes. But as home ownership was increasing, wages remained stagnant. Those who could own property and still live within their means steadily decreased. Low interest rates, and the rise of subprime loans made housing available to more people, and kept demand and prices artificially high. Most home owners believed that prices would continue to climb, which would allow them to refinance risky loans when their mortgages adjusted to very higher rates.

Mortgage lenders reaped the benefits of these loans through fees, and closing costs, while they carried virtually none of the risks. As lenders assumed loans, they quickly sold them to investment houses that bundled them into mortgage backed securities. Monthly mortgage payments were essentially used as revenue streams to pay investors who bought pieces of these securities.

The scheme began to unravel when, even with liberal lending policies, the number of people who could afford the ever-increasing home prices began to dwindle. As decreased demand exerted a downward force on home prices, people saw the equity in their homes quickly evaporate. The inability to pay adjusted 5-year interest rates, along with a steady increase in unemployment created a wave of foreclosures not seen since the depression era. The Center for Responsible Lending estimated that by the first half of 2009, over 1,000,000 foreclosures were filed in the U.S. The center also predicted that by 2012, 9 million foreclosures will be filed, which will cost families a total of $1.9 trillion.

Aside from the financial and emotional effects that the housing crisis has had on individuals and families, foreclosures have had huge effects on society at large, including lost tax revenue, lowered property values and an increase in blight and crime. The crisis has also created less predictable effects. A 2008 study conducted by the Centers for Disease Control found that foreclosures increased the spread of the West Nile Virus in California neighborhoods where neglected swimming pools became breeding grounds for mosquitoes (Carroll, B. D., Quiring, R., Reisen, W. K., and Takahashi, R. M.,).

The response from CSR scholars to the economic crisis has been minimal at best. At the height of the recession, scholars were still publishing studies based on the performance-based models, without mention of the corporate irresponsibility that nearly brought down the world economy. These authors were wholly unobservant, and/or uncritical of the obvious dichotomy between what they considered advances in the CSR literature, and the economic and environmental context that existed when their articles were published. It is unreasonable to expect academics to respond to every corporate sin, but it is surprising that the most recent ethical failings of business have to date, received barely a mention in the CSR literature.

A New 'Old' Research Agenda: Returning to Our Roots

Because a uniform definition of corporate social responsibility still eludes us, industry has been free to translate CSR in ways that have been best suited to create the most financial and strategic gain. As discussed earlier, this creates a two sided coin where business can be philanthropic and irresponsible at the same time. For example, In July of 2010, *the San Francisco Business Times* rated Bank of America among the top 60 corporate givers in the Bay area. However, the company has refused to pay employee healthcare costs, and plans to lay off 35,000 workers in the next three years, despite the fact that the corporation received 25 billion in bailout money from the federal government. Nike corporation provides another example ethical dualism. The company has made an effort to create strong employee empowerment programs in China, while quietly moving their operations to Indonesia because of an increase in Chinese labor costs.

The minimal behavioral standard (MBS) is more than a moralistic imperative to do no harm. As just demonstrated, it is a realistic approach to our social-industrial system, which is organic by nature. As we have seen, setbacks or progress in one aspect of the system can have profound effects on others. Campbell (2007) argued that CSR literature within the past thirty years has virtually ignored the symbiotic nature of this relationship, and calls for a revival of a do-no-harm perspective in its most basic form. He explained:

> "...we can array examples of socially responsible corporate behavior along a continuum ranging from minimally responsible behavior, as I have defined it, to increasingly more responsible behaviors as others have defined them. Granted, it might be difficult for everyone to agree on which specific instances of corporate social responsibility fit where along this continuum. But the point is that virtually all of the literature on corporate social responsibility has neglected the minimum end of the continuum, focusing instead on behaviors located toward the other end. This is both surprising and important given the fact that some firms may score quite high on corporate social responsibility by conventional definitions but very low by my definition" (2007, pp. 951).

A research agenda that takes up MBS as a unifying definition, and explores viable areas of research and practice are necessary. Several questions need to be addressed: How can we develop a multidimensional framework for MBS? What does it mean to "do no harm"? What are the various cultural interpretations of MBS? What is a viable analytical model for predicting possible harm? What would a continuum of harm look like? How can harm be rectified? What are the conditions that best enable MBS? What is the role of institutions, government, industry groups, nongovernmental organizations, and the educational system in enabling MBS? How is MBS applied in different socio-cultural and political contexts? How can an organization implement and measure MBS across the supply chain? Studies that address these research questions can potentially result in a revival of normative approaches to CSR.

In addition, case studies that examine companies that have behaved ethically, according to MBS principles, would be highly useful. For example, The SA 8000, which is a measurement tool based on the findings from 13 international human rights conventions, measures how well a company has protected the health and well-being of its employee-stakeholders. The eight elements of the tool include health, safety, working hours, child labor, forced labor, discrimination, freedom of association, collective bargaining, wages and discipline. Some of the organizations that have met the SA 8000 standards include Beraca (Brazil), a company that develops raw materials for use in the cosmetic industry, Rosy Blue Diamond (Thailand), a diamond plant, Sabaf (Italy), which produces components for gas cooking appliances, TDE (Bolivia), a utility company, TNT Express (Argentina), a global shipping company, and Yesim (Turkey) a textile company. These are considered medium-sized entities (by international standards), and are viable, profitable companies. A thorough study of these and other companies that have achieved similar ratings would provide a model for those who desire to bring their business into line with minimal behavioral standards.

Conclusion

The field of corporate social responsibility currently lacks a uniform definition, and is narrowly focused on corporate performance outcomes. These conditions have provided opportunities for business to distort the theory and practice of CSR. This paper calls for a return to a minimal behavioral standard or a "do no harm" research agenda suggested by Campbell. This is not a moralistic agenda. The recent examples of corporate negligence and the societal outcomes of poor corporate behaviors have demonstrated that MBS is a realistic area of research that acknowledges the true symbiotic nature of the social-industrial relationship. In developing MBS as a central construct in the field, it is necessary to build a comprehensive theoretical framework that can be used to create an active and applied research agenda. Given the economic and environmental disasters of the last decade, the current need for such an agenda is particularly pressing.

References

Ackerman, R. W., (1973). How companies respond to social demands. *Harvard Business Review*, 88-98.

Barnard, C. J. (1938). *The Functions of the Executive.* Cambridge, MA: Harvard University Press.

Blumberg, P. I. (1976). *The Megacorporation in American Society.*(Englewood Cliffs, N. J.: Prentice-Hall.

Brancato, C. K. (1995). *New Corporate Performance Measures*. New York: The Conference Board.

Business Roundtable Institute for Corporate Ethics (2004). Mapping the terrain. Retrieved from
http://www.corporate-ethics.org

Business Roundtable Institute for Corporate Ethics (2006). Corporate governance survey key Findings. Retrieved from http://www.businessroundtable.com

Bowen, H. (1953). *Social Responsibilities of the Businessman.* New York: Harper.

Campbell, J. L. (2007). Why would corporations behave in a socially responsible way?: An institutional theory of corporate social responsibility. *Academy of Management Review, 32,* 946-967.

Carroll, A. B. (1979). A three-dimensional conceptual model of corporate performance. *Academy of Management Review, 20,* 92-117.

Center for Financial Marketing Integrity and the Business Roundtable Institute for Corporate Ethics Symposium Series on Short-Termism (2005). Breaking the short-term cycle: discussion and recommendations on how corporate leaders, asset managers, investors, and analysts can refocus on long-term value.

Center for Responsible Lending (2009). Continued decay and shaky repairs: The state of subprime loans today. Retrieved from http://www.responsiblelending.org/mortgage-lending

Clark, J. M. (1930). The socializing of theoretical economics. In R. Tugwell (Ed.) *The Trend of Economics.* New York: F. S. Crofts & Co.

Clarkson, M. B. E. (1995). A stakeholder framework for analyzing and evaluating corporate social performance. *Academy of Management Review, 20,* 92-117.

Cohn, J. (1970). Is Business Meeting the Challenge of Urban Affairs?" *Harvard Business Review, 48* (March-April).

Davis, K. (1973). The case for and against business assumption of social responsibilities. *Academy of Management Journal, 16,* 312-322.

Deetz, S. (1995). *Transforming communication transforming business.* Cresskill, NJ: Hampton Press.

Fitch, H. G. (1976). Achieving corporate social responsibility. *Academy of Management Review, 1,* 38-46.

Friedman, M. (1962). *Capitalism and Freedom.* Chicago: University of Chicago Press.

Freeman, R. E. (1984). Str*ategic Management*: *A Stakeholder Approach.* Boston: Pitman.

Galbraith, J. K. (1967). *The New Industrial State.* Boston: Houghton-Mifflin.

Gray, R. (2000). Current developments and trends in social and environmental auditing, reporting and attestation: A review and comment. *International Journal of Auditing, 4,* 247-268.

Jones, T. M. (1995). Instrumental stakeholder theory: A synthesis of ethics and economics. *Academy of Management Review, 20,* 404-437.

Kanter, R. M. (1999). From spare change to real change: the social sector as beta site for business innovation. *Harvard Business Review, 77,* 122-132.

Keim, G. D. (1978). Corporate social responsibility: An assessment of the enlightened self-interest model. *Academy of Management Review, 3,* 32-39.

Kreps, T. J. (1940). *Measurement of the social performance of business.* Washington, D.C.: U.S. Government Printing Office. Retrieved from http://openlibrary.org/books/OL6429139M/Measurement_of_the_social_performance_ofbusiness

Linowes, D. (1975). *The Corporate Conscience.* New York: Hawthorn Books.

McWilliams, A., Siegal, D. S. & Wright, P. M. (2006). Corporate social responsibility: Strategic implications. *Journal of Management Studies, 43,* 1-18.

Michel, L. R., Bernstein, J., & Shierholz, H. (2009). *The State of Working America: 2008-2009.* Ithaca, N.Y. ILR Press.

Meehan, J., Meehan, K., & Richards. (2006). Corporate social responsibility: The 3C-SR model. *International Journal of Social Economics. 33*(5/6), 386-398.

Min-Dong, P. & Lee, P. (2008). A review of the theories of corporate social responsibility: Its evolutionary path and the road ahead. *International Journal of Management Review 10*(1), 53-73.

Moyer, R. C. (1974). Efficiency and corporate social investment. *Business and Society, 14,* 5-11.

Murray, E. A. (1976). The social response process in commercial banks: An empirical investigation. *Academy of Management Review, 1,* 5-15.

North, D.C. (1990). *Institutions, institutional change and economic performance.* New York: Cambridge University Press.

Ostrom, E. (1990). *Governing the commons: The evolution of institutions for collective action.* New York: Cambridge University Press.

Paine, L. S. (2003). *Value Shift: Why Companies Must Merge Social and Financial Imperatives to Achieve Superior Performance.* New York: McGraw-Hill.

Pisarek, T. (2010, July 16). Our review yielded a complete view of giving. *San Francisco Business Times.*

Porter, M. E. & Kramer, M. R. (2002). The competitive advantage of corporate philanthropy. *Harvard Business* Review, *84,* 78-92.

Reisen, W. K., Takahashi, R. M., Carroll, B. D., & Quiring, R. (2008). Delinquent mortgages, neglected swimming pools, and West Nile virus in California. Atlanta, GA. Centers for Disease Control. Retrieved from www.cdc.gov/eid/content/14/11/pdfs/1747.pdf

Streeck, W. (1997). Beneficial constraints: On the economic limits of rational voluntarism. In J.R. Hollingsworth & R. Boyer (Eds.) *Contemporary capitalism: The embededness of institutio*ns. New York: Cambridge University Press.

The Aspen Institute (2009). Overcoming short-termism: A call for a more responsible approach to investment and business management. Retrieved from http://www.aspeninstitute.org/publications/overcoming-short-termism-call-more-responsible-approach-investment-business-management

Vogel, D. (2005). *The Market for Virtue: The Potential and Limits of Corporate Social Responsibility*. Washington, D.C. Brookings Institution Press.

Wallich, H. C. & McGowan, J. J. (1970). Stockholder interest and the corporation's role in social policy. In Baumol, W. J. (Ed.), *A New Rationale for Corporate Social Policy*. New York: Committee for Economic Development.

Wolfe, R. (2009). *Capitalism hits the fan: The global economic meltdown and what to do about it*. New York: Olive Branch Press.

Wood, D. J. & Jones, R. E. (1995). Stakeholder mismatching: a theoretical problem in empirical research on corporate social performance. *International Journal of Organizational Analysis*, *3*, 229 –267.

Chapter 16: Moving Beyond CSR

From Corporate Social Responsibility to the Democratic Regulation of Transnational Corporations

David Humphreys

Abstract: This publication examines the role of transnational corporations in governance and critically evaluates the dominant self-regulatory approach of corporate social responsibility (CSR). By placing the onus for change on the corporation, CSR represents an agent-led approach to a systemic problem, and as such it is deeply flawed. After distinguishing between the ideas of CSR and corporate accountability, the latter of which emphasises the answerability of the corporation to public authorities and citizens, the publication then offers an original model for the democratic regulation of the corporation. The model proposes, first, the negotiation of a new corpus of international law to be agreed by states but ratified by those corporations that wish to trade or invest internationally and, second, the reinvigoration of the public charter as an active instrument of public control. It aims to provide a nested framework within which corporations can trade and compete, while restoring to local communities final decision making authority on the conditions under which corporations may, or may not, operate. Some possible objections to the model are anticipated and addressed.

Introduction

Those who work in the public education sector and are funded from the public purse should contribute to public debate on matters of public importance. As Edward Said argued in his 1993 Reith Lectures, the public intellectual is 'someone whose place it is publicly to raise embarrassing questions, to confront orthodoxy and dogma (rather than to reproduce them), and to be someone who cannot easily be co-opted by governments or corporations' (Said 1996: 11). To Said, the public, broadly defined, is the intellectual's natural constituency. In this respect scholars can arguably find no more pressing contemporary public welfare issue on which they should speak than global environmental degradation.

One of the drivers of environmental problems is the transnational corporation. This publication analyses the increasing ease with which corporations are now able to evade public oversight. It seeks to move beyond analysis to address the normative question of what policies, political systems and governance structures are necessary if corporations are to be brought under democratic public control. Grappling with normative issues raises the question of whether public scholars should engage in advocacy; and if so on whose behalf should we claim to speak? In line with Said I would suggest that academics should be free to engage in advocacy providing that the advocacy in question is expressly intended to promote human rights or otherwise enhance the public interest. The public interest is, of course, an essentially and perpetually contested concept. The spatial scale at which we analyse 'the public' may vary significantly between communities, while in sustainability discourse the notion of 'the public' should include the needs of generations that have yet to be born.

This publication first outlines why we should study the role of transnational corporations in environmental governance. It then introduces and critiques the idea of corporate social responsibility (CSR), differentiating between CSR and corporate accountability. The final substantive section presents an original model for the democratic regulation of corporations.

The Transnational Corporation and Environmental Governance

A transnational (sometimes called multinational) corporation is 'a company that operates in a number of different countries, either in terms of productive or service activities or in terms of having subsidiaries or affiliates in several countries' (Thompson 2009: 406). The last fifteen years has seen the emergence of a burgeoning literature within the academic and activist communities on corporations, the power they wield and how they may evade public oversight, especially in the majority world of Latin America, Africa and Asia (for example, Bakan 2004; Bollier 2003; Christian Aid 2004; Clapp and Utting 2008; Cromwell 2001; Derber 2002; Drutman and Cray 2004; Gates 2001; Korten 1995, 1999, 2006; Litvin 2003; Monk 2008).

The modern business corporation was originally conceived to serve public needs. There are three attributes of the corporation that affect its role in environmental governance. First, corporations have a legal personality. The legal right of a corporation to exist and raise money through issuing shares is provided by public authorities in a charter. In 1886 a US court case, *Santa Clara County v. Southern Pacific Railroad*, ruled that a corporation should be considered a legal person with the same constitutional rights as a US citizen, thus giving to corporations a status that is equal to people (Korten 1995: 1; Drutman and Cray 2004: 63). Second, corporations have a fiduciary responsibility to act in the interests of their shareholders. The doctrine of shareholder primacy was established in the Michigan court case, *Dodge v. Ford Motor Company* 1919.

Third, the shareholders of corporations have a limited liability, a principle first introduced in England in 1851. If a corporation is sued shareholders are liable only for their initial investment, and not for any damages greater than this. For limited liability corporations it is the personality of the corporation that is liable, not its directors or managers. Corporations can divide themselves into legally separate entities, such as holding companies and subsidiaries, so that if successfully sued any damages will be confined to a small 'firm' within a larger organisational structure. This makes it more difficult for plaintiffs to obtain legal redress for any environmental damage corporations may cause.

Sustainability, however defined, cannot be attained unless corporations actively promote it. If the world's largest economies are measured by either the annual GDP of a country, or the annual turnover of a corporation, then over half of the world's largest economies are corporations. Transnational corporations are major users of natural resources and owners of industrial and agricultural land. They generate a significant percentage of global carbon dioxide emissions. The 200 largest corporations control approximately 30% of global gross domestic product (GDP), while the largest 500 control approximately 80% of foreign direct investment and 70% of world trade (Elliott 2004: 117). Environmental standards may be driven down as countries compete to offer more attractive investment terms to transnational corporations, the so-called 'race to the bottom'. Yet many corporations operate with no effective control from their shareholders or from governments; indeed increasingly it is corporations that influence governments. Some corporations effectively conduct their own diplomacy, with political and legal departments that specialise in negotiating with governments (Ross 2007: 216). Big businesses have become standard setters rather than standard takers. Corporate alliances such as the World Business Council for Sustainable Development, the European Round Table of Industrialists and the US Council for International Business have prepared the first drafts of international legal agreements tabled in intergovernmental negotiations (Humphreys 2001; Derber 2002). The increased influence of corporations in international negotiations has led to what may be termed the 'privatisation' of the United Nations, in which international law increasingly reflects the interests of business (Lee, Humphreys and Pugh 1997).

Deregulation has freed corporations from public oversight. Most now function with little, if any, commitment to the spaces and communities within which they operate. They increasingly operate not only beyond local community control but beyond the control of national governments, wielding enormous power yet protected from the worst consequences of their action by limited liability law. They have rights, including some important rights in international law, but without concomitant responsibilities. If corporations are growing in size and political influence then how can local communities regain democratic control over them?

From Corporate Social Responsibility to Corporate Accountability

In the contemporary neoliberal era mandatory national and international environmental legislation is eschewed in favour of voluntary and market-based initiatives (Harvey 2003). Corporate social responsibility (CSR) fits comfortably within neoliberal logic. CSR refers to the wide range of voluntary initiatives by corporations, sometimes in conjunction with other stakeholders, 'to promote ethical corporate behaviour and minimise the negative impacts of business activity on society and the environment' (Clapp and Utting 2008: 1). CSR is based on the assumption that corporations themselves best know how to improve their social and environmental performance. There are various forms of CSR including voluntary statements of principles from individual businesses, schemes agreed jointly by several corporations (such as the UN Global Compact), and market-based certification and labelling schemes. While it originated from business, CSR has been accepted by many developed governments and by the European Union as the dominant approach to business (self-)regulation (European Commission 2002).

Companies may adopt CSR schemes for a variety of reasons, including improving resource and energy efficiency, public relations, demands from stakeholders and to ward off tougher mandatory regulation. Some corporations adopt CSR schemes for more altruistic and ethical reasons (Thompson 2009). CSR schemes vary enormously but typically include commitments against sweatshop or child labour and the promotion of gender equality, fuel efficiency, waste management, nature conservation and carbon dioxide emission reduction. Proponents argue that CSR helps to fill a global regulatory vacuum by exerting a normative pull on business that raises standards. Corporations that take a lead in CSR can set new standards that laggard businesses will later adopt in order to avoid reputational damage (Assadourian 2006). To John Ruggie, schemes such as the Global Compact signify 'the emergence of a new advocate for a more effective global public sector: business itself' (Ruggie 2003: 115).

But CSR has many critics. CSR may be seen as a contradiction in terms; under the law the corporation has no social responsibility, only the fiduciary duty to maximise its shareholders' interests. Corporations often evade the voluntary commitments they make (Christian Aid 2004). Commitments are usually vague, often taking the form of generalised principles. Timebound and quantifiable targets and verifiable performance benchmarks are the exception rather than the rule. Because of the voluntary nature of CSR schemes there is no mandatory verification, no obligation for independent auditing and no penalty for corporations that fail to adhere to their commitments.

One argument against joint CSR schemes such as the Global Compact focuses on the relationship between the strength of standards and the number of participating corporations. The standards of such schemes have to be weak to induce participation. Schemes with strong standards will have low uptake; they will achieve significant impacts for the limited number of corporations that adopt them, but low impact overall. Schemes with weak standards will achieve high uptake, but because they promote only minor changes in corporate practices, again there is only a limited overall impact. Uptake is uneven, both by sector and across space, with some types of business and some countries more active on CSR than others. There remain regulatory gaps through which unscrupulous businesses can slip.

However, CSR schemes have had some impact in ratcheting up standards for some firms. But whether CSR schemes may be considered effective depends on how 'effectiveness' is defined. If effectiveness is defined as behavioural change that would not otherwise occur then some CSR schemes should be considered effective. But if effectiveness is defined as solving the problem at hand, such as maintaining or enhancing environmental quality, then CSR must be seen as fundamentally ineffective, as environmental problems have worsened since CSR was first adopted in the early-1990s. CSR leaves the onus on responding to environmental problems to corporations; it is an agency response to systemic problems that can only be solved with a coordinated system level response. CSR did not emerge primarily as a response to global environmental and social problems, and has thus failed to grapple meaningfully with them. CSR schemes focus primarily on changes that will benefit the corporation, such as providing predictability in an uncertain policy environment and improving resource efficiency. But there is no reason to conclude that simply improving corporate efficiency will arrest broader systemic problems, such as nature conservation and decarbonisation of the global economy. Foundational questions such as does sustainability require a reduction in international trade, a macro-level restructuring of global financial markets or a worldwide reduction in resource-intensive modes of production modes are not admitted into CSR discourse.

CSR constitutes a weakening of the public sphere at the national and international levels. Governments have, in effect, passed responsibility for standard setting from the public to private sectors. At the international level the Global Compact enhances the status of the UN secretary-general, but bypasses, and thereby diminishes, intergovernmental bodies within the UN system. It presumes that the era of state regulation has ended, supplanted by a new era of global governance in which the state is just one actor amongst many. As David Coleman has argued, by appealing directly to corporations to adopt global standards and thus, in effect, inferring that states and international organisations are the laggards at standard setting, the Global Compact has subverted the idea of global public regulation (Coleman 2003: 353).

So there are problems with both the means of CSR (often untransparent and profoundly undemocratic) and the ends (simply not fit for the purpose of arresting environmental degradation and achieving sustainability). CSR is a surface phenomenon: it does not penetrate deep into corporate governance structures. Under limited liability law corporations can impose environmental externalities on society by, for example, clearfelling forests, polluting waterways and dumping toxic waste, while internalising the financial benefits, leading to huge imbalances between private profits and social welfare. In a neoliberal policy environment it is often 'rational' to degrade the environment for private gain. The work of Arild Vatn on rationality is relevant here. Vatn argues that rationality is best understood as a plural concept that encompasses the 'I' rationality of self-interested utility maximising states and corporations, and 'we' rationality that focuses on cooperation and collective gains (Vatn 2008). Institutions are guided by different types of rationality, and whatever notion of rationality is internalised in an institution will shape the behaviour of those who work within it. As Elinor Ostrom (1990) shows, institutions can be designed that prevent commons tragedies, at least at the local level. But the modern corporation is the result of the progressive weakening of collective 'we' rationality and the strengthening of individualistic 'I' rationality leading to a weakened public sphere and the utilitarian/neoliberal theory that the common good is best realised by the interaction of buyers and sellers in 'free markets' (Vatn 2008: 74).

To Vatn, therefore, the behaviour of corporations is in large part determined by the particular socio-historical context in which it operates. The voluntarism of CSR generates a free rider problem: businesses that do not sign up to CSR, or sign up but do not implement, avoid environmental costs that more principled businesses incur. A corporation motivated by a strong notion of 'we' rationality will inevitably suffer a comparative disadvantage relative to those governed by a ruthless and instrumentalist 'I' rationality. From this argument it follows that if the notion of rationality that governs corporations has evolved as it has due to changes within the socio-political environment that have led to neoliberalism, what is needed in order to promote corporate behaviour that serves the common good is a fundamental shift in this broader environment.

This is what corporate accountability advocates. Proponents of corporate accountability seek to stipulate the duties and obligations of corporations, emphasise the answerability of corporations to stakeholders and publicly accountable authorities and reassert the role of public policy in governance (Clapp and Utting 2008: 17). The next section develops an original model for corporate accountability. Drawing from and building upon earlier work (Humphreys 2006) the model seeks to reconcile two pressing governance challenges: to uphold tough international standards that provide a framework within which corporations can compete fairly, while passing the final decisions on corporate activities back to local communities.

Towards the Democratic Regulation of Transnational Corporations

Local responses can promote and enhance environmental, cultural, social and economic sustainability, but even the best local responses will ultimately fail if they take place within a neoliberal economic system that places the rights of investors above those of communities. To be effective, local responses need to be embedded within an international framework dedicated to the enhancement of what John McMurtry calls life values (1999, 2003). The democratisation of globalisation and the democratisation of local spaces should thus be seen as symbiotic and mutually reinforcing processes.

Central to the model proposed in this section is the democratic regulation of the corporation. The social and environmental consequences of corporate practices should no longer be subordinated to the quest for profit. The fiduciary duty of corporations to maximise shareholders' interests – a duty that from a legal standpoint currently trumps all moral and ethical considerations – should be replaced by an explicit legal responsibility for the corporation to act *pro bono publico* (for the public good). To infuse accountability into corporate practices, the notion should be revived that the right of the corporation to operate is conditional upon its satisfying public needs as stipulated in public charters. The final arbiters on the standards to which corporations should adhere should be local public bodies.

Under the Westphalian system of international law that has emerged over the last four centuries, states both make international law and are subject to it. However, the state is no longer the main international actor. To ensure minimum global standards a new corpus of international law is needed that regulates corporations rather than states. States, as the legitimate representatives of national publics in international politics, will negotiate this corpus of law, which will stipulate the standards to which corporations should adhere if they are to be permitted to trade and invest internationally. This new body of law should be agreed free of interference from corporations, which, as regulatees rather than regulators, would be denied access to the legislative process.

The first step would be the negotiation of a Convention on Transnational Corporations outlining the responsibilities and duties of corporations. This would set a raised plateau of tough obligations and standards for corporations. Whereas an individual state adopts a treaty by signing and ratifying it through its domestic legislature, a corporation would adopt the convention by endorsing it through its board of directors and shareholders' meetings. No corporation could trade or invest internationally without first adopting the convention. By doing so corporations would recognise that their right to engage in transnational economic activity is conditional upon the observance of obligations to the global public. These obligations would, at a minimum, include commitments to uphold environmental quality, respect the precautionary principle, undertake environmental and social impact assessments, allow independent environmental and social auditing and respect community rights and traditions. Corporations ratifying the convention would receive an international charter permitting them to trade internationally. In terms both of intent and content, the convention would be the opposite of the contemporary corpus of international trade law, which outlines the rights of investors rather than their duties.

To invest in a country, a corporation would then need to obtain a country-level charter from a public authority in the host country. This would stipulate the terms and standards that the corporation should observe. The granting or withholding of country-level charters would be a matter of public debate, with the final decision being made by the national government. The conditions stipulated in a country charter could be stronger, but not weaker, than those outlined in the convention. A corporation would need a charter from every country in which it operated. Inevitably the contents of charters would vary as different corporations would be admitted to different countries under different circumstances to meet different publicly-defined needs.

A corporation with a country-level charter would then be free to find a locality in which to invest. Publicly accountable groups at the sub-state level would have the right to determine which corporations invested in their space. The conditions would be stipulated in a local charter. The provisions contained in a local charter could strengthen, but not weaken, those laid out in the country-level charter. Actors at the sub-state level charged with upholding the public interest will come in many guises, reflecting the rich diversity of local cultures, economies and commons regimes that are to be found in most countries. They will include, for example, democratically elected local councils and more traditional local community governance structures. Irrespective of the form of governance at the local level, a local group or authority would be under no obligation to issue a charter if it did not consider this to be in the interests of its public.

The revitalisation of the charter as an instrument for public accountability will stimulate citizen engagement and participatory democracy. Citizens' views would now count. Corporations would have to adjust to the needs of local communities rather than, as now, communities being forced to adjust to intrusions from big business playing by international trade rules. In a post-neoliberal world, a new mode of doing business would emerge based upon the needs of the local economy. This will benefit, for example, those communities that wish to conserve local fishing and forest resources and those that do not want large superstores or 'global brands' disrupting the cultural distinctiveness of the local economy. If local communities exercise greater control over their economies then a greater share of the income from the local economy will flow to the local level where it can be used to fight poverty and social exclusion.

But the local level cannot entirely dominate. Global targets should be set on public good provision. Targets would be necessary on, for example, forest cover and greenhouse gas emissions. Multilevel coordination between the different layers of governance would then be needed to ensure that these targets were met. Agreement would need to be reached at the intergovernmental level on the responsibilities of individual countries with respect to global targets. Similarly, within countries, coordination will be necessary between the state and sub-state authorities on the responsibilities that local spaces should make to public good provision.

Corporations adopting the Convention on Transnational Corporations would be obliged to ensure its implementation by all subsidiary companies and to undertake to trade only with businesses that respect and implement the convention. This would reinforce standards amongst market players. Standards adopted by one business would thus be passed along supply chains which would act as transmission belts along which rules are passed and enforced. Insisting that a corporation know its supply chains is not unreasonable, but it would call for mandatory international certification schemes. Some reform of international financial markets would also be necessary, including a minimum period for holding shares. This would promote shareholder activism in corporate governance, encouraging shareholders to monitor the social and environmental performance of the business. There is no public interest in share dealers buying shares and selling them at the click of a mouse a few minutes later to earn a 'margin'. A minimum period of, say, five years would ensure that shareholders took an active interest in corporate management and invested only in socially responsible businesses.

If the courts were to find that the convention had been violated then a corporation would be liable to penalties, such as fines, suspension of the international charter or, in severe cases, the revocation of the international charter and the dissolution of the corporation's assets. Similarly, if a corporation were to violate a national or local charter it would answer to national and local authorities, and may suffer financial penalties or the withdrawal of its charter. Where a corporation causes environmental damage due unsustainable, unscrupulous or negligent corporate practices, then it should be required to make good (as far as possible) on the damage caused and to pay a financial penalty. Should the corporation have insufficient funds to pay these costs, the courts should have the power to dissolve the corporation and seize its assets. Limited liability legislation should be repealed and the courts should have the power to seize the private assets of company directors.

Some will argue that this is draconian. In response four points should be made. First, in most countries the law can be used to pursue assets gained from illegal and immoral activities, such as drug smuggling and prostitution. There is no reason to deal differently with those enrich themselves from the degradation or asset stripping of nature. Second, the principle of limited liability has enabled corporations to shifts risks and costs from the corporation to society as a whole. The repeal of limited liability legislation will mean that those whose policies generate environmental and social externalities will be those who pay for them. Third, the risk of financial penalties accruing to corporations and directors would provide a strong financial incentive for corporate policies that promoted long-term sustainable practices. Fourth, financial penalties would co-opt the world's financial markets into promoting environmental, cultural and social sustainability. Financial investors want profitable businesses. If knowledge emerged that a corporation had engaged in unsustainable practices that violated a charter, the result would be a fall in the value of the corporation's stock as the markets reacted in anticipation of heavy fines or the dissolution of the corporation. Financial investors would thus have an incentive to monitor corporate environmental practices. This would help to repair the problem of what Robert Nadeau (2003) has termed the absent feedback loop, whereby the depletion of natural capital simply does not register with corporations and international financial markets.

A further objection may be that international rules outlining the obligations of corporations are 'impractical'. Yet business leaders and their political allies have consistently pressed for international rules on neoliberal objectives, such as trade, investment and intellectual property rights. On what basis can it be claimed that international rules for sustainability and human rights are, in some way, impractical? It may also be claimed that a multilevel system of charters would be 'bureaucratic' and 'protectionist', both of which are pejorative terms for neoliberals. But if bureaucratisation is the price of accountability, then let these charges be made, as the social and environmental costs of allowing corporations to penetrate new spaces without effective public oversight have already proved too large. And it is hardly protectionist to point out that local and, sometimes, national businesses are at a significant disadvantage when competing with powerful transnational corporations. A nested system of public charters would help to equalise the huge power asymmetries between local communities and corporations. Indeed, on what basis would anyone seek to deny public authorities the right to decide which corporations can have access to their economies and which should not?

It may also be claimed that if environmental and social standards are set 'too high', then corporations will stop investing in local communities. But given that a key driving force of environmental degradation is investment that is not constrained by strong safeguards, this argument should be dismissed. Irrespective of the regulatory environment, corporations will continue to search for investment opportunities. They will soon learn to adjust to the needs of local communities if the alternative is not to invest at all. With effective public safeguards in place, only environmentally and socially irresponsible investment will be blocked.

Finally, it may be argued that it is utopian, even naive, to argue that corporate-driven environmental degradation can be reversed using the same institutions – the state and intergovernmental organisations – that so far have failed. In response, it should be asked that if publicly accountable bodies, such as the state and intergovernmental organisations, are not going to represent the interests of citizens and promote public goods, then who, precisely, will do this? The problem is not so much with publicly accountable bodies, but with their penetration by corporate interests. The solution is to reform and strengthen public bodies rather than to agree with the neoliberal view that, premised on the notion that a weakened state is 'inevitable' under globalisation, searches for new forms of governance which hand more power to business, such as CSR. Far from being abandoned, public government and intergovernmental organisations should be reclaimed, revitalised and democratised.

Conclusions

Public authorities have both the right and the duty to govern business in the public interest, yet economic decision making is in large part driven by corporations whose sole duty is to serve private shareholders. This represents an unreconciled tension in global governance, one that often passes unrecognised. The model of corporate accountability proposed here would reconcile this tension by establishing as paramount the collective public interest to which all other considerations, including corporate policy and shareholder value, should be firmly subordinated. It would reinvigorate the principle that corporations should be free to operate if, and only if, they provides benefits for the public good. It would render CSR obsolete, restore full political authority to a dynamic, inclusive and democratically accountable public domain and reconnect corporations to the communities within which they were previously embedded.

There will, admittedly, be huge costs to corporations if they are to adopt more sustainable and responsible practices. But the environmental and social costs that have arisen from predatory and exploitative corporate practices – including massive displacement of communities, species loss and climate change – have also been vast, although they have not been accurately chronicled. Simply put, nature and communities are currently paying the costs of corporate enrichment. In any case, the governance reforms advocated here will be minimal and small scale compared to the massive interventions and curbs on corporate activity that will be necessary in, say, another half-century if global environmental degradation continues unchecked.

Under the system of nested and differentiated governance proposed here, countries and communities would not adopt identical rules, although they would adopt minimum rules. The system would promote universal values and standards while respecting and promoting the diversity and right to self-determination of countries and communities. It would seek to govern corporations in the interests of environmental sustainability, at both the local and global levels. It would enable local spaces to sustain their cultural and social diversity while also providing a non-discriminatory framework within which corporations can compete in global markets. As such, the proposed model could provide an embryonic framework within which the interconnected fundamentals of environmental, social, cultural and economic sustainability can flourish and thrive. It is in this spirit, and in line with Said's entreaty to scholars to seek to speak on behalf of the public at large, that this proposal is offered for criticism and debate.

References

Assadourian, Erik (2006) 'Transforming Corporations', in Worldwatch Institute, *State of the World 2006*, New York: WW Norton.

Bakan, Joel (2004) *The Corporation: The Pathological Pursuit of Profit and Power,* London: Constable.

Bollier, David (2003) *Silent Theft: The Private Plunder of Our Common Wealth*, London: Routledge.

Christian Aid (2004) *Behind the mask: The real face of corporate social responsibility*, London: Christian Aid.

Clapp, Jennifer and Utting, Peter (2008) 'Corporate Responsibility, Accountability, and Law: An Introduction', in Peter Utting and Jennifer Clapp (eds), *Corporate Accountability and Sustainable Development: Ecological Economics and Human Well-being*, Oxford: Oxford University Press, pp.1-33.

Coleman, David (2003) 'The United Nations and Transnational Corporations: From an Inter-nation to a 'Beyond-state' Model of Engagement', *Global Society: Journal of Interdisciplinary International Relations*, Vol.17, No.4, pp.339-357.

Cromwell, David (2001) *Private Planet: Corporate Plunder and the Fight Back*, Oxfordshire: Jon Carpenter Publishing.

Derber, Charles (2002) *People Before Profit: The New Globalisation in an Age of Terror, Big Money, and Economic Crisis*, London: Souvenir Press.

Drutman, Lee and Cray, Charlie (2004) *The People's Business: Controlling Corporations and Restoring Democracy*, San Francisco: Berrett-Koehler.

Elliott, Lorraine (2004) *The Global Politics of the Environment* (Second Edition), London: Palgrave Macmillan.

European Commission (2002) COM(2002) 347 final, 'Communication from the Commission concerning Corporate Social Responsibility: A business contribution to Sustainable Development', 2 July 2002.

Falk, Richard (2001) 'Humane Governance and the Environment: Overcoming Neo-Liberalism', in Brendan Gleeson and Nicholas Low (eds), *Governing for the Environment: Global Problems, Ethics and Democracy*, Basingstoke: Palgrave, pp.221-236.

Gates, Jeff (2001) *Democracy at Risk: Rescuing Main Street from Wall Street*, Cambridge MA: Perseus.

Harvey, David (2003) *The New Imperialism*, Oxford: Oxford University Press.

Humphreys, David (2001) 'Environmental Accountability and Transnational Corporations', in Brendan Gleeson and Nicholas Low (eds) *Governing for the Environment: Global Problems, Ethics and Democracy*, Basingstoke: Palgrave, pp.88-101.

——— (2006) *Logjam: Deforestation and the Crisis of Global Governance*, London: Earthscan.

Lee, Kelley; Humphreys, David and Pugh, Michael (1997), '"Privatisation" in the United Nations System: Patterns of Influence in Three Intergovernmental Organisations', *Global Society: Journal of Interdisciplinary International Relations,* Vol.11, No.3, pp.339-357.

Litvin, Daniel (2003) *Empires of Profit: Commerce, Conquest and Corporate Responsibility*, London: Texere.

Korten, David C. (1995) *When Corporations Rule the World*, London: Earthscan.

——— (1999) *The Post Corporate World: Life After Capitalism*, San Francisco: Berrett-Koehler.

——— (2006) *The Great Turning: From Empire to Earth Community*, San Francisco: Berrett-Koehler.

McMurtry, John (1999) *The Cancer Stage of Capitalism*, London: Pluto Press.

——— (2003) *Value Wars: The Global Market Versus the Life Economy*, London: Pluto Press.

Monks, Robert A.G. (2008) *Corpocracy*, Hoboken NJ: John Wiley and Sons.

Nadeau, Robert L. (2003) *The Wealth of Nature: How Mainstream Economics Has Failed the Environment*, New York: Columbia University Press.

Ostrom, Elinor (1990) *Governing the Commons: The Evolution of Institutions for Collective Action*, Cambridge: Cambridge University Press.

Ross, Carne (2007) *Independent Diplomat: Dispatches from an Unaccountable Elite*, London: Hurst and Company.

Ruggie, John Gerard (2003) 'Taking Embedded Liberalism Global: The Corporate Connection', in David Held and Mathias Koenig-Archibugi (eds) *Taming Globalization: Frontiers of Governance*, Cambridge: Polity.

Said, Edward (1996) *Representations of the Intellectual: The 1993 Reith Lectures*, New York: Vintage Books.

Thompson, Grahame (2009) 'Greening Business', in William Brown, Claudia Aradau and Jessica Budds (eds), *Environmental issues and responses*, Milton Keynes: The Open University, pp.403-444.

Vatn, Arild (2008) 'Sustainability: The Need for Institutional Change', in Peter Utting and Jennifer Clapp (eds) *Corporate Accountability and Sustainable Development: Ecological Economics and Human Well-being*, Oxford: Oxford University Press, pp.61-91.

Part VII: Additional Research in Corporate Responsibility

Part 7 of the book is made up 9 additional CSR research papers on specific topics in specific regions around the globe: (1) CSR in Turkey, (2) CSR Lessons from India, (3) Iranian Culture and CSR, (4) NGO Influence on CSR in China, (5) Intercorporate Social Responsibility, (6) Third-Party Assurance of CSR in Finland, (7) Socially Responsible Lending in Australasian Banks, (8) Teaching Sustainability in Australian Higher Education, and (9) CSR and Potentially Harmful Products in the Gaming Industry.

Research Paper 1: CSR in Turkey

Corporate Social Responsibility in Turkey: A Comparative Research about Current Situation and Future Expectations

Cisil Sohodol Bir, Bahcesehir University, Istanbul, Turkey

Abstract: Today, the approach that the organizations cannot act only with their commercial objectives but at the same time they need to contribute to the social and economical development of the society has been adopted. The idea that the organizations which do not consider their organizational responsibilities as an inseparable part of their work strategy, will inevitably fail whatever the circumstances are, is now becoming a widespread conviction. When approaching the issue from that point of view, it would not be wrong to state that social responsibilities are indispensable implementations of the organizations of our day. Organizational social responsibility has become one of the most talked about, discussed implementations area of business life today. The social responsibility of the organizations are evaluated as a responsibility formed for the benefit of the society, that contributes to the betterment of the human life, without harming the society in all activities from production to consumption. In this article, a detailed evaluation about CSR has been made first , and then a research has been made directed to find out about the current situation and future expectations about CSR in Turkey. The results has been compared with 2007 Resport on European CSR Survey and the data obtained were evaluated with SPSS programme.

Introduction

Across the globe, business leaders are struggling to balance conflicting demands from communities, government, advocacy groups, and others about the role they play in economic advancement, environmental improvement, and social development. No longer is it acceptable simply to make good products that satisfy customers while complying with laws and regulations. Businesses are now called upon to consider – and, indeed, intentionally to manage – the wider social and environmental consequences of their actions, beyond the requirements of the legal and regulatory settings in which they operate. For an increasing number of global and multinational corporations, corporate social responsibility (CSR) has become an important aspect of conducting business (Aquilera et al, 2005; Hummels, 2004; Mackey et al, 2005; Peloza, 2005). Companies that operate globally are being increasing asked to act in a socially responsible manner. In addition to achieving financial returns, they are also expected to care for the environment, their employees and the local community. (Cramer, 2006: 13)

In the recent years, there has been an intriguing appearance of actual research conducted concerning CSR in use. The attempt to move beyond the philosophical, speculative, and prescriptive tendency characterizing most of the literature in CSR seems promising. Several recent studies, some exploratory, others comparative studies and still others empirical in nature address the application of CSR in actual organizations. Of particular importance to the present research are those that address managerial interpretation and use of CSR.(Hussein, 2006: 2)

Although the notion of corporate social responsibility is prominent in some of the current discussions and investigations about the role of business in society, the concept as such is not new. (Hediger, 2010: 529) The concepts of CSR has been discussed, practices and studied for decades. Over the years, corporate social responsibility and its effect on an organization's success has been the subject of much academic debate and criticism. (Footea, Gaffneyb, Evansa:2010, 799) The idea of corporations acting in the public interest is not new and has evolved over time. Corporations in 18th century America were formed explicitly to serve a public purpose and only for that public purpose. By the end of the 19th century, the public purpose of corporations had been transformed into an emphasis on private purpose and private property. The balance between public and private purpose, between collective and individual interests, shifted such that private purpose and individual interests took primacy, replacing the former public interest functions of the corporation (Altman & Vidaver-Cohen, 2000; Hurst, 1956, 1970). Although the CSR concept had existed for decades before (Dodd, 1932), the term was proposed initially in 1953 (Bowen) as a kind of business self-regulation device, a method of ensuring the social control of business without depending on the uncertainties of individual ethics or the coercive authority of governments. (Hussein, 1996; 16-17) Carroll (1999) describes the diverse history behind the concept. It is characterized by changing definitions and interpretations over time, ranging from early expressions of concern about the social responsibility of businessmen in the 1930s to the debates about globalization and the roles of business in society since the 1990s.

Literature Review

The expansive literature on CSR contains numerous definitions of the construct. While there is no single, commonly accepted definition of corporate social responsibility, it generally refers to business decision-making linked to ethical values, compliance with legal requirements, and respect for people, communities, and the environment. Generally speaking, CSR refers to the idea that private firms not only have obligations to their owners, but also to wider society.

One of the earlier academic definitions was by Bowen (1953), who defined corporate social responsibility as an obligation to pursue policies to make decisions and to follow lines of action which are compatible with the objectives and values of society.

McGuire (1963) took the view that the idea of social responsibility supposes that the corporation has not only economic and legal obligations, but also certain responsibilities to society which extend beyond these obligations.

For Davis (1973) CSR begins where the law ends. In other words, it is about what companies do with regards to making a positive contribution to society above and beyond that which constitutes their legal obligations. (Blowfield, Murray, 2008:12-13) Davis (1973) defines CSR as the firm's considerations of, and response to, issues beyond the narrow economic, technical, and legal requirements of the firm to accomplish social [and environmental] benefits along with the traditional economic gains which the firm seeks.

Votaw and Sethi (1975) suggested that these extra responsibilities involved bringing corporate behavior up to a level where it is congruent with the prevailing social norms, values, and expectations. Naylor (1999) defined social responsibility as the obligation of managers to choose and act in ways that benefit both the interests of the organization and those of society as a whole.

Dewitt considered that CSR as the duty of companies to behave in a manner that promotes social, economic and environmental well-being.(Dewitt, 2006) CSR is the broad concept that business are more than just profit seeking entities and, therefore, also have an obligation to benefit society(Werther, Chandler, 2006: 7)

CSR is about businesses and other organizations going beyond the legal obligations to manage the impact they have on the environment and society. In particular, this could include how organizations interact their employees, suppliers, customers and the communities in which they operate, as well as the extend they attempt to protect the environment. (Werther, Chandler, 2006: 8) Proponents of CSR argue that corporations benefit in many ways by operating with a longer term view of their organization and role in society than they do by focusing on just their own short-term profits. (Footea, Gaffneyb, . Evansa:2010: 799)

There is some agreement that corporate social responsibility (CSR) can be thought of as categories of economic, legal, ethical, and discretionary activities of a business entity as adapted to the values and expectations of society (Andrews, 1987; Carroll, 1979; Votaw, Sethi, 1975). The idea of "economic responsibilities" is based on responsibilities such as providing commodities of good quality, employment possibilities, and ensuring good conditions for workers, searching for raw material reserves and new recourses, leading to technological breakthroughs and being regular taxpayers for public expenditure. Novak (1996) summarizes economic responsibility fewer than seven items. These are "to provide customer satisfaction and a fair profit return to investment funds, to create new employments and incomes, make it possible to stride towards higher economic conditions and encourage, to support innovations and to diversify the economic concerns of the citizens. “Legal responsibilities” are enabled by obeying the rules and realizing corporate applications in conformity with the laws. Smitt and Quelch (1993) pointed out that “ethical responsibilities” comprise efforts concerning moral, truthful and fair treatment, respect for humans and prevention of behavior harmful to others. “Philanthropy”, time and support allotted to voluntary corporations and services are included in the fourth phase of social responsibility. McWilliams and Siegel (2001) define CSR as actions that appear to further some social good, beyond the interests of the firm and that which is required by law.

Corporate social responsibility is a form of management that is defined by the ethical relationship and transparency of the company with all the stakeholders with whom it has a relationship as well as with the establishment of corporate goals that are compatible with the sustainable development of society, preserving environmental and cultural resources for future generations, respecting diversity and promoting the reduction of social problems.(Filho et al., 2010:296)

The European Commission (2010) defines corporate social responsibility as ‘‘a concept whereby companies integrate social and environmental concerns in their business operations and in their interaction with their stakeholders on a voluntary basis.’’ Corporate social responsibility concerns are not about *whether* values, but *whose* and *what* values, are represented in business. (Deetz, 2007:269)

CSR has thought as “encompass not only what companies do with their profits, but also how they make them” (Kytle and Ruggie, 2005). Moreover, CSR is seen as a concept which “goes beyond philanthropy and compliance to address the manner in which companies manage their economic, social, and environmental impacts and their stakeholder relationships in all their key spheres of influence: the workplace, the marketplace, the supply chain, the community and the public policy realm.”(Hediger, 2010: 519)

A firm’s survival and success depends on the ability of its managers to create sufficient wealth and satisfaction for its primary stakeholders (Clarkson, 1995). Primary stakeholders of a firm include employees, shareholders, customers, suppliers, communities, and natural environment. If any of the primary stakeholder groups withdraws its support to the firm, the firm’s operation is adversely affected (Clarkson,1995). Firms must take decisions and take action not only in pursuit of their own profit, but also in the interest of stakeholders such as consumers, communities, the environment and employees. Because of that CSR has enormous importance in stakeholder relationships. In today’s highly competitive market environment, many companies have used CSR as a strategic tool to respond to expectations of various stakeholders such as media, public opinion, nongovernment organizations and even consumers, to thus create a favorable corporate image (Jones, 2005). So that CSR should be part of the corporate business plan. (Hawkins, 2006) In recent years, scholars and executives have devoted attention to the implications of CSR policies and practices as well as their relation to business strategy (Mcwilliams, Siegel, & Wright, 2006).

There are numerous reasons underlying organizations’ motivations for engaging in socially responsible endeavors. Firms believe that CSR helps recruit, motivate, and retain employees there are customer-related motivations. CSR may entice consumers to buy a company’s products or services. Companies’ focus on environmental concerns can lead to reductions in production costs. (Sprinkle, Maines, 2010:446)

Many companies are realizing that having a socially responsible corporate image is a valuable strategic asset. (Kim et al., 2010) There are a lot of research which show that firms that perform socially responsible activities enjoy benefits such as customer satisfaction and favorable customer evaluations (Brown and Dacin, 1997; Luo and Bhattacharya, 2006; Sen and Bhattacharya, 2001)

McWilliams et al. (2006: 4) pointed out that CSR ''should be considered as a form of strategic investment'' which ''can be viewed as a form of reputation building or maintenance.'' On the other hand, Fombrun (2005) proposed enhancing corporate reputation as an extrinsic motivation for companies to engage in CSR activities. Garberg and Fombrun (2006) also drew reputation gain as relevant outcomes of CSR programs.(Lai et al., 2010)

Corporate social responsibility is predominantly considered as a western phenomenon due to strong institutions, standards, and appeal systems which are weak in developing countries of Asia (Chapple and Moon, 2005). However, developing countries such as Turkey, the interest in the CSR is increasing day by day. Therefore, the researches about social responsibility is vital for the healthy development of the subject. In this context, the current study aims to contribute to the development of the social responsibility in Turkey.

CSR in Turkey

The experience of the philanthropic stage of CSR in Turkey goes back to the Ottoman times. In the Ottoman era, the "vakif" (foundation) was the premier institutional mechanism for philanthropic provision of public services such as education, health and social security. Today, most family owned conglomerates in Turkey have an associated Vakif. In this sense, the public demand from the companies is shaped within the historical "waqf" philosophy and social responsibility becomes identical to donations and philanthropic actions of the companies.

The assessment of total amount of donations, however, is not easy to identify (Bikmen, 2003) and this puts a limitation on the measurement of impact. Coming to the last 50 years of the political and economic structure; the military coups and an unstable economy with phases of high inflation, it is possible to conclude that the economic and political background in Turkey was not very supportive to long-term planning and thus to concerns of sustainable development. For liberalizing the economy in the beginning of the 1980s,

Turkey took steps to integrate its economy with developed countries. However, this integration process brought new challenges such as competitiveness which certainly acted as an impediment for companies to set up CSR practices mainly due to the price pressure as well as the profitability. The economic role of state has been diminishing for the past 3 decades, but it is still high compared to other EU countries. Nevertheless, the stable inflation and growth rate in the last 5 years created an atmosphere for companies to be more involved with the social issues. Turkey's increased integration with the international bodies, developments, events and campaigns has also been an important element for the country's consciousness on CSR and related issues.

The United Nations Conference on Human Settlements (Habitat II) in Istanbul in 1996, played an important role in terms of enabling the citizens of Istanbul to observe people discussing issues of eradication of poverty and discrimination, promotion and protection of all human rights and fundamental freedoms for all, and provision of basic needs, such as education, nutrition and life-span health care services. This created an atmosphere for the issues related to sustainable development to be discussed and debated in Turkey. in the non-governmental organizations and created a better environment for civil participation. Consequently, both the international issues and the economic and social crises in Turkey created an environment for the discussion of CSR where business had the major role to play and the civil society to monitor and benefit. This analysis is supported by a research of a Canadian based GlobeScan. The research conducted an international survey named CSR Monitor in which the Turkish leg has been conducted by Yontem Research Company. According to the research, corporate citizenship is highly recognized in Turkey, however, the companies are not expected to have operational presence in the fields such as labour rights and environmental issues. The time schedule stated above is also supported by the findings of this research, as the research indicated that CSR as a component of corporate reputation in Turkey has been in an increase since 1999.

In the business environment of Turkey, there is confusion over the definition of Corporate Social Responsibility (and this confusion reflects itself on the practices of CSR. However, on the part of the business community, a strong incentive for efforts developing business and society is observed.

Multinational Companies (MNCs) positively affect the CSR practices in Turkey. The MNCs put positive pressures to their local branches and their suppliers, and this process set trends for Turkish companies. For example, supply-chain issues especially in textile industry, have a positive effect on the application of international labor standards in Turkey.

CSR in Turkey is supported by external drivers such as the international organizations and NGOs. Local initiatives, such as NGOs and customers, are needed to be developed and encouraged to create pressure on companies.

Society's expectations of business are influenced by many factors. In a global study conducted in 2001 by Environics International (www.environics.com), it was found that Turkish consumers valued business ethics, labour practices, environmental impacts and demonstrable social responsibility far less than brand quality when forming an impression of a company. The same study found that in low- to mid-income level countries, the perception of companies as socially responsible is based on reasons which are not CSR related. Society predominantly expects economic performance (jobs) from business in those countries, which is consistent with the findings in Turkey.

Ascigil (2003), in her unpublished survey conducted for TESEV explored management attitudes towards CSR in Turkey. Using Caroll's (1979) and Aupperle's (1994) contextualized questionnaires, Ascigil found that 75% of the managers included in the survey gave priority to economic criteria when making decisions whereas 19.11% gave priority to ethical criteria and only 6% to legal criteria. Ascigil notes that Turkish managers do not differentiate between legal and ethical responsibilities as evidenced by the structural analysis of their responses. Furthermore, the study shows that customers are considered to be the most important stakeholders by 75.8% of managers; employees being the second by 50.8% and the society at large by only 24.3%. According to the same survey, 53.5% of the managers would not give priority to ethical considerations if these would negatively impact economic performance. "Quality" and "Customers" are the most frequently used concepts in companies' mission statements by 61.5%. "Society" is mentioned in only 22.1% of statements whereas "Profitability" is mentioned only in 3.3%. This may be related to the timidity regarding wealth and concerns about the legitimacy of business. Ascigil notes that the mere existence of a mission statement positively affects management attitudes towards CSR and that companies' awareness of CSR increases with post graduate education and with an increased share of foreign capital. She further notes that 49.7% of managers consider themselves as reactive with respect to CSR issues, 13.6% totally ignore the concept and 33.5% believe that they handle CSR as a strategic matter. She concludes that CSR in Turkey has not moved beyond a public relations matter in Turkish companies.

The limitation of cultural drivers is reflected in a low ethical / legal social responsibility performance of corporations in Turkey. In fact, a survey conducted by the Turkish Ethical Values Centre (TEDMER) reveals that 35% of the sample group observed unethical behaviour at work. Most respondents considered fraud, tax avoidance, bribing and discrimination as important ethical issues whereas disclosure quality in informing the public, protecting the environment, valuing diverse opinions and keeping legal records and reports as less important. 57 % of respondents thought that organizations face unfair competition because of being ethical. 92.6 % of the respondents believed that a reconstruction of state and government would be necessary for ethics to be settled. This is comparable to 92.3% who believe economic development would be the necessary precondition. 67.9% of the respondents considered the increased existence of international firms as a very important factor in improving the ethics in Turkey

Research Methodology

In 2007, M. Kaptein, L. Kooning, R.V. Tulder and L.V. Vliet conducted a survey of 200 largest companies in Europe. Companies were questioned on their current involvement in corporate social responsibility as well as their expectation of the importance of CSR future. (Kaptein et al., 2007 Report on European CSR Survey, RSM Erasmus University)

The current research conducted in Turkey based on 2007 Report on European CSR Survey. Questionnaire was adapted from 2007 Report on European CSR Survey results document and sent to 200 companies from 15 different sectors in Turkey. At the end of the period given, return of 110 online questionnaires was provided. Rate of questionnaire returns in the research is 55%. In the data analysis SPSS program was used.

The first objectives of current research is find out the firm's ideas and practices about CSR in Turkey and secondly is to compare the similarities and differences of ideas and practices between European and Turkish firms about CSR implementations.

In this research companies were questioned on their current involvement in Corporate Social Responsibility (CSR) as well as their expectations of the importance of CSR in the future.

The 10 CSR issues that were selected for this survey:

- Corruption prevention
- Ecological diversity
- Education
- Fair trade and fair procurement
- Climate change
- Health and safety
- Income equality and fair wages
- Labor rights
- Poverty
- Transparency of business practice
- With reference to 10 CSR issues (which mentioned above), companies were asked to what extent:
- These issues impact their business;
- They experience pressures from stakeholders to engage responsibly with these issues;
- They have taken measures to address these issues (policies, CSR office, reporting etc);
- They cooperate with stakeholders to deal with these issues; and
- They have developed specific strategies to address the urgent issue of climate change.

This paper corresponds to the perceptions concerning the social responsibility, implementation processes and future expectations of Turkish and European firms. Since the data from the research conducted on European organizations is not available, all the comparisons are made over the published results on 2007 European CSR Survey. Therefore, the results presented as mean scores in that respective research (2007 European CSR Survey) and the data from the research that we conducted on Turkish firms are compared to each other using one-sample test.

The results provided in 2007 Report on European CSR Survey in percentages on the other hand are compared to the data from the research conducted on Turkish firms by employing nonparametric test- binominal test.

Findings

Relevance of Issues

Regarding the 10 CSR issues, companies were asked to indicate the perceived impact of these issues on doing business in Turkey. Respondents could indicate this on a scale from 1 (not at all) to 5 (very much). To compare Turkish and European firms' mean scores one sample t-test was conducted.

Table-1 shows mean scores of relevance of issues both Turkish and European firms and t-test results. According to t-test results for 6 issues Turkish firms' and European firms' opinions about relevance of CSR issues are significantly different. European firms rated greater than Turkish firms about corruption prevention, health and safety, transparency of business practice, climate change, labor rights and income equality and fair wages issues. It means European firms perceived impact of these issues on doing business more than Turkish firms.

Table1: Relevance of Issues

CSR Issue	Europe	Turkey	Mean Difference	t-values	Sig. (2 ~ tailed)
	M	M			
Corruption prevention	4.6	2.1	-2,48	-16,219	,000*
Health and safety	4.5	4.2	-,300	-2,143	,037*
Transparency of business practice	4.5	3.6	-,860	-4,550	,000*
Climate change	4.3	3.5	-,720	-4.934	,000*
Labor rights	4.3	2.6	-1,66	-9,214	,000*
Income equality and fair wages	3.9	2.3	-1,54	-9,554	,000*
Fair trade and fair procurement	3.9	3.8	-,060	-,369	,714
Ecological diversity	3.7	3.8	,140	,937	,353
Education	3.5	3.7	,200	,959	,342
Poverty	3.0	2.6	-,340	-1,782	,081
*p<.05					

Future Urgency of Issues

Companies were asked to indicate the expected increase in urgency of the 10 CSR issues in Turkey. Respondents could indicate this on a scale from 1 (not at all) to 5 (very much).

Table-2 shows mean scores of future urgency of issues both Turkish and European firms. To compare Turkish and European firms' mean scores one sample t-test was conducted. According to t-test results for 7 issues Turkish firms' and European firms' opinions about future of CSR issues are significantly different. European firms rated higher than Turkish firms for 5 of these 7 issues. Turkish firms rated higher score only for health and safety and education. It is an expected result considering that Turkey is a developing country. In Turkey, education and health-related problems could be solved yet so firms expect increase in urgency of these two issues.

Table 2: Future of Issues

CSR Issue	Europe	Turkey	Mean Difference	t-values	Sig. (2~ tailed)
	M	M			
Climate change	4.4	3.6	-,665	-5,570	,000*
Transparency of business practice	3.8	3.3	-392	-2,590	,013*
Ecological diversity	3.7	3.8	,096	,798	,429
Fair trade and fair procurement	3.5	3.6	,071	,471	,639
Corruption prevention	3.5	2.3	-1,153	-8,237	,000*
Labor rights	3.4	2.4	-,951	-6,791	,000*
Health and safety	3.4	3.8	,400	3,212	,002*
Education	3.2	4.1	,940	8,492	,000*
Income equality and fair wages	3.1	2.7	-,324	-2,259	,028*
Poverty	3.0	2.8	-,061	-,375	,710
*p<.05					

Pressure from Stakeholders

Companies were asked to indicate how much pressure they experience from stakeholders to improve their CSR performance in Turkey. The average values on a scale from 1 (no pressure) to 5 (high pressure) are depicted in this table.

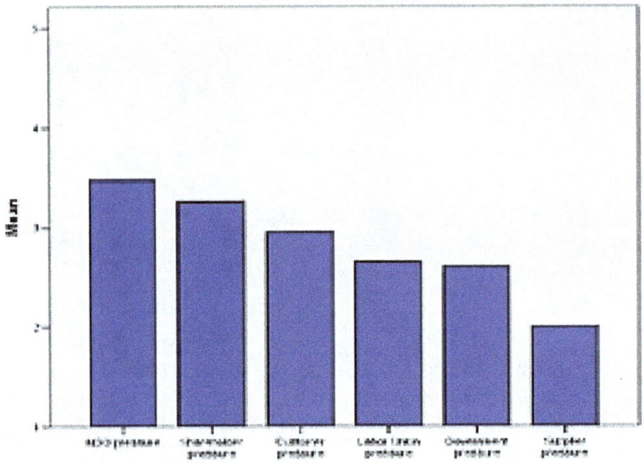

Chart 1: Stakeholder Pressure – European Firms

Chart-1 shows the means scores of European firms pressure they experience from stakeholders to improve their CSR performance and Chart-2 shows the means scores of Turkish firms pressure they experience from stakeholders to improve their CSR performance. When we compare the results it is clear that, in Europe, stakeholder pressure to improve CSR performance more than Turkey. In Turkey, participants rated below the average about all items of stakeholder pressure. European firms mentioned that NGO is the most of the stakeholder group that are pushing to improve firms' CSR performance. Whereas in Turkey, the most compelling group of stakeholders is shareholder. Both in Europe and Turkey the pressure level of the supplier is minimal.

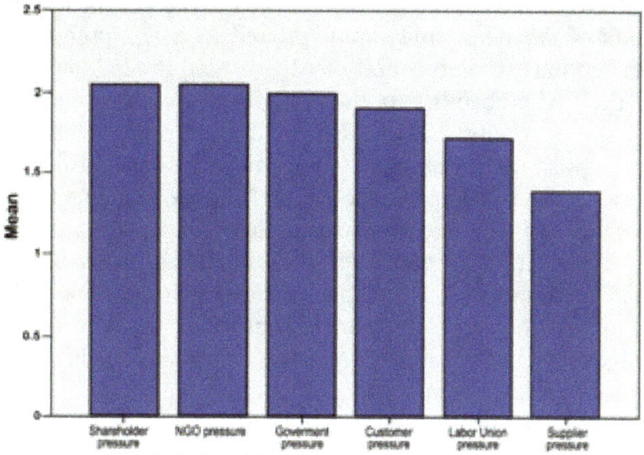

Chart 2: Stakeholder Pressure – Turkish Firms

Expected Increase of CSR Importance

The expected increase in importance of CSR in seven functional areas was measured on a scale from 1 (less important) to 5 (much more important).

Table 3: Expected Increase of CSR Importance

	Europe	Turkey	Mean Difference	t-values	Sig. (2 -tailed)
	M	M			
Reputation Management	4.3	4.2	-,040	-,332	,742
Employee attraction	4.2	3.8	-,380	-2,677	,010*
Competition (in general)	4.1	3.5	-,640	-4,864	,000*
Investor relations	4.0	3.2	-,760	-4,284	,000*
Corporate liabilities/Legal claims	3.8	2.8	-,980	-5,741	,000*
Cost efficiency	3.8	1.9	-1,868	-13,520	,000*
Quality	3.8	2.8	-,960	-5,732	,000*
*p<.05					

Table-3 shows mean scores of expected increase of CSR importance both Turkish and European firms. To compare Turkish and European firms' mean scores one sample t-test was conducted.

According to t-test results for 6 issue Turkish firms' and European firms' opinions about increase in importance of CSR are significantly different. European and Turkish firms have the same opinion only about reputation management.

Official CSR Policy and Quantitative Targets

Companies were asked whether they have official policies in place to address the 10 CSR issues and whether quantitative targets have been defined to measure and improve corporate performance in Turkey.

In this part of the analysis, the binomial test was used because the binomial test of significance is an exact probability test, based on the rules of probability, and it is used to examine the distribution of a single dichotomy when the researcher has a small sample. Besides, the binomial test of significance tests the difference between a sample proportion and a given proportion, for one-sample tests. Results of the other study were entered as a test proportion for the first group ("yes" option). The probability for the second group ("no" option) will be 1 minus the specified probability for the first group.

Table-4 shows results about official policies in place to address the 10 CSR issues for Turkish and European companies and also Table-4 indicate the binomial test results to compare Turkish and European companies. According to results, 7 of the 10 issues about official policies Turkish and European firms are statistically different. 6 of these 7 issues European firms have more official policies than Turkish firms. Only about education issue Turkish firms state that they have more official policy than European firms. It is an expected result because education is the most important CSR subject in Turkey. Most of companies have social responsibility campaigns to improve education in Turkey.

Table 4: Official Policy

CSR Issue	Observed Proportion (Turkey)	Test Proportion (Europe)	Asymp.Sig (1-tailed)
Corruption prevention	,38	,96	,000*
Health and safety	,78	,96	,000*
Transparency of business practice	,77	,86	,000*
Climate change	,44	,63	,005*
Labor rights	,50	,90	,000*
Income equality and fair wages	,17	,71	,000*
Fair trade and fair procurement	,72	,71	,509
Ecological diversity	,58	,53	,277
Education	,66	,41	,000*
Poverty	,17	,18	,495
*p<.05			

Table-5 shows results quantitative targets have been defined to measure and improve corporate performance about the 10 CSR issues in Turkey and Europe. Table-5 also shows the binomial test results to compare Turkish and European companies.

First remarkable result is the having proportion of quantitative targets very low in Turkey. Companies' proportion of ownership quantitative target is below the average all CSR issues. Another important result is differences between Turkey and Europe. 6 of the 10 CSR issues have statistically different results about quantitative targets. European firms have more quantitative targets about corruption prevention, health and safety, transparency of business practice, climate change, income equality and fair wages, fair trade and fair procurement, poverty than Turkish firms.

Table 5: Quantitative Targets

CSR Issue	Observed Proportion (Turkey)	Test Proportion (Europe)	Asymp.Sig (1-tailed)
Corruption prevention	,15	,39	,000*
Health and safety	,43	,69	,000*
Transparency of business practice	,25	,41	,016*
Climate change	,11	,55	,000*
Labor rights	,23	,35	,062
Income equality and fair wages	,12	,28	,011*
Fair trade and fair procurement	,14	,28	,028*
Ecological diversity	,19	,31	,051
Education	,44	,37	,205
Poverty	,00	,4	,000*

Co-operation

Companies were asked to indicate whether or not cooperate with following six stakeholders to improve their performance on the 10 CSR issues in Turkey.

Table-6 and Table-7 show the results of cooperation performance of Turkish and European companies with stakeholders. An also both tables show the results of the binomial test results to compare Turkish and European firms cooperation performance with stakeholders.

When we look at the results it is possible to say that cooperation with stakeholders about CSR issues is low level in Turkey. Firms' highest cooperation percents are with government about transparency of business practice (56%), with competitors about education and corruption prevention (10%), with NGOs about education (66%), with labor union about labor rights (%62), with suppliers about transparency of business practice (50%), with customers about transparency of business practice (56%).

When look at the binominal test results there are some differences between cooperation level with stakeholder between Turkey and Europe. There are statistically differences between Turkish and European firms' stakeholder cooperation about 6 of 10 issues for government, 9 of 10 issues for competitors, 8 of 10 issues for NGO, 2 of 10 issues for labor union, 8 of the 10 issues for suppliers, 5 of the 10 issues for customers.

Table 6: Cooperation with Stakeholders about CSR Issues

	Government			Competitors			NGOs		
CSR Issue	Observed Prop. (Turkey)	Test Prop. (Europe)	Asymp. Sig (1-tailed)	Observed Prop. (Turkey)	Test Prop. (Europe)	Asymp. Sig (1-tailed)	Observed Prop. (Turkey)	Test Prop. (Europe)	Asymp. Sig (1-tailed)
Corruption prevention	,44	,37	,189	,10	,20	,103	,04	,29	,000*
Health and safety	,46	,41	,281	,08	,26	,001*	,30	,33	,385
Transparency of business practice	,56	,39	,011*	,02	,29	,000*	,14	,33	,002*
Climate change	,02	,65	,000*	,02	,47	,000*	,32	,61	,000*
Labor rights	,12	,29	,004*	,06	,16	,031*	,04	,28	,000*
Income equality and fair wages	,00	,20	,000*	,00	,10	,034*	,00	,18	,000*
Fairtrade-fairprocurement	,26	,26	,574	,08	,18	,040*	,12	,26	,013*
Ecological diversity	,06	,31	,000*	,06	,16	,031*	,58	,47	,078
Education	,20	,28	,134	,10	,08	,000*	,66	,28	,000*
Poverty	,04	,18	,003*	,00	,06	,000*	,04	,35	,000*
*p<.05									

Table 7: Cooperation with Stakeholders about CSR Issues

	Labor Unions			Suppliers			Customers		
CSR Issue	Observed Prop. (Turkey)	Test Prop. (Europe)	Asymp.Sig (1-tailed)	Observed Prop. (Turkey)	Test Prop. (Europe)	Asymp. Sig (1-tailed)	Observed Prop. (Turkey)	Test Prop. (Europe)	Asymp. Sig (1-tailed)
Corruption prevention	,08	,12	,268	,02	,26	,000*	,08	,28	,000*
Health and safety	,38	,47	,011*	,38	,43	,286	,40	,20	,006*
Transparency of business practice	,20	,12	,071	,50	,33	,009*	,56	,31	,000*
Climate change	,02	,06	,190	,05	,29	,000*	,28	,47	,005*
Labor rights	,62	,65	,571	,10	,33	,000*	,04	,08	,226
Income equality and fair wages	,20	,51	,000*	,00	,12	,002*	,06	,04	,323
Fairtrade-fairprocurement	,10	,10	,413	,20	,55	,000*	,20	,18	,412
Ecological diversity	,06	,08	,425	,08	,22	,008*	,20	,26	,213
Education	,20	,29	,103	,20	,12	,071	,42	,14	,000
Poverty	,00	,02	,364	,00	,08	,015*	,06	,12	,135*
*p<.05									

Three Measures of CSR Management

With reference to the 10 CSR issues, companies were asked whether they have implemented the following three measures in Turkey.

Table- shows the results of the implementation three measures Turkish and European firms. Table-8 also shows the results of the binomial test results to compare Turkish and European firms' three measures of CSR management.

Firstly, according to code of conduct results 7 of the 10 CSR issues are significantly different between European and Turkish firms. European firms have more proportion for code of conduct almost all CSR issues (except education). All three measures, especially codes of conduct are quite commonly used by European firms. Secondly, according to employee training results 4 of the 10 issues have statistically different between European and Turkish firms. 3 of these 4 issues (corruption prevention, income equality and fair wages fair, trade-/fair procurement) European firms have more proportion than Turkish firms and 1 of these 4 issue (education) Turkish firms have more proportion than European firms. Lastly, according to stakeholder dialogue results 4 of the 10 issues have statistically different between European and Turkish firms.

Table 8: Three Measures of CSR Management

	Codes of Conduct			Employee Training			Stakeholder Dialogue		
CSR Issue	Observed Prop. (Turkey)	Test Prop. (Europe)	Asymp .Sig (1-tailed)	Observed Prop. (Turkey)	Test Prop. (Europe)	Asymp .Sig (1-tailed)	Observed Prop. (Turkey)	Test Prop. (Europe)	Asymp. Sig (1-tailed)
Corruption prevention	,54	,92	,000*	,40	,82	,000*	,46	,43	,385
Health and safety	,68	,82	,012*	,80	,80	,416	,76	,47	,000*
Transparency of business practice	,70	,88	,001*	,64	,65	,494	,74	,49	,000*
Climate change	,38	,43	,286	,42	,37	,276	,50	,65	,021*
Labor rights	,42	,84	,000*	,36	,47	,078	,46	,43	,385
Income equality and fair wages	,16	,61	,000*	,16	,28	,036*	,30	,39	,122
Fairtrade-fairprocurement	,58	,73	,016*	,58	,73	,016*	,50	,45	,284
Ecological diversity	,54	,53	,501	,54	,37	,110	,64	,47	,122

Other CSR Measures

Some other widely used measures to embed CSR were asked to companies. Table-9 shows the results of Turkish and European firms answers. Table also includes binominal test results to compare Turkish and European firms.

According to binominal test results there are significant differences for all 6 items between European and Turkish firms. The firms mostly use information on corporate website to embed CSR in Turkey (92%). The usage of CSR sustainability report and ISO 14001 are rare. Whereas, firms use all items to embed CSR more intensely in Europe.

Table 9: Other CSR Measures

	Observed Prop. (Turkey)	**Test Prop. (Europe)**	**Asymp.Sig (1-tailed)**
Information on corporate website	,92	,98	,018*
CSR/Sustainability report	,30	,90	,000*
ISO 14001	,06	,82	,000*
Section in financial annual report	,60	,80	,001*
CSR in marketing campaigns	,46	,75	,000*
Information brochures	,76	,47	,000*
*p<.05			

CSR Staff

50% of the companies have 1 to 5 people employed to manage CSR and 14% have more than 20 CSR officers in Europe. However 71% of the companies do not have any people to manage CSR.(see charts 3 and chart 4)

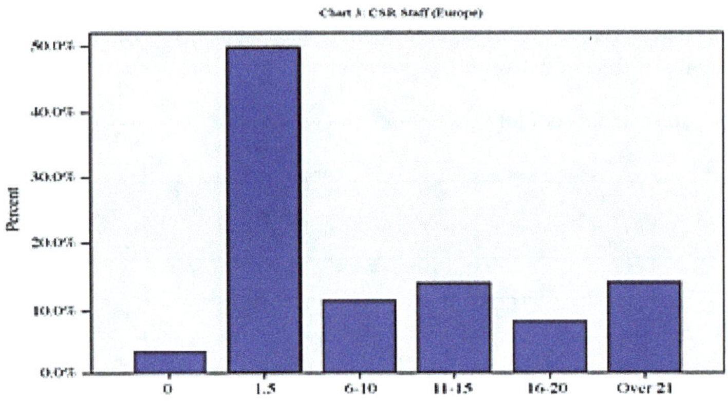

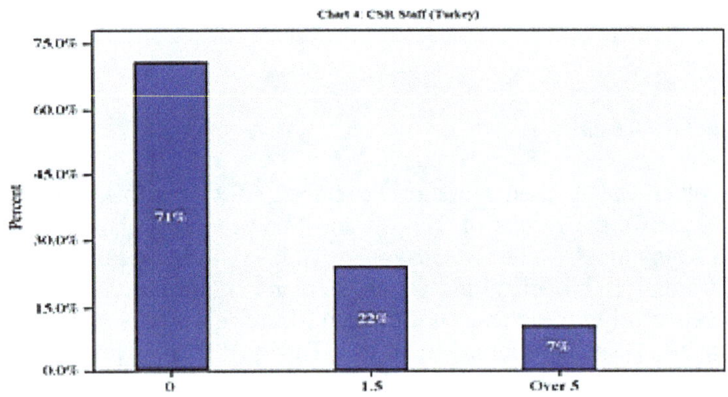

Internal Responsibility

In most cases, either the CEO (33%) or another board member (34%) is ultimately responsible for CSR within the company in Europe. In 8% of the companies no particular person has final responsibility. In Turkey, board member (35%) or CEO (20%) is ultimately responsible for CSR. (See charts 5 and 6)

Chart 5: Internal Responsibility (Europe)

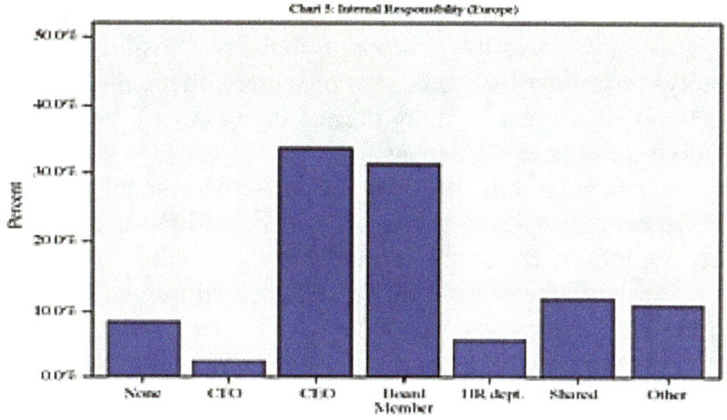

Chart 6: Internal Responsibility (Turkey)

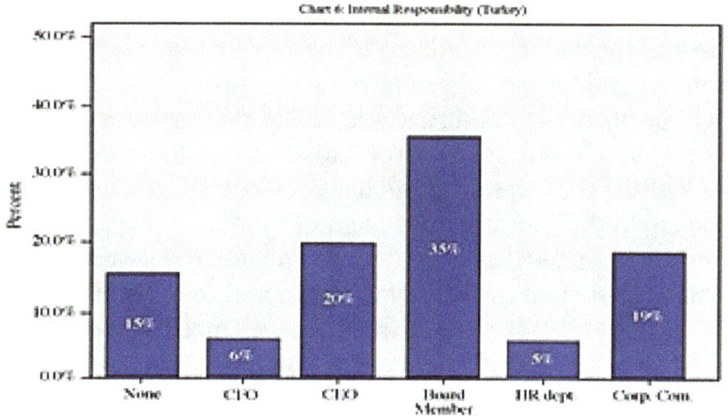

Discussion and Conclusion

Rapid and radical changes which started to be experienced in the world since 1980s brought about significant impacts on business life. Especially the phenomenon of globalization brought about a new layout by altering the way companies transact business. In conjunction with globalization, the perception of competition has changed; in the new global perception of competition , price-orientation has been abandoned, a perception of competition that focuses on the customer has been adopted, the concept of cooperative competition came into question and in creating customer loyalty, common set of values started to become the focus of the discussion. Also, as of this period, the world has become a small village, and everyone has got to be informed about everything together with the developments experienced in information and communication technologies. Together with all these changes, the consumers have also entered in a significant process of change and we came across with a new consumer model who is more judgmental, who makes research, questions and compares.

All developments experienced caused the new concepts to become prominent, and to be mentioned more and to be put into use. Corporate social responsibility has also become one of the most talked about, discussed fields of implementation in business life. Corporate social responsibility is interpreted as a responsibility constituted for the benefit of society, that contributes to human life towards betterment without harming the society in any of the implementations of the company from production to consumption.

Every organization has its own unique environment . The organization affects its environment, and the environment affects the organization. This environment imposes the organization non-ignorable obligations. Therefore organizations are obliged to act in a way to cause minimum harm and maximum benefit to the environment in which they exist. Since organizations are parts of the systems surrounding them, their survival is only possible with the adaptation to the changes that occur in this system. During this adaptation process, one of the most important tools which organizations can benefit from is social responsibility.

Nowadays, the perception that organizations can not only act towards their commercial objectives but they must also contribute to the economic and social development of the society, is adopted. The fact that the organizations that do not deal with their corporate social responsibilities as an integral part of their business strategy will be doomed to failure whatever the circumstances are, is becoming an accepted opinion . It will not be wrong to state that the social responsibility has become one of the most essential implementations for organizations of our day if we approach to the subject from this point of view,

Organizations make a great effort in order to survive in the heavy competition environment in which they exist and to acquire loyal customers for themselves. Consumers of today expect the organizations not to solely produce goods and/or services and sell them but also to make things within the society and add values to it. In addition their customer relationship management , establishing a consistent and healthy communication with other stakeholders concerned, and developing a well-adjusted cooperation have also gained highly great importance. When all these are taken into account together, it is possible to argue that corporate social responsibility implementations offer crucial further developments in terms of bringing further values in the society, maintaining healthy stakeholder relationships, and providing a good and strong reputation for the organizations. Corporate social responsibility offers golden opportunities in terms of providing a steady consistency and cooperation between the organization and its concerning target audience and in this sense, it supports the two-way symmetric approach to the Public Relations. However, in order to make use of the advantages listed above, the organizations must plan, exercise and control the social responsibility projects in a very professional manner. It is important for the social responsibility projects not to be considered as a separate part that is not integrated with other communication activities and its integration to these communication activities is important in terms of reputation management.

Public relations play a key role in the implementation of corporate social responsibility projects, Public relations, as the function of the company responsible for its communication with all concerning target audience and for its reputation , should also undertake the task of performing social responsibility activities, and should plan then exercise these activities just like a communication campaign.

In regards to all these concerns, we have attained some interesting and remarkable findings in the research that we conducted in an attempt to determine what the organizations in Turkey expect from corporate social responsibility, what kind of implementations they perform and the attitude of the public relations employees towards the concerns of social responsibility. When the findings obtained are examined in general, it is possible to state that the organizations in Turkey showed significant differences in their affinity to the 10 basic determined social responsibility concerns accordingly, and that the organizations were not that interested in the concerns other than education, health, safety, and transparency of business practice. Especially the inference that two fundamental social responsibility concerns such as income equality, fair wages and poverty which are often discussed among the important problems in Turkey, did not affect the business strategies of the organizations and the fact that the organizations have always underrated these two subjects among the fields where social responsibility investments would be made, is rather an interesting conclusion. At this point, some remarkable results appear even when the results obtained from the research that we have conducted are compared to results of the research conducted on European companies . So that, the subject of preventing corruption as a social domain which is stated to affect the organizations in the lowest level in Turkey was in the first place for European organizations and became the most important item in their agenda. Nevertheless the differences on the concerns of income equality, fair wages and the labor rights are also important in terms of determining the mental diversity in between.

The most important significant driving force for the betterment of the organizations' performance in social responsibility concerns is that their concerned stakeholders put pressure on them . At this point, it is possible to state the pressure that the organizations which operate in business in Turkey receive from their stakeholder on the development of the social responsibility scopes, ceases to increase in many fields. At this point it is also seen that the stakeholder implementations put the least pressure on the concerns of corruption prevention and the distribution of income. When all concerning stakeholder groups are examined, the group that puts the least pressure on the organization for the betterment of social fields were determined to be the suppliers. This case shows similarities with the results of the research in Europe.

Organizations believe that in the following years, social concerns such as education, health and safety and ecological diversity will become more urgent in our country. At this point it was determined that it is believed concerns such as income equality and fair wages, labor rights and corruption prevention will not gain any urgency and that we come across with these concerns rating the lowest. According to this conclusion of fact, when a social field is mentioned, it is seen that the education is emphasized most and believed to become more important. When we have a look at the results obtained in Europe on the other hand, we see that education could find a place for itself in the lowest ranks among the social concerns that would gain urgency. It is also clearly seen as a significant difference that the organizations in Europe have the urgency for the concerns that climate change would gain in the following years is taken more seriously than the organizations of our country.

One of the most noteworthy results inferred from the research is that the Turkish organizations fell behind the organizations in European setting themselves quantitative goals with regards to social concerns. Also for determination of their formal policy, it is seen that health and safety were given the priority . Even at this point, it is seen that there is a significant difference from the results in Europe. Health and safety concerns which ranked the top in terms of determining the formal policy in our country was seen to be the 8th in results from European and this itself clearly reflects the clear difference between these two groups.

One of the most discussed topics on corporate responsibility concerns is, at what points corporate social responsibility would provide benefits for organizations, and on what it would be effective. At this point, if we have a look at the data inferred from the research, we see that the most significant domain of corporate social responsibility is the reputation management in the organizations. Majority of those who participated in the research stated that the first field of concern was the reputation management that would be affected by corporate social responsibility . At this point, the results we obtained from Turkey and the results from the research conducted in Europe had similar features.

When the answers given by the organizations related to social responsibility projects which they had been conducting were analyzed, the most common field was education. Education takes the lead among the fields to which social responsibility investments are made in our country and is followed by health and safety fields. Fields of poverty and income equality and fair wages seen to be the fields where the organizations made the least social responsibility investments.

A satisfactory improvement in terms of corporate social responsibility implementations on the other hand is that corporate social responsibility is handled by top level management of organizations and general manager, CEO and/or board of the management are involved in making decisions about social responsibility. And this is considered as an indicator of the importance given to the concerns of social responsibility .

When we have a look at the domains which organizations prefer to use while starting and placing such social responsibility campaigns, we see that the internet sites of the companies are confronted most. On this line, informative brochures and posters are also seen among the tools which are often preferred. However, in their sustainability and activity reports, the organizations seem to fail in fulfilling the most important professional requirements of the task such as the part concerning corporate social responsibility and marketing which employs social responsibility. Especially when the results obtained in these fields are compared to the results in Europe, it is clearly seen that the organizations in our country have a very long road ahead of them.

At this point, when we look at the teams which the organizations in Turkey employ to manage corporate social responsibility projects and the number of employees who take part in these teams, the difference between the organizations in our country and the organizations in Europe is brought to the attention once more. When the results of the research conducted in Europe are examined, it was determined that the rate of having a separate team committed to the issue of corporate social responsibility rises up to 95% and in Turkey it remains at 29%, and the number of employees who work in these teams also remain low in a similar way..

When we have a look at the stakeholder communication with stakeholders about social responsibility fields, it is seen that they are reached out mostly for the concerns of transparency of business practice, Civil Society Organizations are reached out for education, unions for health and safety, suppliers for health and safety, and customers are also reached out for the concerns of transparency business practice. The communication with the rivals is almost at the point of zero. In the conclusions inferred from here has also remained quite low compared to the rate of stakeholder communications which the organizations in Europe made.

References

Altman, B.W. & Vidaver-Cohen, D. (2000). "A Framework for Understanding Corporate Citizenship", Business and Society Review, 105(1), 1-7.

Andrews, K. R. (1987). The Concept of Corporate Strategy, New York: Richard D. Irwin, Inc.

Aquilera, R., Rupp, D, Williams, C. & Ganapathi, J. (2007). "Putting the S Back in Corporate Social Responsibility: a Multilevel Theory of Social Change in Organizations, Academy of Management Review, 32(3), 836-863.

Ararat M, (2008). "A Development Perspective for Corporate Social Responsibility: Case of Turkey", Corporate Governance, 8(3), 271-285.

Blowfield M. (2008). Corporate Social Responsibility: A Critical Introduction, Oxford: Oxford University Press.

Bowen, R. (1953). Social Responsibilities of the Businessman, New York: Harper.

Brown, T. J. & Dacin P.A. (1997). "The Company and the Product: Corporate Associations and Consumer Product Responses", Journal of Marketing 61(1), 68– 84.

Carroll, A.B. (1999). "Corporate Social Responsibility: Evolution of a Definitional Construct" Business and Society, 38 (3), 268–295.

Chapple, W. & Moon, J.(2005)., "Corporate Social Responsibility (CSR) in Asia: A Seven Country Study of CSR Website Reporting", Business and Society, 44 (4), 415-441.

Cramer, J. (2006). Corporate Social Responsibility and Globalization: An Action Plan for Business, UK: Greenleaf Publishing,

Davis, K. (1973). "The Case For and Against Business Assumption of Social Responsibility", Academy Management Review, 16(2), 312-322.

Deetz, S. (2007). "Corporate Governance, Corporate Social Responsibility and Communication", in The Debate Over Corporate Social Responsibility, ed: Steve May, George Cheney, Juliet Roper, Oxford University Press: Oxford.

Dewitt J. (2006). CSR to Employees Post-Retirement, Rockhurst University Publication.

Dodd, E. M. (1932). "For Whom are Corporate Managers Trustees?." Harvard Law Review, 45:1145-1163.

Filho J.M., Wanderley L.S.Q., Gómez C.P. & Farache F. (2010). "Strategic Corporate Social Responsibility Management for Competitive Advantage", Brazilian Administration Review, 7(3), 294-309.

Fombrun, C. J. (2005), "The Leadership Challenge: Building Resilient Corporate Reputations", in, Handbook on Responsible Leadership and Governance in Global Business, J. P. Doh and S. A. Stumpf (eds.), Edward Elgar, UK: Cheltenham, 54–68.

Footea J, Gaffneyb N, & Evansa J. (2010). "Corporate Social Responsibility: Implications for Performance Excellence", Total Quality Management, 21(8), 799–812.

Garberg, N. A.& Fombrun C. J. (2006) "Corporate Citizenship: Creating Intangible Assets Across Institutional Environment", Academy of Management Review, 31, 329–346.

Hae-Ryong K., Lee M., Lee H.T.& Kim N.M. (2010). "Corporate Social Responsibility and Employee–Company Identification", Journal of Business Ethics, 95: 557–569.

Hawkins D.E. (2006). "Corporate Social Responsibility: Balancing Tomorrow's Sustainability and Today's Profitability", New York: Palgrave MacMillan.

Hediger, W. (2010). "Welfare and Capital-Theoretic Foundations of Corporate Social Responsibility and Corporate Sustainability", The Journal of Socio-Economics, 39, 518–526.

Hummels, H. (2004). "A Collective Lack of Memory", The Journal of Corporate Citizenship. (14), 18-22.

Hussein M. M. (2006) "Corporate Social Responsibility from The Corporate Perspective: A Delphi Study Of Selected Information Technology Companies", Unpublished Dissertation, Capella University.

Jones, R. (2005). "Finding Sources of Brand Value: Developing a Stakeholder Model of Brand Equity", Brand Management 13(1), 10–32.

Kytle, B., Ruggie, J.G. (2005), *Corporate Social Responsibility as Risk Management*, John F. Kennedy School of Government, Harvard University, Boston.

Lai C.S., Chiu C. J., Yang C.F.& Pai D. C. (2010) "The Effects of Corporate Social Responsibility on Brand Performance: The Mediating Effect of Industrial Brand Equity and Corporate Reputation", Journal of Business Ethics, 95:457–469.

Luo, X. & Bhattacharya C. B. (2006). "Corporate Social Responsibility, Customer Satisfaction, and Market Value", Journal of Marketing 70(4), 1–18.

McGuire, J. B. (1963). Business and society, New York: McGraw Hill.

McWilliams A., Siegel, D. S., & Wright, P. M. (2006). "Corporate Social Responsibility: Strategic Implications" Journal of Management Studies, 43(1), 1-18.

McWilliams, A. & Siegel, D. (2001). "Corporate Social Responsibility: a Theory of the Firm Perspective", Academy of Management Review 26 (1), 117–127.

McWilliams, A., Siegel D. S. & Wright P. M. (2006), "Corporate Social Responsibility: Strategic Implications", Journal of Management Studies 43(1), 1–18.

Naylor, J. (1999). Management, London: Pitman Publishing.

Novak, M. (1996). Business as a Calling: Work and the Examined Life, New York: The Free Press,

Peloza, J. (2005). "Corporate Social Responsibility as Reputation Insurance," presented at the *2nd Annual Corporate Social Performance Conference*, Haas School of Business, University of California, Berkeley, April.

Sen, S. & Bhattacharya C. B. (2001). "Does Doing Good Always Lead to Doing Better? Consumer Reactions to Corporate Social Responsibility", Journal of Marketing Research 38(2), 225–243.

Smith, N., Craig Q.& John A. (1993). "Ethical Issues in Researching and Targeting Consumers," SMITH, N. Craig/QUELCH, John A. (eds.), *Ethics in Marketing* (Illinois: Irwin): 145-195.

Sprinkle G. B. &, Maines L. A. (2010). "The Benefits and Costs of Corporate Social Responsibility", Business Horizons, 53, 445-453.

Votaw, D. & Sethi, S. (1975). The Corporate Dilemma, Englewood Cliff, N.J.: Prentice Hall.

Werther, W.B. & Chandler D. (2006). Strategic Corporate Social Responsibility: Stakeholders in a Global Environment, California: Sage Publication.

Research Paper 2: CSR Lessons from India

Learning From Social Entrepreneurs: A Case Study of Aurolab

Nicola H.J. Swan, U.K.

Abstract

This paper explores how companies can achieve corporate social responsibility (CSR) in communities in developing countries, and achieve their business objectives. An exploratory case study of Aurolab in India is used. Aurolab is an extreme and unique case, which it is hoped is revelatory, so laying the basis for future research in this field.

A review of the literature on CSR in communities is conducted. From this a proposition is put for further investigation. The literature suggests that management practices leading to civil empowerment improve trust, reputation and create core competences and distinctive capabilities, which assist in the generation of competitive advantage. However, it also suggests that this is not sufficient on its own. It is suggested that companies with high levels of CSR should take a leadership position, show sensitivity to cultural issues, local causes, community identity, two-way communication and develop empathy. This is best when exhibited both strategically and operationally with a view to ongoing behaviours and actions.

A desktop review of Aurolab was followed by semi-structured interviews, a site visit by the author for personal observation and many informal interviews. The intention of this process was to establish if the reality of Aurolab (rather than what is written about it) confirmed the outcomes of the literature. Further to see to what extent and under what conditions such outcomes emerge.

On the basis of this field research it was concluded that the proposition was confirmed. Aurolab is a commercial organisation with a legacy of emerging from a social enterprise. They maintain a non-profit status because they return all profits to their social cause. However, possibly

> *due to the legacy of their origins they display all of the attributes of a corporate socially responsible organisation whilst achieving their business objectives.*

This research explores how companies can achieve corporate social responsibility (CSR) in communities in India and achieve their business objectives. An exploratory case study of Aurolab in India is investigated. The intent is to take a unique social enterprise, which operates using a profitable business model, to see if there are lessons which can be learnt by commercial enterprises when addressing their CSR policy in relation to communities in India.

A brief overview of Aurolab's operations is given. This is followed by a review of relevant literature exploring what factors might be expected to be found in a successful CSR model, particularly with relevance to communities in India. From this a proposition is put which is then compared with the reality of findings from Aurolab. This is followed by some conclusions and recommendations for further research.

In 1992 Aurolab started production of Intraocular lenses (IOLs) purely because it was not possible to get IOLs at a price that was affordable in India. The company was developed as an off-shoot of the Aravind Eye Hospital (AEH) run by Dr Venkataswamy. AEH had commenced in 1976 with eleven beds, five for paying patients and six for free patients. The mission, then and now was to eradicate needless blindness. From the start, AEH was set up as a non-profit trust, as was Aurolab. The trusts are separate but work on the same business model of high volume, low cost and high quality. Each organisation makes approximately a 50% profit on turnover and still manages to provide two-thirds of their services free or at reduced cost to the rural poor.

This paper explores Aurolab's business model to see how they integrate CSR into a profitable business model. Aurolab sprang from the social enterprise of AEH and therefore whilst the case study focuses on Aurolab there is an overlap with AEH as they are a key not-for-profit customer and stakeholder of Aurolab.

The paper will now address the components of the literature as relevant to this research, starting with the shareholder and stakeholder debate, particularly focusing on where 'communities' fit as stakeholders. From here the review expands into a more global aspect taking in particular views from India and finally what is said about CSR as either a management or a strategic issue. The literature is summarised by producing a definition for use in the remainder of the chapter which describes what social conditions should be met for the community and what the company can expect in return.

The main tenet of Shareholder Theory is that persons holding shares 'give' this financial capital to company managers, who, acting as agents, maximize the return on investment through 'legal and none deceptive means' (Friedman 1997:56; Friedman 1962). In contrast Stakeholder Theory suggests that managers have a duty to **all** persons who have 'a stake in or claim on the firm' (Evan and Freeman 1988:97). Social Contract Theory, (sometimes referred to as having a licence to operate) involves asking what conditions should be met in order for society to allow a corporation to operate (Donaldson 1982). In effect, Social Contract Theory is an extension of stakeholder theory in that it includes all members of society as stakeholders.

Proponents of Friedman's (1962, 1997) theory can be said to be at the thin end of the wedge of what is morally acceptable (Bradburn 2001). Bradburn (2001) cites an example that corporations could utilise child labour in countries where it is legal to do so to maximise profits, but these extremes would not be accepted in other countries. Arguably current societal pressures about social issues mean many businesses move towards acceptance of Social Contract Theory rather than Shareholder Theory. Particularly so in countries like India where child labour, although illegal, is not uncommon.

Stakeholder Theory, whilst it started in the strategic management field, moved to the normative field of ethics. Within both arenas, there has been a plethora of literature trying to identify and define these stakeholders, or groups of stakeholders as summarized in table 1. There is some agreement on particular groups of stakeholders that are close to organisations, or 'primary stakeholders', such as employees, shareholders, suppliers and customers. However, there is limited agreement on those stakeholders that are slightly more peripheral[1] to the organisation. Various typologies have had more or less influence on management practice but there is no universally accepted model. What can be deduced from the variety of definitions in the literature is that the definition of one company's peripheral stakeholders will vary from another company's, based on the business context and the specific issues at any one time. This makes the development of a definition for 'community' or 'NGO' problematic.

Table 1: Rationales for stakeholder identification

Rationale	Example authors
A relationship exists	Thompson et al. 1991, Freeman 1994, Wicks et al. 1994
Power dependence where the stakeholder is dominant	Stanford Research Institute 1963, Freeman & Reed 1983, Savage et al. 1991
Power dependence where the company is dominant	Freeman 1984, Freeman & Reed 1983, Freeman & Gilbert 1987
Basis for legitimacy of relationship	Cornell & Sapiro 1988, Freeman & Evans 1990
The stakeholder has a claim on the company	Evans & Freeman 1988, Clarkson 1995
The stakeholder has something at risk	Clarkson 1994
The stakeholder has a moral claim on the company	Evans & Freeman 1988, Carroll 1989, Clarkson 1995, Donaldson & Preston 1995
The stakeholder has an interest in the company	Carroll 1989, Savage et al.

[1] For the purposes of this chapter 'peripheral stakeholders' are all stakeholders except employees, suppliers, shareholders and customers, no mater whether they are considered to be close to the organisation or an external group.

but not necessarily with legitimacy to that claim	1991, Clarkson 1995
Depends on the moral vision of the decision-maker and context	Buchholz and Rosenthal 2004
Depends on the organisations life cycle stage	Jawahar & McLaughlin (2001)
Stakeholders are derivative or normative	Phillips et al. 2003

(Source - Adapted from Mitchell et al. 1997 and Laplume et al. 2008)

When analysing Stakeholder Theory further the literature divides stakeholders into groupings – either first and second order (Cooper et al. 2001), where the community is a second order stakeholder; or, by power, legitimacy and urgency of need (Mitchel et al. 1997), where communities come low down the order; or by voluntary and involuntary (Clarkson 1995) where communities are involuntary; or inner and outer (Ridderstrale and Nordstrom 2000) with communities as outer stakeholders. All of these demarcations imply that communities are low down the list of stakeholders. Nevertheless, Ridderstrale and Nordstron (2000) say that all stakeholders have the power of choice and Clarkson (1995) considers all stakeholders to be equal and to have intrinsic value. Mathur and Kenyan (1997) claim that some stakeholders have a stronger influence than others because they are 'top of mind', i.e., families and colleagues, which moves people and hence communities up the importance scale. When looking at the Indian situation there is a far greater acknowledgement that without the commitment to communities and the social infrastructure required in communities business cannot be conducted effectively (CCC (a) n.d.). As a concomitant of this, within India it could be suggested that companies who accept that communities are legitimate stakeholders of prime importance should invest in more than financial capital. Social capital investment highlights the need to balance investment in short-term profit and long-term gain. Chakraborty et al. (2004) purport that businesses that invest in social capital create trust, reciprocity and tolerance ensuring long-term growth for their investors. Indeed other authors consider that CSR in general can improve reputation leading to greater competitive advantage and long-term growth (MacMillan et al 2004). Equally, communities invest their goodwill in companies by tolerating increased traffic, pollution etc and therefore the social investment becomes two-way and potentially improves company risk management.

The linkage between the role of business in the creation of social capital and their role in CSR actually places the company in the role of a civic actor. Being a civic actor is sometimes covered in the corporate citizenship literature and focuses on the normative aspects of CSR. There are two frameworks of note. Firstly, Banyan (2004:337) who proposes that some organisations are 'wired' the right way i.e. civic minded and she terms this as having 'high organisational citizenship'. The second framework is from the Corporate Citizenship Company (CCC (b.) n.d.). They look at a company value chain rather than the behavioural analysis of Banyan (2004). The Corporate Citizenship Company recognise that companies should look backwards and forwards along their value chain taking responsibility for their suppliers being good corporate citizens as well as for what happens to their products at the end of their lifecycle.

National Indian culture impacts heavily on how CSR action is perceived locally. With the legacy of English occupation, foreign companies in India can tend towards operating with a "feudal relationship" towards partners rather than taking a strategic alliance position to communities (Chakraborty et al. 2004). This is especially so when looking at government or company relationships with NGOs. Further, some companies relate to a single local NGO as *the* representative of the community, which may not be the case, as some NGOs are issues based rather than geographically based. Consequently, relationships between NGOs, community organisations (COs) and the companies are particularly important to get right, so no group is excluded. The level of 'power' as a stakeholder held by these NGO/COs varies enormously (CCC (b) n.d.). Further, in view of any so-called feudal relationships it is likely that NGO/COs do not feel empowered. Indeed some NGO/COs have said that globalisation is 'robbing' them of the right to choose their own path both economically and culturally and that this is verging on 'inhumane' (Chakraborty et al. 2004:100). Chakraborty et al. (2004) go further and say that not only does there need to be agreement on CSR issues but also an agreement about what corporate social irresponsibility is.

The extent of this issue goes beyond India with the number of people living in survival economies being approximately 4 billion; mainly within traditional, village based rural areas of Africa, India and China (Prahalad 2004). Further, developing countries account for 90% of the world's population growth (Hart 1997). But India is a fast growing economy, which is attractive for multinational companies (MNC). MNCs need to expand their markets, therefore, not only are they looking at rural communities as a potential labour resource they also view them as potential markets. For some time now outsourcing has linked commerce with the survival economy. Referring to the earlier link between social capital and companies as civic actors, investment in hygiene factors, improving employee retention, productivity and hence production is therefore of importance to these survival ecconomies. However, in developed countries, CSR activities frequently involve employee volunteerism, which is equivalent to a form of self-actualisation (Mazlow 1970). This brings to the fore the concept that corporations might have global CSR policies but they should think about enacting local CSR initiatives as appropriate to the country and even locations within a country. It may be difficult for corporations to adapt to a local culture especially where the company culture reflects the country of origin.

From this brief examination, it can be seen that not only may the MNC attempt to enact a CSR policy that works well in the home country but does not reflect the local culture but it can also be misinterpreted to actually be corporate social irresponsibility.

This review now moves on to examine the CSR debate from the angle of whether it should be a 'management' issue or a 'strategic' issue and how this will impact on business objectives.

As previously mentioned Stakeholder Theory, whilst it started in the strategic management field, moved to the normative field of ethics. Broadly, the focus of the strategic management approach has been to identify people and groups to ensure that business takes advantage of opportunities and minimises risks (Freeman et al., 2010). The ethical approach is to ensure that business mitigates its effects whilst managing those stakeholders that affect it, through incorporating an ethical approach to its decision making (Donaldson and Dunfee, 1994). The link between CSR, community stakeholders and financial goals is seen at various levels from tenuous (Fryxell and Wang 1994), to relevant only as it impacts on primary stakeholders (MacMillan et al. 2004), to a necessity (Chakraborty et al. 2004) and finally as an investment (Schiebel and Pochtrager 2003). Chakraborty et al. (2004:101) particularly take a look at the issues from an Indian perspective. They take the idea of CSR further by referring to 'humane management' and 'corporate spirituality'. This may be a reflection of cultural differences between Indian and the Western culture of other literature reviewed.

Halal (2000) and Vandemoortele (2009) believe that a focus on knowledge sharing between companies and community stakeholders can lead to mutual advantage for all stakeholders; however, Halal (2000) concludes that the collaboration required to achieve the sharing of knowledge should not exist because it is a pledge to society but because it is a factor in competitive advantage. Kay (1993) argued that successful creation and management of a company's distinctive capabilities, one of which is reputation, leads to competitive advantage. Reputation, like knowledge management, is an intangible asset which can be affected by the communities a company works with. A company that enters into joint problem solving processes, which assists the company's performance by increasing its knowledge and reputation, has the corollary effect of empowering the community. Yet only those businesses that go that step further and adopt Corporate Social Leadership (CSL), can sustain this as a competitive advantage (Hilton and Gibbons 2002). Leadership involves setting direction, basing reputation on real customer experience, not spin, and not just complying with regulation but considering how money is generated and how stakeholders are treated (Bradburn 2001, Handy 2002, MacMillan et al. 2004,).

Being first to market is recognised as being a significant business advantage leading to competitive advantage. CSL can therefore also create competitive advantage. As well as constructive relationships with communities leading to two-way knowledge interchange and profitable alliances CSL helps create a motivated workforce who are easy to recruit and retain (Halal 2000, Handy 2002). Collins and Porras (2000) go further and equate the social role of stakeholders to the financial role of shareholders, both being in a loop as they both supply and receive. Others believe that the sustainable development 'end', and appropriate stakeholder management 'means', are driven by fiduciary duty to create shareholder value (Donaldson & Preston 1995, Feltmate and Schofield 1999, BRS 2002). Therefore whatever the driver for co-operation between companies and communities there is a suggestion in the literature that it can be advantageous for both parties.

Summary of Findings in the Literature

Combining the findings on Social Contract Theory, creation of social capital and taking a strategic approach to the management of CSR it can be said that true CSR engagement and embeddedness by companies requires sensitivity to cultural issues, local causes and a form of communication that is two-way, empathetic and comprehensively displayed throughout the organisation. One way to do this may be by collaborating with a local NGO that has the networks and relationships in place (Millar et al. 2004, Murthuri et al. 2009). However, this partnership must be truly representative of the community and one of equals, not feudal (Chakraborty et al. 2004).

CSR can be incorporated integrally into the strategic process of generating added value for the company based on the values held and the stakeholders' views, then embedding those principles within the company culture. For a company to achieve sustainability and balance, it is suggested that their CSR ought to permeate every action from the mission to the strategies through policy, procedure and practice.

When working in India, MNCs must ensure that they fully understand their community's identity and ensure that their actions empower the community not disenfranchise it. This does not necessariliy mean philanthropy, but working with local partners to create sustainable projects. Therefore the following proposition is put:

That 'CSR in Communities' can be defined as a commitment to improve civil society and community wellbeing through business policies and practices which honour ethical values, local culture and respect people and communities, thus generating trust and the respect required to achieve business objectives. It is expected that this approach will produce the following outcomes for business:

1. Improved reputation;
2. Better motivated employees who are easier to retain;
3. Stimulated innovation through knowledge sharing;
4. Better risk management through greater knowledge of the community; and
5. Better stakeholder relationships.

Methodology

The primary objective of the field study was to explore the elements of the business model created by Dr Venkataswamy (affectionately known as Dr V), which saw the growth of Aurolab from AEH. Aurolab is a manufacturing company, developed to achieve a social purpose, but it is reliant on its own profitability to feed this social purpose.

This was qualitative research using a single exploratory case study - Aurolab. The case study methodology was appropriate because a 'how' question was being asked about a contemporary set of events over which the researcher had no control (Yin 1994, 2009). A single case study was appropriate because Aurolab is an extreme and a unique case. Further, Aurolab was a revelatory case in that it was established as a company primarily for social-entrepreneurial reasons. It is however financially sustainable and very successful. Whilst maintaining its profit margins of 50% profit on turnover Aurolab directors and employees have not lost sight of their social origins and all profits are returned to benefit the community.

An investigation of secondary data on Aurolab was conducted. Secondary data was analysed as a first step for practical reasons due to the researcher living in the UK and Aurolab being in India. Following this analysis, fourteen semi-structured interviews were conducted during a site visit. The intention of this process was to establish if the reality of Aurolab (rather than what is written about it) confirmed the outcomes of the literature. Further to see to what extent and under what conditions such outcomes emerge.

Within the semi structured interview framework, open-ended questions were used to produce rich data (Geertz 1973). This style of questioning was appropriate because of the seniority of persons being interviewed and their personal involvement with Aurolab; it was felt they would have sufficient depth of knowledge of the issues and the history of the company. Open ended questions gave the freedom not only to explore in depth the issues arising from the first stage analysis but to add a level of richness and to allow diverse topics to emerge – particularly cultural ones which may not have been thought of by the Anglo Saxon researcher. Many informal interviews were also conducted with production level and administrative staff.

External and construct validity was addressed. External validity was established by interviewing three senior staff from external organisations who had no reason to have a bias about Aurolab. They were however specialists in the field of developing country ophthalmology and knew of Aurolab. Construct validity was established by the use of multiple sources of evidence at data collection stage and establishing a chain of evidence. Further, key informants reviewed the draft case study report for factual accuracy.

Reliability was established by using a case study protocol and a case study database. The same interview schedule was followed for all interviewees who were asked to back up any opinions by examples or evidence of experience. Beyond this the open-ended questions allowed deeper probing into emerging issues.

The data were examined, categorized, tabulated and coded (Miles and Hubberman (1994) to establish if there was evidence that the initial propositions of the study were valid. Within the general theoretical proposition the process of analysis included pattern matching particularly through explanation building (Yin 2009). Based on this, the proposition was refined and compared again with other details in the case. The results were presented following a theory-building approach. This approach was taken as it is especially relevant to examining the facets of a causal argument (Yin 1994, 2009).

Results and Discussion

This section firstly explores the community interventions of Aurolab and the benefits for the rural communities connected with them. Secondly it examine in depth the business model to analyse how they can achieve these community interventions whilst running a consistently profitable business (albeit that the profits are returned to grow the business or provide more free services, and retain its non-profit status). Then lastly it will examine whether Aurolab benefits by the community interventions through improved reputation, retention of employees, innovation, better risk management and better stakeholder relationships as suggested by the literature.

Approximately 45 million people worldwide are blind. 12 million live in India. 80% of this blindness is curable or preventable (Krishnan 2004). In 1976 IOL surgery was state-of-the-art but it was very expensive (Bhandari et al. n.d.). Consequently only 35% of surgeries performed were with IOLs. All other patients received Intracapsular Cataract Extraction surgery (ICCE) meaning they were left requiring glasses. If the glasses were lost or broken, as is often the case in rural farming situations, then the person was left with worse sight than they started with (*ibid.*).

A few suppliers of IOLs dominated the market in the 1980's. The companies would donate IOLs periodically but they would not reduce their prices for consumers in developing countries (*ibid.*). Companies were making approximately 1000% mark up on IOLs. At the end of the 1980's the Health Care Financing Administration, USA (HCFA) placed limits on the price that could be charged for IOLs (Herbst 2003). Working with international NGOs, Dr V had been constantly trying to source IOLs from companies at lower prices. This collaboration of NGOs, lead by Project Impact and Dr V, investigated how to manufacture IOLs at an affordable price but at first the stakeholders were sceptical (*ibid.*). However, following the HCFA intervention, IOL International, a major manufacturer, needed to increase their production capacity and a technology transfer deal was entered into. AEH invested in setting up manufacturing facilities – Aurolab, and IOL International provided the training (Bhandari et al. n.d.).

To achieve this initial collaboration there was considerable stakeholder collaboration that was lead by the NGO Project Impact, and AEH (a non-profit organisation) rather than the company IOL International. This initial drive from the 'third sector' partners allowed them the power of decision-making and ongoing empowerment (interview Dr V). The business model was the innovation of Dr V and his inclusion of community in this business model was central to the success (Interview with Dr V). The CSR interventions and community outcomes for each organisation are summarised in figure 1 to show how Aurolab, the manufacturer, partnered with NGOs/COs at all stages of its development to promote social outcomes.

Figure 1 shows the interconnectivity of Aurolab with key community players and it can be expected that Aurolab's involvement with communities both directly and indirectly through AEHs, and other charitable NGOs it has as its customers, will provide benefits back to them as well. This community involvement is shown to not only help return the blind to a status where they can once again earn a living, but they provide alternative employment to agriculture, training and status (various interviews with staff).

Applying Banyan's (2004) model of organisational citizenship, Aurolab exhibits high corporate citizenship or is 'wired' the right way. When examining the issues involved in Social Contract Theory, Aurolab's culture is based on a two way street of hard work and benefits for all (company and community). This is pervasive throughout both AEH and Aurolab, from the Chairman to the sweepers; you see hard work achieving high levels of efficiency to ensure the maximum patient benefit (author observation). It is evidenced in a different way to Western norms where being busy is often equated with rushing and the rat race. No one rushes, people are calm, but everyone can be seen to be working hard.

Throughout Aurolab there are pictures of a 20th century philosopher, Sri Aurobindo, espousing the need to give to society. A philosophy also held strongly by Dr V and reflected in the serenity you feel within the walls of the buildings. Staff combine hard working ethics with the qualities of peace and tranquillity through the values they espouse and the behaviours they exhibit. Staff at production and management levels were absolutely clear of the vision and philosophy and displayed appropriate behaviours (staff interviews and author observation).

Figure 1: Community Interventions and Outcomes

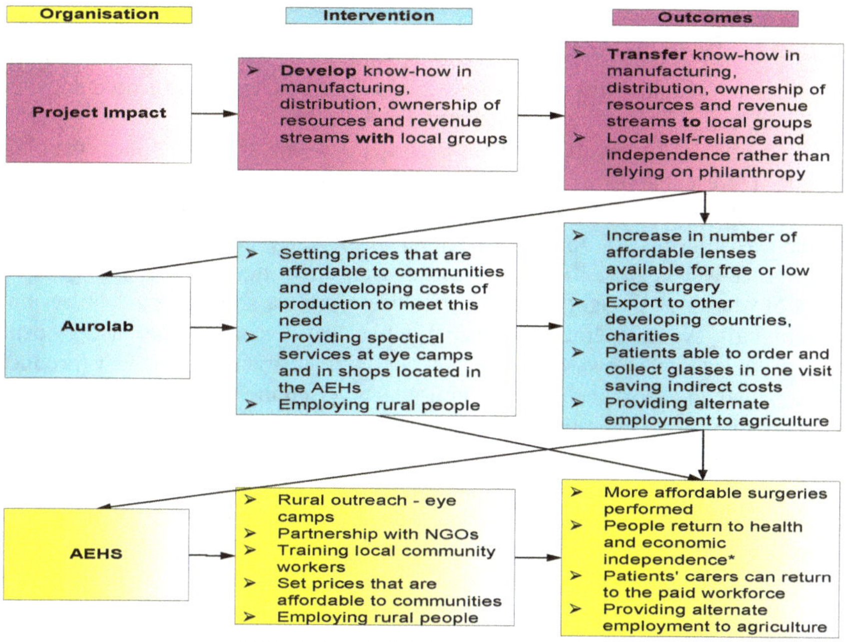

* AEH study of cateract patients showed on average an increase in household income equivalent to 15 times the cost of surgery in the first post operative year (Nirmalan et al 2005)

This analysis of the findings now moves on to discuss how these community interventions and social philosophies, embodied in their corporate culture impact on Aurolab in an operational and strategic sense.

The distinctive capabilities were also shown in the interview stage to be based in the value system and culture. At board level it was said "We also believe that a lot of our real strength comes from our values and philosophies – anything else anybody can get ....it is our key differentiator". From the Chairman downwards the value of the communities' involvement is apparent:

> "What I found when I went into the community, you work with one of them and they will give you support. The community helped always. The same communities help me now. You can't do it without a lot of community support" (Interview Dr V).

The critical linkage between the distinctive capabilities and CSR in Aurolab appeared to the author to be greater than this. It also encompassed the synergy and mutual energy behind the vision held jointly with AEH. This comes from their philosophy and would be hard for others to replicate. It is grounded in the visionary leadership of Dr V. and future leaders embedded throughout Aurolab. The core competencies however are manufacturing, the ability to 'scale up' and grow a model through sheer passion of purpose and innovation of process. Of course, with Aurolab, the social purpose came before the setting up of a manufacturing business. Hence the mission, vision and values of Aurolab and AEH seem so closely entwined.

Even though the philosophy of community involvement being the core of the business model started back in 1961 when Dr V worked for the government, today's board members are working on ways to improve the community involvement. 'Community involvement is a constant but the methodology is constantly being worked upon' (interview Dr Aravind).

There is NGO involvement at a strategic level. The board of Aurolab includes representatives of AEH. This is a legacy of the way they were founded, but Aurolab's board maintain their independence of decision-making. Also the author was informed of an internal retreat in the early part of 2005. AEH, and many other NGOs were there. 'It was quite an open meeting and they gave in terms of what they thought were the priorities, were we should focus' (interview Dr Aravind). At an operational level this two-way exchange was also evident during the site visit by Aurolab's contact with customers over new product development and feedback on existing products. From the above it is evident that Aurolab allows its community stakeholders a high degree of power at an operational and strategic level, which is critical to 'good' CSR (CCC (a) n.d.).

Likewise the business of Aurolab is receiving benefit from this community involvement. For example local marketing costs are negligible because it is assisted at a community level by local NGOs, leading to faster market penetration (interview financial manager and financial statements). Recruitment and retention costs are very low as they are seen as a very desirable employer (Interview with camp manager and various staff). Aurolab gets fast feedback on new and old products (interview - manager product development). Finally, there is a lack of governmental infrastructure in rural areas so the community infrastructure (groups like the local girl guides and boy scouts) assists with distribution and administration particularly in the lead up to eye camps. This two-way virtuous cycle promotes profitable alliances, creating valuable business opportunities as well as community empowerment (Collins and Porras 2000, Halal 2000, Handy 2002).

Analysis of the basic business structures, both hard and soft elements, shows a strong congruence between all organisational elements of Aurolab. Particularly, as has previously been said, the culture of Aurolab penetrates everything. It is therefore unsurprising that it demonstrates strong distinctive capabilities (Kay 1993). Aurolab operates on its reputation for high quality, despite its low prices (Bhandari et al. n.d.). When Aurolab commenced business it was part of AEH, which had a 15-year history, ensuring it had both internal and external networks providing a sound architecture (Kay 1993); and the business model was, and still is, innovative. Despite the fact that Dr V is willing to share his model with other hospitals, they are now recognised as the world's most productive eye care provider. It is fair to say therefore that these distinctive capabilities do indeed assist Aurolab achieve its business objectives.

It is necessary to explore the business model further to see how Aurolab gains other advantages through its community interventions. Aurolab uses on-time accounting practices (Manikutty and Vohra 2004). High volume and capital efficiency are their key drivers of profits. However, raw material costs are similar to companies in the developed world and Aurolab has extra transport costs as the raw materials come from the USA or UK. Their overheads are lower due to no borrowings and labour costs are lower than developed countries; however, staff are paid on a par with people with like qualifications in India (*ibid.*). No compromise is made on production equipment; the best quality equipment is always used. However, cost savings are made on non-essential capital expenditure like waiting areas and staff rooms that are very basic (Manikutty and Vohra 2004 and personal observation). Profit margins are consistently around 50%+ and sales generation at acceptable levels. It is therefore not just as simple as saying that Aurolab can produce at low cost because of 'cheap' labour. Prices of IOLs have dropped considerably. Prior to Aurolab commencing production IOLs were approximately USD$500 each; when Aurolab's production commenced they dropped to approximately USD$5 and now are as low as USD$2. This is purely because Aurolab chose to sell at a price based on cost, not on what the western market would pay. Despite the drop in prices Aurolab still maintains a multi-tier pricing policy so commercial companies are charged more than NGOs or AEH, but not significantly so. The implication of this is that whilst margins have been squeezed increasingly over time, sales generation and turnover have grown through market penetration. Consequently, profit margins of 50%+ have been maintained.

Aurolab has in its customer base over 175 NGOs and charitable or non-profit hospitals and other private doctors and surgeons, with whom it has strong ties. Through its work with them and AEHs, it has an empowering role in helping the communities of blind and poor. Their differential pricing system is the most overt evidence of CSR. Because of their large production volumes this still enables Aurolab to make a 50% profit on turnover.

Prior to Aurolab's existence there was an oligopoly in the market and prices were set based on what people in the developed world were prepared to pay. Since 1992, this has changed dramatically. Because Aurolab works on what patients can afford to pay, it has changed the competitive scene entirely and reduced prices of IOLs worldwide. Equally, it has strengthened civil society by making cataract surgery affordable to all (Elkington 2004, Baue 2004). This first mover advantage and the reputation gained by Aurolab all go towards helping to achieve their business objectives.

It was generally felt by respondents that Aurolab had started trading through the reputation of AEH but now had a solid reputation of its own. A key component of Aurolab's reputation is their transparency as displayed by their declaration of an end-price to the customer. This is not standard procedure for medical manufacturers in India. When asked about transparency, most respondents made the linkage to trust and reputation, in that they felt customers trusted them because of their transparency, their high quality products, and their consistent standards.

Despite Aurolab being an offshoot of AEH, AEHs only contribute 18 – 20% of Aurolab's total sales. Hilton and Gibons (2002) argue that an organisation could not have come this far and remained financially sustainable with such small margins if they had not developed CSL. The involvement of the customers in the growth of the product range and in the ability of Aurolab to trial products has been critical to the company's growth. The Aurolab board acknowledge that to continue this successful leadership they will have to manage the process in full collaboration with their customers and NGOs (various interviews with board members).

As the literature also showed that it would be expected that the business would benefit from improved reputation, retention of employees, innovation, better risk management and better stakeholder relationships a brief overview of these elements is now addressed.

A significant investment in recruitment and training is made by Aurolab at production staff level. At senior level emphasise on self-improvement and growth is also apparent. The constant self-improvement and overpowering work ethic is evident throughout the organisation. Whilst there is some acknowledgement that the production staff find this hard to start with, there is general consensus that in the long run they appreciate it and it increases morale (staff interviews). Staff appear to understand the reasons why they are asked to work in such an efficient but ordered manner. Staff turnover and morale can therefore be seen, within the cultural context[2], as being low turnover and high morale as expected from the proposition.

There were two views on innovation – one being that Aurolab was not innovative and the other that it was very innovative. However, when the stories told and examples given were examined they were closer to agreement than it originally appeared. The consensus was that they did not innovate new products but were very innovative in their manufacturing processes to achieve affordability. This was not just due to the availability of cheap labour but because of true ingenuity of the business model and again the linkage to the social purpose and mission was paramount:

Probably as a reflection of their secure financial position risk management is not a top of mind issue by many mid level and production staff. In fact, other than the senior board members most people were rather vague about what it meant. However, it was clear from interviews with board members that the method they use to minimise risk in large ventures is to partner with likeminded NGOs and if the project works they scale it up which is consistent with a stakeholder approach. Further examination of the stakeholder approach revealed that whilst most respondents in Aurolab at production level and middle management level did not feel they had direct contact with the community this was because they equated community with individual patients rather than the wider connotation of communities of the blind, NGOs/COs and specific geographic rural communities.

---

[2] Arranged marriages are the norm in this area of Tamil Nadu so many female employees will be expected to leave work to live in a new town with their husbands on marriage.

There was however wide acceptance that they partnered with NGOs and the partnerships were always that of equals. The author felt that this lack of identity with community was because they compared themselves to the AEH staff who have daily communication with patients, rather than comparing themselves to other manufacturers who have virtually no community interaction (Interview production manager).

To establish a form of external validity to these findings three persons from external organisations were interviewed. All respondents spoke highly of the reputation of Aurolab. There appeared to be no doubt that the products from Aurolab where 'trusted products' amongst surgeons. All respondents felt that the Aurolab model was socially responsible and could benefit many other regions of the world. There was also recognition of the first mover advantage obtained by Aurolab. The connection with social responsibilities was also mentioned as '*...spreading the wealth. Not only does Aurolab do the right thing by making IOLs affordable, but they employ many people and generally enrich Madurai and the surrounding villages that they get their staff from.*'

Conclusions

In addressing this research a number of key themes were identified in the literature. From the empirical analysis, the proposition put in the literature appears to be confirmed. At the very least, the key elements identified as CSR within Aurolab can be said to show that they are not corporately socially irresponsible (Chakraborty et al. 2004). At best it confirms a CSR agenda that is so ingrained (or as Banyan (2004) would say Aurolab is wired the right way) that it is not really identified as such but just seen as 'business as usual'.

Aurolab is legally a separate entity from AEH, able to make its own decisions and critically it is a manufacturer, albeit one with a social cause at the heart of its being, not part of the hospital. This places Aurolab in an unique position in that as a manufacturer it could be construed as 'commercial'. In fact, on its profit margins, it is a successful commercial operation. However, it is set up as a non-profit trust; consequently all profits are returned to grow the business or to provide more free services. Despite this it is also easy to see Aurolab as part AEH. It is the author's contention that this cement between Aurolab the manufacturer and AEH the community-focused organisation, and other like-minded NGO's and charitable hospitals (of which there are about 175 on the customer list), is the true verification of the unwritten CSR policy. One could argue that Aurolab only follows this path to maintain its tax-free non-profit status but this misses the point. The founders of AEH did not want to become manufacturers, they where ophthalmic surgeons. The only way they could achieve their mission was if someone would manufacture IOLs at an affordable price. No one would, so they were virtually forced into manufacturing or accepting the status quo. The directors of Aurolab made a conscious choice, not only to grow their business, but also to do it in such a way that it fits with all of its customer's social missions. From the support of the rural communities to create demand at eye camps, to their pricing policy and their strategic involvement of community partners in decision-making, everything points to an embedded CSR policy as described in the literature. In fact they would reach CSL standard. However, it is so ingrained in the organisation that they do not refer to it as CSR, purely the way they do business.

The business model used in AEH (a service company) was transferred to Aurolab (a manufacturing company). This is the unique aspect of this case study. A business model that worked for a social enterprise is also working for a 'commercial' manufacturer. From a business point of view the model has also been very successful in achieving distinctive capabilities, reputation, retention of employees, good risk management and excellent stakeholder relationships. Also, and not least, it has been consistently profitable. From a community point of view, there is an employer of rural people as an alternative to agriculture, there are many blind people restored to economic empowerment, plus their carers can return to paid employment, there is infrastructure put in place in rural communities, but possibly most importantly there is building of social capital in the communities and empowerment of many female members of their society who are the primary employees of Aurolab.

However, for the lessons from Aurolab, the case study, to be transferable to other commercial organisations more research would be needed. But on the question of whether lessons can be learnt from this case study, it is the author's contension that the answer is yes. There is the argument that shareholders would not accept the 'thin' margins that Aurolab operates with, even if high volumes can be achieved, but this does not necessarily hold water. Not only is it accepted as a generic strategy (Porter 1980) that many companies follow, it also assumes the presence of shareholders. The majority of companies in the world are small to medium size enterprises, most of which are not public companies.

Limitations and Recommendations for Further Research

This research has focused on a business model with little attention given to philanthropic endeavours or assessment of the value chain both forward and backward. It is therefore limited in that it only looks at one aspect of what could be a three-pronged CSR portfolio (CCC (b) n.d.). Further, whilst the methods employed by Aurolab to value staff were mentioned, it was only as they impacted on staff generally. Staff satisfaction was not measured specifically. Equally, because of the cultural norms (both geographic and religious), the methods may not be transferable but it is felt that the philosophy of valuing staff is. A final limitation is that the community outcomes were not investigated empirically. AEH conducts regular community research and the results of this were taken as accurate. Further independent research could verify these facts.

Aurolab is a manufacturer. However, it was born from the legacy of a social enterprise. This places the CSR cart before the manufacturing horse. Further practical research would be required to investigate if commercial organisations can use the elements of Aurolab's business model to help generate an integrated CSR policy. This would place the new research in a different context whereby the commercial imperatives may come first but investigating under what circumstances it is possible to 'wire' the social philosophies into the organisations to achieve the commercial outcomes.

References

Banyan M.E. 2004 Wiring Organisations for Community Governance: Characteristics of High Organisational Citizenship Administrative Theory & Praxis Vol 26 No 3 pp 325-344

Baue W 2004 A Brief History of Sustainability Reporting available at www.socialfunds.com/news/print.cgi?sfArticled=1459 July 2nd 2004 accessed 04/03/2005

Bhandari A. Ibrahim M & Sandhu J.S n.d. The Aurolab Model for Enabling Access to Medical Technologies http://bridge.berkeley.edu/pdfs/aurolab_India_report.pdf accessed 15/07/2005

Bradburn R. 2001 Understanding Business Ethics Continuum London

Business for Social Responsibility 2002 White Paper available at www.brs.org/CSRResources accessed 11/07/2005

Chakraborty S.K., Kurien V., Singh J., Athreya M., Maira A., Aga A. & Gupta A.K. 2004 Management

Paradigms Beyond Profit Maximisation Vikalpa Vol 29 No 3 July – September pp 97 - 117

Clarkson ME 1995 A Stakeholder Framework For Analysing and Evaluating Corporate Social Performance

Academy of Management Review Vol 20, No 1, pp 92-117

Collins J.C. and Porras J.I. 2000 Built to Last Random House Business Books London

Cooper S., Crowther D., Davies T. and Davis M. 2001 Shareholder or Stakeholder Value CIMA UK

Corporate Citizenship Company (CCC) n.d. (a) Citizenship: Defining Terms and Scoping Key Issues

www.corporate-citizenship.co.uk/social/default.asp accessed 11/04/05

Corporate Citizenship Company (CCC) n.d. (b) The Monitoring, Measuring and Reporting Corporate Social

Responsibility available at www.corporate-citizenship.co.uk/social/default.asp accessed 11/04/05

Donaldson T.J. 1982 Corporations and Morality Prentice-Hall, Englewood Cliffs NJ

Donaldson T. J. and Dunfee T. W. 1994 Towards a Unified Conception of Business Ethics: Integrative Social Contracts Theory Academy of Management Review Vol 18, Iss 2 252 - 284

Donaldson T. and Preston L.E. 1995 The Stakeholder Theory of the Corporation: Concepts, Evidence and

Implications Academy of Management Review Jan Vol 20 Iss 1 pp 65-91

Elkington J, 2004 The Triple Bottom Line: Does it all add up? Earthscan Publications Ltd UK

Evan W.M. & Freeman R.E. 1988 A Stakeholder Theory of the Modern Corporation: Kantian Capitalism in

Ethical Theory and Business (3rd Ed) Beauchamp T.L. and Bowie N.E. (Eds) Prentice-Hall, Englewood Cliffs NJ

Feltmate B.W. & Schofield B.A. 1999 Elevating Shares and Saving the Planet CMA Management

Jul/Aug, Vol. 73 Iss 6, pp 20 - 25

Freeman R. E., Harrison J. S., Wicks A. C., Parmar B. L. and De Colle S. 2010 Stakeholder Theory: The State of the Art Cambridge Cambridge University Press

Friedman M. 1962 Capitalism and Freedom University of Chicago Press

Friedman M. 1997 The Social Responsibility of Business to Increase its Profits in Ethical Theory and

Business (5th Ed) Beauchamp T.L. and Bowie N.E. (Eds) Prentice-Hall, Englewood Cliffs NJ

Fryxell G.E. & Wang J. 1994 The Fortune Corporate 'Reputation' Index: Reputation for What? Journal of

Management Vo 20, No. 1, pp1-14

Geertz C. 1973 Thisck Description: Towards and Interpretivist Theory of Culture IN Geertz C. (ed) The Interpretation of Cultures: Selected Essays New York Basic Books

Halal W. 2000 Corporate Community: a Theory of the Firm Uniting Profitability and Responsibility

Strategy and Leadership March-April 2000 Vol 28 Iss 2 pp10 - 17

Handy C. 2002 What is Business for? Harvard Business Review December Vol 80 Iss 12 pp 49 - 56

Hart S.L. 1997 Beyond Greening: Strategies For a Sustainable World Harvard Business Review Jan – Feb

Vol. 75 Iss 1, pp 66 -76

Herbst K. 2003 Compassionate Manufacturing: Aurolab Does Business with the Poor http://www.changemakers.net/journal/03january/herbst.cfm accessed 05/03/2005

Hilton S. & Gibbons G. 2002 Good Business: Your World Needs You Texere Publishing USA

Kay J. 1993 Foundations of Corporate Success: How Business Strategies Add Value Oxford University

Press Oxford UK

Krishnan P. 2004 Infinite Vision Dr Govindappa Venkataswamy Aravind Eye Care System Madurai India

MacMillan K., Money K., Downing S. & Hillenbrand C. 2004 Giving Your Organisation SPIRIT: An

Overview and Call to Action for Directors on Issues of Corporate Governance, Corporate Reputation and Corporate Responsibility. Journal Of General Management Vol 30, Iss 2 Winter pp 15 – 42

Mathur S.S. & Kenyon A. 1997 Creating Value: Shaping Tomorrow's Business Butterworth-Heineman

Oxford

Mazlow A. 1970 Motivation and Personality, 2nd ed., Harper & Row New York

Millar C.C.J.M., Choi C.J. & Chen S. 2004 Global Strategic Partnerships Between MNEs and NGOs:

Drivers of Change and Ethical Issues Business and Society Review Vol 109 Iss 4 pp 395-414

Mitchell R., Agle B. and Wood D. 1997 Towards a Theory of Stakeholder Identification and Salience:

Defining the Principle of Who Really Counts Academy of Management Review Oct Vol 22 Iss 4 pp 853-886

Murthuri J. N., Matten D. and Moon J. 2009 Employee Volunteering and Social Capital: Contributions to Corporate Social Responsibility British Journal of Management Vol 20 Iss 1 75 - 89

Porter M 1980 Competitive Strategy: Techniques for Analyzing Industries and Competitors The Free Press

Prahalad C.K. 2004 Fortune at the Bottom of the Pyramid: Eradicating Poverty Through Profits Wharton

School Publishing NJ

Ridderstrale J. and Nordstrom K. 2000 Funky Business: Talent Makes Capital Dance FT.com., London

Schiebel W. & Pochtrager S. 2003 Corporate Ethics as a Factor for Success - The Measurement Instrument of the University of Agricultural Science (BOKU), Vienna Supply Chain Management Vol 8, part 2 pp 116-121

Vandemoortele . 2009 The MDG conundrum: Meeting the Targets without Missing the Point Development Policy Review Vol 27 Iss 4 355 - 371

Yin R.K. 1994 Case Study Research Design and Methods 2nd ed Sage Publications London

Yin R.K. 2009 Case Study Reseearch Design and Methods 4th ed Sage Publishing London

Research Paper 3: Iranian Culture and CSR

The Role of National Culture in Corporate Social Responsibility: Case Study: Iran

Bahram Ranjbarian, University of Isfahan, Isfahan, Iran (Islamic Republic of)

Hadi Teimouri, University of Isfahan, Isfahan, Iran (Islamic Republic of)

Abstract: Business leaders have consensus that managing in times of turbulence and accelerating change challenges their traditional views of competitiveness and success factors needed for survival and profitability. Today's managers must deal with globalization of markets, increasing intensity of competition, rapid technological changes, a shift from an industrial economy to a knowledge, human capital, demographic changes, environmental challenges, changing value systems and consumer preferences. In addition the changes in society are forcing companies to consider standpoint of various interest groups in decision making. Building relationships with customers, suppliers, employees, communities and other stakeholders can become central to competitiveness and form the foundation for a new, progressive and people centered corporate strategy which attacks the sources – not the symptoms – of challenges facing business today. This brings us to the increased importance of corporate social responsibility. Corporate social responsibility (CSR) is a strategic decision whereby an organization undertakes an obligation to society in the form of sponsorship, commitment to local communities, attention to environmental issues and responsible advertising. The major aim of this paper is to study the role of national culture in corporate social responsibility. The research methodology is descriptive and for collecting theoretical aspects of the research scientific books and journals are used. The results of this paper indicate that national culture among other factors plays a more substantial role in corporate social responsibility in particular in Islamic countries.

Introduction

Globalization has resulted in the proliferation of new laws and regulations that direct business activities to address diverse social problems. The long-term impact of these social policies is a sea change in the ''rules of thumb'' by which business is expected to operate in harmony with social environment (Sharma and Talwar, 2005). The firm's external environment manifested in public policies and expectations is becoming a key factor in major strategic business decisions. In addition, change in social values and ideologies have tremendous implication for the role that business is expected to play in the society. Growing concern about the ethical dimensions by corporations has become a practice. In this scenario, it is no wonder that the attention of top management, Government and society are being directed towards corporate governance and corporate accountability (Hazarika, 1998).

Corporate social responsibility (CSR) is, regardless of specific labeling, any concept concerning how managers should handle public policy and social issues (Windsore, 2006). On the other hand, corporate social responsibility (CSR) is fundamentally an ethical concept. It involves changing notions of human welfare and emphasizes a concern about the social dimensions of business activity that have a direct concern with quality of life in the society. The concept provides a way for business to concern itself with social dimensions and pay some attention to its social impacts. The word ''responsibility'' implies that business organizations have some kind of obligation towards the society in which they function to deal with social problems and contribute more than just economic services (Sharma and Talwar, 2005).

As per Peter Drucker, ''the enterprise is an organ of society and its actions have a decisive impact on the social scene. It is thus important for management to realize that it must consider the impact of every business policy and business actions upon society. It has to consider whether the action is likely to promote the public good, to advance the basic belief of society, to contribute to its stability, strength and harmony'' (Drucker, 1954). Many factors influence on corporate social responsibility, and firms have several factors to consider with respect to choosing appropriate CSR strategies.

In this paper the main line of argument has been that the concept of corporate responsibility is inherently context-specific, as national culture playing an important part in influencing how society expects businesses to behave. This context is very new and in previous any researches have been not done in this context.

History of Corporate Social Responsibility (CSR)

Society's Rising Expectations for Business

The notion that business has duties to society is firmly entrenched, although in the past several decades there has been a revolution in the way people view the relationship between business and society(Lantos,2001). Archie Carroll (1979) and other researchers believe that we should judge corporations not just on their economic success but also on non-economic criteria. Carroll (1979) proposed a popular four-part definition of CSR, suggesting that corporations have four responsibilities or "four faces" (Carroll, 2000) to fulfill to be good corporate citizens: economic, legal, ethical, and philanthropic.

Economic responsibilities. Ever since the industrial revolution, we have depended on business as a major economic institution for producing want-satisfying goods and services; providing jobs and fair pay for workers; seeking raw materials supplies; discovering new resources, technological improvements, and products; paying taxes for public needs; generating the investment capital necessary for economic growth; all while earning a profit for the owners and serving as an investment opportunity . Previously, if a firm did all of this while obeying the law, it was praised (Lantos, 2001).

Eighteenth-century Scottish philosopher Adam Smith, in The Wealth of Nations, provided us with a framework for modern business and its relationship to society. Smith proposed that capitalism, by encouraging the pursuit of gain and efficiency, works to create greater wealth than any other economic system, and maximizes liberty by allowing individuals freedom of choice in employment, purchases, and investments, thereby benefiting the common good. Endeavoring to beat one's rivals, and toiling to produce better work to earn the next promotion, if done ethically, will result in high personal development and therefore excellent use of one's time and talents and the firm's treasury (Johnson, 1990). The manager's role is to act as a fiduciary or trustee to a principal, the owners or shareholders, being their steward in effectively and efficiently managing the organization's assets.

Economic responsibility, then, is to be profitable for principals by delivering a good quality product at a fair price is due to customers. Novak (1996) more fully delineated a set of seven economic responsibilities. These are to: (1) satisfy customers with goods and services of real value, (2) earn a fair return on the funds entrusted to the corporation by its investors, (3) create new wealth, which can accrue to nonprofit institutions which own shares of publicly-held companies and help lift the poor out of poverty as their wages rise, (4) create new jobs, (5) defeat envy though generating upward mobility and giving people the sense that their economic conditions can improve, (6) promote innovation, and (7) diversify the economic interests of citizens so as to prevent the tyranny of the majority. Lantos call these duties economic CSR. Societal expectations in this realm have appeared to hold steady over the years (Lantos, 2001).

Legal responsibilities. Legal duties entail complying with the law and playing by the rules of the game. Laws regulating business conduct are passed because society does not always trust business to do what is right. However, laws have certain shortcomings to ensure responsible behavior: they are of limited scope (they can't cover every possible contingency); merely provide a floor or moral minimum for business conduct; are reactive, telling us what ought not to be done, rather than proactive, telling us what ought to be done; and might be followed involuntarily out of fear of punishment rather than voluntarily out of internal moral conviction (Lantos, 2001).

Ethical responsibilities. Ethical duties overcome the limitations of legal duties. They entail being moral, doing what is right, just, and fair; respecting peoples'' moral rights; and avoiding harm or social injury as well as preventing harm caused by others (Smith and Quelch, 1993). Ethical responsibilities those policies, institutions, decisions, or practices that are either expected (positive duties) or prohibited (negative duties) by members of society, although they are not necessarily codified into law (Carroll, 2001). They derive their source of authority from religious convictions, moral traditions, humane principles, and human rights commitments (Novak, 1996). Today, virtually all members of the business system agree, at least in theory (although, unfortunately, often not in practice) with this third set of "social responsibilities that Lantos call ethical duties ethical CSR.

Prior to the 1960s, business ethics was not a major concern of business people. Rather, it was left to theologians to discuss issues of fair wages, unfair labor practices, and the morality of capitalism. The Protestant work ethic taught people to work hard and be successful—this was the essence of business' social responsibility.

Beginning in the 1960s ethical issues in business were raised on an unprecedented scale. There was a heightened realization that repressive labor practices could be found at even some of the most admired corporations, unsafe products were being sold, the business system was taking a toll on the natural environment, society was not succeeding in elevating those most economically deprived, bribery was occurring on an international scale, and morality was being compromised in the pursuit of money and power. Liberal consumerist media portrayed business as evil, implying that almost any business activity is morally reprehensible. Consequently, we heard consumer outcries against insensitive and immoral business practices. As a reaction to the negative publicity, by the mid-1970s, the concept of raising corporate America's consciousness was in vogue in both corporate boardrooms and college classrooms. The idea was that enterprises should not single-mindedly pursue profit without regard to morality.

Thus, since the 1970s, society's expectations of business ethics have been climbing. Unlike yesteryear, productivity alone is no longer considered sufficient to morally justify a business organization. Also important is how wealth generation affects non-economic aspects of society, such as the welfare of employees, customers, and other members of the business system, as well as other outside groups and the natural environment (Lantos, 2001).

Altruistic responsibilities. Carroll's discretionary or philanthropic responsibility—"giving back" time and money in the forms of voluntary service, voluntary association, and voluntary giving—is where most of the controversy over the legitimacy of CSR lies. Over the past half century, business increasingly has been judged not just by its economic and its moral performance, but also by its social contributions. Henry Ford II identified this when he spoke at the Harvard Business School as far back as 1969: "The terms of the contract between industry and society are changing...Now we are being asked to serve a wider range of human values and to accept an obligation to members of the public with whom we have no commercial transactions" (Chewning et. al, 1990).

CSR actually has its roots in the thinking of early twentieth century theologians and religious thinkers, who suggested that certain religious principles could be applied to business activities. For example, Andrew Carnegie devised a classic twofold statement of corporate social responsibility based on religious thinking. First, was the charity principle, which required more fortunate individuals to assist less fortunate members of society. Second, was the stewardship principle, a biblical doctrine that requires businesses and wealthy individuals to see themselves as stewards or caretakers, not just of shareholders' financial resources, but also of society's economic resources, holding their property in trust for the benefit of society as a whole.

Thus, there was a concern for the macro-level outcome of business decisions in ways that went beyond the loyal agent's argument that a manager's duty is solely to loyally serve the employer by contributing to profit maximization. Now, it was suggested that stewardship of the corporation's resources somehow be melded with a view of stewardship of society's resources to more broadly serve society. Business was said to have stewardship responsibilities not just to shareholders, but also to so-called "stakeholders" (a.k.a. constituencies or publics), notably employees, customers, competitors, suppliers, distributors, the local community in which the enterprise operates, the general public, and the natural environment. When corporations make business decisions they have both short- and long-term effects on many sectors of society (Lantos, 2001).

Benefits of CSR

Any company with ambitions regarding CSR clearly must display all the hallmarks of a learning organization. While the journey is invariably difficult, tangible rewards can make all the effort worthwhile (Strategic Direction, 2005). The payoff can include:

- Enhanced reputation: Bearing in mind almost two-thirds of UK adults allegedly mistrust business leaders, any boost to reputation can be worth its weight in gold.
- Satisfaction and loyalty among employees when organizational values mirror their own.
- Innovation: Evidence suggests that responsible companies are more creative. It can have significant long-term benefits if a company is able to introduce effective practices that also positively impact on society or the environment.
- Greater prospect of attracting investment: Investors are now looking beyond the figures towards those organizations noted for their responsible business practices. Analysts believe this trend will grow even more because investors have their own reputations to consider. Pressure from investors can also help bring other companies into line.

- Interaction with a wider audience that increases knowledge and helps to improve risk management.
- Enhanced product lifecycles with better management of materials and waste combining to lower operational costs.

National Culture

Hofstede (1980, 1991) defines national culture as the collective mental programming of the people of any particular nationality. Hofstede suggests that people share a collective national character which represents their cultural mental programming. This mental programming shapes the values, attitudes, competences, behaviors, and perceptions of priority of that nationality.

National culture is defined by Fukuyama (1995) as inherited ethical habit. An ethical habit can consist of an idea or value, or of a relationship. Ideas, values, and relationship patterns constitute the ethical codes by which societies regulate behavior. They are nurtured by repetition, tradition, and example. They are re in forced through images, habits, and social opinions.

National Culture Dimensions in Hofstede's Study

In Hofstede's (1991) study, the dominant value patterns among the countries differed in five main dimensions: Individualism/Collectivism, Power Distance, Uncertainty Avoidance, Masculinity/Femininity (recently called Quantity of Life vs. Quality of Life (Robbins, 2003)) and Long/Short-term Orientation.

Individualism/Collectivism: (the way in which people live together and the relationship that exists between individuals and the community): This dimension represents 'the degree to which people in a country prefer to act as individuals rather than as members of groups'.

- **Power Distance**: the extent of inequalities in such areas as prestige, wealth and power: 'It represents the degree of inequality among people which the population of a country considers as normal'.
- **Uncertainty Avoidance**: the extent that cultures cope with uncertainty through technology, law and religion. This dimension represents 'the degree to which people in a country prefer structured over unstructured situations'.
- **Masculinity/Femininity**: the sex roles socialized in families, schools, peer groups and through the media. It represents 'the degree to which values like assertiveness, performance, success and competition, which in nearly all societies are associated with the role of men, prevail over values like the quality of life, maintaining warm personal relationships, service, care for the weak, and solidarity, which in nearly all societies are more associated with the role of women'.
- **Long/Short-term Orientation**: is a measure for the degree of long- or short-term orientation in a country's culture.

Iran's Profile of Work-related Values in Hofstede's Study

Table 1 indicates the findings that emerged from Hofstede's study. It shows the countries at the two extremes of each dimension. It also indicates Iran's rank order among the 53 countries and regions included in the study (latifi, 2006).

Table 1: Iran's Rank Order in Hofstede's Study

Dimensions	**Countries as the extremes and Iran's position**
1- Individualism/Collectivism	*-Most individualist cultures: USA, Austria, Great, Britain* *- Most collectivist cultures: Guatemala, Equador, Panama* *- Iran: 24 out of 53, Medium*
2- Power Distance	*- Highest power distance: Malaysia, Guatemala, Panama* *- Lowest power distance: Austria, Israel, Denmark* *- Iran: 29/30 out of 53, Medium*
3- Uncertainty Avoidance	*- Strongest Uncertainty Avoidance: Japan, Portugal, Greece* *- Weakest Uncertainty Avoidance: Singapore, Hong Kong, Denmark* *- Iran: 31/32 out of 53, Medium*
4- Masculinity/Femininity	*- Most masculine cultures: Japan, Austria, Venezuela* *- Most feminine cultures: Sweden, Norway, the Netherlands* *- Iran: 35/36 out of 53, somewhat feminine*

Source: adapted from Hofstede (1980; 1991)

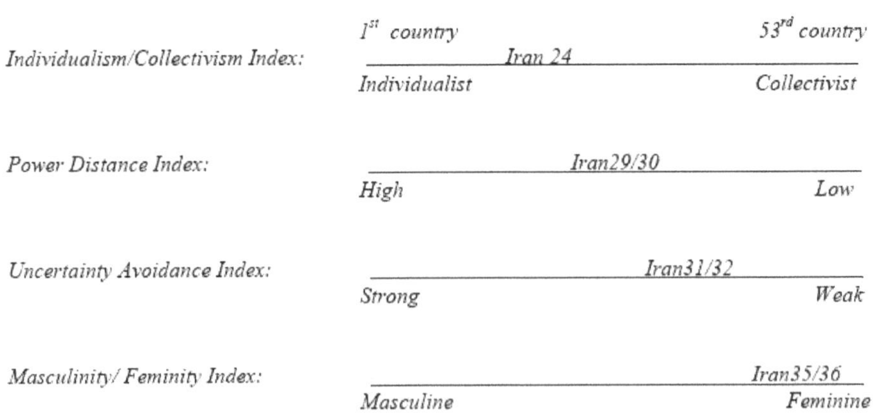

Figure 1: Iran's Position among the Countries Studied by Hofstede (1980, 1991)

Figure 1 illustrates that, in most of the dimensions, Iran lies in the middle of the two extremes. It is almost mid-way in Individualism/Collectivism, Power Distance and Uncertainty Avoidance. Iran is a somewhat feminine society based on Hofstede's results (latifi, 2006).

The Facets of Iranian Culture

Being one of the oldest civilizations in the world, the settlers in the plateau of Iran were affected by different cultures, and can be considered as a multi-faceted culture.

According to Bani-Asadi (1984), Iranian culture is a mixture of three different cultures which have coexisted for many years in Iran. As indicated in Figure 2, they are:

1. Ancient Iranian Culture, with about 6,000 years of history.
2. Islamic Culture, with about 1,400 years of history; and
3. Western Culture, with about 200 years of history in Iran.

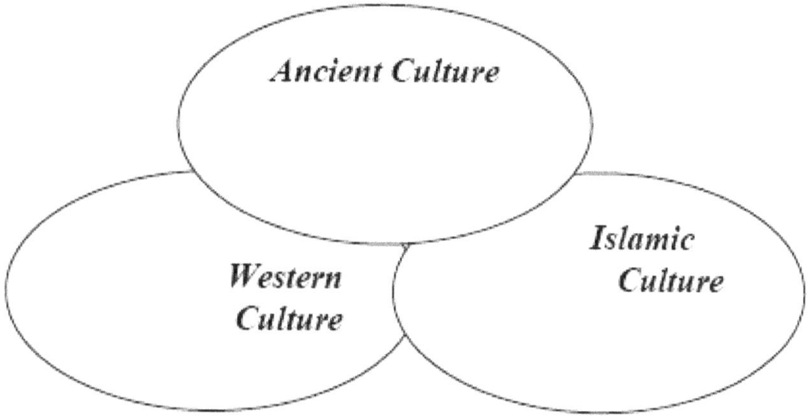

Figure 2: Three Facets of Iranian Culture

To facilitate understanding, it is appropriate here to distinguish the term 'subculture' from the term 'facet'. In the case of Iran, subcultures can be applied to Turkish, Kurdish or Arabic subcultures. They are equivalent to English, Welsh or Scottish subcultures within the UK. The subcultures are rooted in the geographical settlements of a nation.

However, the facets of Iranian culture carry a broader and deeper concept than the subcultures. In fact, all of Iranian subcultures have been more or less influenced by these cultural facets over time. The following sections describe briefly the characteristics of these cultural facets based on Hofstede's dimensions (latifi, 2006).

Ancient Culture Characteristics based on Hofstede's Dimensions

As the Ancient Culture has been lived and developed through the long history of Iran it has been highly influenced by the conditions mentioned above. Therefore, according to the points noted earlier, its characteristics, based on Hofstede's dimensions, could be summarized as follows:

1. **Collectivist**: Interested in socializing with others. Iranian people are very well known for their hospitality.
2. **High power distance**: Preferring dependence in the form of autocratic or paternalistic superiors (teacher, parent or boss).
3. **Weak uncertainty avoidance**: Based on their historical and territorial conditions (continuous threat of attacks, and dependence on rainfall which is an uncertain source of water) the people are used to tolerating ambiguity and uncertainty.
4. **Masculine**: Traditionally, most early societies were masculine, since the power source was mostly based on muscle power and men were those who benefited more from the source of power. It could also be caused by the necessity to work under harsh climate, which includes assertiveness and aggression that is masculinity.
5. **Short-term orientation**: The feeling of deep insecurity and unpredictability, mentioned above, might cause people to value whatever produced instantaneous results.

Islamic Culture

The influence of Islam on Iranian Culture has to be studied through the Islamic ideology backing it. It is obvious that any age-old ideology could be interpreted differently in any given society and in different eras regarding its various social, cultural, and environmental backgrounds. Islamic culture as a major ideology has not been exempt from this. Passing through ages and different societies, it has been mixed, or sometimes misinterpreted, with the existing traditions and values of societies.

Therefore, looking at an Islamic country and examining some characteristics of Islamic culture cannot be bias-free in terms of the country's traditions and social values. Instead, in this respect, we need to consider some fundamental Islamic concepts and their potential effects on a culture from the present study's point of view.

Islamic World-view and Fundamental Concepts

In the Islamic value system, as in the Judeo-Christian faith, God is the central theme. In the Islamic world view, God is the Meta ideal of every part of the Universe. Not only are all parts of the Universe created by God, but they all form an integrated whole (monism), in which every individual part is directed towards Him, except humankind, who due to his/her 'free will' may or may not accept God as his/her creator and ideal. One progresses towards Him only because of his/her own purposeful acts. Faith and piety are the essential elements in this progress (Shariati, 1349) Faith is absolute reliance on God, the only absolute ideal; while piety is the 'selfcontrolling force' that keeps man directed towards God by preventing him from deviations (Bazargan, 1346). Therefore, piety is the most essential element for perpetual progress, and thus, it has the utmost value.

The mechanism of progress is human's 'action' based on the intention to attain proximity towards God, by creating helping relationships and rendering services to others. In order to render desired services effectively, familiarity with, knowledge of, and skill in solving man's problems are needed. Thus, in addition to devotion and sacrifice, knowledge, in its broadest sense, is also highly valued.

One's efforts and actions in the aforementioned direction result in her/his own development, which will be carefully evaluated in the Resurrection, where he/she sees the long-term consequences of his/her past actions. Thus, according to this world-view, the present bounded life of humankind is essentially considered as a means for one's development in order to enter the other stages of life. Present neglect produces hindrance, lack of development, deviation, or a fall (Bani-Asadi, 1984).

Islamic Culture Characteristics based on Hofstede's Dimensions

In this section Iranian culture dimensions are reviewed briefly from the Islamic point of view:

Individualist and collectivist (individual responsibility and evaluation within a cooperative society) There are many verses (e.g. 6.164, 40.17, 16.111) in the Quran stating that the people's deeds are evaluated individually:

> "Now have ye come unto Us solitary as We did create you at the first, and ye have left behind you all that We bestowed upon you, and We behold not with you those your intercessors, of whom ye claimed that they possessed a share in you. Now is the bond between you severed, and that which ye presumed hath failed you"(6.94).

On the other hand, Islam persuades people to co-operate in righteousness:

> "help ye one another unto righteousness and pious duty. Help not one another unto sin and Transgression"(The Holy Quran, 5.2).

It also persuades them to socializing and care for other people, both relatives and no relatives, (e.g. 16.90, 4.135, 2.83, 6.152). Therefore, both extremes in this dimension are considered in Islam.

Low power distance: It is believed that mankind is created from a single couple (The Holy Quran, 49.13, 2.213) and all people are sisters/brothers and equal in nature.

Thus, Islam believes in equality of people regardless of their gender, race, social class, job, etc. (e.g. verses 80.1–12, 16.97). Piety is the only criterion upon which they are evaluated by God:

> "O mankind! Lo! We have created you male and female, and have made you nations and tribes that ye may know one another. Lo! the noblest of

> you, in the sight of Allah, is the best in conduct. Lo! Allah is Knower, Aware"(The Holy Quran, 49.13).

Consultation with subordinates is also emphasized in Islam. In this regard Hazrat Ali advised his governor:

> "Try always to learn something from the experience of the learned and the wise, and frequently consult them in state matters so that you might maintain the peace and good will which your predecessors had established in the land"(Nahjul Balagha: Section 3).

Given all this and bearing in mind Hofstede's definition of power distance dimension, we can come to the conclusion that a low power distance society is recommended by Islam.

Weak uncertainty avoidance associated with time-awareness/hard work: Time pressure is the main potential source of anxiety for a Muslim. Time and the life in the present world are counted the invaluable assets for human beings to build their future in the next world.

In the Islamic world view, people will be asked about their affluence (including time), hence, any individual should make the best use of every minute of her/his life for developing herself/himself and others. The main source of pressure in the procedure is the limitation of time and the uncertain time of death and the Resurrection.

Hofstede (1991) argues that uncertainty is a source of anxiety, and 'religion helps in the acceptance of the uncertainties one cannot defend oneself against'. In fact, this happens as religion can calm down the anxiety caused by uncertainty. The Holy Quran says:

> "Who have believed and whose hearts have rest in the remembrance of Allah. Verily in the remembrance of Allah do hearts find rest"(13.28).

Referring to the stability that is another criterion in Hofstede's Uncertainty Avoidance Index, Islam asks the people to leave any place or position in which they are unable to discharge their responsibilities:

> "Lo! as for those whom the angels take [in death] while they wrong themselves, (the angels) will ask: In what were ye engaged ? They will say: We were oppressed in the land. [The angels] will say: Was not Allah's earth spacious that ye could have migrated therein? As for such, their habitation will be hell, an evil journey's end"(4.97)

Therefore, we may conclude that in an Islamic culture the uncertainty avoidance could be fairly low. But, not only must it not be associated with any kind of time wasting or laziness but also must encourage people to be hardworking. Hazrat Ali in the letter writes:

> "For every department of administration, let there be a head, whom no trying task might cause worry and no pressure of work annoy"(Nahjul Balagha: Section 10).

Masculine and feminine: Again in this dimension Islam does not locate on an extreme or may do on both. Because on one hand the people are taught to care about each other, to sympathize with the weak: The Holy Quran says:

> "And forget not kindness among yourselves"(2.237).

And:

> "Do good to parents, kind folk, orphans, those in need, neighbors who are near, neighbors who are strangers, the companion by your side, the wayfarer [ye meet], and what your right hands possess: For Allah loveth not the arrogant, the vainglorious"(4.36).

From a planning point of view, in which this dimension is confined to competition and motivation in the business area, it seems that the tendency of Islam is still toward a feminine society.

Long-term orientation: In this dimension the 'quick/long result expected' (Hofstede,1991) Islam has a very long-term world view and believes in eternal life after death.

There is a tight linkage between what people do and achieve and their expectation in the eternal life. The Holy Quran says:

> "So Allah gave them the reward of the world and the good reward of the Hereafter. Allah loveth those whose deeds are good"(3.148).

Concerning 'respect for tradition', which is a characteristic of a 'short-term orientation' culture (Hofstede, 1991), Islam respects the good tradition as Hazrat Ali wrote:

> "Do not disregard the noble traditions set by our forebears which have promoted harmony and progress among the people; and do not initiate anything which might minimize their usefulness. The men who had established these noble traditions have had their reward; but responsibility will be yours if they are disturbed"(Nahjul Balagha: Section 3).

Further, Islam rejects following unfavorable traditions:

> "And when it is said unto them: Follow that which Allah hath revealed, they say: We follow that wherein we found our fathers. What! Even though their fathers were wholly unintelligent and had no guidance?"(2.170)

Given all this, Islam locates in a long-term orientation position.

Western Culture

The failure of Iran in its wars with Russia in the early years of the 19th century, which was parallel with the Industrial Revolution and scientific progress in Western societies, caused greater attention to the importance of Western technology and civilization to empower the country against enemies. This, in turn, led to the importation of Western and industrial values into the country and into the national culture.

Western and Industrial Values

While there are obvious differences between the culture of one Western country and another, there are some certain values which are perceived as Western culture in Iran and they have influenced Iranian culture. The dominant values of Western culture are mostly derived from a secular world view. Economic growth, security, individualism, democracy, comfort and enjoyment are regarded as Western values among Iranians.

Having reviewed Western and industrial values, Western culture characteristics can now be summed up. The main reference in this regard was Hofstede's study (1991).

- **Individualist:** The ties between individuals are loose, and everyone is expected to look after herself/himself and her/his immediate family.
- **Low power distance**: Power is expected to be distributed equally. A preference for a consultative style of decision making.
- **Strong uncertainty avoidance**: Discomfort with uncertainties in life. Preference for structured rather than unstructured situations matching the industrial life style.
- **Masculine**: Values such as competition, success and performance are more prevalent than values like warm social relationships, quality of life and care of the weak.
- **Short-term orientation**: Based on Michael Bond's study (Chinese Cultural Connection, 1987), Hofstede (1991) listed 23 countries according to their Long-Term Orientation (LTO) scores. Western countries were ranked 12th to 20th, starting with Sweden (12th) and ending with Canada (20th).

Table 2 summarizes the characteristics of the three facets (described in the previous sections), and the value profile of Iranian culture in Hofstede's study.

In considering Table 2 one should keep in mind that there is a difference between the traits shown in the first row (Hofstede's study results) and the rest. The first is extracted from an experiment and comparative research and, therefore, bears relative values while the others derive from a theoretical study and carry absolute and expected values.

Table 2: Value Profile of Iranian Culture in Hofstede's Study and a Dynamic Map of the three Facets of Iranian culture

Dimensions	Individualism/ Collectivism	Power Distance	Uncertainty Avoidance	Masculinity/ Femininity	Long/Short Term Orientation
Hofstedes Study	Medium	Medium	Medium	Somewhat feminine	*-
Ancient	Collectivist	High	Weak	Masculine	Short term
Islamic	Individualist And Collectivist	Low	Weak and Time-awareness	Masculine & Feminine	Long term
Western	Individualist	Low	Strong	Masculine	Short term

Note: *This dimension was added in 1991. The index is not available for Iran.

The second point regarding the table is that, as mentioned earlier, Iranian culture is a mixture of the three cultural facets coexisting and interacting for several hundred years.

Thus, mapping clearly the characteristics of each one, regardless of their possible influences on each other, is neither easy to do nor realistic.

Hence, base on the figure 2, different people, organizations, or the whole country's culture in different periods of time to behave according to the different combinations of the three cultural facets.

Conclusion

Globalization has resulted in the proliferation of new laws and regulations that direct business activities to address diverse social problems. The long-term impact of these social policies is a sea change in the ''rules of thumb'' by which business is expected to operate in harmony with social environment. The firm's external environment manifested in public policies and expectations is becoming a key factor in major strategic business decisions. In addition, change in social values and ideologies have tremendous implication for the role that business is expected to play in the society. Growing concern about the ethical dimensions by corporations has become a practice. In this scenario, it is no wonder that the attention of top management, Government and society are being directed towards corporate governance and corporate accountability (Hazarika, 1998).

Corporate social responsibility (CSR) is, regardless of specific labeling, any concept concerning how managers should handle public policy and social issues.

In this paper the main line of argument has been that the concept of corporate responsibility is inherently context-specific, as national culture playing an important part in influencing how society expects businesses to behave.

Research finding suggests that companies which are located in countries characterized by higher levels of power distance, individualism, masculinity, and uncertainty avoidance exhibit lower levels of social responsibility (Ringov and Zollo ,2007). Hence with regarding different Iranian culture aspects and domination Islamic culture; we can conclude that in Iran and similar countries social responsibility levels are high.

References

Special Category

The Holy Quran, Translated by Mohammed Marmaduke Pickthall, Available on: gopher://wings.buffalo.edu:70/00/student-life/sa/muslim/isl/Quran/pickthall/000.README pickthall.

Nahjul Balagha: Sermons, Letters and Sayings of Imam Ali Ibn Abi Talib (as), Translated by Askari Jafri (1994), Eleventh Revised Edition, Islamic Seminary Publications.

Others

Bani-Asadi, H. (1984) 'Interactive Planning on the Eve of the Iranian Revolution', PhD Dissertation, The University of Pennsylvania.

Bazargan, M. (1346 PC) Taghva: Tormoz Ensan. Tehran: Noor.

Carroll, A.B. (2000), "The four faces of corporate citizenship," in Business Ethics 00/01, Richardson, J.E. (Ed)., Dushkin/McGraw-Hill, Guilford, CT, pp. 187-191.

Carroll, A.B. (1979), "A three-dimensional conceptual model of corporate performance", Academy of Management Review, Vol. 4 No. 4, pp. 497-505.

Chinese Culture Connection (1987) 'Chinese Values and the Search for Culture-free Dimensions of Culture', Journal of Cross-cultural Psychology, 18: 143–64.

Drucker, P.F. (1954), The Practice of Management, Harper Perennial Publications, NewYork, NY.

Fukuyama, F. (1995), Trust: the social virtues and the creation of prosperity. Hamish Hamilton, London.

Hazarika, A. (Ed.) (1998), Corporate Social Responsibility and the Oil Industry: Global Experiences, Tata McGraw-Hill Publications, New Delhi.

Hofstede, G. (1980), Cultures' Consequences. Sage, London.

Hofstede, G. (1991), Cultures and Organisations. McGraw- Hill, London.

Johnson, T.S. (1990), "How the notion of a calling manifests itself in the world of business: one viewpoint," America, Vol. 162 No. 5, February 10, pp. 117-120.

Lantos, G.P. (2001), The Boundaries of strategic corporate social responsibility, Journal of Consumer Marketing, Vol.18, No.18, pp.595-630.

Latifi, F. (2006), A dynamic model interpreting work-related values of multi-faceted culture: the case of Iran, The International Journal of Human Resource Management, Vol.17, No.12, pp.2055-2073.

Novak, M. (1996), Business as a Calling: Work and the Examined Life, The Free Press, New-York.

Ringov, D. and Zello, M. (2007), the impact of national culture on corporate social performance, Corporate Governance, Vol.7, No. 4, pp.476-485.

Robbins, S.P. (2003) Essentials of Organizational Behavior. New York: Prentice Hall.

Schwartz, S.H. (1992), "Universals in the content and structure of values: theoretical advances and empirical tests in 20 countries", in Zanna, MP. (Ed.), Advances in Experimental Social Psychology, Academic Press, San Diego, CA.

Shariati, A. (1349 PC) Islamshenasi. Tehran: Shamaa.

Sharma, A.K. and Talwar, B. (2005), Insights from practice corporate social responsibility: Modern vis- a- vis vedic approach, Measuring Business Excellence, Vol.9, No.1, pp.35-45.

Smith, N.C., and Quelch, J.A. (1993), Ethics in Marketing, Irwin, Homewood, IL.

Strategic Direction. (2005), Vol. 21, No. 7, pp. 24-28, Emerald Group Publishing Limited, ISSN 0258-0543.

Windsor, D. (2006), Corporate social responsibility: Three key approaches, Journal of Management Studies 43:1, 0022-2380.

Research Paper 4: NGO Influence on CSR in China

The Importance of Non-Government Organizations in the Corporate Social Movement in China

Maria Lai-Ling Ling, Malone University, Ohio, USA

Alice Lai-Heung Lam, Hong Kong, China

Lewis Hon-Chung Lam, Hong Kong, China

Abstract: The authors discuss how Chinese environmental non-government organizations (NGOs) can thrive as effective stakeholders through market power. The research is based on extensive literature review, four years' field work in China, in-depth interviews of twenty-six Chinese business executives coming from seventeen different foreign multinational enterprises, five staff of three national Chinese environmental NGOs, and personal reflections. Chinese environmental NGOs are very localized and embedded in party-state relationships. They always struggle for financial support, credibility from the public and enterprises, and government approval. They are limited to be service providers in a contested space defined by a cautious legal system. Ironically, the Chinese government and foreign multinationals (MNEs), not the Chinese environmental NGOs, are the key actors in the corporate social responsibility (CSR) movement in China. The authors argue that the Chinese environmental NGOs must use leverage on their unique resources and strengthen their capacity through participating and learning in some available corporate social responsibility (CSR) programs. The basic strategy for the Chinese environ- mental NGOs is to increase their networking with corporations, government-owned non-government organizations, and international non-government organizations in selected environmental projects in China. When foreign MNEs are committed to provide opportunities for the Chinese environmental NGOs to be potential partners, these corporations will perform much better in a global market economy. The success of corporate social responsibility movement initiated by the Chinese government will be attained when there are balanced relationships among the Chinese government, local Chinese environmental NGOs, and corporations. When the capacity of the Chinese environmental NGOs is strengthened, the charity and stewardship principles of the CSR movement will be implemented.

Introduction

Environmental issues in China are a serious concern to the Chinese government[1] and the international community. Corporate Social Responsibility (CSR) related to environmental aspect is initiated by the Chinese government and is mandated by buyers in the global supply chain. The Chinese government has set up rigorous environmental regulations that stress government support, economic incentives, and voluntary actions by enterprises (Ho, 2005; van Rooij, 2006). The "government has started to explore new ways to tackle carbon emissions and pollution, including reforms to the taxation system" (Financial Times, 2008). The Chinese government expects foreign multinational enterprises (MNEs) to be good models for Chinese enterprises because foreign MNEs are capable of installing "clean and efficient technologies" and developing their institutional capacity of their Chinese subsidiaries and suppliers in China to enforce international and Chinese environmental regulations (Soete, 1985). Several foreign MNEs with strong global supply chains are committed to equipping their Chinese suppliers to address environmental issues through their CSR programs (A White Paper from the Business Roundtable, 2000; Wood and Kaufman, 2007). Many foreign MNEs present environmental welfare as an important sustainable strategy in their corporate social responsibility or environmental reports. Many inter-government organizations command MNEs to follow international environmental guidelines.[2] The media monitors the environmental practices of some prominent foreign MNEs in China.

The key actors in the environmental CSR movement[3] in China are the Chinese government and foreign MNEs, not Chinese non-government

[1] Through many public speeches in 2008, the central-government policy makers affirmed that inflation and the environment as the biggest obstacles to the economic growth. Environment protection is now not treated as a distraction from economic growth and is part of the future China.

[2] OECD Guidelines, Revision 2000, Part V (Environment) provides that "Enterprises should, within the framework of laws, regulations and administrative practices in the countries in which they operate, and in consideration of relevant international agreements, principles, objectives, and standards, take due account of the need to protect the environment, public health and safety, and generally to conduct their activities in a manner contributing to the wider goal of sustainable development."

[3] The corporate social responsibility (CSR) movement seriously addresses the proper relationships between people and corporations in the international economic system (Zerk,

organizations (NGOs) or the local consumers (Lam, 2007, 2008, 2009a, 2009b). Chinese environmental NGOs in China do not command the same degree of organizational autonomy as NGOs in democratic countries (Ma, 2006:9).[4] They must continually negotiate with the Chinese government for political power and resources through "self-censorship" and personal ties (i.e., *guan-xi*). Many Chinese environmental NGOs in China have less financial, informational, and managerial power than do those in other foreign multinational corporations. The public prefers to rely on the government rather than NGOs in solving environmental problems (Ho, 2008:28). When the Chinese environmental NGOs are still struggling to be accepted by the public, the government, and foreign MNEs, what is the contribution of the Chinese environmental NGOs in the CSR movement? Under what conditions can the local Chinese environmental NGOs thrive to be effective stakeholders? To what extent can the local Chinese environmental NGOs work with Chinese government and foreign MNEs so that these three key actors can pursue the truth and goodness of the CSR in China?

This article is organized as follows: The first section describes and discusses the characteristics of Chinese environmental NGOs in the CSR movement and their impact on the CSR movement. The second section discusses possible strategies for the Chinese environmental NGOs to thrive as effective stakeholders in the CSR movement and the implications for effective stakeholder management.

Methodology

This research is based on extensive literature review, personal reflections, and four years' field work in China. It also builds upon the authors' study on human rights movement organizations in Hong Kong, China (Lam, Lam & Lam, 2006) and one author's studies about the transfer of corporate social responsibility from foreign multinational enterprises to Chinese subsidiaries (Lam, 2007, 2008, 2009a, 2009b). This article draws on secondary data, a content analysis of Chinese environmental NGOs' web sites, foreign corporations' corporate environmental performance reports, and in-depth interviews of twenty-six Chinese business executives coming from seventeen different foreign multinational enterprises, five dedicated staff of three Chinese environmental NGOs in Beijing, and five executives of one government-owned environmental organizations in Beijing. Seven interviewees are responsible for corporate environmental projects in their corporate social responsibility programs. The authors interviewed two staff members of Chinese environmental NGOs and two corporate social responsibility

---

2006:18-23). Companies are expected to protect the interest of the less privileged people and to consider the interests of those affected by business. They have to go beyond the legal requirements and the interest of shareholders (McWilliams & Siegel, 2001) and fulfill their social, ethical, discretionary responsibilities when they are creating wealth (Carroll, 1979). Two basic ethical principles of CSR are charity and stewardship (van Tulder & van der Zwart, 2008:139).

[4] Ma (2006:9) quoted several studies and verified that very few Chinese organizations met the Western conceptions of NGOs. She also quoted the definition of NGOs given by Salamon and Anheier (1992:134). NGOs are "not only formal, private, and non-profit-distributing, they are also self-governing and voluntary."

officers twice in Beijing during 2008 and 2009. Environmental NGOs in Beijing are significant as they are operating close to the political center of China and are regarded as **opinion leaders** among Chinese environmental NGOs. One author listened to the voices of environmental advocates in a one-day conference at Beijing University in March 2008 and two-day corporate social responsibility conference at Beijing in June, 2009. The authors studied in depth two national environmental NGOs in Beijing in-depth and discussed the issues with their staff members for more than two hours in 2008 and 2009. The authors also discussed with knowledgeable professors about their work in the area of non-government organizations in China in Beijing and Tianjin cities. The authors read the graduate students' dissertations about Chinese environmental NGOs. The literature of environmental NGOs can illustrate what NGOs should be and could do in the CSR movement in China.

During May and June 2006, May and June 2007, March and April 2008, and May and June, 2009, the authors talked with more than one hundred Chinese executives and graduate students about their expectations for government, foreign multinational enterprises, and non-government organizations in various cities of China including Chongqing, Dalian, Qingtao, Zhejiang, Nanjing, Shanghai, Tianjin and Beijing. Several graduate Chinese students also shared their working experiences in their foreign MNEs in China. One hundred fifty Chinese graduate students and executives in Chongqing University, Qingtao University of Technology, and Dalian University of Technology were invited to discuss the impact of foreign MNEs upon communities in China. One author also read the published Chinese documents, articles, and Chinese students' dissertations about corporate responsibility, multinational corporations, and Chinese environmental NGOs. The authors had firsthand experience about the challenges of enforcing environmental regulations in various cities of China.

As China is presently in a similar situation as Japan was in the 1970s economically and environmentally. Japan is always expected to provide an excellent road map for Chinese policy makers and managers to know how to solve the environmental problems during the next decade (Emmott, 2008). The authors interviewed five Japanese expatriates about their experience of transferring Japanese environmental programs in their Chinese subsidiaries. The authors also validated some findings of Japanese MNEs' environmental policies in China by interviewing seven Japanese executives, who are implementing corporate social responsibility practices in their Chinese subsidiaries, three Japanese researchers, a Japanese consultant, Japanese professors and students in Tokyo when one author was working as a research fellow in an institution in Japan during April and May 2008. One author also sought to validate her findings about American corporations' environmental practices by talking with more than twenty American executives in international professional conferences such as Academy of Management, International Center for Corporate Accountability, and Corporate Responsibility Officers during 2007.

Characteristics of Chinese Environmental NGOs in China

Chinese environmental non-government organizations (NGOs) emerged in the mid-1990s. There are three thousand core environmental NGOs in China. The creation of many new social organizations in China is mainly due to the fact that some government roles were relinquished to government organized NGOs (GNGOs) and non-government ones as China's economy is moving from a planned economy toward a market economy. Many Chinese intellectuals attribute the expansion of local Chinese NGOs and deep changes in the relationships between the state and the NGOs to the development of market economy (Ma, 2005:207). In this paper, the authors will focus on both registered and unregistered local environmental NGOs in China. GNGOs will not be discussed as they are similar to the second government. These local Chinese environmental NGOs are not directly under the control of the Chinese government and are facing very harsh operating conditions. They are localized, small, and fragmented. They are still accustomed to relying on the government for media coverage and political resources. They are involved in a wide range of environmental challenges: environmental education, biodiversity protection, energy conservation and efficiency, air and water pollution. They mainly focus on environmental education (Economy, 2005:29) and manage their embedded relationships with the party-state through "self-censorship." The actual practices of NGOs in China are very clouded and unclear (Watson, 2008). They always struggle for financial support,[5] credibility from the public and enterprises, and government approval in a transient economy in which there is poor legal enforcement of environmental laws in China.

According to the present Chinese legal and administrative system, only non-profit organizations, registered at the Ministry of Civil affairs, are recognized as NGOs (*feizhengfu zushi)*. There are three types of registered NGOs: social organization (*shetuan*), foundations (*jijinhui*), and private non-profit enterprises (*minban feiqiye danwi*). As the registration process is very demanding and bureaucratic, some associations register under the Industrial and Commercial Bureau or disguise their identities as units within universities or government organizations. Indeed, some associations are incapable of registering under the existing legal framework (Wang, 2000). According to a recent survey about environmental NGOs in China, 11.2% of environmental NGOs did not register (China Environmental NGOs Survey and Report, 2005). There are about three thousand core environmental NGOs, registered and unregistered, in China (one interviewee's research data).[6] Many registered environmental NGOs are mainly students' associations, and industry and trade associations. All registered NGOs in China are said to have a special relationship with the government officials or

---

[5] About 76.1% of environmental NGOs do not have a fixed revenue and their workers are not frequently paid. Finance is always regarded as a key factor to limit the development of environmental NGOs. A few well-known environmental NGOs still cannot obtain stable revenue from the international donors. Some NGOs raise money through some projects that attract international donors but are not practical to the local Chinese. (read the voice of environmental NGOs' leaders from http://www.nanfangdaily.com. cn/2m/20060323/xw/szxw2/200060323 or http://news3.xinhuanet com/banyt/2004-04/07/content_1406170 htm.)

[6] It is difficult to know the exact figure of Chinese environmental NGOs because some are unregistered and some registered as for-profit business entities. Economy (2005) estimated there were 2000 Chinese environmental NGOs. One interviewee estimated that there were 3000 Chinese environmental NGOs in year 2008.

the government units that approve the registration.[7] Inside dealing is quite a common practice in China and should be dealt with.

China is still a one-party state system and "does not have a social organization law to protect NGOs from the abuse of power by official agencies and office holders" (Ma, 2005: 6). NGOs in China are expected not to offend the state because they are regulated and supervised by the state. "It is clear that the Party-state will not tolerate the emergence of groups that are potentially antagonistic to it" (Watson, 2008). In Ma's study of many non-government organizations, it was found that "Chinese NGOs in general enjoy more autonomy than it seems on the surface" (Ma, 2006:205). Ru and Ortolano (2008) find that the state does not exercise much control over eleven national and eleven Beijing municipal environmental NGOs in China since these NGOs' leaders are extremely well-connected to Party and State and adopt self-censoring to comply with the state requirements and pursue their organizational goals. The interactions between NGOs and the state are carried on through traditional connections and informal interactions. Thus, many environmental NGOs in China are embedded in party-state relationships and adopt a conscious strategy to "de-politicize environmental politics" (Ho, 2008: 29). Many elites and organized environmental groups do not unify into a specific group of pollution victims to the antipollution movement: "the anti-development overtones of such efforts; the personal preferences of organized environmental social organization members; the lack of communication between pollution victims and the more elite and organized environmental groups; and the threat of repression from authorities" (Barttell, 2008:138). Thus, many Chinese environmental NGOs stay closely to the government's environmental agenda (Turner, 2003) and have to struggle to be independent through being cooperative with the government or "self-censorship." These NGOs need to gain legitimacy and power from the public by conforming to the government agenda of developing economic progress and providing social stability.

"Most environmental NGOs are permanently short of financial resources" and consequently do not have human resources with environmental knowledge and skills (Ho, 2008:32). Many Chinese environmental NGOs have a very short life-span and cannot deliver the services they promised. They are in the stage of getting financial resources from corporations and earning social recognition and support from the government in environmental projects. The Chinese environmental NGOs must know how to overcome many psychological hurdles, including mistrust from the public and misunderstanding of their NGOs' intensions.

Chinese Environmental NGOs in the CSR Movement

The Chinese environmental nongovernment organizations (NGOs) cannot exert much pressure on foreign MNEs and the local government when the local NGOs

---

[7] See the critique of the registration process of NGOs from the web sites of Advisory Center for Non-Profit Organizations (http://www.npo.com.cn/cindex.asp, April 20,2008) and the web site of NGO Research Center at Tsinghua University (http://www.ngorc.org.cn, April 20, 2008).

are restricted by current regulations, their own capacity, and local social trust. The authors find that many corporate executives can treat their corporate social responsibility (CSR) corporate programs as a gesture of public relations which are irrelevant to their corporate strategies. Many corporate social responsibility programs and international codes are criticized as marketing devices used to mask the problems of environmental degradation and social injustice in China (Sum & Ngai, 2005; Yu, 2006). Some corporations appear to pay only lip service to environmental welfare within their CSR programs and do not like the involvement of local NGOs. Tension between the companies' social compliance auditing programs and their buying behavior in China contribute to many false reports (Harney, 2008:205).

When the Chinese environmental NGOs do not affect the success of the foreign corporations in China, the voices of Chinese environmental NGOs can easily be disregarded. Managers of foreign MNEs do not need to be proactive to manage the relationships with the local Chinese NGOs in their CSR programs. Foreign MNEs' environmental programs in China mainly focus on their *local production efficiency and economic return.* Their CSR practices are not integrated with other functional areas (Lam, 2007, 2008, 2009a, 2009b). Their CSR practices are used as a means to reduce their operational risk and develop good relationships with the Chinese government when the Chinese government has aggressively promoted CSR for seeking "harmonious society" during the past five years.[8]

Some foreign multinational enterprises (MNEs) are found to focus more on reporting CSR activities rather than managing relationships with Chinese environmental NGOs or other local stakeholders even though they fulfill international environmental standards such as ISO 140001 and the Global Reporting Initiative Sustainability Reporting Guidelines. Their CSR initiatives are to fulfill the demand from international NGOs or customers and investors from developed countries rather than local NGOs in China. Foreign MNEs are found to increase their emphasis on the developed countries' CSR principles and to decrease their emphasis on the Chinese CSR principles when they are faced with more pressure from their consumers and investors in developed countries as Schepers (2006) proposed.

There is information and financial asymmetry between corporations and local environmental NGOs. Some CSR staffs of several leading foreign MNEs not only have personal experience in running NGOs but also have a good understanding about local and international environmental policy and regulations. These CSR people could have made more of a contribution to the Chinese government than

---

[8] Since 2005, the Chinese government kept on promoting CSR committee, forums, and standards. CSR is also framed by the Chinese government sponsored organizations as "soft competitive advantage" or "important market opportunities." The Chinese government expects foreign multinational enterprises (MNEs) to be good models to Chinese enterprises as foreign MNEs are capable to increase the awareness of corporate social responsibility and improve the corporate social responsibility practices of their affiliated companies and suppliers in China (Murdoch & Gould, 2004; Tateisi, 2004; CSR in China Report, 2006; Report of Chinese Entrepreneurs' Growth and Evolution, 2007; Wood and Kaufman, 2007).

the local NGOs in advocating environmental policy and regulations. It is also risky for foreign MNEs to share information with Chinese environmental NGOs when these foreign MNEs perceive that these NGOs are opportunistic. According to the transaction cost approach (Williamson, 1981), foreign MNEs prefer to develop their own internal expertise by running their own environmental programs. Three corporate executives affirmed that their environmental expertise is a specific asset to their companies and has been used to negotiate better positions with the Chinese government in environmental policies.

Many foreign MNEs do not trust local environmental NGOs as their credible partners. They prefer to work with the international NGOs such as World Wide Fund for Nature (WWF) or the Chinese government-owned environmental organizations, including government-owned environmental non-government organizations (GNGOs). Many foreign MNEs rely on local environmental NGOs to plant the trees and pick up refuse in some local community projects. Many environmental NGOs are accepted by corporations to carry out social service and advocate positions which match with the government agenda. Chinese environmental non-government organizations (NGOs) often merely supplement the basic services provided by the Chinese government. For example, The Global Village of Beijing, a Chinese environmental NGO, helps organize garbage sorting in Beijing's residential communities in the Green community project supported by ExxonMobil (Corporate Social Responsibility Report of American companies in China, 2007: 16). Twenty out of thirty environmental projects done by Japanese companies in China were planting trees in local communities (Corporate Social Responsibility Report of Philanthropic Activities by Japanese companies in South China, 2008:90-93). In summation, many Chinese environmental NGOs do not have the opportunity to contribute any high-value-added service such as research or consulting to foreign MNEs. Several staff members, who are responsible for corporate social responsibility programs in China, made the following critique toward environmental NGOs:

> Interviewee 1: NGOs should ask support from government, not corporations.
>
> Interviewee 2: Many NGOs like to chase the wind. CSR programs are like fashion. They propose us many projects for getting quick money from our corporation.
>
> Interviewee 3: Many NGOs are incapable and do not understand corporate positions and procedures.

Many Chinese environmental NGOs are very small and compete against each other for funding from a few large corporations. One interviewee, directed corporate social responsibility programs, indicated that he was overwhelmed by NGOs' fund raising approach and did not trust these NGOs' intentions. Several business executives, including corporate social responsibility officers, stated that their business was for profit-making and corporate social responsibility (CSR) work should be implemented by government and NGOs. They generally indicated that the government, not the corporation, was responsible for the future development of NGOs. The cooperation between MNEs and local Chinese environmental NGOs is still limited in China because "Chinese NGOs have insufficient capacity, most international donors and NGOs do not consider NGO-business partnership a priority, and local governments and industries are unwilling to institute green production processes" (Turner, 2003).

The legal enforcement of environmental laws is very weak in China. Many stakeholders' interests and legitimacy are at stake when the laws are enforced (van Rooij, 2005). When some Chinese environmental NGOs request the local government to enforce some environmental regulations that are against the local government's immediate economic interest, they will receive extraordinarily hostile reactions from the local government. One Chinese environmental NGOs had been threatened by a corporate lawyer to withdraw its critique against the corporation's environmental damages for three years. Eventually, the Chinese environmental NGO stopped the accusation when the corporation documented new facts to support its environmental practices. Indeed, these new facts were misleading because the new trees planted there were much inferior than the hundred-year-old trees being cut in the area and the death of the old trees was attributed to the natural disaster instead of corporate greed (an interview's lament). In reality, the Chinese environmental NGOs can easily lose their legitimacy, power, and reputation in their local provinces. Many Chinese environmental NGOs' reports about the violation of environmental laws were discarded as unscientific when these reports were against the economic interest of local government and corporations (an interviewee's comment).

Chinese environmental NGOs are limited to be service providers in a contested space defined by a cautious legal system. They seldom have opportunities to participate in policy making or to monitor the implementing of environmental laws in China. Their development is still constrained by the registration process and the lack of support from the Chinese government. All interviewees from environmental NGOs stated that government registration was the major obstacle to founding Chinese environmental NGOs. The current regulations only allow one NGO of specific domain to be registered in a particular area. The regulations also specify the size of memberships and financial investment. Two interviewees, working in the area of environmental NGOs, commented that Chinese government was very concerned about money launderings through NGOs and tax evasion practices done by corporations. Thus, the strict regulations upon the local environmental NGOs discourage grassroots' initiatives and horizontal linkages among local NGOs (Ho, 2008:22). As a result, only few local NGOs whose leaders having close government connections can go through the registration process and earn special favor in the Chinese system.

How Can Chinese Environmental NGOs Thrive to be Effective Stakeholders in the CSR Movement in China?

Chinese environmental NGOs must gain their power from the market economy, not from social power or existing political system. Chinese environmental NGOs must use leverage on their unique resources and strengthen their capacity through participating and learning in some available corporate social responsibility (CSR) programs or sustainable development programs. Their basic strategy is to increase their networking with corporations, government-owned non-government organizations, and international non-government organizations in some projects which cannot be done by government.

Actively participate in foreign MNEs' corporate social responsibility (CSR) or sustainable development programs

As many leading foreign enterprises advocate their commitments to sustainability and improve the Chinese suppliers' sustainable development practices in the coming ten years (Sustainability in Business, 2010), many local environmental NGOs can provide training and education to these corporations' employees and suppliers in China. These environmental NGOs can also gain financial and managerial resources by participating in some foreign internationals' corporate social responsibility (CSR) or sustainable development projects before they can move toward equitable exchange relationships. These four projects are necessary: support key Chinese NGO-building groups, sponsor Chinese environmentalists working and training in international environmental NGOs, aid Chinese environmental groups to promote green activism, and award environmental programs (Turner, 2003). For example, more than 60 Chinese environmental grassroots organizations in Southwest and East China improve their organizational capability and development through two training sessions provided by Ford Motor Company's Ford Motor Conservation and Environmental Grants (Corporate Social Responsibility Report of American Companies in China 2007:18). One environmental NGO developed partnerships with corporations and trained these corporations' leaders to know how to be volunteers in the local community and to have closer relationships with the natural environment in their corporations' corporate social responsibility (CSR) programs. In return, the staff in the Chinese environmental NGOs also learned how to communicate with corporate executives and strengthen the capacity of their organizations (two interviewees' comments).

Leverage on unique resources

The more goodwill the environmental NGOs generate, the easier for them to generate government approval and mobilize corporations to be their partners. The goodwill can be generated from the reputation of the founder of an NGO or the specific expertise of an NGO. For example, the Chengdu Giant Panda Breeding Research center has numerous accomplishments in panda preservation and reproduction. The organization can attract domestic and international institutions to do joint research for protecting wild animals. It also attracts the involvement of the staff of Kimberly-Clark, a globally well-known tissue paper making company, to care for the growth of the panda (the Corporate Social Responsibility Report of American companies in China 2007:24). Thus, environmental NGOs need to leverage their unique resources and develop their expertise in-depth. When they can provide training to government officials in their particular area of expertise, they can earn more social recognition and mobilize more people to be interested in their projects. When there is more and more collaborative work done between foreign MNEs and environmental NGOs, more and more corporations will model the collaborative work and create certain social norms of cooperation between business and NGOs according to institutional theories (DiMaggio and Powell, 1983).

Gain power from market economy

Chinese environmental NGOs must enable enterprises practicing CSR to have better competitive advantages. They can improve many corporations' manufacturing process and enable corporations to enjoy first mover advantages by setting higher environmental business practices and industry standards. These strategies are essential. Keep trade associations transparent, explore the niches of Chinese environmental NGOs in the foreign MNEs' environmental programs, and use market economy to monitor the activities of foreign MNEs.

The Chinese environmental NGOs can balance the relationships between these associations and the Chinese government by developing their ability to understand the positions of the trade associations of foreign corporations and examine the relationship between lobbying expenditure and new regulations in their NGO reports (Henriques, 2007: 154-156). These associations are highly trusted by foreign MNEs in the CSR movement. The associations are independent of the Chinese government and are highly self-regulated for the interests of their members. Chinese government officials are not held accountable to a particular company when they consult with the entire associations. Through the associations, executives can assist the Chinese government to draft environmental regulations by providing comprehensive corporate data and sharing its company's research on environmental issues. For example, an association of foreign enterprises has assisted the Chinese government for the recent past five years to draft the new regulation on controlling certain polluting substances. The five-year process of consultation and relationship building between the association and the Chinese government improves the enforceability and the acceptance of the new regulations. In return, members in the association can easily comply with the new regulations and ask for the Chinese government's support in other environmental regulations (From an interview of a CSR director of a leading global company).

Chinese environmental NGOs can help foreign MNEs to reach out to local communities by localizing *(han-huo)* their environmental philosophies and practices in the context of the Chinese operating environment. The environmental NGOs can frame their claims as the "third party" when they collaborate with the trade association of foreign MNEs. When there are conflicts between environmental NGOs and foreign MNEs, the environmental NGOs should use the existing environmental regulations and research data to support their positions. Thus, the framing strategy of environmental NGOs is to use an extensive environment data to rationalize their claims and also use collective interpretations to present their messages.

Implications for Effective Stakeholder Management

Foreign MNEs must develop some programs to strengthen the capacity of Chinese environmental NGOs and nurture these NGOs to be good local partners if they want to have sustainable competitive advantages through CSR programs in China. They must initiate some innovative collaborative projects with the Chinese environmental NGOs in the market when they want to actualize economic or political opportunities provided by the Chinese government.

One interviewee, working in the environmental area for a foreign MNE, works extra hours to nurture a few NGOs for his company's environmental programs. He has worked in the China environmental agency for more than 10 years. He plans to select and develop a few environmental NGOs to learn the operation of his enterprise and the Chinese government regulations. When these selected NGOs are capable of carrying out his company's environmental policies in the local community, his company's factories can be open to the public in the future. The interviewee perceives that developing the capacity of NGOs is more effective and less expensive than running an advertising campaign about his company's environmental activities in China.

As the Chinese government is taking serious environmental actions, some NGOs can quickly follow the government agenda and interrupt the activities of foreign MNEs in China. For example, Friends of Nature, China's first legally registered NGO, uses the market economy to monitor the activities of some companies and prohibits some companies to issue their stock as they continually pollute the environment (Friends of Nature Report, 2008). The Chinese NGOs can be very confrontational to foreign MNEs if foreign MNEs are not responsive to the local needs. It is better for foreign MNEs to be proactive and develop relationships with the Chinese environmental NGOs in order to reduce many external uncertainties and actualize their environmental movement opportunities in China.

Foreign MNEs must communicate their environmental programs to the Chinese environmental NGOs and invite them to develop some niche in the foreign MNEs' environmental policies. These enterprises can invite the Chinese environmental NGOs to provide environmental education to their corporate executives and Chinese suppliers in China through partnerships or volunteer programs. Foreign MNEs can integrate their environmental commitment and financial bottom lines through being responsive to local needs. When foreign MNEs are committed to provide opportunities for the Chinese environmental NGOs to be potential partners, they will be better performers by collaborating with selected Chinese NGOs or transferring their partnership experience with local environmental NGOs to their Chinese suppliers and Chinese partners. In return, the collaborative work can be specific resources that can sustain the reputations of these foreign MNEs in the global supply chain and in China. Foreign MNEs' CSR programs can be relevant to their corporate strategies when their corporate executives are involved in the local community and natural environment through the collaborative work with local Chinese environmental NGOs in China. The more engagement of local Chinese environmental NGOs in these corporations' CSR programs, the better business performance will be attained!

Chinese environmental NGOs need to develop their learning capabilities when they are co-evolving with the changing government and corporations (Vaill, 1996). They must work toward equitable partnerships with corporations and find a way of engaging corporations so that environmental NGOs would not be trapped in being part of a name only "green-washing" activity of foreign MNEs. They should explore CSR programs that can balance the relationships among foreign MNEs, the Chinese government, and environmental NGOs. The balanced relationships are essential for keeping the truth and merit of the CSR movement in China.

Conclusion

The above discussion, about the challenges of Chinese environmental non-government organizations (NGOs) in the corporate social responsibility (CSR) movement and some possible strategies for them to be effective stakeholders in a contested legal space, has attempted to change the relationships among the Chinese government, local environmental NGOs, and foreign MNEs. The success of a CSR movement must build on the balanced relationships among government, NGOs, and corporations. The authors argue that CSR programs will be relevant to corporations and be sustainable in China when foreign MNEs have serious dialogues and collaboration with the local Chinese environmental NGOs. Foreign MNEs are recommended to take proactive collaborative relationships with the Chinese environmental NGOs and enable the Chinese environmental NGOs to be more dependent on the MNEs rather than the government. When the public is still not so enthusiastic for the Chinese environmental NGOs' projects, the Chinese environmental NGOs need to earn social recognition through the support of Chinese intellectuals, businesses, and the Chinese government. They must create a political space through market power.

When the Chinese environmental NGOs have more financial resources, political autonomy, and social recognition, they can develop better relationships with the local Chinese government and foreign MNEs. When these NGOs can illuminate the corporations' CSR practices and increase the competitive advantages of corporations that implement integrated and holistic CSR management, Chinese environmental NGOs' voices and expertise will be respected. Through the contribution of Chinese environmental NGOs, CSR programs will enable corporations to have sustainable competitive advantage in a sustainable operating environment. When the capacity of the Chinese environmental NGOs is strengthened, the charity and stewardship principles in the CSR movement will be implemented. Chinese environmental NGOs can gradually develop themselves from being social service providers to policy advocates through lobbying. Hopefully, the Chinese environmental NGOs can develop specific organization forms and fulfill their function as the "third party" in China with "small government, big society" characteristics.

Acknowledgements

The authors thank Dr. Peter B. Vaill, Dr. Martha J.B. Cook, Dr. Georgia L. Eshelman, Dr. Chuen-jin Tao, Gretchen Sudar, Simon Lam, and writers' group of Malone University for their helpful feedback.

References

A White Paper from the Business Roundtable (2000). *Corporate social responsibility in China: Practices by U.S. companies.*

Barttell, A. (2008). Channeling dissent: the institutionalization of environmental complaint resolution. In P. Ho, & R. L. Edmonds (Eds.), *China's embedded activism: Opportunities and constraints of a social movement* (pp. 111—150). U.K.: Routledge.

Carroll, A.B. (1979). A three-dimensional conceptual model of corporate performance. *Academy of Management Review*, 4(4), 497-505.

China environment NGOs survey and report (in Chinese) (2005). China environmental association.

CSR report in China (in Chinese) (2006). The annual report of the Chinese Institute of Business Administration, 2005—2006. Published by China Finance Economic company, Beijing, China.

Corporate Social Responsibility Initiatives of AmCham-China Member Companies 2006. Partnering for Progress (2006). The American Chamber of Commerce People's Republic of China.

Corporate Social Responsibility: Philanthropic Activities by Japanese Companies in South China (in Japanese) (2008). Japanese Foundation Beijing Office.

DiMaggio, P.J., and W. W. Powell. (1983). The iron cage revisited: Institutional isomorphism and collective rationality in organizational fields. *American Sociological Review*, 48, 147—160.

Emmott, B. (2008). What China can learn from Japan on cleaning up the environment. The Mckinsey Quarterly. http://www.naider.com/noticias/detalle, accessed 20 September 2008.

Economy, E. (2005). Prepared statement of Elizabeth Economy. *Environmental NGOs in China: Encouraging action and addressing public grievances.* Roundtable before Congressional-Executive Commission on China one hundred ninth Congress. Washington, U.S.

Financial Times (2008). China explore new ways to tackle its environmental challenges. Oct. 9, p.4

Friends of Nature (in Chinese) (2008). http:www.fon.org.cn, accessed 5 September 2008.

Harney, A. (2008). *The China Price.* New York: The Penguin Press.

Henriques, A. (2007). Corporate truth: The limits to transparency. Earthscan, U.K. and USA.

Ho, P. (2005). Greening industries in newly industrializing countries: Asian-style leapfrogging? *Int. J. Environmental and Sustainable Development*, 4(3), 209—226.

__________ (2008). Self-imposed censorship and de-politicized politics in China: green activism or a color revolution? In P. Ho, & R. L. Edmonds (Eds.), *China's embedded activism: Opportunities and constraints of a social movement* (pp. 20—43). U.K.: Routledge.

Lam, A., Lam, M., & Lam L. (2006). A study of human rights non-government organizations (NGOs) as social movement organizations (SMOs) in

Hong Kong, China: Implications for higher education. *International Journal of the Humanities*, 3(9), 105—117.

Lam, M.L.L.(2007). A study of the transfer of corporate social responsibility from well-established foreign multinational enterprises to Chinese subsidiaries. In J.Hooker, J. Hulpke, & P. Madsen (Eds.), *Controversies in international corporate responsibility.* International Corporate Responsibility Series, Volume 3, 343—363. Pittsburgh: Carneige Mellon University.

_________. (2008) "Being Innovative by Doing Good." *Proceedings of Academy of Innovation and Entrepreneurship 2008*, Tsinghua University, Beijing, China.

_________. (2009a) "Beyond Credibility of Doing Business in China: Strategies for Improving Corporate Citizenship of Foreign Multinational Enterprises in China," *Journal of Business Ethics*, 86(1).

_________. (2009b) Sustainable development and corporate social responsibility of multinational enterprises in China. In Ivanaj and McIntyre (Eds.) *Multinational Enterprises and the Challenge of Sustainable Development, 230—244* . Cheltenham, UK and Northampton, MA, USA: Edward Elgar.

Ma, Q. (2006). *Non-governmental organizations in contemporary China: Paving the way to civil society?* U.K.: Routledge.

McWilliams, A., & Siegel, D. (2001). Corporate social responsibility: a theory of the firm perspective. *Academy of Management Review* 26(1): 117-127.

Murdoch, H. & Gould, D (2004). Corporate social responsibility in China: Mapping the environment. *A study commission by the Global Alliance for Communities and Workers.* GA Publication Series: Baltimore.

OECD (2000). *OECD Guidelines for Multinational Enterprises: 2000 Review.* http://www.oecd.org., accessed 15 September 2008.

Report on Chinese Entrepreneurs' Growth and Evolution (in Chinese) (2007). China Machine Press.

Ru, J. & Ortolano, L. (2008). Corporatist control of environmental non-governmental organizations; a state perspective. In P. Ho, & R. L. Edmonds (Eds.), *China's embedded activism: Opportunities and constraints of a social movement*, 20—43. U.K.: Routledge.

Schepers, D. (2006). The impact of NGO network conflict on the corporate social responsibility strategies of multinational corporations. *Business & Society*, 45(3), 282—299.

Soete, L. (1985). International diffusion of technology, industrial development and technological leapfrogging. *World Development,* 13(3), 409—422.

Sum, N.L. & Ngai, P. (2005). Globalization and paradoxes of ethical transnational production: Code of conduct in a Chinese workplace. *Competitive & Change*, 9 (2), 181—200.

Sustainability in Business (2010). Retrieved Jan. 18, 2010 from the conference website, at: http://www.regonline.com/builder/site/tab1.aspx?EventID=723660

Tateisi, N. (2004). *Corporate social responsibility leads to sustainable economic growth in China—Observations from the leader of the CBCC Dialogue mission on CSR in the People's Republic of China*. Retrieved Sept. 8, 2006 from http://www.keidanren.or.jp/CBCC/english/report/2004.

Turner, J. L. (2003). Cultivating environmental NGO—Business partnerships. *The China Business Review*, 22—25.

Vaill, P. (1996). *Learning as a way of being: Strategies for survival in a world of permanent white water*. San Francisco: Jossey-Bass Publishers.

van Rooij, B. (2006). Implementation of Chinese environmental law: Regular enforcement and political campaigns. *Development and Change*, 37(1), 57—74.

van Tulder, R., & van der Zwart, A. (2006). *International business-society management*. Oxford: Routledge.

Watson, A. (2008). Civil society in a transitional state: The rise of associations in China. In Jonathan Unger (Ed.). *Associations and the Chinese State: Contested spaces*. Armonk, N.Y; M.E. Sharpe, pp.14—46.

Wang, M. (ed.) (2000) *Zhongguo NGO Yanjiu* <Research on NGOs in China>, no. 38, Beijing: UNCRD Research Report Series.

Williamson, O. (1981). The economics of organization: The transaction cost approach. American Journal of Sociology, 87, 548—577.

Wood, C. H., & Kaufman, A. (2007). The communication of corporate social responsibility (CSR) through the supply chain: an SME perspective. In Gerald I. Susman (ed.), *Small and Medium-Sized Enterprises and the Global Economy*, 140—153. Cheltenham, UK and Northampton, MA, USA: Edward Elgar.

Yu, X.M. (2006). *Putting corporate codes of conduct regarding labor standards in a global-national-local context: A case study of Reebok's athletic footwear supplier factory in China*. Unpublished dissertation, The Hong Kong University of Science and Technology.

Zerk, J. (2006). *Multinationals and corporate social responsibility: Limitations and opportunities in international law*. Cambridge University Press, UK.

Research Paper 5: Intercorporate Social Responsibility

From Corporate Social Responsibility to Intercorporate Social Responsibility: A Case Presentation

Michela Cortini, University G. D'Annunzio of Chieti - Pescara, Abruzzo, Italy

Abstract: The present paper presents the innovative concept of intercorporate social responsibility. The theoretical frameworks we make reference to are, on one hand, the International literature on Corporate Social Responsibility (CSR), social in nature, and, on the other one, the economic literature on externalities. Generally speaking, the most recent international literature by "Corporate Social Responsibility" means some virtuous behaviour performed by a single and specific corporation, as, for example, a way of production sensitive and respectful toward the environment. The idea of intercorporate social responsibility, instead, stresses the potentiality, in terms of corporate virtuous behaviours, of a network of different organizations. In other words, the core idea of our paper is that "together it is possible to perform better and even in a more ethical way". The idea of intercorporate social responsibility took origin thanks to a project by which we developed a new way to solve production externalities, that is to say externalities exchange among corporations. Production externalities, which generally represent a challenge that has to be managed to prevent performing in a non ethical way, if exchanged, become a CSR source. In particular, we have developed a technological platform by which a consortium of 60 Italian enterprises (named Costellazione Apulia) may exchange externalities (otherwise origin of waste) within a European funded project. The idea has been that one of observing how SMEs exchange not only material externalities but also technological and knowledge externalities, verifying the Marshall vs Jacobs model of economic development supported by externalities and observing the development of a special interactive and inter-organizational social responsibility. The paper presents the idea of intercorporate social responsibility within the most recent literature on Corporate Social Responsibility and reflects, in a more general way, on externalities as a way to support organizational development and corporate virtuosity.

From Corporate Social Responsibility to Corporate Social Performance

An interesting change has occurred recently within the International literature on CSR, with a growing number of researchers (among others, Basu & Palazzo, 2008; Raar, 2002; Doh & Teegen, 2004; Waddock, 2000) calling for more concrete way of thinking about CSR that has been named *Corporate Social Performance*. In this sense, it is particularly meaningful to remember the much cited work by Fredrick titled "From CSR1 to CSR2: the Maturing of Business-and-Society Thought" (1978) according to which firms were no longer involved, or not simply involved, in academic debates around the notion of CSR but rather they had to respond pragmatically and in a concrete way to various social pressures. The above mentioned article was in line with Sethi's work on the construct of Corporate Social Performance (1975), later developed by Carroll (1979) and Wartick and Cochran (1985).

Such a thereotical shift in favour of a more pragmatic view of CSR has not meant actually, a united way of viewing CSP. Actually, two different points of view exist: one, which may be called the "classical view" (Clarke, 1998; Lantos, 2001), derives from the neoclassic economic theory, and stresses the importance of shareholders' profit; the second one is concerned with all the stakeholders' interests, including both primary and secondary stakeholders (Branco & Rodrigues, 2007).

On the other hand, the stakeholders' perspective states the firms have to respect and consider the interests of all parties affected by their actions and decisions, the so-called stakeholders. These latter include "group and individuals who benefit from or are harmed by, and whose rights are violated or respected by, corporate actions" (Freeman, 1998, p.17). In contrast to the classical view, the stakeholder perspective states that "the goal of any company is or should be the flourishing of the company and all its principal stakeholders" (Werhane & Freeman, 1999, p. 8).

In the first CSR literature there has been a sort of communicative prejudice according to which only individuals may be called stakeholders, while in recent papers it is becoming more and more clear that also mute stakeholders, like for example, the environment or future generations or potential victims (Capron, 2003) do have the right to be labelled as stakeholders, with all the consequences of the case.

Our paper makes reference to CSP framework within the stakeholders' perspective, and it takes as central stakeholders the environment and the future generations, what we have called elsewhere mute stakeholders (Cortini, in press).

Waste Management as a Way to Perform Corporate Social Responsibility

To fully understand what we mean, we have to think that by the term "performance" we make reference to a way of doing, of producing, of managing every little resource, from money, to employees, to environment, and so on.

In this line, it is clear that a first challenge is represented by waste management.

It is fuzzy that, generally speaking, when common people (but mass media as well) talk about CSR, make reference actually only to corporates' behaviour during the phase of production, without taking into considerations what comes after. So that, the focus is on the present time and the most important thing is to not use child work nor produce air pollution. Actually, when we look at corporates' behaviour, things become more and more complicated, so that even when an organization respects their employees and the social environment where it is located, it is possible that it does not perform in an ethical way, for example without having full consciousness of the future effects of its production.

The effects of production are, on a first step, linked to waste and by-products corporations produce with their core business.

Waste management is an important issue especially with an increasing climate of scrutiny toward corporate behaviours, which are controlled by local government, society and mass media. In this sense, "even if a corporation adopts cleaner production totally, it will still generate waste. So, the other indispensable element is to make a loop, considering waste products as raw materials, circulating them in industrial activities just as a substance in biosphere" (Yang & Feng, 2008, 814).

Perhaps the most ethical way to manage waste is to find the way by which what is meant as waste by an organization A may become a resource for a second organization B.

This recycle, which is the basis of several experiences of industrial symbiosis, has a condition, and here is our concern: waste may become an important resource only when organizations stop thinking about themselves as monads and, rather, conceive themselves as a part of a network.

From Waste Management to Circular Economy

When put in a network, different corporations may exchange waste and byproducts, in order to perform an efficient use of resources, taking reducing, reusing and recycling as aims and closed materials cycles and recycled use of energy as principles (Yang & Feng, 2008). For such a reason, some researchers belonging to the field of industrial symbiosis and industrial ecology prefer to use the label "circular economy".

Our proposal, in brief terms, is to image an industrial district where different corporations exchange waste and by-products, which in no way would be used in commercial terms. This is possible because what is seen as simply waste by an organization may be seen as an important resource for another one.

Viewed in these terms, waste and by-products are externalities, non-voluntary effects of production and consumption; effects for which nobody pays (when they are positive) or nobody is paid for (when they are negative). In other words, an externality occurs when a decision or an act causes costs or benefits to third party stakeholders (Pigou, 1954).

The most part of the International literature concerning externalities have melt such a concept with that one of external diseconomics, underlining the negative character usually associated to externalities which someone calls market failures since there is not a market for externalities. Such a last characteristic derives from the fact that externalities do not have a link with *core business* or *core activity* of their producer; to give an example, think about industrial pollution in some sense necessary to produce cement, pollution which is not on the market, nor the positive effects of bees for some agriculture farmers.

Even if externalities are not pursued by the producer nor the receiver, they may be nevertheless so deep as to generate political issues and efforts of correction (Hey, 2003).

Since externalities violate pareto optimum, they need to find some social solutions, at least when one of the social actors involved becomes conscious of the role externalities may play. The different solutions include: transforming external effects in something internal, developing a private negotiation between the parties (Coase Theorema), and finally Pigovian taxes.

Actually, since we live by a specialization economy, it is pretty rare to solve externalities by transforming them in something internal; generally they are solved by private negotiations or by state interventions.

A Pigovian tax is a tax levied to correct the negative externalities of a market activity; for example, a Pigovian tax may be levied on producers who pollute the environment to encourage them to reduce pollution, and to provide revenue which may be used to counteract the negative effects of the pollution.

Beside the intervention by the state, we may think about a private negotiation between the parts having as an aim to reach a social equilibrium; the final scope of the Coase theorema is to maximize the use efficiency of a given resource, on the basis of market bargaining, in turn developed thanks to the property rights. The sole condition to let the model works lies in the null cost of transactions and in a perfect competitive market.

Classical solutions to externalities have been criticized; first of all the inglobation of external effects implies being able to manage at least two different competencies, a condition not often expressed by contemporary markets, devoted to specialization.

Pigovian corrections, standing their basis on the pareto model, need an a priori property right and are pretty ingenuous in believing to distinguish always and in a clear way between who produces and who receives externalities (Vatn & Bromley, 1997). In addition, their efficacy is ex post, because of the novelty they represent (think about the fact that an externality is always found out) so that it is pretty impossible to prevent them. In other words, it is difficult to image all the laws replying to all the possible externalities, standing that externalities are often hidden to the people who produce or receive them.

The critics of Coase model refer the poor realism which defines null costs of transactions and the confusion that may arises between property rights and private uses of specific resources.

The project we present can be seen as a new way to solve externalities or, in other way, as a new way to manage waste, that is to say: exchanging externalities or recycling resources thanks to an electronic platform.

As we have already underlined, exchanges and recycles are possible thanks to a network of corporations; and it is for such a reason that we prefer to talk about Intercorporate Social Responsibility, which is the core idea of our paper.

By proposing the concept of intercorporate social responsibility we would like, on one hand, for what concerns theoretical speculation, to anchor our proposal to the stakeholders' perspective and, on the other one, in more pragmatic terms, we invite corporations to think about themselves and to conceive themselves not only as an isolated entity in a never-ending struggle with other competitor corporations but rather as a part of a network. And, going on, we believe that for a network of corporations will be easier to perform CSP's activities in comparison to what happens for isolated firms.

From Corporate Social Responsibility to Intercorporate Social Responsibility: A Case Presentation

The case we would like to present here is based on a technological platform by which a consortium of 60 Italian enterprises may exchange externalities (otherwise origin of waste) within a European funded project called *Avanzare, Developing*. The Italian name of the project, *Avanzare*, means at a time "to develop" and "to remain"; a rest, when well recycled, is transformed in money saving and richness.

Avanzare would like to give value back to all the energies SMEs use for their core business, developping virtuous intercorporate behaviors and supporting externalities' exchanges so as to impact in a less invasive way on the environment and to create corporate wellbeing, since the project has proved to support psychological wellbeing of employees (Tinelli, Pagano, Cortini, 2007) and to promote organizational commitment.

The gain corresponds to the single firm environmental and social sustainability and in addition to the gain derived by externalities' exchanges; in other terms, we will have less production costs, more product quality, less environmental impact for each singular corporate social responsability act and in addition for each externalities' exchange.

On such a basis we propose the project *Avanzare, Developing*, proposed by the Consortium Costellazione Apulia[1]. Consortium Costellazione Apulia was born in December 2001 and put together 50 family firms with the shared interest

---

[1] For further information http://www.costellazioneapulia.net/

in cooperation and innovation. In particular, with *Avanzare*, the Consortium Costellazione Apulia has meant to test a new way, beside the traditional economics, based on externalities' exchanges so as to make the Italian region Puglia context more competitive and sustainable.

Avanzare is a project co-funded by the European Union (793.000 euro) under the intervention 6.2 of POR Puglia 2000-2006 and realized by Consortium Costellazione Apulia with the aid of the University of Bari and Politecnico of Bari, and it aims to promote the first portal to support interorganizational externalities' exchanges.

When SMEs belong to the same industrial sector we will have an endogenous growth in Marshallan terms; in this circumstance, family firms will exchange human and social capital externalities, information and knowledge, beside technological externalities exchanges which, in turn, will represent dynamic externalities.

On the other hand, when firms of the Consortium will belong to different industrial sectors, we will have a development similar of that one described by Jacobs for urban areas (1969), with exchanges primarily concerning the material dimension.

The gain of such an exchanges' project will be not only on a singular firm level (more profit, more credibility) but also at a social level in terms of economic growth, as some researchers have well shown (Matveenko, 1995 on Russian endogenous growth; de Lucio, Herce, Goicolea, 2002 on Spanish context).

In a different way in comparison to what happens in industrial eco-parks and industrial symbiosis (2003), the SMEs involved in the project do not exchange externalities one another always in the same way, but rather they "offer" their externalities to an information centre which has the role to let all the other corporations know about the new available resource.

Our system is more flexible and able to recycle also new waste, new byproducts, new externalities, while in industrial symbiosis corporations recycle among themselves always the same externalities but such a difference brings some management problems.

These concern the ease of being in touch and knowing immediately about an externality, about an opportunity and, on reverse, concerns the ease in saying what rests at the moment and may be offered; of course if there were huge costs, both in economic terms and in time, in letting the others know about own externalities and knowing what others' externalities rest, the projects could not work. For the above reason we have developed an electronic platform by which the consortium of SMEs may exchange information on rests and externalities.

When and if the externality is represented by some information, we will have in the meantime the externality exchange; when the externality is represented by something material we will have the consciousness of such an availability which is fundamental for the exchange itself. It is important to underline that in this case what allows externalities' exchange is once more the proximity between two firms (the idea of the Consortium), otherwise the costs related to exchange will outperform the benefits.

We have chosen as mass media supporting the externalities' exchange the Internet and the mobile phone, thanks to the ease in sending and receiving messages concerning the different availabilities, artefacts' price, usability and mobility.

In addition, with internet and mobile phones externalities can be recognized rapidly (some externalities may be used best before).

Finally, an important reason why in favour of the Internet and mobile phone concerns the diffusion tax of these mass media, easy to be used in terms of both coding and decoding messages. In this sense, traditional mass media, television and radio, even if are quite easy to use in order to receive messages, do not express usability in terms of messages coding. In other words, what we did look for was an IC technology small as to be mobile, easy to use, shared.

Since generally third millennium economic agents have both a PC with Internet access and at least one mobile phone, we would have, without additional costs (so that the condition of Coase Theorema will be respected), economic gain and growth and environmental and social sustainability (Tanucci & Cortini, 2008).

Conclusion

We have presented the project *Avanzare* that we have developed in Puglia, a region in Southern Italy, with the purpose of supporting a more sustainable way of doing business, related to the idea of intercorpoorate networks. In particular, our idea is that it is easier to perform in a more ethical way when different corporations are put together in a network; something we have called *intercorporate social responsibility*. This theoretical construct refers to the possibility of corporate social responsibility performed by a network of firms, which, if they were isolated, would otherwise produce more production externalities and waste.

In this sense, it seems to us that intercorporate networks may do well not only in business efficiency terms but also in green management terms, meaning, first of all, a less impact on the environment.

Such green and sustainable solution has been possible thanks to a technological platform which allows partners to mutually exchange with ease their production externalities.

References

Bird, B., Welsh, H., Astrachan, J.-H., Pistrui, D. "Family Business Research: the evolution of an academic field", *Family Business Review,* 2002, XV(4), pp. 337-350.

Bourdieu, P. *The forms of capital.* Westport, CT: Greenwood Press, 1983.

Burt, R.S. "Cooptive corporate actor networks:Areconsideration of interlocking directorates involving American manufacturing". *Administrative Science Quarterly*, 1980, *25*, 557–582.

Burt, R.S. *Structural holes: The social structure of competition.* Cambridge, MA: Harvard UniversityPress, 1992.

Carlaw, Kenneth I. and R. G. Lipsey "Productivity, Technology and Economic Growth: What is the relationship?" *Journal of Economic Surveys*, 2003, 17(3).

Cortini, M. "Le esternalità: di che cosa si tratta", in Cortini, M. & Ligorio, B. (eds) *Economia del dono. Aspetti psicosociali nello scambio delle esternalità tra imprese*. Roma, Aracne, 2007.

Filion, L. J. *Visions et relations : clés du succès de l'entrepreneur*, Montréal : les éditions de l'entrepreneur, 1991.

Fu, S. "Smart cafè cities: testing human capital externalities in the Boston metropolitan area", *Journal of Urban Economy*, 2007, 61, 86-111.

Gali, J. "Keeping up with the Joneses: consumption externalities, portfolio choice, and asset prices". *Journal of Money, Credit, and Banking*, 1994, 26, 1-8.

Glaeser, E. L., , Kallal, H. D., Scheinkman, J. A., Shleifer, A. "Growth in cities". *Journal of Political Economy,* 1992, 100, 6, 1289-1304

Henderson, V.J. "When does an industry locate?" *Journal of Urban Economics*, 1992, 35, 83-104.

Hey, J. D. *Intermediate Microeconomics: People are Different*, McGraw-Hill, 2003.

Jacobs, J. *The Economy of Cities,* Random House, New York, NY, 1969.

Jaffe, A. B., Trajtenebrg, M., Henderson, R. "Geographic localization of knowledge spillovers as evidence d by patent citations". *Quarterly Journal of Economics*, 1993, 63, 3, 483-499.

Liu, W. F. & Turnovsky, S. J. "Consumption externalities, production externalities, and long-run macroeconomic efficiency". *Journal of Public Economics,* 2005, 89, 1029-1097.

Matveenko, V. "Development with positive externalities: the case of the Russian Economy", *Journal of Policy Modeling*, 1995, 17, 3,207-221.

Miller, D., Le Breton-Miller, I., & Lester, R.H. "*Family involvement, agency and performance in the Fortune 1000"*. Paper presented at the Academy of Management Annual Meetings, Honolulu, HI, August 2005.

Morris, M.H., Williams, R.W, Nel, D. "Factors influencing family business succession", *International Journal of Entrepreneurial Behaviour & Research*, 1996, Vol. 2 No.3, pp.68-81.

Nahapiet, J. & Ghoshal, S. "Social capital, intellectual capital, and the organizational advantage", *Academy of Management Review*, 1998, *23*(2), 242–266.

Pigou, A. C. *The Economics of Welfare*, London, Macmillan, 1954.

Putnam, R. "The power of balance: Transforming self, society, and scientific inquiry". *Administrative Science Quarterly*, 1993, *38*(1), 146–149.

Sharma, P. "An overview of the field of family business studies: Current status and directions for the future", *Family Business Review, 2004,* XVII(1), pp. 1-34.

Tanucci, Giancarlo, Cortini, Michela "Externalities' Exchange for developping family business", *Global Conference on Business and Finance Proceedings*, 2008, Volume 3, Number 1, pp. 241-248.

Tinelli, A., Pagano, M. & Cortini, M. "Il progetto "Avanzare"" , in Cortini, M. & Ligorio, B. (a cura di) *Economia del dono. Aspetti psicosociali nello scambio delle esternalità tra imprese*. Roma, Aracne, 2007.

Turnovsky, S. J. & Monteiro, G. "Consumption externalities, production externalities, and efficient capital accumulation under time non-separable preferences". *European Economic Review*, 2007, 51, 479 – 504.

Vatn, A. & Bromley, D.W. "Externalities – a market failure". *Environmental and Resource Economics*, 1997, 9, 135-151.

Villalonga, B. & Amit, R. "How do family ownership, control, and management affect firm value?" *Journal of Financial Economics*, 2006, *80*(2), 385–417.

Yang, S. & Feng, N. "A case study of industrial symbiosis: Nanning Sugar Co., Ltd. In China", *Resources Conservation & Recycling*, 2008, 52, 813-20.

Research Paper 6: Third-Party Assurance of CSR in Finland

Third-Party Assurance Practices of Corporate Social Responsibility Reporting: Experiences from Large Finnish Listed Companies

Ulla Kotonen, Lahti University of Applied Sciences, Finland

Abstract: This research analyses third-party assaurance of corporate social responsibility (CSR) reporting from large Finnish listed companies' point of view. The emprical study focuses on questions: 1) what kinds of motives and objectives appear behind third-party assurance, 2) how third-party assurance procedures are organised, 3) who act as a third-party assurance provider, and 4) what kind of information is presented in the assurance statements. Finally, the large Finnish listed companies' assurance practices are compared to corresponding international studies. The empirical research shows that only few of large Finnish listed companies use third-party assurance. The third-party assurance provider is either public accountant company, csrnetwork or both of them. Regardless of an assurance provider, the assurance processes are almost identical and follow the typical steps of third-party assurance process presented in previous researches. The biggest differences between assurance statements are related to the extent of assurance statement and specificity of reported information. Csrnetwork reports in their assurance statements more detailed descriptions, for example recommendations for future reporting, than auditors. Companies' motives and objectives behind third-party assurance are mostly same as presented behind CSR reporting. It is seen that third-party assurance increases credibility and reliability as well as transparency of CSR reporting. On the other hand, companies realise third-party assurance as a possibility to develop their CSR reporting practices. From this point of view, the third-party of assurance providers have also a consulting role.

Keywords: Corporate Social Responsibility, CSR, Reporting, External Assurance, Third-party Assurance, Listed Companies, Finland

Introduction

Companies, including Finnish listed companies, are paying increasing attention to demonstrating their commitment to corporate social responsibility (CSR) by including it in the information they provide to stakeholders. The previous theoretical and empirical research on CSR reporting has focused on the extent and nature of CSR reporting, whereas the CSR auditing and assurance practices have received clearly less attention. At the same time, internal and external auditing of reported financial information and reporting values such as transparency and reliability have received increasing attention. Against this background, it is surprising that the CSR assurance has been given very little attention. However reliability is one of the most important characteristics of information, also in CSR reporting.

For this reason, I focus on assurance of CSR information, in this paper. The paper is focused especially on the experiences of and views on third-party assurance as well as used third-party assurance methods and practices on the large Finnish listed companies' points of view. Based on previous theoretical and empirical studies, I first summarize i) definations and regulations of CSR assurance, ii) assurance process, iii) assurance providers, iv) assurance statements, and v) international practices of third-party assurance. The research material consists mostly of previous theoretical and empirical researches published in international scholarly journals and in scientific publications over the past two decades. The empirical part of study is focused on analyzing the CSR assurance practices of the large Finnish listed companies. From this point of view, the key research questions are: 1) what kinds of motives and objectives appear behind third-party assurance, and on the other hand why some of the companies don't use third-party assurance, 2) how the third-party assurance procedures are organised, 3) who act as a third-party assurance provider, and 4) what kind of information is presented in the assurance statements. Finally, the idea is to compare the large Finnish listed companies' assurance practices to corresponding international results.

Definations and Regulations of CSR Assurance

While there is no single, commonly accepted definition of corporate social responsibility or corporate social responsibility reporting, there is no commonly accepted definition of CSR assurance. Otherwise, CSR assurance has been discussed in terms of 'social auditing or audit' (e.g. Gao & Zhang 2006; Gray 2001; Owen et al. 2000), 'verification" or "validation" (e.g. Deegan et al. 2006). Also several definitions of CSR assurance (e.g. NEF 1995; Elkington 1997; Vinten 1990; Gao & Zhang 2001; Zhang et al. 2003) have been offered by scholars and practitioners. Even if definitions emphasize differently most of them see assurance as a process that aims at making an organization more transparent, accountable and open to stakeholders (cf. Zadek & Raynard 1995; Hill et al. 1998; Gao & Zhang 2001; Zhang et al. 2003; Rotheroe et al. 2003).

Currently, there are two recognised professional standards of assurance: the AA1000 Series provided by the Institute for Social and Ethical Accountability (AccountAbility), and the International Standard on Assurance Engagements (ISAE 3000) provided by the International Audit and Assurance Standards Board (IAASB), as a part of the International Federation of Accountants (IFAC). The purpose of the ISAE 3000 is to establish the basic principles and essential procedures and also to provide guidance for professional accountants in public for the performance of assurance engagements other than audits or reviews of historical financial information. The AA1000 Series are principles-based standards including the AA1000 AccountAbility Principles Standard (AA1000APS) 2008, the AA1000 Assurance Standard (AA1000AS) 2008, and AA1000 Stakeholder Engagement Standard (AA1000SES) 2005. In addition, GRI (Global Reporting Initiative) and the G3 guidelines (GRI 2009) include demands concerning assurance.

According to the G3 the assurance can be based on the above mentioned professional standards for assurance or it may involve approaches that follow systematic, documented, and evidence-based processes but are not governed by a specific standard. The AA1000AS 2008 defines sustainability assurance as the methods and processes employed by an assurance provider to evaluate an organisation's public sustainability disclosures about its performance as well as underlying systems, data and processes against suitable criteria and standards in order to increase the credibility of public disclosure. And assurance statement is seen as an important part of this process. Despite some differences between standards as well as internal varieties of standards related for example used principles and levels of assurance they all include activities designed to result in published conclusions on the quality of the report and the information contained within it. Regardless assurance standards developing an applied CSR assurance procedure is a challenging task (Morimoto et al. 2005).

Assurance Process

The literature review by Morimoto et al. (2005) indicates that the assurance procedures are not uncommon but vary quite a lot. In practice the assurance consists of formal monitoring and evaluation procedures of CSR reporting by checking corporate disclosure against predetermined reporting elements based on current CSR reporting guidelines (e.g. GRI). Due to differences in the scope and objectives of the assurance, the criteria used, the type of assurance and the level of assurance given, the assurance process and assurance statement varies.

In addition to external third-party assurance, different internal assurance practices as well as scoring protocols, quality assessments, benchmarking and award schemes are used for analyzing and evaluating existing CSR reporting (see e.g. Hammond & Miles 2004).

There exist several attempts to develop CSR assurance processes (e.g. Kok et al. 2001; Gao & Zhang 2006). The assurance processes can normally be divided into following main steps: 1) engagement, 2) planning, 3) the assurance work, and 4) the assurance statement (Adams & Evans 2004). Gao and Zhang (2006) have presented a more detailed ten staged assurance process including 1) policy and strategy review, 2) defining assurance boundaries, 3) stakeholder-based design, 4) defining indicators, 5) stakeholder consultation, 6) internal audit and document review, 7) preparation of accounts and external support, 8) external verification, 9) publication of statement, and 10) stakeholder dialogue (cf. Wallage 2000). As Park and Brorson (2005) have noted companies are not directly ready for a third-party assurance, but companies need to pass certain steps before they are ready for a complete third-party assurance process with stakeholder involvement.

It seems that the major difficulty of developing CSR assurance systems is related to the derivation of appropriate indices. According Morimoto et al. (2005) the two major obstacles are "bias in choosing categories against which an organization's performance may be measured, and the difficulty in identifying indices applicable to all sectors". As crucial points of developing a CSR assurance system, Morimoto et al. (2005) mention issues such as the inclusion of all significant stakeholder groups in the assurance process, diversity in individual perceptions of CSR, the problem of negative screening, the shortcomings of the 'tick-box' approach to assurance CSR, the requirement that the measurement of CSR should be both quantitative and qualitative in nature, and the achievement of CSR six key elements. The last of these is connected to the lack of one broadly accepted definition of the CSR concept. Together these (differences in assurance practices and definitions of the CSR concept) bring out a question about an expectiation gap.

In CSR assurance case, the gap arises due to many different issues for example a lack of technical competencies, the timeliness and relevance of auditor communication (Swift & Dando 2002), a lack of legal requirements (Adams & Evans 2004), a lack of one single set of widely agreed standards on which to report (Lewellyn 2000), a lack of guidelines specifying what type of assurance opinion should be issued in what circumstances (Kamp-Roelands 1999), a board range of stakeholders with different and often competing interests (Adams & Evans 2004), a lack of determination of the assurance scope and appropriate assurance methods and evidence (Lewellyn 2000), and qualitative nature of reported information (O'Dwyer 2001; Swift & Dando 2002).

Assurance Providers

Gao and Zhang (2006) divide assurance providers into two different categories: 1) stakeholders who are involved in participation of decision-making and dialogue process (opinions about stakeholder engagement see e.g. Owen et al. 2001), and 2) professionals or specialists. The stakeholders' important role is supported by standards (e.g. AA1000) but also by the global PwC (2007) empirical survey that gives evidence of stakeholder panels as a link between stakeholders' expectations and companies CSR reporting. The stakeholder panels' role is primarily related to the question "whether the company is reporting the right thing", whereas assurance providers' role is concentrated on the question "whether a company is reporting things right".

Despite recognition of the stakeholders' important role, the majority of CRS assurance is still audit-based. This is largely caused by the fact that in most of cases assurance providers are members of IFAC which encourages assurance providers to use the ISAE 3000 standard for non-financial assurance. However, several smaller assurance providers, such as JustAssurance and csrnetwork, using AA1000AS are becoming more and more popular (SustainAbility 2009).

In both cases, stakeholder and professional assurance provider, competences and professionals' skills and capabilities play an important role. This is also highlighted by launching the AccountAbility Assurance Provider Member and Licensing program and a training program with the Certified Sustainability Assurance Practitioner (CSAP) qualification. The program highlights competences such as an understanding of sustainability assurance, an understanding of stakeholder engagement, an understanding of sustainable development, and the ability to make informed professional judgements on an organization's sustainability performance. As Adams and Evans (2004) remind, assurance providers must provide useful and valued service both to stakeholders as well as to clients.

Assurance Statements

Both assurance standards, AA1000AS and ISAE 3000, include detailed descriptions about information that should be included in assurance statements. In practice it seems that AA100AS users provide much more information in their assurance statements than others, and this significantly raises the value of their statements for readers (SustainAbility 2009). Despite the guidelines of assurance statements the previous studies (e.g. Deegan et al. 2006 & 2005) show that there is much ambiguity and variation inherent within the contents of the assurance statements. Also the title of assurance statements varies. (Deegan et al. 2006)

Among others, Park and Brorson (2005) have been concerned about the quality of assurance and assurance statements. As a future development point of view, Adams and Evans (2004) emphasise that the nature of assurance opinion and how it should relate to the scope of the assurance and findings of the assurance with respect to the inclusivity of stakeholders, completeness, credibility and accuracy of data.

International Practices of Third-party Assurance

Against some assumptions (e.g. SustainAbility 1996), the previous empirical studies (e.g. KPMG 2002; AcountAbility 2004) establish that the number of companies using third-party assurance was for many years quite low. In the early 1990s, CSR reports were not accompanied by a third-party assurance, and until the mid to late 1990s the incidence of third-party assurance statements started to increase in some industries (Deegan et al. 2006). It appears that over the last few years, the use of third-party assurance has increased. According KPMG survey (2008), in 2007, about 56 percent of the top 250 of Global Fortune 500 (G250) companies that issued a CSR report included some form of third party assurance, and almost half of the top 100 of national companies (N100) did the same. In

2002 and 2005, only 30 % of the G250 companies published third-party assured reports. Instead of a formal assurance statement, some companies include the views or commentary of other external parties such as stakeholder panel, academics, individual experts or NGOs, in their CSR reports. (KPMG 2008; see also KPMG 2005 & 2002).

The increasing interest in third-party assurance raises questions about companies' motives to assure their CSR reports. Based on the KPMG survey (2008) the most important drivers seem to be to improve quality of reported information, to reinforce credibility among stakeholders as well as to improve reporting practices. The other motives mentioned in previous studies (e.g. Park & Brorson 2005) are for example maintaining the position as frontrunners, benchmarking with other companies, awards, responding to the questions from stakeholders as well as integration of the CSR reporting into the annual financial reporting.

Research Context, Data and Methods

This empirical study of third-part assurance practices of CSR reporting in large Finnish listed companies is focused on analysing 1) what kinds of motives and objectives appear behind third-party assurance, 2) how the third-party assurance procedures are organised, 3) who acts as a third-party assurance provider, and 4) what kind of information is presented in the assurance statements. Finally, the idea is to compare whether the assurance practices of the large Finnish listed companies are consistent with the previous international studies reviewed in this study.

The study is based on the analysis of qualitative data consisting of special CSR reports, especially assurance statements as a part of them. This means that the empirical analyses are based on formal CSR information that companies have published in 2006 and 2007. Thus, I do not take up assurance practices of web-based information or other information such as newsletters, brochures or press releases etc. for consideration when I analyze the assurance practices. The paper is focused on the used CSR assurance forms and motives behind existing third-party assurance practices, the internal assurance and verification processes are omitted from this research. The empirical research material was collected during autumn 2007 and spring 2008. The empirical analyses are supplemented with interviews with four company representatives (corporate responsibility/sustainability managers of Fortum, Kesko, Outokumpu and Stora Enso) and with two sustainability advisors of two public accountant companies (PricewaterhouseCoopers and KPMG). The interviewed sustainability advisors represent the view of third-party assurance, and both have gained wide and long-term experience from CSR reporting in Finland. The interviews were made in author's guidance and control by Terhi Hyvärinen as a part of her Master's Thesis during spring 2008. The idea of having four managers responsible for CSR in the case companies was to reflect on the reporting as well as the underlying experiences of their organizations' CSR assurance practices. The aim of the thematic interviews was to deepen the understanding of the views on CSR reporting and especially third-party assurance in the case companies.

Based on the above mentioned principles the empirical research data consists of CSR information published by 31 large Finnish companies listed at OMX Nordic Exchange Helsinki. Large listed companies mean companies that belong in the Large Cap segment of the Nordic Exchange, their market value is over one billion euros. For industry classification the Global Industry Classification Standard (GICS) is used. Fourteen of those 31 companies (written in italics in Table 1) have published a special CSR report or published CSR information as an individual part of annual reports, and only a few (four in 2006 and five in 2007) of those fourteen companies have used third-party assurance.

When evaluating the validity, reliability and generalization of the results presented in this study, four aspects have to be noted. First, the research is based on interpretative understanding and qualitative analyses are always more or less subjective. Second, the analysis is based on CSR information produced by large Finnish listed companies. Thus the study doesn't give an extensive description of the CSR assurance practices in all Finnish listed companies or in non-listed companies. Third, the study focuses only on third-party assurance and only briefly mentions other assurance or verification methods. Fourth, the research is a cross-sectional study based on CSR assurance practices in two specific years. Thereby the analysis gives a snapshot of Finnish CSR third-party assurance practices. Meanwhile, the analysis doesn't tell about history, development or future of CSR reporting assurance practices of the large Finnish listed companies. Thus the reality reconstructed in this study must not be generalized but used to understand third-party assurance practices of CSR reporting in this context.

CSR Reporting in Large Finnish Listed Companies

The motives behind responsible behaviour and at the same time for voluntary CSR reporting of large Finnish listed companies are quite the same kind as presented in international studies (e.g. Graham et al., 2005; Hemingway & Maclagan 2004; Menon & Menon, 1997; McWilliams & Siegel, 2001; Moon, 2001; Skinner 1994 and 1997; Francis et al. 1994; Diamond & Verrecchia 1991; Kim & Verrecchia 1994; Bushee et al. 2003; Healy & Palepu 2001). The large Finnish listed companies understand responsibility as a duty to act responsibly towards their stakeholders and CSR reporting as a response to stakeholders' expectations and demands (Kotonen 2008). Companies' experiences about special CSR reports seem to support the integration of CSR and annual reports (cf. Jones et al. 2005; Line et al. 2002). The reporting amount and quality of reported information vary considerably in the large Finnish listed companies. Even if only less than half of large Finnish listed companies publish a special CSR reports, almost all the companies have included some kind of responsibility information in their annual reports. It seems that most of the large Finnish listed companies define corporate social responsibility based on Elkington's triple bottom line (TBL) model. In addition, companies follow more or less GRI guidelines. Despite that, their reporting practices are diverse and are thus non comparable.

Third-party Assurance Practices in Large Finnish Listed Companies

Of the 14 large Finnish listed companies studied deeply in this research only four had their 2006 CSR report verified through a third-party assurance process by an independent assurance provider. Two of these companies used a public accountant company as their external assurance provider, one made use of csrnetwork and one of the both.

Table 1: Third-party Assurance in Large Finnish Listed Companies in 2006 and 2007

Name of company	Industry	CSR reporting in 2006 and 2007	Third-party assurance	
			2006	2007
Amer Sports	Consumer Discretionary	a part of annual report		
Cargotec	Industrials	a part of annual report		
Elisa	Telecommunication	a part of annual report		
Finnair	*Industrials*	*a special CSR report*	no	no
Fiskars	Consumer Discretionary	a part of annual report		
Fortum	Utilities	a part of annual report		
Kemira	Materials	*a special CSR report*	no	no
Kesko	*Consumer Staples*	*a special CSR report*	yes	yes
Kone	Industrials	a part of annual report		
Konecranes	Industrials	a part of annual report		
Metso	*Industrials*	*a special CSR report*	no	no
M-real	*Materials*	*a special CSR report*	yes	yes
Neste Oil	Energy	a part of annual report		
Nokia	*Information Technology*	*a special CSR report*	no	no
Nokian Renkaat	Consumer Discretionary	a part of annual report		
OKO	*Financials*	*a special CSR report*	no	no
Orion	Health Care	-		
Outokumpu	*Materials*	*a special CSR report*	no	yes
Outotec	Industrials	a part of annual report		
Pöyry	Industrials	-		
Ramirent	Industrials	a part of annual report		
Rautaruukki	*Materials*	*a special CSR report*	no	no
Sampo	*Financials*	*a special CSR report*	no	no
SanomaWSOY	Consumer Discretionary	a part of annual report		
Stockmann	Consumer Discretionary	a part of annual report		
Stora Enso	*Materials*	*a special CSR report*	yes	yes
TietoEnator	*Information Technology*	*a special CSR report*	no	no
UPM-Kymmene	*Materials*	*a special CSR report*	no	no
Uponor	Industrials	a part of annual report		
Wärtsilä	*Industrials*	*an individual part of annual report*	yes	yes
YIT	Industrials	a part of annual report		

M-real as a part of Metsäliitto Group had its CSR report assured by PricewaterhouseCoopers, Wärtsilä by KPMG and Stora Enso by csrnetwork. Kesko's Corporate Responsibility Report has been assured by third-party assurance provider since 2002. For the last two reporting cycles, Kesko has used two assurance providers: csrnetwork and PricewaterhouseCoopers. In addition in 2006 AccountAbility and csrnetwork benchmarked Kesko's previous Corporate Responsibility report using Accountability benchmark RatingTM (www.accountabilityrating.com). This benchmarking measured Kesko's performance in six domains (stakeholder engagement, governance, strategy, performance management, assurance, and public disclosure) and its results was reported as follows:

> "The Assurance domain looks for a rational approach to securing appropriate assurance for the claims made in the company's external reports.
>
> Kesko's scoring for the 2005 assurance cycle is 21 points. Assurance has emerged as a key issue in the Accountability Rating with just 27 of the G-50+ companies having their reports externally verified. The average score for the G-50+ companies is 10 points and for the Top 10 companies 34 points.

A summary of the main findings:

> The 2005 statement does not disclose clearly whether the assurance provider was free to select sites and interviews. Furthermore, it does not assess Kesko's processes for identifying material issues, responsiveness to stakeholders or the company's performance against targets." (Kesko 2006, 2)

In addition to the four companies mentioned above also Outokumpu had its CSR report verified externally in 2007. Respectively OP-Pohjola Group (2007, 3) states in its responsibility report: *"Separate audit functions do not exist for the different sub-areas of corporate responsibility; instead, issues related to corporate responsibility are taken into account as part of the general audit"*. Other companies have not had their CSR reports assured externally during the period in question or do not report activity in their CSR reports, annual reports or on/at their websites.

Although the international and Finnish trend in assuring CSR reporting is towards third-party, contradictory behaviour can also be seen. An example of the opposite trend is Fortum, which earlier (in the years 2000 to 2004) used external assurance for its separate CSR report, but when giving up a separate CSR report, it also gave up third-party assurance. External assurance was no longer used as it was not considered very important based on the results of a stakeholder survey the company had carried out.

When there is no external assurance, companies often make use of internal verification, or in some instances such certification method as a certified ISO 14001 environmental management system (e.g. Rautaruukki) or an auditing system (e.g. Stockmann) to verify the information. In addition, several companies have joined different organisations or sustainability indexes (e.g. Dow Jones

Sustainability Index) that encourage companies towards responsible behaviour and transparent reporting. For example Stockmann is a member the Business Social Compliance Initiative (BSCI). In most cases internal assurance focuses especially on verifying environmental information while the assurance of social responsibility receives less attention. In some cases, like Nokia for example, some areas of reporting may have been subject to third-party assurance.

> "Ecofys Germany GmbH has reviewed Nokia's methodology and procedures of data collection, accounting and reporting of Greenhouse Gas (GHG) emissions as described in the internal directive "Greenhouse Gas Reporting Methodology in Nokia." ... "Our responsibility, in accordance with Nokia's management instruction, is to carry out a limited assurance engagement on the approaches outlined in chapter 4 and 5 of the Methodology, in order to provide conclusions on the conformity with the principles and requirements of the WBCSD/WRI Greenhouse Gas Accounting Protocol for the scope of activities and emissions agreed with WWF for the Climate Savers Programme". (Nokia 2008, 1)

When it comes to reporting on economic responsibility, a reference is often made to closing of accounts and their statutory auditing by the company auditors. E.g. Rautaruukki (2009) states at its website that their CSR reporting has not been verified by a third party but the financial data are subject to auditing. In some cases an outside consultant has been used in an internal assurance process. This is true for example in the case of Metso:

> "With the exception of the information based on the financial statements, the information in the report (Sustainability Report) has not been audited by an independent party. The quality of the environmental information in the financial statements has been assessed in collaboration with an independent consultant." (Metso 2007, 37)

Internal assurance procedures are largely company specific and depend on the internal verifier. In most companies internal assurance means comparing data over a period of time and finding reasons for possible deviations without specific internal assurance processes. Also companies that use third-party assurance verify their reports internally as well.

Assurance Providers in Finland

In practice, based on the interviews, an almost unanimous view prevails among the large listed Finnish companies, being that the provider of third-party assurance must be reliable, independent, professional and reputable in the eyes of the general public. It is also considered an asset that the provider adheres to a set of assurance instructions and that the work of the third-party assurance provider is supervised. An external assurance provider should also try to develop his/her expertise and ways of working all the time.

The choice of a public accountant company as a third-party assurance provider is justified, among other things, with strict rules and their experience in auditing and verifying the correctness of presented data. The use of auditors as third-party assurance providers is often also supported by their current knowledge of the company, which results in lower assurance expenses. The assurance services provided by public accountant companies are, however, considered to focus more on the assurance of economic responsibility while the social and environmental responsibilities receive less attention. To improve the assurance of these sectors a sustainability expert has been appointed to work as an assurance provider together with a Chartered Accountant.

Should a third-party assurance provider of CSR reporting then be rotated like auditors? The view of corporate responsibility/sustainability managers is that it is good to use one and the same assurance provider for several years in order that the assurance process could be developed on a long-term basis. On the other had changing the assurance provider at intervals is considered to be in compliance with good reporting practices.

Motives and Obstacles of Third-party Assurance in Large Finnish Listed Companies

According to the views of the sustainability advisors interviewed in this study the motives for external assurance are first of all to be found in the companies' efforts to show proof of the transparency, reliability and correctness of the data reported. The assurance process is used as if to increase the completeness, accuracy and comparability of the data. The company managers' interviews revealed that the use of third-party assurance improved the credibility of the reported data. Stakeholders are also believed to appreciate external assurance.

On the one hand companies also find third-party assurance a learning process and/or management tool. It is not seen so much as a means of spotting mistakes but as a kind of development project, where special attention is paid to CSR reporting, to improving business related weaknesses as well as to development opportunities. Thus assurance is considered a way to promote the continuous development of social responsibility management and reporting:

> "Independent assurance promotes the continuous development of the processes behind corporate responsibility management and improves the reliability of reported information and the accuracy of individual" (Kesko 2007, 29).

When considered like this the companies highlight internal developing. This kind of approach to the third-party assurance is desirable but often difficult to put into practice.

The expense of a third-party assurance as well as other resources, such as the staff time input it requires, constitute obstacles of third-party assurance. The sustainability advisors interviewed estimated that smaller companies in particular emphasise the cost-benefit ratio achieved through a third-party assurance process. In some cases the lack of third-party assurance is a clear management decision whereas in others the companies do not have sufficient knowledge of the third-party assurance process and thus fail to see the benefits it may yield. Assurance can also be considered a cumbersome and time consuming process.

Interviews also indicated that companies may find the development of their CSR report somewhat incomplete and therefore do not wish to use a third-party assurance provider to assess their reporting. Stakeholders do not always require a company to assure its reporting either. Occasional CSR report readers do not even necessarily know what third-party assurance means or do not simply pay any attention to the whole matter. Thus there might also be misunderstandings about third-party assurance (cf. more generally audit expectation gap by e.g. Gay et al. 1998; Humphrey et al. 1992). Analysts and major investors, however, appreciate sustainable development indexes (e.g. Dow Jones Sustainability Index), which in turn often presuppose third-party assurance.

Legislation may also be used to justify the lack of third-party assurance. This is illustrated in the case with Metso:

> "The modernization of the Finnish Accounting Act's general guidelines does not add new key performance indicators regarding personnel and environment to the sphere of information to be audited at Metso." (Metso 2009)

The above mentionned obstacles are consistent with those four main types of arguments: 1) high level of the assurance fee, 2) uncertainty about the value, 3) priority given to other work, and 4) no external pressure, presented by Park and Broson (2005).

Should third-party assurance be compulsory? Although the companies interviewed did not see it necessary to have their CSR reports assured by a third party, they were not quite unanimous about the matter. Especially public accountant companies consider that in future CSR report assurance should be compulsory, however not yet, not before reporting practices develop and obtain their established forms. There are still several unsolved questions related to the assurance process being compulsory, such as what is considered social responsibility reporting.

Third-party Assurance Processes in Large Finnish Listed Companies

As stated above, there are no established procedures when it comes to third-party assurance and thus the scope and assurance processes often vary a lot. Based on the interviews it would seem that in all the four large Finnish listed companies that used third-party assurance in 2006 the process is, however, quite similar. This might be a consequence of a low number of assurance providers as well as compliance with assurance standards.

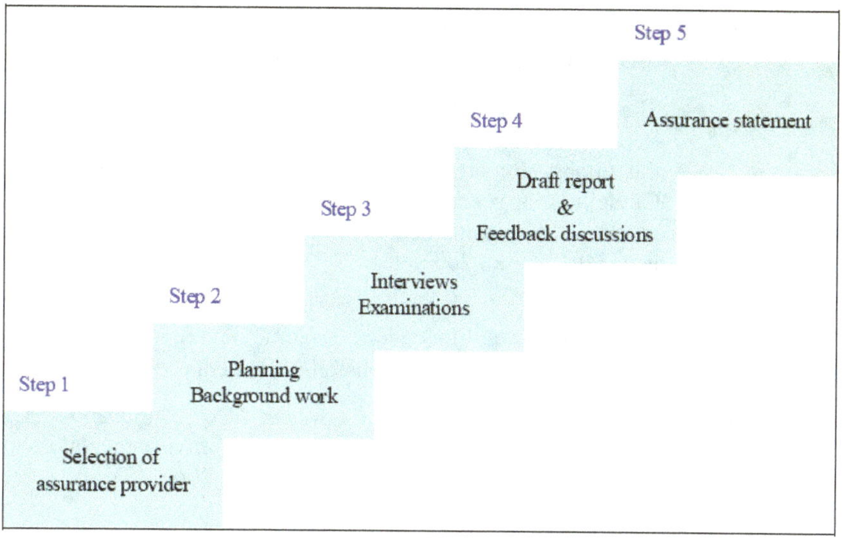

Picture 1: Third-party Assurance Process of Large Finnish Listed Companies

The above described CSR assurance process of large Finnish listed companies would seem to comply with the five-step assurance process model, including planning of the assurance process, background work, interrogation of the database, examination of the draft report and feedback meeting between the assurance provider and the reporting organization, presented by Park and Brorson (2005). Regardless the general uniformity of processes, there is one substantial difference between assurance processes carried out by different assurance providers. The assurances carried out by csrnetwork seem to include more stakeholder interviews than those by public accountant companies. And due to differences in business operations there are some company specific emphasis in assurance work. Based on the interviews, the differences are considered problematic, companies and auditors alike would appreciate common instructions that would be binding for all the assurance providers.

Assurance Statements of Large Finnish Listed Companies

The analysed assurance statements are poorly comparable. Especially differences in the scope of the assurance process are considered a factor that reduces comparability. In practice this means that the assurance activities of public accountant companies and csrnetwork are directed at different things and are also different in scope. For example in the case of Kesko the assurance carried out by a public accountant company has been restricted to deal with economic responsibility information only:

> "We have been engaged by the management of Kesko Corporation to provide assurance on their 2007 Corporate Responsibility Report ('the Report') for the year ended 31 December 2007, with respect to the following information therein:

- The corporate responsibility performance in the area of economic responsibility, as reported in the section titled 'Economic performance' on pages 31-43; and
- The comparison of the economic responsibility indicators in the Report with the economic responsibility indicators outlined in the Global Reporting Initiative Sustainability Reporting G3 Guidelines, as reported in the section titled 'Comparison of the report with the guidelines of the Global Reporting Initiative' on page 90." (Kesko 2007, 96)

Correspondingly the emphasis in the Stora Enso CSR report provided by csrnetwork on environmental and social responsibility elements.

> "The objective of the assurance process was to check claims and review the arrangements for the management of social and environmental issues and the systems for collection of data." (Stora Enso 2006, 52)

The reasons for the differences in the focus and emphasis of the assurance are various. A company does not even want to have, or is not even prepared for having, the whole report assured. The assurance provider's special competence also affects the assurance focus. From the reader's point of it is, however, desirable that the whole CSR report would be assured.

Differences in assurance reports can also be seen in how the assurance providers describe the assurance process, its realization as well as the methods used in their statements. The assurance statements prepared by public accountant companies are more limited than those provided by cscnetwork, in which observations have been explained more widely and in greater detail. For example csrnetwork has in its Kesko 2007 assurance statement taken up three observations concerning materiality, six with regard to completeness as well as two related to responsiveness. In addition to these the statement lists a couple of observations from the previous year. Respectively the statement provided by PwC reads:

> "nothing has come to our attention that causes us to believe that the subject matter information of the assurance engagement does not give a balanced and appropriate view of Kesko Corporation's corporate responsibility performance in the area of economic responsibility, in all material respects, based on the above mentioned assurance criteria". (Kesko 2007, 96)

What is essential from the point of view of CSR reporting is that in addition to the actual assurance statement the companies also receive for their internal use a development report, which deals in great detail with all the observations made and presents recommendations on how to amend things as well as analyses the respective risk levels. Besides reliability of CSR reporting, this brings internal added value that companies are waiting from third-party assurance providers.

Conclusion

Assurance of CSR reporting is a very complex issue. Even if assurance has been a part of discussions since the existence of CSR reporting it has not been highlighted until the last two decades. During this time CSR reporting has become more sophisticated and stylish with a wider scope of issues. Also stakeholders' demands and expectations for CSR reporting have changed and increased. As a response to increasing demands and problems of voluntary reporting different kinds of reporting policies, guidelines as well as assurance guidelines are created. Despite attempts at standardization CSR assurance practices still vary between organizations, industries and assurance providers. This is partly due to different corporate characteristics, general contextual and internal contextual factors influencing the extent and nature of corporations' CSR reporting. Also several additional motives as well as barriers for third-party assurance of voluntary reporting are presented. Increasing costs is one of the most important barriers to use of third-party assurance. In some cases also the lack of experience and knowledge are seen as significant impediments to the implementation of assurance practices. Despite increasing interest in a third-party assurance, the assurance practices are still in the early stages of its evolution and this is seen also in the empirical results.

As a conclusion, the study indicates that the CSR assurance practices of large Finnish listed companies are mostly consistent with reported in responsible international studies. The empirical analysis establishes that only precious few Finnish listed companies verify their CSR reports and information by independent third-party assurance provider. In these few companies CSR assurance is based on ISAE 3000 or AA100AS assurance standards, and public accountant companies play the most important role as assurance providers. In two of them the third-party assurance provider is the auditor, in one case csrnetwork and in the other both auditor and csrnetwork. That's mostly because chartered accountants are seen to be more independent than other assurance providers. On the other hand, chartered accountants are criticized for focusing foremost on financial and other numerical information. Regardless of assurance provider, the assurance processes are almost identical and follow the typical steps of third-party assurance process presented in previous research. In many cases the process scheduling and timing to the busiest time of year were seen to be problematic. The biggest differences between assurance statements are related to the extent of the assurance statement and specificity of reported information. csrnetwork reports in their assurance statements more detailed descriptions, for example recommendations for future reporting, than auditors. Companies' motives and objectives behind third-party assurance are on the other hand same as the presented behind CSR reporting (e.g. stakeholders' expectations and demands). It is also seen that third-party assurance increases credibility and reliability as well as transparency of CSR reporting. Regardless of whether CRS reports are or are not assured, Finnish companies' CSR information is seen to be reliable. It seems that some companies realise a third-party assurance as possibility to develop their CSR reporting practices. From this point of view, the third-party assurance providers have also a consulting role.

The CSR assurance, especially third-party assurance, needs further theoretical and empirical research. This research proves some evidence and experiences from large Finnish listed companies' point of view. Because of the small sample size of this study it doesn't tell the whole picture of third-party assurance in Finland. Thus it is necessary to extend the research into medium and small size Finnish listed companies in the future.

References

AccountAbility (2004) The accountability rating 2004: encoding accountability. Available: http://www.accountabilityrating.com/client/area2/downloads/2004_AR_report.pdf, Accessed: 29.12.2008

———. (2006) Accountability rating 2006: summary report of results. Available: http://www.accountabilityrating.com/client/area2/downloads/2006_AR_report.pdf, Accessed: 29.12.2008

Adams, C.A. & Evans, R. (2004) Accountability, completeness, credibility and the audit expectations gap, *The Journal of Corporate Citizenship*, Summer 2004, 14, 97-115

Bushee, B., Matsumoto, D. & Miller, G., (2003) Open versus closed conference calls: the determinants and effects of broadening access disclosure, *Journal of Accounting and Economics*, 34 (1-3), 149-180

Deegan, C., Cooper, B.J. & Shelly, M. (2005) An investigation of TBL report assurance statements: Australian evidence, *Australian Accounting Review*, 16(2), 2-19

———. (2006) An investigation of TBL report assurance statements: UK and European evidence, *Managerial Auditing Journal*, 21(4), 329-371

Diamond, D. & Verrecchia, R. (1991) Disclosure, liquidity, and the cost of capital, *The Journal of Finance*, 66, 1325-1355

Elkington, J., (1997) *Cannibals with forks: the triple bottom line of 21st century business*. Oxford: Capstone Publishing

Francis, J. & Philbrick, D. & Schipper, K. (1994) Shareholder litigation and corporate disclosures, *Journal of Accounting Research*, 32, 137-165

Gao, S. & Zhang, J. (2001) A comparative study of stakeholder engagement approaches in social aditing, In: Andriof, J. & McIntosh, M. (eds.) *Perspectives on corporate citizenship*, Greenleaf Publishing, Sheffield

———. (2006) Stakeholder engagement, social auditing and corporate sustainability, *Business Process Management Journal*, 12(6), 722-740

Gay, G., Schelluch, P. & Baines, A. (1998) Perceptions of messages conveyed by review and audit reports, *Accounting, Auditing & Accountability Journal*, 11(4), 472-494

Graham, J.R., Harvey, C.R. & Rajgopal, S. (2005) The economic implications of corporate financial reporting, *Journal of Accounting and Economics*, 40, 3-73

Gray, R. (2001) Thirty years of social accounting, reporting and auditing: what (if anything) have we learnt?, *Business Ethics: A European Review*, 10(1), 9-15

GRI (2009) G3 Guidelines, Available: http://www.globalreporting.org/NR/rdonlyres/ED9E9B36-AB54-4DE1-BFF2-5F735235CA44/0/G3_GuidelinesENU.pdf, Accessed 2.2.2009

Hammond, K. & Miles, S. (2004) Assessing quality assessment of corporate social reporting: UK perspectives, *Accounting Forum*, 28, 61-79

Healy, P.M. & Palepu, K.G. (2001) Information asymmetry, corporate disclosure and the capital markets: a review of the empirical disclosure literature, *Journal of Accounting and Economics*, 31(1-3), 75-102

Hemingway, C.A. & Maclagan, P.W. (2004) Managers' personal values as drivers of corporate social responsibility, *Journal of Business Ethics*, 50, 33-44

Hess, D. (1999) Social reporting: a reflexive law approach to corporate social responsiveness, *Journal of Corporate Law*, Fall 25(1), 41-85

Hill, W.Y., Fraser, I.A.M. & Cotton, P. (1998) Patients' voices, rights and responsibilities – on implementing social audit in primary health care, *Journal of Business Ethics*, 17(13), 1481-97

Jones, P., Comfort, D. & Hillier, D., (2005) Corporate social responsibility and the UK's top ten retailers, *International Journal of Retail & Distribution Management*, 33(12), 882-892

Kamp-Roelands, N. (1999) Audits of environmental reports: are we witnessing the emergence of another expectation gap?, Nederlands Instituut van Registeraccountants

Kim, O. & Verrecchia, R. (1994) Market liquidity and volume around earnings announcements, *Journal of Accounting and Economics*, 17, 41-68

Kesko (2006) Corporate responsibility report 2006. Available: http://www.kesko.fi/modules/upndown/download_file.asp?id=797E2430 E58D4CCB9E7A0A563774C678&itemtype=UPNDOWNFILE, Accessed: 29.12.2008

———. (2007) Corporate responsibility report 2007. Available: http://www.kesko.fi/modules/upndown/download_file.asp?id=E4EEDE6 68DAE4030B7414275C33125A8&itemtype=UPNDOWNFILE, Accessed 29.12.2008

KPMG (2002) International survey of corporate sustainability reporting 2002. Available: http://www.gppi.net/fileadmin/gppi/KPMG2002.pdf, Accessed: 29.12.2008

———. (2005) International survey of corporate responsibility reporting 2005. Available: http://www.kpmg.nl/Docs/Corporate_Site/Publicaties/Internatioanl_Survey_Corporate_Responsibility_2005.pdf, Accessed: 29.12.2008

———. (2008) KPMG International survey of corporate responsibility reporting 2008. Available: http://www.kpmg.com/SiteCollectionDocuments/International-corporate-responsibility-survey-2008.pdf, Accessed: 29.12.2008

Kolk, A., Walhain, S. & Van de Wateringen, S. (2001) Environmental reporting by the fortune global 250: exploring the influence of nationality and sector, *Business and Strategy and the Environment*, 10, 15-28

Kotonen, U. (2008) Formal corporate social responsibility reporting in Finnish listed companies, Paper presented at 7th International Conference on Corporate Social Responsibility, 3-5 September 2008, Durham Business School, Scotland

Lewellyn, P.G. (2000) Sustainability auditing: issues for the AICPA, *AccountAbility Quaterly*, 13, 30-34

Line, M., Hawley, H. & Krut, R. (2002) The development of global environmental and social reporting, *Corporate Environmental Strategy*, 9(1), 69-78

McWilliams, A. & Siegel, D, (2001) Corporate Social Responsibility: A theory of the firm perspective, *Academy of Management Review*, 26(1), 117-127

Menon, A. & Menon, A. (1997) Environpreneurial marketing strategy: The emergence of corporate environmentalism as market strategy, *Journal of Marketing*, 61 (January), 51-67

Metso (2007) Sustainability report 2007. Abailable: http://www.metso.com/corporation/home_eng.nsf/fr?readform, Accessed: 29.12.2008

———. (2009) Non-financial reporting. Available: http://www.metso.com/corporation/home_eng.nsf/FR?ReadForm&ATL=/corporation/sd_eng.nsf/WebWID/WTB-060307-2256F-C7A10, Accessed: 29.12.2008

Moon, J. (2001) Business social responsibility: a source of social capital?, Reason in practice 1(3), pp. 35-45

Morimoto, R., Ash, J. & Hope C. (2005) Corporate social responsibility audit: from theory to practice, *Journal of Business Studies*, 62, 315-325

NEF (1995) Social auditing for community and co-operative enterprises, Paper presented at workshop 1, The New Economics Foundation, Edinburgh

Nokia (2008) Independent Assurance Statement to Nokia Corporation. Available: http://www.nokia.com/NOKIA_COM_1/Environment/Our_responsibility/Environmental_strategy/Ecofys_Short_Independent_Assurance_Statement_2008-10-15.pdf, Accessed: 29.12.2008

O'Dwyer, B. (2001) The legitimacy of accountants' participation in social and ethical, accounting, auditing and reporting, *Business Ethics: A European Review*, 10(1), 27-39

OP-Pohjola Group (2007) Corporate responsibility report 2007. Available: https://www.op.fi/media/liitteet?cid=150830097&srcpl=3, Accessed: 29.12.2008

Owen, D.L., Swift, T.A., Humphrey, C. & Bowerman, M. (2000) The new social audits: accountability, management capture or the agenda of social champions?, *European Accounting Review*, 9(1), 81-98

Owen, D.L., Swift, T. & Hunt, K. (2001) Questioning the role of stakeholder engagement in social and ethical accounting, auditing and reporting, *Accounting Forum*, 25 (3), 264-282

Park, J. & Brorson, T. (2004) Experiences of and views on third-party assurance of corporate environmental and sustainability reports, *Journal of Cleaner Production*, 13, 1095-1106

PwC (2007) The right combination. Available: http://www.pwc.com/extweb/pwcpublications.nsf/docid/68143387B9B287ED8525707B004AF554/$file/PwC_assurance_on_cr.pdf, Accessed: 29.12.2008

———. (2008) Fresh eye on CSR reports, *World Watch*, 1, 22, Available: http://www.pwc.com/gx/eng/about/svcs/corporatereporting/WW1_08.pdf, Accessed: 29.12.2008

Rautaruukki (2009) Content and scope of the report. Available: http://www.ruukki.com/www/corporate.nsf/documents/8655D18E5A57594EC2257404004677FE!Opendocument&lang=1, Accessed: 29.12.2008

Rotheroe, N., Keenlyside, K. & Coates, L. (2003) Local agenda 21: articulating the meaning of sustainable development at the level of the individual enterprise, *Journal of Cleaner Production*, 11, 537-548

Skinner, D.J. (1994) Why voluntarily disclose bad news?, *Journal of Accounting Research*, 32, 38–61

———. (1997) Earnings disclosure and stockholder lawsuits, *Journal of Accounting and Economics*, 23, 149-282

SustainAbility (2006) United Nations Environmental Programme. *Engaging stakeholders volume 2: the case studies*, London

———. (2009) Assurance. Available: http://www.sustainability.com/researchandadvocacy/issuebriefs.asp?id=308, Accessed: 29.12.2008

Stora Enso (2006) Stora Enso's Sustainability 2006 report. Available: http://www.storaenso.com/media-centre/publications/older-annual-reports/Documents/SR_en_vsk06.pdf, Accessed: 29.12.2008

Swift, T. & Dando, N. (2002) Form methods to ideologies: closing the assurance expectations gap in social and ethical accounting, auditing and reporting, *Journal of Corporate Citizenship*, Winter 2008, 81-90

Vinten, G. (1990) The social auditor, *International Journal of Value-Based Management*, 3(2), 125-136

Wallage, P. (2000) Assurance on sustainability reporting: an auditor's view, *Auditing: A Journal of Practice and Theory*, 19, 53-65

Zadek, S. & Raynard, P. (1995) Accounting works: a comparative review of contemporary approaches to social and ethical accounting, *Accounting Forum*, 19(2/3), 164-175

Zhang, J., Fraser, I. & Hill, W.Y. (2003) A comparative study of social audit models and reports, In: Andriof, J., Waddock, S., Husted, B. & Rahman, S. (eds.), *Unfolding Stakeholder Thinking 2*, Sheffield: Greenleaf Publishing, 244-66

Research Paper 7: Socially Responsible Lending in Australian Banks

Socially Responsible Lending in Times of Crisis: An Exploratory Study of Australasian Banking Practice

Thomas Kern and Nicholas McGuigan, Department of Accounting and Corporate Governance, Macquarie University, Sydney, Australia

Abstract: This paper provides an exploratory study of how socially responsible Australasian banking corporations are and if recent events, such as the global financial crisis, have enabled them to learn lessons in regards to responsible lending practice. Evidence was gained primarily through an analysis of corporate disclosures of two major Australasian banking corporations operating in New Zealand. The data were analysed to see if a change in lending practice occurred to be more in line with corporate social responsibility (CSR). The findings suggest a strong verbal commitment to CSR by the banking corporations, even through tough economic times. However, only when specific goals, achievements and their relation to the overall sustainability agenda are disclosed in a consistent and continuous manner, will real social and responsible banking practice occur. This paper adds to the limited literature of CSR reporting in the financial sector, informing from a public policy perspective on disclosure of banking corporations' lending practices, thus contributing to a global dialogue on CSR within the financial industry.

Introduction

It is common knowledge that the global financial crisis is immense in its economic scope having far-reaching social impacts for industry, business, households, individuals and the financial profession. The impact on the banking industry has been immense through asset write-downs, tighter funding and increased market volatility. The most significant impacts for banking corporations in Australasia have been higher funding costs, weaker global investment markets and the deteriorating credit environment (Westpac, 2008b).

Recent actions taken by governments and regulators around the world have begun to alleviate this pressure through restoring confidence in the financial system resulting in the improved access to funding for banks. These have included significant decreases in the official cash rates, government issued guarantees for bank liabilities, provisions of liquidity facilities, state recapitalisations and even nationalisations of banks. All of the measures taken have the goal to improve the liquidity position of banking corporations, ultimately stabilising the financial system and thus fostering an economic recovery.

In terms of corporate social responsibility (CSR), we have to ask ourselves the question "has this improved access to funding been utilised by banking corporations to lend money in a more socially responsible and sustainable manner?" The benefits of these government-initiated measures are evident in the short term. However, will this facilitate a sustainable economic recovery that can be passed on to future generations? Or did the banks simply fail to learn from their mistakes, continuing along an irresponsible lending route, heading for another crisis with adverse social impacts?

This research attempts to investigate how socially responsible Australasian banking corporations lending practices are and if these recent global events enabled them to learn sustainable lessons. Data for the study were collected by means of corporate disclosure analysis. Documents reviewed included the corporations' CSR reports, independent assurance statements, annual reports, media releases and websites through the period 2006 – 2009. The disclosed data were analysed in order to investigate whether the current economic crisis has led to a change to their lending practices to be more in line with CSR.

The rest of the paper is organised as follows. Relevant literature on the global economic crisis and the irresponsible lending practices of financial institutions, corporate social responsibility and its role within financial institutions is reviewed next. This is followed by a description of the research methodology employed. The findings of the study are then discussed and analysed, with the conclusion and limitations presented in the final section.

Literature Review

This section commences by reviewing literature relating to the causes of the global economic crisis, followed by an analysis of the social impacts arising from the crisis. The section concludes by reviewing the important role corporate social responsibility has to play within financial intermediaries.

Global Financial Crisis and the Irresponsible Lending Practices of Financial Institutions

The U.S. Government policy of deregulation of the commercial and investment banking industries and their subsequent failed regulation were important contributors to the global financial crisis (Immergluck, 2009). In 1982, the U.S. Congress passed the Alternative Mortgage Transactions Parity Act, resulting in a change to banking laws that enabled new mortgage products to be introduced and ended the traditional practice of banks issuing conventional fixed-rate mortgages (Birger, 2008). This coupled with the United States Securities and Exchange Commission's (SEC) loosening of regulations in 2004 enabled many investment banks to significantly increase their debt levels. This resulted in a growth in Mortgage-backed Securities (MBS)[1], which led to the creation and widespread use of subprime mortgages (Labaton, 2008).

It is generally thought that the concrete causes in the economic downturn can be traced back to two major factors, namely, irresponsible home lending practice particularly in the U.S. and the interrelated securitisation of mortgages (Taylor, 2009). The worldwide engagement of financial institutions in this sub-prime market has lifted the impacts to a global level. Recent events have proven that money has been lent and invested by financial institutions in an irresponsible and unsustainable manner, driven by private greed and kept relatively unchecked by a failing regulatory system (Banktrack, 2008).

U.S. financial institutions' lending policies had significantly relaxed in the lead up to the financial crisis with very little financial screening procedures being implemented (Immergluck, 2009). Lenders were increasingly offering loans to high-risk borrowers, including, illegal immigrants, minority groups and consumers who could not afford the mortgage repayments from the beginning (Schwarz, 2007). These irresponsible home lending practices were compounded with the offering of increasingly risky loan options. For example, median deposit requirements in 2005, for a first time homebuyer in the U.S. was 2%, with 43% of those borrowers producing no deposit at all (Knox, 2006).

The criteria for obtaining a U.S. home loan consistently weakened in the period 2003-2006. Firstly, the Stated Income Verified Assets (SIVA) loan was introduced where a borrower did not need to prove their respective income, they simply had to 'state' and provide evidence that they had money in the bank. The No Income, Verified Assets (NIVA) loan then superseded this, where an individual no longer required proof of employment. These guidelines continued to loosen, resulting in the creation of No Income No Asset (Ninja) loans where the borrower did not have to state nor prove any owned assets (Connon, 2007). This was further fuelled by the use of automated loan approvals, allowing loans to be made without appropriate review and documentation.

Mortgage products presented by financial institutions became increasingly complex to the average borrower (Immergluck, 2009). Interest-only adjustable-rate mortgages (ARM) were offered allowing homeowners to pay the interest

---

[1] A mortgage-backed security, first issued by the Government National Mortgage Association (Ginnie Mae) in 1970, is a debt obligation that represents a claim on the cash flows from mortgage loans on residential property (Ross, Westerfield and Jordan, 2004).

payments during an initial period with no contribution to the principal amount. A third of ARM loans offered between 2004 and 2006, provided a 'teaser' interest rate of 4% which increased significantly after an initial period resulting in a doubling of a borrowers monthly mortgage payment. A growing proportion of subprime ARM loans were being offered, at the request of financial lending institutions, to borrowers with credit scores high enough to qualify for conventional mortgages with more favourable terms and conditions (Brooks and Simon, 2007).

Irresponsible lending practices of financial institutions can be extended to the facility of credit card debt for consumers. The growing amount of credit card debt in the U.S. has resulted in a level of $962 billion in July 2008, with a median credit card debt of U.S. $3,000 per citizen and an average number of two credit cards held per person (Korkki, 2008). This phenomenal growth in credit can be attributed, in part, to attractive credit products being offered by financial institutions. These include low interest rate credit cards, low-rate interest being offered for a short period, no interest being charged for a minimum 'start-up' time period and no bank fees being offered on credit facilities. The introduction of attractive credit products, coupled with the financial institutions' fee structure of credit defaults, dishonour fees and credit card inactivity fees has led to a large increase in debt borrowing for average homeowners.

Taylor (2009) argues the interrelated securitisation of mortgages in the U.S. by financial institutions has proved a significant factor in the global financial crisis. The securitisation of home loans essentially enabled banks to sell these loans in a repackaged form of mortgage-backed securities (MBS) to investors, therefore distributing the associated credit risk. Securitisation enabled those banks to replenish their funds, with no obligation to hold the debt until maturity, allowing them to issue further loans and generate further fee income. Problems arose as these complex repackaged mortgages contained adjustable-rate sub-prime and other problematic mortgages.

Financial disclosures in relation to the valuation of MBS and their associated risks and credit rating have proved insufficient in recent times. Schwarcz (2008) states the disclosures describing the MBS and their risks generally comply with SEC regulations. It is the growing complexity of this market, he argues, that led to ineffective disclosure. The risks giving rise to the collapse of the market for securities backed by subprime mortgages were disclosed, the disclosure was insufficient, in part because complexity made the risks very difficult to understand. Therefore "a lot of institutional investors bought [the subprime mortgage-backed] securities substantially based on their ratings [without fully understanding what they bought]..." (Schwarcz, 2008, p. 1110). The risk associated with the MBS was underestimated by rating agencies through a lack of competition, poor accountability and the inherent difficulty in assessing this risk due to the products complexity. Thus, securitisation created an inherent financial risk in the balance sheets of financial institutions (Taylor, 2009).

The process of securitisation enabled foreign investors and financial institutions to invest in the U.S. housing market, creating a global impact. As U.S. housing prices declined, major global financial institutions that had borrowed and invested heavily in subprime MBS reported significant losses. This created a domino effect leading to defaults and losses on other loan types increasing significantly as the crisis expanded from the housing market to other parts of the economy (Immergluck, 2009). Irresponsible lending practices of financial institutions and a lack of independent regulation exacerbated this crisis leading to a highly leveraged society, resulting in major social impacts within a global context.

Societal Impacts of the Global Financial Crisis

The boom and inevitable bust in the U.S. housing market resulted in severe and widespread financial impacts and costs. The spillover effect of the housing collapse in the U.S. into broader credit and financial markets resulted in widespread distress for borrowers, lenders and investors (Immergluck, 2009).

Impacts on Borrowers

The irresponsible lending practice of financial institutions leading up to the financial crisis meant that a great number of subprime mortgages were being offered to borrowers who could not have previously afforded home ownership and to those who had adequate credit ratings. Through lenders' weakened home loan criteria of, no initial deposit requirements, no income screening process nor verification of employment, individuals were able to access subprime mortgages at high financing costs with very little equity to cushion any unforeseen event. These high-risk loans, with more debt to equity, increase the financial risk of moving from a rental to owned accommodation (Foote, Gerardi and Willen, 2008).

The devaluing of house prices and eventual collapse of the housing market, along with high imposed interest rates and fees on subprime mortgages led to defaults of debt repayments and forced foreclosures (Immergluck, 2009). Belsky, Retsinas and Duda (2005) illustrate high-risk borrowing can significantly reduce the financial return to investments in homeownership. The costs to borrowers through foreclosure can include loss of substantial owner equity and a worsening of credit history and lowering of credit score.

Beyond the immediate financial loss to borrowers of high-risk loans there can be longer-term costs incurred, including those relating to weakened credit histories and lower credit scores. Diminished social and economic opportunities can result from weakened credit histories, in particular, job applicant evaluations, potential tenant assessments, underwriting insurance, provision of future credit and provision of utilities such as power, gas, water and phone (Immergluck, 2009).

Borrowers being forced to exit homeownership may suffer socially, emotionally and psychologically. These costs are often less transparent and more complex to measure than the financial costs inherent in foreclosure. These costs include, loss of borrowers social network and social support system through relocation (Briggs, 1998; Dawkins, 2006), complexity associated with relocation of children to schools (Haveman and Wolfe, 1994), humiliation associated with foreclosure and bankruptcy (Ronson, 2005; Fletcher, 2006; Armour, 2008) and psychological effects such as fear, anxiety, tension and stress (Fields, Justa, Libman and Saegert, 2007).

Impacts on Lenders and Investors

High-risk lending can produce an amount of financial costs to lenders and investors, especially when investing in MBS. Greenlaw, Hatzius, Kayshap and Shin (2008) provide an estimated $400 billion in direct investment losses in MBS and related instruments. The Organisation for Economic Estimates provides supporting evidence in 2008 with an estimate of $350 to $420 billion (Blundell-Wignall, 2008). Highly leveraged U.S. banks, investment banks and government sponsored entities account for approximately $200 billion in direct losses, causing a large flow through impact on the lack of financial capacity in the U.S. credit market (Greenlaw et.al, 2008).

Financial institutions did not solely experience financial losses, they were also experienced by smaller more socially oriented investors. Triple-A credit ratings assigned to associated securities and financial instruments led to a number of conservative institutional investors investing in MBS and suffering significant losses. These included local and state government finance agencies, used to fund local governments and school boards, and public pension funds (Evans, 2007).

Impacts on Global Economy

Financial losses were experienced in many parts of the world due to investments in the U.S. subprime market by foreign investors. Blundell-Wignall (2008) estimates that one-third of mortgage-related securities losses will accrue to overseas investors. Baily and Elliott (2009) state that U.S. consumption accounted for more than a third of the growth in global consumption between 2000 and 2007. "The US economy has been spending too much and borrowing too much for years and the rest of the world depended on the U.S. consumer as a source of global demand" (Baily and Elliott, 2009, p. 21). A current U.S. recession and an increased savings rate of U.S. consumers, declines in growth elsewhere have been dramatic. For the first quarter of 2009, the annualised rate of decline in GDP was 14.4% in Germany, 15.2% in Japan, 7.4% in the UK, 18% in Latvia, 9.8% in the Euro area and 21.5% for Mexico (Bailey and Elliott, 2009).

The collapse of the U.S. housing market and its ensuing financial crisis has led to a global recession. Secondary societal impacts resulting from this recession include decreased property valuation (Been, 2008), increased crime rates (Immergluck and Smith, 2006), rental eviction, unemployment (Mortished, 2009) and political unrest (Jolly, 2009; Maltezou, 2009; Schwirtz and Levy, 2009). These secondary impacts have reinforced the more direct impacts to the financial markets resulting in a global recession with long lasting effects.

Corporate Social Responsibility Role in Banking Corporations

The banking industry, in recent times, has received a considerable amount of adverse media coverage for allowing the current expansion of debt and their intransparent disclosure (Fletcher, 2006). Coulson (2007) argues that banking corporations' play a large intermediary role in a modern financial system, having widespread impact on local communities, individuals and businesses.

CSR involves organisations' taking into account the economic, environmental and social impacts of their activities when making decisions therefore providing information for a variety of external stakeholders. CSR therefore extends beyond a traditional shareholder approach to business (Ullman and Herbohn, 2005). CSR enables organisations to act responsibly and to consider the wellbeing of all stakeholders not just their shareholders (Birch, 2003; Husted and Allen, 2000). Furthermore, CSR reporting can act as a vehicle of transparency, allowing banking corporations a direct means to inform their external stakeholders of their business strategies, actions and plans with regard to topical environmental, social and economic issues.

In recent times there has been an increase in the adoption of CSR practice within banking corporations, in particular, the reporting of socially responsible issues. This increasing adoption has been partially assisted through an increase in CSR reporting instruments including, ethics, principles and guidelines, codes and voluntary standards (Goel, 2005). Key organisations have endorsed sustainable development within the financial sector both in New Zealand - New Zealand Stock Exchange, Reserve Bank of New Zealand - and internationally - United Nations, Organisation for Economic Cooperation and Development (OECD), Global Reporting Initiatives, Dow Jones Sustainability Index and the Equator Principles (Banktrack, 2009).

CSR reporting is currently voluntary for New Zealand financial institutions with no immediate regulatory move to mandate such disclosure. Despite current voluntary practice and the relatively recent impact CSR reporting is having on financial institutions, New Zealand banking corporations have become active in producing separate published CSR reports to that of their annual report. These reporting initiatives have been extended in recent times to incorporate external, independent verification and assurance reports of banking corporations CSR activities.

Solomon (2007) argues for improved corporate accountability through greater disclosure of all types of risks to stakeholders, including financial – credit market and liquidity, and non-financial – legal, environmental and social. Harte, Lewis and Owen (1991) found that annual reports were not adequate in providing information to screen companies on a socially responsible basis. Friedman and Miles (2001) reported an increase in the importance placed on environmental and social issues within business leaders. Solomon and Solomon (2003; 2007) provide further support through the conducting of extensive interviews with the institutional investment community. The research indicated that social and environmental concerns are being treated as mainstream issues and that fund managers are dissatisfied with the level of disclosure. Stihele (2004) states financial institutions need to be more transparent in their credit policies especially those that relate to their social and environmental impact.

A need for more transparent disclosure is evident within financial institutions. Solomon and Solomon (2002) call for 'active dialogue' to take place amongst stakeholders. Active dialogue will result from improvements in the quality and quantity of social and environmental disclosure and the development of longer and stronger communication, thus constituting a 'virtuous circle of CSR' (Solomon, 2007, p. 287). We have to ask ourselves the question 'has the improved access to funding, through governmental and regulatory assistance, been utilised by banking corporations to lend money in a more socially responsible and sustainable manner?' The benefits associated with these government-initiated measures are evident in the short term. However, 'will this facilitate a sustainable economic recovery that can be passed on to future generations?' Or 'did the banks simply fail to learn from their mistakes, continuing along an irresponsible lending route, heading for another crisis with adverse social impacts?'

This exploratory research attempts to investigate how socially responsible Australasian banking corporations are and if these recent global events enabled them to learn sustainable lessons in regards to lending practice. This research aims to provide an insight into whether financial institutions are responding in form as well as in spirit to the ever-growing needs of socially responsible investors.

Research Methodology

An exploratory analysis of corporate disclosures from two Australasian banking corporations operating in New Zealand was used to investigate whether the current economic crisis has led to a change in their lending practices, bringing them more in line with CSR. Corporate disclosures include: CSR reports and their independent assurance statements, annual financial reports, media releases and information contained within the financial institution's website during the period 2006-2009.

Westpac Banking Corporation (Westpac) and Australia & New Zealand Banking Group Limited[2] (ANZ) were chosen as the two exemplars for analysis as they are regarded as pioneers and global leaders in the field of financial institutional CSR reporting. Westpac has undertaken proactive CSR reporting since 2002 for its Australian operations and 2004 for its New Zealand counterpart. In 2009, they achieved gold status within the Dow Jones Sustainability Index (DJSI) being one of only two financial institutions worldwide to gain this status. Westpac follows the Global Reporting Initiative (GRI) Guidelines to produce its CSR reports. In 2009, Westpac achieved the highest quality assurance level, A+ as assessed by an independent assurance provider (Westpac, 2009a). Similarly, ANZ started their CSR Reporting on a group level in 2005 and has been named, for the assessment period of 2009-2010, Global Supersector Leader within the DJSI for the third successive year. Furthermore, both banking groups are comparable in regards to common total assets and have a similar scope of business.

The analysis has been limited to consumer lending practices, especially to home loans and credit card debt. The corporate disclosures were searched utilising key words, such as social responsibility, responsible banking,

[2] The research has utilised corporate disclosures at the national level, from Westpac New Zealand Limited and ANZ National Bank Limited, and at the group level, from Westpac Banking Corporation and Australia & New Zealand Banking Group.

responsible lending, lending policies, lending standards, financial literacy, financial hardship, financial inclusion, financial crisis, financial turmoil. All relevant disclosure was then entered into a spreadsheet, categorised by institution, keyword, year and source. Using the frequency of occurrence, five key areas were determined from this raw data, credit risk management (lending criteria), financial assistance programmes, credit card debt measures, financial literacy programmes and responsible lending principles.

Results and Discussion

It is evident that both institutions are aware of and explicitly state the responsibility the banking industry has for the financial crisis and the resulting link to CSR. This is best reflected by the Chairman of Westpac Banking Corporation who states "… it's an uncomfortable reality for some in our sector that values are indeed part of this current crisis, through unethical decision-making, misaligned incentives and poor corporate disclosure" (Westpac, 2008b, p.3), while ANZ affirms CSR is more important than ever before (ANZ, 2008b).

The preliminary results of the analysis indicate a clustering of activity around the start of the global financial crisis, mid 2007. This is followed by an increase in disclosure through CSR reports, media releases and website information during 2008, remaining constant throughout the timeframe to October 2009. A more in-depth analysis of the Banks' corporate disclosures in relation to consumer lending practices enabled the development of five key areas of discussion, namely credit risk management (lending criteria), financial assistance programmes, credit card debt measures, financial literacy programmes and responsible lending principles. The research findings for each of these areas are now discussed.

Credit Risk Management

Credit risk is generally defined as the potential that a borrowing customer will fail to meet its obligations in accordance with the agreed borrowing terms. The credit risk management of financial institutions aims to avoid exceeding impairment losses by maintaining credit risk exposure within acceptable parameters. This is critical for the long-term success of any banking organisation. Credit risk management involves the establishment of an appropriate credit risk framework, a sound credit approval process and the maintenance of an appropriate credit administration, measurement and controlling process. The major reason for failures of financial institutions continues to be directly related to loose credit standards and the inability to adapt these to economic changes (Basel Committee on Banking Supervision, 2000). Therefore a socially responsible financial institution's natural reaction to a recession is to tighten credit risk management policy.

In 2008, ANZ instinctively reacted to the recession through a tightening of their credit risk management. This can be illustrated in their CSR disclosure "Specifically we have monitored, and when required, adjusted our capital levels, improved 'stress testing' of our various customer portfolios, tightened credit risk management and insured our risk management team is involved in business decisions even earlier than usual" (ANZ, 2008b, p. 13). The tightening of lending criteria was further referenced in relation to home lending: "given the shift in economic conditions, we have tightened lending standards for some prospective borrowers, especially in areas where there is evidence of falling house prices" (ANZ, 2008b, p. 14). Westpac made no disclosures in relation to the tightening of neither credit risk management nor loan criteria during this period. It is a reasonable assumption that Westpac, faced with the same economic environment, would have also taken measures to restrict their credit risk.

Interestingly, despite a tightened credit risk management practice there has been substantial growth in consumer lending. In 2008, ANZ report a 12% ($17.0 billion) growth in lending mainly attributable to housing loans from mortgages (ANZ, 2008c). Westpac report a similar growth in consumer lending during this period, 13% ($17.8 billion) predominantly within the housing market (Westpac, 2008a).

A lack of detailed disclosure statements, as indicated above, prevents stakeholders from being able to assess whether a financial institution is acting in a socially responsible manner. In order for meaningful disclosure to occur financial institutions need to be more transparent in their credit policies especially those that relate to their social and environmental impact (Stihele, 2004; Solomon and Solomon, 2002; Solomon, 2007).

Financial Assistance Programmes

The continuing increase in consumer debt levels in many developed countries coupled with recent economic events have created cause for concern. Such high levels of household debt dramatically reduce consumers' future disposable income making households particularly vulnerable to a volatile economy, as recently experienced in the U.S., thus hindering sustainable development. Specifically in New Zealand, the total household debt to disposable income ratio has increased from 59% in 1991 to 162% in 2008, while 93% of consumer debt is related to housing (RBNZ, 2009).

This level of household debt, from both sides of the Tasman, has resulted in rising levels of overdue consumer debt, as indicated in Table 1 below.

Table 1: Proportion of Overdue Consumer Debt Customers in Australia and New Zealand for Westpac and ANZ

	Westpac		**ANZ**	
	2008	**2007**	**2008**	**2007**
	%	%	%	%
Australia				
Mortgages	0.29	0.28	0.40	0.25
Credit Card	0.33	0.37	1.49	1.30
New Zealand				
Mortgages	0.47	0.21	0.75	0.25
Credit Card	1.25	0.90	1.70	1.40

Westpac's financial assistance programme, 'Westpac Assist' was first introduced in late 2007 in Australia and followed in New Zealand, early 2009. Through this programme Westpac has found that the causes of customers' financial difficulties are highly complex and personal, often relating to illness, unemployment or a death in the family. It is for this reason they are proactively promoting early intervention in order to obtain the best outcome for customers and shareholders (Westpac, 2008b).

Furthermore, Westpac New Zealand introduced custom designed principles to assist customers in financial hardship that are unable to meet their contractual obligations. Examples of which include, extending the period of the contract, interest only repayment options and postponing of payments with interest to be capitalised to the loan (Westpac, 2009b).

Similar actions in response to rising overdue consumer debt were undertaken by ANZ. In 2008, 'Customer Connect' was introduced, a programme which is designed to give retail customers in financial difficulty more repayment flexibility in order to bridge periods of financial instability with deferred or reduced repayment arrangements of up to twelve months. Greater support for retail customers facing financial difficulty was also the goal in the enhancement of staff training through their implemented 'Financial Wellbeing' programme (ANZ, 2008c).

Both banking corporations showed a willingness to assist in times of financial hardship with the implementation of innovative programmes of assistance for their retail customers. It is important to note that these financial assistance programmes were designed to bridge a period of economic difficulty, often through the provision of more flexible repayment options. This had the effect of easing a pressurized situation by removing a debt obstacle in the immediate term and replacing this with an even greater obstacle in the future. It is evident that these measures provide debt consumers assistance in the short-term but do very little to create a long-term sustainable solution.

Credit Card Debt Measures

In response to mounting credit card debt repayments not being met, as indicated in Table 1, both financial institutions provided incentives for credit card management. ANZ introduced in November 2007 (Australia) and August 2008 (New Zealand) a new type of credit card product rewarding participants, through a bonus point system, for making repayments rather than on purchases made (ANZ, 2007a; 2008b).

Westpac introduced a DebitPlus Visa card in 2007, allowing customers all the benefits associated with a credit card, but making use of a consumer's cheque account (Westpac, 2007a). Contradicting evidence can be found under the heading 'Westpac credit card offer takes pain out of Christmas shopping' when during the 2007/2008-holiday period Westpac introduced an interest-capped credit card (4.99%) for Christmas purchases. After six months the interest rate reverted back to the standard 'Westpac Low Interest MasterCard rate' (12.95%) (Westpac, 2007d). This action seems to promote the consumption of credit card debt therefore contradicting responsible lending practice and contributing to the increased overdue credit card debt levels in New Zealand as seen in table 1.

Financial Literacy Programmes

Financial literacy, the ability to make informed judgements and to take effective decisions regarding the use and management of money, is a prerequisite for personal sustainable development. The New Zealand Retirement Commission has recognized the importance of enhancing financial literacy with the commission of the Centre for Financial Literacy in 2008. The Centre provides a platform for the implementation and monitoring of a National Strategy for Financial Literacy implemented in June of that year. This has recently been extended to include a financial literacy education programme within the New Zealand school curriculum.

Westpac believe "[that] as financial experts, we ... recognise our corporate responsibility to share our knowledge, skills and information to help New Zealanders manage their money better" (Westpac, 2007c). Westpac launched an innovative financial literacy workshop programme, 'Managing Your Money', in 2006 (Westpac, 2007a). This programme was further enhanced through web-based tutorial information being provided and an increase of workshop deliveries in 2008 (Westpac, 2008b; 2008c).

Similarly, ANZ disclosed the implementation of a financial literacy programme, 'MoneyMinded', combined with their 'SaverPlus' to promote money management skills in both Australia (2004) and New Zealand (2007) (ANZ, 2007b). 2008 saw ANZ enhancing this programme to include topics on superannuation, home ownership, tenancy and investment basics, with a goal set for 2009 to enhance the overall financial literacy programme (ANZ, 2008c).

The analysis shows that both ANZ and Westpac have clearly illustrated a solid and ongoing commitment to financial literacy. The banks' financial literacy programmes commenced prior to the financial crisis, Westpac in 2002 and ANZ in 2004. The CSR reports of both banks disclose goals towards the enhancement of participation in their respective financial literacy programmes. For example, ANZ have disclosed rates of participation at 15, 000 Australians in 2006, 20, 000 Australians in 2007 and 30, 000 Australians and New Zealanders in 2008 and 2009 (ANZ, 2007b, 2008c, 2009b). If these disclosures are used as a benchmark then it is probable that between both banks 60, 000 individuals would have the opportunity to participate in their programmes. Although, this provides some indication of reinforcement of socially responsible practice, with a combined total population of 26, 206, 600 this would equate to a 0.23% impact on Australia and New Zealand consumers, suggesting plenty of room for further enhancement (Australia Bureau of Statistics, 2009; Statistics New Zealand).

Responsible Lending Principles

Until financial literacy programmes have a significant impact on the behaviour of borrowers, banks should consider lending responsibly in order to protect their own reputation and the wellbeing of their customers (Richards, Palmer and Bogdanova, 2008). Responsible lending means that credit products are appropriate for consumers' needs and are tailored to their ability to repay. This can be achieved through the provision of suitable lending policies that enable banks to act in a fair, honest and professional manner before, during and after the lending transaction (European Commission, 2009). This level of socially responsible banking practice coupled with financial literacy education enables consumers to make informed and sustainable borrowing decisions. An internationally growing trend for financial institutions to implement responsible lending principles is present (Banktrack, 2009).

In 2005, ANZ implemented responsible lending principles within their Australian practice. However, these principles were limited to consumer credit card debt (ANZ, 2006). Their implementation assisted ANZ to act in a more socially responsible manner by: not offering a credit card limit increase if poor credit performance or inability to meet repayments was found; not offering a credit card limit increase if a consumer is receiving governmental benefits; providing information about easy and efficient ways to reduce the credit card limit; ensuring the minimum monthly credit card repayments do not fall below 2% of the outstanding balance; providing transparent information in regards to any increase in credit card limit offers, for example, outlining how much the minimum monthly repayment would increase if the offer was accepted and including information about how to request a lower offer; and explaining in clear and simple terms how interest on credit cards is calculated and charged, what fees may apply, and the consequences of late repayments (ANZ, 2009a). The financial recession triggered a review of these principles in 2008, changes to this policy have not yet been disclosed (ANZ, 2008c; 2009b).

Westpac implemented more holistic principles for responsible lending within Australia in 2007, namely to, seek only to lend what our customers can afford to pay, market our products and services responsibly, support customers facing financial difficulty and improve financial literacy (Westpac, 2007b). In response to the financial crisis, Westpac disclosed a goal in 2007 to establish responsible lending principles in New Zealand during 2008. These principles were targeted at consumer home lending and credit card debt (Westpac, 2007a). The principles are currently disclosed as a work in progress, having been drafted and discussed internally with the need to engage further internal and external stakeholders prior to their launch (Westpac, 2008b).

Conclusions, Limitations and Further Research

"As the global nature of the 'credit crunch' has shown, banks play a pivotal role in the economy and in the whole sustainability agenda. One bank's own impacts may not be significant, yet through its financing and lending activities the indirect impacts are" (Corporate Citizenship, 2008, p. 5). Through the above mentioned government and regulator led measures a restoration of confidence in the financial system has resulted. This improved access to funding for banks places the power for sustainable change again in the hands of banking corporations to make ethically responsible lending decisions.

This paper has undertaken to provide an exploratory study into the financial disclosures of two Australasian banking corporations, Australia & New Zealand Banking Group Limited and Westpac Banking Corporation. The study utilizes the disclosures of both institutions during the commonly accepted global financial crisis timeline of 2006-2009 to try to establish whether Australasian banking corporations have learnt sustainable lessons in regards to their lending practice.

The evidence presented in both banks has indicated a strong verbal commitment to CSR, even more so through tough economic times.

Evidence suggests that both institutions are taking responsible measures, however weaknesses in their specific disclosures are evident. In terms of the banks' credit risk management practice a lack of specific disclosure, especially in relation to lending criteria, does not allow stakeholders to conclude whether the banks' adjusted their credit approval process to match the changed economic environment. The examination of their financial assistance programmes illustrated that both banks recognized their social responsibility towards customers in financial hardship. However, their economic responsibility towards their shareholders appears to prevent long-term sustainable solutions for those customers being found.

In terms of social responsibility, the least convincing disclosures were found in the area of credit card debt measures. ANZ introduced a system rewarding customers on their repayments rather than on their credit purchases. The fact that rewarding repayments require purchases in the first place has not been mentioned in their disclosure. Thus, it remains a questionable measure for reducing credit card debt levels. Westpac behave in a similar socially irresponsible manner having promoted a credit card product with a teaser interest rate during the holiday period of 2007-2008. This action directly contradicts previous efforts to reduce credit debt levels, with the introduction of a DebitPlus Visa card.

Financial literacy education programmes provide one of the most important means of enhancing consumer understanding and thus achieving a more sustainable borrowing behaviour (Retirement Commission, 2009). A strong commitment by both banks has been made to the development and, in the light of the financial crisis, enhancement of financial literacy programmes. However, due to highly aggregated disclosure stakeholders are unable to assess the efficiency of these programmes. The research findings indicate, even with generous estimates of participation planned, there is plenty of room for enhanced coverage. The self-imposed CSR goals, to develop and disclose responsible lending principles, have shown both banks' acknowledgement of the importance of socially responsible lending practices. However, the results found were disappointing. ANZ has confined their responsible lending principles to credit card debt while Westpac NZ have not yet managed to disclose responsible lending principles within the three year period 2007-2009. Overall, these results indicate a need for a heightened level of detailed disclosure to create transparency within the market, in order for individuals to make more informed decisions.

This exploratory research is confined to the analysis of consumer lending disclosures as presented in the banking institutions media releases, CSR reports, annual reports and website. Further investigation into the implementation of socially responsible banking practice through interviews with banking personnel and key external stakeholders such as customers, shareholders and community interest groups is planned. Further research presents itself in the conducting of a comparative analysis of socially responsible banking practice between Australasian efforts and those taking place in the European Union.

The lending practices that contributed to the U.S. sub-prime crisis remind us that banks must ensure that their products are responsibly sold and easy to understand by consumers (Immergluck, 2009). A need for more transparent disclosure is evident within financial institutions, such as ANZ and Westpac, in order to create a more informed market. This level of discourse between banking corporations and their external stakeholders has to remain 'active' through enhanced quality and quantity of disclosure (Solomon and Solomon, 2002; Solomon 2007). Only when specific goals, achievements and their relation to the overall sustainability agenda are disclosed in a consistent and continuous manner, will real social and responsible banking practice occur. The power for real sustainable change is with the banking corporations. Let us see if they take up the challenge!

References

ANZ Banking Group Limited. (2006). *What's the Difference?,* ANZ Banking Group Limited.

ANZ Banking Group Limited. (2007a). *ANZ launches new credit card that rewards customers for repayments*, 26 November 2007, ANZ Banking Group Limited.

ANZ Banking Group Limited. (2007b). *What's the Difference? Corporate Responsibility Report 2007,* ANZ Banking Group Limited.

ANZ Banking Group Limited. (2008a). *2008 Annual Report*, ANZ Banking Group Limited.

ANZ Banking Group Limited. (2008b). *ANZ launches New Zealand's first credit card that rewards repayments*, 11 August 2008, ANZ Banking Group Limited.

ANZ Banking Group Limited. (2008c). *Corporate Responsibility Review 2008*, ANZ Banking Group Limited.

ANZ Banking Group Limited. (2009a). *ANZ Customer Charter*, ANZ Banking Group Limited. Last accessed: 25 September 2009: http://www.anz.com/australia/aboutanz/CustomerCharter/popup/popup.asp?popup=Responsible

ANZ Banking Group Limited. (2009b). *Corporate Responsibility Interim Report 2009,* ANZ Banking Group Limited.

Armour, S. (2008). Foreclosures Take an Emotional Toll on Many Homeowners. *USA Today*. Last accessed: 21 September 2009: http://www.usatoday.com/money/economy/housing/2008-05-14-mortgage-foreclosures-mental-health_N.htm.

Australia Bureau of Statistics. (2009). *Australian Demographic Statistics*, Australia Bureau of Statistics.

Banktrack, (2008). Bank to the Future: El Escorial Statement on Banks and the Financial Crisis. Last accessed: 18 September 2009: http://www.banktrack.org/download/bank_to_the_future_el_escorial_statement/escorial_declaration_final.pdf.

Banktrack, (2009). http://www.banktrack.org. Last accessed: 18 September 2009.

Bailey, M. N. and Elliot, D. J. (2009). *The US Financial and Economic Crisis: Where Does it Stand and Where Do We Go From Here?* The Brookings Institution. Last accessed: 21 September 2009:

http://www.brookings.edu/~/media/Files/rc/papers/2009/0615_economic_crisis_baily_elliott/0615_economic_crisis_baily_elliott.pdf.

Basel Committee on Banking Supervision, (2000). *Principles for the Management of Credit Risk*, September, Basel Committee on Banking Supervision.

Been, V. (2008). External Effects of Concentrated Mortgage Foreclosures: Evidence from New York City. Testimony before Committee on Oversight and Government Reform Subcommittee on Domestic Policy. Last accessed: 23 September 2009: http://domesticpolicy.oversight.house.gov/documents/20080522105505.pdf.

Belsky, E., Retsinas, N. and Duda, M. (2005). The Financial Returns to Low-Income Homeownership. Harvard University Joint Center for Housing Studies, Working Paper W05-9. Last accessed: 21 September 2009: http://www.jchs.harvard.edu/publications/finance/w05-9pdf.

Birch, D. (2003). Corporate social responsibility: Some key theoretical issues and concepts for new ways of doing business, *Journal of New Business Ideas and Trends*, 1(1), p. 1-19.

Birger, J. (2008). How Congress helped create the subprime mess, *Fortune*. Last accessed: 16 September 2009: http://money.cnn.com/2008/01/30/real_estate/congress_subprime.fortune/.

Blundell-Wignall, A. (2008). The Subprime Crisis: Size, Deleveraging and Some Policy Options. Financial Market Trends Paper ISSN 0378-651X. Last accessed: 21 September 2009:
http://www.oecd.org/dataoecd/36/27/40451721.pdf.

Briggs, X. (1998). Brown Kids in White Suburbs: Housing Mobility and the Many Faces of Social Capital, *Housing Policy Debate*, 9, p. 177-221.

Brooks, R. and Simon, R. (2007). Subprime debacle traps even very credit-worthy, *The Wall Street Journal*. Last accessed: 20 September 2009: http://www.realestatejournal.com/buysell/mortgages/20071204-simon.html.

Connon, H. (2007). Why Ninja mortgages could wreak havoc, The Observer. Last accessed: 20 September 2009: http://www.unc.edu/~salemi/Sub-prime%20Crisis/Ninja%20Mortgages%20Observer%209_30_07.pdf.

Corporate Citzenship. (2008). *ANZ Corporate Responsbility Report 2008 – External Assurance Statement and Commentary*, 4 December 2008, Corporate Citzenship.

Coulson, A. (2007). Environmental and Social Assessment in Sustainable Finance, in Unerman, J., Bebbington, J. and O'Dwyer, B. (Eds) *Sustainability Accounting and Accountability*, Routledge, Oxon, p. 266-282.

Dawkins, C. (2006). Are Social Networks the Ties That Bind Families to Neighbourhoods? *Housing Studies*, 21, p. 867-881.

European Commission. (2009). *Public Consultation on Responsible Lending and Borrowing in the EU*, 15 June 2009, Brussels: European Commission, Internal Market and Services DG, Financial Institutions retail issues, consumer policy and payment systems.

Evans, D. (2007). Montana, Connecticut Hold Downgraded by Moody's. *Bloomberg*. Last accessed: 21 September 2009: http://www.bloomberg.com/apps/news?sid=anQ2BNJxVVM8&pid=20601087.

Fields, F., Justa, F., Libman, K., and Saegert, S. (2007). American Nightmare. *Shelterforce* No. 150. Last accessed: 21 September 2009: http://www.nhi.org/online/issues/150/americannightmare.html.

Fletcher, D. (2006). Debt Suicides, *The Mirror*. Last accessed 16 September 2009: http://www.mirror.co.uk/news/tm_objectid=16708338&method=full&siteid=115875&headline=d-pound-bt-suicides-name_page.html.

Foote, C., Gerardi, K., and Willen, P. (2008). Negative Equity and Foreclosure: Theory and Evidence, Federal Reserve Bank of Boston. Public Policy Discussion Paper No. 08-3. Last accessed: 21 September 2009: http://www.bos.frb.org/economic/ppdp/2008/ppdp0803.htm.

Friedman, A. L. and Miles, S. (2001). Socially responsible investment and corporate social and environmental reporting in the UK: An exploratory study, *British Accounting Review*, 33, p. 523-548.

Goel, R. (2005). *Guide to instruments of corporate responsibility: an overview of 16 key tools for labour fund trustees*. York University. Last accessed: 21 September 2009: http://ipe.77.evous.fr/IMG/pdf/goel_guide_to_instruments.pdf.

Greenlaw, D., Hatzius, J., Kayshap, A. and Shin., H. (2008). Leveraged Losses: Lessons from the Mortgage Market Meltdown. Unpublished manuscript. Last accessed: 21 September 2009: http://www.chicagogsb.edu/usmpf/docs/usmpf2008confdraft.pdf.

Harte, G., Lewis, L. and Owen, D. (1991). Ethical investment and the corporate reporting function, *Critical Perspectives on Accounting*, 2, p. 227-253.

Haveman, R. and Wolfe, B. (1994). *Succeeding Generations: On the Effects of Investments in Children*. New York: Russell Sage Foundation.

Husted, B. and Allen, D. (2000), Is it ethical to use ethics as strategy? *Journal of Business Ethics*, 27, p. 21-31.

Immergluck, D. and Smith, G. (2006). The Impact of Single-Family Mortgage Foreclosures on Crime, *Housing Studies*, 21(6), p.851-866.

Immergluck, D. (2009). *Foreclosed: High-Risk Lending, Deregulation, and the Undermining of America's Mortgage Market*, New York: Cornell University Press.

Jolly, D. (2009). Hundreds of Thousands Protest in France. The New York Times. Last accessed: 23 September 2009: http://www.nytimes.com/2009/01/29/world/europe/29iht-france.4.19789187.html?_r=1.

Knox, N. (2006). 43% of first-time home buyers put no money down. USA Today. Last accessed: 20 September 2009: http://www.usatoday.com/money/perfi/housing/2006-01-17-real-estate-usat_x.htm.

Korkki, P. (2008). Watching that balance grow … and grow, The New York Times. Last accessed: 20 September 2009: http://www.nytimes.com/2008/07/13/business/13count.html.

Labaton, S. (2008). S.E.C. Concedes Oversight Flaws Fueled Collapse. *The New York Times*. Last accessed: 16 September 2009: http://www.nytimes.com/2008/09/27/business/27sec.html?_r=1&em.

Maltezou, R. (2009). Greeks Shut Airports, Services to Protest Economy. Reuters. Last accessed: 23 September 2009: http://www.reuters.com/article/newsOne/idUSLP45582720090225.

Mortished, C. (2009). Global Unemployment Heads Towards 50 Million. *The Times*. Last accessed: 21 September 2009: http://business.timesonline.co.uk/tol/business/industry_sectors/banking_and_finance/article5607656.ece.

Reserve Bank of New Zealand. (2009). C6: Total household claims - Money, credit & financial statistics. Last accessed: 23 September 2009: http://www.rbnz.govt.nz/statistics/monfin/

Retirement Commission. (2009). National Strategy for Financial Literacy, Retirement Commission. Last accessed: 23 September 2009: http://www.financialliteracy.org.nz/sites/default/files/webfm/National%20Strategy/National-Strategy-full-report.pdf.

Richards, M., Palmer, P. and Bogdanova, M. (2008). Irresponsible Lending? A Case Study of a U.K. Credit Industry Reform Initiative, *Journal of Business Ethics*, 81, p. 499-512.

Ronson, J. (2005). 'Who Killed Richard Cullen?', *The Guardian*. Last accessed 16 September 2009: http://money.guardian.co.uk/creditanddebt/creditcards/story/0,1456,1529921,00.html.

Ross, S. A., Westerfield, R. W., and Jordan, B.D. (2004) *Essentials of Corporate Finance*, New York: McGraw-Hill.

Schwarz, M. A. (2007). Minorities hit hard by rising costs of subprime loans. *USA Today*. Last accessed: 20 September 2009: http://www.usatoday.com/money/economy/housing/2007-04-25-subprime-minorities-usat_N.htm.

Schwarcz, S. L. (2008). Disclosure's Failure in the Subprime Mortgage Crisis. Utah Law Review, p.1109-1122, Duke Law School Legal Studies Paper No. 203. Last accessed 16 September 2009: http://epubs.utah.edu/index.php/ulr/article/viewFile/78/70.

Schwirtz, M. and Levy, C. J. (2009). As Economy Sinks, Russians Protest. The New York Times. Last accessed: 23 September 2009: http://www.nytimes.com/2009/02/01/world/europe/01iht-01russia.19832483.html.

Solomon, A. and Solomon, J. F. (2002). The SRI dilemma for pension fund trustees: Some perceptions of their evolving role, *Business, Relationships, Accountability, Sustainability and Society* (BRASS), Working Paper Series No. 7, p. 1-45.

Solomon, A. and Solomon, J. F. (2003). Commentry: Pension fund trustee payment debate, *European Financial Services Regulation*, July, 14-16.

Solomon, J. F. (2007). *Coporate Governance and Accountability*, West Sussex, England: John Wiley and Sons Limited.

Statistics New Zealand. (2009). *National Population Estimates: September 2009 Quarter,* Statistics New Zealand.

Stihele, M. V. (2004). *Critical issues in the financial industry, Somo financial sector report*. Amsterdam: Somo.

Taylor, J. B. (2009). The financial crisis and the policy responses: An empirical analysis of what went wrong. *NBER Working Paper No. w14631*. Last accessed 30 August 2009: http://ssrn.com/abstract=1327252.

Ullman, A. E. and Herbohn, K. F. (2005). A full cost environmental accounting experiment, *Accounting, Organizations and Society*, 30(6), p. 519-536.

Westpac Banking Corporation, (2007a). *New Zealand Stakeholder Impact Report 2007*, Westpac Banking Corporation.

Westpac Banking Corporation. (2007b). *Westpac 2007 Stakeholder Impact Report*, Westpac Banking Corporation.

Westpac Banking Corporation. (2007c). *Westpac CEO Supports Campaign for Financial Literacy*, 15 May 2007, Westpac Banking Corporation.

Westpac Banking Corporation. (2007d). *Westpac credit card offer takes pain out of Christmas shopping*, 4 October 2007, Westpac Banking Corporation.

Westpac Banking Corporation, (2008a). *Annual Report 2008*, Westpac Banking Corporation.

Westpac Banking Corporation, (2008b). *Stakeholder Impact Report 2008*, Westpac Banking Corporation.

Westpac Banking Corporation, (2008c). *Taking money skills to Manukau youth*, Media Release, 5 September 2008, Westpac Banking Corporation.

Westpac Banking Corporation, (2009a). *Customer Brandwidth: The Westpac Group Annual Review and Sustainability Report*. Westpac Banking Corporation.

Westpac Banking Corporation, (2009b). *Westpac New Zealand's approach for assisting borrowers facing financial hardship*, Media Release, 13 April 2009, Westpac Banking Corporation.

Research Paper 8: Teaching Sustainability in Australian Higher Education

Sustainability in Higher Education: The Australian Experience

Mei-Leng Rankin, Northern Melbourne Institute of TAFE, Victoria, Australia

Abstract: There has been a growing interest in environmental issues for the past 30 odd years. The world at large is becoming more socially conscious about the impact of environmental issues such as global warming, achieving sustainable growth and development. On a corporate level, businesses are slowly recognising the need to be more accountable in their pursuit of higher profit margins, and that good business practice and sustainability go hand in hand. Education in sustainable development has become fairly topical amongst educators. In Australia, while there have been many courses in environmental and sustainability studies, there are to date, still limited courses available in the field of sustainable business, and when taught they are often conducted at the subject level in post graduate courses. Within industry there appears to be limited knowledge as to what sustainability is let alone its implementation in a business context. This paper will investigate the current trend and initiatives taken by the higher education sector in Australia in promoting education for sustainability and compares this with the rest of the world. In particular, the paper will investigate the shortcomings at the higher education sector incorporating sustainability in the business studies curriculum at higher education sector. If Australia is to be in the forefront of the promotion of sustainable business practices by equipping current and future graduates to be sustainable specialists, then a lot more need to be done today or the country will find itself with a serious shortage of skills in the near future.

Introduction

In the past thirty years, there has been an increasing global interest in environmental issues. The world at large is becoming more socially conscious about the impact of environmental issues such as global warming and ozone depletion; depletion of natural resources; and waste disposal, resulting from the pursuit of economic growth and development on society. There is international recognition that to continue in the pursuit of economic growth and development without any consideration of the environment and proper stewardship of our natural resources would jeopardise the needs and welfare of future generations. On a corporate level, businesses are recognising the need to be more accountable to stakeholders and society in general in their pursuit of higher profit margins. Increasingly, a number of companies worldwide have taken initiatives and proactive steps to alter their business practices to accommodate sustainability, but this adaptation process is slow compared to other sustainability initiatives.

As a result of the growing awareness of environmental protection and accountability, the pursuit and promotion of sustainability for the future has gained a tremendous global momentum, leading to many global initiatives to work together towards a sustainable future. Since the1980s, global summits and conferences have been held by various organisations to make the world aware of environmental threats and to discuss global cooperative initiatives and action plans towards a sustainable future. One of the key action plans that have been widely endorsed is the education for sustainability to promote public awareness. Chapter 36 of Agenda 21 of the Rio Summit of 1992 states: "education is critical for promoting sustainable development and improving the capacity of the people to address environment and development issues"[1] . Agenda 21 has given the stimulus for leaders of the world, in particular, educators to take a significant leading role in the promotion and education for sustainable development.

Even prior to the Rio Summit, the drive towards education for sustainability has moved actively along the corridors of higher education. The formation of the Talloires Declaration of University Leaders for a Sustainable Future (ULSF) in France, 1990, was a major significant move towards the promotion and education for sustainability in higher education.[2] This Declaration outlines a 10-point action plan for incorporating sustainability and environmental education in all areas of a teaching institution. In 2008, signatories to this Declaration have grown from the original 22 universities to 378 universities and colleges in 2008, covering 50 countries across 5 continents[3].

The establishment of the Global Higher Education for Sustainability Partnership (GHESP) in 2000 is another of such initiative. This partnership brought together like-minded academics around the world to work for the common goal of making education for sustainability the focal point in the overall culture or ethos of institutions of higher education.

---

[1] UN Conference on Environment and Development, Agenda 21, UN Doc. A/CONF, 151.26 (1992)

[2] There have been many other declarations and charters such as the COPERNICUS Charter (1993), Kyoto Declaration (1993), but the Talloires Declaration is the more popular one.

[3] Tallories Declaration Institutional Signatory List, Association of University Leaders for a Sustainable Future (ULSF)

The period 2005 – 2014 was declared as the United Nations Decade of Education for Sustainable Development (UNDESD, Johannesburg Summit, 2002). At this Summit it was acknowledged that education would be the key to changing and reshaping society's attitude towards achieving a sustainable future. Global co-operations and sharing of ideas within the education arena of teaching and research would help to effectively disseminate knowledge on sustainability to a global society, and transform society towards a sustainable future.

We are now entering the half way mark of the UNDESD. Without doubt, there have been numerous initiatives and cooperation between academic leaders around the world to educate and promote sustainability for the future. How successful have these initiatives been? Have we implemented action plans that are indeed directing our mind set, actions and behaviour towards a sustainable future? Are the current and future graduates of higher education well equipped to deal with the diversity and complexities of sustainable development? Are some countries more vocal and active in the promotion of sustainable development than others? In short, are we there yet in the pursuit of a sustainable future?

The general consensus amongst leading academics around the world is that despite all the talks and initiatives generated by numerous summits and conferences, when it comes down to the ground level, generally, universities that are slow to embrace sustainability as part of their culture are those who are faced with a resistance force to change which makes integration of sustainability into higher education a challenge. This is brought about by the fact that the structure and culture of institutions of higher education are more complex (and often very conservative), and the integration of sustainability into the structure and culture becomes a significant challenge. In contrast, the integration of education for sustainability at the formative years of learning (from primary to secondary schooling) and community education have been generally more receptive and effective.

Australia as a nation has been a keen participant in the pursuit of sustainability for the future. Since the 1980s, the Australian government has been proactive in the promotion of education for sustainability at all levels of governance. They have encouraged close ties and partnerships between institutions of learning and research, industries and businesses, and the community at large. While Australia is on par with the rest of the world in environmental studies at higher education levels, there is still a significant gap in the education for sustainability in the field of business studies.

This paper will present a survey of the current situation in Australia relating to the incorporation of sustainability at higher education level and investigate the current trend in education for sustainability in Australia. It will seek to identify the gap that exists, and provides a discussion for future direction, to ensure that Australia is on the road to equipping graduates with appropriate skills to take the nation to a sustainable future. The paper will start with an overview of the importance of a holistic approach to education for sustainability. It will then investigate the initiatives that have been implemented in Australia and analyse the current trend of education for sustainability at the higher education sector in Australia. The paper concludes with a recommendation for action plan to fill in the gap.

Education for Sustainability at Higher Education Sector

The road towards achieving sustainability is an ongoing learning process of educating, motivating and equipping current and future generations. The UNDESD recognises that universities and other institutions of higher education have a pivotal role in educating and preparing current and future graduates towards securing a sustainable future. Graduates of tomorrow must be equipped and empowered with skills and knowledge that will help them create a more sustainable future, taking into consideration environmental integrity, economic viability and an equitable society for current and future generations.

Education for sustainability must be approached in a holistic manner, embracing the three pillars[4] of sustainability.

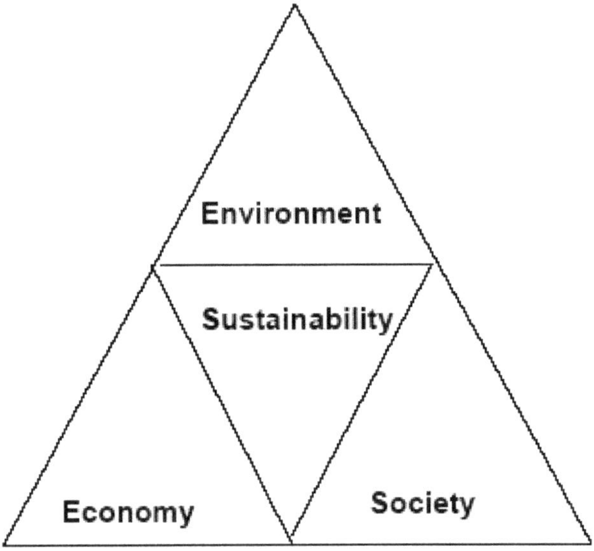

Figure 1: The Three Pillars of Sustainability*,
*The Cultural Aspect of Sustainability has been implied in the 'Society' pillar. This is not discussed here as it is not Central to overall discussion of Paper

It should go beyond merely creating an awareness of environmental threats and problems, but instead should provide the stimulus for mind change and attitudes, challenging set behaviour, understanding the root causes of environmental threats, and providing the necessary skills for seeking solutions and being proactive in creating a sustainable, equitable future. Future leaders of the world need these skills to take society towards a sustainable future, and institutions of higher education have an important role in preparing competent, highly skilled graduates worthy of leading current generation towards creating a sustainable future for generations to come.

To understand what education for sustainability really entails, one must first have a grasp of what 'sustainability' or 'sustainability for development' really

[4] Vierdemann (1996) refers to the environment, economy and community(society) as the three pillars of sustainability

means. The concept of sustainability is not one that can be succinctly and easily captured by a simple phrase. It is a complex concept that seeps into all aspects of society, interlinking the environment, economy and community. There have been many attempts to capture the essence of sustainability or sustainable development and to clearly define its meaning. The definition that has most widely been referenced is that which came out of the Brundtland Report (1987), which states that sustainable development is: "development that meets the needs of the present without compromising the ability of future generations to meet their own needs." While this definition implies a balance of actions between current and future generations, it is still rather vague in its meaning. Professor Cairns of McGill University, Montreal (2006), said that the notion of sustainability should encompass goals as diverse as "... environmental protection, climate stability, elimination of poverty, concern for the well-being of future generations, good corporate and social governance, social inclusiveness, maintenance of small communities and ways of life..."

While, teaching and research are the major functions of institutions of higher education, to effectively embrace sustainability, they must integrate this concept in a comprehensive way in all functional aspects of an institution of higher education. Blackburn (2008) said that these institutions are no different from any other organisations, and have both an operational as well as service and product side to their activities that have significant impacts on sustainability. To effectively promote sustainability in higher education is to embrace sustainability in all aspects of university life – from operational, and management functions to the teaching and advancement of research, and working together with stakeholders and the community at large.

The Australian Experience

At the end of 2008, there were 105 registered higher education providers in Australia. Of these, 41[5] are of university status, and the remainder are non-university institutions like the TAFE institutions, and other specialist areas.[6] In 2008, 13 of the 41 Australian universities have become signatories to the Talloires Declaration, reaffirming their commitment to the education and integration of sustainability in the culture of their institutions.

The Australian government has long been a key supporter and promoter of education for sustainability at all levels of education. It has encouraged, funded and supported many initiatives into sustainability education and research projects. In 1997, the then Federal Minister of Environment and Heritage, the Honourable Robert Hill, commissioned a study to identify the environmental education needs for Australia and this culminated in the National Action Plan of 2000. This Plan

---

[5] 30 of these universities are public funded and two are privately funded. All the universities and certain number of the non-university providers are self-accrediting institutions (68 self-accrediting institutions altogether in 2008).

[6] TAFE – stands for technical and further education. These institutions of higher education, unlike the traditional universities, focus on vocational based learning, but also offer traditional degree courses. In Australia, TAFE institutions are mainly (State) government funded and the courses are accredited by the respective State.

outlined the key principles towards an effective education for sustainability framework and many key initiatives that have been successfully implemented in all sectors of education even before the start of the UNDESD.[7] These initiatives put Australia in a strong position to confidently move through the decade. One of the many significant initiatives was the establishment of the National Environmental Education Council (NEEC) in 2000. The primary role of the Council was to identify key priorities in education for sustainability and acts as an advisory to the Minister for the Environment and Heritage.

Another initiative was the establishment of the Australian Research Institute in Education for Sustainability (ARIES) in 2003 in conjunction with Macquarie University and the Department of the Environment, Water, Heritage and the Arts. ARIES was formed with the primary aim to be the leading edge in research and education for sustainability across many sectors in Australia.

In 2005, ARIES published a number of national reviews of environmental education and its contribution to sustainability in various educational sectors in Australia. The review identified the gaps needed to make education for sustainability effective in further and higher education, and outlined 13 recommendations towards this end. The findings in the review were consistent with findings observed by global counterparts. At the time of the review, it was found that despite the many efforts and initiatives taken by leading academics in promoting education for sustainability, institutions of higher education were faced with greater challenges in gaining in roads in embracing sustainability in their overall institutional culture, due to the stringent and traditional conservative mind set of those in institutional governance. The review essentially found that for an institution to effectively embrace sustainability there must be a whole of institution approach, from the top level of governance, flowing down to the management and operational side, to the teaching and research side, as well as fostering partnerships and close links with the larger community.

The Australian Vice-Chancellor's Committee (AVCC) [8] in 2006 acknowledged the leading role of universities in promoting the goals outlined in UNDESD, and declared a commitment to education for sustainable development. In the policy statement, AVCC declared that, "by 2020, the university sector in Australia will be playing a key role in promoting sustainability in the community through research and building capacity to achieve change for sustainability."[9]

As we enter the second half of the UNDESD, *"are we there yet?"* in our pursuit of a sustainable future, and how does the Australian case for education for sustainability at the higher education sector fare in comparison to its global counterparts?

Majority of the higher education sectors in Australia that have embraced sustainability has adopted the whole of institute approach.

---

[7] In 2006, a new National Action Plan for Education for Sustainability was developed and is currently being formalized.

[8] The AVCC is the council of Australia's university presidents.

[9] AVCC Policy on education for sustainable development, August 2006

Governance, Operational and Management Side

Institutions of higher education in Australia are by and large self-governing institutions, dictating their own policies and directions. In 2008, of the 41 universities, 56% have specific strategic plans incorporating policies and directions towards a sustainable institution, taking into consideration, social and corporate responsibilities. Some of the non-university providers, for example, the vocational based institutes like Kangan Batman; Holmesglen and NMIT[10] also have policies that support sustainable practices in their operational and management functions. Some institutions like Swinburne University and Kangan Batman have signed voluntary agreements with EPA.[11] Policies of sustainable practices directing campus greening programs through recycling and waste disposal management; reduction of effluent and greenhouse gas emission; efficient water and energy management; and sustainable procurement decisions have been widely and enthusiastically adopted across campuses in these institutions that have embraced sustainability in the institutional ethos. The increase in employment of staff to coordinate environmental improvement and compliance, and the encouragement and support of professional development of academic and support staff have been significant initiatives undertaken by these institutions. The incorporation of comprehensive sustainability reporting and audits into the annual reports has made these institutions accountable to their stakeholders and the wider community.

On the operational and management side of things, it would seem that the institutions of higher education in Australia are comparable with many of its counterparts around the world. Even the smaller institutions have taken proactive actions in incorporating sustainable practices.

However, in comparison to global counterparts, there is still alot that can be done to fast track the path towards a sustainable future. Given the considerable number of higher education providers in Australia, the number of institutions that have explicit policies and practices incorporating sustainability practices is less than 40%. As we move towards the second half of the UNDESD, there are still a large portion of institutions that are still resistant to the change to integrate sustainability into the organisational structure. In the long run, these institutions must realise that to be in the competitive leading edge of providing quality education they will need to be willing to change and adapt way of thinking to befit current trend.

Research Activities

The research arm of institutions of higher education is a key instrument in the promotion of education for sustainability and the practices of sustainability in the wider community. Through its various research activities, new ideas and solutions can be found to pave the way to a sustainable future and collaborative research

---

[10] Northern Melbourne Institute of TAFE

[11] The higher education sector in Australia like other business organisations are subjected to government regulations such as those imposed by EPA to ensure proper resource and waste management are consistent in achieving a sustainable future for the country.

with industries. Government and non-government bodies' support and collaborations also can help advance the course towards sustainability.

In Australia, the calibre of research in the field of environmental and sustainability studies by highly qualified staff and post graduate students are highly regarded in the international scene. Major awards such as the Nobel Prize awarded to acclaimed Australian researchers have raised the profile of leading academics in environmental research in Australia. Many of the leading universities have created specific cross disciplinary centres or institutes of research specialising in environmental and sustainability studies, and fostering partnerships with government and non-government organisations, corporate businesses and international organisations- all with the view of promoting and sharing knowledge and skills towards achieving a sustainable nation. Examples of some of these institutions are shown in Table 1.

Table 1: Centres of Research in Environmental and Sustainability established within the Confines of Institutions of Higher Education

Universities	Sustainability/Environmental Research Centres/Institutes
Monash	Monash Sustainability Institute
RMIT	Global Sustainability@RMIT
Swinburne	National Centre of Sustainability
Victoria	Inst of Sustainability and Innovation
Macquarie	Sustainability @MQ
ANU	ANU Green-Sustainability Office
University of New South Wales	Institute of Environmental Studies
University of Technoliogy Sydney	Institue of Sustainable Future
Griffith	Griffith School of Environment
Murdoch	Insitute of Sustainability and Technology Policy
Curtin	Centre of Excellence in Cleaner Production
Sunshine Coast	Regional Sustainability Research Group
Queensland Insitute of Technology	Institute of Sustainable Resources

The areas of research are diverse and varied, ranging from climate studies, biodiversity and ecosystem studies, natural resource management, pollution prevention, integrated transport solutions, corporate and social responsibilities and governance.

The research institutes of sustainability and environmental studies set up by the key institutions of higher education in Australia are amongst the best in the world. The ability to attract and retain staff of varied and extensive experience in sustainability research is a credit to the institutions. The ability to share knowledge, train, equip and mentor student researchers will ensure Australia will be a nation that has the ability to lead the nation to a sustainable future. The momentum and motivation for sustainability need to be maintained and kept on going. To do so, requires institutional support at the highest level and funding of staff as well as research projects. Unfortunately, Australian institutions of higher education face the same problem of funding deficiencies like universities worldwide. Institutions of higher education in Australia are by and large self-funded, highly dependent upon student population. Regardless of the source of funding, CEOs of these institutions face the dilemma of how to slice up the annual budget amongst its various departments and faculties, as each department reasons for a bigger share. Collaboration and partnership with industries have helped boost the funding for most of these institutions. Obviously, the more renowned and established institutions gained greater funding and publicity at the expense of the smaller institutions. As such, the spread of research capabilities across the many higher education providers in Australia is sorely skewed towards the few.

Teaching Activities

In the area of teaching and learning, environmental education has been part of the curricula in higher education in Australia ever since the 1970s. These studies have tended to be very much scientific, usually in the domain of the sciences. At the end of 2008, a survey of the current trend in education for sustainability has not progressed far. Of the 105 listed higher education providers, 38 institutions offer under 400 courses [12] (both undergraduate and postgraduate levels) in environmental/sustainability studies, and these 38 institutions are universities. Table 2 shows that in 2008, the focus of environmental or sustainability studies are still heavily biased towards the environment pillar of sustainability, with majority of the courses monopolised by the Science, Arts and Engineering faculties of these institutions. Nearly 58% of courses are in environmental science studies.

However, when we consider the amount of students enrolled in the various field of studies, the sciences and engineering enrolment make up about 16% of total enrolment, whereas the amount of students enrolled in the fields of management and commerce, and social and culture, account for over 51% of full time student enrolment in higher education institutions in Australia (see Figure 2). While the majority of the higher education student population is centred in the business and social /cultural fields, the integration of sustainability in these fields of studies are sorely lacking. And yet, these two fields cover the other two important pillars of sustainability.

[12] Note: These do not include the courses and subjects taught at MBA levels.

Table 2: Distribution of Courses which has Environmental or Sustainability Content Incorporated, *Source: Department of Education, Employment and Workplace Relation:* www.goingtouni.gov.au *Course Finder, 2008*

Types of Environmental Studies	Level of studies	
	Undergraduate	Postgraduate
Environmental Science	97	20
Environmental Management/Policy	20	54
Environmental Engineering	18	8
Environmental Studies/Humanities	1	6
Environmental Education	0	3
Environmental Tourism	3	1
Environmental Economics	0	1
Environmental Health	10	19
Environmental Law	0	27
Environmental Design/Planning/Technology/Restoration	14	6
Environmental and Sustainability	0	7
Natural Resource Management and Sustainability	2	3
Sustainable Studies and Developmen	0	18
Sustainable Management and Corporation	0	6
Others (technology, outdoor	3	5

Future corporate leaders and enterprises traditionally come from within these fields of study, especially the business stream. The realisation that profitability and accountability to society and the environment are intertwined, have made sustainable business practices a topical issue. Professor Hart of Kenan-Fagler Business School, USA said, "Like it or not, the responsibility for ensuring a sustainable world falls largely on the shoulders of the world's enterprises, the economic engines of the future."[13] And yet sadly, there appears to be a limited knowledge as to what sustainable accounting is let alone its implementation in a business context.

Sustainability seeps into all facets of the business world, including sound economic management, resource and waste management, corporate finance, ethics and governance, and many more. Businesses are primarily responsible to stakeholders and to the wider community and therefore, to educate the corporate world to address sustainability challenges and fast track the path towards tangible sustainable outcomes, graduates moving into the business sector must be equipped with the skills and knowledge to lead business organisations to achieving a viable sustainable economy that is accountable and socially just.

[13] Hart, S, 1997, Beyond Greening: strategies for a sustainable world, Harvard Business Review, p67-76

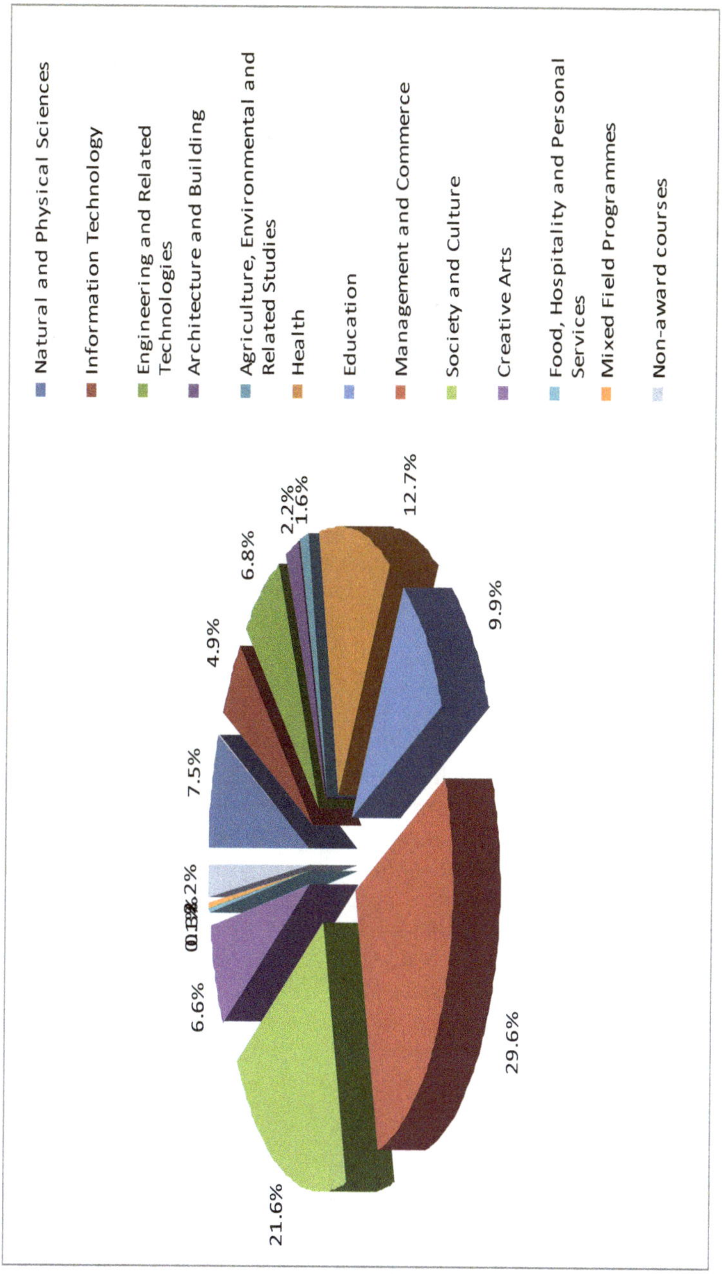

Figure 2: Statistics on full time Student Enrolment in Broad field of Studies in Higher Education, 2007*, Source: Selected Higher Education Statistics (DEEWR).
*At time of Publication, 2008 Numbers were not available but the trend is likely to be the same.

Effective education for sustainability goes beyond tagging a handful of subjects on sustainability studies in traditional curriculum.

In 2008, there are still limited courses available in the field of sustainable business or accounting, and when taught they are often conducted at the subject level in post graduate courses, and often as part of the MBA curriculum[14]. While Graduate business schools provide an opportunity for business professionals to upgrade or "green" their qualifications, there is a greater role for institutions of higher education to provide base level undergraduate education for mainstream students to equip them in all areas of business practices that promote sustainable development and meets environmental standards.

Currently, the only undergraduate course that attempts to cover the social cultural aspects of sustainability is the Bachelor of Development studies offered by the University of Newcastle[15]. The University of Southern Queensland also offers a four years full time Bachelor of Accounting and Sustainable Business (BASB). Apart from these two courses, the integration of sustainability in traditional undergraduate business/commerce/accounting courses are sorely lacking in the corridors of institutions of higher education in Australia.

A survey of universities around the world also indicate that this is also very much in the infant stage of development while there are ample post graduate level courses in business sustainability. In part, this slow take-off is not because of the lack of interest of institutions of higher education. After all, most institutions will only offer courses that are in demand and will attract students. If businesses who realise the importance of changing business habits to incorporate sustainability fail to communicate the importance and need of a skilled workforce to higher institutions, universities around the world will fall short.

In a survey of 500 US business executives[16], it was found that even among corporations noted for sustainability, 'nearly 33% of these claimed their management does not have much faith in the business case for sustainability and does not actively support the concept internally – many executives do not fully appreciate what a pursuit of sustainability can mean to business success and society: still fewer know how to approach it in a systematic way that realises its maximum business value. Business people often see sustainability programs as outside the circle of things essential for success –only a few would embrace.'

In 2006, a research report[17] found that climate change is a major business risk and will have significant repercussions on the economy. The report also indicates action needs to be taken now to reduce risk, rather than to try and fix the problem after the event, with the costs associated with taking actions to reduce risks substantially lower. In the current work market, skills in sustainability concepts and practices are in demand.

---

[14] In 2006, the National Review of MBA programs in Australia (by ARIES) indicated that majority of these programs did not include sustainability in core units or as elective units. Even the professional courses did not explicitly address educaton for sustainability. In 2008, the position is still the same. There is no comprehensive integrated course that deals with issues of sustainable business practices.

[15] This degree is offered by the Faculty of Science and Technology in conjunction with Faculty of Business and Law, and Faculty of Education and Arts.

[16] Blackburn, 2008, p7

[17] Australian Business Roundtable on Climate Change Report, April 2006

In the short term, businesses have to retrain their staff to deal with "green" business practices and reporting. While the recognition of corporate and social responsibilities towards a sustainable future is acknowledge by Australian business corporations, the implementation of sustainability reporting still lags in relation to international standards. In part this is due to the lack of qualified graduates who have the confidence to lead businesses into a sustainable mindset and business practices and accountability. In the long run, for Australian businesses to remain competitive in the global market, institutions of higher education must fast track the incorporation of sustainability studies into business curriculum at the undergraduate level where over 80% of student population are in.[18]

Engagement with the Wider Community

In the area of research and overall institutional culture, there have been numerous successful engagements with the wider community. Collaborations of projects with industries, government bodies and NGOs have been effectively pursued in diverse fields. Funding, sponsorship and student involvement in community projects have also been strongly supported. By working together with the wider community, there is greater opportunity to promote sustainability awareness through mutual vision, and sharing of resources.

Future Direction and Conclusion

The world we live in is no longer the same as that of past generations. The social, economic and environmental issues and problems that we face are changing and in many ways are different than before. Increased consumerism, chasing the higher profits of business corporations, depletion of natural resources, violation of the natural bio and eco systems aggravates the environmental problems we face today. We have come a long way in making the world aware of environmental threats and coming up with solutions to deal with these threats. However, it is time that the focus on sustainable education is shifted towards the other two equally important pillars. Greed and unsustainable business practices have brought about recent global financial crises.

To protect our world and to ensure a sustainable future for the next generation requires a change in mindset. There is a need to instil in current

---

[18] In 2009, the University of Canberra offers a sustainability major/minor attached to a three year traditional undergraduate degree, as an attempt to 'green' one's qualification.
In 2008, NMIT has taken steps to develop a comprehensive three year undergraduate degree which integrates sustainability within all aspects of the curriculum to provide a multi-disciplinary approach to the study of sustainable business and accounting. The degree identifies and meets an industry, government, professional bodies and community need in providing graduates with skills and knowledge to apply contemporary sustainable practices within a business context. The course provides knowledge and skills in sustainability reporting including the Global Reporting Initiative (GRI) and the National Greenhouse and Energy Reporting Act (2007), and international obligations requiring adoption of sustainable business practices.

generation the social and corporate responsibilities towards the three pillars of sustainability. New solutions need to be found, and new knowledge and life long skills need to be developed. Value driven profitable sustainable business practices need to be taught. Businesses who are leaders in embracing sustainable practices are coming to terms with the lack of expertise in current business graduates. In the short term, MBA programs to "green " or retrain current graduates in sustainability skills may suffice, but in the long run, there will be an adverse shortage of skilled graduates. In this regard, institutions of higher education have a vital and significant role in preparing future leaders of the world with expertise in sustainability.

In order to create a "green-collar" workforce to drive the economy to a sustainable future, there is a need to fast track the education of our current graduates, especially at the undergraduate level. The teaching of sustainable business and accounting practices is still in the infant stage. It is time that more undergraduate business degrees with sustainability incorporated are developed. And this should be more than simply tagging a unit or two to a traditional business degree. The concept of sustainability must be seeping through the veins of all traditional business units – where graduates are not only aware of the three pillars of sustainability, but are trained to be ethical leaders and have ethical management practices, and are aware of the balance of profitability with the quality of life and environment.

It is expected that in the next two decades, the workforce in Australia will expand to about 3.4 million jobs.[19] And, as Australia moves towards being a keen participant of the carbon emission trading scheme, there is a need for graduates with sustainability skills to lead key businesses towards a sustainable, responsible future. As a nation, we need to fast track the already well established framework of education for sustainability to equip graduates to take us on the path of sustainable economic growth and prosperity and have a competitive edge in the global world.

Acknowledgement

I would like to express my gratitude to John Grech, Di Holman, Rima Sungkar and the Faculty of Business (Higher Education), NMIT, for all the support they have given me in making this paper a possibility. A special thank you to my colleague, Shriley Wong, for taking the time to proof read the paper.

References

Austrlalian Business Roundtable on Climate Change Report, April, 2006

Blackburn, William, *The sustainability handbook: the complete management guide to achieving social, economic, and environmental responsibility*, 2008, Earthscan.

[19] Finanacial Review, July 2008

Cairns, Robert, *On accounting for sustainable development and accounting for the environment*, Resources Policy, Volume 31, Issue 4, December 2006, Pages 211-216.

Education Section, Financial Review, July 14th, 2008

Hackett, Steven, *Environmental and natural resources Economics: Theory, Policy and the Sustainable society*, 2006, Armonk, NY: M.E. Sharpe

Hunting, SA., Mah, J. and Tilbury D., *'Education About and For Sustainability in Australian Business Schools: Embedding Sustainability in MBA Programs'*, 2006, Australian Research Institute in Education for Sustainability (ARIES) for the Australian Government Department of the Environment, Water, Heritage and the Arts, Sydney: ARIES.

Hart, S, *Beyond Greening: strategies for a sustainable world*, 1997, Harvard Business Review, p67-76

Tilbury D., Keogh, A., Leighton, A. & Kent, J. *A national review of environmental education and its contribution to sustainability in Australia: further & higher education*, 2005, Vol 5, Canberra, Australian Government Department of the Environment, Water, Heritage and the Arts and ARIES

UN Conference on Environment and Development, Agenda 21, UN Doc. A/CONF, 151.26 (1992)

Vierdeman, S, *Sustainability's Five Capitals and Three Pillars, in building sustainable societies: A blueprint for a post-industrial world*, ed, D Pirages, 1996, Armonk, NY: M.E. Sharpe

www.goingtouni.gov.au

Research Paper 9: CSR and Potentially Harmful Products in the Gaming Industry

The Marketing of Legal but Potentially Harmful Products and Corporate Social Responsibility: The Gaming Industry View

June Buchanan, Macquarie University, New South Wales, Australia

Gregory Elliott, Macquarie University, New South Wales, Australia

Lester W Johnson, The University of Melbourne, Victoria, Australia

Abstract: A number of industries sell products (or services) such as tobacco, alcohol and gambling that, although legal, are considered potentially harmful to some members of society. Unlike other that attract no attention when using strategies to increase market share, many of these potentially harmful products attract criticism from concerned members of society and often governments when their markets increase. Corporate scandals in recent times have led to greater calls for social responsibility to be embraced by all businesses, but the call is most pronounced towards organisations providing products that are detrimental to certain members of society. This paper investigates gaming industry perceptions of compliance with the precepts of corporate social responsibility (CSR) in the marketing of electronic gaming machines (EGMs). Thirty-eight face-to-face and/or telephone interviews were undertaken with EGM manufacturers, gaming consultants,managers of gaming establishments and casino operators in Nevada (USA) and New South Wales (Australia), along with management of the gaming regulatory authority in New South Wales (NSW). In spite of a much tighter regulatory environment in NSW, it was found that the major gaming operators in Nevada appear to be aware of, and practice, CSR to a noticeably greater extent than do gaming operators in NSW. Notwithstanding this however, EGM operators both in Nevada and NSW need to implement socially responsible marketing strategies and tactics to a significantly higher degree than is currently practiced in order to enhance their reputation, decrease criticism from key stakeholders and minimise the potential threat of increased regulatory constraints.

Introduction

Marketing managers are responsible for increasing profits through customer satisfaction as a result of offering quality products at the right price, in the right place, providing pertinent information and, in the case of services, in an appealing environment (also referred to as the 'servicescape'). When these products are legal but potentially harmful however, that is often accompanied by criticism from the community, government and other concerned stakeholders, particularly when company profits rise. Increased pressure on all organisations to operate in a socially responsible manner has arisen during the past ten years as a result of such infamous operations as Enron, Tyco, WorldCom and Parmalat. It is even more important, therefore, for industries that market legal but potentially harmful products to adopt socially responsible processes and practices that go beyond legal requirements only. These respective organisations need to be seen to be genuinely responsible rather than using corporate social responsibility (CSR) for the purposes of public relations (PR) or window dressing.

Well-documented evidence on the potentially harmful effects of tobacco, alcohol and gaming products, raises the question of: "why are they legal?". One could argue that, in addition to the substantial fiscal contribution these industries make to government coffers, cultural factors also play a part. Australia for example has traditionally been a nation where 'a drink, a smoke and a bet' is part of the national psyche. Although over-consumption of any of these products invariably results in harmful effects, Doughney (2007a) argues that the gaming industry is less ethical than the tobacco industry because the victims of the former can be more readily identified. The purpose of this paper is to extend the predominant focus on the tobacco and alcohol industries to consider another potentially harmful product, namely electronic gaming machines (EGMs), from within the gaming industry itself. Although there is a substantial body of research into EGMs, this paper will specifically examine the views of the gaming industry in terms of EGMs, marketing and CSR.

Increasing concern exists about the negative social costs associated with those who over-indulge and over-spend their own budgetary limitations as a result of becoming addicted to playing EGMs. Although Australia has only 0.3 per cent of the world's population (and almost 14.5 million adults aged 18 and over (ABS 2008) - the legal age for gambling in Australia), it has more than 20 per cent of the world's 'high intensity gaming machines' (Productivity Commission 1999), increasingly referred to as EGMs but also known colloquially as 'pokies' in Australia and 'slots' or 'video poker machines' in the USA. New South Wales (NSW) has half the number of EGMs in Australia and "has the highest number of gaming machines per 10,000 people anywhere – including Las Vegas" (Miserable Odds, 13 February 2006, p.22). Recent figures (Australian

Gambling Statistics 2006) show that total Australian gambling turnover for 2005-06 was almost $108 billion (with NSW at almost $57 billion). Gambling expenditure (gamblers losses) was more than $10 billion for Australia and $5 billion for NSW. Australia has 200,850 gaming machines, of which NSW has 100,034 (Australian Gambling Statistics 2006). Star City is the only legal casino in NSW and has 1,500 EGMs. Other EGMs are in NSW registered clubs and 'pubs'. Much negative perception exists regarding not only access issues and the high prevalence of EGMs in Australia, but also controversies regarding their placement in low socio-economic areas where customers can least afford it (Doughney 2007b; McMillen et al. 2004; Marshall and Baker 2002; Mellor 2005). Others (Livingstone and Woolley 2007) criticise the lack of effective legislation in protecting problem and at risk gamblers and accuse the government and the gaming industry of being collaborators in the obfuscating, rhetorical discourse of 'business as usual'.

Given the negative perception of EGMs by many in Australian society and the increased interest in CSR globally (see for example de Bakker et al. 2005), the focus of this research is on the question: 'to what extent do operators of EGMs consider that they incorporate CSR into their marketing strategies?'. Accordingly the perspective in this paper is on how gaming operators view themselves in terms of being socially responsible, as opposed to the identified existing literature that predominantly looks from the 'outside in'.

Corporate Social Responsibility (CSR)

Definition

Widespread consensus that the concept of CSR is fraught with a multitude of terms and definitions appears to exist (Aupperle et al. 1985; Campbell 2007; Carroll 1998; de Bakker et al. 2005; Lantos 2001; McWilliams et al. 2006; Valor 2005). Some feel that this should not be an impediment however, with Dahlsrud (2006) stating that, although there is still confusion about how CSR should be defined, the existing definitions "are to a large degree congruent" (p. 1). Further, he considers that it is not the lack of a universally accepted definition so much as it is "about how CSR is socially constructed in a specific context" (ibid). Nevertheless, others consider the many "paradoxes inherent in the phrase 'corporate social responsibility'" and that, "until these paradoxes are properly addressed, corporate social responsibility can legitimately be branded an invention of PR" (Frankental 2001, p.18; Campbell 2007; Friedman 1970; Roberts 2003). An extensive review of the CSR literature by de Bakker et al. (2005) finds that McWilliams and Siegel's (2001:117) definition of CSR, being "actions that appear to further some social good, beyond the interests of the firm and that which is required by law", has gained prominence in the management literature (pp. 383-384). This definition is also supported in kind by much of the existing CSR literature and is the one adopted by the authors of this paper.

What is CSR?

In accord with the above definition, many writers now consider that, although being profitable is in a sense socially responsible (providing jobs, paying taxes etc.) and adhering to the law is paramount (unlike the aforementioned disgraced corporations), firms cannot be considered to be adopting the tenets of CSR unless they act beyond these components – i.e. to also include the ethical and discretionary/philanthropic components of Carroll's CSR Pyramid (1991). It is now widely accepted that, whilst the core function of a business is to make a profit within legal boundaries, firms also need to be socially aware and responsible

Gaming

A large body of academic and public policy literature on gambling exists, but the majority of it focuses on issues relating to problem gambling. Work by Hing and others (Hing 2000; Hing 2001; Hing and McMillen 2002; Hing 2003; Hing and Mackellar 2004) examines problem gambling as a social issue in the context of NSW registered clubs, however, no literature has been identified that deals specifically with the issue of how gaming operators market, or should market, EGMs, particularly with the legal impediments that are in place in Australia to restrict such promotion. Our paper builds on Hing's work by including hotels (colloquially known as pubs in Australia) and the casino in NSW as well as casinos in Nevada. Given that controversy continues to exist in the NSW media regarding EGM operations in NSW, it appears that many of the issues raised by Hing in terms of social responsibility in the late 1990s, still exist today. Accordingly, given increasing EGM turnover, their widespread availability in pubs (since 1997 in NSW) in addition to registered clubs and the casino along with continued controversy, this research would appear to be pertinent and timely.

CSR and Marketing

Many scholars appear to agree that the ethical and altruistic components of CSR should be strategic in nature (The Asia-Pacific Centre for Philanthropy & Social Investment 2006; Dentchey 2004, Haigh and Jones 2006; Lantos 2001; Salia et al. 2003; Wulfson 2001) whereby both the firm's bottom line and its stakeholders benefit. Marketing scholars such as Asongu (2007) specifically view CSR as a powerful marketing tool, if used strategically. Many others (such as Luo and Bhattacharya 2006; Maignan and Ferrell 2004) endorse the important role that marketing can play in CSR, with others developing a stakeholder model specifically for implementing social responsibility in marketing (Maignan et al. 2005). In addition to the increasing awareness of the importance of including stakeholders in social responsibility theory and practice, the seminal article by Vargo and Lusch (2004) has had a paradigmatic shift effect in marketing meta-theory by viewing marketing as a service function whereby *all* stakeholders benefit. A conceptual paper developed by El-Ansary and Cerne (2005) integrates CSR into a marketing strategy framework, which includes the role that pressure from the media, NGOs, regulators and other stakeholders exerts on the firm to be socially responsible.

Legal but Potentially Harmful Products

Normal free-market pressures such as competition, consumer fickleness and financial considerations affect all businesses; however marketers of legal but potentially harmful products have additional challenges of political, regulatory and social opposition (Davidson 2003). The tobacco, alcohol and gambling industries have enjoyed substantial profits for many decades, achieved in part by the employment of marketing strategies and tactics that encourage ever-greater consumption of their products.

In the past, these powerful industries have successfully lobbied governments in order to avoid legislation designed to inhibit their marketing activities. Because of outcry from various stakeholders however, these industries have become heavily regulated, particularly in Australia. Davidson (2003, pp. 141-143) presents three caveats that concern marketers of legal but potentially harmful products at all points in time, namely (1) marketers must never target their products to vulnerable groups; (2) product management decisions must never be aimed at increasing *overall* usage, either from new users or from existing users, and (3) marketers dare not offer 'bigger, better, more efficient, more exciting' products without expecting substantial backlash from concerned members of society. Certainly, the degree of backlash from many in Australian society towards the availability and marketing of EGMs, along with the disproportionably high amount of money spend on EGMs by problem gamblers, is substantial and enough to warrant serious concern by EGM manufacturers and operators.

The perception by many in society is that CSR is either being ignored or, if it is being claimed at all, is window dressing only (Campbell 2007; Frankental 2001, Friedman 1970, Roberts 2003). This scepticism has led to lobbying efforts by concerned community groups against the tobacco, alcohol and gambling industries. In addition, the three caveats referred to earlier (Davidson 2003) appear to be flouted to varying degrees by these industries. This further endorses the vital importance of marketing legal but potentially harmful products with a strong adoption of socially responsible principles, processes and practices.

The Present Study

Research Objective

Against the background of the discussion of the general principles of CSR along with gaming and its potentially harmful consequences and other socially harmful products, this study sets out to explore and document the phenomenon of EGMs and the marketing practices of gaming operators against the prescriptions of CSR (based on Carroll's CSR Pyramid components).

Methodology

Qualitative research was conducted due to the "large volumes of exceedingly rich data obtained from a limited number of individuals" (Walker 1985, p.3) and the fact that such data are "a source of well-grounded, rich descriptions and explanations of processes occurring in local contexts" (Miles and Huberman 1984, p.15). Furthermore, given the lack of publicly available information relating specifically to the marketing of EGMs in a socially responsible manner, in-depth interviews were considered to be the most effective way of obtaining information and understanding in this area. Accordingly, a purposeful sample was chosen.

Interviews, observational and secondary data were collected intermittently over a two-year period (2005 and 2006), with secondary data continuing to be collected. Semi-structured interviews were conducted during May-July 2005 and May 2006 in Nevada and during 2005 and 2006 in NSW. These two jurisdictions were chosen because Las Vegas has long been considered the 'gambling capital of the world' and NSW has more EGMs than any other state or territory in Australia, has more than double the turnover from EGMs than the next highest state, Victoria (Australian Gambling Statistics 2006) and has the highest number of EGMs per head of population in the world (Miserable Odds, 13 February 2006, p.22 2006).

Respondents

A series of one to two hour in-depth interviews was undertaken with thirty-eight gaming consultants, gaming machine manufacturers and gaming operators in NSW and Nevada and gaming legislators in NSW, as can be seen in Table One. The gaming operator venues ranged in size from the large 'super casino' conglomerates on the Las Vegas Strip and the large 'locals' casino operators in Nevada, to the smaller not-for-profit registered clubs and privately owned 'pubs' in NSW. Respondents consisted of business owners, senior government personnel and senior managers. Access to respondents was through introductions from personal contacts.

Instrument

The semi-structured interviews covered nine topic areas: (1) Reputation; (2) Supply Chain; (3) Purchase of new and/or second-hand EGMs; (4) Financial considerations (ability to offer incentives); (5) Social considerations; (6 – for casinos only) Percentage of revenue from EGMs vis a vis table games; (7) Percentage of revenue from EGMs vis a vis rooms and restaurants etc.; (8) Allocation of promotional budget; (9) Target market. Many of these were sensitive questions on which not much is known and it was felt that the results would enable the authors to become the first to make comparisons and develop conclusions in this area. The following convention will be used for referencing, as all respondents have been assured of utmost confidentiality: NSW respondents will be referred to as NSW1, NSW2, etc. and respondents from Nevada will appear as NEV1, NEV2, etc.

Table 1 Respondent Classification

Location	**Category**	**No. of Respondents**
Reno (Nevada)	Gaming consultant and gaming conference organiser	1
Las Vegas (Nevada)	Gaming consultant	1
Las Vegas (Nevada)	Gaming Machine Manufacturers	4
Las Vegas (Nevada)	Management of International Casinos	7
Las Vegas (Nevada)	Management of 'Locals' Casinos	2
Lake Tahoe (Nevada)	Gaming Machine Manufacturer	1
New South Wales	Gaming Legislators	3
New South Wales	Gaming consultants	6
New South Wales	Gaming Machine Manufacturers	2
New South Wales	Casino	1
New South Wales	Owners and Managers of Hotels (Pubs)	6
New South Wales	Management of Registered Clubs	4

Results/Findings

Our research indicates that the corporately owned large casinos in Las Vegas report a much stronger awareness of, and focus on, social responsibility than does the gambling industry in NSW. The large Nevada casino corporate owners actively monitor the smaller casinos to ensure that they do not attract the attention of the gaming regulators by acting in a socially irresponsible manner. These large corporations realise if any of the smaller casinos 'step out of line', the entire gaming industry will receive increased regulation. Explicit evidence of the heightened focus on socially responsible operations is the expense and professionalism with which the social responsibility statements and brochures of some of the largest corporations are presented. Some respondents seem to be proactive in terms of social responsibility, with one from a large gaming corporation stating that there is a "very strong focus on social responsibility" by them (NEV2). This would appear to be endorsed by having a full-time 'Responsible Gaming' staff member in their organisation. Another respondent stated that one of the largest EGM manufacturers in the USA has "a fantastic program in terms of responsible gaming" (NEV5). If this is the case, it may explain why there appears to be a lot less legislation in the Nevada gambling market than in the NSW jurisdiction.

CSR is vital to having a good reputation. One respondent stated that the EGM manufacturers and operators "have to have a good reputation with regulators in Nevada, much more so than in Australia" (NEV3). This was explained during an interview whereby the respondent had informally attended a certain casino some months earlier and was advised a few days later by the regulators not to go there any more due to the presence of certain criminal identities, or, following that, the respondent's organisation would lose its licence. Perhaps this adherence to observing the regulations and presenting the appearance of strict ethical conduct is why the Nevada regulatory gambling environment is substantially more relaxed than in NSW in terms of advertising, promotion and self-regulation. This might also be the reason why the popular press in Nevada does not extensively report on the 'social evils of EGMs' as happens in NSW. An alternative interpretation might also be that Nevada is much more tolerant of gambling because of its greater economic dependence on gambling than in the more economically diversified economy of New South Wales.

In spite of the seemingly stronger awareness of, and adherence to, CSR in Nevada than in NSW, there is no room for complacency in either jurisdiction. The Strip casinos are potentially in a time bomb, with one respondent (NEV17) stating that the management of the various casinos are very concerned about potential litigation from either an individual, or class action against them for unethical practices, such as continuing to send out marketing materials to people who have requested self-exclusion. Given the watershed situation in the tobacco industry with multiple class and individual actions resulting in billions of dollars in payouts, gaming operators have much to be concerned about.

Marketing Mix for Gaming Services

Unlike less 'controversial' businesses, if gaming operators try to increase consumption of EGMs, they tend to face a backlash by concerned community groups. The manager of a gaming venue in NSW stated, "There is hysteria around EGMs." (NSW6). This appears to be borne out by the regular number of media articles highlighting the 'evil' effects of EGMs, along with the strong focus on problem gambling in the academic literature.

Product

In services marketing, it refers to the intangible elements offered on top of the core product. In terms of gaming venues, the core product is the EGM, which the customer is essentially leasing for the duration of time spent playing the machine. This core product is subject to certain mandatory restrictions, such as restrictions on reel speed and limits on note acceptors. In spite of this however, controversy remains in Australia as to the effectiveness of existing regulatory restrictions and current EGM features.

An important issue regarding EGMs and CSR is that many consider that the choice of EGMs compared with other gambling products is the most addictive to the player (see for example Becoña 1996), making the marketing of EGMs the most financially lucrative. Most gambling revenue in Australia comes from EGMs (Australian Gambling Statistics 2006), with a small percentage of players providing most of the profits. In spite of this, controversy exists over the accusation that EGMs are the 'crack cocaine of gambling' (Barker and Britz 2000, p. 164) with Dowling et al. (2005) finding that

> "Despite overwhelming acceptance that gaming machines are associated with the highest level of problem gambling, the empirical literature provides inconclusive evidence to support the analogy likening electronic gaming to 'crack-cocaine'." (p. 33)

A concern expressed by one of the respondents relates to the technology of gaming machines, with a much higher amount of money going through EGMs due to the increased number of bets compared to the previous mechanical reels. This lends support to Sharpe et al.'s (2005) study showing that a reduction in maximum bet levels is an effective harm minimisation strategy. This same respondent stated, "EGMs are basically selling time (for entertainment). They're terrible instruments for stealing people's money. All complaints from players were not in terms of losing money, but losing it too quickly. Even problem gamblers appear to realise, by and large, that they're not going to win big time" (NSW7). This highlights the need for EGM service providers to act in a socially responsible manner by focusing on the entertainment aspect for the player, rather than solely on profits. This could be achieved by offering 'more bang for the buck' ", i.e. greater time spent on the EGM for the same amount of money input by the player, than is currently offered.

In addition to being concerned about the 'value for money' aspect, another respondent stated that: "Managers don't want to offer EGMs that are harmful to players, any more than people selling cars want to sell death traps, otherwise they'd soon go out of business. That's the last thing the club would want to do." (NSW6).

Customer relationships are an integral part of business success. One of the respondents stated that in the past there was a much stronger focus on the relationship with the customer, whereas now the focus is on maximising profits (NSW11). Support is offered by Hing's (2000) findings that NSW Registered Clubs (with their not-for-profit status) had subsumed their community-based charter for an economic imperative. One of the tenets of corporate social responsibility is to develop strong relationships with customers, suppliers and other pertinent stakeholders, in addition to broader societal considerations. As important as the economic component of CSR is, EGM marketing managers would be well advised to develop stronger relationships with key stakeholders, including their customers, in order to close expectational gaps.

Price

The price paid by the EGM customer and the benefits returned to them helps determine the 'value for money' and hence customer satisfaction. In NSW, the legislated minimum return to player (RTP) from EGMs is 85 percent, whereas in Nevada, the minimum is 75 per cent. Gaming venues in both jurisdictions are able to offer a RTP above this level if they choose. "NSW clubs have always set RTP around 90%, both before and after legislation" [NSW 2001 Gaming Machines Act and subsequent legislation] (NSW7). Respondents in Las Vegas stated that operators set their RTPs higher (90% plus) than the legislated minimum, in order to be competitive (NEV1; NEV7).

A NSW respondent, in an attempt to demonstrate the value-for-money aspect of EGMs, stated "RTP is about 90% overall in any one venue compared to 50% for scratchies." (NSW8). Whilst EGMs may well return almost double the RTP vis a vis scratch-off lottery cards, the overall amount spent on EGMs is significantly higher. An alternative and perhaps cynical perspective to this view of price would be to ask, "How fast does the average customer lose money"?

Place

Distribution channels ensure that the product is available at the right time, in the right quantity and at the right place for the final customer.

Community members who are on social benefits and/or on a very low income appear to have a propensity to play EGMs. Typically, these are the people who also have 'time on their hands'. As a result, controversy exists regarding availability of EGMs in lower socio-economic areas. (Breen et al. 2002; Doughney and Kelleher 1999; Marshall and Baker 2002; O'Neil and Whetton 2002). Others however question (a) the validity of methodological approaches, (b) whether or not problem gambling is more prevalent amongst lower socio-economic groups and/or (c) the effectiveness of the introduction of reduced caps of EGMs in lower socio-economical areas (AC Neilsen 2007; Doran et al. 2007; McMillen and Doran 2006; S.A Centre for Economic Studies 2005). Nevertheless, the NSW Government has recognised the very real threat posed to those on welfare benefits in low socio-economic areas in terms of spending their payments on EGMs instead of basic necessities such as rent, food and clothing.

In order to act in a socially responsible manner, EGM operators in low socio-economic areas need to ensure that their clients are not spending all, or most, of their welfare payments on EGMs. Marketing managers should take extra care on known times when welfare payments are made to ensure that the message to 'gamble responsibly' is particularly emphasised. Staff also need to observe the length of time spent playing, and the amount of money put into, EGMs by their customers on these days and, where deemed excessive based on certain criteria, management should limit and control for this. A number of instruments exist through which to ascertain whether or not gambling is excessive to the point where the player could be classified as a problem gambler (for example the 4 Es by Rockloff et al. (2007) and the well-known South Oaks Gambling Screen (SOGS) test and Canadian Problem Gambling Index (CPGI)). A perhaps more practical test (eight questions taking less than a minute to complete), namely the EIGHT (Early Intervention Gambling Health Test) screen, has recently been validated for use by untrained personnel to successfully identify Level 2 (moderate) and Level 3 (severe) problem gamblers in a variety of settings and cultures (Sullivan 2007). One way to protect EGM players from over-spending would be in the form of a signed agreement where, on entering the venue, customers would be asked in set a pre-determined limit on the amount spent during their time there in the form of a signed document. Expenditure could be monitored through the use of a tracking card, such as TITO (ticket-in, ticket-out). Obviously, EGMs would need to be set to only accept TITO cards, not cash.

Promotion

Marketers aim to communicate the benefits of the service offering to their existing, and potential, customers. Normally, this is achieved through a variety of promotional tools, such as advertising, sales promotion, personal selling, direct mail, internet advertising, telemarketing and public relations.

EGM marketing managers in NSW face limitations through which they can communicate their service offering. A blanket ban on all external advertising of gaming machines by hotels, registered clubs and to a large extent the casino, has existed since the introduction of the 2001 NSW Gaming Machines Act. EGMs can however, be advertised internally (jackpots, links etc.) (NSW3). EGM manufacturers are allowed to advertise in trade magazines and at trade exhibitions.

Whilst there has not been any banning of gaming machine advertising in Nevada, there are rules regarding 'truth in advertising', where any claim in the advertisement needs to be substantiated. A restriction on advertising to children, or including them in any advertising message, also exists and there is an expectation of good taste in advertising, with the Hard Rock Casino (Las Vegas) having been fined in the past for unacceptable advertising.

Interestingly, the emphasis of the majority of casinos in Nevada and the majority of registered clubs and pubs in NSW is on the promotion of the non-gaming aspects of the venue. In NSW, this is due to the outright ban of all external advertising of EGMs, which means that gaming venues can only advertise food, entertainment and facilities (apart from Star City Casino which can show table games, but not EGMs, in their advertisements). In Nevada, the tourist casinos on the Las Vegas Strip now obtain more revenue from their rooms, beverage and entertainment than from their gaming floor, in spite of there being no advertising ban other than adhering to the principle of 'truth in advertising'. The local casinos in Nevada also advertise the facilities they offer in addition to advertising their gaming machines. In NSW, the marketing of the facilities and entertainment provided within the pubs and registered clubs is designed to attract patrons to the premises. NSW hotel proprietors (albeit a small number) have been known to attempt to circumvent some of the regulations relating to the blanket ban of the external advertising of EGMs.

Given the blanket ban on all external advertising of EGMs in NSW, it may be tempting for some operators to try and 'skirt around' the restrictions by adhering to the law in a literal sense, but perhaps not spirit. It is vital therefore that EGM service providers go beyond legal requirements and adhere to the principles of transparency and honesty in their communication efforts in order to develop a good reputation and hence be thought of as acting in a socially responsible manner.

People

Customers' perceptions of service quality are strongly influenced by their interaction with the firm's personnel (Lovelock et al. 2004). One NSW respondent stated that their club puts a lot of emphasis on staff training and on the culture of the organisation, which flows on to the way people (customers) are treated by staff. Their club has a strong 'customer is king' philosophy. The club tries to look after customers by providing good service, such as tray service to players. They have 380 staff on the lookout for problem gamblers (NSW6). NSW legislation states that venues must provide the same tray service to all patrons in their venue, not just EGM players.

Many of the super casinos in Nevada employ attractive females in eye-catching costumes (low neck-lines, short skirts, stilettos) who walk around the gaming tables and gaming machine areas offering free drinks to patrons. The authors recognise that this may act as an inducement for the patron to either gamble, or, if already doing so, spend a longer time in the venue.

The importance of strong ethical values and applied training throughout all levels of the organisation, cannot be under-estimated. This also exposes a more fundamental point regarding CSR and that is that CSR is (presumably) more than what businesses *say*; it's what they *do*. This point also exposes the flaw in measuring CSR based solely on businesses' self-reporting.

Process

Service personnel rely on efficient and accurate 'backstage' processes in order to function effectively and deliver a high quality service experience to the customer. When processes fail, front-line staff often bear the brunt of the customer's anger and frustration (Lovelock et al. 2004).

The introduction of TITO technology in Nevada, and more recently in NSW, has facilitated the process by which EGM customers can insert and collect their money. Instead of having to walk over to a payout section on the gaming floor to collect larger size winnings, and instead of having to insert cash into each machine (inserting credit cards is banned in NSW), players can now have their credits transferred from machine to machine through their TITO card (with a limit of $2000 value in NSW), without having to withdraw remaining credits from one machine and re-insert the money into another. Accordingly, one could argue that one of the potentially addictive features of the EGM, that of the sound of the rush of coins falling into the EGM tray, is taken away by TITO, although the authors are also cognisant of the fact that TITO may actually facilitate the ease with which players can lose up to $2000 in one sitting.

Physical Evidence

Tangible cues become an important part of the overall service experience. Customers evaluate such factors as the physical layout of the premises, quality and comfort of seating and other furniture, lighting and music, dress standard of employees, quality of the food and beverages and promotional materials (Lovelock et al. 2004). "There is no difference between running a restaurant and running a gaming floor – criteria: location, ease of parking, security, what's the food like, what's the customer service like. The club has good décor, safety and security and the best and latest machines". (NSW6). A variety of casinos exist in Nevada, ranging from the shabby, run-down casinos, to the mid-range 'ordinary' casinos through to the super luxurious, opulent, high standard casinos offering world-class restaurants, entertainment and accommodation. It should be noted that, whereas NSW legislation demands EGM venues to have clocks that are clearly visible to every EGM patron, this is not the case in Nevada. Accordingly, the absence of clearly visible clocks and natural lighting in the Las Vegas casinos means players are shielded from any sense of time of day and even, at the extreme, how many days have passed.

A potential issue concerns the layout of the gaming floor. Gaming marketing managers need to ensure that players are not entrapped in any way. Large casinos have vast numbers of strategically placed EGMs, which can make it difficult for customers to find their way out. EGM marketing managers also need to ensure they are not providing an environment that encourages people to stay longer and play EGMs beyond their original intention.

In terms of being socially responsible, whilst it is perfectly acceptable for marketing managers to offer a pleasant environment on their gaming floor, it is important not to encourage an impulsive or compulsive response.

Conclusion and Implications

In sum, we found that operators of electronic gaming machines (EGMs) surveyed, particularly those in Nevada, considered that they operate within the tenets of corporate social responsibility. Evidence exists however to indicate that EGM operators may not be as socially responsible as they believe. Although the majority of operators satisfy legal/regulatory compliance, we found that very few go beyond this to incorporate voluntary ethical and philanthropic/discretionary principles into their marketing and other business function processes and programs.

Given the strong community backlash over the unprecedented growth in legalised gambling and the increased awareness of, and concern for, the resulting problems to a significant number of regular EGM players, operators in NSW and Nevada would be wise to adopt strategies that address and ameliorate these community concerns.

Fundamentally, the extreme 'Pareto effect' (also known as the 80/20 rule), which sees that the most profitable customers are the problem gamblers, exposes a serious ethical dilemma. Thus, given the extraordinarily high proportion of profits provided by problem gamblers, CSR recommendations may well be strongly resisted by the EGM industry unless there is some dramatic shift in perspective within the industry. Irrefutable statistics showing the extraordinarily high proportion of EGM profits that are derived from problem and at risk gamblers (see for example Livingstone and Woolley 2007; Symond 2007) means that any inaction on the part of the gaming industry would surely be unconscionable.

In spite of one NSW respondent's assessment that gaming operators could not do anything in addition to the heavily regulated environment in terms of being socially responsible (a highly questionable assertion!), companies would be well advised to go beyond the mandated requirements and adopt a philosophy of proactive social responsibility that in turn is imbued within every employee. At the same time it should be recognised that many gambling operators may see such a move towards a proactive social responsibility stance as tantamount to madness, as it would be seen as fundamentally challenging their *raison d'étre*.

Notwithstanding, many in the marketing community would see such a stance as far-sighted and ultimately more sustainable. Furthermore, given the increasing evidence of a positive link between CSR and profitability in much of the literature, any cries by the industry of potential loss of profit as a result of becoming more socially responsible should be treated with healthy scepticism. In marketing terms, a proactive social responsibility move would represent the adoption of the "societal marketing concept" (for example, Kotler et al. 2001), an advance beyond the familiar "marketing concept". However, while the adoption of the societal marketing concept has been advocated in the marketing literature for over thirty years, any sober assessment of the gambling industry would suggest that movement to such a position is highly improbable in the short term. Nevertheless, with the potential threat of rolling back the number of EGMs in Australia by the Federal Government, along with a regular diet of negative media stories, the predominance of focus on problem gambling in the academic literature and seemingly widespread negative sentiment in society, gaming operators may well find their resistance to CSR adoption will adversely affect their business survival in the longer term.

In order to maintain or increase the legitimacy of EGM operators and to change their marketing orientation from being 'market driven' to that of a 'market driver' (see for example El-Ansary and Cerne 2005), the following recommendations for marketing in a socially responsible manner are offered:

1. *Product*: EGMs should not contain seductive sounds or graphics. Nor should they include any misleading 'odds of winning' signage on the machine or on electronic boards above the machines.
2. *Price*: EGM operators should ensure that their patrons are not able to feed large amounts of money through the EGMs. The 'value for money' and entertainment aspects need to be emphasised.
3. *Place*: Whilst it is not suggested by the authors that there should be a total ban on EGMs in low socio-economic areas, it is strongly recommended that there not be a higher than average prevalence in these areas. This might well be an issue for the regulators. It is also recommended that staff in these areas take particular note of any patrons seen to be spending their welfare payments or wages on gambling.
4. *Promotion*: Although all external promotion of EGMs is banned in NSW, operators must ensure they don't try to 'skirt around the edges' of these legal restrictions. Whilst promotional mail-outs are banned in NSW, some concern exists in Nevada regarding inappropriate mail-outs with promotional inducements to patrons who have for example 'self-excluded'. It is also recommended that EGM operators implement the philanthropic component of Carroll's CSR Pyramid through donating a percentage of their profits to charities.
5. *People*: All gaming staff are required to undertake government mandated training in the socially responsible provision of gaming services in NSW. Anecdotal evidence suggests that many staff are told by their managers to basically ignore their training. Management need to strongly endorse and support the socially responsible delivery of service throughout all levels of the organisation.

6. *Process*: EGM operators need to monitor the impact of TITO and take action if it is seen that patrons are losing money more easily than they would without a TITO card.
7. *Physical Evidence*: Whilst all service providers have a fundamental right to provide high quality and attractive physical cues, it is incumbent on EGM operators to ensure that issues of 'entrapment' and 'enticement' are not exacerbated by the layout of the gaming floor or any other unreasonable inducements.

Having set out the above prescriptions it should also be aknowledged that these are concerned with risk mitigation, since prohibition is demonstrably unworkable and harmful consequences in such an industry are inevitable. Ultimately the solution that emerges will be one that the casino, clubs, pubs and the community are willing to live with. As with all gambling generally, at the end of the day it is not possible to please all of the people. It's a matter of striking a balance between (social) risk and (social) return.

References

ABS: Australian Bureau of Statistics: 2008, "3201.0 - Population by Age and Sex, Australian States and Territories, Jun 2008" http://www.abs.gov.au

AC Neilsen: 2007, "Prevalence of Gambling and Problem Gambling in NSW: A Community Survey 2006", NSW Office of Liquor, Gaming and Racing, Department of the Arts, Sport and Recreation http://www.olgr.nsw.gov.au/pdfs/rr_prevalence_gambling.pdf accessed 11 February 2008

The Asia-Pacific Centre for Philanthropy & Social Investment: 2006, Swinburne University - Australian Graduate School of Entrepreneurship, 11 October

Asongu, J.: 2007, "The Legitimacy of Strategic Corporate Social Responsibility as a Marketing Tool", Journal of Business and Public Policy, Vol. 1, No. 1 pp. 1-12

Aupperle, K.E., A.B. Carroll and J.D. Hatfield: 1985, "An Empirical Examination of the Relationship between Corporate Social Responsibility and Profitability", Academy of Management Journal (2), 446-463

Australian Gambling Statistics: 2006, Office of Economic and Statistical Research, Queensland Treasury, 23rd edition.

Barker, T. and M. Britz: 2000, Jokers Wild: Legalized Gambling in the Twenty-first Century (Praeger, USA)

Becoña, E.: 1996. "Prevalence Surveys of Problem and Pathological Gambling in Europe: The Cases of Germany, Holland and Spain", in J.J. Marotta, J.A. Cornelius and W.R. Eadington (eds.), The Downside: Problem and Pathological Gambling, 2002, Vol. 1, Reno, Nevada: Institute for the Study of Gambling and Commercial Gaming

Breen, H., N. Hing and P. Weeks: 2002, "Machine Gaming in Sydney Clubs: Characteristics of the Supporting Resident Populations", Journal of Gambling Studies 18(3), 283-312

Campbell, J. L.: 2007, "Why Would Corporations Behave In Socially Responsible Ways? An Institutional Theory of Corporate Social Responsibility", Academy of Management Review 32(3), 946-967

Carroll, A.: 1991, "The Pyramid of Corporate Social Responsibility: Toward the Moral Management of Organizational Stakeholders (balancing economic, legal and social responsibilities), Business Horizons, July-August 34(4), 39-49

_________ 1998, "The Four Faces of Corporate Citizenship", Business and Society Review 100(1), 1-7

Dahlsrud, A.: 2006, "How Corporate Social Responsibility is Defined: An Analysis of 37 Definitions", Corporate Social Responsibility and Environmental Management 15(1), 1 - 13

Davidson, D. K.: 2003, Selling Sin: The Marketing of Socially Unacceptable Products, 2nd edition (Praeger Publishers, USA)

de Bakker, F., P. Groenewegen and F. den Hond: 2005, "A Research Note on the Use of Bibliometrics to Review the Corporate Social Responsibility and Corporate Social Performance Literature", Business & Society 45(1), 7-19

Dentchey: 2004, "Corporate Social Performance as a Business Strategy", Journal of Business Ethics, Vol. 55, No. 4, pp. 395-410

Doran, B.J., D. C. Marshall and J. McMillen: 2007, "A GIS-based Investigation of Gaming Venue Catchments", Transactions in GIS 11(4), 575–595.

Doughney, J. and T. Kelleher: 1999, "The Impact of Poker Machine Gambling on Low-Income Municipalities: A Critical Survey of Key Issues" Workplace Studies Centre Victoria University, Australian Government Productivity Commission http://www.pc.gov.au/inquiry/gambling/docs/finalreport accessed 4 March 2008

Doughney, J.: 2007a, "Ethical Blindness, EGMs and Public Policy: A Tentative Essay Comparing the EGM and Tobacco Industries" International Journal of Mental Health Addiction 5, 311–319

_________ 2007b, "Lies, Damned Lies and 'Problem Gambling' Prevalence Rates: The Example of Victoria, Australia" Journal of Business Systems, Governance and Ethics 2(1), 41-54

Dowling, N., D. Smith and T. Thomas: 2005, "Electronic Gaming Machines: Are They the 'Crack-Cocaine' of Gambling?", Addiction 100, 33-45

El-Ansary, A. and Cerne, A.: 2005, "An Integrative Framework for Evolving a Socially Responsible Marketing Strategy", Lund Institute of Economic Research Working Paper Series http://www.lri.lu.se/en/publications/workingpapers?item=73 last accessed 6 June 2009

Frankental, P.: 2001, "Corporate Social Responsibility – a PR Invention?", Corporate Communication: An International Journal 6(1), 18-23

Friedman, M.: 1970, "The Social Responsibility of Business is to Increase its Profits", New York Times Magazine, September 13 http://www.colorado.edu/studentgroups/libertarians/issues/friedman-soc-resp-business.html accessed 10 September 2007

Haigh, M. and M. Jones: 2006, "The Drivers of Corporate Social Responsibility: A Critical Review", The Business Review, Cambridge, Vol 5 (2). Ashridge Business School UK,
http://www.ashridge.org.uk originally accessed 27 August 2007

Hing, N.: 2000, "Changing Fortunes: Past, Present and Future Perspectives on the Management of Problem Gambling by New South Wales Registered Clubs". Unpublished doctoral dissertation, University of Western Sydney, Maccarthur, Sydney, Australia

_________ 2001, "Changing the Odds: A Study of Corporate Social Principles and Practices in Addressing Problem Gambling ", Journal of Business Ethics 33(2), 115-144

_________ 2003, "An Assessment of Member Awareness, Perceived Adequacy and Perceived Effectiveness of Responsible Gambling Strategies in Sydney Clubs", Report, Centre for Gambling Education and Research, Southern Cross University, Lismore Australia for the NSW Department of Gaming and Racing. http://www.dgr.nsw.gov.au/pdfs/rr_hing.pdf accessed 15 November 2007

Hing, N. and J. Mackellar: 2004, "Challenges in Responsible Provision of Gambling: Questions of Efficacy, Effectiveness and Efficiency", UNLV Gaming Research & Review Journal 8(1), 43-58

Hing, N. and J. McMillen: 2002, "A Conceptual Framework of the Corporate Management of Social Impacts: The Case of Problem Gambling" Business and Society Review 107(4), 457–488

Kotler, P., S. Adam, L. Brown, G. Armstrong: 2001, Principles of Marketing, (Prentice Hall, Pearson Education Australia)

Lantos G.: 2001. "The Boundaries of Strategic Corporate Social Responsibility", Journal of Consumer Marketing 18 (7), 595-630

Livingstone, C. and R. Woolley: 2007, "Risky Business: A Few Provocations on the Regulation of Electronic Gaming Machines", International Gambling Studies 7(3), 361-376

Lovelock, C., P. Patterson and R. Walker: 2004, Services Marketing: An Asia-Pacific and Australian Perspective, 3rd edition (Pearson Education Australia)

Luo, X. and Bhattacharya, C.B.: 2006, "Corporate Social Responsibility, Customer, and Market Value", Journal of Marketing, Vol. 70, October, pp. 1-18

McMillen, J., D. Marshall, E. Ahmed and M. Wenzel: 2004, "2003 Victorian Longitudinal Community Attitudes Survey", Gambling Research Panel Report No. 7, Melbourne, State of Victoria http://hdl.handle.net/1885/45189 accessed 9 January 2008

McMillen, J. and B. Doran: 2006, "Problem Gambling and Gaming Machine Density: Socio-spatial Analysis of Three Victorian Localities" International Gambling Studies 6(1), 5-29

McWilliams, A., D. Siegel and P. Wright: 2006, "Guest Editors' Introduction – Corporate Social Responsibility: Strategic Implications", Journal of Management Studies 13(1) 1-18

Maignan, I. and O.C. Ferrell: 2004, "Corporate Social Responsibility and Marketing: An Integrative Framework", Journal of the Academy of Marketing Science, Vo. 32, No. 1, pp. 3-19

Maignan, I., O.C. Ferrell and L. Ferrell: 2005, "A Stakeholder Model for Implementing Social Responsibility in Marketing", European Journal of Marketing, Vol. 39, No. 9/10, pp. 956-977

Marshall, D.C. and R. G. V. Baker: 2002, "The Evolving Market Structures of Gambling: Case Studies Modelling the Socioeconomic Assignment of Gaming Machines in Melbourne and Sydney, Australia ", Journal of Gambling Studies 18(3), 273-291

Mellor, N.: 2005, "The Rise of EGM's in the Sunshine State – A Case Study of the Discounting of the Public Interest in the Name of Evidence Based Practice", Program leader, Gambling Help Services, Relationships Australia, PowerPoint slides downloaded from http://www.ijma-journal.com/ppt/c05p00046.ppt on 9 January 2008

Miles, M.B. and A.M. Huberman: 1984, Qualitative Data Analysis (Sage Publications, Beverly Hills), p.15

Miles, M., L. Munilla and J. Darroch: 2006, "The Role of Strategic Conversations with Stakeholders in the Formation of Corporate Social Responsibility Strategy", Journal of Business Ethics 69(2), 195-205

Miserable Odds: 2006, Editorial, The Daily Telegraph, Sydney 13 February p.22

O'Neil M. and S. Whetton: 2002, "An Assessment of the Impact of Gaming Machines on Small Regional Economies", The South Australian Centre for Economic Studies, Adelaide and Flinders Universities, Economic Issues No. 3

Productivity Commission: 1999, "Australia's Gambling Industries", Peter Costello, Federal Treasurer http://www.pc.gov.au/inquiry/gambling/docs/finalreport accessed 4 March 2008

Roberts, J.: 2003, "The Manufacture of Corporate Social Responsibility: Constructing Corporate Sensibility", Organization 10(2), 249-265

Rockloff, M., T. Signal and V. Dyer: 2007, "Full of Sound and Fury, Signifying Something: The Impact of Autonomic Arousal on EGM Gambling", Journal of Gambling Studies 23(4), 457-465

SA Centre for Economic Studies: 2005, "Study of the Impact of Caps on Electronic Gaming Machines", Final Report, commissioned by the Victorian Gambling Research Panel, funded by the Victorian Government through the Community Support Fund

Salia, D., Carroll, A. and Buchholtz, A.: 2003, "Philanthropy as Strategy – When Corporate Charity 'Begins at Home'", Business & Society, Vol. 42, No. 2 pp. 169-201

Sharpe, L., M. Walker, M. Couglan, K. Enersen and A. Blaszczynski: 2005, "Structural Changes to Electronic Gaming Machines as Effective Harm Minimization Strategies for Non-Problem and Problem Gamblers", Journal of Gambling Studies 21(4), 503-520

Sullivan, S.: 2007, "Don't Let an Opportunity Go by: Validation of the EIGHT Gambling Screen", International Journal of Mental Health and Addiction 5(4), 381-389

Symond, P.: 2007, Principal of Betsafe, www.betsafe.com.au and author of: 'How to Stop Gambling' (2003), Bantam Books. Information obtained through personal communication (email) on 16 November

Valor, C.: 2005, "Corporate Social Responsibility and Corporate Citizenship: Towards Corporate Accountability", Business and Society Review 110(2), 191-212

Vargo, S. and R. Lusch: 2004, "Evolving to a New Dominant Logic for Marketing", Journal of Marketing, Vol. 68 (January), pp. 1-17

Walker, R.: 1985, "An Introduction to Applied Qualitative Research" in Robert Walker (ed.), Applied Qualitative Research (Gower, Aldershot, England) p.3

Wulfson, M.: 2001, "The Ethics of Corporate Social Responsibility and Philanthropic Ventures", Journal of Business Ethics, Vol. 29, Nos 1-2, pp. 135-145.

www.ingramcontent.com/pod-product-compliance
Lightning Source LLC
LaVergne TN
LVHW052022200926
848481LV00005B/1554